FODOR'S

JAPAN

1985

Area Editors: JAN BROWN, DR. MICHAEL COOPER, DAVID JONES, MIRANDA KENRICK, K.V. NARAIN, TOMATSU OGATA, CLIFF PARFIT, PETER POPHAM, JOHN TURRENT, MICHIKO YOSHII

Editorial Contributors: STUART ATKIN, SIR HUGH CORTAZZI, DR. JOHN HANSON-LOWE, DOUGLAS MOORE KENRIGK, VIVIENNE KENRICK, PATRICIA MASSY, WALTER MILLER, AMAURY ST. GILLES, NORMAN SKLAREWITZ, DR. ALAN TURNEY

Editor: DEBORAH JURKOWITZ

Editorial Associates: ELENORE BODIE, DIANNE CLARK

Drawings: KAMIMURA KYOICHI, TED BURWELL

Maps and City Plans: PICTOGRAPH, C.W. BACON

FODOR'S TRAVEL GUIDES
New York

Copyright © 1985 by FODOR'S TRAVEL GUIDES
ISBN: 0-679-01126-9
ISBN: 0-340-36275-8 (Hodder & Stoughton)

All the following Guides are current (most of them also in
the Hodder and Stoughton British edition).

**FODOR'S COUNTRY
AND AREA TITLES:**

AUSTRALIA, NEW
 ZEALAND AND
 SOUTH PACIFIC
AUSTRIA
BELGIUM AND
 LUXEMBOURG
BERMUDA
BRAZIL
CANADA
CANADA'S MARITIME
 PROVINCES
CARIBBEAN AND
 BAHAMAS
CENTRAL AMERICA
EASTERN EUROPE
EGYPT
EUROPE
FRANCE
GERMANY
GREAT BRITAIN
GREECE
HOLLAND
INDIA, NEPAL, AND
 SRI LANKA
IRELAND
ISRAEL
ITALY
JAPAN
JORDAN AND HOLY
 LAND
KOREA
MEXICO
NORTH AFRICA
PEOPLE'S REPUBLIC
 OF CHINA
PORTUGAL
SCANDINAVIA
SCOTLAND

SOUTH AMERICA
SOUTHEAST ASIA
SOVIET UNION
SPAIN
SWITZERLAND
TURKEY
YUGOSLAVIA

CITY GUIDES:

AMSTERDAM
BEIJING,
 GUANGZHOU,
 SHANGHAI
BOSTON
CHICAGO
DALLAS AND FORT
 WORTH
GREATER MIAMI
HONG KONG
HOUSTON
LISBON
LONDON
LOS ANGELES
MADRID
MEXICO CITY AND
 ACAPULCO
MUNICH
NEW ORLEANS
NEW YORK CITY
PARIS
ROME
SAN DIEGO
SAN FRANCISCO
STOCKHOLM,
 COPENHAGEN,
 OSLO, HELSINKI,
 AND REYKJAVIK
TOKYO
TORONTO
VIENNA
WASHINGTON, D.C.

FODOR'S BUDGET SERIES:

BUDGET BRITAIN
BUDGET CANADA
BUDGET CARIBBEAN
BUDGET EUROPE
BUDGET FRANCE
BUDGET GERMANY
BUDGET HAWAII
BUDGET ITALY
BUDGET JAPAN
BUDGET LONDON
BUDGET MEXICO
BUDGET
 SCANDINAVIA
BUDGET SPAIN
BUDGET TRAVEL IN
 AMERICA

USA GUIDES:

ALASKA
CALIFORNIA
CAPE COD
COLORADO
FAR WEST
FLORIDA
HAWAII
NEW ENGLAND
PACIFIC NORTH COAST
PENNSYLVANIA
SOUTH
TEXAS
USA (in one volume)

GOOD TIME TRAVEL GUIDES:

ACAPULCO
MONTREAL
OAHU
SAN FRANCISCO

MANUFACTURED IN THE UNITED STATES OF AMERICA
10 9 8 7 6 5 4 3 2 1

CONTENTS

CONTENTS

FOREWORD

Japan, a country roughly the size of California with almost half the population of the entire United States, is not an especially easy country for the Western visitor—and yet the cultural and other rewards *far* outweigh any small and temporary difficulties. And the legendary Japanese hospitality is a fact.

Fodor's Japan is designed to enable the independent traveler to gain the widest access to—and understanding of—Japan's scenery, religious and historical sites, entertainments, cuisine, architecture, crafts and art, and above all her people.

The book is also structured to offer the practical details needed to take the visitor not only through the usual Tokyo–Kyoto axis, but beyond, to such extremely impressive cultural and scenic areas as old Kanazawa and Takayama, the Japan Alps, Matsushima, the Kyushu hot springs, and so many others. For the entire country, we offer the widest possible **range** of activities and, within that range, present you with **selections** of events and places that will be safe, worthwhile, and of good value. The descriptions we provide are just enough to enable you to make your own informed choices from among our selections.

All selections and comments in *Fodor's Japan* are based on the editors' and contributors' personal experiences. We feel that our first responsibility is to inform and protect you, the reader. Errors are bound to creep into any travel guide, however. We go to press in the winter, and much change can and will occur in Japan even while we are on press and certainly also during the succeeding twelve months or so when this edition is on sale. We cannot, therefore, be responsible for the sudden closing of a restaurant, a change in a museum's days or hours, a shift of hotel ownership (for the worse), and so forth. We sincerely welcome letters from our readers on these changes, or from those whose opinions differ from ours, and we are ready to revise our entries for next year's edition when the facts warrant it.

Send your letters to the editors at **Fodor's Travel Guides, 2 Park Avenue, New York, NY 10016.** Continental or British Commonwealth readers may prefer to write to Fodor's Travel Guides, 9-10 Market Place, London W1N 7AG, England.

We are grateful to officers of the Japan National Tourist Organization (JNTO), both in the United States and in Japan—especially Etsuko Penner and Isokazu Tanaka—for their help on the book, and the various prefectural tourism offices, especially Kagoshima's, for their help in the amassing and checking of information for the book.

FACTS AT YOUR FINGERTIPS

 FACTS AND FIGURES. Four main islands—Honshu, Shikoku, Kyushu, and Hokkaido—and hundreds of smaller ones make up the Far Eastern nation of Japan. About 119 million people live in a land of about 378,000 square kilometers that curve, long and thin, through temperate zones in the north to the subtropical in the southwest. Japan is a mountainous country, subject to earthquakes, with hot springs and several volcanoes that are still very much alive. The coasts are irregular, indented with bays and studded with offshore islands. Although the cities are heavily populated and rural areas are becoming increasingly urbanized, Japan remains a beautiful, unusual country.

Tokyo, the capital city, is on the Pacific coast of the main island of Honshu, with Kyoto, the ancient capital, 600 kilometers away in the west-central district. An express motorway links the two cities, and the fastest Shinkansen bullet trains put them less than three hours apart. Honshu is replete with compelling places of interest, scenic, historical, industrial, commercial.

Even in just a short visit to Tokyo, it is possible to make day trips that will immeasurably enrich your Japan experience. Nikko has the grandeur of magnificent shrines and the wonder of mountains, lakes, and waterfalls. Yokohama, a harbor city only 30 kilometers away, has a slight un-Japanese flavor left over from last-century influences and in its Chinatown. Kamakura unfailingly appeals with its monuments of 700 years ago, and Hakone, a year-round mountain resort, excels in hot springs, the wide outdoors, and superlative scenery.

Grouped in the west-central district, ancient heartland of Japan, are Kyoto, Nara, and Ise, each one a treasury of history, culture, and the arts. No visit to Japan is complete without at least one of these centers being explored. West of this grouping spread the industrial center of Osaka, and Kobe, which is residential and charming. This is also the eastern end of the Inland Sea, no longer unspoiled and unpolluted, but still lovely with its rocky coasts and innumerable islets.

Now that superexpress bullet trains are extended to Northern Honshu and the Japan Sea coast, districts that used to be remote are much more accessible. The Tohoku region, less frequented in the past, is enjoying stepped-up popularity now that people can get there more readily. Kanazawa, not directly served by bullet trains, still gains in closer approach. Longer-staying visitors usually want to go on from Kanazawa, capital of the Japan Sea coast region, to Gifu's special old town of Takayama and to the special old village of Shirakawa. To be in these localities is like walking into a scene on an old woodblock print.

The smallest of the four main islands of Japan, Shikoku, has the strong attraction of rural simplicity, as well as good beaches, popular shrines and temples, and several castle towns. Across the Inland Sea from the southern shores of western Japan, Shikoku is being linked to Honshu by a series of bridges for trains and motor vehicles that will supplement the older ferry boat and air services.

Mountainous Kyushu, third largest island and cradle of Christianity in Japan, has numerous national parks and scenic and historic attractions. The foremost place of interest here is Nagasaki, oldest open port in Japan. Beyond Kyushu lies a string of islands, the Ryukyu chain, leading down to the main island of Okinawa. This is a subtropical region of checkered history and distinctive character. Resort islands, the Ryukyus are known for clear, blue seas and yellow sands, and brilliant sunsets probably unparalleled elsewhere in Japan.

1

The northernmost island of Hokkaido, next to Honshu in size, is, again, different in personality. Hokkaido attracts lovers of mountains and snow, of untamed nature and space. The Ainu people of Japan live in Hokkaido. Their arts and crafts and cult of the bear offer major interest to visitors.

Japan today is many faceted. The old-world image of flowers, the kimono, and the tea ceremony, though it fades in fact, is still clear in the spirit. The woodblock print depiction of wooden houses, shrine festivals, and a temple in the snow is still an actuality, overlaid though it is with apartment blocks, concrete high-rise office buildings, and expressways. The age-old sense of service and hospitality to guests is still prevalent.

In ways that matter to international visitors, Japan is no longer old Asia at all, but modern cosmopolitan. Hotels compare with the world's best and range in price to accommodate different budgets. They are subject to very strict safety standards imposed by the Fire Prevention Law. Japan's domestic transport systems could serve as models for the world. Japan's shops and restaurants overflow with the good things of life.

For many reasons, Japan should hold no terrors at all for the independent traveler. It is one of the safest countries in the world and one of the most honest. Even the language is a much lower hurdle than it used to be. The Japan National Tourist Organization is instrumental in smoothing the way in several practical directions. It has produced an effective finger-pointing dictionary, entitled *The Tourist's Handbook,* that facilitates communication. It has instituted a goodwill guide service program, under which 11,000 qualified volunteer guides who wear special badges help you out of your difficulties. Its Japan Travel-Phone is another information and rescue device. Its Home Visit Program sets up opportunities for you to be received in any of 450 family homes in a dozen Japanese cities. And there is almost no tipping in Japan.

The Japanese National Railways' Japan Rail Pass enables holders to use the railways, including the Shinkansen superexpress lines, at substantial savings throughout the entire network. With these considerations, it is no surprise that year by year the numbers of tourists to Japan increase.

THE JAPANESE COST OF LIVING. The average young family in early 1984 had an income of about ¥270,000 per month. This salary has to be multiplied by about sixteen to arrive at the annual income figure, as it is customary in Japan for an employee to receive a summer bonus equal to about two months' salary, and a year-end bonus equal to about two months' salary.

In recent years since high-rise buildings have succeeded the previous one- or two-story dwellings, city living patterns have changed. Young families nowadays often live separately from the older generation, often in apartment blocks. Many young families are buying their own condominiums, described as 1LDK or 2LDK or 3LDK. The number gives the count of bedrooms, and the letters refer to the one living room and combination dining-kitchen. A 3LDK condominium costs about ¥25 million, obtainable by housing loan, and a young family pays back about ¥50,000 each month for 35 years or so. Additionally, the family has to pay about ¥10,000 a month for a janitor. Apartment blocks are often very far from the city center, and working commuters normally spend one hour or more traveling from their homes to their jobs.

A family of four spends about ¥72,000 a month on food, and ¥20,000 a month for heating, lighting, and water. If a car is bought on the installment plan, repayments for it have to be budgeted. A washing machine, a refrigerator, and a color television set are normal pieces of household equipment, and every family has at least one superior camera.

 WHEN TO GO. The tourist season in Japan is generally thought to begin in March, to carry on in strength through November, and to taper off by the following February. That is, although spring and autumn are top favorite seasons, Japan is a year-round tourist country.

Climate. Japan has four clear-cut seasons of equal length, each one with its own character and customs, and each with much to commend it. Generally, spring is described as being warm, summer as hot, autumn as cool, and winter as cold.

Since Japan stretches from lat. 45°33' N. to lat. 20°25' N., a broad generalization calls for modification. Northern Japan and the Japan Sea coast have heavy snowfalls, whereas snow is unknown in Okinawa. Rain may fall at any time, but is usually heaviest in Honshu from mid-June until about four weeks later. This rainy season begins a month earlier in Okinawa, and moves steadily northeast. Hokkaido has no summer rainy season.

Spring is the season for flowers, beginning in Okinawa and moving northeast through the islands. Cherry blossoms open in Tokyo at the beginning of April. Summer is the season for seeking out beach and mountain resorts. In most of the country late summer is very hot and steamy. Autumn is spasmodically tempestuous when typhoon winds and rains hit the islands. After each storm, summer heat retreats to make way for sunshine and serene clear skies. Winter is usually dry and bright, and the focus of interest shifts to the ski slopes.

Average temperatures, in centigrade

	January	April	July	October	Annual Average
Sapporo	−5.1	6.1	20.2	10.4	7.8
Kanazawa	2.6	11.5	24.8	15.8	13.7
Tokyo	4.1	13.5	25.2	16.9	15.0
Kyoto	3.5	13.1	26.1	16.7	14.8
Nagasaki	6.2	15.0	26.4	18.8	16.6
Naha	16.0	20.8	28.2	24.1	22.3

Average rainfall (in milliliters) and humidity percentage (in parentheses)

	Spring	Summer	Autumn	Winter	Annual Average
Sapporo	118(68)	64(80)	90(74)	104(75)	1,141(74)
Tokyo	49(66)	122(79)	140(74)	203(57)	1,503(69)
Kyoto	56(67)	145(76)	239(74)	122(72)	1,638(73)
Naha	122(79)	142(82)	174(74)	149(70)	2,118(78)

 PACKING. Your first consideration will be the season, and in this regard Japan makes it easy for you. The four seasons are models of their kind, so dress accordingly. Winter clothes for December to February; spring clothes, including rainwear and folding umbrellas, for March to May; summer clothes, including swimsuits and some light rainwear, and umbrellas that double as parasols, for June to August; and autumn clothes and rainwear for September to November.

Remember that cities, even in summer, call for city dress. The best bet is to dress conventionally. For convenience, wash and wear, noncrushable fabrics are recommended. For ladies, pantsuits are acceptable in the cities, but shorts or beachwear are not. Hats are not necessary, and cocktail dresses can see you through evening occasions. Comfortable footwear is essential, and the simpler the shoe the better. As shoes are not worn inside the Japanese home nor in certain temples, being able to get in and out of your shoes gracefully and quickly is a decided advantage. If you plan to be in Japan in winter, and if you suffer from cold feet, bring your own woolen socks to help you over these shoeless occasions. A pair of airline slippers also may be handy to carry with you. Sandals with open toes are not the best for walking along graveled paths, and there are many of these in Japanese temples and parks.

Nowadays you can buy almost anything you need in the big cities, but be sure to bring with you a sufficient supply of anything that is important or special to you. You may also at times be glad to have with you a picnic set, can and bottle opener and corkscrew for your days or nights of self-catering. It does no harm to have pocket tissues with you to tide you over the unexpected. A traveler's alarm clock and a flashlight are sometimes helpful. Sunglasses are a necessity since the sunlight in Japan is bright. A supply of extra passport photos is a good idea—you may need them for documents if you impulsively rearrange your schedules. In this no-tipping country, you may like to be prepared with suitable little gift items, such as handkerchiefs or perfume sachets, to reward someone who has been attentive to you.

TOURIST INFORMATION. There is a plethora of informative leaflets and pamphlets put out by the *Japan National Tourist Organization*. Your nearest Japanese Embassy or Consulate or office of Japan Air Lines is also well equipped to answer general questions. For specific advice, stay with JNTO. Main offices are at the following addresses:

Tokyo Kotsu Building, 10th floor, 2–10–1 Yuraku-cho, Chiyoda-ku, Tokyo;

630 Fifth Avenue, New York, NY 10111;

333 North Michigan Avenue, Chicago, IL 60601;

1519 Main Street, Dallas, TX 75201;

1737 Post Street, San Francisco, CA 94115;

624 South Grand Avenue, Los Angeles, CA 90017;

2270 Kalakaua Avenue, Honolulu, HI 96815;

165 University Avenue, Toronto M5H 3B8, Ontario, Canada;

167 Regent Street, London W.1, England;

115 Pitt Street, Sydney, N.S.W., Australia;

Peter Building, 58 Queen's Road, Hong Kong;

56 Suriwong Road, Bangkok, Thailand.

Travelers' Aid. The *Japan Association of Travel Agents*, headquarters at Nippon Building Annex, 2–7–1 chome, Otemachi, Chiyoda-ku, Tokyo 100 (270–5461), aims at the development of the tourist industry in Japan. It will deal with any tourist's complaints concerning services handled by JATA members. JATA has branch offices in Nagoya, Osaka, and Fukuoka.

Guides will be provided by a travel agent, or if you prefer, you may telephone the *Japan Guide Association Headquarters*, Shin Kokusai Bldg. (213–2706). The association is closely related to JTB, the nation's semi-official Japan Travel Bureau.

WHAT WILL IT COST? Japan has a long-standing reputation for being expensive, and it's not getting any cheaper, but other countries have been growing more pricey, so that gaps in costs tend to narrow. A survey conducted in November 1983 announced that out of seventeen major world cities Tokyo ranked eighth halfway down, in costliness for travelers. The Japan National Tourist Organization, which conducted the survey, points out, however, that prices in Tokyo are still cheaper than in many U.S. and some European cities.

With Tokyo's price level set at 100 in the travelers' cost index, the results of the survey placed New York at the top of the index at 155.71; and Mexico City, at 68.23; and San Paulo, at 66.38, came bottom lower than Tokyo. The items considered in the cost survey were a single room with breakfast in a hotel, a steak dinner with house wine in a restaurant, restaurant beer, hotel whisky, a fast-food lunch, and a 5-kilometer taxi ride.

To begin at the top: A Tokyo super deluxe hotel room for one costs from ¥15,000 to ¥25,000 per night. Usually it is advantageous to be a couple, for whom a double or twin room costs from ¥20,000 to ¥35,000 per night. Tax and service charges are additional. Usually no discounts for long stays are offered. JNTO also pointed out in its survey that because Tokyo is a safe city, its hotels are well patronized by local people and so are not exclusive, and therefore excessively costly, places.

A super deluxe Japanese inn is not cheaper, and in fact can be more expensive. Usually, the rates for Japanese inns include dinner and breakfast. Tax and service charges are added and rates for long stays are not discounted.

Prices at the top in other major cities and in popular resorts are not markedly different. However, as you go down the price scale you will find that it is still possible, even in Tokyo, to find clean, unadorned rooms in simple hotels and inns for as little as ¥4,000 per head per night. If you don't mind bunks or dormitory accommodations, you can pay even less.

For dinner in a super deluxe restaurant, whether in a top hotel or in an independent establishment, there is hardly any limit on what you can spend. But cheap restaurants exist everywhere in Japan. They have show windows with wax models of the dishes they offer, and their prices are clearly marked. You can call a waitress to the show window, and point to anything that catches your fancy. She will do the rest, promptly, cheerfully, and honestly. And she does not expect a tip.

Here are a few money-saving tips you might want to keep in mind:

1. Get out on your own. Use local transportation. Japanese cities are among the safest in the world, and someone always pops up to help you if you look lost.

2. Eat the local food: the Japanese diet is a delight.

3. Cash your traveler's checks or foreign currency at banks, never at hotels, shops, restaurants or—God forbid—nightclubs.

4. Have a little Japanese currency on you when you arrive in the country, so that you can tip properly or pay the baggage charge, airport bus fare, or taxi fare properly and without having to surrender dollars or pounds at a disadvantageous rate.

5. Change your Japanese coins before you leave—use the bank at the departure terminal when you depart.

The Japan National Tourist Organization's useful manual, "Budget Travel in Japan" is unfortunately both out of date now and hard to obtain. However, here are the prices of everyday goods and services listed in the manual, adjusted for inflation.

A simple, clean, central hotel, per person in a double room.
Tax and service charges included   ¥ 6,200
Breakfast in a coffee shop, "Morning Service"
of coffee, a boiled egg and toast   400
Lunch in a simple restaurant   1,000
Dinner in a restaurant   3,700
One subway fare, basic   100
One taxi ride, basic (2 kilometers)   470
Cinema ticket, first-run movie   1,500
One pack of cigarettes   200
One coffee   300
One beer in a popular bar   500

                             ———————
                           ¥ 14,370

This means that, without straining, you should stay within about US$65 a day. Add to this the cost of a Japan Rail Pass, ¥ 25,000 for seven days, for example, and you will be able to include long-distance touring within Japan in your calculations.

HOW TO GET THERE. Japan is reachable by air and by sea. The two major international airports are the New Tokyo International at Narita, which is actually in the neighboring prefecture of Chiba and at least an hour's journey, by road, from the Tokyo City Air Terminal; and Osaka (Itani) International Airport. The Tokyo Airport at Haneda mostly caters to domestic flights, with the notable exceptions of certain flights from Taiwan, and of carriers bringing V.I.P.s.

Other airports handling international flights are at Sapporo on Hokkaido, Nagoya on Honshu, Fukuoka and Kagoshima on Kyushu, and Naha on Okinawa.

International seaports are at Yokohama, Nagoya, and Kobe on Honshu, and at Nagasaki and Kagoshima on Kyushu.

Travel Agents. A reliable travel agent is necessary to your well-being. She or he can tell you what is and what isn't available, and what the current travel bargains are. (These change all the time.) She can handle your individual requirements, or attach you to a group. You will have to allow for the fact that she will tie you in with her own business connections. There's nothing wrong with that so long as she and they are reputable.

BY AIR

Flight time from Honolulu to Tokyo is seven hours, from Los Angeles to Tokyo is 9½ hours. The Polar flight from London to Tokyo is 17 hours. Via Moscow, the London to Tokyo flight time is 14½ hours. By the southern route, more than 26 hours are taken. Sydney to Tokyo takes 9½ hours.

First-class, executive-class and economy-class cabins are available on many major carriers. If you are an independent traveler paying full fare (not in a group or using any kind of discount ticket), you may change your carrier for different sectors of your trip. Some trans-Pacific airlines have arrangements with steamship companies to fly passengers across, join a cruise ship for part of the itinerary (among the islands of Indonesia perhaps, or into Korea or Mainland China), then return by plane.

Group rates for package and charter tours remain the most economical. It is always worth enquiring into "excursion," "APEX," and any other special fares. Even typical economy fares between Los Angeles and Tokyo, for example, can vary by several hundred dollars depending on how long in advance the reservation is made (and paid for), how long a stay is involved, whether any land arrangements are tied in, how many stopovers are included, and other factors.

Some charter tour packagers simply block-book seats on major airlines at reduced prices. Some major airlines offer special charter-like prices in order to boost travel on certain routes during certain periods. Regardless of formal status, all flights must meet the same U.S. federal government standards of aircraft maintenance and safety, crew qualifications, and reliability.

Given the distance and cost involved in any trip to Japan, many travelers try to maximize the time and money spent by taking in other locales in the area. Korea is only a short, separate trip away from Japan. A popular sweep through Southeast Asia would include Taiwan, Hong Kong, Bangkok, and Singapore. Between Bangkok and Singapore, a stop may be made at Kuala Lumpur, capital of Malaysia.

If you are so ambitious as to decide upon a visit to the South Seas, from Japan you may fly to Manila, Bali, then go on to Sydney, Australia, and Auckland, New Zealand. As well as all the hinterland of these countries opening up for you, you are also placing yourself well for advancing into the islands of Micronesia and Melanesia.

Luggage. Regulations for air travelers from the United States base baggage allowances on size. Economy-class passengers may each take two pieces of baggage provided that the sum of their dimensions is not over 2m. 70cm., or 106 inches (neither piece being more than 1m. 58 cm., or 62 inches, combined height, width, and length). First-class allowance is two pieces up to 1m. 58 cm., or 62 inches, overall dimensions each, total 3m. 16 cm., or 124 inches. There is also a 32-kilogram (70-pound) limit for each piece of luggage. Penalties for regulation contravention are severe.

To and from Britain. If you're traveling to Japan on a scheduled airline ticket, you'll realize the return fare is equal to a round-the-world fare, as Tokyo is halfway around the globe from London. You may wish, therefore, to take advantage of a wide number of stopovers allowed on such a ticket. These, on the Southern route, represent nearly every major tourist destination in the northern hemisphere. You can pop in to the Middle East, India, Singapore, Bangkok, Hong Kong, Taiwan. From Tokyo, you can return the same way to stop at different cities, or continue around the world to Hawaii and North America, before crossing the Atlantic to home.

More than 30 airlines operate international services to Japan. Their counters are divided, at Narita Airport, into two wings. The airlines are listed below, with their code letters, under the building wings where they are located.

North Wing		South Wing	
Japan Airlines	JL	Air France	AF
Air India	AI	Alitalia	AZ
Civil Aviation Administration of China (CAAC)	CA	British Airways	BA
Continental Airlines	CO	Canadian Pacific Airlines	CX
Garuda Indonesian Airways	GA	Cathay Pacific Airways	CX
Iran National Airlines	IR	Korean Airlines	KE
KLM Royal Dutch Airlines	KL	Lufthansa German Airlines	LH
Malaysian Airlines	MH	All Nippon Airways	NH
Egypt Air	MS	Northwest Orient Airlines	NW
Pakistan International	PK	Pan American World Airways	PA
Philippine Airlines	PR	Varig	RG

North Wing		*South Wing*	
Qantas Airways	QF	SAS Scandinavian Airlines	SK
Sabena Belgian Airlines	SN	Singapore Airlines	SQ
Aeroflot Soviet Airlines	SU	Swiss Air	SR
UTA French Airlines	UT	Thai Airways International	TG
Iraqi Airways	IA	Japan Asia Airways	EG
Air New Zealand	TE	Finnair	AY
United Airlines	UA		

BY SEA

An increasing number of passenger ships as well as freighters having limited accommodation for passengers are calling at ports in the Far East. Since schedules are extremely variable, it is advisable to make your inquiries and bookings well in advance.

Among the American travel agencies handling travel by sea are: *Air and Marine Travel Service,* 501 Madison Avenue, New York, NY 10022; *Pearl's Freighter Tips,* 175 Great Neck Road, Great Neck, NY 11021; *Freighter Travel Service,* 201 E. 77th Street, New York, NY 10021.

The following list gives some of the possibilities of travel by sea.

Pearl Cruises of Scandinavia, with an office under this name in San Francisco, regularly schedules cruises to China aboard this company's flagship, the one-class M/S *Pearl* of Scandinavia. The *Pearl,* 12,456 tons, cruises from Hong Kong to China, Korea, Kobe in Japan, and back to Hong Kong. Tours are sold in both the U.S. and Europe for twelve two-way cruises on the route annually.

Royal Viking Sea, of the Royal Viking Line, 1 Embarcadero Center, San Francisco, CA 94111, sails from California to the South Pacific, Indonesia, Singapore, Hong Kong, Japan, and Hawaii.

The Cunard Line's *Queen Elizabeth II* calls at 30 ports from New York, on round-the-world cruises.

P. and O. Cruises have *The Princess Diana,* the world's latest luxury liner, going into round-the-world service. *The Princess Diana,* 40,000 tons, is claimed to be the most technically advanced deep-sea passenger ship ever built.

Hapeg-Lloyd's new cruise ship, M/V *Europa,* sails east from Genoa, taking 115 days to go around the world, calling at Kobe, Nagoya, and Yokohama in Japan.

The *Pacific Princess,* 20,636 tons, takes 70 days to travel around the world. She calls at Kobe and Yokohama in Japan. Celebrated as television's "Love Boat," filmed in Far Eastern locations.

Knutsen Line of Norway, has three vessels that ply between Western Australia and Japan, calling at Nagoya, Yokohama, Osaka, and Moji. They are the M/S *Lloyd Bakke,* the M/S *Anna Bakke,* and the M/S *Ragna Bakke.*

Once a month, a Soviet passenger ship sails from England via the Atlantic and Pacific to Yokohama, where time permits visits to Kamakura and Hakone. The *Mikhail Lermontov,* 20,000 tons, one of five "writer class" passenger ships named after famous Soviet writers, takes 96 days to sail around the world.

EXTENDED TOURS. Package tours save you time, money, and hassle, although they restrict you to a greater or lesser degree to the group itinerary—depending on the type of tour and how rigidly you choose to stay with it. You don't have to stay with it at all times, unless it suits you. Most package tours to this part of the world combine several East Asian countries into one trip. Obviously the cost of travel escalates as the number of days and stops increases, but this can be an effective and relatively economical way to get an overview of the region and a feel for the various cultures in it.

Your travel agent is likely to be familiar with most of the tour operators listed below or should be able to obtain any specific information you might wish to have. We urge you to check the specifics, particularly as fluctuations in currency rates in recent years have greatly affected package operators. Please remember that a solo traveler is always charged more, and the supplemental charge may be significant.

Maupintour, 408 E. 50th St., New York, NY 10022, offers an ambitious 17-day "Grand Japan" tour that covers the highspots for approximately $3,200 plus airfare (round-trip economy APEX fare: about $900).

American Express, American Express Plaza, New York, NY 10004, goes to Tokyo, Hakone, Kyoto, Taipei, and Hong Kong on a 15-day "Asian Highlights" tour for approximately $948 plus airfare; a 17-day tour, "The Asian Affair," covers roughly the same spots for $1,098 plus air fare. Add $1,300–1,500 for airfare, round trip from Los Angeles.

Airlines offering their own tour packages include *Singapore* (SIA), which incidentally is frequently the airline used by other tour packagers; *Pan Am, Japan, Northwest Orient,* and *Philippine.* Check the white pages for telephone numbers or consult a travel agent for specific details.

Other reliable tour operators with experience in travel to Japan include:

Four Winds, 175 Fifth Ave., New York, NY 10010.

Hemphill/Harris, 16000 Ventura Blvd., Encino, CA 91436.

Japan & Orient Tours, 250 E. 1st St., Los Angeles, CA 90012.

Lindblad, 8 Wright St., Westport, CT 06880.

Orient Holiday, 1211 Avenue of the Americas, New York, NY 10036.

Pacific Delight, 132 Madison Ave., New York, NY 10016.

Shogun, Suite 312, 1235 Weller, St., Los Angeles, CA 90012.

Sita World Travel, 3932 Wilshire Blvd., Los Angeles, CA 90010.

In the United Kingdom:

Bales Tours, Bales House, Barrington Rd., Dorking, Surrey, offers a 15-day package covering Tokyo, Kamakura, Kyoto, Hiroshima, Kumamoto, and Beppu. Priced at £1,890, there are two departures a year, in April and Sept. Fully escorted.

Kuoni Travel Ltd., Kuoni House, Dorking, Surrey, have put together a selection of packages to Japan and the Orient. For example, to Tokyo and Kyoto, then on to Hong Kong, Singapore, and Bangkok. 18 days (15 nights) either £1,228 or £1,281, depending on season. An extra week in Thailand, at Pattaya, is available.

Serenissima, 2 Lower Sloane St., London SW1 8BJ, another culture-vulture organization, has a specially guided art-treasure tour—19 days at £2,295.

W.F. and R.K. Swan, 237 Tottenham Court Rd., London W1P OA1, do an art-treasures tour of Japan. It lasts 18 days with a cost of £1,995. Expert guest lecturer.

JAPANESE TRAVEL AGENCIES AND TOURS. (Addresses for the agencies and companies below are given at the end of this section.) The *Japan Travel Bureau* claims to be the oldest travel agency in the Far East. This bureau offers an extensive variety of tours, conducted in English, under the legend "For People Who Like People." JTB's well-established Sunrise Tours cover Tokyo and vicinity, Kyoto and vicinity, Osaka, and Kyushu. Tours from three days to eleven days proceed from Tokyo over either the Kamakura or the Hakone routes to Kyoto. Eight- and nine-day tours include cruises through the incomparable Inland Sea. Two alternative routes in Kyushu occupy eleven and thirteen days.

JTB offers a choice of two-grade tours (Standard and Deluxe) on many of its Sunrise Tours. The tours take care of hotels, trains, coaches, sightseeing, and escorts. Any Sunrise Tour may be joined from major hotels. Most depart daily, year-round.

JTB's Sunrise Super-Saver package, designed to coincide with the Japan Rail Pass, is suggested as a way to save time and money while designing your own tour. The program covers 56 hotels in 41 cities. JTB makes the first hotel reservation; you do the rest. Upon arrival at the first hotel, travelers pick up hotel coupons for either seven or fourteen nights, along with a tour kit guidebook. Hokkaido and Okinawa participate in this program. A seven-night coupon costs ¥35,000 for half a twin room; a fourteen-night coupon costs ¥70,000.

The Fujita Travel Service calls itself Japan's largest bus tour operator. The Fujita Group owns several modern hotels along the routes of its tours; its tourists naturally stay in them. Fujita's itineraries are similar to those of JTB. Fujita's Imperial Coachman Tours are listed as regular and superexpress, traveling eastbound as well as westbound, all of varying lengths of time.

Hankyu Express and *Tobu Travel Company,* Nichido Yaesu Building, 3–4–12, Nihonbashi, Chuo, Tokyo (tel. 272–1421) offer Japan Holiday Tours on more limited scales. *Japan Gray Line* sets up the "only golf tour available in Japan."

Japan Air Lines, Tokyo Building, 2–7–3, Marunouchi, Chiyoda-ku (tel. 456–2111) has a variety of tours of Okinawan resorts. It uses its own hotels with sporting facilities that focus on the sea.

If you have a particular interest in factory inspection, cultural tours, or specialized travel, make your first approach to the *Japan National Tourist Organization,* 10th floor, Tokyo Kotsu Kaikan, 2–10–1 Yurakucho, Chiyoda-ku, Tokyo.

The following travel agencies and companies are equipped to handle all or some of your travel and related problems should you come to Japan on your own.

American Express International, Halifax Bldg., 3–16–26, Roppongi, Minato-ku, Tokyo; *Air Voyages Co.,* 1–14–4, Jingumae, Shibuya-ku, Tokyo; *Everett Travel Service,* Kokusai Bldg., 3–1–1, Marunouchi, Chiyoda-ku, Tokyo; *Fuji Tours International,* Ryuwa Bldg., 2–3–5, Yurakucho, Chiyoda-ku, Tokyo; *Fujita Travel Service,* 7–2–22, Ginza Chuo-ku, Tokyo; *Hankyu Express International,* 3–3–9, Shimbashi, Minato-ku, Tokyo; *Hanshin Electric Railway,* 2–6–20, Kyobashi, Chuo-ku, Tokyo; *Japan Gray Line,* Pelican Bldg., 3–3–3, Nishi-Shimbashi, Minato-ku, Tokyo; *Thomas Cook/Wagons-Lits,* No. 20 Mori Bldg., 2–7–4, Nishi Shimbashi, Minato-ku, Tokyo.

Japan Air Lines has an information service at 457–111 in Tokyo; *Japan Travel Bureau,* Foreign Tourist Department, 3rd fl., Goyo Kensetsu Bldg., 1–13–1, Nihonbashi, Chuo-ku, Tokyo; *Kinki Nippon Tourist,* Kintetsu Bldg., 19–2, Kanda-Matsunagacho, Chiyoda-ku, Tokyo; *Kuoni Travel,* Asahi Tokai Bldg., 2–6–1 Otemachi, Chiyoda-ku, Tokyo.

New Orient Express, Tanaka-Tamuracho Bldg., 2–12–15, Shimbashi, Minato-ku, Tokyo; *Nippon Express,* Nittu Bldg., 3–12–9, Sotokanda, Chiyoda-ku, Tokyo; *Nippon Travel Agency,* Shimojima Bldg., 1–2–17 Higashi-Shimbashi, Minato-ku, Tokyo; *Overseas Travel Service,* Shin-Yurakucho Bldg., 1–12–1, Yurakucho, Chiyoda-ku, Tokyo; *Shosenkoku,* Toyokawa Bldg., 8–12–13 Ginza, Chuo-ku; *SITA World Travel,* Hibiya Park Bldg., 1–8–1, Yurakucho, Chiyoda-ku, Tokyo; *Joe Grace's Travel Center,* 1404 Chateau Bunkyo, 1–15–19, Nishikata, Bunkyo-ku, Tokyo; *Unitours Nippon Ltd.,1–11–2, Nihonbashi, Kayaba-cho, Chuo-ku, Tokyo. Yusen Air & Sea Service,* Sanshin Bldg., 1–4–1, Yuraku-cho, Chiyoda-ku, Tokyo.

TRAVEL DOCUMENTS. Your first essential document is your passport, without which you cannot leave your own country. **U.S. residents** must apply in person to their nearest U.S. Passport Agency, or to their local county courthouse. In some areas, selected post offices are also equipped to handle passport applications. If you still have your latest passport issued within the last eight years, you may use this to apply by mail. Otherwise, take with you: (1) a birth certificate or certified copy thereof, or other proof of citizenship; (2) two identical photographs, 2½ ins. square, full face, black and white or color, on non-glossy paper and taken within the past six months; (3) $15 ($10 if you apply by mail); (4) proof of identity, such as a driver's license, previous passport, any governmental ID card. Social Security and credit cards are *not* acceptable. U.S. passports are valid for five years. If it gets lost or stolen, immediately notify either the nearest American Consul or the Passport Office, Dept of State, Washington, D.C. 20524.

If you are **not an American citizen,** but are leaving from the United States, you must have a Treasury Sailing Permit, Form 1040D, certifying that all federal taxes have been paid. Apply to your District Director of Internal Revenue for this. You will have to present various documents: (1) blue or green registration card; (2) passport; (3) travel tickets; (4) most recently filed Form 1040; (5) W-2 forms for the most recent full year; (6) most recent current payroll stubs or letter; (7) check to be sure this is all!

To return to the U.S., you need a re-entry permit *only* if you intend to remain abroad more than 364 days. If abroad less, your Alien Registration Card will get you in on return. Apply for the Re-entry Permit at least six weeks before departure in person at the nearest office of the Immigration and Naturalization Service, or by mail to the Immigration and Naturalization Service, Washington D.C. This permit entitles the noncitizen resident to stay abroad a total of two years. (Naturalized American citizens may now stay abroad an unlimited length of time, even in the country of their origin.)

Canadian citizens entering Japan must have a valid passport. In Canada, apply in person to regional passport office in your area. Or write to the Passport Office, Dept. of External Affairs, Ottawa, Ontario K1A 0G3. A $10 fee and two photographs are required. Canadian citizens living in the U.S. need special forms from their nearest Canadian consulate.

Visas. The nationals of Canada and several non-English speaking countries are exempted from visa requirements so long as they do not stay for longer than three months (six months in the case of Austria, Germany, Ireland, and the United Kingdom, among others), nor seek employment in Japan. Visas are also not required for transit passengers continuing their journey by the same or first connecting flight within 72 hours, nor for steamship passengers on overland tours of under 15 days between two ports.

Americans must obtain a visa, from any Japanese consulate. Passport photographs and confirmed air or sea passage may be required; visas are either commercial or tourist. Tourist visas are granted for varying periods (90, 120, or 180 days), allowing multiple entry and exit. Business visas will often allow a longer stay, depending on the business at hand. Tokyo Immigration Offices are at 3-3-20, Konan, Minato-ku, and on the 6th floor, World Import Mart, Sunshine City, Ikebukuro.

Tourists with permission to stay longer than 90 days must register with their local ward offices within the 90 days of entry. They are then issued with their Registration Cards. This registration is mandatory. All non-Japanese must carry their passports with them at all times until receiving Alien Registration Cards, which must then always be carried. Alien Registration Cards have to be surrendered upon leaving Japan.

CUSTOMS ENTERING. Japan is strict about firearms, pornography, and narcotics other than alcohol or tobacco. Anyone caught with drugs is liable to detention, deportation, and refusal of re-entry into Japan. The maximum sentence for possession and trafficking is five years. Certain fresh fruits, vegetables, plants, and animals are also illegal.

Duty-free allowances for nonresidents are: 3 bottles of alcohol; 200 cigarettes, 50 cigars, or 500 grams of tobacco; two ounces of perfume; two watches or clocks, each worth less than ¥30,000; and goods other than the above with a total market value not above ¥100,000. If you have possessions following you, you must fill in on arrival a "declaration of unaccompanied goods."

HOW TO GET AROUND. There is nowhere you cannot get to in Japan, where the network of air, sea, and land transport is reliable and usually comfortable. **By air.** The three major domestic airlines are *Japan Air Lines, All Nippon Airways,* and *Toa Domestic Airlines.* JAL is a major-city line; the others serve similar spots and act as feeder lines to smaller towns. The airlines try to provide English-speaking hostesses aloft and JAL, in particular, has bilingual employees at each of its terminals. Additionally, JAL staffs an Overseas Visitors' Service in the office of the Daini Tekko Building, next to the Hotel Kokusai Kanko, near the Yaesuguchi entrance to Tokyo Station. This service helps solve problems of getting around, and of getting in and out of Japan.

Both JAL and ANA use Super Jumbo (B747SR) as well as smaller aircraft. Sample fares and travel times are: Tokyo-Sapporo, ¥25,500 one way, 1 hour 30 minutes; Tokyo-Osaka, ¥15,600 one way, 55 minutes; Tokyo-Okinawa, ¥37,300 one way, 2 hours 40 minutes.

Toa Domestic Airlines (TDA) and *Nihon Kinkyori Airways* cover all-Japan routes, many of them short-hauls. *Southwest Air Lines* (SWAL) hops among the islands in the Ryukyu chain.

By boat. Japan's ferryboat and steamer network offers extensive service along coastal waters. The Inland Sea is, of course, thoroughly covered by steamer, ferry, and hydrofoil between all points. Other routes include Tokyo to Kyushu in 26 hours; Osaka to Kyushu in 14 hours; Kyoto Prefecture to Hokkaido in 26 hours; Tokyo to Kobe, Nagoya to Kyushu, and Tokyo to Hokkaido. In all, about 100 long-distance ferries operated by twenty-two companies cover twenty-eight major routes. Ferries have grades of accommodation, from cabins with private bathrooms to dormitory rooms with public facilities.

By rail. Japan is famous for having one of the finest rail systems in the world. The *Shinkansen* "bullet trains," that travel at speeds of up to 210 kilometers per hour, are reputed to be the fastest, most punctual, and safest trains in the world.

Special features of the fastest *Hikari* superexpresses include compartments for wheelchair passengers, and dining as well as buffet cars. The trains do not have baggage cars, and only limited overhead rack space. Nonsmoking accommodation is very limited.

The *Hikari* travels between Tokyo and Osaka in 3 hours 8 minutes, stopping only at Nagoya and Kyoto on the way. The *Kodama,* slower express, makes eleven stops before reaching Shin Osaka, and takes an hour longer. Neither stops for more than two minutes at any station, so you have to hurry to get on and off.

Forty-five *Hikari* superexpress trains operate daily between Tokyo and Hakata, taking 6 hours 26 minutes. Slower *Kodama* trains take 7 hours 48 minutes.

Shinkansen superexpress trains also run on the Tohoku and the Joetsu lines, both beginning from Ueno in Tokyo. The *Yamabiko* on the Tohoku line corresponds to the *Hikari,* and the *Aoba* corresponds to the *Kodama.* The *Asahi* on the Joetsu line corresponds to the *Hikari,* and the *Toki* is the equivalent of the *Kodama.* On the Tohoku line, the *Yamabiko* goes to Morioka in Iwate Prefecture, taking 3 hours 17 minutes for the 505-kilometer distance. Some *Yamabiko* trains terminate at Sendai. All *Aoba* trains terminate at Sendai except the last one of the day. On the Joetsu line, both the *Asahi* and the *Toki* terminate at Niigata. The faster *Asahi* takes 1 hour 45 minutes to cover the 303-kilometer distance.

All superexpress trains have frequent departures. Should your superexpress ever be more than two hours late, you are entitled to a refund of the express charge. An announcement in English informing foreign passengers of the refund is made on the train. If a delay of more than two hours occurs, superexpress fares are reduced 50 percent.

Hikari fares with express charges are: *Tokyo–Kyoto,* ￥11,800; green, or first class, costs an additional ￥5,400. *Tokyo–Hiroshima,* ￥16,100; green is an additional ￥7,800. *Tokyo–Hakata,* ￥19,400; green is an additional ￥7,800.

Yamabiko fares with express charges are: Ueno–Sendai, ￥8,900; green is an additional ￥4,200. Ueno–Morioka, ￥11,700; green is an additional ￥4,900.

Asahi fares with express charges are: Ueno–Nagaoka, ￥7,200; green is an additional ￥4,200. Ueno–Niigata, ￥8,700; green is an additional ￥4,200.

Telephone calls may be made to and from the bullet trains. From Tokyo or Yokohama, the number is 248–9311. The minimum charge is ￥300 for the first three minutes.

Calls made to the Tohoku and Joetsu lines from Tokyo are made by dialing 248–9311. From other areas, the number for the Tohoku line is 0222 67–6131; for the Joetsu line, it is 0252 22–9191.

Leisurely rail trips can be made on the older lines, which provide credible cover of the Japanese islands. So long as you get a seat, which on the long-distance trains is only a question of reserving in advance, railroad travel has much to commend it.

Several private railroad lines in the Tokyo and Kyoto–Osaka areas offer excellent service, mostly to resort areas, occasionally also to distant cities. Around Tokyo are two popular private lines, the **Tobu** line to Nikko, and the **Odakyu** route to Hakone, both using air-conditioned "romance" cars. These, like other private lines, are on an all-reserved, one-class basis and have refreshment stands on each train.

In the Kansai area, the **Kinki Nippon Railway** provides service between Osaka and Nagoya through a scenic route, and operates a fine train from Osaka to Nara.

Japan Rail Passes for tourists coming to Japan are sold at overseas offices of JAL, JTB, and Nippon Ryoko. Holders of the tickets may travel on any JNR train to anywhere in Japan for seven, fourteen, or twenty-one days. These tickets cost ￥25,000, ￥41,000, and ￥53,000 for regular coach travel. Green car passes cost ￥35,000 for seven days, ￥58,000 for fourteen days, and ￥76,000

By car. Foreign tourists with international driving licenses may drive in Japan. Few want to, because of the congestion on the roads, unfamiliarity with local road customs, and paucity of English-language signs. Japan observes a driving-on-the-left rule of the road. The Japan Automobile Federation does have a "Manual for Drivers and Pedestrians" printed in English, and road maps in the Roman alphabet are available at large bookstores.

A continuous freeway drive exists between Tokyo and Kumamoto Prefecture in Kyushu. This consists of three expressways known as the Tomei (Tokyo to Nagoya), the Meishin (Nagoya to Kobe), and the Chugoku (Kobe to Kano) that then link with the Kyushu Expressway. When two additional sectors are completed, the entire freeway system will run from Aomori, the northernmost prefecture in Honshu, to Kagoshima, the southernmost prefecture in Kyushu.

Tolls for a medium-size car traveling on the continuous freeway between Tokyo and Kumamoto are ¥20,700. When the fuel cost is added, the 16-hour drive costs more than ¥40,000. This is about ¥10,000 more than the air fare between the two points.

Japan has over 150 rent-a-car agencies, and a very wide variety of vehicles is available. Rental rates, excluding gasoline and mileage charges, are from about ¥5,000 for half a day. There are plenty of gasoline stations everywhere, selling regular gasoline at ¥160 per liter. They are closed on Sundays and national holidays, and it is illegal to carry containers of spare gasoline in your car.

Hiring a car with a driver is expensive, about ¥5,000 per hour, but possible. Usually drivers do not speak English. If you want to use a car with driver and an English-speaking escort for a day's sightseeing trip, your hotel can make arrangements for you.

By bus. Japanese National Railways operate all-night bus services on expressways, setting out from the Yaesuguchi side of Tokyo Station. From Tokyo to Osaka takes about 9½ hours and costs ¥8,200 for a reserved seat. To reserve, call 215–0489.

Pedestrians please note: When you are crossing a road in Japan, look to the right first and then to the left before stepping out into traffic. Keep-to-the-left is the rule for vehicles and for pedestrians, except where there is no sidewalk; then you walk on the right so that you face vehicular traffic.

Public transportation. City trains, subways, and buses are highly organized and efficient in Japan. They are also always crowded. It can be really difficult finding your way to the line you want in the mazes of big interchange stations in the biggest cities. Buying your ticket can also be a hurdle. Never hesitate to ask when you need guidance. Although Japanese people often stumble in their attempts at English, they always want to help and somehow will find a way.

At least most railway stations have names in English. Buses rarely do and are much more difficult for strangers to use.

Taxis. Taxis can be essential to your comfort during some part of your stay. Minimum charge for the first 2 kilometers is ¥470, with an ¥80 increase for every 405 meters, and a time charge when held up. After 11:00 P.M., the rate increases by 20 percent. There are taxi stands at designated points, or you can flag a cruising taxi. Pick one with a red sign in the windshield; this indicates that the cab is vacant. The driver opens and closes the passenger door by remote control, so take care to stand clear.

Note: Taxi drivers often genuinely do not know destinations, so you have to be able to direct them. It is better to set out with written instructions from your hotel. Drivers do not expect tips. It's also a good idea to carry a card from your hotel so that you can get back without trouble.

Some terms in general use in addresses:

-ken	prefecture (state)
-shi	city
-ku	ward
-machi	district within a ward, or a town
-chome	a block or group of blocks within a *ku* or a *machi*
-ban	"number," meaning a house or building number

Some other common geographical terms:

-kawa or *-gawa*	river
-wan	bay
-bashi or *-hashi*	bridge
-ko	lake
-yama	mountain
sen	line (rail, bus, or subway)
eki	station
kita	north
minami	south
nishi	west
higashi	east

MONEY. Japanese currency floats without a fixed official exchange rate between the yen and the U.S. dollar or the pound sterling or other currencies. Foreign currencies can be converted at banks and hotels and some shops. You may reconvert from Japanese yen to your original currency.

Traveler's checks and credit cards are safe and simple ways to carry money. Personal checks are completely useless in Japan. Many establishments honor the credit cards of organizations such as American Express, Barclaycard, Diners Club, MasterCard, Visa, and Carte Blanche. Traveler's checks are sold by banks and agencies. Amongst those widely used are those of the Bank of America, Cook's, and American Express. Japan's Bank of Tokyo and Fuji Bank sell traveler's checks in yen at their offices in the United States.

Japanese money is issued in ¥10,000, ¥5,000, ¥1,000, and ¥500 notes. There are silver ¥500, ¥100, and ¥50 yen coins. The ¥10 yen coin is copper in color, and the ¥5 bronze. ¥1 coins, that are practically without value, are aluminum.

It is a good idea upon arrival in Japan to acquire a good stock of 100 yen and 50 yen coins. You'll need these constantly for local transport fares and vending machines.

Note: All prices mentioned in this book are indicative of costs at press time. We suggest that you keep an eye open for fluctuations in exchange rates while planning your trip—and while on it. Presstime, U.S. $1.00 = ¥235.

HOTELS AND INNS. Hotel reservations should be made well in advance to avoid any disappointment with a room which you have to take on short notice. A good rule is to have your travel agent request your hotel accommodation at least three months prior to arrival. It is possible to make quick bookings up to seven days before arrival at several of Japan's top hotels, through Japan Travel Bureau International in the U.S., New York, Los Angeles, San Francisco, Honolulu.

You can confidently expect to find service and accommodation superlative in the upper categories of hotels and inns, and accommodation good and clean in the lesser-priced establishments that don't offer service. Hotel construction continues apace in Japan, resulting in superb buildings with advanced facilities. Japan's best luxury hotels without doubt qualify for leading world class status in terms of service and elegance.

Except for the super deluxe class of hotels, prices in major cities and in popular resorts are not markedly different from Tokyo's. Our listings in each chapter offer a range of prices from top to bottom.

Cheaper travel has two important elements to recommend it: the unfailing sense of hospitality of the average person, and the acceptable standards of sanitation that are the norm in Japan. Cheaper travel carries you closer to the people in everyday life, and is very likely to open up the way for you to have more fun as you gain deeper insights. It is still possible, even in Tokyo, to find clean, unadorned rooms in simple hotels for as little as ¥4,000 per head per night. If you don't mind bunks or dormitory accommodation, you can pay even less.

Business hotels, hostels, and cheaper inns usually include tax and service charges in their rates. Major hotels do not. The tax levied is 10 percent of your total bill, minus ¥1,500 per head per night, and service charges are 15 percent. Tax is not levied on bills under ¥4,000. If your dining bills are separate and paid after each meal, you are not liable for tax until you go over ¥2,500.

The descriptions below will give you some idea of the types of low-cost accommodation available in Japan.

Business Hotels. These are connected with the Japan Business Hotel Association and provide convenient and inexpensive accommodation for pleasure travelers as well as for business people. Service is not provided. Expect to pay ¥5,000 per person per night, and be pleased if you get a lower rate.

Minshuku. These are private homes that accept paying guests for overnight stays. Each visitor or group is accommodated in a private room, but all guests come together around the family dining table. Guests are expected to lay their bedding at night, to provide their own toilet gear and nightwear, and to tidy up in the morning. Minshuku charge about ¥5,000 per person per night with two meals. Reservations have to be made in advance, and that is not easy to do until you get to Japan. You could begin by communicating with the *Japan Minshuku Association* at 201, New Pearl Building, 2–10–8, Hyakunin-cho, Shinjuku-ku, Tokyo, and asking for a list of their 25,000 minshuku throughout Japan and the addresses of different reservation centers.

Inns. Those registered with the Japanese Group Inns are moderately priced —not high-class, but friendly, hospitable, and economical. You touch the Japanese way of living here, since the rooms are floored with straw tatami mats, and you sleep on quilts on the floors. You join in the Japanese bathing habit, too (see under *Staying in a Ryokan,* below). Expect to pay ¥4,500, and to buy breakfast and dinner separately.

Kokumin Shukusha. These are public lodgings built in scenic places or national park areas known for their natural beauty. Many are operated by the Ministry of Health and Welfare, and some are privately operated lodgings authorized by the National Park Association. Lodging is a standard ¥4,800 a day with two meals. Advance reservations can be made through the Japan Travel Bureau.

Kokumin Kyuka Mura. Vacation villages established in a number of different locations, they are government run, they usually offer recreational facilities, and they are open to foreign visitors. Overnight stay with two meals is about ¥6,000. Advance reservations should be made through a Japan Travel Bureau office or, once you are in Japan, through a Kokumin Kyuka Mura Service Center. The *Tokyo Service Center* is on the 1st floor, Tokyo Kotsu Kaikan, 2–13, Yurakucho, Chiyoda-ku; the *Osaka Service Center* is on the 1st floor, Sho Daimaru Building, 2–12, Shinsaibashisuji, Minami-ku; the *Nagoya Service Center* is on the 1st floor, Chunichi Building, 1–6, Shin Sakaecho, Naka-ku.

Youth Hostels. Visitors who are not already members in their own countries ṇay apply for international guest cards, which cost ¥ 3,000, at the *Japan Youth Ĩostels* national office, Hoken Kaikan, 1–1, Sadohara-cho, Ichigaya, Shinjuku-:u, Tokyo 162. There is no upper age limit for people wanting to stay at youth ;ostels. Advance booking is indicated, and travelers should be checked in before 9:00 P.M. Stay in any one hostel is restricted to three consecutive nights. The standard overnight charge is around ¥ 2,700, with sheet rental, baths, supper, and breakfast costing extra.

Temples. Japan Travel Bureau offices accept reservations for lodgings in temples, called *shukubo.* The charge is about ¥ 5,000. In a temple you expect to have a simple, tatami-matted room and be served vegetarian dishes, similar to the priests' regular fare, for supper and breakfast. You will be offered a shared bathroom, and will sleep on quilts spread on the floor. You will be invited to join in the early morning Buddhist service, but it is not compulsory.

Pensions. These constitute another type of low-cost accommodation in the countryside. They usually are small-scale Western-style hotels with about 10 bathless rooms. The average charge per person is ¥ 6,000 for bed and breakfast. Apply through the *Japan Pension Center,* 6–3–9, Minami Aoyama, Minato-ku, Tokyo; 407–2333.

Camping. A limited number of "auto camping sites" exist across the nation. Apply to the *Japan Auto Camping Association,* New Ueno Building, 7th floor, 1–24, Yotsuya, Shinjuku-ku, Tokyo, for details.

It is unlikely that you will find much English spoken in any of the money-saving facilities listed above. JNTO's dictionary, "The Tourist's Handbook," can be of inestimable help together with goodwill, which goes a long way to breaking down the language barrier.

 STAYING IN A RYOKAN. Japanese inns, conjuring up the atmosphere and sentiments of bygone days, illustrate the uniqueness of old-style Japan. You should try to spend at least one night in a traditional Japanese inn and experience the kind of living that otherwise you only read about. But forget about the notion that inns are cheaper than Western-style hotels!

In the truly traditional inn you will be surrounded by the exquisite simplicity of Japanese design: translucent paper windows, sliding doors, mat floors, alcoves, corridors of polished natural wood, delicate gardens. Everything will be immaculate. A Japanese inn is an expanded version of the typical old-fashioned home in this country. With the exception of the modern structures, the inn will be constructed of wood, stucco, and tile, the only paper in evidence being that used to cover the window panes and the dividing panels between rooms. Usually one or two stories in height, the rooms are all traditional style with matted flooring, sliding walls, and low-slung furniture.

Certain practices remain constant whether you stay in an expensive or a cheap inn. You leave your shoes at the entrance and wear the slippers that the inn provides. You leave your slippers at the entrance to your room, and inside the room wear just your socks or stockings, or go barefoot. Probably in the room you will be asked to sign the inn's register and be given green tea. You wear your slippers again when you go to the toilet, where once more you leave the slippers outside the door and wear the footwear provided inside the toilet.

Should you have a room with its own toilet, you should similarly observe this footwear-changing custom. It has its origins in cleanliness and hygiene, and is strictly followed in the home as in the inn.

The inn provides you with its own *yukata* (summertime cotton kimono) plus, in cold weather, a heavier overjacket. You may change at once out of your own clothing and wear the inn's garments in your room, along the passages, in the public rooms, if there are any, and even out in the street if you have the nerve. If you do venture outside, you should wear your normal underwear under your yukata, and complete your outfit by wearing the inn's wooden clogs (geta). The yukata serves also as your sleep garment.

Bathing. The inn probably expects you to check in late in the afternoon and to have your bath as soon as you've settled in. Many inns have large public bathrooms as their main attractions. Some have private bathrooms attached to the rooms. In either case, you are expected to follow the Japanese bathing practice. Undress, and leave your clothing in baskets, or lockers, in the changing room outside the bathroom. Take your towel (a small one, provided by the inn) and your soap, and go through the door into the bathroom, closing the door behind you.

Especially in hot-spring resorts, bathrooms are big and often very beautiful with rock surrounds and ingenious decorations. The bath can resemble a small, ornate swimming pool. Nowadays, sexes are usually segregated, but not always. There is no need to be reluctant to go to a public bathroom. No one takes any notice of anyone else, so accustomed are the Japanese to their bathhouses and bathing procedures. Innkeepers, however, have become used to the hesitation of non-Japanese and, if they are able, perhaps will arrange for you to have a bathroom to yourself for half an hour or so. This kind of special consideration depends upon the nature of the inn and its facilities.

Inside the bathroom, everyone behaves as modestly as possible and gets on with the important task of getting clean. You have the use of small stools on which to sit and small tubs that you fill with washing water. You do all your washing and rinsing, from top to toe, on the tiled floor outside the bath, and pour away your used water there. Only when you are squeaking clean and free from any trace of soap do you get into the bath, just to sit and enjoy.

Japanese people like their bathwater to be hot, usually much hotter than Westerners are used to. The trick of getting into scalding water is to avoid disturbing it too much. Just slide in and keep still; and don't stay too long.

Since bathwater is heated once a day, toward late afternoon, bathrooms are freshest—and hottest—at this time. Unless your inn has a hot spring, you should not expect the bathroom to be functioning in the morning. The evening is for bathing.

In many ryokans you can order a masseur or masseuse for after your bath.

Dining. By the time you get back to your room from your bath, your room maid will be setting up your dinner. This is usually served in your room on the low table. You sit on cushions on the floor (some inns provide back rests) and use chopsticks for the variety of food spread before you. You don't get a menu. Dinner courses are set.

Japanese inns with their peculiarities are having to find ways of solving modern problems. Old ways have the tug of nostalgia, but running an inn in the old way is becoming economically unviable. Labor is the prime difficulty. The work of an inn, maintained in an old way, is hard, and the ratio of maids to numbers of guests and rooms is high. Among the interesting compromises quite often encountered nowadays is the use of a public dining room for breakfast. Breakfast always used to be brought to the room as, in most cases, dinner still is. Labor is saved in the mornings if everyone goes to the food, instead of the other way around.

Many establishments are willing to give you a Western-style breakfast. You'll be better off staying with a Japanese breakfast, which is surer ground for innkeepers. Among local horror stories is that of the eggs and bacon fried the night before, kept in the refrigerator, and carried frozen hard straight to the breakfast table.

In the evening. After dinner, the maid clears away everything, including the table itself, and takes bedding from a cupboard. She makes up your beds, one for each person in your family, on the floor, wishes you a good night, and goes away. You will be sleeping on two or more mattresses, which may be of cotton or foam rubber, and under one or more layers of Japanese quilts, called futon. The pillow is usually small and hard. If it doesn't suit you, you may take the cushion you have been sitting on, fold it double and wrap a clean towel around it, fastening it with a pin.

You are left to your own devices for the rest of the evening. There may be a television set in your room, perhaps one into which you will have to feed ¥100 coins for one-hour programs. There is unlikely to be a bilingual service.

Modernization. In many ways, modernization means improvement. Japanese people themselves can no longer tolerate the extremes of heat and cold that they used to. So unless you are out to rough it, you can be hopeful of temperature-controlling devices in Japanese rooms, if not yet in the passageways. Rooms are normally screened, also, to keep the insects outside. And quite often room doors are outfitted with locks; that never was the case in the past. Flush toilets are more common than they used to be; again, it depends on where you are staying.

Cost. Costs in Japanese inns are capable of wide variations. An innkeeper himself has a hard time explaining his system. The charges for a room depend, understandably, upon its size, decor, and the view it commands. But these charges change with season, time of the month, and even day of the week. This practice is not chicanery. It's just the way it's done.

The charges for dinner and breakfast are similarly subject to change. You may be quoted an A course, a B course, and a C course, for room and two meals, per head, from, say, ¥12,000 to ¥20,000. The differences between the courses will be accounted for by the number of dishes or the kinds of foods. It is hard to find out exactly what these differences are. It is better for you to decide by price and take what comes. Your innkeeper will always want to impress you by serving the best. He thinks you deserve it.

Of course anything you order separately, such as sake or beer, will be charged separately. Conversely, inns will sometimes allow you to stay without taking meals at all. Then you will be charged only the room price, plus tax and service charges.

LAUNDRY. Top-class hotels take care of your laundry and dry cleaning in 24 hours if it is urgent, in two to three days otherwise. Coin-operated laundries exist in residential districts. Often public bathhouses have a washing machine or two, where your laundry gets swished around while you're in the tub.

DINING OUT. Restaurants often have set lunches which are much cheaper, and quicker-served, than both à la carte dishes and dinners. Exquisite Japanese food is as costly as gourmet Western food, but everyday Japanese dishes, available everywhere, are inexpensive, low in fat content, and moderate in calories. Japanese green tea is usually included with ordinary Japanese fare. Cheap restaurants have show windows with attractive wax models of the dishes they offer, and prices are clearly marked. Scout around among the dining rooms of department stores, restaurants in big office buildings, and in underground shopping arcades.

 TIPPING is not customary in Japan. The service charge that is added to hotel and restaurant bills takes the place of individual tipping. Taxi drivers are not tipped. Prices are set for porters. Some beauty parlors post notices asking patrons not to tip. Japanese people dislike being treated as if they were beggars, and tipping, to them, places them in this category.

On the other hand, little gifts are never wrong as tokens of appreciation for any special services willingly given. Never forget to say "thank you." Simple politeness goes a long way.

 BUSINESS HOURS, HOLIDAYS, AND LOCAL TIME. Banks, business houses, and government offices are closed on Sundays each week. Banks are open from 9:00 A.M.–3:00 P.M. from Monday to Friday, and until noon on Saturdays. They are not open on the second Saturday of the month. Business houses and government offices are open from 9:00 A.M.–5:00 P.M. from Monday to Friday and until noon on Saturdays. Some business houses observe a five-day week; and the post office does not handle money or insurance business on the second Saturday of each month. Department stores are open from 10:00 A.M.–6:00 P.M. and usually take a weekday holiday instead of Sunday. Local shops often stay open until 9:00 P.M. and do not take regular holidays.

Japan has twelve national holidays in a year. These are:

January. *New Year's Day,* January 1. In most cities and towns, the ladies put on their best kimonos and go out to their family shrines, or else the most fashionable temples, and pay their respects to their ancestors, and admire each other's attire. Children go out with their fathers to fly kites. National holiday. Most shops, stores and offices closed through January 3.

Adults' Day on the 15th, to honor youth who have reached voting age, which is 20 in Japan. National holiday, but no special observances, usually.

February. *National Foundation Day,* on the 11th. National holiday celebrating accession to the throne of the first emperor, Jimmu.

March. On the 3rd, *Girls' Day,* while not a holiday, is observed in most homes, the girls displaying sets of expensive dolls (never played with), and receiving congratulations from the relatives. You will see sets of these dolls in some public places on display.

Vernal Equinox Day, a national holiday to celebrate the coming of Spring. Visit to ancestral graves. Celebrated on the 20th or 21st.

April. *The Emperor's Birthday,* on the 29th, is a national holiday, and the beginning of "Golden Week." There being two more national holidays in the space of a week, business comes to a standstill at this time, and everyone tries to go touring around the country.

May. *Constitution Day* to commemorate promulgation of the country's new, peaceful, basic law, a postwar creation. National holiday held on the 3rd.

Children's Day, formerly called Boys' Day. From bamboo poles families hang cloth streamers in the shape of the carp, which symbolize strength. Also a national holiday.

September. *Respect for the Aged Day.* National holiday, on the 15th.

Autumnal Equinox Day, to celebrate the first day of autumn and to venerate one's ancestors. National holiday, held on the 23rd.

October. *Sports Day.* A new national holiday, on the 10th, commemorates the Tokyo Olympics of 1964.

November. *Culture Day,* on the 3rd, is a national holiday which is supposed to encourage the people to love peace, freedom and culture, but on which nothing much happens except that the people rest. Before the war, this day was celebrated as the Emperor Meiji's Birthday, and many older people today still visit Meiji Shrine in Tokyo to pay respect to the memory of the great man who brought Japan into the community of nations.

Labor Thanksgiving Day, also a national holiday held on the 23rd. Frequently combined with celebrations of a good harvest in the countryside but in itself merely a special day of rest. Before war's defeat brought about the disestablishment of the Shinto religion, this day was a national holiday of Thanksgiving only. Then as now, the emperor offers new rice wine (sake) fermented from this year's crop, to the gods.

Time in Japan is 10 hours ahead of Greenwich Mean Time, and 15 hours ahead of Eastern Daylight Savings Time.

THE JAPANESE CALENDAR. The Japanese year is often indicated by the reign of the emperor. This year is the 60th year of the Showa (the formal name for Emperor Hirohito).

CHERRY AND PLUM BLOSSOMS. Here is our list of recommended blossom-viewing spots and dates: **Plum blossoms:** *mid-February to mid-March*—Tokyo area, especially Yushima Tenjin Shrine in Bunkyo Ward, and Okutama-Yoshino on the Tama River: also at Baien in Atami; *late February to late March*—Kairakuen Park in Mito City, just north of Tokyo about 3 hours by train. Irises and hydrangeas bloom in June. Chrysanthemums flower and maple leaves turn color in October/November.

Cherry blossoms: *late January*—Okinawa; *late March*—Shikoku Island, especially Dogo Spa, Kochi Park and Kotahira Shrine. Duration 3 weeks; *late March*—Kyushu, especially Kijima Plateau near Beppu; *beg. April*—Tokyo area, especially suburbs at Koganei, Tama Cemetery, and Inokashira Park. About 2 weeks. In downtown Tokyo, Shinjuku and Ueno parks, Aoyama Cemetery, Yasukuni Shrine, and the new Garden Road promenade near the Fairmont Hotel). *Beg. April*—Shonan, especially Kinugasa Park near Yokosuka. 2 weeks; *mid-April*—Kyoto, especially Heian Shrine, Ninnaji Temple, and Arashiyama Park. About 2 weeks; *mid-April*—Chiba-Kanto area, especially Lake Sayama, Nagatoro Gorge, and Sanrizuka (near Narita). Duration about 2 weeks; *3rd week of April*—Fuji-Hakone area, especially Mt. Horai at Kowakidani, Sengokuhara, and Miyanoshita. Duration 3 weeks; *late April*—Mt. Yoshino near Nara, and Ise Shrine. About 3 weeks; *late April*—Tohoku, especially Matsushima and Morioka. Duration 3 weeks; *early May*—Hokkaido, especially at Hakodate's Goryokaku Park.

COMMUNICATIONS. Telephones. Along the streets you'll find blue and green public pay telephones in booths, and red pay telephones in front of some shops. A local call costs ¥10 for 3 minutes. Insert another ¥10 coin before the time is up to keep going. The larger red telephones are for long distance calls, and they accept up to ¥60 at a time. There is no time limit on domestic long-distance calls, but you must keep feeding in ¥10 coins at intervals of a few seconds. Yellow long-distance telephones take ¥100 coins at a time. Green telephones accept special telephone cards as well as coins. If you do not know the area code, dial 100 for long-distance service, and 104 for information, in Japanese.

Overseas calls: book your calls at your hotel through the operator. From area codes 03 (Tokyo), 045 (Yokohama), 052 (Nagoya), 06 (Osaka), 075 (Kyoto) and 078 (Kobe), dial 0051 only. From area codes beginning 072–074, 076–079, and 082–089, dial (06) 945–1122. From Okinawa, dial (0988) 66–0011. From other area codes, to Asian countries, dial (03) 211–4211. To U.S.A., Europe and other areas, dial (03) 211–5511. For station-to-station calls, rates are lower than personal calls. For a collect call, give the number and the operator will connect you if the party agrees to pay the charge. This service is available between Japan and U.S.A., Canada, Korea (Republic of), Hong Kong, Taiwan, Australia and European countries. Charges to Europe are ¥2,490 on weekdays for 3 minutes, to the U.S.A. ¥1,980. Sunday calls to the U.S.A. are discounted a few percent. Subscribers registered with KDD can make calls much cheaper through direct dialing, with a charge unit of six seconds. Check with your hotel.

Mail rates vary according to destination. These are:

	Asia, Australia	Canada, U.S.A.	Europe
Air mail letter			
up to 10 grams	¥130	¥150	¥170
for each extra 10 grams	¥70	¥90	¥110
Air mail post card	¥90	¥100	¥110
Aerogram	¥120	¥120	¥120

Ordinary **cablegrams** are ¥118 per word to the United States, and almost ¥200 per word to most of Europe. Seven words is the minimum. Urgent telegrams may be sent at double the ordinary rate. Letter telegrams, somewhat slower, are about half the ordinary rate. Minimum of 22 words.

ELECTRIC CURRENT. Hotels usually have outlets for 100 volts only. Eastern Japan including Tokyo is on a 50-cycle basis, western Japan including Kyoto and Osaka is on 60 cycles. The dividing line between eastern and western is roughly halfway between Tokyo and Nagoya, near the city of Shizuoka.

HINTS TO HANDICAPPED TRAVELERS. Language Service Volunteers of the Japanese Red Cross have published a book: *Accessible Tokyo.* A copy of this, from 1–1–3, Shiba Daimon, Minato-ku, Tokyo, will be of great assistance to a traveler on crutches or in a wheelchair.

MEDICAL TREATMENT. The *International Association for Medical Assistance to Travelers* is a worldwide association offering a list of approved English-speaking doctors, whose training meets British and American standards. Write to IAMAT, 736 Center St., Lewiston, NY 14092. In Japan IAMAT has member hospitals or clinics in Tokyo, Yokohama, Osaka, Kyoto, Kobe, Hiroshima and Okinawa. The fixed fees are: office calls $20; house and hotel calls $30; weekends, holidays, nights $35. Other IAMAT offices are: in Canada at 123 Edward Street, Toronto, Ontario MGE 1B9; in Europe at Gotthardstrasse 17, 6300 Zug, Switzerland; in Australia at St. Vincent's Hospital, Victoria Parade, Melbourne 3065.

SECURITY. In this country of low crime rate, you still need to take reasonable precautions. Leave your valuables in hotel safe-keeping—there is no sense offering temptation. Lost property often finds a way back to the owner if it is clearly labeled with name and address; small items are often recoverable from where they were left (if you can remember where you put them down), from Lost Property offices of railways and taxi companies, or from local police boxes.

Emergency numbers, dialed without charge from public telephones, are: 110 for police; 119 for fire services and ambulances. Such calls have to be made in Japanese.

 CUSTOMS DEPARTING. Americans who are out of the United States at least 48 hours and have claimed no exemption during the previous 30 days are now able to bring in $300 worth of purchases duty-free (up from $100). For the next $600 worth of goods beyond the first $300, inspectors will assess a flat 10 percent duty, rather than hitting you with different percentages for various types of goods. The value of each item is determined by the price actually paid (so keep your receipts). All items purchased must accompany the passenger on his return. Every member of the family is entitled to this exemption, regardless of age, and the allowance can be pooled.

Not more than 200 cigarettes, or one carton, may be included in your duty-free exemption, nor more than a quart of wine or liquor (none at all if your passport indicates you are from a "dry" state or are under 21 years old). Only one bottle of perfume that is trademarked in the U.S. may be brought in, plus a reasonable quantity of other brands.

Antiques are defined, for customs purposes, as articles manufactured over 100 years ago and are admitted duty-free. If there's any question of age, you may be asked to supply proof.

It is illegal to bring into the U.S. foreign meats, plants, fruit, soil, etc., without permission as they can spread destructive diseases. Write for the pamphlet, *Travelers' Tips,* Program Aid 1083 to: Treasury Department, Office of Regional Commissioner of Customs, Region II, Custom House, New York, NY 10048. In the last several years a large number of birds, animals and marine mammals have also come under protection as endangered species, and cannot be brought into the U.S.

British Customs. British subjects may import the following goods, duty-free: 200 cigarettes, or 100 cigarillos, or 50 cigars, or 250 grams tobacco; plus one liter of alcohol of more than 22 percent proof, or 2 liters of alcohol not more than 22 percent proof, or 2 liters of fortified or sparkling wine and 2 liters of still table wine; plus 50 grams of perfume and ¼ liter of toilet water; plus other goods to the value of £28.

Canada. Residents of Canada, after 7 days away, may, upon written declaration, claim an exemption of $150 per calendar year plus an allowance of 40 ounces of liquor, 50 cigars, 200 cigarettes, and 2 pounds of tobacco. For details ask for Canada Customs brochure, "I Declare."

Australia. Duty-free allowances include 200 cigarettes or 250 grams of cigars and tobacco, and one liter of liquor. Dutiable goods to the value of A$200 included in personal baggage are also duty free. Additional items to the value of A$160 are dutiable at 20 percent. New Zealand regulations are similar.

Everyone. If you have brought with you any foreign-made articles such as cameras, binoculars, expensive timepieces, it is wise to have receipts from the retailer showing that the items were bought in your home country. If you bought such articles on previous holidays abroad, and have already paid duty, carry with you those relevant receipts. Otherwise, on returning home, you may be charged duty again—and for British residents, VAT as well.

As you leave Japan, you must not carry anything with you that resembles a weapon, even if it is a pair of scissors. All baggage is searched to reduce hijacking risks.

"Using the airport" fee, collected at the check-in counters, is ¥2,000 per adult and ¥1,000 per child aged 12 years and under.

CONVERTING METRIC TO U.S. MEASUREMENTS

Multiply:	by:	to find:
Length		
millimeters (mm)	.039	inches (in)
meters (m)	3.28	feet (ft)
meters	1.09	yards (yd)
kilometers (km)	.62	miles (mi)
Area		
hectare (ha)	2.47	acres
Capacity		
liters (L)	1.06	quarts (qt)
liters	.26	gallons (gal)
liters	2.11	pints (pt)
Weight		
gram (g)	.04	ounce (oz)
kilogram (kg)	2.20	pounds (lb)
metric ton (MT)	.98	tons (t)
Power		
kilowatt (kw)	1.34	horsepower (hp)
Temperature		
degrees Celsius	9/5 (then add 32)	degrees Fahrenheit

CONVERTING U.S. TO METRIC MEASUREMENTS

Multiply:	by:	to find:
Length		
inches (in)	25.40	millimeters (mm)
feet (ft)	.30	meters (m)
yards (yd)	.91	meters
miles (mi)	1.61	kilometers (km)
Area		
acres	.40	hectares (ha)
Capacity		
pints (pt)	.47	liters (L)
quarts (qt)	.95	liters
gallons (gal)	3.79	liters
Weight		
ounces (oz)	28.35	grams (g)
pounds (lb)	.45	kilograms (kg)
tons (t)	1.11	metric tons (MT)
Power		
horsepower (hp)	.75	kilowatts
Temperature		
degrees Fahrenheit	5/9 (after subtracting 32)	degrees Celsius

INTRODUCTION TO JAPAN

by
JOHN B. HANSON-LOWE

A retired exploration geologist who has lived in Japan for 23 years, John B. Hanson-Lowe has been a book reviewer for the Japan Times, *is a fifth kudo at judo, and has published articles on judo in several countries.*

High travel costs and limited leisure compel many tourists visiting Japan from afar to join tours led by guides who are competent but shackled by fixed schedules and itineraries; and even visitors less restricted in their means often tend to visit only standard localities that "must be seen." Despite the fact that they realize so much in Japan is westernized, contemporary, many people have the feeling that it is a vaguely mysterious country with a fearsomely difficult language and writing system, strange customs such as sleeping on the floor, and repellent foods such as raw fish—and they find every inducement to go only where customary creature comforts and people who can speak their language can be found: to Tokyo, Nikko, Kyoto, perhaps Hiroshima. Rather than return home with blurred memories, limited only to the safest tourist destinations, why not take courage and explore areas outside the major cities as well?

26

Tokyo and Kyoto need little introduction, and are covered in detail later in this book. Below, we have tried to provide a brief introduction to some of Japan's less frequented, but thoroughly worthwhile, tourist destinations.

Geography and Climate

Before deciding where to travel in Japan, consider for a moment some major geographical features of the country. Japan consists of a long chain of about 3,900 islands and islets on the eastern margin of Asia, stretching roughly 1,730 miles from the north of Honshu to the southernmost island of Yonaguni east of Taiwan, almost on the Tropic of Cancer. A second line of small islands stretches from southeastern-most Honshu to the Ogasawara Islands, although the easternmost island, Minamitori, lies just north of that Tropic. By far the largest islands are Honshu, followed by Hokkaido, Kyushu, and Shikoku, covering in all some 140,000 square miles, with an *average* elevation of almost 1,000 feet and some 80 percent of them very mountainous. Mountain chains strike approximately along the axial lines of the islands, and are studded with volcanoes, active ones numbering about sixty. There is very little flatland; coastlines are highly indented.

A map of the *entire* western chain of islands, if superimposed on a map of eastern North America at the same latitudes, would stretch from Montreal well into the southwestern part of the Gulf of Mexico; and if superimposed on Western Europe and Africa it would stretch from Lyons to northeast Mauritania. Other major climatic factors apart, such a great latitudinal distance would guarantee very marked differences in climate between the northernmost and southernmost islands of Japan. Major elements in controlling Japan's climate are: the fact that the trend of the mountain chains is at right angles to the direction of the prevailing winds (the cold northwest monsoon in winter and the warm, humid southeast monsoon in summer); the presence of both warm and cold sea currents passing along Japan's shores; and the typhoons that are generally active between July and September. During the gradual change from the northwest to the southeast monsoon from early June until mid-July, the occasionally heavy "plum rains" *(tsuyu* or *baiu)* are unpleasant for the traveler, although important for rice farming.

Areas facing the Pacific exhibit marked climatic contrasts compared with those facing the Sea of Japan. Broadly speaking, Hokkaido is characterized by a humid, continental (i.e., having a large annual temperature range) climate; most of Honshu has a very humid, continental climate; that of Kyushu and Shikoku together with the Kinki district of Honshu is moist continental, becoming increasingly subtropical toward the south, and definitely so in the southernmost islands, including the Ogasawaras.

As there is a high annual *average* rainfall of 70 inches, it is not surprising that most of the country is forest covered. The north is a boreal (having short summers and snowy winters), coniferous zone; farther south, a zone of cool temperate, broad-leaved deciduous trees extends, and yet farther south there is a zone of warm, temperate evergreen (laurel) vegetation. Obviously, change in elevation of the land in a given zone modifies this simplified description. Southernmost Kyushu, as well as the Ryukyu and Ogasawara islands, are characterized by subtropical vegetation. Natural forests in Honshu and to the south have been replaced to a considerable extent by cryptomeria, Japanese cypress, pines, and so forth.

During the last phase of the Pleistocene glaciation, which ended some 10,000 to 12,000 years B.C., so much seawater was locked up in the ice that worldwide sea level was sufficiently lowered to expose land bridges between Siberia and north Japan, and between south Korea and south Japan. It is thus conceivable that Neolithic people crossed into Japan from mainland Asia; in any case, the earliest relics found are of that age. It must be stressed that there is no Japanese race, but an ethnic complex including Mongolian groups, Malay Negritos, and bearded Caucasian Ainus—round eyed, light skinned and with flattened cheekbones.

Hokkaido

To return to the matter of finding off-the-beaten-track areas, it is clearly not possible to do more here than indicate just a few; but certainly Hokkaido, Japan's "Far West," must rank high in any list. This island, unique in the country, is ideal territory for the lover of the open air, the hiker, the fisherman, the swimmer, the climber, the birdwatcher, and in winter the skier. There are splendid mountains, active volcanoes (e.g., Io, Esan, and Showa Shinzan, dating from 1945), glorious mountain lakes, forests that occupy some 70 percent of the area, green pastoral meadows with horses and cattle; and when the winter snow melts, the wildflowers are dazzling. There are bears and wild deer, and a few hundred red-crested cranes in the Kushiro plains. The people generally are much more expansive, speaking and laughing more loudly and heartily than the folk in Tokyo. They are less inhibited and concerned with social graces, and the visitor, if he or she is gregarious, can have an immensely enjoyable time here.

Many festivals can be seen throughout the year, for example, the Snow Festival at Sapporo with its gigantic, beautifully carved ice sculptures; and the Fire Festival at Abashiri in July, a grand opportunity to see the Ainu in costume, with their dances and tamed bears. You may, however, find something melancholy about the gaiety of a dying race.

Don't forget to take strong footwear and some warm clothing. Remember that midsummer temperatures *average* no more than 70°F and that there is no set plum-rain season. Typhoons are not frequent, but sea fogs are common in summer on the southeastern coasts. Food presents no problem. In the bigger centers there are western-style restaurants; seafood is plentiful (salmon, for example), and there is first-class farm produce. The deer are now protected, so you are not likely to taste venison soba (noodles).

Northern Honshu

Visitors on standard tours to Kyoto and Nikko can picture to themselves something of what the life of the cultured was like during some
thousand years of Japanese history; those who have ventured to Hokkaido have experienced a vibrant, contemporary frontier land; but to
linger awhile in Tohoku (the northern part of the main island of Honshu) is to discover a very different world indeed.

This is a land with rugged, north-south mountain ranges, volcanoes
(some of them active), colored caldera lakes, green fertile basins, and
rocky coasts—an environment where tough, cheerful, friendly Japanese, although encroached upon by the modern world, live in a traditional rural way: farmers working in ballooned trousers and quilted
working jackets with billowy sleeves, recounting their legends, expend-
ing much of their energy on sports of many kinds (hunting for instance)
and in relaxing in ubiquitous and splendid hot-spring baths.

Temperatures in the Tohoku region are generally lower than in
southwest Japan, summers shorter and snowfalls very heavy, especially
in the western coastal areas. Most arable land is devoted to rice growing, but orchards and mulberry fields are commonly seen. Travel by
train and bus if you must, but you'll see a lot more if you hire a bicycle
or hike around to enjoy, for example, the Tono Basin—there are very
few such places left in Japan—where you can sample the rural lifestyle
of Japan's feudal past.

In the main cities are modern hotels, but don't pass up the opportunity to experience a *ryokan* (traditional Japanese hotel), *minshuku*
(family-run overnight boarding house where the guest is made to feel
as one of the family), or *kokumin shukusha* (people's lodge), and
partake of authentic Japanese meals.

There will, of course, be difficulties over language out in this countryside, but remember that even Tokyoites meet with dialects unintelligi-
ble to them, sometimes referring to the Goshogawara inhabitants in
Aomori province as "country bumpkins." So do what everybody else
does and try using sign language.

A word of warning: be sure to draw up your itinerary in Tokyo
before setting forth, especially regarding trains and buses.

Shikoku

Apart from a few major cities and industrial centers on its coast, the
island of Shikoku, one of the earliest inhabited parts of Japan, is very
secluded and one of the least visited areas on tourist circuits, even
Japanese ones. It has, moreover, a low population density, which is
diminishing. The chief visitors are the some 100,000 pilgrims who go
there annually, clad in white, intent upon making the round of the 88
temples scattered over the island's mountain backbone and beautiful
fringing coasts facing both the Inland Sea and the Pacific.

Shikoku's highest mountain is Ishizuchi San, reaching 6,500 feet.
Fine forests of cedar, pine, and camphor cover much of the island
surface. Southern Shikoku is one of the warmest regions in Japan, with

mild winters. The northern shores tend to be sunny throughout the year and have low rainfall. The inhabitants are, in general, traditional, unsophisticated, and very hospitable, the descendants of seafaring folk not averse in olden times to engaging in piracy. But so seldom are foreigners seen today that they tend to be looked at as curiosities, though always with a touch of deference. Do not be surprised if you are taken to see special local sights not mentioned in the guidebook, or even invited to dinner.

The island's rail network is limited, though there are plenty of buses. Once again, armed with a good map, the best way to enjoy Shikoku is on foot. This is such a splendid region for the lover of the outdoors that virtually everywhere delights will be found, not least in the many islets of the Seto Inland Sea to the north. In southwesternmost Shikoku is the fine Ashizuri-Uwakai park with its superb granite cliff scenery and its remarkable marine park where the corals and fish of the reef-bound seacoast may be viewed from glass-bottomed boats. Naturalists will not wish to lose the chance to see the flying squirrels at Raidakuji near Yoshida, in the west, or the extraordinary onagadori roosters, in the southern city of Kochi, with tails at least 20 feet long. On Shodo Island in the Inland Sea is the largest monkey colony in Japan.

Unless you are very fastidious you can enjoy simple Japanese food everywhere. There is fine fish, and, especially at temples, delicious mountain vegetables and rice. You may even be able to try some *itadori* (great knotweed), which is somewhat like rhubarb and eaten with a pinch of salt.

Kyushu

The extraordinarily interesting island of Kyushu is also largely unexplored by the visitor. The Kyushu mountain range, centrally placed and high and rugged, stretches in a NE–SW direction across the island, while the roughly parallel but lower Tsukushi range crosses the northwest. Between these ranges lies a volcanic region with the world's largest crater basin, Mount Aso, encompassing five extinct vents and the very active Nakadake (4,341 feet). To the south of the Kyushu range is another volcanic area, which includes the famous Sakurajima volcano (some 3,640 feet high) surrounded by *shirasu,* upland plains of volcanic ash and pumice. Kyushu has a highly indented coastline with rugged peninsulas, numerous bays and gulfs, and characteristic rias in the strait between Kyushu and Shikoku.

Thanks to a more southerly location and to warm sea currents, the climate is on the whole relatively warm with mild winters. There is greater rainfall in summer than winter, but the wettest period comes in the *baiu* season, when flooding and high winds are common. The climate of northern Kyushu does not differ greatly from that of western Honshu. In southern Kyushu it tends to be subtropical, warm, and humid throughout the year. Of course, elevation modifies climate and, consequently, vegetation. In the southeast portion of the island you may be surprised to find subtropical trees and plants at low altitudes, while sugar cane grows on the island of Tanegashima just to the southeast of southernmost Kyushu. In the interior much of the high land is under forest.

Kyushu holds a prominent place in Japanese mythology, and a fascinating history has led to its being considered the cradle of Japanese civilization. The first recorded contact with the West was here, and in 1549 St. Francis Xavier brought Christianity to Japan at Kagoshima in southern Kyushu. Given their long history of contact with the West, one is not surprised to find that the inhabitants do not exhibit the embarrassment toward foreigners noted in Shikoku; indeed they show a certain inquisitiveness. Friendly and open, with a love of initiative, they are more animated than the Japanese in other parts of Japan and not afraid to be themselves.

Rail and bus reach most places of interest here; yet, once again, the most beautiful and striking points of interest often ultimately have to be reached on foot. And what splendid variety there is! Magnificent national parks—Sobo Katamuchi, for example, with its extensive forests, great gorge, and strange rock formations, wild boar, deer, and antelope. Lovely gardens such as the Iso Gardens at Kagoshima and the superb Suizenji Park in Kumamoto, Japanese in style and entirely manmade (as is the famous Moss Garden at Kyoto), with a magnificent castle nearby. Fine shrines abound, as well as grand scenery and innumerable spas. Nor must one forget the grandiose lunar landscape of Mount Aso nor the "hells" of Beppu with their fumaroles, solfataras, and geysers—all the essentials of the best infernos. And try not to miss seeing some of the island's striking festivals.

There are attractions galore for the trencherman: *satsuma ryori* cuisine found only in Kagoshima: *tonkatsu,* spare ribs of pork cooked in miso (bouillon made from fermented soy beans); batter-covered minced fish deep fried; local lollipops made from yams and rice. Elsewhere look for *mizutake,* chicken cooked in a broth of ginger, soy sauce, and sake; skewers loaded with tofu (bean curd) then browned over charcoal and spread with sweet bean paste; *karashi-renkon,* bean paste and mustard placed in the holes of a lotus root, then dipped in flour and deep fried; and, unless one is squeamish, *uma-sashi,* sliced raw horse meat, with sake to drink.

In a brief introduction it has been possible to suggest only in very bold terms the great variety of travel possibilities for the more adventurous visitor. Consult the pages of the guide carefully, and you're likely to discover even more.

THE JAPANESE WAY OF LIFE

ALAN TURNEY

*Alan Turney is chairman of the department of English Literature at Seisen Women's College in Tokyo. He is the author of two collections of essays—*Japan: A World of Difference *and* Other Lands, Other Customs—*and the book* Foreigners in Japan. *Mr. Turney has also written extensively on Japanese literature and translation, and has translated several works by the Japanese author Natsume Soseki.*

If you arrive in Japan from the United States or Europe, the chances are that your first sight of the country will be Narita International Airport, virtually indistinguishable from any other international airport in the world. From Narita there are two major ways of getting to downtown Tokyo: by the TCAT (Tokyo City Air Terminal) bus, or on a high-speed train called the Skyliner. If you opt for the former, you will find yourself carried along a network of recently completed freeways, somehow isolated from the surrounding countryside, and you will feel that you are in a very modern, efficient society. If you take the Skyliner, you will have the same impression, but from the window of the train you will see a thatched farmhouse here and there, since Chiba Prefecture, in which Narita is situated, is a largely agricultural area. You may find that the sight of people working in rice paddies, viewed

32

from the window of a smoothly gliding, well-appointed train, gives you cultural indigestion, and you may be forgiven for wondering which is the real Japan. If such is your reaction, you are not alone; the Japanese themselves sometimes have trouble in coming to terms with the eclectic nature of their culture.

Perhaps as recently as twenty years ago the image that the average American or European had of Japan was of a country of geisha, cherry blossom, and Mt. Fuji. This was certainly the image that the Japanese felt Westerners had of their country and it tended to irk them, since, even at that time, they were a highly industrialized nation and were already beginning to move ahead in some technological fields. Their attitude was, and still is to some extent, like that of the Englishman who takes a fierce pride in his heritage, feeling vaguely irritated that tourists should find his country quaint because of the old customs that are still preserved. Similarly, the Japanese, not wishing their country to be thought backward or old-fashioned, will go out of their way to offer proof of its modernity at every opportunity, forgetting perhaps that the visitor wishes to see the more traditional aspects of their culture.

There has been a Japanese boom in the United States in recent years, with great interest being taken in a vast array of things Japanese, from business methods to the martial arts. There is no doubt that the West is much better informed about Japan than it was (although one is still asked occasionally whether the Japanese live in paper houses), but there is still an element of mystery about the country and it is difficult to reconcile the modern and traditional aspects of the culture. One wishes to know what sort of people have produced this culture and what contingencies have caused things to develop as they have.

Japan has traditionally been the end of the line with regard to cultural flow. Buddhism, for instance, which originated in India, found its way to Japan via China and Korea and evolved into something distinctly Japanese. However, there was nowhere for it to be passed on to, and this has been true of other cultural phenomena as well. The results are twofold. The first is that throughout history many streams of thought and culture have flowed into Japan, where they have mixed with the current culture, thereby adding to it and modifying it. The second result is, briefly, that the Japanese have come to regard it as quite natural that they should import culture, but tend to assume that their own culture cannot be exported. They are, therefore, excellent students of the culture of others, but poor teachers of their own.

The fact that so many streams have swirled together in Japanese cultural waters is readily apparent to a person visiting the country for even a short time. It is not uncommon, for instance, to find a Shinto shrine within the compound of a Buddhist temple, something that is rather startling at first to those who are used to thinking of religions as being separate entities. Moreover, strolling down a back street in a residential area, you might find the front garden wall of a house hung with black and white striped cloth, with large wreaths mounted on black and white legs standing against it. This would mean that someone in the family had died and that a wake was being held inside. If you listened carefully, you might hear the sound of a priest intoning the Buddhist sutras coming from within the house. Seeing and hearing this, you would be entitled to assume that the family were practicing Buddhists, and indeed they might be. However, in Japan things are rarely as simple as they seem. There is very often a duality, or even a plurality, involved in a situation. And it is very likely that a person who is buried according to Buddhist rites would have been married in a Shinto ceremony. There is a Buddhist ceremony for marriage, but comparatively few people are married according to it. There seems to be a feeling that Shinto is concerned with the "here," while Buddhism concerns itself with the hereafter. Hence the general custom of being married Shinto and buried Buddhist.

This situation is indicative of how Japanese people think in general. On the positive side, it means that they tend to be rather tolerant, insofar as they do not feel that there is any one "right" way to do something—what is right for one person may not be right for another. It also means that what appear as paradoxes to a Westerner may not bother them and they may see no need to resolve them, hence situations like that mentioned above where there is a Shinto shrine within the compound of a Buddhist temple.

However, the obverse side of the coin is that the Japanese are often unwilling to be specific and to give clear-cut answers, and this is often a source of frustration for the visitor. It is quite difficult, for example, to obtain concrete information of a general kind with regard to visa requirements. I remember phoning the immigration office some years ago when my parents were due to come to Japan for a visit. I had heard that someone coming from Britain could get a six-month tourist visa at the port of entry, and phoned to confirm this. The official I spoke to was very courteous, but no matter how I phrased the question, I was told that no general rule could be given and that the passport in question would have to be seen before any decision could be made. In any event, when my parents actually arrived in Japan they were given a six-month visa with no trouble at all.

This lack of clarity which often exists with regard to rules means that much is left to the discretion of the person responsible for implementing them, a fact that can operate in one's favor. Indeed, in some cases there may be no rule, only precedent, something which is not lightly disregarded in Japan. Not too long ago, I was standing in line behind a Canadian missionary at the immigration office in Tokyo. This man had come to pick up visas for himself and his wife. The immigration official, while going through the necessary paperwork, remarked that the man's wife would have to come and pick up her visa herself. The missionary mentioned that he had been told on a previous visit that this would not be necessary. The official completed the paperwork and said once again that the lady concerned would have to come herself. Very quietly, the missionary explained that he lived quite a long way away and asked if there was no way that he could be given his wife's visa, as he had her passport with him. The official said that the lady *should* come herself. The missionary said that, yes, he understood that, but ... The official finally said that because the man had been told that his wife need not come in person, he would make an exception and give her visa to her husband.

This quiet exchange and its satisfactory outcome were highlighted by the fact that at another window some distance away another Westerner of indeterminate nationality was yelling at an official about his rights. Ten minutes after the Canadian left, this man left too, still shouting and presumably without having achieved what he had set out to do. The moral is a trite one, but nevertheless worth stating. The Japanese are, in general, very sympathetic and genuinely consider foreigners as guests in their country. Because of this, they will often go out of their way to help a foreigner, and they will make exceptions and let him get away with things that they would not allow another Japanese to do. However, yelling and trying to bully one's way through are invariably met with a quiet but stony resistance that nothing will shake.

Orientals are often described as being inscrutable. I do not find this true at all. Westerners tend to think that the Japanese are phlegmatic. Nothing could be further from the truth. They are, in fact, very emotional. However, one must learn to read the Japanese face. Gestures and expressions differ in meaning from culture to culture, and what may be a smile in one country may be construed as a hostile baring of the teeth in another. What, then, of the Japanese smile? The first thing to note is that it is not always connected with humor. The Japanese do smile when they are amused or happy, of course. But they also use a smile as a means of concealing their feelings. Occasionally it will mask sadness. Many a Westerner has been taken aback at hearing a Japanese announce a bereavement with a smile on his face. To the uninitiated, this appears to be a sign of callousness. In fact it is not. It is considered very bad form in Japanese society to thrust oneself upon others, or even to talk too much about one's personal affairs. The reason for the smile in the above case is that the speaker does not wish to burden the listener with his own personal sorrow, and so appears to make light of it.

A smile can, of course, conceal anger. "Face" is still very important in Japanese society. And if a Japanese thinks that he has been insulted or slighted in some way, he will resent it bitterly. Moreover, offense is easily taken. It is for this reason that discussion and not debate is the preferred method of decision making. In the West, two people might become quite heated in the course of a debate and make some fairly unflattering remarks about each other's opinions and intelligence. This would not stop them, however, from having a drink with each other afterwards. But in Japan, such remarks would lead to animosity. However, because harmony in society is so highly prized in Japan, people have developed higher flashpoints (at least in public) and may smile at such times. But this smile may conceal a smoldering inner resentment.

This "grin and bear it" attitude, the idea that one may only resort to physical retaliation after repeated and intense provocation, paradoxically gives rise to a great deal of apparently gratuitous violence in Japanese movies. In a Western, the hero takes one punch on the jaw from the villain and then proceeds to wipe the floor with him. In a Japanese movie, the hero is beaten again and again and subjected to humiliation and indignity. All this he must suffer in order to win the sympathy of the audience, so that when he finally does explode and wreak havoc among his enemies his action is seen as being justified.

While on the subject of the Japanese character, it is appropriate to mention their honesty and kindness. The *Japan Times* has a letters-to-the-editor column entitled "Readers in Council," in which foreign residents let off steam and air grievances (real and imagined) that stem from living for an extended period in a foreign country. However, letters from tourists and those on short business trips are almost invariably positive. There are any number of accounts of how helpful people are and how honest. Stories abound of forgotten wallets or cameras being returned to their owners, even though tracking them down took a great deal of time and trouble.

Although Japan does have a crime problem, the Japanese are in general law-abiding people, and even the big cities such as Tokyo are, by and large, safer than their counterparts in North America and Europe. However, the increase in violence in junior high schools is seen as a cause for alarm, and the gangs of hotrodders who roar around some areas at night give the police considerable trouble. These phenomena are viewed as symptomatic of juvenile rebellion against the pressures of an education system which, in line with the extremely competitive nature of Japanese society in general, puts children in competition with each other as early as the kindergarten level in some cases.

Worrying as these tendencies are, their ill effects are rarely apparent to the short-term visitor. People who work in stores are generally extremely polite, and if you ask someone the way on the street, the chances are that they will take you to your destination rather than merely telling you the way. Some Westerners become impatient in shops because of the time it can take to get served. Things are not hurried, and when a purchase has finally been made, the customer may ask for it to be gift wrapped, which the clerk will happily do. Try not to be impatient on these occasions. Remember that when your turn comes you will receive the same undivided attention. Don't let this give you the impression that it will take you an hour to buy a loaf of bread. When it comes to buying food and everyday household goods, in Japan, as in the West, supermarkets are the rule rather than the exception.

A well-known British journalist on her first visit to Japan remarked to me recently that her initial impression of the country was how happy the people looked. This surprised her, as she had not expected such lightheartedness in a country whose people are renowned for being workaholics and economic animals. Her observation is quite true. The Japanese, although they are hard workers, have a lively sense of fun and laugh often. There are, of course, many festivals throughout the year and these are delightful to see. But it is not only on these occasions that gaiety prevails. The Japanese love a party and have the ability to instill any social function with a festive spirit. Even a mundane car trip can turn into a party, and no family would set out on one without a good supply of rice crackers, rice balls, oranges, and the like. Not so different from a picnic, except that the excitement of the moment is likely to mean that the party will start before the car has gone more than two or three hundred yards. If you have the chance, try to mix with the Japanese socially, as well as taking in the more formal events. The chances of a tourist being invited home by a casual acquaintance are not very great, but semi-official programs do exist whereby a Japanese family will entertain overseas visitors at home, so it might be worth contacting your local Japanese Consulate to see if they have any information.

If you are in Japan on business, you are bound to be the subject of an introduction at some time or other. On these occasions name cards are exchanged, something which is uncommon in the West, perhaps, but nevertheless not too strange. What might strike you, however, is the length and degree of detail of the introduction. Depending on the circumstances, not only your name, but also such information as where you were born and what college you went to may be given, as well as much more besides. This is because Japanese society functions very much on the principle of personal introduction. The expression "it's not what you know but who you know" might have been coined in order to describe Japanese society. People go through a chain of acquaintances to get things done to a far greater extent in Japan than they do in the West.

Take, for instance, getting a teaching place at a college or university. No academic would write a letter to a college asking if they had a position vacant that might suit him. He would know that, even if there were such a position, he would not get it, because in Japan there is something suspect about a person who would, so to speak, advertise himself in this way. If he knew there was a position open at the college, he would try to find someone in his chain of acquaintances who could mention his name in the right ear. Then the college might, all things being equal, contact him and ask if he would consider teaching there. This is why in Japan one speaks not of hiring teachers but of inviting them to teach. Whether it is getting a college position, setting up a business venture, or submitting a manuscript to a publisher for consideration, nobody walking in off the street is likely to be successful, no matter how worthy he may be.

Another fact that accounts for the long introduction is that a great deal of day-to-day business is done on the basis of trust. Thus, if you give someone your name card with an introduction to somebody on it, you are effectively lending him your good name. The same is true on many occasions with a verbal introduction, too. By going into great detail about a person's background, you are showing the other party that there is not, as far as you know, anything suspicious about him. After such an introduction, depending upon your own reputation, he will probably be taken on trust as a friend of yours by the person to whom you have introduced him.

An introduction, then, is not made lightly or in irrelevant circumstances. That is why if you are with a Japanese and he bumps into a friend on the street, he will stop and chat for a minute or two without introducing you at all, unless he feels that it might be a good thing to establish a relationship between you for some future purpose. In these circumstances you are left to look up in the air and pretend that you are elsewhere. This is not impoliteness on his part, just a question of relevance.

But to return to the subject of culture, the mixture of native Japanese and Western, the old and the new. From early times there was, as we have seen, a steady flow of culture into Japan from China and Korea. As time passed, Europeans, too, came to Japan, bringing their culture with them. The missionaries, led by St. Francis Xavier, brought Christianity, and with the Dutch traders came the by-product of Western medicine, while people such as the Englishman Will Adams brought with them a variety of skills and techniques—in the case of Adams, shipbuilding. Just when it seemed, however, that Japan might move into the international current, the Tokugawa Shogunate closed the country to outsiders. This was in the mid-17th century. And from then until the middle of the 19th century the only legal contact with Europeans was with the handful of Dutchmen who were allowed to remain on a small island in Nagasaki harbor.

The reasons for this closure are many and complex, but in a nutshell one can say that the Tokugawas, who had lately consolidated their power in the country after a period of civil war, were afraid that the European cultural influx was a prelude to political penetration, in the same way, for example, that the British East India Company proved to be the thin end of the wedge in India. This isolation continued for about two hundred years. In 1853 Commodore Perry arrived in Japan, demanding the opening of the country. The Tokugawas lacked the power to deal with the ramifications of this demand and the Shogunate collapsed in the face of opposition by some of the major clans about a decade and a half later. The Emperor Meiji moved to Edo, which was re-named Tokyo (Eastern Capital), and thus, with the Meiji Restoration of 1868, began the modern history of Japan.

The Meiji Period was one of frenetic activity. Not everybody, of course, was in favor of opening up the country to foreigners and adopting Western ways. The slogan of one movement, *sonnojoi* (revere the Emperor and expel the barbarians) speaks for itself. However, those who went abroad and gained firsthand experience of just how far advanced the West was industrially, realized that Japan, if she was not to be left behind, must modernize, and that this would mean studying Western methods and techniques. There were even those who, in their infatuation with things Western, suggested that Japanese be abolished and English substituted as the national language. Even today there is an element that slavishly and unthinkingly adopts any and every Western fad and that seems to have lost its cultural roots. However, the mainstream of cultural development has always reflected an attempt to adopt those aspects of Western culture and technology which would benefit the country, while preserving what is best in Japanese culture. The pendulum has occasionally swung hard to the right, sometimes disastrously, as with the swing toward nationalism and ultimately militarism in the thirties. But the general trend has been toward modernization, and this has meant, particularly at the material level, importing a great deal that is Western.

Although there is a temptation to regard Japan as being a "Western" nation, particularly after a visit to one of the large cities, to do so is to overlook the fact that, underneath the glass and concrete exterior, many traditional values still hold sway. Indeed, the Japanese often seem to feel that only that which is old is Japanese. I can remember being asked to appear on a television program in Tokyo some years ago.

The subject was life in Japan and life in England. I was rather amused when the producer came to me a few days before the program was to be recorded and said that he had encountered a problem. He was finding it very difficult, he said, to find a Japanese house in Tokyo. By a Japanese house, he meant one of traditional design, which is single-storied with a verandah running along two sides (you can still find them in country areas).

Now it *is* true that this is a Japanese house. But, as I pointed out to the producer, if millions upon millions of Japanese people are living in some other kind of house, then those too must presumably be Japanese. There is a tendency to polarize when trying to describe Japanese society and say, for example, that old houses exist side by side with modern buildings, the old coexisting with the new. This is of course true. But to view things entirely in this way is to see Japanese society as being made up of disparate and undigested phenomena, and would suggest that only that which is traditional is Japanese, which is certainly not true.

The Japanese have earned the reputation of being copiers, and with good reason. As we have seen, it was only by dint of copying, some-times down to the tiniest detail without necessarily understanding what they were doing, that they were able to emerge as a modern, industrial-ized nation. However, although this process of modernization has often caused the Japanese to feel a crisis of identity, the more perceptive have seen right from the beginning of the Meiji Period that, technology aside, in cultural areas what was necessary was not copying but adapta-tion. Consequently, much of what you see in Japan is a synthesis of East and West. The houses are a case in point. Typically, a Japanese house will have at least one *tatami* room, while the plumbing will probably be what you would expect to find in the West. Again, the bathroom will have a deep tub and a completely tiled floor so that you can wash and splash before getting into the hot water. All in all, despite its Western aspects, not the kind of house that you would expect to find in the States or Europe. Moreover, you will find that a residential area in the city has about it a look and a feel which, although different from that of a village in the countryside, is no less distinctively Japanese. The point is, Japan is what it *is* and not only what it *was*. One must view the society both diachronically and synchronically, for to ignore the synthesis of Oriental and Western, ancient and modern, and to think only in terms of their coexistence, is to ignore a very positive and stabilizing element in the development of Japanese society and culture.

It is not only with Japanese houses that what appears to be Western at first sight is, in fact, not exactly so. There is, for example, a distinctly Japanese quality about the clothes that young children wear. One would have to describe the clothes as Western, I suppose, since they are not kimono. But they are not exactly what you would see on the streets of London or New York.

Sometimes such a synthesis can appear very subtly, almost indiscern-ibly. Most Japanese men possess a black, formal suit. As you are walking through the town, particularly on a Sunday or national holi-day, you may see a man so dressed, carrying, perhaps, a purple, cloth-tied bundle in one hand. This man is probably on his way to or from a wedding. If anything strikes you at all, it will most likely be that, although the man is wearing a Western suit, he is carrying not a bag but a traditional *furoshiki*. And you might see this as one more example of the coexistence of East and West in Japan. But there is something you could not know unless you accompanied the man to the wedding, and that is that virtually every other man present will be wearing an identical suit (or perhaps a formal morning suit). Younger men tend to wear single-breasted suits, while older men largely opt for the double-breasted version, generally with cuffs on the trousers. Other than this, there is little or no variation in cut. Everyone will be wearing an identical white necktie (for which he will substitute a black one when attending funerals). The above is true for the rich and the not so well-off in both city and country.

On consideration, you will realize that the suit has become stylized. It is a style that has not changed since such a suit became *de rigueur*, and that will probably not change in the years to come. It is a *Japanese* suit. Moreover, the fact that almost everybody at the function is wearing the same suit reflects a love of formality and conformity which is truly Japanese. The ethnic nature of the suit itself may be open to argument, but the fact of the suit being worn by people en masse unmistakably has its roots in Japanese rather than Western soil.

The Japanese language, too, is a synthesis. With the adoption of Chinese ideographs to write native Japanese words *(yamatokotoba)*, there gradually came into the language words of Chinese origin *(kango)*. Thus the language today is basically a mixture of *yamatokotoba* and *kango*. However, you will not have been in Japan long before you realize that many of the words you hear have a familiar ring to them. In the midst of a stream of otherwise incomprehensible language you will hear a word that sounds more or less English—*pen* (pen), *biiru* (beer), *erebeta* (elevator), *naifu* (knife) and so on, the list is endless.

Back in the Meiji Period when the country was opened to foreign influence, it was found that on many occasions there was no word to describe a thing or an institution found in the West—a bank, for instance—and so a new vocabulary item had to be coined. This was normally done by taking two or three Chinese characters whose combined meanings were descriptive of the thing concerned and putting them together. A car, for example, became *jidosha* (literally, self + moving + wheel). Some words, however, were taken directly from English or other European languages. Gradually, as the rate of progress accelerated, it became impracticable to continue coining new words, and so it became the rule to take loan words direct. The result is that in technological literature the text is saturated with such vocabulary items.

It is not only in the field of technology, however, that these words exist. They took root in the everyday language and, there being no equivalent of the Academie Française in Japan, they have proliferated to a tremendous degree. This is something that worries traditionalists, who feel that, by adopting foreign loan words, the Japanese are somehow de-Japanizing their language. Such a reaction is understandable, particularly in a country that was cut off from the outside world for two centuries. However, language is a living thing and, as such, is bound to change. Indeed, not only is Japanese changed by the inclusion of foreign loan words, but the loan words themselves are changed. They become Japanese. If you were walking past a building and saw the words "morning service," you might conclude that the building was a church. You would be wrong. It would be a coffee shop, and the morning service would refer to the toast and perhaps a hard-boiled egg which you could get with a cup of coffee at an especially low price between certain hours of the morning.

How truly Japanese loan words can become is illustrated by something that happened when my wife and I were thinking of buying our present house. The estate agent who showed us around said that, although there was no *sentoraru hiichingu* (central heating), it would be easy to install. He then asked me if I knew what *sentoraru hiichingu* was. He intended no irony. He was not conscious of using English words. For him, they constituted a Japanese technical term.

It is true that many of these words are no more than affectations used to impress, particularly by the young, and that they will quickly disappear, as have many before them. Many, however, will not, since they are legitimate and often show a consciousness of fine distinctions in meaning. The most obvious examples are those that refer to a Western, as opposed to a native Japanese, object. *Tsukue* is the low table used in a Japanese *tatami* room, while *teburu* (table) is a Western-style table. A slightly different example is when the word *doraiba* (driver) is used instead of *untenshu* (which also means driver). The former refers to a person who is driving his family car for pleasure, while the latter refers to somebody like a bus driver. Again, a word may be used to express a concept hitherto unfamiliar, such as *boranteia* (volunteer), used in the sense of one who does community work.

As you are walking along the street, not only will you hear familiar words, you will also see English everywhere—on T-shirts, shopping bags, and on storefronts. English expressions and slogans are used in the world of advertising to give a chic and modern image to a product. The problem is that most of this English is not produced by native speakers, and the results are often very interesting. You will see something that looks like English at first sight, but on consideration you will probably be at a loss as to what it means. Such expressions range from *For beautiful human life*, the slogan of a large corporation, which is almost English, to the *Drive me crazy—Camellia*, uttered by a famous American actress in a TV commercial, which is almost not. Such utterances drive teachers of English to drink, but sanity can be saved if you regard them, like loan words, as being culturally Japanese. They have emigrated and no longer belong to Britain or America.

Speaking of English: How much can you expect to be able to communicate in this language while in Japan? In country areas, your chances of finding anybody who speaks English are very slim, and if the truth be known, even in large cities there is not much chance of finding anyone who can speak more than a smattering, despite the fact that English is taught in public schools for six years. Those most likely to be able to help you in English are high-school students, easily recognizable by their school uniforms. In fact, they may even approach you in a park or on a train and ask if they can practice their English conversation.

English is now an elective subject at school. But since it is impossible to get into any department of any university without passing an examination in English, it is, de facto, a compulsory subject for anyone who wants to go on to higher education. This means that the object of the exercise is to enable students to get into a university and not to converse with native speakers. The result is that the emphasis is on grammar and translation, although much more conversational English is being taught nowadays.

To any suggestion that English be dropped from college entrance examinations and English for special purposes be taught at college, the Japanese are likely to reply that English is not taught as an examination subject only, but as a means of giving students a broader perspective and making them more international. This sounds fine in principle, but the learning of English at the junior- and senior-high school levels does not, in fact, seem to have led to a high state of internationalization, any more than five years compulsory study of French under the old English grammar-school system guaranteed that the student would be able to order a cup of coffee in Paris with any degree of success or would come to feel any closer to the French in particular or the international community at large.

A great deal is said about internationalism in Japan today, and no chance is lost to host an international conference. There is no doubt that the Japanese have become cosmopolitan, as even a short stay in a large city will demonstrate. But are they truly international? There have, of course, always been true internationalists in Japan and there still are. However, internationalism to date tends to have been Japano-centric, and it would seem that much that is done in its name is actually aimed at having foreigners "understand" Japan, which means accepting the image the Japanese have of themselves. The Japanese are invariably kind and considerate toward foreigners. But in Japanese society, treating a person as a guest is a subtle way of keeping him at arms' length. It would seem that the Japanese feel somewhat threatened if their culture is studied too much, as though something were being stolen from them. On the other hand, they are delighted that somebody should be interested enough in their country to want to study it. However, many real changes have taken place in the past two or three years and things look promising for the future.

The problem when writing about a country as fascinating as Japan is that the topics one could cover are endless. What should be included and what omitted? How is it possible to paint a word picture that will conjure up the feel of the country for someone who has never visited it? Should one speak of the sounds of the seasons—the cicadas in summer, the cry of the man selling hot potatoes through the streets as autumn moves on toward winter; or of the cherry blossom in spring and the glorious fall colors? Whatever else is left out, no essay on Japan would be complete without mentioning something about space.

Much has been written about the fact that the Japanese live in rabbit hutches, and it is quite true that the average Japanese house is small by American or European standards. This is only natural because with a population about half that of the United States and twice that of Great Britain and with large areas of the country occupied by mountains, living space is at a premium. The Japanese, however, are extremely good at overcoming such disadvantages and, in the process of coming to terms with the limitations that lack of space imposes, they have developed an exquisite sense of proportion and an ability to work as designers within a very small space. The art of growing *bonsai* is an example of this, as is the creation of the *tsuboniwa* (a one *tsubo* garden). A *tsubo* is about 36 square feet and, although such a garden need not be literally as small as this, the term refers to quite a tiny area of land within which perhaps a few bamboos, a rock, and a stone lantern create a delightful view to look at out of one's window.

Both the tea ceremony and *ikebana* (flower arranging) are examples of Japanese art forms in which three-dimensional space and the relationship between objects in that space are extremely important. In the tea ceremony, it is the position of the various utensils which, together with many other factors, helps to create an ambience of serenity.

Although the tea ceremony is not so widely practiced as *ikebana,* it still plays a role in the education of young women and is very much a part of the establishment, as witness the October 1983 wedding between Princess Masako, a niece of the Emperor, and the eldest son of the Headmaster of the Urasenke tea ceremony school. There is a hierarchy within each of the schools of the tea ceremony, as there is within the schools of *ikebana,* traditional dancing, sumo wrestling, or any activities having their roots in antiquity. They are, in fact, all feudal in nature and the headmastership of a school is generally passed on within the same family from generation to generation.

The tea ceremony was never a popular pastime and, relatively speaking, there is probably little difference in the number of people who practice it today, compared with those in days gone by. It is far from defunct, however, as testified to by the fact that every department store has a section that carries a selection of tea ceremony paraphernalia, usually with inordinately high price tags attached. It is, as it always has been, the preserve of the educated and privileged classes. Indeed, if one joins a tea ceremony school, or a school of flower arranging or Japanese dance, a great deal of money will be required if the individual is to make a name for himself or herself.

In the tea ceremony, probably far more than in *ikebana,* there is an inherent paradox, namely the coexistence of a spirituality, which derives from Zen Buddhism, with a materialism, which derives, in part, from the appreciation of art objects associated with the ceremony. This paradox, apparent or real, is one that any student of Japanese culture has to come to terms with. The coexistence of an undeniable, and much vaunted, spirituality and a very clear materialism symbolizes, perhaps more than anything else, the problem that foreigners have in understanding Japan.

One reason why *ikebana* has been able to gain greater popularity than the tea ceremony—even spreading to foreign countries—is that it can be performed by an individual in the absence of any onlookers and can be appreciated by one or more people later, whereas the tea ceremony needs to be performed by one person for one or more people at a given time. Moreover, the end product of *ikebana* is more concrete and rather less ephemeral than that of the tea ceremony. However, both have as their common objective the tranquility of mind of both the performer and the observer and, therefore, far from being mere stylized relics of a bygone age, they have more relevance than perhaps ever before in that pressure cooker that constitutes Japan's contemporary society.

Perhaps another reason that the Japanese are so conscious of space and of mass balanced by mass is that their written language is spatial rather than linear. Whereas Western children are taught to write in terms of lines—the *d* must be sitting on the line and the tail of the *g* goes down to the next line—Japanese children learn to form each character within a square, and consequently become aware very quickly, not only of the relationship of each part of the character to the others, but of the relationship of the character itself to the unoccupied space around it. It is for this reason that the Japanese will say, when speaking of calligraphy, that the empty spaces are as important as the characters themselves.

It is possible that it is this spatial view of things that enables the Japanese to hold several apparently conflicting concepts in their minds at the same time, seeing the relationship between them, without perceiving any necessity to "resolve" the situation, whereas Western logic, as represented by the syllogism—major premise, minor premise, conclusion—demands resolution. If you realize before you arrive in Japan that you will be confronted with a large number of apparent paradoxes and incongruities, you may avoid cultural indigestion to some degree. Enjoy the rice paddies. Enjoy the well-appointed trains. Which is, I believe, where we came in.

THE HISTORY OF JAPAN

DOUGLAS KENRICK

Douglas Kenrick is the author of a number of books, and has contributed many articles about Japan to periodicals in several countries. A long-time resident of Japan, he is Past President of the Asiatic Society of Japan.

Japan's recorded history is remarkable. Until 1945, the Japanese could claim that, in historic times, their island home had never been overrun by a foreign army. Twenty miles of waves between Dover and Calais blocked Napoleon and Hitler. Similarly the narrow Sea of Japan engulfed Kublai Khan's Mongol hordes in the 13th century. The sea barrier between their islands and the neighboring Asian mainland has molded the history of the Japanese people as effectively as the soil, the climate, and the terrain.

Until about 300 B.C. Japan's earliest inhabitants, the Jomon, lived by hunting, fishing, and food gathering. Their origin is obscure. They could have come from the south or the north, or migrated through nearby Korea from deep in Asia. Even their name, Jomon, has been adopted from their cord-marked pottery, which was first described, and named, by an American, Edward Morse, as recently as 1874. What little is known about them comes from the analysis of the Japanese

45

language and studies of artifacts that have survived. They were most populous in the central region north of Tokyo. The International Christian University (I.C.U.) in suburban Tokyo has built a fine museum which houses a number of Jomon artifacts, some estimated to be about 10,000 years old, excavated on its own campus within an hour of the center of today's metropolis. The I.C.U. museum is but one of many liberally scattered in every population center throughout Japan. Whatever part of the country being explored, the interested visitor will find numerous displays of ancient artifacts.

Then, from Korea, came the Yayoi people, so named for their distinctive pottery, first classified during excavations in 1878 in the Yayoi suburb of Tokyo. The Yayoi brought knowledge of farming and metallurgy and they did not have to fight their way ashore. Northwestern Kyushu near today's Fukuoka, their first landfall, had few inhabitants two thousand years ago, but over the course of six hundred years, from 300 B.C. to A.D. 300, more and more immigrants arrived from the war-torn mainland and seized the best rice-growing land. As this land was settled, farmers alternated as warriors to hold their acres against ambitious neighbors, or new arrivals, or both. Slowly the scattered settlements were united, at first in the rich Kansai plain around today's Osaka, Kobe, Nara, and Kyoto.

One tribe, or "kingdom," the Yamato, extended and consolidated its power by conquering its neighbors or by making alliances with them. From the Kansai they slowly expanded westward to absorb the older established "kingdoms" in Kyushu. The Yamato leaders, who claimed to be the descendents of the Sun Goddess, Amaterasu, took the title of emperor around the 5th century A.D. In the mid-6th century, Buddhism, introduced from China by way of Korea, was accepted by the Yamato court.

Rulers had no permanent capital, perhaps because superstition required a new leader to move from a place defiled by the death of his predecessor, but as the country became more unified, a stable center was needed from which to govern. In the 8th century the first capital city, modeled on the Chinese metropolis, Ch'ang-an, probably the largest city in the world at that time, was laid out at Nara with wide straight roads. However, within a hundred years the capital was moved from Nara, partly, it is often said, because of the power of the Buddhist clergy there. Several magnificent Nara temples, said to be the oldest wooden buildings in the world, still function. They reveal the architecture of 8th-century T'ang China and survive to give a picture of old Japan, because after fires new structures were rebuilt as replicas of the old.

After a ten-year stopover at Nagaoka, only about 80 miles away, a more permanent capital was founded at Heian (now called Kyoto), another few miles west. Again a well-laid out, grand city was planned and partly constructed. It endured as the capital of Japan, in name if not always in fact, for over a thousand years—from 794 to 1868.

The Rise of the Shoguns

At first the central government had claimed ownership of all land, but over the years courtiers progressively acquired large personal estates. These, which they left to the supervision of local managers, became semi-independent, and the government's income diminished.

A noble family, the Fujiwara, by acquiring vast lands and by intrigue and intermarriage with the imperial family, dominated the court. Despite occasional challenges, they overshadowed the emperors and held a monopoly of high court posts for centuries. The emperors retained their religious status and large personal estates, but gradually lost political power.

While the court excelled in lavish ceremony and artistic accomplishments, economic and political control slowly devolved to the provincial estate managers who strengthened and held their positions by their military prowess. Two warrior groups consolidated their control of much of the country—the Minamoto in the region around what is now Tokyo, and the Taira along the Inland Sea from today's Osaka throughout most of western Honshu.

A struggle between court factions in the middle of the 12th century brought the Taira into the capital. Their leader, Kiyomori, took the Prime Ministership, married his daughter to the Emperor, and put her son on the throne. The Minamoto challenged Taira supremacy and crushed it in 1185. Minamoto Yoritomo took for himself the rank of *Shogun* (military leader), and settled in Kamakura, some thirty miles from today's Tokyo. With strong military forces at his command, Yoritomo effectively ruled the land while leaving the emperor his title and a court with purely notional powers in Kyoto.

The Minamoto line did not last long. Yoritomo started the heads falling by disposing of his younger brother, chief general in the defeat of the Taira. He eliminated other members of his family and, soon after his death in 1199, his wife's relatives, the Hojo family, finished off Yoritomo's remaining heirs. The Hojos made themselves hereditary regents of puppet shoguns whom they selected, first from the Fujiwara and then the imperial family. Real government by the Hojos, camouflaged behind this imposing array of figureheads, was exerted through a loose control over semi-independent warrior lords each with his own local domain.

As far back as the 8th century, even when the imperial court was in control of a centralized government, aggressive Buddhist priests had resisted and even threatened the imperial line. By the Kamakura era (1185–1333), Buddhism had become a widespread religious movement with fortified monasteries and large estates. It embraced commoners as well as military aristocrats. From the late 12th century a new sect, Zen, was introduced by Japanese monks returning from China. Its emphasis on intuitive enlightenment, achieved by rigid self-discipline, which made book learning and logical thought unnecessary, appealed to the warrior class.

Kublai Khan, grandson of Genghis Khan, leader of the Mongols who overwhelmed China, Central Asia, and much of the Near East in the 13th century, conquered Korea in 1259, and ordered the Japanese to submit to his authority. The Kamakura warriors defied him by beheading his envoys. In 1274 Kublai Khan sent a strong fleet to enforce his will. It seized some small islands and landed in Hakata Bay near today's Fukuoka, but the threat of tempestuous weather persuaded his army to withdraw back to Korea. In 1281 the Mongols sailed a second time with a huge army of 150,000 men. They again reached Hakata Bay, but before their full force was ashore the fleet and most of its men were destroyed by a typhoon, named and praised in Japanese history as a "divine wind," or *kamikaze*, sent by the gods to protect their sacred land.

The End of the Kamakura Era

The defeat of the foreign invaders led also to the overthrow of the Kamakura Shogunate. An emperor, Godaigo, felt that an emperor should govern. In 1331, supported by discontented warriors of western Japan, who had depleted their resources in resisting the Mongols and gained no spoils of war or monetary reward from the shogunate, Godaigo led a revolt to reestablish imperial government. Ashikaga Takauji, commanding a shogunate army from eastern Japan to put down the revolution, changed sides in 1333. A general of a second eastern army, instead of fighting Ashikaga, joined him, seized Kamakura, and eliminated the Hojo family. But Ashikaga then drove Godaigo from Kyoto, named another member of the imperial family emperor, and had himself appointed shogun. Godaigo retreated into the mountains south of Nara and set up an alternative, but powerless, court at Yoshino. His successors continued their resistance for sixty years until the Ashikaga promised that their line would alternate on the throne, a promise that was not kept.

Life Under the Ashikaga

Although the Ashikaga family, who settled at Muromachi in Kyoto, inherited the title of shogun through to 1573, it never ruled the whole country as effectively as Kamakura had done. Ashikaga were, however, important patrons of the arts. Painting, landscape gardens, flower arrangement, and the tea ceremony, all brought originally from China by Zen monks, flourished and were molded into what have become typically Japanese forms. In their simplicity and closeness to nature the genius of that age found high expression. Manufacturing—textiles, metal wares, paper—also expanded and merchants guilds were organized to speed the movement of goods from place to place. Osaka grew as a purely commercial city, dominated by merchants who cooperated with a great Buddhist temple stronghold of the True Pure Land Buddhist Sect (Jodo-Shinshu). Osaka's sailors traded by sea along Japan's indented coastline, and imported goods and coins from China. (The coins were needed because there was no locally minted currency and money was increasingly taking the place of rice and cloth as a medium of exchange.) By the 15th and 16th centuries the Japanese were playing an important role in shipping and commerce on the East China Sea.

Japanese pirates, often working with Chinese, plundered Chinese coastal cities.

Economic progress was achieved despite the almost continuous wars that racked the country, waged between warrior clans fighting to expand their domains. Alliances changed intermittently. Central control disintegrated as the local warrior-lords established effective political units, some large, some small, but none paying taxes to Kyoto. The Ashikaga shoguns became powerless figureheads and the imperial family and its attendant nobles were without the income to pay for elaborate funerals or ceremonies. One emperor, whose calligraphy was beautiful, copied poems and sold them for a pittance. Though titles and court rankings were retained, on three occasions in the 16th century a new emperor was not properly invested.

An End to Civil Wars

In 1568 Oda Nobunaga, who ruled a large area around Nagoya, overpowered the imperial court and the Ashikaga shogun in Kyoto. He expanded his control, capturing monasteries and other centers of resistance. (The Jodo-Shinshu temple stronghold in Osaka held out for a long ten years before falling.) Before he had subdued all Japan, Nobunaga was assassinated in 1582.

His ablest general, Hideyoshi, restored the Osaka fortress and built himself a palace and castle in Kyoto. He subdued all opposition and brought to an end the long period of civil wars. With his huge armies unemployed, and no further opposition in Japan, he set out to conquer China. In 1592 with 160,000 men he invaded and overran Korea but was forced back by Chinese armies. At Hideyoshi's death in 1598 his armies promptly withdrew from the mainland.

The Tokugawa Reign

In 1600 Tokugawa Ieyasu, who had been Hideyoshi's general in eastern Japan, defeated other contenders in a great battle and became undisputed ruler of all Japan. He set out to consolidate his power, to enforce political stability, and to ensure that control would remain in the hands of his descendants. Ieyasu made his castle at Edo, now Tokyo, the center of government. He took the title of shogun but left the emperor and his court undisturbed with nominal authority in Kyoto. He reserved for the Tokugawa family direct control of all major cities, ports and mines, and large personal estates, thereby appropriating a rice yield of about 7 million koku (one koku is about five bushels) out of a national total of about 26 million. The rest of the country he divided into fiefs (han), each supervised by the Tokugawa but governed autonomously by a lord (daimyo). A hierarchy of four social classes—in order, from the top down: aristocrats, warriors, farmers, and townspeople (merchants)—was strictly enforced. A powerful bureaucracy included the world's first large-scale secret police system, which spied on everyone. While important positions, from shogun down, were established on a near-hereditary basis, the holders of these posts were largely figureheads with councils or officials behind them. Collective decision making was entrenched. The Tokugawa political system was to remain unchanged for two and a half centuries.

The first Europeans, the Portuguese, had reached Japan in 1543. Christianity was introduced by St. Francis Xavier who stayed for two years, 1549–1551, and despite Buddhist opposition, made many converts. It has been estimated that there were 150,000 Christians in Japan by 1580 and double that number in the early 17th century. Profitable trade, particularly in firearms, came at the same time as the missionaries. Hideyoshi and the Tokugawa saw advantage in trade with Europe and had no religious aversion to Christianity. They were, however, worried that the missionaries could be the advance patrols of foreign armies that might try to put Japan under a colonial yoke. In 1587 Hideyoshi decreed that all Christian missionaries should leave Japan, but he did little to enforce this until, in 1597, he had six European priests and twenty Japanese Christians crucified. At first Ieyasu was friendly toward the missionaries and tried to persuade Spanish merchants to trade directly with Edo but then, in 1609, the Dutch established a trading post at Hirado, an island off the northwest coast of Kyushu. Ieyasu found that religion and business could be separated. In 1617, the Tokugawa re-enforced Hideyoshi's decree. Within a few years all missionaries were killed or forced to leave and thousands of Japanese Christians renounced the faith or were killed.

In 1636 the Tokugawa ordered, on pain of death, that no Japanese should go abroad and that no Japanese already abroad should return. The construction of large, ocean-going vessels was prohibited. Only one link with the outside world was allowed. The Dutch were permitted residence, as virtual prisoners, on a small island which is now an almost indistinguishable part of Nagasaki, and Chinese merchants, under strict supervision, were also allowed to visit and trade at that port.

Until the 19th century Japan remained strictly regulated and at peace. Two great cities, Edo (Tokyo) and Osaka, grew as centers of commerce. Industry—weaving, pottery, lacquerware—became significant, the economy more sophisticated. The four social classes stayed rigidly divided but the lowly merchants accumulated wealth and power far beyond their status. The arts catered to them and relied on their support. Painting and literature reflected urban life. The stage entertained the city dwellers. In the countryside, farmers, the majority of the population, subsisted on the verge of starvation, but even in remote *hans* some local lords encouraged craftsmen and artists. Pottery kilns in the south of Kyushu, around Kagoshima, in the northwest of Kyushu at Arita (near Fukuoka), and on the Japan seacoast of Honshu at Kanazawa, challenged the central potteries near Nagoya (and particularly those of Seto). The quality of the ceramics has made the names of their wares world famous. Beyond tight Tokugawa centralization, their industries mushroomed as far distant as the Satsuma *han* (with its port and capital of Kagoshima). The visitor who travels beyond the great cities will still find rewarding evidence of the cultural and industrial developments of old Japan, which supplement the treasures to be seen in Tokyo, Kyoto, Osaka, and other central repositories of old arts and crafts.

The End of Tokugawa Rule and the Samurai Era

In the first half of the 19th century, America, Britain, and Russia sent envoys to Japan requesting that foreign trade by permitted. Their pleas rejected, America, in 1853, sent an intimidating four-ship fleet under Commodore Perry. The shogunate appealed to the Kyoto court and the largest *daimyo* for guidance but, against vocal and widespread urgings to repel the barbarians, realized the weakness of its defenses. The Edo Shogunate bowed to the foreign guns and signed a treaty permitting a small, regulated trade.

The court refused to confirm the shogun's action. Opposition took concrete form. The warriors of the Choshu *han* (at the southern tip of Honshu) defied the shogunate. In 1866 the shogun's military action to subdue their revolt failed. In 1868 a coalition of the Choshu, Satsuma, and Tosa *hans* announced the "restoration" of imperial rule. Further battles were bloody but short. The Tokugawa shogun handed back his authority to the emperor.

Emperor Meiji was still a boy. He followed long established tradition and left the control of government to his new "court." The low-ranking but vigorous provincial samurai who had propelled the emperor to the throne were only too pleased to govern in his name. The Meiji era marked Japan's entry into the international sphere and the beginnings of her modernization, which developed with remarkable speed throughout the forty-four years of the new emperor's reign.

The emperor's capital was moved from Kyoto to Tokyo, the new name for Edo. The principal *daimyo* were persuaded to relinquish their domains and were, temporarily, made governors of their old fiefs. The lesser *daimyo* had to follow their example. The new centralized government created Western-style ministries for specific tasks but perpetuated many of the traditional methods of controlling the country. It appropriated the income of the shogunal and *daimyo* domains and obtained loans from rich merchants. The new leaders from Satsuma assumed control of the navy, and their peers from Choshu took over the army and the supervision of internal affairs.

By 1873 the new administration felt strong enough to strip the warrior caste of its prestige and power by granting rather small stipends (which were soon converted into lump-sum payments) and by decreeing universal military service. In 1876 the samurai were ordered not to wear swords, their erstwhile badge of superiority. Many samurai enlisted as officers in the new army, others joined the police force or became leaders in educational establishments and businesses, but the majority lost their elite status and became ordinary citizens. Some samurai refused to accept the new regime and revolted—the most serious uprising being in Satsuma, led by one of the men (Saigo Takamori) who had done much to establish the new government. The rebels were crushed bloodily by the new conscript army.

Industrialization and Western Influence

The emperor had been brought to power with the slogan "sonnojoi" ("repel the barbarians") but his new advisors realized they did not have weapons to resist the West. They decided instead to match Western industrialization with the slogan "rich country, strong military." Factories were subsidized and, when successful, were turned over to private enterprise, the rich merchants on whom the new government relied for financial support and who, in the course of time, became the *zaibatsu*, or financial empires. Industry grew and prospered.

For two decades the Japanese leaned heavily on Western knowledge. The government sent students abroad and brought in a host of Western experts. As Japan acquired the new knowledge and techniques, a reaction set in. Many foreign teachers were dismissed. Japan settled down to assimilate the foreign knowledge and adapt it to suit her needs.

As one step to obtain international recognition, a constitution was created in 1889. It established a parliamentary organization which followed Western democratic precedents, at least superficially. A German model was followed, with nominal power in the hands of the "sacred and inviolable" emperor. Below the apparently democratic surface of an elected Diet (parliament), the real control of government remained in the hands of a small group of elder statesmen who dominated the Imperial Household Agency, the Privy Council, the House of Peers, the Armed Forces, and the bureaucracy. Prime Ministers were appointed from on high, not by the members of the Diet. The House of Representatives put up an energetic but unsuccessful running battle for a say in government.

Japan Becomes a Military Power

By 1899 Japan had succeeded in her efforts to abolish the "unequal" treaties that had been forced on her by the foreign powers when they established diplomatic relations more than thirty years before—treaties which excluded foreigners from prosecution under Japan's laws and restricted Japan's power to levy duties on imports. In 1894 Japan had followed the example of the European powers, had gone to war with China and had defeated her giant neighbor. China had to pay a large indemnity, grant Korea independence, and hand to Japan various territories—Taiwan, the Pescadore Islands, and the Liaotung peninsula in southern Manchuria. Almost immediately Russia, France, and Germany joined diplomatically and forced Japan to return the Liaotung peninsula to China. Three years later Russia seized this peninsula for itself. In 1902 Japan won Britain to her side with an Anglo-Japanese Naval Alliance and attacked Russia in 1904. The Russians were defeated. They had to acknowledge Japan's paramount interest in Korea, transfer to Japan their lease of the Liaotung peninsula and their railways in southern Manchuria, and cede the southern half of Sakhalin, an island north of Hokkaido. In 1910 Japan annexed Korea. During the First World War she acquired German possessions in China and the North Pacific. She had become a world power.

When the elder statesmen *(genro)* passed on, power remained with their protégés, who were closely linked with the armed forces and the *zaibatsu*. In the 1920s it seemed that Japan's parliamentary system might influence the behind-the-scenes government but, by the thirties, economic depression, aggressive nationalism, and the strength of the leaders of the armed forces curbed more liberal tendencies. The military men were deeply dissatisfied with governments that curbed their allocation of state funds and limited their say in foreign policy. Thought to be more "sincere" than the rich leaders of industry and self-seeking politicians, the military officers had wide support. Most of the farming population had received army education as young conscripts. Farm families had never benefited during times of national prosperity and the starvation wages of the urban poor were threatened by the world depression.

In 1928 in Manchuria, the army took independent action. Young officers blew up a train to kill a Chinese warlord. In 1931 middle-grade officers, claiming that Chinese had destroyed a section of the Manchurian Railway, overran all Manchuria. The army closed ranks and defied government endeavors to punish the offenders. Manchuria was made a puppet state, Manchukuo. The League of Nations sent a commission and condemned Japan. She withdrew from the League. In 1932, young army men assassinated government leaders, including Prime Minister Inukai. In 1936 they committed another massacre of parliamentary leaders. Progressively the political parties lost all influence over the government. Prime ministers came and went until, in October 1941, General Tojo, as Prime Minister and head of the army, established open military control.

In 1936 Japan had joined an Anti-Comintern pact with Germany. By 1938 she had captured all of China's main cities and ports, though the Chinese fought on. In that year she went to war with the Soviet Union on the eastern border of Manchukuo and was defeated. Three years later she had taken military control of French Indo-China. America restricted scrap iron and oil sales to Japan and, in 1941, with the British and Dutch, imposed an oil embargo.

World War II and Its Aftermath

With war in Europe, Japan could have withdrawn from China, resumed friendly relations with America, and developed her industries to take over the whole Eastern and much of the world market, as she had done during the First World War. Economically she would have gained immeasurably. Instead she chose to go to war with America.

At dawn on Sunday, December 7, 1941, Japan attacked the United States at Pearl Harbor without warning. Four years of fighting in China had developed her armed forces and their industrial support to their fullest extent. Within six months she conquered Malaya, Singapore, the Dutch East Indies, the Philippines, and Burma. Siam had become her ally. However, within a year her advance was halted. By 1945 her overseas forces were isolated and her cities in ruins. She was exhausted and surrendered unconditionally on August 14, 1945, a week after atom bombs had been dropped on Hiroshima and Nagasaki.

Japan was occupied by a foreign army for the first time in her history. A Far Eastern Commission of eleven (later thirteen) countries in Washington, and an Allied Council for Japan of the four major Allies in Tokyo, were empowered to make policy. However, the American armed forces, under General Douglas MacArthur, with the title Supreme Commander of the Allied Powers, took over the Occupation to the virtual exclusion of the Allies. To his American subordinates, and to the Japanese, MacArthur was, almost literally and certainly in common parlance, God.

Japan was demilitarized and stripped of her overseas possessions. Her soldiers and civilians, over six million of them, were brought home. Repressive laws were scrapped. Political prisoners were released, militaristic and ultranationalistic organizations dissolved. Shinto ceased to be a state-organized religion. War criminals were brought to trial. About 200,000 persons who had held positions of responsibility in carrying out the war were "purged," not as individuals but by category—military officers, military police, politicians, civil servants, businessmen, teachers.

The Occupation policies were, however, remarkably lenient. The actual government of the country was left in Japanese hands. Reforms were instituted with the aim of creating a democracy rather than penalizing a defeated enemy. A new constitution amended the old one of 1889. It deprived the emperor of all political power but he remained as "the symbol of the State and of the unity of the people." He declared that he was not "divine" and was not tried as a war criminal. The new parliamentary system gave government to an elected House of Representatives, no longer subordinate to the military, the Privy Council, or the House of Peers (which became an elected House of Councillors). The judiciary was made independent. The fundamental rights of the individual were legalized. Japan renounced war and the maintenance of military forces "forever."

Wealth was redistributed by a crippling capital levy, as well as graduated income and inheritance taxes. The huge commercial and industrial conglomerates (the zaibatsu) were broken into smaller units. Absentee landlords were abolished and tenants enabled to buy the land they cultivated. The noblity lost their titles. Education and the school system were restructured along American lines. Labor unions were encouraged.

Industry was almost nonexistent, inflation horrific. The urban population, swollen by returnees, was impoverished. Only farmers had reasonable incomes. By 1948 economic recovery became a major objective for the Occupation authorities, and the war in Korea in 1950–1951 made the supply of American troops a top priority. A peace treaty was signed by 48 nations (but not by Mainland China or the Soviet Union) on September 8, 1951, in San Francisco and the Occupation terminated April 28, 1952. On the same day Japan and America signed a security pact.

External trade flourished, first in textiles and in products with a high labor content such as cameras, binoculars, and a huge range of "sundry goods." The manufacture of ships, steel, and cement progressively expanded. Then came motorcycles, radios, and TVs. The government supported industry at the expense of the home consumer. Inadequate social services forced the people to save. Industries retained profits and ploughed them back into the latest plants and equipment. As a result, Japan's economy was "miraculously" successful in the late fifties, and proceeded to expand at an evergrowing pace. The gross national product grew at a rate of 10 percent or more each year.

Japan Today

Privation during hostilities and the shock of the nuclear bombs on Hiroshima and Nagasaki created a deeply rooted revulsion against war. American army bases throughout the country became reminders of what everyone wanted to forget. In 1960 a new treaty with America was signed, providing that the United States would consult with Japan before using its bases for combat and that nuclear weapons would not be brought in without consultation. During the 1980s the United States has been pushing Japan to expand her no longer insignificant "defense" forces. A new generation of Japanese is still reluctant, but Japan's defense budget has been increased substantially.

Recent economic developments are well known. To enable its war-torn industries to reestablish themselves, imports were virtually prohibited for the first two postwar decades. These restrictions caused worldwide resentment and have been progressively relaxed during the last decade. Nevertheless, Japan remains a difficult market for overseas manufacturers. Her success in exporting high quality products competitively causes great irritation in many countries where world depression has led to unprecedented unemployment. Japan's success has boomeranged to such an extent that the principle of free trade is being challenged by workers and the owners of industry in many countries whose economies are threatened. Is Japan on a peak or a plateau, or has she more heights to scale? Each of the three possibilities has its advocates.

(See also the Historical and Art History Chronologies at the back of the book.)

THE CRAFTS AND HANDWORK OF JAPAN

by
PATRICIA MASSY

Patricia Massy has lived in Japan since 1965. Her column "Crafts and Craftsmen" is a popular feature of the Japan Times, *and among her publications is* Sketches of Japanese Crafts, *about folkcrafts existent today.*

Despite its overwhelming achievements in modern technology, Japan has retained a surprising number of its traditional crafts, even adding to them new Western techniques and concepts. At a time when industrialized societies are struggling to accommodate human skills to robotized mass production, this has placed Japan in a preeminent position. Here there is such an abundance to learn and to enjoy that the visitor interested in handwork invariably feels the need to return again and yet again.

The endurance of the traditional arts can only be partially explained by Japan's long cultural heritage. These arts were brought precariously close to extinction when after the overthrow of the shogunate, in their eagerness to catch up with the West, the Japanese readily destroyed

56

whatever was valued in the past. At the same time, the artisans who had operated under the protection of the feudal lords or who had supplied their needs, suddenly found themselves unemployed and, still worse, unemployable. Who, for instance, needed the braided cords called *kumihimo* that were made exclusively for samurai armor?

The *kumihimo* makers eventually solved their dilemma by innovating a new use for the cords as ornamental accessories for the woman's obi. Although many crafts were rescued by such do-or-die ingenuity, which did not always prove as successful aesthetically as it did economically, other crafts slowly sank into oblivion. On the other hand, export industries—Kyoto's brocades, Arita's porcelains—flourished through the introduction of European production methods. Likewise, new crafts derived from the West, such as hammered copperware, were born, eventually becoming traditions in themselves.

In every field at least one dedicated person could be found who kept faith in the ancient skills of Japan. These rare few were among those chosen in 1955 by the Agency for Cultural Affairs as recipients of the title "Holder of an Important Intangible Cultural Property," an honor that requires them to preserve the traditional skills and to convey them to the next generation. Among the present recipients, who are popularly called Living National Treasures *(ningen kokuho),* thirty-three work in the hand arts. Eleven groups of craftspeople have also been awarded special status for maintaining a local craft such as the spinning of floss silk and *kasuri* dyeing (see under *Textiles,* below) of Yuki in Saitama Prefecture. Encouraging artists and artisans to persevere, the IICP program has stimulated interest in and respect for their work among the general public. It has also inadvertently served to boost the prices of their creations to astronomical heights. As original work seldom dips below the million yen mark, the average collector must be satisfied with studio pieces or the work of a student of the master.

Folk Art

Initially an even greater impetus for good craft work was sparked by Soetsu Yanagi, a thinker and critic, who, finding the greatest beauty in simple things, launched a handcraft movement in the 1920s that soon gained more momentum than any other in the world. To differentiate the work of the unknown craftsman, which he considered self-less, from that of the artist, which was self-conscious, Yanagi coined a new Japanese word, *mingei,* meaning the art of the people.

Siding with Yanagi were several potters who later rose to the foremost position in contemporary pottery: Shoji Hamada, Kanjiro Kawai, Kenkichi Tomimoto, and the Englishman Bernard Leach. Their work can be seen at the *mingei-kan* (folk art museum) in Tokyo and Kurashiki. Even a short visit to one of these museums is inspiring.

Unfortunately, Yanagi's message was misinterpreted by many as approval of anything amateurishly handmade, especially things with a rustic or regional look. Shoddy articles of straw or fake *kasuri* and cheaply conceived knickknacks are labeled *mingei* in souvenir shops throughout the country. True *mingei* shops are now changing their names to *kogei* (handwork) or *zakkaya* (a shop selling sundry domestic wares).

The Mingei Association includes numerous craftspeople who adhere to Yanagi's aesthetic concepts and who look toward the pieces produced in preindustrialized times for inspiration rather than for imitation. In October each year the *mingei-kan* in Tokyo holds an exhibition of their new work. Most pieces are for sale.

Fine Crafts

Those whose interest lies more in elegant examples of handwork should visit the *Dentokogei-ten,* an exhibition of the work of craftspeople who strive toward the ultimate in perfection and skill. Held on a national scale starting in mid-September in Tokyo and regionally in April, it displays work in every category of fine crafts from figurines and silverwork to basketry and kimono. Some of the Living National Treasures enter their pieces as well. As can be expected, prices are far beyond the reach of the ordinary pocketbook. That a goodly amount is bought reveals the Japanese appreciation for the intrinsic value of fine workmanship.

The *Dentokogei-ten* schedule varies slightly from year to year, usually starting in Tokyo (Mitsukoshi Department Store) in mid-September, then traveling on to Nagoya, Osaka, Kanazawa, Okayama, Takamatsu, Fukuoka, and Hiroshima with a two-week display at each location. It winds up in Kyoto around mid-February.

Most craftspeople belong to one or more associations that give them an opportunity to exhibit. Watch the newspapers for an extensive listing of individual and group shows, many of which are presented in the department store galleries. Among these are *Nitten,* which attracts the avant-garde, and *Kokugakai* (its exhibition is billed as *Kokuten*), which is an off-shoot of the Mingei Association. Craft Center Japan is unique in being an association of individual crafts people that has a permanent showroom at Maruzen Book Store in Tokyo and Kyoto. Oriented more towards design than technique, this group's work is marked by simplicity and function in form.

In 1975 the government promulgated the Law for the Promotion of Traditional Craft Industry, qualifying regional handcrafts with a history of 100 years or more to receive official recognition upon meeting the established standards. Over 100 crafts have won admittance to this select membership, allowing them to display a special mark. An excellent showroom has been established in Tokyo: Japan Traditional Craft Center (Zenkoku Dentoteki Kogeihin Senta) near the Gaienmae subway station on Aoyama-dori, closed Thursdays. Besides biweekly displays, it also offers dozens of videotapes (some in English), a library of craft-related books and magazines (mostly in Japanese), and helpful information service. Held around the second week of January at Seibu Department Store in Tokyo's Ikebukuro, association's annual exhibition has the air of a great fair, as craftspeople from all over the country show their wares and demonstrate their skills. A similar exhibition occurs in mid-September in Osaka. The choices offered at those times are bewildering in number, reasonable in price, and unique in opportunity.

Choose Carefully

Craft shops abound—some good, some just so-so—giving the visitor here plenty of exercise in sorting out what is of true value and plenty of frustration when the budget finally demands a limitation in spending. Although it is difficult to generalize, the clever shopper would probably shun the arcades and souvenir spots in favor of specialty shops such as Takumi or Ginka Corner. In department stores, too, articles not displayed in the galleries and craft sections should be carefully scrutinized. What appears to be wood might not be so at all. Some rather pretty "lacquerwork" is being done with cashew lacquer on plastic. If the price is considerably lower than other pieces, chances are you have found a good imitation. As Hideyoshi is supposed to have said back in the 16th century, you get what you pay for. This does not necessarily mean that highly priced articles are good—here is where the discriminating eye must be put to play—but Japanese labor now costs as much as it does in other industrialized countries. For this reason, the majority of bamboo baskets sold for household use come from China. A quick comparison with a Japanese basket will show that the imported examples are poor in quality and workmanship—the bamboo tends to be splintery and the rim sloppily finished. Of course, China does produce fine bamboo work; it will be found in reputable craft shops.

Regional Crafts

During the rule of the Tokugawa, the provinces were administered by the *daimyo* like integral countries, kept separate by economic and physical barriers. The outcome was the development of local cultures of such variety in form and content that even after over 100 years of free intercourse, unique characteristics are evident in each district. This is especially true of the crafts, many having been established or encouraged by the feudal overlords for trade with other provinces or for tribute to the shogun in lieu of rice. The list includes Wajima lacquerware, Echigo ramie (a linen-like cloth), Nanbu iron tea kettles, Gifu paper lanterns and umbrellas, Satsuma pottery, and Nabeshima porcelain, among many others. Employing a great number of people who performed specialized tasks, these crafts were considered the prime industries of the time.

Besides such crafts produced primarily for "export," others sprang from local needs (sake and pickle barrels, chests of drawers, fishing and farming tools) and from local festivals and religious beliefs (kites, masks, talismans). Another source was the home (textiles for everyday wear or for mattress covers, snowboots, and backpacks of straw). Finally we come to souvenirs made by people catering to the traveling merchant, the pilgrim, the hotspring guest, the samurai on his way to and from Edo. These include pâpier-maché and clay figurines, woodblock prints, lathe-turned bowls and *kokeshi* dolls, wooden combs, and tie-dye cotton fabric.

Today whoever buys any one of these traditional crafts is taking home a fragment of the life of old Japan.

Pottery. Contemporary pottery is fascinating to student and collector alike because in it are found the many styles that have emerged since the Yayoi people brought the potter's wheel and the tunnel kiln from Korea sometimes between A.D. 200–300, supplanting the remarkable, but primitive, hand-coiled and rope-impressed work of the prehistoric Jomon period. Masterful hand-coiling and paddling have continued uninterrupted in such folk kilns as Tamba, Otani, and Tsuboya, and some Shigaraki and Shino potters have reestablished the tunnel kiln for its wondrous effects of fire and ash that are beyond the range of human power. From the tunnel kiln evolved a more controllable type of sloped kiln called *noborigama*. For over 1,000 years the potters of Bizen in Okayana Prefecture have been producing *noborigama* pieces famous for their firemarks and accidental glazes formed by the soft ash that is swept through the kiln by the searing flames of the pine fire. A visit to the private museum of the late Kei Fujiwara, a Living National Treasure, will reveal the awesome potential of Bizen pottery. For a look at *noborigama*, the two most convenient kiln sites are Mashiko near Tokyo and Shigaraki near Kyoto. The memorial museum of Kanjiro Kawai in Kyoto also contains a *noborigama*. Although the kiln is no longer in use, the dwelling and its furnishings, both designed by Kawai, and the pottery shaped by his hands provide a glimpse into the life and heart of a potter.

Porcelain production began around 1600 in the Arita area of Kyushu, marking a turning point in Japanese pottery. About this time the tea cult had attained such influence among the rich and powerful that a number of Kyushu *daimyo* abducted hundreds of potters from Korea in order to produce Korean-style teaware in their own fiefs. Karatsu and the folk kilns of Onda and Koishibara are among those that show glaze and forming techniques of Korean origin. Arita also owes much to advanced Korean skills. The beautiful blue and white Arita porcelain with overglaze enamels came to be treasured throughout Japan and even in faraway Europe, for, along with silks, it was the most important article of overseas trade in the feudal era. Kurita Museum outside Tokyo houses an extensive collection of Imari and Nabeshima ware produced in the Arita area. Porcelain kilns were also established in Seto near Nagoya (of Noritake ware fame), in Kanazawa (Kutani ware), and in Kyoto. It was in Kyoto that the art of applying overglaze enamels to earthenware was first successfully accomplished, and the ancient capital has ever since been famous for its elegant porcelains and colorfully enameled earthenware. A National Treasure tea jar by Ninsei, who invented the enameling technique, is owned by the MOA Museum in Atami.

Seto saw the development of Oribe ware, admired by tea devotees for its fanciful green and iron-brown brush painting, and another earthenware coated with a thick white-pocked feldspathic glaze called Shino, which was also a favorite for the tea ceremony. At the same time ash glazes improved by leaps and bounds in both Kyoto and Seto. The best celadon and *tenmoku* glazes, which originated in Sung China, now are produced by Japanese master potters. In this way, through the creative application of old methods and an eagerness to attempt new ones, Japanese potters have reached the pinnacle in achievement.

CRAFTS AND HANDWORK 61

As there are well over 100 kiln sites with innumerable potters work-ing in innumerable styles and no one knows how many more working independently, this brief survey will have to act merely as a point of reference for a journey into the world of Japanese pottery. Whether you discover perfection-conscious artisans or imaginative modern artists, mass production or one-of-a-kind, it is an intriguing trip.

Textiles. Because the kimono encourages the use of contrasting weaves and patterns and subtle color combinations, the Japanese have a keen appreciation of handmade textiles. Although kimono dealers no longer enjoy a large turnover, formal occasions still inspire women to don their best Japanese attire. Western clothes, too, sometimes are made of handweaves. Accordingly, the textile arts attract a significant number of young people, some working in the big Kyoto textile indus-try, some doing creative work. The modern creative work is not imme-diately noticeable, however, as it appears primarily in private and group shows.

The most conspicuous textile art is the formal kimono. Most origi-nate in Kyoto where they are hand-dyed in the painstaking *yuzen* process. The design may be applied with outlines of rice paste resist or by means of dozens of stencils. The fascinating process, which is brought to completion with gold and silver foil and delicate silk em-broidery, can be seen at the Yuzen Kaikan.

Worn with *yuzen* kimono, the brocade *obi* are produced on jacquard looms in the Nishijin area of Kyoto. Scintillating metallic yarns and foil highlight the brilliant patterns, which are visible to the weaver only from the reverse side to prevent soiling the fabric. Tapestry weave is the most tedious work. The weaver manipulates up to 40 shuttles at one time and pushes the weft yarns into the silk warp by means of his or her fingernails, which are kept filed like a comb for this purpose. Demonstrations of brocade weaving are held at the Nishijin Kaikan and the Dentosangyo Kaikan, where the many refined handcrafts of Kyoto are on display.

In the countryside, women in prewar days would weave the regional fabrics for their simple kimono, but today very few face a loom except to make an income. Floss silk *(tsumugi)*, cotton, and ramie fiber are woven in stripes, plaids, and *kasuri,* a technique whereby the yarns are tie-dyed before weaving so that when woven they produce a pattern. The "picture *kasuri*" of Kurume and Yumigahama are particularly admired. Bought by the bolt, which is one kimono length (i.e., about 12 meters by 33 centimeters), kimono fabrics can run into quite a lot of money. At antique shops and shrine fairs, however, one can easily acquire an old kimono in a fairly good regional weave. Sometimes examples of *kasuri* weaves are made especially for cushion covers and wall hangings.

In the northern prefecture of Iwate some excellent homespun is being woven into mufflers, ties, and piece goods. Also locally produced are tie-dye patterns on silk in natural red madder and purple dyes. Nearby in Aomori there is an unusual type of counted embroidery called *kogin,* made with white cotton yarn on dark blue hemp or wool. The embroid-erer counts the yarns of the dark blue wool or hempcloth as she carefully works the white cotton stitches into geometrical patterns. *Kogin* is so incredibly precise that it is often mistaken for a weave.

The casual summer kimono is a crisp blue and white cotton *yukata.* Although the traditional manner of dyeing with paste resist is now reserved for the connoisseur, the clean-cut stenciled lines of the *yukata* patterns are irresistible in their Japaneseness. Blue and White, a creative boutique in Tokyo, specializes in adapting these *yukata* fabrics for practical modern apparel and accessories.

Another stencil art, the bright *bingata* of Okinawa, has become world-famous through the work of the late Living National Treasure Keisuke Serizawa. A leader of the folk art movement, Serizawa blended flowing Okinawan motifs with the stylized approach characteristic of folk art, and, with the spark of his boundless imagination, brought to life patterns that are stunning in their bold use of form, line, and color. His popular calendars and cards on handmade paper are stocked at Takumi Craft Shop in Tokyo, where it is also possible to obtain a *noren* (short curtain hung in doorways) or screen from his studio. A visit to the Serizawa Museum, a 20-minute bus ride from Shizuoka, is highly recommended. Viewing his works and his private collection of folk textiles in the tranquil setting of the exquisitely designed museum is an uplifting experience.

Woodwork. Blessed with great forests of hardwoods with beautiful grain (horse chestnut, *keyaki,* persimmon) and straight evergreens that split well *(hinoki* and *sugi),* the Japanese have since earliest times relied on wood for their dwellings and domestic needs and have learned to understand its potential as a material for fine craftsmanship. In the domestic field, cooperage still plays an important role. The coopers of Kyoto and Akita produce fine-drawn basins and pails that are too pretty to be kept out of sight. Bentwood lunch boxes (*bento-bako*) made of *sugi* and laced with cherrybark once were a common lunchtime sight but now are more often seen on the coffee table. *Bento-bako* and *jubako* (stacked boxes) coated with a golden transparent lacquer called *shunkei* are a well-known craft of Takayama. Good woodwork usually is given a coat of lacquer, either transparent or opaque, and many lacquerware areas exist, Wajima at the tip of Noto Peninsula having the highest reputation. Noted for *maki-e* (designs in gold and silver and nacre) and *chingin* (etched designs inlaid with gold and silver) executed on a thick coat of glossy black lacquer, the products of Wajima represent the acme in elegance, but many other interesting and beautiful techniques have equal value. Although lacquer is resistant to heat and chemicals, direct sunlight spoils the color, and the dryness of heated rooms may cause cracking of the lacquer and warping of the wood.

Tansu, the Japanese chest of drawers, have acquired widespread popularity abroad for their strong, simple lines and stout iron fittings. Tansu may be constructed of *keyaki* (prized for its burly grain), cherry, pine, or *kiri* (prized for its lightness). Traditionally *tansu* are produced in the cities of Sakata, Sendai, and Matsumoto, the latter specializing in dark-stained furniture combining elements of both East and West. Because of the price of modern pieces, however, most visitors prefer to buy antique furniture.

Finally, a word must be put in for the distinguished cabinetmakers of Kyoto and Tokyo. Working with choice wood and toylike tools, they skillfully create traditional pieces of furniture, stationery boxes, cosmetic boxes, tea cabinets, sets of drawers for valuables, and so on, all showing the refinement demanded by the wealthy townspeople of old.

Paper. Although the number of papermakers has diminished in recent times, over fifty papermaking locations remain active today, producing paper coveted throughout the world for its loveliness and durability. Papers with a shiny surface are made from *gampi* or *mitsumata*, both growing wild in mountainous areas. *Kozo,* a kind of mulberry, produces a rustic paper of such incredible strength that it can be treated like cloth. For an enjoyable outing to see the papermaking process, visit Ogawa near Tokyo or Kurodani near Kyoto. Charming stenciled and tie-dyed paper products are made from Kurodani paper. In Gifu, too, the existence of a good local paper led to the development of the famed Gifu lanterns and umbrellas. Ozeki Company, which also manufactures the sculptural paper lamps of American artist Isamu Noguchi, allows visitors in its workroom to view the clever construction of the delicately painted traditional summer lanterns called *Gifu chochin.*

While Kyoto is famous for its elegant papers and paper fans (stop by Miyawaki Baisen's perfumed shop to discover the delights of a fan, only one of which is to make a cooling breeze), Tokyo is known for *chiyogami,* gaily patterned woodblock-printed papers. Used to decorate boxes and to fold into *origami* crafts, *chiyogami* come in a tantalizing variety of designs. The leading *chiyogami* maker, Isetatsu, has a shop close to Sendagi Station on the Chiyoda subway line where one can pick up folded paper dolls called *anesama ningyo,* miniature notebooks, *chiyogami*-style paper napkins, and other charming articles of old Tokyo, as well as a selection of *chiyogami* patterns.

Figurines. The traditional Japanese doll is not meant to be played with. Whether a folk object or an example of fine art, *ningyo* are for display. The origin of the majority of folk figurines can be traced to a wish for protection against harm and illness, for fertility, for success in business, or for prosperity. The roly-poly pâpier-maché *daruma,* for instance, represents a Zen monk who sat so long in meditation that his legs withered away. Because the toy arights itself when knocked over, it signifies recovery from misfortune. The figures of an old man and woman symbolize long life and conjugal happiness. The superbly crafted Kyoto dolls of little boys and girls originally were intended as decoys should harm approach the real child. *Hina ningyo* of the Doll's Festival are thought to have evolved from such substitution figures. It can be understood why the Japanese treat dolls so respectfully and speak of the doll as having a soul. The costume dolls, which range from the gorgeous to the sublime, also are instilled with symbolic or poetic meaning. The very best of these truly attain the level of fine art: two dollmakers have been designated National Treasures. The pearly white finish on the dolls is achieved by several applications of oystershell paint, a skill that in itself takes years to acquire.

Metalwork. Even if jewelry making has blossomed late in Japan, there being no traditional jewelry outside of Okinawa, other fine metalwork has more than made up for this deficiency. Of international fame is the Japanese sword. One should not overlook the fact that not a few swordsmiths turned to the manufacture of scissors and knives at the end of the feudal period; so these commonplace articles are far from common. Forged of iron for resilience and steel for sharpness, Japanese edge tools have no equal. In metal casting, too, the Japanese artisans are supreme, whether in the production of colossal temple bells or in the forming of tea kettles. Their skill in metal inlay, which caused wonderment when first seen in Europe a century ago, once embellished tea kettles and sword guards. Now it is more often seen on decorative pieces and small ornaments.

JAPAN

64

Recommended shops. *Moyai* in Kitakamakura (turn right after coming out main exit of Kitakamakura Station) has excellent examples of folk pottery (Onda, Koishibara, Shuzai) and baskets (bamboo, *akebi,* wild grape, wisteria).

Ginka Corner. run by the Bunka Publishing Company which puts out the fantastic magazine *Ginka* (Silver Flower), offers a continuously changing selection of sophisticated art and craft work. The main gallery is located near Keio Hotel.

Takumi, down from Ginza's Sony Building towards Shinbashi Station, was the first *mingei* shop in Japan and is known for its Mashiko pottery and regional crafts.

Tsukamoto, a few blocks toward Tameike from the Roppongi intersection, specializes in Mashiko pottery.

Bingoya, at Wakamatsu-Cho, Shinjuku-Ku, has the most extensive collection of folk crafts in Tokyo. As it was originally a doll shop, it is especially strong on *kokeshi* and other folk figurines.

Kogensha in the city of Morioka in Tohoku is famous for its extensive collection of northern Japan crafts; excellent coffee shop.

Tsugaru Kogei Ten in Hirosaki (also in Tohoku) is small but well-stocked with *akebi* baskets, *kogin,* and other crafts of Aomori Prefecture.

Uoza, in Tsuruya Department Store in the city of Kumamoto on Kyushu and Hitoyoshi, also in Kumanoto Prefecture, features the work found in southern Japan.

Kura, located in an old *godown* across the street from the Kurashiki Folk Art Museum, is known for its carefully chosen crafts from Japan and other parts of Asia.

Kogei Kudaka in Naha city offers a better choice in Okinawan crafts than any other place in Japan.

THE PERFORMING ARTS IN

JAPAN

by
STUART ATKIN

Stuart Atkin is a writer, actor, and narrator, living in Tokyo. He runs the only resident British professional theater group in Japan, "Albion-za," which gives regular performances in Tokyo and around the country. Mr. Atkin has also written a humorous book about Japan, and has been a regular columnist for the Mainichi Daily News.

Japan is a land of performers. This is hardly surprising, as so much of the Japanese history of manners and relationships is based on rituals both complex and simple.

There is perhaps no better way to enjoy a visit to Japan than to adopt the "man-watching" approach of the British zoologist, Dr. Desmond Morris. On a recent visit to Japan he wandered around observing the Japanese interact with one another. He noted the persistent ritual of bowing: a skillfully choreographed and well-timed mode of behavior full of meaning. He watched the subtle psychological rituals that surround sumo wrestling and commented on the deliberate avoidance of facial expression. He sat in the theater and watched the melodramatic extensions of daily behavior that are enacted in Kabuki: the exaggerated suggestions of deep emotion presented in a symbolic fashion. He joined the cheerleaders at a high school baseball tournament and noted that the well-synchronized chanting and drumming corresponds exactly to the normal heartbeat, only accelerating and finally breaking up into a thousand individual reactions during moments of great excitement.

These are just a few examples of the great panoply of rituals and performances to be found in Japanese life, on stage and off. Ritual is at the heart of all performance and so many of the detailed body movements and behavior patterns of the Japanese stem directly from Buddhist training, Shinto ceremonies, and the ancient code of samurai behavior. Over the centuries these rituals were refined and simplified into the ascetic disciplines so well known today in the West: Zen, the Tea Ceremony, *ikebana, kendo,* calligraphy, and many others. But these rituals are only one aspect of the wealth of performing arts to be discovered in Japan.

It is not necessary to pay anything to witness the Japanese in performance. Tokyo's big Western-style hotels would appear to be the least likely places to experience anything intrinsically Japanese, and yet every day they are the venue for wedding parties, celebrations of all kinds and meetings that demonstrate all the ritualistic elements of behavior that oil the workings of society. A ride on any train will soon display many more: in particular, the performances of men who take a pride in their work and see the control of a train full of passengers as a role of great responsibility. The guards (conductors) wear white gloves and salute their colleagues on the platform. Stationmasters salute express trains as they whistle through the station. Join any tour by bus or boat and the performance will go on endlessly. The guide will sing and carefully explain the delights of the surrounding scenery whether or not the weather permits vision of it and, indeed, whether or not there are any Japanese-speaking customers present. Visit a department store and the story is the same. Arrive at 10:00 A.M. as the doors open and you will be greeted like royalty at a film premiere by ranks of bowing sales assistants; ride up and down in the elevator a few times to experience the extraordinary singsong delivery of girls with their bland expressions—a performance that is the result of many rehearsals in the elevator-girl training department. The show even extends to the girls who stand outside the elevator. It is a delight to watch the skill with which they can bow to the customers and manage to extract head and obligatory hat from the doorway just before the doors close. Another well-rehearsed detail of life can be found in all kinds of shops: the art of gift-wrapping. If you say that the tin of biscuits or electric toilet-seat heater you are buying is a present, you may even get a choice of ribbon.

The list of such daily rituals is endless. Some of them look unnecessary at first glance, but they do promote a sense of well-being and order and help to smooth the daily interactions of Japan's 119 million people.

One rung up the performing ladder brings us to those informal performances in which the Japanese take such great delight. Many Westerners have a basic image of Japanese people as being either poker-faced, sober, conservative, and uncommunicative as individuals or outrageously noisy in tour groups. In fact the Japanese are a gregarious and raucous nation on home territory and in familiar situations. Both the stresses of city life and the rigors of rural life are dissipated by way of the joys of party-giving, drinking, dancing, and singing. Most Japanese love to get up and perform and will therefore find any excuse for a party. Sometimes the excuse is seasonal—end-of-year, Christmas, start-of-year, cherry-blossom-viewing, etc.—or it may be for birthdays, coming-of-age, arriving, leaving, moving, anniversaries. In fact, it is possible to find 365 different excuses for having a good time.

Few visitors have the chance to witness the traditional wedding party with its blend of unsmiling inter-family contractual agreement and riotous singing and jokes full of innuendo. But everyone has the chance to see one of the dozens of street festivals that happen every day all over the country—happily uniting the rhythms and rites of the past with the loudspeakers and lifestyles of the present.

To see the drinkers in action, all you have to do is visit some medium-sized *akachochin,* a kind of bar-cum-restaurant distinguished by a red lantern hanging beside the entrance. These places serve Western-style food as well as Japanese delicacies and have a free-and-easy, noisy atmosphere. The ability to speak Japanese is not essential and invitations to join in the general carousing are frequent. Have some old favorite song up your sleeve—whether you can really sing or not—and you could make friends for life. Any song will do: anything from "Old Macdonald Had A Farm" to "Yesterday" will be acceptable, or even your national anthem if all else fails.

The same preparation (one simple song) is also useful for experiencing a recent cultural phenomenon, the *karaoke* bar. The word *karate* means "empty hand," and *karaoke* stands for "empty orchestra." This is a special kind of mixer/cassette player which provides the musical backing for whoever wants to stand in the spotlight at the microphone and sing along. In some establishments you automatically pay for this privilege on the bill, in others you pay a small amount for every song you render. Even if you decline all invitations to perform, you can still spend an hour or two watching the antics of the eager amateur songsters of Japan in thousands of karaoke bars or "snacks" across the nation.

Another recent performing attraction is the gathering of young people on weekends in such places as Yoyogi Park, near Harajuku in central Tokyo, or beside Osaka Castle. Out come a hundred portable cassette players and around them weave the representatives of a weird selection of groups, ranging from the "Takenokozoku" ("Bamboo-Shoot Tribe") with their pseudo-Chinese frippery to the "Amegurazoku" ("American Graffiti Tribe") and their passable imitations of the Presley era. Once again it is all free entertainment.

Behind all of these informal performances lies the weight of centuries of formal entertainment, many forms of which are still very much alive. One look at any of the English-language newspapers or weekly and monthly guides to what is happening in all the major cities will indicate the huge variety of performing arts available in Japan to suit all tastes and all budgets. A Horowitz concert, a foreign ballet or opera performance, or a Julio Iglesias dinner show could cost you up to $200 a head, or roughly the same as a private geisha show. On the other hand, you can sit right next to the *hanamichi* or "flower path" at the National Theater in Tokyo and smell the perfumed actors and see every stitch in their elaborate kimonos for as little as $8.

The National Theater

The spacious and elegant National Theater, across the moat from the Imperial Palace in Tokyo, should certainly be included on the itinerary of anyone interested in the traditional performing arts of Japan. It is a big complex with three separate auditoriums: the main one for Kabuki and other large-scale performances; the Small Hall, which specializes in Bunraku performances; and the more recent intimate theater largely devoted to the popular art of comic story-telling called Rakugo. The National Theatre differs from, say, the British National Theatre complex in two ways: first, you cannot just wander around buying souvenirs or posters or drop in for a drink without a ticket for a performance; second, the main purpose is very clearly stipulated: to present, and thereby help to preserve, the traditional performing arts from all corners of Japan. National Theatre programs regularly include folk dancing, Buddhist chanting, Gagaku (Imperial Court Music), regional drumming, and concerts using traditional musical instruments, as well as Kabuki and Bunraku. Special lecture-demonstration performances are given regularly. Although designed primarily for school children they are well worth seeing for their explanations of Japanese theater techniques. Modern plays are also presented, but only if they have been successfully performed elsewhere, vetted, and regarded as suitable. The National Theatre's policy is essentially conservative, so expect nothing shocking.

Kabuki

The Japanese are fond of describing the great playwright of the Edo Period (1600–1868) as the "Shakespeare of Japan." His name was Chikamatsu Monzaemon and he was very much responsible for molding all kinds of source material into the poetic dramas we can still see today under the general title of "Kabuki." Although he began writing for actors, he developed an interest in the popular puppet theater, Bunraku, and many of his plays began as puppet dramas before being transformed into Kabuki epics.

But the real origins of Kabuki were laid 50 years before his birth, around the time that Shakespeare was writing *King Lear* and *Othello*. Taking advantage of the peace recently established by the first Tokugawa Shogun, Tokugawa Ieyasu, a group of female performers began producing dancing and singing shows of a distinctly lewd nature for the masses. The performers also made money on the side as prostitutes. These wild performances rapidly gained popularity and were referred to as "Kabuki" ("avant-garde"). The same name is used now, but is written using the characters for "song-dance-skill."

Eventually the military regime took exception to these shows and banned female performers in 1629. This lead to the birth of the all-male Kabuki form we still have today. Kabuki gradually developed into a real theatrical art during the late 17th century and early 18th century, at the same time as the puppet-narration art of Bunraku. Both theatrical forms differed from the traditional performing arts in that they were created by and for the lower strata of the feudal society, in particular the merchant townsmen. As a result, they suffered from various restrictions imposed by the ruling military regime not unlike those imposed on Shakespeare's actors. With the continuing ban on female performers, the Kabuki actors developed the *onnagata* (female impersonators) whose ideal representations of feminine grace and beauty still serve as models today; indeed, several leading actors are the principals of *buyo* dancing schools.

Chikamatsu and the other playwrights were fascinated by topical stories, many of them to do with the finacial troubles of the "gay quarters," love suicides, murders, and the like. Elaborate sets and costumes were produced to depict the Edo world in detail, and performances today closely resemble those portrayed in woodblock prints of 150 years ago. Dramas that involved the upper levels of society were thinly disguised as fictional stories set in medieval Japan. In this way the actors could escape censure even though they were really presenting contemporary dramas using contemporary language. Some themes were taken from Noh or Kyogen plays, but they were transformed into a readily accessible theatrical form.

Kabuki has become much better known around the world in recent years thanks to the efforts of popular actors such as Ichikawa Ennosuke, Nakamura Utaemon, and Bando Tamasaburo. Kabuki tours rightly consist of attractive or exciting fragments, generally much shorter than the performances in Japan. But the pruning of plays and concentration on spectacular effects has also been happening at home, and although it raises many eyebrows among conservatives, it has led to something of an upsurge of interest in Kabuki, particularly among young people. A young and very talented *onnagata* (player of female roles) such as Bando Tamasaburo has a following much like a pop star's.

It is difficult to categorize Kabuki because it encompasses a tremendous variety of themes, styles, and effects drawn from all branches of Japan's traditional performing arts. In many ways it resembles the Peking Opera, although Japanese actors lack the acrobatic brilliance of their Chinese counterparts. Certainly the word "opera" might be more appropriate to describe Kabuki than "theater." In fact, Kabuki, Bunraku, and Noh all depend for their pace and emotional effect on music, and although Kabuki actors rarely burst into song, the general effect is much more of a stylized operatic performance than pure drama. In Kabuki, silence is not of the essence and there are even well-rehearsed shouts from the audience at dramatic moments (usually paid for by the actors themselves) to give an unusual 3-D feeling to what is basically a 2-D form of staging.

It should be mentioned that many Japanese have some difficulty understanding the language of Kabuki, much of which is 18th century, and this has led to the introduction of an earphone service, which provides a running interpretation in modern Japanese. At the National Theatre this service is available in English, too. Elsewhere the ample information in the English language programs ensures that visitors manage to follow at least the outline of the action.

The interaction of Kabuki, Noh, and Bunraku is extraordinary. Many of the plays in the Kabuki repertoire began their lives as puppet plays (Bunraku), and even now particular scenes on the Kabuki stage are accompanied by narrators and *shamisen* players from the world of Bunraku. In a few plays, Kabuki actors even behave like puppets. Noh is another basic source for Kabuki material, and Noh-based performances retain the general atmosphere and format of the Noh stage as well as the music, although the dozen or so players and singers of Noh performances are replaced by up to fifty in the Kabuki version. This interaction means that it is possible to visit one Kabuki performance and get a real taste of all three major theatrical forms, with perhaps a certain amount of Japanese dance *(Buyo)* thrown in for good measure. If the program seems to include several unrelated items, there is likely to be greater variety of effect and style.

Bunraku

Bunraku is actually a fusion of three separate performing arts: puppeteering, recitation, and musical accompaniment. Puppet dramas probably first entered Japan from China in the 7th century A.D. These early puppet performances were related to primitive beliefs and religious performances. Wandering troupes of puppeteers came to Japan via Korea in the early 8th century. Just as the medieval religious plays of Europe slowly developed into popular drama, so these semi-religious puppet performances became more sophisticated, but the art of Bunraku was not born until two other skills were added to those of the puppeteers: the arts of *joruri* story-telling (from the 15th century) and *shamisen*-playing (mid-16th century). The form crystallized around 1600, shortly before the birth of Kabuki. During the course of the 17th century Bunraku developed into an extremely popular adult theatrical art, at times even more popular than Kabuki.

Bunraku is well known for its unique three-man puppet operation, and the effects produced can be extremely moving. Certainly the idealized versions of children played by puppets are more interesting than the real young boys with their whining voices in Kabuki. However, the main puppeteers have a strong desire to display their faces to the audience for most of the time and a considerable ability in the suspension of disbelief is required to forget that the puppets are being manipulated. The real tour de force of the Bunraku performance is the vocal virtuosity of the *tayu* narrators. Bunraku puppeteers never speak; instead, a narrator sits on a rostrum projecting from stage left (the audience's right) and not only tells the story but provides the voices for all the characters as well, accompanied by a *shamisen* player. It is a wonderful sight to see the narrator in full passionate flow, complete with vivid facial gestures, as the *shamisen* player sits beside him betraying not an iota of emotion. Because of the physical strain involved, narrators change for each scene. The secret of getting the most from a Bunraku performance is to sit within ten rows of the stage. From this vantage point you will see exactly what the puppets are doing and be in a position to watch the narrator without getting a stiff neck.

Noh Drama

The minimal theater form of Noh has a history of over 1,000 years. It developed from popular plays on religious themes, which were performed in Buddhist temples and Shinto shrines. But it took on its characteristic form only with the continued patronage of the shoguns and noble classes during the 14th century. The most distinguished poet and playwright of the period was Zeami Motokiyo (1363–1443). He was encouraged to include more and more esoteric court poetry in the plays, and the art of Noh gradually became the exclusive property of the upper levels of society, using sophisticated language and abstract movement.

For those interested in the ethereal, Noh should be experienced in a real Noh theater. It is the least accessible of Japan's theater arts: its effect is built up from the subtle combination of ancient poetic lines chanted rather than sung, symbolic dance movements, and the representation of characters long dead and actions that took place long ago. Action on stage is minimal, the pace is slow and controlled, and there are no lighting changes. To many the effect is soporific. However, because of the large number of Western scholars interested in ancient Japanese literature—and Noh has a history of over one thousand years —there are many published translations of Noh plays. Most Japanese members of Noh audiences will follow the score-script, because the language is extremely archaic and a great percentage of the audience is somehow involved in the study of Noh music or dance. There are far more performances of Noh today than there used to be, thanks to the introduction of air-conditioning, but there is a general feeling that the quality of performance is dropping. However, it is also said that only experts can distinguish between amateur and professional performances of Noh, so the best way is to find the nearest theater and let the wave of stifled emotion and deep passion wash over you.

Kyogen

Much more accessible are the comic interludes known as "Kyogen," which have recently become so popular that they are presented as programs in their own right. They consist of simple and amusing situations designed to demonstrate the foibles of humanity. Simple props and mime techniques make them very easy to understand even if you only have the barest idea of the story.

The origins of Kyogen are as ancient and obscure as those of Noh. The stories clearly developed from early forms of song and dance, but include Buddhist parables, folktales, and funny sketches that are really a form of social satire. It is likely that they were improvised by actors long before they ever came to be written down. Some are as short as ten minutes.

Gagaku and Bugaku

Gagaku literally means "elegant, authorized music" and it encompasses dancing, singing, and instrumental playing. It has always been the special preserve of the Imperial Household, with origins that go back at least 1,500 years. The musicians of the Music Department of the Imperial Household today are mostly descendants of the original performers. They give performances inside the Imperial Palace in Tokyo twice a year as well as at the National Theatre and at special events. "Bugaku" is the term used when dancing is included, and "Kangen" is used when the pieces are only instrumental. Although some of the pieces performed could be described as original Japanese music, many are based on pieces imported centuries ago from India, China, Korea, and Indo-China.

Performances are slow and extremely colorful. Costumes are ornate, utilizing many varieties of helmet and mask. Bugaku was originally intended to be performed in the open air, and there are performances at shrines around the country, particularly during major festivals. Perhaps the most spectacular setting is the stage built out over the sea at Itsukushima Shrine on Miyajima near Hiroshima in Western Japan. Bugaku performances are given there on payment of a fixed fee.

Gagaku and Bugaku still enjoy a following, and many foreigners find inspiration in the music provided by the assorted wind, string, and percussion instruments of Gagaku. The atmosphere of a Gagaku performance is very ritualistic: the musicians file slowly on, followed by several dancers (all men). The movements of the dancers are slow and graceful as they depict fragments of an old tale or simply a dance of celebration. The stage itself is colorful, with a green damask covering and red-lacquered railings with gold ornaments. At the back of the stage are two enormous drums covered with ornamentation. The audience sits or stands on three sides of the stage.

Geisha

Traditional dancing (Buyo), singing, and the art of playing the *shamisen* and *koto* (a kind of horizontal harp) have always been part of the training of perhaps the best-known of all Japanese performers, the geisha. Originally geisha were selected at a very young age: indeed, many of them were girls from the country or orphans who were sold to geisha houses. There are still many geisha of all varieties, but the term, originally used only for highly trained performers, is sometimes used loosely these days to include more casual entertainers at hot-springs resorts. An evening with high-class geisha can only be arranged through Japanese contacts and tends to be disappointing. A traditional geisha performance will include an assortment of tidbits culled from the traditional performing arts, mixed with modern songs and titillating games. The geisha tend to work nowadays much as a girl in an office does, with regular hours, but they must attend many dancing and singing classes to polish their act. Some of them are supported by patrons, mostly middle-aged businessmen. The most qualified performers are far from young, the humor of various silly games and songs is often lost on foreigners, and the pricetag can be phenomenal. The idea of geisha as prostitutes, which is still part of the *Oxford Dictionary* definition, is also misleading. Some may well provide a variety of personal services, but that kind of performance is more easily found in the neon-lit side streets than within the somberly traditional walls of the real geisha "teahouse."

Contemporary Japanese Drama

Watch any modern samurai drama on stage or on television and you soon become aware of the great debt all young actors owe to the traditional theatrical and musical arts. Most of them have never seen live Kabuki or Noh, but the movements and speech patterns have entered the Japanese performing psyche. This is also true of a lot of contemporary Japanese drama, even the most experimental. Exaggerated eye movements, shouting from the throat, and melodramatic gesture are so much a part of Japanese stage life that if is difficult for directors to tone down their actors' performances to suit contemporary plays or television closeups. Although there is something of a dearth of significant young playwrights, there is no shortage of theater activities. Unfettered by union problems, theaters spring up everywhere and performers put on a show wherever there is room to pitch a tent or take over an empty basement. There are original Japanese plays performed in tiny rooms, and the audience is provided with a plastic bag in which to put their shoes. The actors make no money from it, especially as most groups are heavily overstaffed, and they have to work in bars or as taxidrivers to keep their artistic activities going. The same is true of many dancers and musicians, who often teach children between rehearsals. From an audience point of view the majority of small-scale Japanese performances could be summed up as the Theater of Discomfort, worth experiencing once but certainly not too often.

On any day of the year there will be a multitude of theatrical and musical performances in any Japanese town or city. Many of these will be by foreign artists, whether they be opera singers, pianists, ballerinas, or rock stars. By some quirk of international cooperation very few foreign theater groups visit Japan; perhaps because of the unbelievable quantity of foreign plays performed in Japan in translation. There are over thirty translations into Japanese of both *Hamlet* and *Romeo and Juliet* and there is always a performance of Shakespeare going on somewhere in Japan. One group in Tokyo regularly works through the whole repertoire, and because the translations it uses are modern Japanese, a variety of fresh and contemporary interpretations are possible. All significant playwrights are performed in Japanese, whether they are American, French, German, Russian, or indeed any other nationality. Large professional groups often produce huge box-office successes with foreign plays and musicals. Recently *Jesus Christ Superstar, My Fair Lady, Amadeus, The Elephant Man* and *Cats* have all transcended cultural differences to play to packed houses.

The desire to study European opera, ballet, and classical music is widespread in Japan these days, and there is a corresponding number

of opera companies, ballet groups, and orchestras, many of high quality. This enthusiasm also means that visiting groups have very successful tours of Japan. During a single year it was possible to see La Scala,
the Royal Ballet, the Bolshoi Ballet, and the Wiener Burgtheater in
Japan, as well as innumerable American dance companies and musicians from around the world.

The same is true in the world of pop music and jazz. Few groups or
solo artists will miss the chance to appear in front of large Japanese
audiences and promote record and video sales to an increasingly affluent young generation. With this enthusiasm for foreign music goes a
corresponding interest in jazz dance and aerobics. Few Japanese popular singers ever make much impact abroad, but there is a huge market
for local talent, very much tied in with television programming, which
makes or breaks *tarento* at an alarming rate.

The scope of the performing arts in Japan seems limitless. A loose
description of Japanese theater might also include sumo wrestling, the
popular all-female revues, amateur performers on television, mul-
timedia presentations, soft porno movies, and bullfights—all part of the
Japanese performing maelstrom.

JAPANESE FOOD AND DRINK

by
DAVID JONES

David Jones is the former head of Pan American World Airways Public Relations Department for Asia. He is a member of numerous wine societies, a member of the Japan chapter of the International Wine and Food Society, and founder and president of the Japan chapter of the Amities Gastronomique International.

Japan can boast of foods to fit any taste, from the finest to the junkiest, and no traveler, not even the confirmed meat-and-potatoes addict, will starve here. There is plenty of beef available and it is among the best in the world (and most expensive), although the potatoes won't necessarily accompany it. Most Japanese steakhouses prefer to serve bean sprouts and beef fried rice, instead of potatoes—not a bad combination. If roast beef is what you want, you need not leave your hotel. It is served at most of the top hotels in Japan's major cities, as well as at special restaurants elsewhere. Then you will get your potatoes, but baked; the Japanese consider baked potatoes and roast beef the ideal combination.

For the gourmet, Japan is an exhilarating experience, an exciting adventure in exotic flavors as well as in tasting recognizable dishes done with a uniquely Japanese flair. The Japanese meal aims not at stuffing

75

the stomach, but at pleasing the eye and the palate while taking the edge off hunger. It not only concentrates on flavor, trying to adhere as closely to the natural taste as possible, but also on beauty of service. The vessel in which the food is served must match and complement it, as should the surroundings. Thus, ambience takes on special meaning in a Japanese meal. The food is an integral part of the environment.

It is because of its sense of the gastronomically esthetic that gourmets claim that Japanese cuisine is at least the equal of the French and the Chinese, widely regarded as the best in the world. They say that of the three, the Chinese is the most basic, for it concentrates only on flavors. French cuisine moves up the scale a bit, because it does pay attention to presentation. But it is the Japanese cuisine that makes a complete art out of a meal by appealing to the eye and the palate—and even sometimes to the ear, as in the pleasant sound the meat makes when swished through the boiling bouillon in the preparation of *shabu-shabu,* giving rise to the onomatopoeic derivation of the name.

Dining in a Ryotei

One finds the best Japanese food at high-class restaurants called *ryoteis,* where a variety of foods is available, served in a pattern that has a fairly rigid order. A typical meal could start with an hors d'oeuvre like *sansai nitsuke,* a small dish of flowering mountain fern boiled in fish bouillon and seasoned with soy sauce and *mirin,* a type of Japanese liqueur, and served with sake; to be followed by *sashimi* or slices of raw fish; a boiled green vegetable, flavored with soy sauce and sesame seed or shavings of dried bonito; and then the main course, which would be a whole fish purchased that day at the market and grilled *shioyaki*-style, where the entire fish is coated with salt and broiled over charcoal until the skin is crisp. *Suimono,* or clear soup made from delicately flavored fish bouillon to which boiled vegetables, a mushroom, and a fish cake have been added, will begin the coda of this gastronomic symphony. It would be continued with rice, brought in a dark lacquered bowl to set off its sparkling whiteness. The final chords would be struck by a dessert, consisting nowadays of seasonal fruit like melon.

It must be emphasized that such a menu would be just one possibility of the innumerable combinations available. The soup, instead of suimono, could be *dobin mushi,* which consists of bits of chicken, gingko nuts, whole or sliced mushrooms and a few vegetables in a fish bouillon seasoned with mirin and served in an earthenware teapot. In this elegant and unique service, the lid of the teapot is used as the soup bowl. Or the sashimi dish could be *aji tataki,* where a section of pompano or saurel is chopped and mixed with onion or leeks and ginger and re-placed on the whole fish, which lies curled on a bed of seaweed or sliced *daikon,* the Japanese radish. *Yaki-hamaguri,* or broiled clams served in their shells on a bed of salt with a slice of lemon, could also be included in the menu.

Some ryoteis serve their own form of *kaiseki-ryori,* a set menu which originated in the simple fare of Buddhist monks whose practice of carrying heated pebbles or kaiseki in their habits to keep warm gave rise to the name. On the way to its present elaborate, highly sophisticated and expensive version, it became a part of *ocha-no-yu* or the tea ceremony, where it is still customary to serve kaiseki snacks at the end of the ritual.

Two variations of kaiseki-ryori have evolved: *kyo-ryori* or the kaiseki of the Kansai or Osaka area, and *shojin ryori*, which consists of vegetarian dishes. Shojin ryori is served mainly in Buddhist temples, but is also found in special vegetarian restaurants. Kyo-ryori is characterized by a lighter taste and color than that found in the Kanto or Tokyo area, the difference coming from the lighter soy sauce and white miso or fermented soybean paste used in the Kansai.

The portions in kaiseki-ryori are small, reflecting their former existence as snacks at the end of the tea ceremony. Depending on the restaurant, as many as a dozen dishes could be included in the menu, consisting of *omuko*, or hors d'oeuvres, like *sansai nitsuki; shuto*, or salted fish gut; *hassun*, a dish made of ocean fish and vegetables; *nimono*, a cooked dish, usually fish; *yakimono*, a grilled fish; *takiawase* or a mixture of boiled vegetables with tofu or bean curd; *sunomono*, or salted fresh vegetables mixed with small pieces of raw fish and seasoned with sugar and vinegar; *agemono* or a fried dish like tempura; *tsukemono* or Japanese pickles; rice; and *maccha*, or green tea, accompanied by tea cakes.

Ryoteis usually look like traditional Japanese inns or even private homes. A small garden is almost a necessity, even in the busiest, most crowded sections. It makes the restaurant seem like a haven far from the madding crowd—and Japanese crowds can be very madding. Service is always on a low lacquered table set on a *tatami* floor and performed by a young kimonoed woman whose sole responsibility during the service is the guests in that particular *zashiki* or Japanese room.

Nowadays, some ryoteis are taking cognizance of the desire of foreigners to try their foods and are setting up in major hotels, like Kitcho in Tokyo's Imperial Hotel. It is a branch of a very famous ryotei and serves its own kaiseki-style food. It is available to guests of and visitors to the hotel, although its price of ¥ 12,000 may seem a bit steep. Compared to other kaiseki prices, though, it is quite reasonable.

Itamae-Ryori

If ¥ 12,000 seems a bit much, one can find a substitute in *itamae-ryori* where the food is like that found in a ryotei but less expensive and less elegantly served. Itamae literally means "in front of the board," but is Japanese for a chef of the highest rank, who not only has the necessary talent but has trained for at least ten years to attain his position. Those who do not have the money to open their own ryotei and who wish to work for themselves operate such restaurants. A la carte and table d'hôte menus are available, with most clients preferring the latter. The diner sits at the counter where he or she has the added pleasure of watching the chef create the delicacies to be eaten. The prices are a fraction of those in ryoteis, but, of course, the embellishments are absent. The beauty of the serving plays a subordinate part to the flavor of the food.

Nabemono

In the winter time dishes of the *nabemono* variety are popular, as the warmth exuded by the boiling pot and imparted by the food on a cold night adds to the joy of eating. There is a range of such dishes, from the delicious and thrillingly dangerous *chirinabe* to the popular, especially among foreigners, shabu-shabu.

Chirinabe is made with fugu, which is the puffer or globefish, but can be made with others. Fugu is by far the most interesting, gastronomically and otherwise. Certain of its organs contain a poison, tetrodotoxin, which, if consumed, is fatal in 60 percent of the cases. This gloomy statistic in no way diminishes its popularity among Japanese gourmets, who have faith in the ability of the fugu chef to keep them alive and happy gastronomes. To be a fugu chef, an aspirant must pass a stiff examination not only on his ability to cut and serve the fish properly but also on his knowledge of how to avoid the poisonous parts.

The first course in a fugu meal is *sashimi,* where the tastiest parts of the flesh are thinly sliced and set in the shape of a flower or waves on the sea on a matching plate, with color added to the white, almost transparent slices by tiny stemmed vegetables, seaweed and a mixture of grated daikon and red pepper. Served with it is a dip made of *dashi,* which is the essence of seaweed and dried bonito extracted by boiling and mixed with soy sauce and sake. To spice the dip the daikon-red pepper mixture is blended into it.

After the sashimi comes the *nabemono.* The beauty of this dish is found essentially in the raw ingredients that are brought in a bowl. They are carefully arranged with an eye toward contrasting and complementary colors and shapes and consist usually of leeks, Chinese cabbage, mushrooms, tofu, and the rest of the fish. When the pot of bouillon begins to boil, a kimonoed waitress puts the fish, the vegetables and the bean curd into it with a pair of long chopstocks. As each morsel is done, she takes it out and places it on a diner's plate.

Another type of nabe is *dotenabe.* It consists of oysters, leeks, tofu, chrysanthemum leaves, and sweet miso paste.

When pieces of chicken are substituted with the addition of *harusame,* or spring rain, which is a poetic term for thin noodles made out of vegetable protein, the nabemono is called *mizutaki,* another favorite cold-weather dish.

Shabu-shabu, which vies with *sukiyaki* in popularity with foreigners, is also like chirinabe, with very thin slices of beef replacing the fugu. A sauce similar to that used in chirinabe and called *ponzu,* whose base is *daidai,* a sour orange-like fruit, is served as a dip. If a milder kind is desired, *gomadare,* a sauce based on miso and sesame seeds, is available. One pleasant addition to shabu-shabu, especially welcome on a cold winter night, is the soup that is made from the broth in which the meat and vegetables are cooked. The waitress seasons it, cooks some noodles in it and serves the resultant up as very tasty noodle soup.

Then there is the *chankonabe* of the sumo wrestlers. Many people entertain the erroneous notion that chanko is fattening, because the wrestlers are so huge. However, if anyone were to feed on the dish for a month, he would slim down to sylphlike proportions. Although chankonabe is closely identified with the athletes, their hugeness actually comes from the large portions of rice and tremendous amount of alcohol they put away.

The chanko served at restaurants is different from that produced at sumo stables by young hopefuls who learn the art of cooking it before they are taught the rudiments of their chosen profession. At a restaurant there are different types of chanko served at different prices, with the most expensive consisting of beef and an assortment of vegetables similar to those served in other nabes. Less expensive would be a combination of beef and fish, and the cheapest a combination of chicken and fish. On the other hand, beef is seldom found in a sumo stable's nabe. Those chankos have an excess of vegetables with the meat limited to parts of a scrawny chicken and fish.

With nabemonos, which are numerous, varying with the chef, restaurant, region, and season, the best drink is sake. A variation, called *hirezake,* where the fin of the fugu is steeped in the sake until it imparts a sweetness to the flavor, is served with chirinabe. Some people prefer beer or whiskey with nabemono, both of which are acceptable. Wine of any sort would be wasted, just as sake would be wasted on a fine French meal.

Sometimes classified as a nabemono, sukiyaki, which many foreigners believe is the Japanese national dish, has been and may still be the best known of the extensive Japanese cuisine. Actually a latecomer to the gastronomic scene (it came into being in the late Edo Period, which was from 1603 to 1868), it consists of thin slices of beef cooked together with assorted vegetables in an iron pan over gas heat, although sometimes an electric skillet is substituted, to which sake or mirin, sugar, soy sauce, and dashi have been added. Chicken sometimes replaces the beef to appeal to the economy minded.

Sushi and Sashimi

Before Japanese food or a form thereof was spread abroad by enterprising entrepreneurs, foreigners looked askance at items such as sushi and sashimi. They were—ugh!—raw fish. Today, it is not the gastronomically adventurous who indulge in them, but those who were introduced to the foods under less than ideal conditions in the United States and elsewhere and who wish to try the real thing on its home grounds. If they have any sort of palate, they should soon discover the difference. For sushi and sashimi, Japanese gourmets argue, cannot be duplicated away from Japan. The difference, they say, lies in the freshness of the fish, plus, as regards sushi, the care with which the rice is prepared. Abroad, the chefs are less exacting, probably because their clientele is not so demanding.

The origin of sushi dates back well over a thousand years. It existed in Japan in the Nara Period, which was in the 7th century, developing as a means of preserving beef and fish, which were salted and placed in a tub of steaming rice, where they remained until the rice became sour and had imparted its flavor to the meat. In preserving the meat, the Japanese discovered that it became tastier. Much later, sushi makers used vinegar to sour the rice quickly. This was called *hayazushi* or quick sushi. Today, beef is no longer used—it went out when Buddhism came in—but the rice and fish have reversed positions. Now the fish is used as flavoring for the rice, which plays the more important role in sushi. That should come as a surprise to connoisseurs outside Japan.

In the Edo Period, sushi split into the *oshizushi* of the Kansai (Osaka area) and the *nigirizushi* of the Kanto (Tokyo area). In oshizushi, the fish is marinated or boiled and then placed with rice into a rectangular mold, somewhat harking back to its origin. The block of rice and fish is then cut into smaller serving pieces. In nigirizushi, the rice is molded by hand into little oblong shapes on which a dab of *wasabi* or Japanese horseradish is rubbed lightly. The slice of raw fish is then placed on the wasabi. The best of the sushiyas use only the finest rice, which is flavored with vinegar, sugar, and salt. Nigirizushi today is by far the more popular kind and is found all over the country as well as in the sushiyas abroad. Oshizushi is mainly found in the Kansai.

Sushi connoisseurs sit at the counter or bar, pointing out what fish they want from the display in the glass section in front of them. They maintain that the time that elapses between the cutting of the fish and its consumption is critical, for the fish loses its freshness rapidly. They usually stick their noses up at chopsticks and pick the sushi up with their fingers, claiming that the wood of the chopsticks interferes with the flavor.

Here are a few sushiya terms:

O-toro. The finest grade of tuna, cut from the belly of the fish and well larded with fat. Sushi connoisseurs order extra wasabi with this, asking for "sabi kikashite," otherwise, the fat will overcome the wasabi, destroying the happy balance of sushi, rice, wasabi, and soy sauce flavors.

Chu-toro: Medium-grade tuna with less fat than o-toro. It is still very tasty. It has the same effect on wasabi.

Maguro: Plain tuna, taken from the back and with much less fat. It is the cheapest grade.

Tekkamaki: All "makis" consist of rice with seaweed wrapped around it, the name differing with what is in the rice. Tekkamaki has maguro in the center. If there is cucumber inside, it is *kappamaki.* With Japanese pickle as the filling, it is *norimaki.*

Odori ebi: Sushi experts call a shrimp that was lively just before its demise a dancing shrimp or odori ebi. The livelier it is, the sweeter it tastes, they say.

Wasabi: Called Japanese horseradish, it comes from the root of a mountain plant and is very spicy. It is either grated or made from the powdered form.

Hirame: Sole. Gourmets ask for *engawa,* which is from the side of the filet and is firmer and tastier. It is like the bavette steak of the French.

There are many other terms, but the best sushi houses have translations of the Japanese names for the fish and shellfish available.

Sashimi is something different. It stands on the flavor and texture of the fish alone, because it is served only with a dip of soy sauce in which some wasabi is mixed. When ordered as *sashimi teishoku,* which means a complete meal, the sashimi is served with soup, rice and pickles. It is always decorated with *tsuma,* or raw vegetables, which are a part of the meal. However it is ordered, as main course or hors d'oeuvres, it is served in a bowl or on a flat porcelain or wooden plate.

Nowadays sashimi refers to anything served raw. At certain restaurants, one can find beef sashimi (in no way resembling tartar steak), chicken sashimi, and even whale sashimi. The last can only be obtained at special restaurants, where it is served chilled almost to the freezing point with a ginger sauce. It is considered a delicacy by many Japanese and foreigners. Anyone wishing something even more exotic could try fried bees or stewed snake, which is supposed to be invigorating.

Sake is by far the best alcoholic drink to accompany sushi and sashimi, although some customers ask for beer. There has been an attempt, now and then, to try to match a white wine, with unsatisfactory results. If not in a frame of mind for alcohol, the diner can restrict himself to *agari,* the sushiya term for its delicious green tea.

As for other specialized restaurants, there is one that serves only tofu, but in an infinite variety of ways; another where sardines are the specialty; and one where only *soba,* the noodles made of buckwheat flour, are available, but in about 150 different forms.

Eel as a Specialty

Then there are *unagiyas,* where only *unagi,* or freshwater eel, is served. No true gourmet would turn his nose up at this exquisite version of the ubiquitous eel; for it is one of the greatest dishes of its kind in the world. In the best unagiyas only the wild variety is used, for flowing water improves the texture and flavor of eel flesh. Cultured eel, if one may use that term, are also available. They are raised in still water—in ponds and lakes—after being captured on their way to fresh water from their unknown birthplace somewhere out in the Pacific. Both cultured and wild eel are kept alive until their moment of glory, when they are sacrificed for the sake of gourmet palates. Dispatching an eel is a tricky business. With sudden death, sudden rigor mortis must set in. To accomplish this, the itamae must place his victim in precisely the right position so that he can get at the right nerve to make the eel stiffen at the moment of its instant demise. Obviously, it takes a chef of great talent and long training to perform such an anatomically exacting task.

At unagiyas, eel is served as a complete course, which would begin with a seasonal vegetable, followed by grilled eel liver, sashimi of a fish other than eel, grilled unagi, soup, rice, and fruits. Eel can be had in a much cheaper form, as in *unagi domburi,* where it is grilled and laid on a bed of rice, or *kabayaki,* which is grilled eel with rice on the side.

Although it is available throughout the year, there are certain times when eel becomes the traditional food, the food one *must* eat. One such time is during the *Doyo-no-hi* of summer, translated roughly as the hottest day of the year (the date changes annually, as it is part of the lunar calendar). During the Doyo-no-hi all restaurants that serve eel in any form are crowded with customers, for the Japanese believe the fatness of the eel restores energy drained from the body by the heat.

Unagi is prepared differently in the Kansai and Kanto regions. In the latter, it is first steamed, a process which removes some of the fat and tenderizes the fish, and then grilled. In the Kansai, it is merely grilled. Which is better is a matter of taste.

The O-bento

He who has an adventurous palate but not the means to support its curiosity may well find satisfaction in the Japanese o-bento or lunchbox. It used to be what workmen brought from home in light, shallow boxes for their noonday meal. It has since developed into a variety of o-bentos at prices ranging from cheap to moderate and has branched out into the eki-ben, which are the specialized o-bentos that can be purchased at various railroad stations. O-bentos are complete meals unto themselves, with various contrasting foods sectioned off into smaller compartments within the container. The number of dishes that can make up an o-bento is too numerous to list, but a usual combination would consist of rice, salmon eggs, fish cake, carefully carved raw and boiled vegetables and other delicacies, artfully arranged to make an appetite-appealing picture.

Eki-ben are available at station platforms and shops. Passengers who know their eki-ben will wait until the train stops at a certain station before buying one. Some of them have achieved a fame that has spread throughout the country, like Chiba's *Yakihama Bento,* or clams served over rice; Yokohama's *Shumai Bento,* or Chinese meatballs; Yamagata's *Hanagasa Zushi,* or shrimp with various vegetables; and Okayama's *Nuku Zushi,* another arrangement of shrimp and vegetables. It is almost worth it to buy an eki-ben just to see the pretty picture it makes.

O-bento, the generic term, may take some getting used to, but once one has acquired a taste for rice with some sort of fish or seafood and bits of cooked vegetables, it will be difficult to go for long without having lunch out of a Japanese lunchbox.

Less Expensive Ways to Dine

But if o-bento also puts a strain on one's purse, there is still *okonomiyaki.* It means, roughly, "do-it-yourself" cookery, although some foreigners, because of its price, pronounce the name, "economy-yaki." It is a pancake that you cook yourself, the batter and fixings having been provided by the restaurant. Chopped bits of vegetables are usually in the batter, but the customer selects the filling out of a choice of meat, like chicken or beef, and seafood, like shrimp or squid. Sometimes fried noodles, the cheapest of the fillings, are provided. As they say, in an okonomiyakiya, criticism of the chef gets one nowhere.

If you are wandering the streets at night (almost all streets in Japan are comfortingly safe except for the automotive traffic) and find yourself suffering the pangs of unbearable hunger, look for a food wagon or listen for the sound of a Japanese flute announcing the presence of a wagon serving *ramen.* Ramen are Chinese noodles served in pork broth with soy sauce. A steaming bowl of ramen will help allay the hunger, and is especially good for drink-sodden stomachs.

Another wagon food is *oden,* consisting of fish cakes, seaweed, hard-boiled egg, and sometimes octopus cooked in a broth and served with a dab of very hot mustard. *Yaki-imo,* or baked potato, which is actually yam, is served from a picturesque cart with a crooked stovepipe coming out of the top. Baking of the yam is done with pebbles warmed by a wood fire beneath. Anyone can locate such wagons by listening for the long drawn out, "Y-a-a Ki-i-i-i Mo-o-o."

A word to those sensitive to sanitary conditions: The Japanese, if anything, are oversanitized, being even more conscious of germs than the Americans. Japanese who go to the United States sometimes complain about the water there. If one is looking for the state of the art in sanitation, Japan is the place.

A Sampling of Regional Cookery

There has already been some mention of seasonal foods, of which there are many, such as bamboo shoots and bonito in spring, fugu in winter; in fact, they are too numerous to list. But Japanese restaurants specialize in seasonal foods. They will always have some kind, like the sansai nitsuke already described, available somewhere in a meal. There are all sorts of regional foods as well as particular regional ways of cooking them, too numerous to mention in their entirety. Suffice it to name just a few.

The northern island of Hokkaido has a specialty of frozen salmon sashimi, called *ruibe.* Satsuma, on the island of Kyushu, is proud of its *sake zushi,* or rice steamed in sake. *Chawanmushi* is a sort of custard made from fish broth, eggs, and other ingredients. It is sometimes described as poached soup and is so delicious that even the most xenophobic of palates would take to it. One of Nagasaki's specialties is chawanmushi, double its normal size and containing nine different kinds of food, like fish cake, gingko nut, eel, chicken, marsh parsley, and so forth.

For the Less Daring

If your sense of the gastronomically proper is offended by what has been described so far, remember what was said in the beginning of this essay—there are foods in Japan that the nervous palate will embrace like long-lost friends.

One of these is *yakitori,* bits of chicken grilled on a skewer à la shish kebab. Practically all the chicken, except the bones, is used. At the better yakitoriyas large cups of warm sake are served with the chicken, an excellent combination.

Tempura will also probably make a squeamish palate happy. Bits of seafood and vegetables are dipped in a batter of egg and flour and deep-fried. Served with grated daikon mixed with shoyu and raw egg, tempura usually constitutes a meal in itself. Tempura teishoku, the complete meal, generally includes shrimp, squid, white fish, eggplant, green pepper, string beans, onion, and *nori,* or crisp dried seaweed.

Tempura, like sushi, should be eaten at the counter—the farther it travels from the deep iron pot filled with hot oil in which it is fried, the less tasty it becomes and sogginess tends to set in. As in all deep-fried Japanese foods, the oil must be the right temperature in order to cook the food to the proper degree of color and crispness. Oil that is not hot enough results in food that is soggy and too light; if too hot, it over-browns the morsel. The batter, too, must be of the correct consistency, otherwise it interferes with the flavor of the food instead of enhancing it.

Not as well known as the other two but at least as popular with foreign residents and Japanese is *tonkatsu,* the Japanese version of breaded pork cutlet. One can best describe it as pork cooked in the tempura way, for it is similarly deep-fried. But in addition to being dipped in batter, the pork is also rolled in bread crumbs. There are three kinds available: *rosu,* which is loin of pork sliced fairly thickly; *hire,* which is the Japanese version or pronunciation of filet; and *hitoku-chikatsu,* or very lean pork.

Yakitori (grilled basted chicken chunks or parts on a small wooden spit) is another popular food, often found in smoke-filled yakitoriyas seating only a dozen or so customers, most at a counter. Gizzards, livers, and other parts alternate with the meat, sometimes enlivened with scallions or flavored with the fabulous *shiso* leaf.

Then, of course, there is steak. The most popular way of broiling steak in Japan is *teppanyaki*-style, where it is cooked in front of the customer along with the vegetables to be served with it, which usually include onion, bean sprouts, and green pepper. Beef fried rice, which is delicious, or a bowl of plain boiled rice can be ordered at the end of the meal; the latter is the usual choice of the Japanese.

Something similar to teppanyaki-style steak was introduced to the United States, where it became very popular. Upon its introduction, however, something new was added: the so-called Ballet of the Blades, where the chef does a juggling act with his wicked-looking knife. Many Americans, on coming to Japan, are disappointed when such entertainment is left out of the menu. But so self-respecting steak chef would deign to adulterate his art with such shenanigans.

Western-style Cuisines

If the Japanese way of cooking steak, chicken, and pork is still a bit exotic for the palate, one can have recourse to the various sorts of restaurants in Japan serving genuine Western-style cuisines, restaurants that could more than hold their own in their home countries.

There are several French restaurants in Tokyo operated by French chefs who would be recognized as masters of their craft in such gastronomic edens as Lyons and Paris. Although the bulk of them is in Tokyo, there are a few in the Kansai area. To list some and not all would be unfair to those left out; hence, let it be sufficient to say that there are genuine French restaurants to match every purse, where anyone hankering after a budget-designated menu will find satisfaction.

There is also a growing Franco-Japanese cuisine, started by Japanese who have studied their craft in France. Unrestricted by tradition, they are very imaginative and create dishes that sound familiar but reflect a Japanese heritage rather than French. Gourmets familiar with this cuisine predict that, though merely a variety now, it will eventually develop into a completely different species.

Japan also can boast some fine Italian restaurants, as well as several Italo-Japanese establishments whose relationship to Italian cuisine is the same as that of the Franco-Japanese to the French. In addition, Japan has a range of German, English, Swiss, Spanish, Russian, Indian, Korean, and innumerable Chinese restaurants. There is even an African restaurant (Rose de Sahara) in Tokyo's Shibuya ward that serves an African chicken so spicy that if a guest completely consumes a serving, he gets his name on the restaurant's roll of honor.

Alcoholic Beverages

Alcoholic beverages are usually a necessary adjunct to satisfactory dining, and the Japanese, who are by no means adverse to drinking, have their share. They even make Japanese wines, which have been improving through the years to the point where some of them are palatable. But the soil and climate of Japan are not conducive to creating acceptable alcoholic levels. Japanese producers import East European wines in bulk and mix them with the domestic output to achieve a 12 ½ percent alcohol level, which the Japanese consumer apparently demands.

On the other hand, Japanese whiskey is quite good, although the only thing Japanese about it is the neutral spirits used in the blend. It is based upon Scotch whisky shipped in bulk from Scotland. There are those who prefer Japanese to Scotch and bourbon, however. Of course, it is all a matter of taste, but one does tend to think that, in such cases, the neutral spirits must be pretty good, since the Scots keep their best Scotch for bottling themselves.

When it comes to Japanese beer, there are few complaints. Although it is a matter of opinion as to whether the Japanese product can compare with the best the Germans have to offer, there are even Germans who will support such a claim. Japanese beer is certainly at least as good as anything that can be obtained outside of Germany.

Sake, though, is the Japanese drink. It may even be dubbed the national drink. Popularly called "rice wine," it is a brew rather than the product of vinification. It dates back to the days before grain was known in Japan, when a fermented drink made of nuts and berries was produced. It came into its own in the Nara Period, when malt is believed to have been introduced. Sake is served on important occasions and is the drink offered in ritual libation to the gods. It is drunk by the champion of a sumo tournament in celebration of his triumph, at weddings when vows are pledged, and on other ceremonial occasions; and it is just drunk. Attaining as much as 20 degrees alcohol, its average alcoholic content is around 15 degrees. There are three grades: *tokkyu-shu,* the best, which has an alcoholic content of 16 to 17 degrees; *ikkyu-shu,* the middle grade with an alcoholic content of 15.6 to 16.5 degrees; and *nikkyu-shu,* the lowest grade, which has an alcoholic content of 15 to 16 degrees. Sake is best drunk young, the sooner after brewing, the better, according to aficionados. It goes with all Japanese foods and is used in Japanese cooking. When ordering sake, one usually gets a rather sweet kind, called *amakuchi*. This is now prevalent because it is the favorite of women and the younger generation. Sake connoisseurs demand *karakuchi* or dry sake, however, instead of asking for a certain grade of sake—the best restaurants carry only tokkyu-shu. Sake is usually served at body temperature, sometimes a little warmer. It is drunk cold at times, depending on the food. If you want it cold, of course you may ask for it. But usually it is better warmed.

Japan's only native distilled liquor is *shochu*, made from millet, potatoes, and sake lees. Its proof can get as high as 90 degrees. It is looked down upon by many Japanese much as gin was sneered at in England in the last century as the laborer's drink. Shochu, because of its more powerful kick, is favored by men who want its strength after having worked a full day at some energy-demanding job like construction.

Mirin, mentioned earlier, is made from a mixture of shochu and a sweetened fermentation of rice. It is used mainly in cooking.

Other alcoholic drinks are *umeshu*, inaccurately called plum wine, and *toso*, which is served traditionally on New Year's Day. Umeshu is made by steeping green Japanese plums or ume in shochu for at least a year. Toso is made by mixing sake with mirin and what may well be called a bouquet garni.

SHOPPING IN JAPAN

by
MICHIKO YOSHII

A founding editor of Tour Companion, *a weekly newspaper for foreign tourists, Michiko Yoshii was formerly a reporter and the entertainment editor for* The Daily Yomiuri. *She currently works as a freelancer specializing in the traditional performing arts of Japan.*

When it comes to business, the Japanese are systematic and pay the closest attention to fine details. Thus, for tourists, shopping in Japan has been made easy, convenient, safe, profitable, and exciting.

What makes shopping in Japan exciting is the tremendous range of products available—everything from traditional folkcraft items and antiques to the most advanced electronic products and fashion goods, not to mention quality products imported from other countries. Unfortunately, as a rule, the tourist is denied the excitement of bargaining in Japan because prices are just as they are marked clearly on the merchandise, in universal Arabic numerals. This, however, makes it safe. They don't have one set of prices for the natives and another for tourists.

If you should even so much as suggest that the shop should give you a discount, the answer usually is a polite smile and a barely perceptible shaking of the head. Sometimes the clerk just walks away as if to infer

that this is not a store for the likes of you. However, there are a few
exceptions where an attempt to bargain is not rejected outright. One
is the Akihabara district in Tokyo where every shop is a wholesale or
discount outlet dealing in electronic goods. Other exceptions are the
antique and curio shops where you may suggest that your budget is
only so much. But even in these places, price negotiations are not
allowed to drag on endlessly; everything is settled with finality after one
or two exchanges.

The practice of clearly marking prices is convenient because you
don't have to ask a clerk each time and you can swiftly settle on an item
that is within your budget. What's more, you don't have to calculate
in your head how much the price will be with the sales tax, because the
marked price is everything.

One might expect that the convenient shops set up for the tourist
trade—tax-free centers and arcades—would be a place for haggling.
But even shops in these places will rarely entertain your desire to
bargain. These places have ordinary Japanese customers as well, and
they don't bargain.

The tax-free shops and centers are places where you can make profitable purchases. However, not everything in their showcases is tax free.
The principal authorized tax-free items are pearls; watches; precious
metals; articles decorated with precious metals; articles made of tortoise shell, coral, amber, and ivory; cloissoné ware; furs; portable TV
sets; record players; stereo equipment; radio sets; magnetic tapes; cameras; and projectors, including their parts and accessories. For some
items, however, there is a minimum price below which tax is *not* discounted. Moreover, the tax-free percentage differs according to the
kind of item; therefore it is not possible to say here in general terms
how much you can save on tax. You just have to go to the store, pick
out an item and then ask the clerk.

A word of caution: you must have your passport with you in order
to qualify for a tax discount. The clerk will prepare the documents
necessary for showing to customs when you leave the country.

Selecting the Store

Knowing the categories of shops will make shopping easy for the
first-time visitor to Japan. First, all major hotels have shopping arcades
whose shops are branches of reputable stores and where sales clerks are
bilingual and are accustomed to foreign tourists. For quick shopping,
the hotel arcades are unexcelled, but their range of products is limited.
Then, in a large city like Tokyo, there are tax-free shopping centers,
which are easily accessible from most centrally located hotels. Here,
too, language is not a problem, but the range of goods they offer is
necessarily limited as in the case of hotel arcades.

Offering a wider range of goods are the one-stop shopping centers.
Such one-stop shopping centers as the International Arcade in Tokyo
and the Kyoto Handicraft Center in Kyoto are tourist-oriented and
thus have clerks who speak English. Some tax-free purchases are possible. Others, like the Sukiyabashi Shopping Center in Tokyo, are not
tourist-oriented and thus do not have any tax-free shops and clerks

normally do not speak English. The range of merchandise on display, however, is much wider than in the hotel arcades or tax-free shopping centers. Some one-stop shopping centers operate year-round.

Many of the shops in the shopping centers are specialty shops, quite often branches of specialty shops with main stores in individual locations in districts such as the fashionable Ginza. In a big city like Tokyo there are specialty shops for almost any item, from paper to pottery and toys to optical goods. These are, of course, the best places to look for the widest choice in any particular kind of product. Language in such stores is not too much of a problem because the goods on display and the marked prices speak for themselves.

The widest variety of goods can be seen at the big department stores, which are numerous in big cities like Tokyo, Osaka, and Nagoya. Regional cities, too, have well-stocked department stores. The bigger department store companies have branches in a number of cities and one or two even in the same city. Among the best known department stores are Mitsukoshi, Takashimaya, Daimaru, Sogo, and Hankyu.

Japanese department stores have many features that set them apart from those in other countries. They not only boast that they have everything the consumer needs from cradle to grave (one department store recently sold a second-hand train locomotive), but they also go to great lengths to provide entertainment and culture as well. They put on first-class art exhibits, sometimes imported from abroad, and they have theaters, tea ceremony rooms, rooftop playgrounds for children, and cultural classes, mainly for housewives.

In general, Japanese department stores have a similar layout—foodstuffs in the basement; handbags, shoes, neckties, accessories, cosmetics, etc., on the first floor; clothes for men, women, and children on the second, third and/or fourth floors; kimono, obi, beddings, kimono accessories, zori footwear, etc., on the fifth floor; furniture, interior goods, household implements, tableware, chinaware, toys, stationery, jewelry, cameras, etc., on the higher floors; and tea parlors and restaurants on the seventh floor or above. Bargain sales usually take place close to the top floor.

Every major department store in the big cities provides an information sheet in English, showing each floor's displays and the services available. As soon as you enter the store, go to the main information desk on the ground floor and ask for this sheet.

English-speaking guides are usually on hand on each floor. Many salesgirls at major department stores can understand simple English. If your inquiry is complicated, she will link you by telephone to an English-speaking guide.

Services to facilitate shopping for foreign tourists include currency exchange (only in central department stores in big cities), usually at a counter close to the ground-floor information desk. Another service is packing and shipping of your purchase to your home address for a charge.

First-aid and lost-and-found (including stray children or adults) services are also available.

All department stores stay open on Sundays and national holidays but close on different days of the week. Make sure before you go that the one you want to visit is open on that day. Business hours are generally 10:00 A.M. to 6:00 P.M.

Money

Japanese stores do not accept currency other than yen. Most stores patronized by tourists accept international credit cards, such as Diner's, American Express, MasterCard, and Visa. And they will not accept personal checks.

While we are on the subject of money, it should be mentioned that you might find the Japanese inconsiderate in the way they give you your change. The clerk will not hand you the change in the Western way, adding up the coins and notes on top of the purchase price, starting with the smallest denomination. She will just hand you the lumped change, usually on a small tray, with an "Arigato gozaimasu" (Thank you). You might fear that you are being short-changed. However, if you observe Japanese shoppers, you will note that hardly any of them check the change before putting it away. They trust the clerk's integrity and mathematical ability.

Something Japanese

Japan's modern manufactured consumer products require no introduction because aggressive Japanese businessmen have made them familiar to people all over the world—cameras, watches, audio equipment, VTRs, and so forth. The best brands are known just as widely in other countries as in Japan. Just in case, the leading camera names are Nikon, Canon, Konica, Asahi (Pentax), Ricoh, Mamiya, Minolta, and Fujica. The big five in electronic products are Hitachi, Matsushita (National), Toshiba, Sony, and Standard, but there are a host of other top-quality makers. In watches, you can't go wrong with either Seiko or Citizen. The products of these manufacturers are beyond reproach in quality and can be bought for less than in your own country, with the possible exception of Hong Kong, where a few items are actually cheaper than in Tokyo. Except for highly specialized items, you don't have to go farther than the hotel arcade or the tax-free shops for the consumer products of modern industry.

But if you are going shopping for things traditionally Japanese, some suggestions may be in order.

Kimono and Accessories

The heavily embroidered, brilliantly dyed kimono you've seen in pictures of Madam Butterfly are meant to be worn only by brides, young girls, or geisha. When a Japanese married woman—or any respectable lady over 25—dresses up in a kimono, it's generally a fairly subdued, *shibui* affair. The Japanese businessman has learned that the foreign woman would be sorely disappointed with the real thing suitable to her age and station, and so an industry of "kimono for tourists" has sprung up. These kimono are inexpensive, bright, and cheerful (gaudy in Japanese eyes), and the shops selling them will gladly fit you up with an easy-to-tie *obi* (the wide sash worn around the waist), *zori* (sandals) and other necessary accessories. Or you can simply use these kimono as dressing robes.

The *happi* coat is another bit of Japanese clothing popular with foreigners. The real *happi* coat is a hip length, loose jacket made of heavy dark blue cotton. *Happi* coats are worn by firemen, carpenters, gardeners, and other workmen. The *mon* (crest) of the employer (or fire station) is printed on the back of the jacket. Foreigners found these working-class symbols made snappy beach coats, and the tourist industries soon leapt into the fray. They began turning out *happi* coats in all sorts of textures, materials, colors, and designs. Some would look good on the beach, some look ghastly anywhere.

These *happi* coats are standard tourist items you'll find everywhere, but it's not always so easy to get the genuine article. The International Arcade in Tokyo has them, as well as heavy dark blue workmen's aprons. Westerners have discovered these make good conversation-piece barbecue aprons.

Haori are hip length jackets worn over the kimono. Silk *haori* are more for fashion than warmth, and some people use these as evening coats. Winter knitted *haori* make fine sloppy sweaters, good for either ski lodges or elderly aunts.

By far the favorite Japanese garb of foreigners who live in Japan is the summer *yukata*. These informal cotton kimono are inexpensive, gay, and wonderful for lounging. The department stores sell *yukata* only in the summer but you can buy ready-made *yukata* in Western sizes, for both men and women, throughout the year at arcade and other tourist kimono shops. Westerners have found all sorts of new uses for *yukata* material, from dresses to curtains and table mats.

For *tabi* (the short, bifurcated socks worn with Japanese sandals), in various colors and large Western sizes, go to the tourist kimono shops.

A *furoshiki* makes a fine small gift to take home. It is a large silk or cotton square, which the Japanese use for bundling things. Furoshiki come in an infinite variety of colors and designs, including reproductions of famous old woodblock prints, and make wonderful neck or head scarves. They can be found at any kimono shop.

Furnishings

"Chow" tables (known as *chabudai* in Japan, these are the low tables off of which the Japanese eat their meals), antique Sendai *tansu* chests, and old oblong wooden *hibachi* (charcoal braziers) converted into low tables with the brass-lined charcoal heating section turned into a planter, are just about Japan's only contributions in the furniture field. Department stores are the best places to shop for new tables and rattan furniture; antique and curio shops for old pieces.

Zabuton, the large cushions Japanese use on their *tatami* straw mat floor where chairs are taboo, make handsome accessories for any home. *Zabuton* generally come in sets of five, but oversize models are sold singly. Winter *zabuton* are covered in silk, summer ones in cotton, linen, or straw. *Tenugui,* small hand cloths made of rough cotton cloth, are attractively colored and printed with designs. You can use them as hand towels, or as luncheon place mats, or as scarves. Some foreign residents stitch several together to make summer tablecloths.

The Japanese have such a genius for working bamboo that some modern craftsmen have elevated their wares to the status of art objects —and price their creations accordingly. But don't let that put you off. The country still abounds in inexpensive and imaginative bamboo products of all shapes and sizes. Department stores are a good place to find them, both in the household tableware department (trays, baskets, etc.) and in the flower-arranging sections (bamboo vases).

Paper, Pottery, Ivory, Lacquerware

Paper and Paper Products. Japan's lovely handmade papers are world renowned. Incidentally, "rice paper" is a misnomer. Japanese paper is made from wood pulp, just like paper everywhere. Widely available and inexpensive are bright rice-paper billfolds that have cover reproductions of traditional woodblock prints.

Fans. Fans are vital props in Japanese dance and theater. The theatrical fans are bigger and more elaborate than the everyday variety used by both men and women as a decorative and cooling hot weather accessory. In the summer months the department stores have large fan sections, where you can buy beauties for very little. Foreign women, incidentally, generally prefer the men's fans, as they tend to be more *shibui* (restrained and subtle) than those favored by Japanese ladies.

Pottery and China. Japan has long been famous for its beautiful porcelain. Antique and curio shops are the places to look for the products of the great old kilns—Imari and Kutani ware are among the best known. In recent years foreigners have also discovered the charms of Japanese folk pottery, and Japan's inexpensive Western-style china is familiar to all.

Lacquerware. Lacquerware is one of the best buys in Japan, both for beauty and price. Every department store has a large lacquer section, where you can find lovely trays, boxes, and bowls of all shapes and sizes. Lacquer soup bowls are wonderful additions to the Western table, and even the inexpensive ones hold up well under daily use. Every curio shop will have some fine old lacquer in stock, but fine old lacquer, especially the gold pieces, gets quite expensive. The Japanese also turn out a good bit of lacquer allegedly designed for foreigners, which is sold in hotel arcades and other tourist centers. It is generally garish, tasteless, and best avoided.

Cloisonné, Damascene, Ivory. Cloisonné enamel, called *shippo* in Japanese, is happily undergoing a design renaissance. While the old-fashioned flowers, birds, and bees designs are still being turned out in quantity, cloisonné artisans are also successfully experimenting with a new modern look more appealing to today's taste.

You'll find new and old ivory pieces in many of the arcades and curio shops. Probably Japan's best known and most interesting ivory carvings are the small *netsuke* ornaments, formerly used to attach tobacco pouches to the *obi* belt. *Netsuke* collecting is a favorite Japanese sport. Luckily the supply is so plentiful that this is still a game the average collector can afford.

The Sword. The Japanese sword remains for most Japanese the symbol of the whole warrior cult of the past, and the process of making one is a semireligious undertaking in Japan. The sword comprises a complete mystique in itself and is regarded as an art object of the first rank. Today good swords are hard to come by. The blade itself, with its inscriptions and individual qualities, is the main object of the mystique. Most Westerners are not interested in the qualities of the blade, but find the sword ornaments or accessories fascinating. They are miniature sculptures of a sort rarely seen in the West. They include the *tsuba* (sword guard), the scabbard, and the *menuki* on the hilt, in all of which the art of metal and lacquer working rose to an incredibly high standard. *Menuki* hilt ornaments have been converted into earrings, cuff links, and brooches, and are a popular souvenir item.

Yardstick for Selecting Pearls

Cultured pearls are Japan's most famous product, and unhappily one of the most difficult to give advice on. Color, luster, shape, size, and flaws determine a pearl's value, but it often takes an expert's eye to detect the subtle distinctions in these qualities. All other things being equal, the luster is the most important factor. And the luster, say the experts, is "undefinable but unmistakable—a clear, almost translucent coloring with a subdued but warm glow." The wisest move for the nonexpert is to compare various pearls in your price range, and do your best to spot this elusive "luster" quality.

As for shape, the perfectly round pearls fetch the highest price, but the irregular baroque pearls, having zoomed into fashion prominence, are also rising in price. For the record, the experts list fifty-four natural pearl "colors" ranging from silvery white to a steely dark gray.

A reputable dealer is your safest guide in this complicated field. Don't expect, however, to buy a rock-size necklace for peanuts. "Many tourists come in demanding a 10 millimeter choker," laments one leading dealer. "These are almost impossible to find, and if you can find one it would be terribly expensive." A string of pearls can cost anywhere from ¥100,000 to ¥4,000,000 and more. Be prepared to pay at least ¥100,000 to ¥200,000 for a string of decent quality.

Caution on Antiques

In Japan, as in every other country, you should seek expert advice before investing heavily in any serious work of art. Forgeries and frauds in Orientalia are unhappily prevalent, and extremely difficult to detect.

The National Cultural Properties Protection Law, designed to keep the best of Japan's artistic heritage safe on home soil, requires an export certificate for any antique art object. The law is vague about just when an object qualifies as an "antique," so the final say remains with government authorities. Most curio shops don't bother to tell you about this law, and anyway, most of the things found in these shops certainly wouldn't qualify as national treasures. But dealers in first-class antiquities will advise you to go through the formalities. They will handle the red tape for you.

A Word on Silk Fabric

The most original designs and interesting textures of Japanese silk are reserved for the kimono silk and obi brocades. Kimono material comes in rolls, about 12 inches wide and 10 yards long, just the amount required for one kimono. Obi material comes in two widths, about 9 and 21 inches, and is about 10 feet long. The fabulous obi brocades make stunning evening jackets or sheath dresses. To use this material for Western clothing, however, takes a skillful dressmaker. Rolls of soft pastel silks, often delicately patterned with flowers, are used for the *nagajuban,* the undergarment that serves the function of a slip. *Nagajuban* alone make pretty dressing gowns.

Regional Shopping

The best shopping towns in Japan are Tokyo, Kyoto, and Osaka. Kyoto is the center of Japan's traditional culture and art. Tokyo and Osaka are best for modern industrial products. The home of traditional industrial art objects and folkcraft are the provincial areas. Tokyo has just about everything. Almost all the famous and long-established stores in other parts of the country maintain branch stores in Tokyo.

Kyoto is the home of Japan's beautiful handwoven Nishijin brocade, colorful and elegant *yuzen-zome* kimono fabrics. It is famous for Kiyomizu-yaki ceramics, lacquerware, elegant Kyo dolls, dancing fans, screens, antiques, and art objects.

Both Nikko and Hakone, two of Japan's most popular tourist spots, have several good antique and curio shops.

Just about every town and region in the country is noted for some local product or other, either handicraft or foodstuff. If you travel in the countryside, or pay a visit to a hot-spring resort, you will find these regional specialties at local souvenir shops. They are good places to find amusing and inexpensive little gifts.

Also there are folk toys native to certain localities, representative of which are *kokeshi* dolls of the Tohoku district in northern Honshu, wooden carved toys modeled after the horse or the cow also of the Tohoku district, Kyo dolls of Kyoto, and Hakata dolls of Kyushu.

Below is a list of localities and the products for which they are famous.

Hokkaido. Wooden carvings of bear and handicraft items by Ainu people.

Sendai (Miyagi Prefecture). Lacquerware, *kokeshi* dolls, bamboo ware.

Fukushima Prefecture. Soma-yaki pottery with horse designs, double-bottomed tea kettles and tea cups designed to prevent heat from escaping.

Mashiko (Tochigi Prefecture). Mashiko-yaki pottery rich in pastoral flavor.

Kiryu (Gumma Prefecture). Meisen plain-weave silk fabric.

Yuki (Ibaraki Prefecture). Yuki *tsumugi* silk pongee.

Kasama (Ibaraki Prefecture). Kasama-yaki pottery of daily utensils rich in rural flavor.

Kamakura (Kanagawa Prefecture). Kamakura-bori carved wooden trays, soup cups, saucers, plates, covered boxes, etc.

Shizuoka Prefecture. Green tea.

Yamanashi Prefecture. Crystal necklaces, pendants, seal chops (a seal chop has a person's name engraved on the end and is used in Japan instead of a signature), etc.

Niigata Prefecture. Ojiya cotton crepe, silverware (Tsubame City), comical *noroma* folk dolls (Sado Island).

Ishikawa Prefecture. Wajima-nuri lacquerware, multi-colored Kutani porcelain (Kanazawa), colorful and elegant Kaga-yuzen dyed silk fabric, and elegant Kaga dolls.

Nagoya (Aichi Prefecture). Seto-yaki porcelain, lacquerware, cloisonné, curios, and toys.

Gifu Prefecture. Mino-yaki pottery, including *Shino, Oribe,* yellow and black *Seto;* hand-made *washi* paper, paper lanterns, paper umbrellas and other paper products.

Mie Prefecture. Pearls (Shima), Tokoname brown pottery.

Nara Prefecture. Articles made of deer horns, dolls, fans, reproductions of Noh masks.

Okayama Prefecture. Bizen-yaki pottery.

Takamatsu (Kagawa Prefecture, Shikoku). Lacquerware, engravings, wooden articles, bamboo ware, Japanese-style parasols, etc.

Fukuoka Prefecture (Kyushu). Hakata *Obi,* Hakata dolls.

Arita (Saga Prefecture, Kyushu). Arita-yaki porcelain internationally known for its superior quality.

Nagasaki Prefecture (Kyushu). Articles made of tortoise shell, coral ware, Koga folk dolls.

Kagoshima Prefecture (Kyushu). Satsuma-yaki porcelain, Satsuma-*gasuri* fabric.

Fukuoka Prefecture (Kyushu). Kurume-*gasuri* fabric.

Beppu (Oita Prefecture, Kyushu). Bamboo and wooden articles.

Okinawa. Bingata stencil-dyed silk fabric, linen, *bashofu* cloth made of banana fiber, Tsuboya-yaki porcelain, coral articles.

Useful Japanese Expressions

Although tourists will have little difficulty in communicating with shop clerks in Tokyo, knowledge of a few short Japanese expressions will be helpful when you do shopping in the provinces.

I-ku-ra de-su-ka? (what's the price?); *kai-te kuda-sai* (please write it down); *ko-re* (this); *a-re* (that); *mi-se-te kuda-sai* (please show it to me); *motto oh-ki-i-no* (a larger one); *motto chi-i-sai-no* (a smaller one); *motto yasu-i-no* (a cheaper one); *motto ta-ka-i-no* (a more expensive one); *chi-gau-iro* (different color); *issho-ni* (together, when you want your purchase packed in one bundle); *be-tsu be-tsu* (separately); *i-ri-ma-sen* (I will not take it); *ko-re wo kuda-sai* (give me this one); *Ari-ga-to* (Thank you).

SIGHTSEEING CHECKLIST FOR JAPAN. In preparing this list, we hope to encourage you to go out and about on your own in Japan. The following enumeration of places and events, presented as a kind of "Several Top Tens," is designed to get you going. Remember it is only a selection, to which you'll undoubtedly make additions of your own. Wherever you go, don't forget your camera. For details, see the individual chapters that follow.

TOKYO

Generally, you can go anywhere and everywhere for the beguiling blend of old and new, East and West. Be sure to take in an ultramodern hotel or two, a sophisticated department store or two, a landscaped garden or two. Particularly: the Imperial Palace Plaza. This is a wide thoroughfare of trees and lawns, regarded as the "heart" of the entire nation. The palace itself is not in sight. It is hidden by trees, and is well within the private grounds.

Ginza is the city's fashionable, main shopping district.

Asakusa gives you a look at the old downtown and the Kannon Temple. The Bean-Throwing Festival of February 3 is an exciting one here. The Sanja Festival of May 17–18 is exceptionally elaborate and vigorous.

Visit a temple, such as Zojoji in the Shiba district.

Visit a shrine, such as Meiji in the Harajuku district. In June, the Inner Gardens have irises in bloom along a winding ravine. The Seven-Five-Three Festival of November 15 is particularly appealing here, with children of these three ages out in their very best.

Tokyo Disneyland has a magic of its own, the Disney Kind. It is at Urayasu, thirty minutes from central Tokyo by subway and bus.

CHIBA-KANTO

Narita. If you arrived at Tokyo International Airport, there's no need to go again until you leave. But Narita Shinshoji Temple is worth a visit. Pilgrim time is in January, when the temple and the small town are particularly festive.

Mito. Kairakuen Park is one of Japan's most celebrated three. February is a favorite time, when the plum trees blossom.

Mashiko. Pottery town, home of the late famed Shoji Hamada. Kilns, workshops, and retail shops stacked with folkcraft pots and plates.

Omiya. Hikawa Shrine is perhaps the oldest and largest shrine in this region. It is an ideal and popular setting for wedding parties, usually in evidence in spring and autumn.

Ogawa. Paper-making village, where every craftsman's cottage has its doors open so you can see men at work, and watch the processes.

Chichibu. Has a spectacular Night Festival on December 3. Drums, bells and flutes, lanterns and fireworks, and big, decorated floats, all on a cold winter night.

YOKOHAMA

Yokohama's Chinatown is something a little bit different, with its Chinese shops and restaurants. Motomachi is the shopping street that has sister ties with London's Bond Street. The harbor reminds of the more leisured past when everyone came and went by sea. Ocean-going liners, as well as container vessels, still put in here.

KAMAKURA

Great Buddha. A huge, bronze figure, in the open since the 15th century when a typhoon and then tidal waves carried away the temple building around it.

Tsurugaoka Hachimangu Shrine. The existing buildings date from 1828, but the shrine was founded in 1063. September 15 and 16 are the dates of its festival, with mounted archery performed on the 16th.

Kenchoji Temple is the headquarters of the Kenchoji branch of the Rinzai sect of Buddhism, and the greatest of the Five Great Zen Temples of Kamakura.

Engakuji Temple is headquarters of the Engakuji school of the Rinzai sect of Buddhism.

Meigetsu-in Temple has to be seen in June, when hydrangeas turn its approach lane and its entire precincts blue.

FUJI-HAKONE-IZU

Mt. Fuji. Japan's most sacred mountain, with a dramatic presence at any time of year. Five lakes lie at its foot, in a beautiful resort area.

Hakone. Chokoku-no-Mori in Hakone is an Open-Air Museum of modern sculptures.

Shimoda. On the Izu peninsula, preserves the Gyokusenji Temple that was home for Townsend Harris, America's first consul to Japan. May 17 is the date of the Black Ship Festival here, commemorating the arrival of Commodore Perry in 1854.

NIKKO

Toshogu Shrine, the mausoleum of Ieyasu, founder of the Tokugawa Shogunate, is the main attraction among many. Brilliant and dazzling, it is set amidst majestic scenery, and is both grand in scope and attentive to the smallest detail. The Shrine's Grand Festivals are on May 17 and 18, and October 17. The mountains behind Nikko and the woods around Lake Chuzenji are brilliant in autumn when the maples change color.

ALPS, SNOW COUNTRY, SADO ISLAND, KANAZAWA, TAKAYAMA

Karuizawa. For summer holidays. Cool woodlands nearly 1,000 meters above sea level. Horses and cycles for rent. Mt. Asama, active volcano, for spectacle.

Kusatsu. For winter holidays. Snow and mountains outside, hot springs inside.

Tokamachi has a snow festival in mid-February. Snow carvings on the streets, and ice caves where the children play house.

Sado, Japan's sixth largest island, has an old gold mine where prison laborers used to work. Now underground tableaux recreate the mining past.

Kanazawa, capital of the Japan Sea coast region, is an old castle town, formerly the seat of the Maeda family, wealthiest of all families of the Edo Period. The Hyakumangoku Festival takes place in mid-July. Kenrokuen is another of Japan's three most famous landscape gardens.

Takayama is another old castle town and a "little Kyoto." Many old buildings and a general sense of the past persist here. Takayama Festival, full of color and enthusiasm, is scheduled twice a year: April 14 and 15, and September 9 and 10.

Shirakawa hamlet is famous for its houses that are four stories high, made of stout wood, heavy beams, and thick thatch. Each house, built in the gassho-zukuri style, used to accommodate up to 50 people united in a large-family system, headed by the family patriarch.

Tsumago and Magome, on the old Kiso Road, are ancient post towns, now model villages kept in a traditional manner.

NAGOYA AND ISE-SHIMA

Nagoya. Nagoya Castle, dating from 1610, was a World War II casualty that is now rebuilt. The factories that make Noritake china and Ando cloisonné are open to visitors. The Television Tower gives a wide panoramic view of Nagoya and district. The Tokugawa Art Museum holds 7,000 works of art, historical relics, and heirlooms of the family that ruled Japan for 265 years.

Inuyama. Meiji Mura is an outdoor village on the outskirts of Nagoya that preserves buildings of the Meiji Era, 1868–1911.

Gifu. An old-fashioned town, noted for its production of paper lanterns and paper umbrellas. Cormorant fishing, held nearly every night of summer, from mid-May to mid-October, can be viewed here on the Nagara River. Gifu is about 45 minutes from Nagoya by train.

Ise. Uji-Yamada railway station is access point for the Great Shrines of Ise, Japan's most holy. The Outer Shrine is called Ge-ku; it enshrines the Goddess of Grain. The Inner Shrine, Nai-ku, enshrines the Sun Goddess, divine ancestress of the Imperial Family and creator of Japan.

Toba. At Pearl Island, in Toba Harbor, you can see demonstrations of the process of culturing pearls, as worked out by Kokichi Mikimoto, the original Pearl King. Mount Koya is a leading religious, historical, scenic, and artistic center. Kobo Daishi, founder of the Shingon Sect of Buddhism, established in 816 this great complex of temples and monasteries that is a pilgrimage site.

KYOTO

Everyone's dream of Old Japan, where just to walk the back streets takes you back into an earlier time. Three Imperial Palaces require permits to view. These are: Kyoto Gosho, Katsura, and Shugakuin.

Heian Shrine. Built in 1895 on the occasion of Kyoto's 1100th anniversary.

Kiyomizu, at the top of "Teapot Lane." This Clear Spring Temple has a wide, stilted platform commanding spectacular views.

Nijo Castle, built in 1603, as the opulent residence of Ieyasu, first shogun of Japan.

Kinkakuji, the Temple of the Golden Pavilion, which began as a shogun's villa.

Ginkakuji, The Silver Pavilion, was also a shogun's villa. It is now a Zen temple.

Sanjusangendo (formally, Rengeoin). A National Treasure, this temple houses a Thousand-Armed Kannon figure (also a National Treasure), and 1,000 smaller Kannon images.

Ryoanji, the Temple of the Peaceful Dragon, is world-renowned for its garden of fifteen stones. For your meditation.

Saihoji, the Moss Temple, has a unique garden where more than forty species of mosses grow.

Higashi and Nishi Honganji are two headquarters of the Jodo Shinshu Sect of Buddhism. Nishi Hoganji is where the sect originated, and is one of the finest temples in Kyoto.

For pageantry in the streets, visit Kyoto during any of the following festivals: May 15; the Aoi, or Hollyhock Festival. July 16–24; the Gion Festival. October 22; the Jidai, Festival of the Eras. **N.B.** Cherry blossoms in April. Maple leaves in color in November.

NARA

Kasuga Shrine of 3,000 lanterns is set in extensive wooded grounds. Deer wander at will in the surrounding park. All 3,000 lanterns are lit in the festivals of February 3 and 4 and August 15. Kofukuji is the five-story pagoda that is a calendar picture of Nara.

Todaiji, the East Great Temple, was founded in 745. Deserving of close scrutiny for its myriad details. Daibutsuden, the Great Buddha Hall, is the largest wooden structure in the world. It houses the Great Buddha that is the world's largest bronze statue.

Shoso-in is the log-cabin Imperial Repository that, for over 1,200 years, has preserved a priceless collection of objects, including jewels, clothing, silverware, masks, and writing materials.

Nigatsu-do (February Hall) and Sangatsu-do (March Hall) are outstanding for themselves and their treasures, and for the rural nature of their surroundings.

Horyuji, a few kilometers west of Nara, is the marvelous temple founded in 607 by Prince Shotoku. This was the center of art and scholarship during Prince Shotoku's time, and the place where Buddhism in Japan first began to thrive.

OSAKA

There's a castle, and two towers that provide city views. As a big industrial city, Osaka keeps its citizens amused in entertainment centers. The main ones are at Shinsekai, Umeda, Dotombori, and Sennichi-mae. Shinsaibashi-dori is a shopping area.

INLAND SEA COASTAL AREAS

Kobe. Port Island is a new man-made complex of many facilities. Ijinkan, also in Kobe, are the residences of early foreign inhabitants, interesting for historical sidelights.

Himeji. Shirasagi-jo is the famed and beautiful Castle of the White Heron.

Okayama. Korakuen, the third of Japan's top three landscaped gardens, is here.

Kurashiki. Its old houses and Edo-Period rice granaries date from feudal days when this was a port for shipping rice.

Hiroshima. The Atom Bomb Dome remains in its devastated state. The Peace Memorial Park, the Hall, and Museum have to be seen, along with the Memorial Cathedral for World Peace.

Miyajima. This is where the shrine seems to float on the sea.

Matsue. As well as an exceptionally well-sited castle, Matsue has writer Lafcadio Hearn's house as a main attraction.

Tottori. Sand dunes and sunsets make for picture postcard views, unlike any others in Japan.

Amanohashidate. The pine tree covered sandbar is thought to look like a bridge leading up to Heaven.

Naruto Straits. The whirlpools between Awaji and Shikoku become ferocious four times a day as tides change.

Takamatsu has two claims to fame: Beautifully landscaped Ritsurin Park, and Kompira Shrine, which protects the men who go to sea in ships.

Matsuyama is the island of Shikoku's largest city, and a castle town. Dogo Spa here is a very old one.

KYUSHU

Beppu. Bathing in colored hot springs and baking in hot sand are special attractions.

Fukuoka. Renowned for its silk textiles and Hakata clay dolls. Dontaku is the big festival of May 3–5.

Nagasaki. Glover House is the romantic and fictitious site of Madame Butterfly's waiting and watching. View of the harbor.

Nagasaki Peace Park, laid out to commemorate the August 9, 1945, atomic bombing.

Megane-bashi, Spectacles Bridge, has been in daily use since 1634. It had to be rebuilt recently after being damaged in a storm.

Peiron is Nagasaki's boat race, exciting and noisy. Held either the first or second Sunday of June.

Unzen National Park, east of Nagasaki, year-round attractions.

Mt. Aso, between Beppu and Nagasaki, is noted for its crater basin, which is the largest of its kind in the world.

Kagoshima is dominated by its active volcano, Sakurajima. Lava flow has formed a peninsula linking the volcano, which used to be on an island, to the mainland.

Arita. This pottery town has the kilns and shops of Kakiemon, Ima-emon, and Gen-emon.

TOHOKU

Sendai. Hundreds of strangely shaped pine-clad islands, north of the city of Sendai, make up the glory of Matsushima. The Tanabata Star Festival of August 6–8, in Sendai, is famous nationwide.

Yokote has an appealing Kamakura Festival on February 15 for three days. Snow sculptures are made in the streets, as well as little snowhouses for children to play in, and have parties with cakes and sweet drinks.

Morioka. The festival of June 15 is called Chagu-Chagu Umakko, or Horse Festival. Caparisoned horses are led to Sozen Shrine where their owners seek blessings for them.

Soma. Also spotlights horses, on July 23–25, during Nomaoi, or Wild Horse Chasing. Ancient armor, shrine flags, and thudding hooves.

Hirosaki stages its Nebuta Festival, from August 1–7. A picturesque lantern festival.

Akita has a lantern-balancing festival from August 5–7. Participants are skillful and the festival is very beautiful.

HOKKAIDO

Sapporo. Hokkaido University is north of Sapporo Station. Dr. William S. Clark of Massachusetts established the Sapporo Agricultural College here in 1876.

Clock Tower Building, south of the station, is the only Russian-style building in Sapporo.

O-dori Promenade stretches east to west in the center of Sapporo. The television tower at the eastern end gives a panoramic view of the city and environs.

Maruyama Primeval Forest, four kilometers southwest of the station, has many different kinds of trees, and is designated as a "Natural Monument."

Teine Olympic Ski Grounds, 45 minutes by bus from Sapporo, were the site of the Winter Olympic Events in 1972.

Hakodate. The third-largest city in Hokkaido, Hakodate has a Trappist Convent that produces butter and candy marketed as specialties of Hokkaido.

Shikotsu-Toya National Park. At Shiraoi, within the park, is an Ainu Village that is one of the best in Hokkaido.

Noboribetsu, also within the park, is famed for its hot springs that feed all the local hotels and inns.

Daisetsuzan National Park. This is the largest mountain national park in Japan. Sounkyo Gorge and Tenninkyo Gorge are renowned for the beauty of their cliffs and waterfalls.

Kushiro. Along the river inland from Kushiro on the southeast coast of Hokkaido is a natural park noted as the habitat of red-crested cranes.

Akan National Park. Has three large lakes: Akan, known for the green weed marimo that is a "Special Natural Monument"; Kutcharo, with thermal springs bubbling up at its southern end, and many spas along its sandy shores; and Mashu, a crater lake with no inlet nor outlet. Mashu has clear water allowing a view to a depth of more than 40 meters.

Rishiri-Rebun-Sarobetsu National Park. Rishiri and Rebun are islands reached by ferry from Wakkanai, Hokkaido's northernmost city on the western tip. Both islands are the haunts of wild sea birds.

Sarobetsu, south of Wakkanai, is known for its garden of hundreds of subarctic-zone wild flowers.

THE RYUKYU ISLANDS

Okinawa. Wartime memorials include the Himeyuri-no-to (Lily Tower) and the Shiraume-no-to (White Plum Tower) where schoolgirls died; and the Kenji-no-to where schoolboys committed suicide.

Gyokusendo, southwest of Naha, has more than 400,000 stalactites and stalagmites in vast underground caverns.

Okinawa's biggest festival is Eisa, a lively mass dance, held from July 14–16.

Iejima. The island where American war correspondent Ernie Pyle was killed.

Taketomi, in the island chain, is rural and untouched.

Iriomote, another island, is the habitat for a primitive wild cat, believed to be unique to the island's forests.

EXPLORING TOKYO

by
JOHN TURRENT

John Turrent was on the editorial staff of The Japan Times *from 1978 until 1984, writing regularly for the daily newspaper,* The Student Times, *and* The Japan Times Weekly. *He is now working as a freelance writer and translator in Tokyo. Mr. Turrent is co-author and author, respectively, of the guidebook* Around Tokyo, *volumes 1 and 2.*

The first impression many people have of Tokyo is of a city teeming with people and traffic, a concrete jungle of modern office buildings stretching as far as the eye can see. The rush-hour crush for which the capital of Japan is notorious is a fact of life here. To experience it at first hand, head for Shinjuku Station in western central Tokyo between the hours of 8:00 and 9:00 in the morning and try changing trains there. Several railway lines pass through Shinjuku, including the green-colored Yamanote loop line, the Chuo line, which runs from Tokyo Station out to the western suburbs, and the private Keio and Odakyu lines, both of which start at Shinjuku. And as if that weren't enough, Marunouchi subway line trains also stop there.

The squeeze, accompanied by plenty of pushing and shoving and heaving, should be enough to convince you that Tokyo, with a population of over 11 million people, is indeed an overcrowded city. The

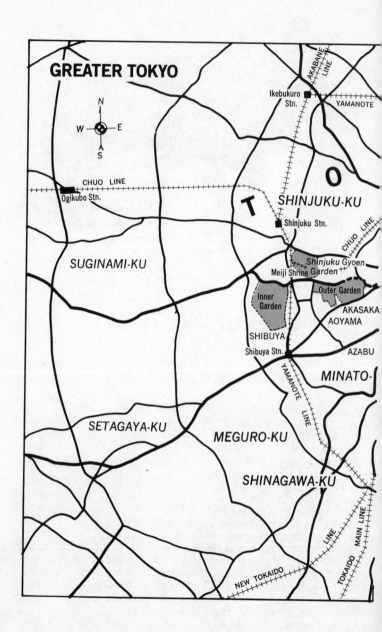

GREATER TOKYO

N
W — E
S

CHUO LINE
Ogikubo Stn.

SUGINAMI-KU

T   O

SHINJUKU-KU

Ikebukuro Stn.

AKABANE LINE

YAMANOTE

CHUO LINE

Shinjuku Stn.

Shinjuku Gyoen
Meiji Shrine Garden

Inner Garden

Outer Garden

AKASAKA
AOYAMA

SHIBUYA
Shibuya Stn.

AZABU

MINATO-

YAMANOTE LINE

SETAGAYA-KU

MEGURO-KU

SHINAGAWA-KU

NEW TOKAIDO

LINE

TOKAIDO MAIN LINE

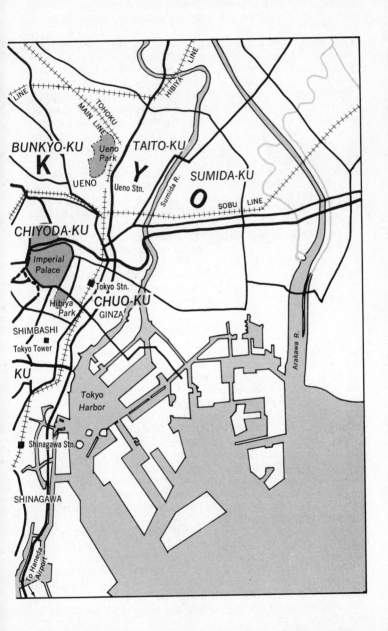

Shinjuku experience is repeated at various degrees at many other stations around the capital, especially the main Tokyo, Shinagawa, Shibuya, Ikebukuro, and Ueno stations on the Yamanote line, all starting points for other lines fanning out into the suburbs. While recovering your composure after being bundled off the train, spare a thought for the many citizens of the capital who have to suffer the rush hour every working day of the week.

Fortunately, first impressions do not have to be lasting ones. Having got over the worst aspect, it is a good idea to take a look at the city from a different angle by climbing to one of Tokyo's high spots, of which there are several possible choices. Your hotel might rise high enough to offer a panoramic view of the capital. If not, head for the nearest skyscraper with an observation floor.

The biggest cluster of skyscrapers in Tokyo is a 10-minute walk from the west exit of Shinjuku Station—within this grouping the Keio Plaza Hotel, Center Building, Nomura Building, and Sumitomo Building all have observation floors. Other possibilities are Kasumigaseki Building, near Toranomon Station on the Ginza subway line, the World Trade Center Building near Hamamatsucho Station on the Yamanote line, and Sunshine 60 (the largest of them all at 240 meters) near Ikebukuro Station on the Yamanote line. Last but not least, there is Tokyo Tower, which, when it was built in 1958, was the tallest independent steel tower in the world at 333 meters. It has two observation platforms, at 150 and 250 meters, and is located at Shiba Park, not far from the World Trade Center Building. As in the case of some of the skyscrapers, an entrance fee is required at Tokyo Tower.

From the observation platform of your choice, you will be able to enjoy spectacular views of the capital and its surroundings. On a clear day, especially after a good rainfall has cleared away all the smog, you should be able to see Mount Fuji to the south, and the hills and mountains of Chichibu to the west. To the southeast you can see Tokyo Bay, particularly fine views of which can be had from the World Trade Center Building and Tokyo Tower, which rise nearby. To the north, you might be able to make out the hills of Nikko in Tochigi Prefecture.

In this way, the mammoth city can be put into perspective. You can picture it as a small village by the sea, which is what it was when Ota Dokan built the first castle stronghold in the area in 1457. That first castle, which was located in today's Hibiya district, did not last long, but the town of Edo (as Tokyo was then known) began to develop and prosper in the 17th century, most notably under the guidance of the first Tokugawa shogun, Ieyasu.

Edo, which was modeled after Kyoto, was chosen by Ieyasu as his capital because of its situation near the sea, with mountains nearby. It is said that Edo had already developed into the largest city in the world by the mid-18th century, when it had a population of about 1 million. Edo became the capital of all of Japan in 1868 when the shogunate was overthrown and imperial rule restored throughout the nation. It was then that the city's name was changed to Tokyo, which means "eastern capital."

Tokyo continued to expand rapidly after 1868, when a period of Westernization brought in a new look in the form of red-brick, Western-style architecture. However, Tokyo has been reduced to rubble on two occasions in the 20th century: in 1923 by a huge earthquake and in 1945 by wartime air raids. This is the reason why Tokyo today appears to be such a thoroughly modernized city.

Except for part of the Tokyo Station building and the occasional structure hidden among glass and ferro-concrete, the red-brick architecture of the Meiji Period has largely disappeared now. Beneath the skyscrapers, though, there are still many traces of Tokyo's past to be seen, and it is these that make up the capital's attractions. The concrete jungle image is a true one if you limit yourself to central areas such as Marunouchi and Shinjuku, but Tokyo is actually a city with a wealth of history and culture, greenery, and even has islands to offer. Its high spots are certainly not limited to its skyscrapers.

Getting Around the City

Tokyo consists of 23 central wards, 26 cities, 6 towns, and 9 villages. Its farthest point, which cannot be seen even from the top of the tallest skyscraper, is the Ogasawara, or Bonin, island group, located in the ocean to the southeast and reached in about 30 hours by boat. The central point is the Imperial Palace, a long-standing favorite among tourists.

Despite the size and congestion involved, Tokyo is quite an easy city to get around in. Nearly all the famous spots are accessible by overground train or subway, or a combination of both. The central area is served by the Yamanote loop line, which runs from Tokyo Station in the east down south to Yurakucho, Hamamatsucho, and Shinagawa, then up the western side of the city's central area via Shibuya, Shinjuku, and Ikebukuro, then back to Tokyo station via Ueno in the northeast. There are a total of twenty-nine stations on the Yamanote line.

The other main line that you'll be using in the central Tokyo area is the Chuo line, which cuts across the city from east to west, starting at Tokyo Station and operating out into the western suburbs of the capital, passing through Ochanomizu, Yotsuya, and Shinjuku stations on the way. Trains on the Chuo line are painted orange, and those on the Yamanote line green.

Working round the city clockwise from Tokyo Station, the main areas of the city that tourists visit, either for sightseeing or shopping purposes, are Ginza (for its department stores and nightlife), the Roppongi and Akasaka entertainment districts in Minato Ward in the south, Shibuya, Shinjuku, and Ikebukuro in the west for shopping and entertainment, and Ueno and Asakusa in the northeast, for the popular Ueno Park and Asakusa Kannon Temple tourist sights.

Imperial Palace

The palace stands where Edo Castle used to be. After the Meiji Restoration in 1868 brought the Edo Period to an end, construction of a new palace for the emperor was begun on the site and completed in 1888. This Meiji Palace, as it was called, was reduced to ashes in the 1945 air raids, along with much of the rest of Tokyo, although the

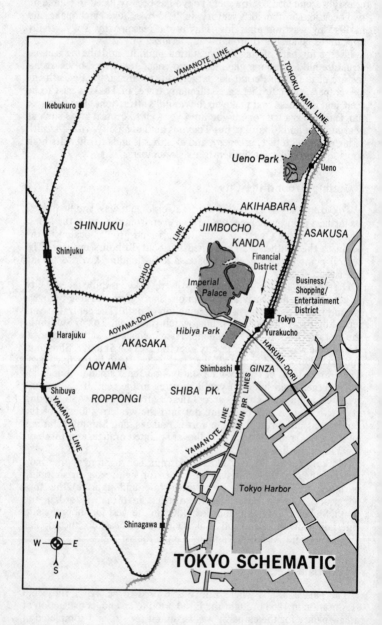

TOKYO SCHEMATIC

moats and stone bridges remained intact. A new palace was completed in 1968, and the path around it has now become a popular jogging course. The public is allowed over the main Nijubashi bridge and into the private grounds on two occasions during the year, at New Year's and again on the Emperor's Birthday, April 29. The palace is located in Chiyoda Ward and is reached from the Sakuradamon, Nijubashimae, Otemachi, or Takebashi subway stations.

The Outer Garden and East Garden are open to the public. The former, which has a giant fountain as its symbol (illuminated at night), can be reached in 5 minutes from Nijubashimae Station on the Chiyoda subway line, while the latter (open only until 4:00 P.M. and closed on Mondays and Fridays) can be reached from Otemachi or Takebashi subway stations. Entrance is free.

DISTRICT BY DISTRICT

Shimbashi–Ginza–Nihonbashi

This is the business, shopping, and entertainment district on the southeast side of the Imperial Palace. Shimbashi Station is distinguished by the steam locomotive displayed outside its eastern exit. There are several hotels located in the vicinity of Shimbashi Station, including Shimbashi Daiichi Hotel, Ginza Daiichi Hotel, Nikko Hotel, and Ginza International Hotel. The Imperial Hotel can also be reached from Shimbashi Station.

The Shimbashi area is a small but popular place to go eating and drinking in the evenings. The many restaurants and bars located on the narrow side streets near the station usually are cheaper than those found in the Ginza area to the north, and the atmosphere of these places tends to be less restrained.

Between Shimbashi and Yurakucho stations are a number of department stores (Matsuzakaya, Hankyu, Mitsukoshi, Matsuya) and other Ginza shops of long-standing fame: Wako, Mikimoto Pearls, Nishi-Ginza Electric Center, and the International Arcade, the latter housing several tax-free shops and quite rightly called one of Tokyo's best bargain centers. It is situated under the railway lines, a short walk from Yurakucho Station.

There's lots to see in this area and, with map in hand, you will be able to plan your own course. For example, a Ginza walking course might take you along Chuo Dori Avenue from Shimbashi Station, past several stores until you reach Matsuya Department Store. Turn left here, and you'll come out at Yurakucho Station. After dropping in to see the Sukiyabashi Shopping Center, Nishi Ginza Electric Center, and International Arcade, cross over to the other side of the railway lines to visit the Imperial Hotel with its arcade of top-class stores, and then on to Hibiya Park and, if time allows, the Imperial Palace as well.

The area around Tokyo Station is mainly taken up by office buildings. It is a busy business district by day, and almost a deserted ghost town at night. Two large bookstores are located near the station, Yaesu Book Center and Maruzen Book Store, which is on Chuo Dori Avenue; both stock English-language books. On the Yaesu exit side of the station, next to Daimaru Department Store, is the Kokusai Kanko

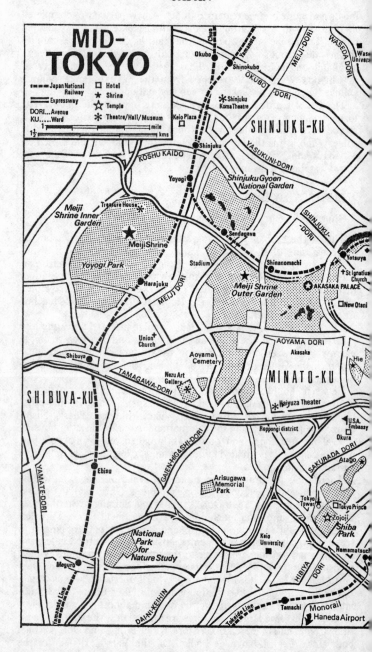

MID-TOKYO

- - - Japan National Railway
—— Expressway
DORI...Avenue
KU.....Ward
1   1/2   mile
|———————|———————| kms

□ Hotel
★ Shrine
☆ Temple
✳ Theatre/Hall/Museum

Chuo
Okubo
Yamanote
Shinokubo
OKUBO DORI
MEIJI DORI
WASEDA DORI
Waseda Univers
✳ Shinjuku Koma Theatre
Keio Plaza □
SHINJUKU-KU
YASUKUNI-DORI
Shinjuku
KOSHU KAIDO
Yoyogi
Shinjuku Gyoen National Garden
SHINJUKU-DORI
Treasure House ☆
Meiji Shrine Inner Garden
★ Meiji Shrine
Sendagaya
Yoyogi Park
Stadium
Shinanomachi
Yotsuya
✛ St Ignatius Church
Harajuku
MEIJI DORI
Meiji Shrine Outer Garden
★
✳ AKASAKA PALACE
□ New Otani
Union ✛ Church
Aoyama Cemetery
AOYAMA DORI
Akasaka
MINATO-KU
Hie ★
Shibuya
TAMAGAWA-DORI
Nezu Art Gallery ✳
SHIBUYA-KU
✳ Haiyuza Theater
Roppongi district
GAIEN-HIGASHI-DORI
U.S.A. Embassy
Okura □
SAKURADA DORI
Atago ☆
YAMATE-DORI
Ebisu
Arisugawa Memorial Park
Tokyo Tower ✳
□ Tokyo Prince
☆ Zojoji
Shiba Park
National Park for Nature Study
Keio University
HIBIYA DORI
Hamamatsuch
Meguro
DAINI-KEIHIN
Tokaido Line
Tamachi
Monorail
➤ Haneda Airport
Yamanote Line

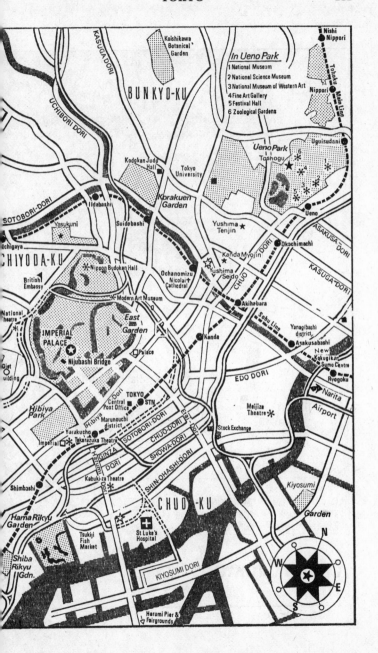

KASUGA DORI

Koishikawa
Botanical
Garden

In Ueno Park
1 National Museum
2 National Science Museum
3 National Museum of Western Art
4 Fine Art Gallery
5 Festival Hall
6 Zoological Gardens

BUNKYO-KU

UCHIBORI DORI

Ueno Park
Toshogu

Nishi
Nippori

Nippori

Tohoku Main Line

Uguisudani

Kodokan Judo
Hall

Tokyo
University

Korakuen
Garden

Iidabashi

SOTOBORI-DORI

Yasukuni

Ichigaya

CHIYODA-KU

British
Embassy

National
Theatre

Suidobashi

Nippon Budokan Hall

Modern Art Museum

IMPERIAL
PALACE

Nijubashi Bridge

Diet
Building

Hibiya
Park

Yurakucho

Imperial
Takarazuka Theatre

GINZA
DORI

Shimbashi

Hama Rikyu
Garden

Shiba
Rikyu
Gdn.

Yushima
Tenjin

Kanda Myojin

Ochanomizu
Nicolai
Cathedral

Yushima
Seido

Akihabara

Sobu Line

Kanda

East
Garden

Palace

Dori
TOKYO
Central STN
Post Office
Hibiya
Marunouchi
district

SOTOBORI-DORI

CHUO-DORI

SHOWA-DORI

Kabuki-za Theatre

SHIN-OHASHI-DORI

CHUO-KU

Tsukiji Fish
Market

St Luke's
Hospital

KIYOSUMI DORI

Harumi Pier &
Fairgrounds

Okachimachi

ASAKUSA DORI

Ueno

KASUGA DORI

CHUO

Yanagibashi
district
Asakusabashi

New
Kokugikan
Sumo Centre

Ryogoku

EDO DORI

Narita

Airport

Meijiza
Theatre

Stock Exchange

Kiyosumi

Garden

N
W E
S

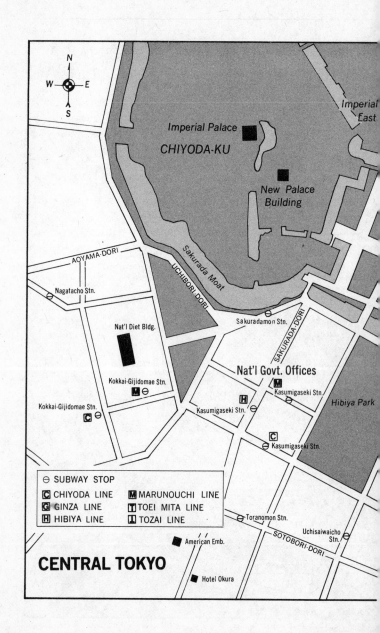

N
W   E
S

Imperial Palace
CHIYODA-KU
Imperial East

New Palace Building

AOYAMA-DORI
UCHIBORI-DORI
Sakurada Moat

Nagatacho Stn.

Nat'l Diet Bldg.

Sakuradamon Stn.

SAKURADA-DORI

Nat'l Govt. Offices

Kokkai-Gijidomae Stn.

Kasumigaseki Stn.

Kokkai-Gijidomae Stn.

Kasumigaseki Stn.

Hibiya Park

Kasumigaseki Stn.

⊖ SUBWAY STOP

C	CHIYODA LINE	**M**	MARUNOUCHI LINE
G	GINZA LINE	**T**	TOEI MITA LINE
H	HIBIYA LINE	**T**	TOZAI LINE

Toranomon Stn.

SOTOBORI-DORI

Uchisaiwaicho Stn.

American Emb.

CENTRAL TOKYO

Hotel Okura

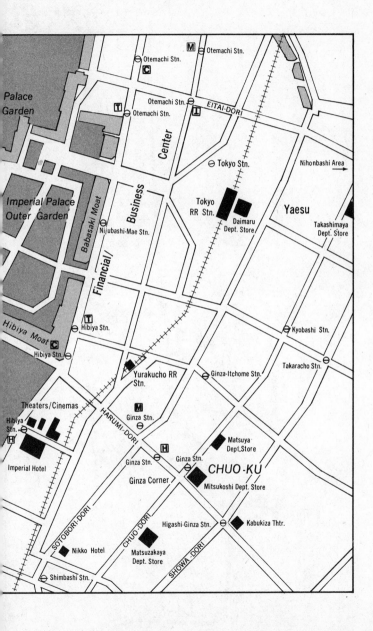

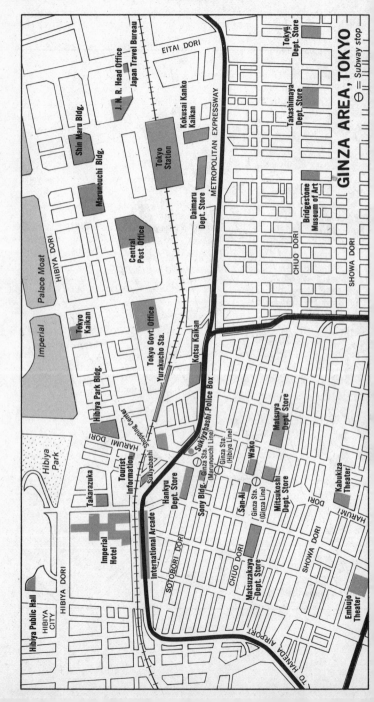

GINZA AREA, TOKYO

⊖ = Subway stop

Hibiya Public Hall
HIBIYA CITY
HIBIYA DORI

Imperial

Palace Moat

HIBIYA DORI

Shin Maru Bldg.

Marunouchi Bldg.

J. N. R. Head Office

Japan Travel Bureau

EITAI DORI

Kokusai Kanko Kaikan

Tokyo Station

METROPOLITAN EXPRESSWAY

Tokyu Dept. Store

Takashimaya Dept. Store

Central Post Office

Daimaru Dept. Store

CHUO DORI

Bridgestone Museum of Art

SHOWA DORI

Tokyo Kaikan

Hibiya Park Bldg.

Tokyo Govt. Office

Yurakucho Sta.

Kotsu Kaikan

HARUMI DORI

Shopping Center

Hibiya Park

Takarazuka

Tourist Information

Sukiyabashi

Sukiyabashi Police Box

Ginza Sta. (Marunouchi Line)

Ginza Sta. (Hibiya Line)

Wako

Matsuya Dept. Store

Hankyu Dept. Store

Sony Bldg.

San-Ai

Ginza Sta. (Ginza Line)

Mitsukoshi Dept. Store

CHUO DORI

HARUMI DORI

Kabukiza Theater

International Arcade

SOTOBORI DORI

SHOWA DORI

Imperial Hotel

HIBIYA DORI

CHUO DORI

Matsuzakaya Dept. Store

Embujo Theater

TO HANEDA AIRPORT

Kaikan Building, whose first through fourth floors house the tourist offices of all of Japan's prefectural districts. Maps and other information can be obtained here. On the Marunouchi side of Tokyo Station, again a predominantly business district, there is the Tokyo Central Post Office, where English is spoken and parcels for international mailing are handled.

One of the most popular temples in Tokyo is Zojoji, located in Minato Ward in the southeastern part of central Tokyo. It is reached in five minutes on foot from Shibakoen Station on the Toei-Mita subway line, or in 10 minutes on foot from Hamamatsucho station on the Yamanote line. Zojoji Temple is said to date from the 14th century, although the main hall had to be rebuilt after the war. The red-lacquered main gate was originally constructed in 1605.

Nearby is Tokyo Tower—you won't miss it, as it rises 333 meters and dwarfs all else below. In addition to the observation points, there is a waxworks on the third floor. From the tower you can look over Shiba Park, which sprawls below.

Hibiya Park and Kitanomaru Park both border the grounds of the Imperial Palace. The former is on the south side. Because it is situated near the Kasumigaseki, Shimbashi, and Yurakucho business districts, it is a popular place for office workers to rest during their lunchtime break. Kitanomaru Park is on the north side of the palace and can be reached in 5 minutes on foot to the west from Kudanshita Station on the Tozai subway line. Located inside Kitanomaru Park are the Science and Technology Museum, the National Museum of Modern Art, and the Budokan concert hall, while nearby, on the opposite side of Yasukuni-dori Avenue, which runs past the park, is Yasukuni Shrine.

The shrine, which has extensive parklike grounds, is reached in 5 minutes on foot to the west from Kudanshita Station on the Tozai subway line. It is dedicated to the souls of all who fought and died for Japan, and as such is the focus of much debate every time the prime minister attends a memorial service there—is he attending in his capacity as prime minister, and thereby maintaining links with the country's militaristic past, or is he attending in a private capacity?

Yasukuni Shrine boasts some splendid buildings, fine stone lanterns, and handsome *torii* gateways, as well as bronze statues of Yajiro Shinagawa (1843–1900) and Masujiro Omura (1824–1869), both political figures of the 19th century, and a Treasure House of war-related memorabilia.

Akasaka

On the western side of the Imperial Palace is Akasaka, an entertainment district with plenty of clubs, restaurants, and discos. It might also be called a diplomatic village—located in the area are the National Diet building; the Ministry of Foreign Affairs; the embassies of the U.S.A., Brazil, Canada, and Mexico; and the Geihinkan Akasaka Palace, where foreign dignitaries stay. The Metropolitan Police Department, the National Theater of Japan, and the Suntory Gallery also have addresses in this area. Local hotels include such big names as the Hotel Okura, the Hotel New Otani, the Akasaka Prince, the Akasaka Tokyu

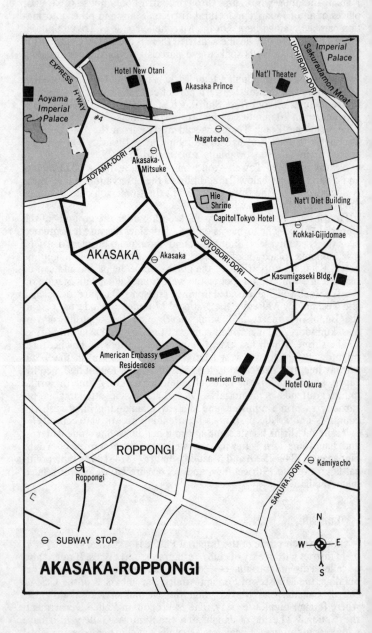

Hotel New Otani

Akasaka Prince

Nat'l Theater

Imperial Palace

EXPRESS H'WAY

Aoyama Imperial Palace

#4

AOYAMA-DORI

Akasaka-Mitsuke

Nagatacho

Hie Shrine

Capitol Tokyo Hotel

Nat'l Diet Building

Kokkai-Gijidomae

AKASAKA

Akasaka

SOTOBORI-DORI

UCHIBORI-DORI

Sakuradamon Moat

Kasumigaseki Bldg.

American Embassy Residences

American Emb.

Hotel Okura

ROPPONGI

Roppongi

Kamiyacho

SAKURA-DORI

⊖ SUBWAY STOP

N
W · E
S

AKASAKA-ROPPONGI

Hotel, and the Capitol Tokyu. And right in there with them all is Hie Shrine. However international it is, a Japanese neighborhood wouldn't be complete without a shrine or temple, after all. If you happen to be in town in June, then be sure to visit the shrine's festival which takes place from the 10th to the 15th of that month every year. It is one of the largest and most colorful annual festivals in Tokyo.

The National Diet Building, which stands on Kasumigaseki Hill in Nagatacho, was completed in 1936. The central tower of the 65.5-meter-high structure has become one of the main landmarks of Tokyo. As you face the building, the right half is taken up by the House of Councillors and the left half by the House of Representatives.

The main entertainment districts in this area are Akasaka-Mitsuke and Roppongi, both of which have convenient subway stations and are well frequented by the foreign resident and tourist communities.

Shibuya

Along with Ginza, Roppongi, Shinjuku, and Ikebukuro, Shibuya, in Tokyo's western quarter, is one of the leading shopping and entertainment districts in the capital. The symbol of the area, however, is neither a main department store nor a nightclub spot, but the bronze statue of a dog called Hachiko that sits outside the north exit of Shibuya Station. Hachiko lived in the Shibuya area from 1923–1935 together with his master. Every day Hachiko would see his master off to work at the station and return again to meet him in the evening. His master died away from home in 1925, and for 10 years after that Hachiko waited at the station for him to return. The dog's loyalty won the hearts of the people of the area, and after his death the statue was erected on the spot in his memory. The statue has become a popular meeting place for people on their way to the many shops, restaurants, bars, and clubs in the area, while Hachiko himself is preserved in stuffed form in Ueno's Science Museum.

From the Hachiko statue, roads fan out in several directions, all of which offer plenty of opportunities for exploration. A good course is to take the street leading away in the direction in which Hachiko is looking. This street passes Seibu Department Store on the left, and beyond this a turning to the left takes you up Shibuya's Park Avenue (Koen-Dori) toward the NHK Broadcasting Center, on the way passing Parco Department Store on the left and the Tobacco and Salt Museum on the right. Adjoining the broadcasting center is Yoyogi Park, a popular spot among joggers and musicians, and it is possible to walk right through the park as far as Harajuku and the Meiji Shrine.

Omote-Sando, the main boulevard linking Harajuku and Aoyama, began as a solemn, stone-lanterned route for pilgrims. During the early postwar years it swarmed with American Occupation Forces families who lived in nearby Washington Heights, which became Olympic Village in 1964 and is now part of Yoyogi Park. Harajuku is a fashionable district and a favorite haunt for Tokyo's young set.

At the big intersection with Aoyama-dori, turn left. This avenue is another that has changed its character over the last few years. Ultra-

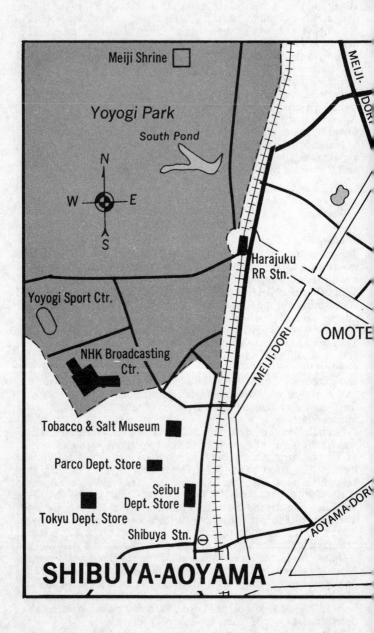

Meiji Shrine □

Yoyogi Park

South Pond

N
W — E
S

Yoyogi Sport Ctr.

NHK Broadcasting
Ctr.

Tobacco & Salt Museum ■

Parco Dept. Store ■

Seibu
Dept. Store

Tokyu Dept. Store

Shibuya Stn.

Harajuku
RR Stn.

MEIJI-
DORI

MEIJI-DORI

OMOTE

AOYAMA-DORI

SHIBUYA-AOYAMA

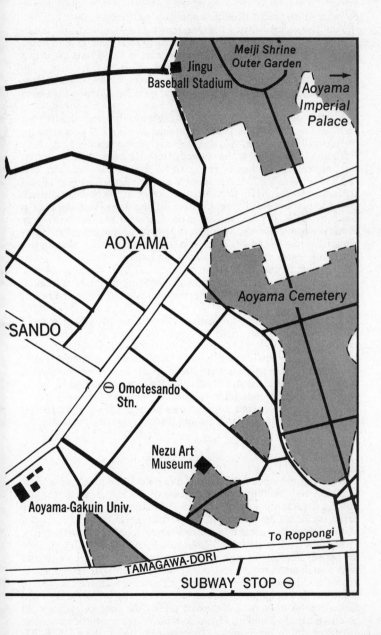

Meiji Shrine
Outer Garden

Jingu
Baseball Stadium

Aoyama
Imperial
Palace

AOYAMA

Aoyama Cemetery

SANDO

⊖ Omotesando
Stn.

Nezu Art
Museum

Aoyama-Gakuin Univ.

To Roppongi

TAMAGAWA-DORI

SUBWAY STOP ⊖

modern, it still tucks away the oddest little remnants of old Japan in between sophisticated boutiques and fast-food restaurants.

You'll see shops that sell flower bowls, multicolored and multi-shaped. You'll see shops that are stacked to their ceilings with *futon*, the quilts that are not only Japanese bedding but also beds. Next to a shop that sells goldfish is a supermarket. Next to this again is an old-style shop that sells tea, colored tea caddies, blue-and-white Japanese teapots, and handleless Japanese teacups. Then there's a high-class store for kimonos.

Aoyama-dori is fashionable, but younger and breezier and trendier than the Ginza. You can reach Shimbashi station from Gaienmae or, if you walk far enough, Aoyama-itchome subway station.

Yoyogi Park can be reached directly from Meiji-jingumae Station on the Chiyoda subway line or Harajuku Station on the Yamanote line, and it is in the immediate vicinity of Meiji Shrine, the Yoyogi National Stadium, and the NHK Broadcasting Center in the Shibuya district. Over the past couple of years the road leading from Harajuku Station down to NHK has become an extra tourist attraction itself every Sunday, when it is closed to traffic and young people engage in everything from dancing to 1950s' rock 'n' roll music to roller skating and practicing tennis against the walls of the bridges.

Meiji-jingu is the main shrine in central Tokyo. It is located near Harajuku Station on the Yamanote line or Meiji-jingumae Station on the Chiyoda subway line. Meiji Shrine, as it is often called in English, was dedicated to the Emperor Meiji (1852–1912) and is still one of the main pilgrimage centers in Japan. Crowds of people visit here from quite distant places, especially on New Year's Day. As well as its *torii* gateways marking the various entrances to the shrine, Meiji-jingu has a splendid inner garden of trees and shrubs, and a particularly outstanding display of irises, which blossom in late June. The wooden *torii* gate of the shrine is the largest of its kind in Japan, standing 12 meters high. The shape of *torii* gates, by the way, is said to derive from the shape of a rooster's perch, because of an old legend in which a rooster crowed, waking the sun goddess and bringing light to the world.

Shinjuku

Walk through one of the exits of Shinjuku Station, ride up a short escalator, and you'll probably find yourself, not out on the street, but inside a department store. Old-fashioned stations serving one purpose only have all but disappeared in Tokyo (one exception being Harajuku Station on the Yamanote line, which is a quaint cottage-like structure). Most of the modern station buildings have literally been built right over the railway lines and house stores, shops, restaurants, coffee shops, and even sometimes cinemas. It is now possible to do your shopping, eat a meal, and have your entertainment without ever leaving the station.

In the case of Shinjuku, the west side is taken up by the Odakyu and Keio department stores and the east side by the appropriately named Shinjuku Station Building. If you do seek to venture outside, the west exit takes you to the Shinjuku skyscraper buildings (the KDD Building, NS Building, Keio Plaza Hotel, Century Hyatt Hotel, Daiichi

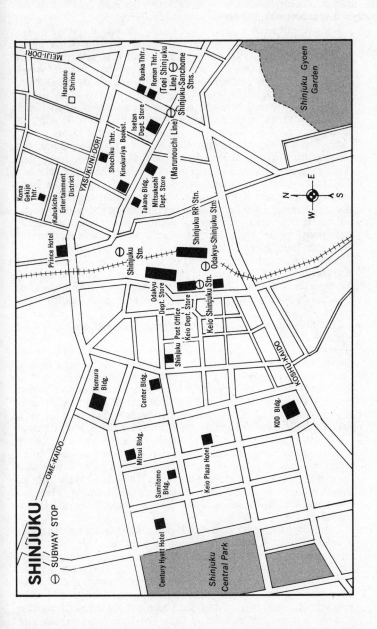

Seimei Building, Sumitomo Building, Mitsui Building, Shinjuku Center Building, Nomura Building, and Yasuda Building).

The east exit leads to the Kabukicho entertainment district which, despite its name, has nothing to do with Kabuki. In the area you'll find, on the safer side, scores of coffee shops, restaurants, discos and pubs, as well as the Koma Gekijo Theater where musicals and variety shows are held. On the "be warned" side, there are lots of strip joints, bars, cabarets, and dark alleyways.

Also to be reached from the east exit are Mitsukoshi and Isetan department stores, Kinokuniya Book Store, the Takano building of boutiques and other shops, which is built on the most highly valued piece of land in Japan, and Hanazono Shrine. This shrine is near the crossing where Yasukuni Dori Avenue and Meiji Dori Avenue meet. It is the scene of a cock fair (*tori no ichi*) every November. The fair is held two or three times in the month, but on differing days, so check with the local press if you're in town around that time. Nearby is "Golden Street," a district of small bars frequented by writers, poets, and others connected with literary world. It is a famous "red-light" area. Many cinemas are located in the two areas near Koma Gekijo and the Isetan Department Store, and Shinjuku Gyoen Garden.

Both the east and west exit areas of Shinjuku have a good selection of smaller stores offering goods at prices cheaper than can be found in the department stores. Discount cameras are a particular attraction. Look for the Sakuraya and Yodobashi stores near the east exit, and the Yodobashi and Doi stores near the west exit.

The Shinjuku district is north of the Shibuya district, and west of the Imperial Palace.

Japan is famous for its parks and landscape gardens, and there are several to be found in Tokyo. One of the best known is Shinjuku Gyoen, which can be reached in 15 minutes on foot from the east exit of Shinjuku Station, or more quickly from Shinjuku-Gyoenmae Station on the Marunouchi subway line. Shinjuku Gyoen has all the attractions of the typical Japanese garden: careful landscaping, artificial hills, ponds, stone lanterns, bridges, plenty of trees and plants, and paths that wind their way throughout. The two main themes of such a garden are serenity and care in arrangement, and after spending a couple of hours inside enjoying the scenery, it comes as quite a shock to step outside again into the crowded and chaotic streets of the capital. Walk through Shinjuku Gyoen as far as the Sendagaya exit, and nearby is the National Stadium, Meiji Shrine Outer Garden, and the Jingu Baseball Stadium.

Two more gardens are located in Bunkyo Ward, in the northern part of central Tokyo. Lying in the shadow of Korakuen, one of the main amusement grounds in Tokyo and also the home of the Yomiuri Giants baseball team, is Koishikawa Korakuen, which can be reached in about 6 minutes on foot from Iidabashi Station on the yellow Sobu line. Like many such gardens, this one was completed in the Edo Period (1603–1868), when Japan enjoyed domestic peace and the shogun demanded that regional lords set up home in Edo (Tokyo) in order to guarantee their loyalty. Koishikawa Korakuen was planned by Tokugawa Yorifusa of Mito (in today's Ibaraki Prefecture). Mito is the site of one of

Japan's three most outstanding landscape gardens, the others being in Okayama and Kanazawa. Such gardens are splendid creations, but more often than not they are full to the brim with groups of tourists following loudspeaker-wielding, flag-waving guides. In this respect, the gardens of Tokyo are what they are intended to be—places of quiet solitude. It is especially advantageous to go on a weekday, but remember that most parks, gardens, zoos, and museums in Tokyo are closed on Mondays.

Also located in Bunkyo Ward is Rikugien, reached in a few minutes on foot to the south from Komagome Station on the Yamanote loop line. Rikugien is a strolling garden set around a central lake; its notable feature is the picturesque view of the lake from whatever angle it is seen. Again, the garden was first landscaped in the 17th century, and like many other such gardens, it consists of artificial recreations of famous scenic spots elsewhere.

Ueno-Asakusa

Ueno Station, to the northeast of the Imperial Palace, is the third largest in Tokyo after Tokyo Station and Shinjuku Station. It is the starting point for railway lines leaving Tokyo for northern Japan, and also the gateway to Ueno Park with all its cultural and natural attractions. It is highly recommended that visitors drop in at the Shitamachi Museum located near Shinobazu Pond, where various exhibits related to the lives of the common people of the area are on display. These include a model of an old tenement house, kitchen and other household utensils, furniture, toys, games that neighborhood children used to play, and photographs.

Tokyo is not a city famous for its statues, but most Tokyoites are well acquainted with at least two, one being the statue of Hachiko the dog outside Shibuya Station and the other being the statue of Saigo Takamori (1827–77), a leading statesman during the period of the Meiji Restoration. The latter is standing in Ueno Park, near Keisei-Ueno Station and not far from Shinobazu Pond.

Ueno Park is located by Ueno Station on the Yamanote and Keihin-Tohoku lines, and includes within its borders Ueno Zoo, Shinobazu Pond, the National Museum of Western Art, the Tokyo National Museum, the National Science Museum, and several other attractions. It is not too much of an exaggeration to say that, while the Imperial Palace is the center of Tokyo, the city's heart is in Ueno. It would be wise to set aside a whole day to see all the attractions of Ueno Park. As well as those mentioned above, there are also Kiyomizu Kannon Temple, which looks over Shinobazu Pond, the five-story pagoda of Kaneiji Temple, which rises 36 meters and dates from 1639, and Ueno Toshogu Shrine, dedicated to the first shogun Tokugawa Ieyasu.

If you don't want to spend the whole day in Ueno Park, one good course for a day's outing would be to visit the park first, then take the special double-decker bus to Asakusa—a 10-minute ride—and after seeing Asakusa Kannon Temple at the end of Nakamise shopping street, take the boat trip down the Sumida River to Hamarikyu Garden, which, in the 17th century, served as the site of a detached palace

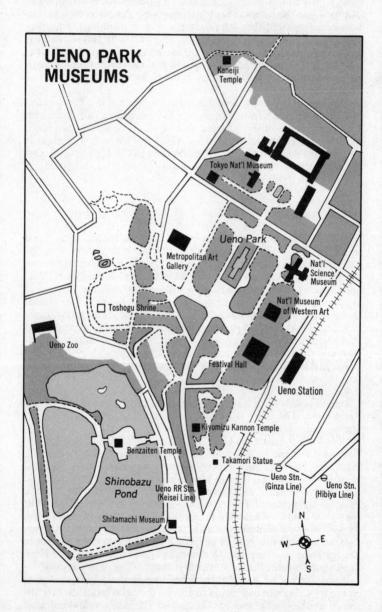

UENO PARK
MUSEUMS

Kaneiji Temple

Tokyo Nat'l Museum

Metropolitan Art Gallery

Ueno Park

Nat'l Science Museum

Toshogu Shrine

Nat'l Museum of Western Art

Ueno Zoo

Festival Hall

Ueno Station

Kiyomizu Kannon Temple

Benzaiten Temple

Takamori Statue

Shinobazu Pond

Ueno RR Stn. (Keisei Line)

Ueno Stn. (Ginza Line)

Ueno Stn. (Hibiya Line)

Shitamachi Museum

N
W E
S

of the shogun. It is an extensive park, and is a 10-minute walk southeast from Shimbashi Station on the Yamanote line. The boats leave from near the bridge just along the road from the Kaminarimon Gate.

As well as being a castle town, Tokyo is a city of many temples and shrines. Temples belong to the Buddhist religion, and shrines, which are characterized by their *torii* entrance gateways, are centers of the Shinto religion.

Asakusa Kannon is the oldest temple in Tokyo, located in a district that has retained much of the atmosphere of its past. Asakusa is a large shopping and entertainment area, consisting of dozens of cross-hatched alleys and covered passageways. Asakusa Station is at the southeastern corner of the district, on the Ginza and Toei-Asakusa subway lines. Take the exit for Kaminarimon Gate, the huge and magnificent entrance to the long and narrow Nakamise shopping street, which leads directly into the grounds of the temple. Nakamise Street is full of colorful souvenir shops offering everything from Japanese-style lanterns and talismans to the latest robot toys for children. By reputation, goods tend to be cheaper in Asakusa, and many Tokyoites come here to shop.

The temple, which is also known as Sensoji, is said to have been founded originally in the 7th century after three local fishermen discovered a small image of the goddess of mercy (Kannon) in their nets. The main buildings in the temple's precincts are the main hall, the front gateway, and a five-storied pagoda, all of which were rebuilt after being burned down during World War II. The temple grounds also seem to be a gathering place for pigeons. Located nearby is a small amusement park, called Hanayashiki Yuenchi.

The western end of Asakusa is dedicated to amusement: theaters, burlesque shows, bath houses, restaurants, tea and snack houses. If you walk along the Sumida River south toward Ryogoku, you will come to the New Kokugikan, the headquarters of sumo wrestling which was opened earlier this year. Sumo tournaments are held there, and a sumo museum is open daily within the building. With any luck on your walk you might meet some sumo wrestlers on theirs. You'll never mistake a sumo wrestler when you see one. Huge, his hair worn in the traditional style, dressed in the traditional style, he makes a picture of old Japan all on his own.

In the industrial area of Koto Ward, to the southeast of Asakusa near the Sumida River, is Kiyosumi Garden. The history of this garden reflects the fate of many Edo-Period gardens and of the aristocracy as well. After the Meiji Restoration, Kiyosumi Garden fell into disuse as feudal lords came upon hard times and all energy was spent on modernizing the nation. Then in 1878 it was purchased by a wealthy industrialist, Baron Iwasaki, who at that time was president of the Mitsubishi Steamship Company. Iwasaki's residence on the site was destroyed in the great 1923 earthquake, after which the garden was donated to the capital, restored and opened to the public. The best way to get to the garden, which is closed on Mondays, is to take a short taxi ride from Monzennakacho Station on the Tozai subway line. Ask the driver for "Kiyosumi Teien."

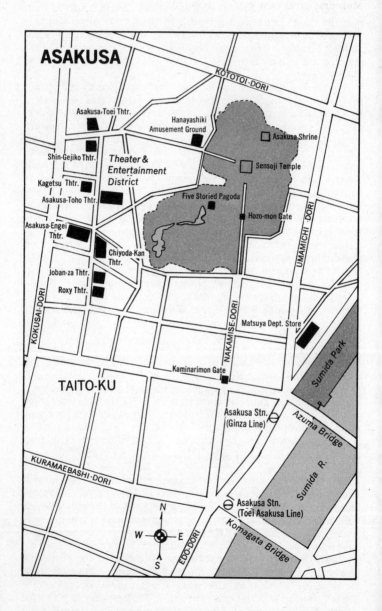

Another oasis of peace and quiet in Tokyo can be found at the Mukojima Hyakkaen garden in Sumida Ward, located a short walk from Tamanoi Station on the Tobu line, which leaves from Asakusa. Make sure you get on the train that stops at every station. Mukojima Hyakkaen, which when translated becomes "Garden of a Hundred Flowers," was a meeting place for poets and writers in the Edo Period and one of its striking features is the many stone monuments standing among the trees and plants with verses written by famous haiku poets engraved on them. It is only a short distance from Mukojima Hyakkaen to the bank of the Sumida River.

One more garden to be noted is the Kyu-Furukawa Garden in Kita Ward. This is a Japanese-style garden, with a difference—it was designed by an Englishman, James Conder, who came to Japan at the beginning of the Meiji Period when Japan was just starting on the road to Westernization. Conder is said to have been responsible for educating the first generation of Japanese architects of the Western school. The residence building of the garden, completed in 1917, is Western-style, and the garden is a typical Japanese *teien*. Kyu-Furukawa Garden can be reached in 10 minutes from Kami-Nakasato Station on the pale blue Keihin-Tohoku line which passes through Tokyo and Ueno stations, or by taxi from Komagome if you want to visit it after seeing Rikugien.

Akihabara-Kanda

Between Ueno and Tokyo stations on the Yamanote line lie Akihabara and Kanda stations, the gateways to two very specialized districts. The Akihabara area is the place to go for discount prices on electric appliances, stereo equipment, tape recorders, radios, and so on. Akihabara is said to be the biggest discount center in the country, and over 50,000 shoppers visit the 600 or so stores every day. As well as being on the Yamanote line, Akihabara Station is also on the Sobu line (for those arriving from the Shinjuku direction) and the Keihin-Tohoku line.

Kanda, together with neighboring Ochanomizu and Jimbocho, is a student town, and the streets are lined with secondhand bookshops, many of them dealing in English-language as well as Japanese books. Taken together with Akihabara, this area makes for a pleasant day's outing, with visits to Kanda Myojin Shrine, Nicolai Cathedral, and the Transportation Museum (5 minutes on foot to the west of Akihabara Station) added to stereo- and book-browsing. On the corner of the Jimbocho main crossing is Iwanami Hall, housing the British Council offices and library.

A recommended walking course in this area is one linking Ochanomizu with Ueno, taking in Nicolai Cathedral, Yushima Seido, Kanda Myojin Shrine, Yushima Tenjin Shrine, Shinobazu Pond, and Ueno Park, in that order. Nicolai Cathedral is a splendid structure, dating from 1891 and a 1-minute walk to the south from Ochanomizu Station. From there, return to the station, and follow the signposts to Yushima Seido, or the Yushima Shrine of Confucius, with its fine gateways and sidewalls built in the original Chinese Ming Dynasty-style.

Across the road is Kanda Myojin Shrine, originally founded in 730 and consisting of several interesting buildings. When leaving this shrine through its *torii* gateway, turn right, walk as far as the first crossing with a police box on the opposite corner, and turn right again. This road leads directly to Yushima Shrine, passing numerous glittering "love hotels" on the way.

Yushima Shrine, founded in the 14th century, is dedicated to scholarly advancement, and it's quite likely that during your visit you'll come across young high-school students offering a prayer there and writing their wishes on special wooden tablets in the hope of gaining a place at university. The shrine is also famous for its plum-blossom festival held every year from late February until mid-March. The shrine can be reached directly in 5 minutes on foot to the west of Yushima Station on the Chiyoda subway line.

To the left of Yushima Shrine's main hall, there are some steps leading down to a road. Turn right at the foot of these steps, and follow the road until you reach the second main crossing. Turn left there, and the road leads to Shinobazu Pond in Ueno Park.

Other Notable Temples

Both Sensoji Temple in Asakusa and Zojoji Temple in Minato Ward appear in the list of 100 most popular spots in Tokyo compiled by the Tokyo Metropolitan Government in 1983 on the basis of a public poll. The place that was voted the most scenic was Takahata Fudo Temple in Hino City, to the west of central Tokyo. It can easily be reached by taking the private Keio line from Shinjuku Station and alighting at Takahata Fudo Station—the temple is just a short walk away, its colorful pagoda showing the right direction. Express trains stop at the station, and the journey from Shinjuku takes about 30 minutes. The grounds house several buildings of cultural and historic importance, and there is also a small hiking course laid out on the hill behind the temple.

Jindaiji Temple is another place worth a short trip outside the center of Tokyo, and it, too, is reached by taking the Keio line from Shinjuku. This time get off at Chofu Station (express trains stop there) and take a bus bound for Jindaiji from in front of the station. The bus journey takes about 15 minutes. In contrast with the urban temples to be found in central Tokyo, Jindaiji has a refreshingly rustic appearance, and behind the temple, which was originally founded in 733, is located the Jindai Botanical Garden with its numerous trees and plants from around the world.

Attractions for Children

Unlike adults who find enjoyment in the unusual, children tend to have universal interests. While adults visiting Japan will probably want to explore temples, shrines, and gardens first, children will delight in a trip to a zoo. The most well-known zoo in Tokyo is Ueno Zoo, located inside Ueno Park. A 3-minute train ride from Takahata Fudo (on the Keio line from Shinjuku) takes you to Tama Zoo, which is of the safari kind with humans riding around in buses and the lions wandering about in relative freedom. Nogeyama Zoo in Yokohama is reached in 10 minutes on foot from Hinodemachi Station, 4 minutes from Yokohama Station by the Keihin-Kyuko line. These zoos are open every day except Mondays.

Amusement grounds will probably be next on the child's itinerary, and there is certainly no lack of these in the Tokyo area. Korakuen amusement park is a short walk from Suidobashi Station on the Sobu line, two stops from Akihabara, which is famous for its many discount electric appliance stores. There is also the small Hanayashiki Park near Asakusa Kannon (Sensoji) Temple, suitable for the younger and less daring.

Toshimaen amusement park is in the northeastern part of central Tokyo and can be reached by the Seibu line running from Seibu-Ikebukuro Station to Toshimaen Station, which faces the park's entrance. A little farther away is Seibuen, reached via the Seibu line, which runs from Seibu-Shinjuku Station and passes through Takadanobaba on the Yamanote line on the way. Located near Seibuen is UNESCO Village, which children should also enjoy. On display in this large park are a number of folk houses from nations around the world.

Other amusement parks, with similar jet coaster thrills and chills as offered by the above places, are Mukogaoka Yuenchi in Kawasaki (from Mukogaoka Yuenchi Station on the private Odakyu line which leaves Shinjuku Station), Yomiuriland (from Yomiurilandmae Station on the Odakyu-Odawara line), and Tama Tech in Hino City, which is located a 5-minute bus ride from Tama Zoo.

Hanayashiki amusement park in Asakusa is closed on Fridays, Korakuen on Mondays, and Yomiuriland on Tuesdays. The other amusement parks are open every day of the week.

The latest addition to entertainment facilities for children visiting or living in Japan's capital city is Tokyo Disneyland, opened in April 1983 on land reclaimed from the sea, in Urayasu, just over the city's eastern border in Chiba Prefecture. Tokyo Disneyland consists of five areas based on separate themes: World Bazaar, Adventureland, Western-land, Fantasyland, and Tomorrowland. They've probably seen it all before, but nevertheless, children are sure to love it. Advance reservations are recommended for people going on weekends or national holidays. See the Practical Information section for details.

Some other places that children should enjoy are the Goto Planetari-um on the 7th floor of the Tokyu Bunka Kaikan, across the road from Shibuya Station on the Yamanote line; the aquarium in the Sunshine 60 skyscraper in Ikebukuro; the Waxworks Museum on the 3rd floor of Tokyo Tower; and Baji Koen, a horse-riding park in Setagaya Ward that regularly holds special meetings and riding sessions for children (a short taxi ride from Chitose-Funabashi Station on the Odakyu line). Local newspapers usually carry announcements of events scheduled at Baji Koen.

DAY TRIPS

Day trips outside the central Tokyo area can be made by using the suburban rail lines that run from several of the main stations on the Yamanote loop line. The main lines and day-trip destinations are as follows:

From Shinjuku

Odakyu line. The Odakyu line runs from Shinjuku to Odawara, special express Romance Cars covering the distance in just over one hour with no stops on the way. Odawara is the site of Odawara Castle, and also the base for excursions into the Hakone hills. The Hakone Tozan railway leaves from Odawara Station for spots such as the Hakone Outdoor Sculpture Museum and Mount Sounzan, while buses depart from outside the station for Lake Ashinoko, on the shores of which are the old Hakone Checkpoint Museum, Hakone Shrine, and nearby Hakone Picnic Garden. See the *Fuji–Hakone–Izu* chapter for more details.

Odakyu line express trains stop at Mukogaoka Yuen Station (20 minutes from Shinjuku), near which are located the Mukogaoka Yuen-chi amusement park and the Nihon Minkaen park in which traditional rural dwellings from different parts of Japan have been reconstructed. This park is located a short taxi ride or a 20-minute walk from Mukogaoka Yuen Station. Two stops down the line from Mukogaoka Yuen is Yomiurilandmae Station, from where it is a 7-minute bus ride to the Yomiuriland amusement park, a huge recreation center that claims to have something for everybody.

Keio line. The Keio line runs west from Shinjuku to Keio-Hachioji, with branch lines on the way for Tama Dobutsuen Zoo and Takaosan-guchi Station, which is located at the foot of the popular and easily conquered Mount Takao. Both the zoo and Mount Takao make excellent day trips, and the former can be visited together with nearby Takahata Fudo Temple, which, as mentioned earlier, was voted Japan's most popular scenic spot in a government poll taken in 1983.

The Keio line also passes through Tsutsujigaoka and Chofu stations, from which buses leave for Jindai Temple and Jindai Botanical Garden.

Seibu-Shinjuku line. The Seibu-Shinjuku line departs from Seibu-Shinjuku Station, which is situated a short walk north from the east exit of the main Shinjuku Station, near the Kabukicho entertainment district. If you're on the Yamanote line, you can also catch a Seibu-Shinjuku line train at Takadanobaba Station, one stop away from Seibu-Shinjuku. The line goes as far as Hon-Kawagoe in Saitama Prefecture, with branch lines on the way for Haijima and Seibuyuenchi stations, and also for Seibukyujomae Station if you're visiting the Seibu Lions Baseball Ground or the UNESCO Village of folk houses from around the world.

Day trips using the Seibu-Shinjuku line include the Seibuen Amusement Ground, a short walk from Seibuyuenchi Station. The amusement ground and UNESCO Village are connected by a special railway line, and the picturesque Lake Sayama and Lake Tama are located nearby. Kitain Temple, with its cluster of about 500 small Buddhist statutes, can be reached from Hon-Kawagoe Station.

From Ikebukuro

Seibu-Ikebukuro line. Seibu-Ikebukuro Station is located a short
walk from the main Ikebukuro Station, and under the same roof. This
line runs westward out to Seibu-Chichibu, where you can catch the
local Chichibu Railway line to popular day-trip destinations such as
Nagatoro Gorge. Special Red Arrow express trains reach Seibu-Chichibu in about 1 hour and 20 minutes from Ikebukuro.

Just before Seibu-Chichibu there is Ashigakubo Station, a 20-minute
walk from Ashigakubo Orchard where there is fruit-picking from
March until November. Strawberries are ready for picking in May,
June, October, and November; plums in July and August; grapes in
August and September. You pick your own and pay for however much
you take.

Nearer to central Tokyo, there is Shakujii Koen Station, a short walk
from Shakujii Park, which offers boating facilities on its lake.

Tobu-Tojo line. The Tobu-Tojo line leaves Ikebukuro Station and
runs out west toward the Chichibu hills, passing through Kawagoe on
the way. Stations to note on the way are Shinrin Koen (1 hour by
express train from Ikebukuro) and Ogawamachi, two stops on. The
former is the station for Shinrin Park, an extensive area of greenery,
which includes cycling courses and playgrounds for children. Bicycles
can be rented from in front of Shinrin Koen Station. Ogawamachi,
meanwhile, is a small rural town that has been a home of paper making
for many centuries. The craft of making Japanese paper is still carried
on in the town, and visitors are welcome to visit the cottages and see
the various paper products. You can also see the paper itself in the
process of being made. See the *Chiba–Kanto* chapter for more information.

From Ueno

Keisei line. Several long-distance trains leave from Ueno, but in
terms of local suburban lines, only the Keisei line need be noted here.
This line runs from Keisei-Ueno Station to Narita, a trip that can be
covered in a day from Tokyo if you just want to visit Narita's Shinshoji
Temple and the park that adjoins it. (See the *Chiba-Kanto* chapter.)
Other stations to note on this line are Horikiri Shobuen, from where
the Horikiri Iris Garden is a 15-minute walk south, and Takasato
Station, where you can pick up a branch line to Shibamata to visit the
hometown and temple (Taishakuten) of Tora-san, the "lovable tramp"
hero of Japan's *Tora-san* film series.

From Asakusa

Tobu-Nikko line. The Tobu-Nikko line from Asakusa reaches
Nikko in about 1 hour and 40 minutes by special express, but although
one-day excursions can be made, the large number of attractions to be
seen in Nikko make it worthwhile for at least a one night's stay (see
our Nikko chapter). Other stops on the Tobu-Nikko line that are
within a day trip's range from Tokyo include Tochigi (2 hours by
limited express), Tobu Zoo (from Tobu Dobutsu Koen Station), and

Nishiarai Daishi Temple, reached by a branch line from Nishiarai Station.

The Tobu-Isezaki line from Asakusa also passes through Tobu Dobutsu Koen Station on its way to Isezaki. En route there is Ashikagashi Station, in the town of Ashikaga. The town's attractions include Bannaji Temple, originally established in the 1190s and containing within its precincts several structures of cultural and historic interest; the site of the Ashikaga Gakko school said to have been founded in the 9th century; and Mount Gyodosan, which rises to 400 meters and provides a pleasant hiking course with another temple, Joinji, as the destination. If you want to do the hiking course, it's best to take a taxi from Ashikaga to Joinji Temple, and from there follow the trail, which leads back into the town. The Ashikaga school, designated as a place of historical importance, lies 600 meters northwest of Ashikaga Station. Bannaji Temple is situated opposite the school.

From Tokyo Station

Chuo line. The orange-colored Chuo line starts at Tokyo Station and runs out to the western suburbs of the capital, passing through Shinjuku on the way. Stations to note for day trips are Kichijoji which brings you within a short walk from Inokashira Park; Takao Station, from which it is possible to reach Mount Takao; and Tachikawa Station, where you can pick up the Ome line to places such as Lake Okutama, Mitake Station for Mount Mitake, and Musashi-Itsukaichi Station for Akikawa Keikoku gorge.

Yokosuka line. The Yokosuka line runs from Tokyo Station south to Kurihama at the mouth of Tokyo Bay, passing Yokohama, Ofuna, Kamakura, Zushi, and Yokosuka on the way. All of these places make for excellent one-day-trip destinations from Tokyo. In particular, Yokohama with its strong traces of Western influence as a port city (see the *Yokohama* chapter), and Kamakura, the ancient capital of Japan with its many temples and shrines and domineering Great Buddha statue, are musts. Kamakura can also be reached from Shinjuku by the Odakyu line, with Katase-Enoshima as the final stop. From Katase-Enoshima, take the local Enoden line to Kamakura. See the *Kamakura–Kitakamakura–Zushi* chapter.

From Shinagawa

Keihin-Kyuko line. The Keihin-Kyuko line runs south from Shinagawa Station down through the Miura Peninsula, ending up at Miura Kaigan Station. Branch lines go to Zushi and to Uraga on the eastern coast of the peninsula. It was at Uraga in 1846 that Commodore Biddle arrived with a letter from the president of the United States asking for the opening of Japan to foreign trade. The request was rejected, but when Commodore Perry appeared at the same port in 1853 with another letter, commercial relations were formally begun.

The Keihin-Kyuko line also passes through Kurihama, where you can take a ferry across Tokyo Bay to Hama-Kanaya in Chiba. Sea bathing can be enjoyed at several spots on the Miura Peninsula's east coast, within range of a day trip from Tokyo, and also at Zushi.

Keihin-Tohoku line. The Keihin-Tohoku line, which passes through Shinagawa, operates between Ofuna in Kanagawa Prefecture, famous for its statue of the goddess of mercy (Kannon) which can be seen from the train, and Omiya in Saitama Prefecture, which is well known for its village of bonsai plants and for Omiya Park, within which stands Hikawa Shrine (see the *Chiba-Kanto* chapter). This line also passes through Yokohama, and therefore can be used to visit that port city. To reach the seafront, take the train to Kannai Station.

Hiking Day Trips

Tokyo is a city with many faces. At the same time that it is a modern business capital, it is also a castle town (albeit without a castle anymore), a port city, a town of temples and shrines, and a haven for garden- and park-lovers. Another aspect of Tokyo that is often forgotten is its mountainous district to the west. The city's tallest mountain is Mount Kumotori, which rises to 2,018 meters and stands on the western edge of the capital, with one foot in Tokyo, one in Saitama Prefecture, and another in Yamanashi Prefecture.

Mount Kumotori is out of the range of day-trippers from the Tokyo area, the ascent requiring a stopover in a mountain lodge on the way. There are two other mountains, however, which can certainly be conquered in day trips. Mount Takao, at 600 meters, is very popular among Japanese people living in the capital. To reach it, take the Keio line from Shinjuku Station to its terminus at Takaosanguchi Station (express trains cover the distance in about 45 minutes). From Takaosanguchi Station it's a short walk to a cable car station, and the cable car then whisks you up to the mountaintop in a couple of minutes. On the summit of Mount Takao there is Yakuoin Temple, and several short nature trail courses which are well laid out. However, the signposts are all in Japanese, so it's advisable not to wander too far off the beaten track unless you are with Japanese friends.

The second mountain that can be easily reached and scaled from Tokyo is Mount Mitake. Take the Chuo line from Tokyo or Shinjuku out west to Tachikawa, and there change to the local Ome line for Mitake Station. It takes about 45 minutes by express train from Tokyo to Tachikawa, and then about 1 hour from Tachikawa to Mitake. A bus leaves from in front of Mitake Station for the foot of the mountain (a 10-minute ride), and then a cable car carries people up to near the top of the 929-meter high mountain. Located a 20-minute walk from the cable car station is Mitake Shrine, the path going through a small mountaintop village of thatched-roof houses.

 TOKYO SIGHTSEEING CHECKLIST. The problem all visitors to Tokyo face is, where to begin? Each person will come up with his or her answer, depending on personal interests, amount of time available, and so on. A recommended starting place, however, is an observation point in one of the city's main hotels or skyscraper buildings. The cluster near the west exit of Shinjuku Station offers your best bet to get a general view of Tokyo from above. Otherwise, try Tokyo Tower in Shiba Park, or the Sunshine 60 building in Ikebukuro, to the north of Shinjuku on the western side of central Tokyo. After enjoying this experience, you can tackle the many parks, gardens, temples, shrines, museums, and shopping areas in the city.

Parks. As many people start a sightseeing tour of Tokyo at the Imperial Palace, the first parks to be visited will be those near there: *Hibiya Park* on the south side and *Kitanomaru Park* on the north. The other parks not to be missed are *Yoyogi Park,* next to Meiji Shrine in the western part of Tokyo, and the immensely popular *Ueno Park* in the northeast. Ueno has it all: fountains, temples, a boating lake, greenery, wild birds, numerous museums—and plenty of tramps as well.

Gardens. Despite its reputation as a concrete jungle, Tokyo has many fine gardens worth seeing. Among them, don't miss *Shinjuku Gyoen* in Shinjuku, in the western part of the city, *Rikugien* in the north (reached from Komagome Station on the Yamanote loop line), and *Hamarikyu Garden* in the south (reached from Shimbashi Station, or taking the stylish route—by boat from Asakusa). These gardens offer tranquility and peace of mind while all else around goes on at a hectic pace.

Temples. To see some of Tokyo's religious architecture, head for the temples. The most famous ones are *Zojoji Temple* in Shiba, near Tokyo Tower, and *Asakusa Kannon Temple,* sometimes called Sensoji Temple, in Asakusa.

Shrines. The main shrines in Tokyo are *Meiji Shrine,* which lies in extensive grounds near Harajuku Station on the Yamanote line, in the western part of the city, and *Yasukuni Shrine,* which is opposite Kitanomaru Park, on the north side of the Imperial Palace.

Museums. There are numerous museums and galleries in Tokyo. Many of them have standing exhibitions (see Tokyo Practical Information). For others, refer to the local English-language newspapers, which carry up-to-date details.

Particularly recommended are the *Shitamachi Museum* by Shinobazu Pond in Ueno Park, which has an exhibition of items related to life in the past in downtown Tokyo; the *Mingeikan,* or Folkcraft Museum, in Meguro Ward, with a fine display on Japanese crafts; and the *Tokyo National Museum* in Ueno Park.

Shopping. Department stores such as *Seibu, Mitsukoshi, Takashimaya, Oda-kyu, Isetan,* and so on can be found in the Ginza, Shibuya, Shinjuku, and Ikebukuro districts. *Harajuku* and *Aoyama* are popular shopping districts among the young. But don't rule out the side streets of *Shinjuku, Shibuya, Shimbashi,* and *Asakusa* when hunting for souvenirs—you'll find many small shops and stores where bargains can be found. For electrical appliance goods, the place to go is *Akihabara,* in the eastern part of the city between Ueno and Tokyo stations. For books, try *Maruzen* in Nihonbashi, *Jena* in Ginza, and *Kinokuniya* in Shinjuku, a 5-minute walk from the east exit of Shinjuku Station.

Night life. The center of night life in Tokyo is *Ginza,* but this is a very expensive district. Most foreigners frequent the *Roppongi* and *Akasaka* districts, which can be reached from subway stations of the same names in central Tokyo. *Shibuya* and *Shinjuku* are also beehives of entertainment, and although they do not cater to the foreign visitor as directly as Roppongi and Akasaka do, there are still many places that welcome foreigners.

Day trips. Many foreigners tour the sightseeing spots of central Tokyo and then take the next train out to such famous places as Nikko or Kyoto, without realizing that many enchanting spots lie within the range of a day trip from the capital. The most popular of these is *Kamakura* to the southwest, with its giant Great Buddha statue and many temples and shrines. If you have time, pay a visit to the nearby *Enoshima Island* as well.

Another recommended day trip involves a circular tour of *Tokyo Bay.* Take the Keihin-Kyuko line from Shinagawa to Kurihama, then a ferry across the bay to Hama-Kanaya port on the Boso Peninsula, and after visiting the Great Buddha statue on nearby Mount Nokogiri (larger than the Kamakura Buddha but not so old), return to Tokyo by train.

Nearer to Tokyo is *Yokohama,* the international port city to the south, which can be reached in about 30 minutes by the Keihin-Tohoku line from Tokyo Station. Do not get off at Yokohama Station, but at Kannai, from where it is a short walk to Chinatown, Yamashita Park, the harbor, the Yokohama Archives museum, and the Foreigners' Cemetery.

Another popular day trip south takes you to *Odawara* to see the city's castle. Odawara is on the Odakyu line, which leaves from Shinjuku Station, and is the entranceway to the Hakone mountains. A day trip to *Hakone* should include visits to Lake Ashinoko, Hakone Shrine, and Owakudani, the boiling valley.

The latest addition to day trips from Tokyo is *Tokyo Disneyland,* which, despite its name, is located in Chiba Prefecture, not Tokyo. The park can be reached by bus from Urayasu Station on the Tozai subway line.

PRACTICAL INFORMATION FOR TOKYO

WHEN TO GO. Tokyo keeps buzzing all year-round, and there will be no season during which you'll find yourself with too much free time on your hands. This is not to say, however, that there are not good and bad times of the year to visit. If you are able to plan your journey, try to keep away from Tokyo in the June–July period when the rainy season hits town. As well as being very wet, the weather is extremely sultry. The next worse time is the summer period from July until late August, when it can be dismally hot for those not used to it. These are definitely the months in which to head north and enjoy Japan's cooler northern districts. The best seasons to visit Tokyo are autumn and spring, although New Year's is also a pleasant time.

HOW TO GET THERE. By air. Tokyo has its main international airport at Narita and its domestic airport at Haneda. A few Japan Airlines flights on domestic routes call at Narita. Two international flights, those of China Airlines and Japan Asia Airways coming in from Taipei, use Haneda. Haneda is also set aside for aircraft carrying state guests.

By bus. It is unlikely that international travelers will arrive in Tokyo by bus. It is possible, though, from Osaka, Kyoto, and Nagoya, on a *Japanese National Railways Highway Bus,* which arrives at Tokyo Central Station, Yaesuguchi side. The journey from Osaka takes more than 9 hours, from Kyoto less than 9, and 6 hours or so from Nagoya.

By train. *Shinkansen* superexpress bullet trains of the Tokaido line pull in at Tokyo Station from Fukuoka, Osaka, Nagoya, and stations in between. Tokyo Station is in central Tokyo, in the Marunouchi district. Those of the Tohoku line arrive at Ueno, near Tokyo Station, from Morioka, and those of the Joetsu line also come to Ueno, from Niigata.

To reach Tokyo from Osaka or Kobe, the best way is by a *Shinkansen* bullet train. You have a choice of many. From Shin Osaka Station, the *Hikari* type takes 3 hours 10 minutes and costs ¥12,200; the *Kodama* type takes about one hour longer. You could fly from Osaka in about 55 minutes, but if you aren't careful you might land at Narita. You would have to specify Haneda. From there you get to Hamamatsu-cho Station in 15 minutes on the *monorail* for ¥270, and complete your journey either by local train or taxi.

From Yokohama Station, local JNR trains take only 30 minutes to reach Tokyo Station.

Be assured that all this sounds more complicated than it will prove to be in fact. All you need to do is survive your arrival and your first day. After that, things will fall into place with surprising ease.

TELEPHONES. The code numbers are 03, for calls made from outside the city. Within Tokyo, a call anywhere costs ¥10 for three minutes. Insert the coin after picking up the receiver and hearing the dial tone, then dial the number. To keep going, insert another ¥10 coin before the time is up.

HOTELS AND INNS. As new hotels rise one after the other, and old hotels add imposing new towers, there is Tokyo talk of "hotel wars." Steady, annual occupancy rates of 85 to 90 percent continue to encourage fresh, innovative construction, as well as constant refurbishing of older buildings. Each new structure sets out to achieve a new high in style and splendor. The stage has been reached where Tokyo's best hotels are, simply, magnificent. It's difficult to imagine what they could think of next to improve in appearance, facilities, or service.

Tokyo's Western-style hotels are very popular places with local people. They supplement the home. Friends are much more likely to meet each other in a hotel coffee shop or cocktail lounge than to entertain each other at home. Dinner parties and business banquets and wedding receptions are popularly held in the hotels. Even Tokyo department stores are likely to hold bargain sales in hotel public rooms. Since Tokyo qualifies as a safe city, Tokyo hotels do not need to be made into exclusive places. Instead they are important community centers.

Western-style hotels usually have some Japanese-style accommodation as well, commanding prices at the dizzying top end of the scale. Completely Japanese-style inns of exquisite quality are rare in Tokyo. There are many lower-priced establishments that are clean, simple, and convenient, and run along the old lines.

Tokyo, which has never been a planned city, has its many splendid hotels in several different areas. In some cases, a new, grand hotel has done a lot toward brightening up an old, unremarkable neighborhood. In other cases, a more modest establishment has been able to hold its ground in a more affluent and noteworthy district. Not so very long ago, Tokyo's best hotels were thought to be in the Ginza-Marunouchi area. Then new buildings began to pull the hotel district along to Akasaka-Mitsuke and Yotsuya. More recently, Shinjuku has been developing as the region for a concentration of new hotels. In a city with Tokyo's idiosyncrasies, location is less important than price when deciding where to stay. Wherever you are, you're likely to find that wherever you want to go is a long way off across town. Tokyo's facilities are dotted all over this huge city. Fortunately local transport is excellent and you can move about readily.

In our *super deluxe* category for **Western-style** hotels is a small coterie of hotels that have everything, and are still getting more. Special features include sauna, gymnasia, swimming pools, panoramic views of the city and distant mountains, and separate, speedy recognition of executive needs. There also will be English-speaking staff. Guest rooms have refrigerators. Hotels in this class have several different kinds of restaurant, as well as 24-hour room service. Their arcade shops are as elegant as any in town. A couple staying in a super deluxe hotel will pay between ¥20,000 and ¥35,000 for a double room. Tax and service charges will be additional.

Our *deluxe* hotels are more numerous, and are only marginally less outstanding than the supers. But, with some overlapping, the room charge is less. Expect to pay between ¥16,000 and ¥25,000 for a twin or double room.

As we go down the scale, the same things have to be said: accommodation and service normally are excellent throughout Tokyo's hotels. The scaling down occurs in the opulence of the surroundings and the exceptional nature of some of the facilities. A couple could expect to pay between ¥14,000 and ¥20,000 for our next category, the *expensive.*

Hotels falling within our *moderate* group have nothing the matter with them. They are just not grand. They are clean, friendly places without the embroidery. A couple would pay between ¥10,000 and ¥14,000.

Business Hotels have their own listings. They are Western-style, efficient, and low cost, without being fancy. You carry your own bags in business hotels, and go out to the nearest cafe for your dinner and breakfast. Most business hotels are conveniently located near railway stations.

Hostels include the youth hostels and dormitory accommodations that round out a city's offerings. For a bed in a dormitory, you can pay as little as ¥1,500. The YMCAs and YWCAs cost more: ¥4,000 should do it.

Tokyo's **Japanese-style** accommodation decreases, except in the inexpensive category. In the *expensive* group, overnight charge per person with two meals would fall within the brackets of ¥12,000 to ¥25,000. Everything would be exquisite in small ways. You would be lucky to find any English spoken.

An inn in the *moderate* group would charge, on the same basis, about ¥8,000 to ¥12,000. An *inexpensive* inn charges anything less than this, and is informal and easygoing.

WESTERN-STYLE

Super Deluxe

Akasaka Prince. 1–2 Kioi-cho, Chiyoda-ku, 102; 234–1111. Designed by Kenzo Tange and rising 40 stories, the Akasaka Prince is proud that every one of its 761 rooms in its new Tower commands a wide, spectacular view of all Tokyo. The Tower has 12 international restaurants, as well as a cocktail lounge, a coffeehouse, a lobby, and parlor. A wide range of services are helpful to business guests, and shopping and entertainment are only minutes away.

Hilton International. 6–6–2 Nishi-Shinjuku, Shinjuku-ku, 160; Opened in 1984, the Hilton has shown its confidence in the west of the city by locating itself in Shinjuku. Its special features include a panoramic view of Mount Fuji, a sauna, gymnasium, indoor swimming pool and tennis court. There seems to be no end to what the Hilton offers, from ordinary guest rooms to meeting facilities and equipment; from massage in the room to interpretation in six languages. Overall, the Hilton touch in service personnel is outstanding.

The Imperial. 1–1–1 Uchisaiwaicho, Chiyoda-ku, 100; 504–1111. Near the Imperial Palace Grounds and the Ginza. This Preferred Hotels Association member is the grande dame of hostelry in Japan. As a guest house for foreign visitors, it opened its doors in 1890 and has flown its flag ever since. Now that it has added the 31-story Imperial Tower, the hotel has a total of 1,135 rooms, with twins, doubles, semisuites, double suites, and full deluxe residential suites. Tower rooms have floor-to-ceiling bay windows. In the shopping arcade are 45 high-quality stores. Its handsome 19th-floor pool is open year-round exclusively for hotel guests. Deserving of every accolade, the Imperial regards itself as developing beyond a "city" to a "metropolis."

New Otani and Tower. 4 Kioi-cho, Chiyoda-ku, 102; 265–1111. With 2,051 rooms, this is the largest hotel in Asia and the fourth largest in the world. The traditional Japanese garden of 10 acres dates back to the 17th century. The New Otani Golden Spa is a health, sports and beauty culture complex. 32 restaurants including the first Trader Vic in the Orient. Crystal Room is a sophisticated restaurant-theater. Special features: *Blue Sky Lounge* atop the hotel, taking one hour for a complete revolution; rooms for businessmen's daytime use; rooms for the physically handicapped; a Tiny Tots' Room, the only one of its kind in Japan providing 24-hour baby-sitting care; a Christian chapel providing "the world's first 24-hour spiritual guidance service in a hotel"; its own orchestra, *The Joyful;* and an automatic money distributor permitting withdrawals of ¥110,000 at a time. 30 rooms on the 21st floor are for ladies only.

The Okura. 2–10–4 Toranomon, Minato-ku, 105; 582–0111. This hotel is known for its supreme, Japanese kind of elegance. It has a traditional garden and two swimming pools, one for the summertime only, and the second for all year. In the ground is the Okura Art Museum, an old Tokyo fixture. Its 980 rooms, many high-class restaurants and banquet rooms occupy the Main Building and South Wing. Membership of the Okura Club International ensures VIP courtesies; while the Executive Service Salon provides the ultimate for business-people.

Deluxe

Capitol Tokyu. 2–10–3 Nagata-cho, Chiyoda-ku, 100; Tel: 581–4511. This used to be the Tokyo Hilton and is now the flagship of the Tokyu Hotel Chain. The setting in Akasaka next to the Hie Shrine is attractive, and it's convenient, with a subway station directly opposite. The hotel has nearly 500 rooms and is distinguished by its Japanese elegance.

Century Hyatt. 2–7–2 Nishi Shinjuku, Shinjuku-ku, 160; 349–0111. Another in the Shinjuku group. Its 28 stories are opposite the Shinjuku Central Park. It has 800 rooms and suites, a heated swimming pool, and a lobby that is a conversation piece: it goes up eight floors.

Keio Plaza. 2–2–1 Nishi Shinjuku, Shinjuku-ku, 160; 344–0111. The tallest in Japan, with 47 stories, 1,500 rooms now that the deluxe annex is open, 20 restaurants, 9 bars and lounges, 800-car garage, 25 elevators, *Sky Restaurant, Sky Promenade,* 7th floor swimming pool, 2 wedding halls (one Shinto, one Christian), all in the middle of Shinjuku. Complimentary Continental breakfast for guests staying in the best rooms. Executive salon and day-care nursery. An Intercontinental Hotel.

Miyako Hotel Tokyo. 1–1–50 Shiroganedai, Minato-ku, 108; 447–3111. This Miyako has 5½ acres of beautifully landscaped Japanese garden. There are 500 rooms, a pool, sauna, health club, along with several restaurants and usual facilities. Its location, that is a bus ride from the nearest station, is a slight handicap that may be compensated for by its ownership: the famous Miyako of Kyoto.

New Takanawa Prince. 3–13–1 Takanawa, Minato-ku, 108; 447–1111. Near Shinagawa Station. This is a 16-story, white building with more than 1,000 rooms and the nation's biggest banquet hall.

Pacific Meridien. 3–13–3 Takanawa, Minato-ku, 108; 445–6711. Near Shinagawa Station. This hotel has 30 stories of 954 well-equipped rooms, restaurants, bars, banquet halls, a swimming pool, and shopping arcade. Its garden is large and beautiful in the Japanese way.

Palace. 1–1–1 Marunouchi, Chiyoda-ku, 100; 211–5211. Just on the edge of the Emperor's palace grounds. Beautiful views of the palace, Tokyo's distinctive skyline, and the Imperial Plaza, the latter especially in the evening. Excellent location for the time-conscious businessman. Arcades and shops, airline offices and all other conveniences. In spite of its central location the surrounding plaza and boulevard keep this hotel in an airy spot. 407 rooms.

Tokyo Prince. 3–3–1 Shiba Koen, Minato-ku, 105; 432–1111. Overlooks Shiba Park and famed Zojoji Temple, a 15-minutes' walk from Hamamatsucho Station. 510 rooms, well equipped, seven restaurants, four cocktail lounges, and unusually pleasant garden restaurants.

Expensive

Akasaka Tokyu. 2–14–3 Nagata-cho, Chiyoda-ku, 100; 580–2311. 566 small but modern guest rooms, Excellent service.

Ginza Tokyu. 5–15–9 Ginza, Chuo-ku, 104; 541–2411. In the busy heart of Tokyo. 420 rooms; 8 Japanese-style, 4 small apartments. Rooms soundproofed have radio and TV. Several grills, bars, restaurants. Excellent Chinese restaurant. Bus to Narita for CPA passengers.

Grand Palace. 1–1–1 Iidabashi, Chiyoda-ku, 102; 264–1111. "An economy-class hotel for businessmen," in the first-class superior bracket. 23 stories, 500 rooms (incl. 131 singles).

Holiday Inn. 1–13–7 Hatchobori, Chuo-ku, 104; 553–6161. 130 rooms, rooftop swimming pool, near Hatchobori.

Kayu Kaikan. 8–1 Sanban-cho, Chiyoda-ku, 102; 230–1111. Near the Imperial Palace. Under Hotel Okura management. 128 guest rooms. Special monthly rates.

Marunouchi. 1–6–3 Marunouchi, Chiyoda-ku, 100; 215–2151. Close to Tokyo Station. Quiet and pleasant, with the atmosphere of a U.S. commercial hotel. Dinner music every night. 210 rooms.

President, Aoyama. 2–2–3 Minami Aoyama, Minato-ku. 107; 497–0111. 212 rooms, suggested for visiting executives.

Takanawa. 2–1–17 Takanawa, Minato-ku, 108; 443–9251. A pleasant smaller hotel, near Shinagawa Station. 217 rooms on the small side. Swimming pool. A regular bus service connects this hotel with Narita Airport, and another with Shinjuku Station.

Takanawa Prince. 3–12–1 Takanawa, Minato-ku, 108; 447–1111. A British Airways Associate Hotel. Ultramodern facilities are mixed with extensive and charming Japanese landscaping. 2 swimming pools. Arcade shops. 500 Western-style rooms, all with bath.

Other Prince Hotels, all recommended, are: **Shinjuku Prince,** 1–30–1 Kabuki-cho, Shinjuku-ku, 160; 205–1111. **Shinagawa Prince,** 4–10–30 Takanawa, Minato-ku, 108; 440–1111. **Sunshine City Prince,** 3–1–5 Higashi Ikebukuro, Toshima-ku, 170; 988–1111. This one has 1,000 rooms in Japan's tallest building.

Tokyo Grand. 2–5–3 Shiba, Minato-ku, 105; 454–0311. In the 15-story Soto Building, business nerve center for the Soto Sect of Buddhism. Japanese, Italian and French restaurants, plus Soto Buddhist vegetarian dinners. Zazen sessions twice a month.

Yaesu Fujiya. 2–9–1 Yaesu, Chuo-ku; 273–2111. A 17-story urban resort-type hotel, near the Yaesu exit of Tokyo Station. 377 rooms, deluxe facilities, and warm hospitality.

Moderate

Atagoyama Tokyu Inn. 1–6–6 Atago, Minato-ku, 105; 431–0109. Very conveniently near Kamiyacho on the Hibiya subway line.

City Pension Zem. 2–16–9 Nihonbashi, Kakigaracho, Chuo-ku; 661–0681. A modern, small hotel, family owned and managed. Walking distance to TCAT. A place to make friends.

Dai-ichi. 1–2–6 Shimbashi, Minato-ku, 105; 501–4411. Fairly comfortable, all conveniences. Close to Shimbashi bar, tavern and nightclub section. Small rooms.

Diamond. 25 Ichiban-cho, Chiyoda-ku, 102; 263–2211. Behind the British Embassy, out of center. Mediocre rooms and service, generous house rules for guests and *their* guests.

Fairmont. 2–1–17 Kudan-Minami, Chiyoda-ku, 102; 262–1151. Also close to the Palace and British Embassy. Quiet, pleasant air of comfortable restraint. Air conditioning. 214 rooms.

Gajoen Kanko. 1–8–1 Shimo Meguro, Meguro-ku. 153; 491–0111. Near Meguro Station. An old-timer still leading a gaudy life.

Ginza Dai-ichi. 8–13–1 Ginza, Chuo-ku, 104; 542–5311. Sister of the Shimbashi Dai-Ichi, this has 817 rooms in a 15-story, H-shaped building near Shimbashi Station.

Ginza International. 8–7–13 Ginza, Chuo-ku, 104; 574–1121. 94 rooms at Shimbashi, adjoining the Ginza. Individual temperature controls in rooms.

Hill-Top. 1–1 Kanda, Surugadai, Chiyoda-ku, 101; Tel: 293–2311. 87 rooms in the student district of Kanda. Popular.

Hotel Den Harumi. 3–8–1 Harumi, Chuo-ku, 533–7111. Seven minutes by taxi from the Ginza district, convenient for the Trade Fair complex at Harumi. Swimming pool as well as more expected facilities.

Hotel Toshi Center. 2–4–1 Hirakawa-cho, Chiyoda-ku, 102; 265–8211. Near the Diet and Akasaka. Very popular.

Hotel Universe. 2–13–5 Nihonbashi, Kayabacho, Chuo-ku, 103; 668–7711. Has the big advantage of being near TCAT.

Ibis. 7–14–4 Roppongi, Minato-ku, 106; 403–4411. 200 rooms on the upper floors of the Ibis Kyodo Bldg., in a fun district.

Kokusai Kanko. 1–8–3 Marunouchi, Chiyoda-ku, 100; 215–3281. Next to Tokyo Station, Yaesuguchi side. Occupies eight floors of one side of an office building. Pleasant.

Miyako Inn. 3–7–8 Mita, Minato-ku, 108; 454–3111. 400 rooms at Tamachi. Brightens a bleak neighborhood.

Shiba Park. 1–5–10 Shiba Koen, Minato-ku, 105; 433–4141. Old favorite with a new annex now has 370 rooms and appropriate facilities.

Shiba Yayoi Convention Hall. 1–10–21 Kaigan, Minato-ku; 434–6841. 156 guest rooms on floors 3–10. Tokyo Bay waterfront.

Takanawa Tobu. 4–7–6 Takanawa, Minato-ku, 108; 447–0111. In Shinagawa. 201 rooms. Interesting neighborhood.

Takara. 2–16–5 Higashi Ueno, Taito-ku, 110; 831–0101. Near Ueno Park and the museums. 100 rooms.

Tokyo Kanko. 4–10–8 Takanawa, Minato-ku, 108; 443–1211. Near Shinagawa station. 102 Western rooms, 56 Japanese.

BUSINESS HOTELS

Akasaka/Roppongi

Akasaka Shanpia Hotel. 586–0811. Nearest station: Akasaka on Chiyoda subway line.

Asia Center of Japan. 402–6111. Nearest station: Nogizaka on Chiyoda subway line.

Ginza/Shimbashi

Ginza Capital Hotel. 543–8211. Nearest station: Tsukiji on Hibiya subway line.

Hotel Ginza Daiei. 541–2681. Nearest station: Tokyo on Yamanote, Keihin Tohoku and Chuo lines.

Mitsui Urban Hotel Ginza. 572–4131. Nearest station: Shimbashi on Yamanote and Keihin Tohoku lines or Ginza subway line.

Tokyo City Hotel. 270–7671. Nearest station: Mitsukoshimae on Ginza subway line.

Tokyo Hotel Urashima. 533–3111. Short taxi ride from Ginza subway station.

Kayabacho Pearl Hotel. 553–2211. Nearest station: Kayabacho on Hibiya subway line.

Shinagawa

Hotel Hankyu. 775–6121. Nearest station: Oimachi on Keihin Tohoku line.

Keihin Hotel. 449–5711. Nearest station: Shinagawa on Yamanote and Keihin Tohoku lines.

Shibuya Area

Hotel Sunroute Shibuya. 464–6411. Nearest station: Shibuya on Yamanote line.

Shibuya Tobu Hotel. 476–0111. Nearest station: Shibuya on Yamanote line.

Shibuya Tokyu Inn. 498–0109. Nearest station: Shibuya on Yamanote line.

Shinjuku

Hotel Sunlight. 356–0391. Nearest station: Shinjuku Sanchome on Marunouchi subway line.

Lion Hotel Shinjuku. 208–5111. Nearest station: Shinjuku on Seibu Shinjuku line.

Shinjuku Park Hotel. 356–0241. Nearest station: Shinjuku on Chuo and Sobu lines.

Shinjuku Sun Park Hotel. 362–7101. Nearest station: Okubo on Sobu line or Shin Okubo on Yamanote line.

Shinjuku Washington Hotel. 343–3111. Nearest station: Shinjuku on Chuo and Sobu lines.

Kanda Area

Akihabara Pearl Hotel. 861–6171. Nearest station: Akihabara on Hibiya subway line.

Akihabara Washington Hotel. 255–3311. Nearest station: Akihabara on Hibiya subway line or Yamanote and Keihin Tohoku lines.

Central Hotel. 256–6251. Nearest station: Kanda on Ginza subway line.

New Central Hotel. 256–2171. Nearest station: Kanda on Ginza subway line.

Satellite Hotel. Korakuen, neighboring the stadium. 814–0202.

Suidobashi Grand Hotel. 816–2101. Nearest station: Suidobashi on Toei Mita subway line.

Tokyo Green Hotel Awajicho. 255–4161. Nearest station: Awajicho on Marunouchi subway line.

Tokyo Green Hotel Suidobashi. 295–4161. Nearest station: Suidobashi on Chuo and Sobu lines.

Ueno Area

Hokke Club Ueno. 834–4131. Nearest station: Ueno on Yamanote and Keihin Tohoku lines.

Hokke Club Ueno Ikenohata. 822–3111. Nearest station: Yushima on Chiyoda subway line.

Ueno Station Hotel. 833–5111. Nearest station: Ueno on Yamanote and Keihin Tohoku lines.

Hotel Ohgaiso. 3–3–21 Ikenohata, Taito-ku. Tel: 828–3181. Nearest station Keisei Ueno Station, Ikenohata exit. Author Ogai Mori (1862–1922) lived here.

JAPANESE INNS

Expensive

Fukudaya. 6–12 Kioi-cho, Chiyoda-ku; 261–8577. Central, just behind Sophia University. 14 rooms, 3 party rooms. Strictly for relaxing. Some Western cooking, but food is primarily Japanese. Price range: ¥ 12,000 to ¥ 25,000.

Moderate

Kin-Ei-Kaku. (Pronounced Keen-ay-kah'-koo.) 2–26 Toyotama Kami, Nerima-ku; 991–1186. In Tokyo's outskirts, far from all hustle and bustle. The air is cleaner than in downtown Tokyo. Western and Japanese food; about ¥ 10,000. Wooden inn.

Seifuso. 1–12–15 Fujimi, Chiyoda-ku; 263–0681. ¥ 6,500 lowest rate for one person, excluding meals. A small, family-run, modernized inn with a separate dining room. No room service.

Yaesu Ryumeikan. 1–3–22 Yaesu, Chuo-ku; 271–0971. Small, central, attractive. About ¥ 12,000 with two meals.

Inexpensive

Chomeikan. 4–4–8 Hongo, Bunkyo-ku; 811–7205. Just to stay, ¥ 4,000 per person. Food and bath extra.

Fujikan. 4–36–1 Hongo, Bunkyo-ku; 813–4441. Just to stay, ¥ 3,000. Food and bath extra.

Hanabusa. 3–30–3 Nishi-Ikebukuro, Toshima-ku; 971–0735. Good prices, quiet and friendly. Discounts for long stays.

Hongokan. 1–28–10 Hongo, Bunkyo-ku; 811–6236. Basically, ¥ 5,500. Extras are extra.

Inabaso. 5–6–13 Shinjuku, Shinjuku-ku; 341–9581. ¥ 7,000 per person with meals and bath.

Kikaku. 1–11–12 Sendagaya, Shinbuya-ku; 403–4501. For two people, ¥ 13,000 with meals, without bath.

Kimi. 2–1034 Ikebukuro, Toshima-ku, 171; 971–3766. Has a Western-style hotel next door, both run by two young and eager traveled brothers. You're lucky to stay here.

Koshinkan. 2–1–5 Mukogaoka, Bunkyo-ku; 812–5291. ¥ 3,500 per person, just to stay.

Nagaragawa. 4–14 Yotsuya, Shinjuku-ku; 351–5892. ¥ 8,000 for two persons, without meals but with bath.

Okayasu. 1–7–11 Shibaura, Minato-ku; 452–5091. ¥ 4,000 per person, overnight only.

Ryokan Fuji. 6–8–3 Higashi-Koiwa, Edogawa-ku. Tel: 657–1062. Only seven rooms; five minutes walk from Koiwa Station.

Sansui-So. 2–9–5 Higashi-Gotanda, Shinagawa-ku. Tel: 441–7475. Small (only nine rooms) five minutes walk from Gotanda Station.

Sawanoya. 2–3–11 Yanaka, Taito-ku, 110; 822–2251. Near Ueno Park, in a district redolent of old Edo.

Shimizu Bekkan. 1–30–29 Hongo, Bunkyo-ku; 812–6285. ¥ 5,000 is the basic charge.

Suigetsu. 3–3–21 Ikenohata, Taito-ku. Tel: 822–4611. Single, ¥ 4,500. Public bath, family bath, showers, coin laundry. Bicycles for rent, cycling and jogging courses nearby.

Yashima. 1–15–5 Hyakunincho, Shinjuku-ku; 364–2534. Every recommendation.

Just for your interest, we're letting you know that Tokyo has "capsule" hotels that are becoming popular for anyone missing the last train home. A capsule is plastic, equipped with a TV set, an intercom, and a radio. Capsules are stacked two or three high in horizontal rows. Patrons crawl in at night and draw a curtain behind them. There's a communal bath or shower, a lounge, and refreshment area as well. For ¥3,000, no one expects much privacy or quiet.

HOSTELS AND DORMITORY ACCOMMODATION

English House. 2–23–8 Nishi Ikebukuro, Toshima-ku; 988–1743. Long-stay arrangements ¥3,000 for two, ¥1,700, and ¥1,900 for one.

Ichigaya Youth Hostel. 1–6 Goban-cho, Chiyoda-ku; 262–5950. ¥1,570, includes sheet and heating.

Japan YWCA Hostel. 4–8–8 Kudan Minami, Chiyoda-ku; 264–0661. For women only.

Okubo House. 1–11–32 Hyakunin-cho, Shinjuku-ku; 361–2348. Dormitory beds, from ¥1,200.

Shin Nakano Lodge. 6–1–1 Honcho, Nakano-ku. 381–4886. Dormitory accommodation, from ¥2,700.

Tokyo International Youth Hostel. 21–1 Kaguragashi, Shinjuku-ku; 235–1107. Bunk beds. ¥1,650.

Tokyo YWCA Hostel. 1–8 Kanda Surugadai, Chiyoda-ku; 293–5421. For women only.

Tokyo Yoyogi Youth Hostel. Bldg. No. 14, Olympics Memorial Youth Center, 3–1 Yoyogi-Kamizono-cho, Shibuya-ku, Tokyo. Tel: 467–9163. ¥1,500, includes sheet. Meals provided, if booked. Members' kitchen.

Tokyo YWCA Sadohara Hostel. 3–1–1 Ichigaya Sadohara-cho, Shinjuku-ku; 268–7313. Has quarters for married couples.

Yoshida House. 1–25–25 Kasuga-cho, Nerima-ku; 926–4563. ¥1,300 per person.

YMCA Asia Youth Center. 2–5–5 Sarugaku-cho, Chiyoda-ku; 233–0611.

 HOW TO GET AROUND. It may be a shock to airline passengers arriving at the new Tokyo International Airport at Narita to find that they still have 64 kilometers to go to reach central Tokyo. Brace yourself for at least another hour of travel before you get to town. This may prove to be the most trying part of your trip.

FROM THE AIRPORT

By bus. When you have passed Customs inspection and reached the arrival lobby, please look carefully at all the announcements and signs in English. Some 30 major Tokyo hotels are served by direct express buses. If you are booked into one of the listed hotels, you can take this bus for a fare of ¥2,700. The journey will take anywhere between 1 and 2 hours, depending upon the time of day and the volume of traffic.

Your next alternative is to take the airport bus to the City Air Terminal (known as TEE-Cat, TCAT) at Hakozaki-cho. You buy your ticket at the *Limousine Bus* ticket counter in the arrival lobby. This bus fare is ¥2,500, and the time allowance to TCAT is up to 1½ hours. Your baggage is carried in a hold on the bus, and delivered to you at TCAT, in exchange for the claim tag given you. At TCAT you can buy another Limousine Bus ticket for ¥200 for the 10-minute run to Tokyo Station; you can get a taxi; or you can go to the nearest subway station, Ningyo-cho, on the Hibiya line, an 8-minute walk.

Children under 12 and the physically handicapped are carried for half price on the Limousine Bus.

By train. Rail travel aboard the *Skyliner* has much to commend it. The Skyliner offers reserved seats only, baggage space, and temperature control. It leaves Keisei Narita Airport Station at half-hourly intervals between 6:30 A.M. and 9:00 P.M., and reaches Ueno Station in exactly 1 hour. You can buy a combination bus/Skyliner ticket for ¥1,660 at the Skyliner ticket counter between the North and South wings of the airport. (Keisei Narita Airport Station is a 6-minute bus ride from the airport.) The Skyliner ticket counter closes at 9:00 P.M. Late arrivals can buy bus tickets for ¥170 each, and Skyliner tickets for ¥1,490 at the Airport Station, for the 10:00 P.M. and 11:00 P.M. trains.

From Keisei Ueno Station you had better take a taxi to your hotel. Alternatively, you can walk for 5 minutes to the *Japanese National Railways* Ueno Station, and take a train of the green Yamanote loop line, or one of the Ginza subway line, to the stop nearest your hotel.

The fares for slower trains from Keisei Narita Airport Station to Keisei Ueno Station are ¥790. A limited express (*tokkyu*) takes 1 hour 15 minutes. An express (*kyuko*) takes 1 hour 30 minutes.

You can get to Shimbashi in central Tokyo from Keisei Narita Airport Station via the *Toei Asakusa* subway line: 1 hour 34 minutes, ¥930. Not every train is direct; you may have to change at Oshiage.

Japanese National Railways have a station, called Narita, that is 25 minutes by bus, a ¥350 fare, from the airport. This line is called Sobu Hon-sen Narita line. A JNR limited express from Narita to Tokyo Station takes 63 minutes and costs ¥1,750 for an unreserved seat. A JNR rapid (*kaisoku*) train takes 75 minutes and costs ¥950.

By taxi. Your final option, unless you are being met or planning on not going any farther, is a taxi all the way. This will cost at least ¥15,000, may take only 1 hour, but, at the mercy of road traffic conditions, it may take longer.

Porter service charges are fixed at ¥200 per piece, and for the longer hauls at ¥300 per piece. Before leaving Narita you can check your heavy baggage at the Air Baggage Service Company (ABC) counter, and have it delivered to your destination the following day. The charge is ¥1,500 for one item under 30 kilograms, and ¥700 for each additional piece.

Passengers **transferring** from Narita to Haneda Airport are taken by the Limousine Bus in, say, 1¾ hours: ¥2,700.

LEAVING BY TRAIN

To leave Tokyo by Shinkansen, you have to go to Tokyo Station. On each of many platforms there is a guide in English, giving a rundown of each line, track number, and the destinations. It points the way also to the JNR Expressway Bus. Tokyo Station has a North, a Central, and a South exit. Each one leads down to a main plaza where, again, everything is clearly indicated in English. Shinkansen tracks are from number 14 to number 19 inclusive. Shinkansen directions are given in blue lettering.

It would be helpful if you asked your hotel to buy your Shinkansen tickets in advance. Otherwise you must go to the windows marked for Shinkansen tickets. Make sure of your carriage number and seat number, train name, and departure time. It is simplicity itself to make all the identifications and to get aboard the correct train.

IN TOKYO

Tokyo sprawls inconveniently and has not one but several business, shopping, and entertainment areas. Each one is accessible by public transport.

By train. JNR operates several electric train services in Tokyo. The *Yama-note* line loops Tokyo with trains going in both directions. Its coaches are green. Fares are calculated by distance, with the shortest distance costing ¥120. Tickets are bought at machines, which give change. Some machines accept ¥1,000 notes. If you know the fare to the station you want to go to, insert coins to cover the fare and press the appropriate button on the machine. If you need change, you will get it delivered along with your ticket. If you don't know the fare, you can try asking somebody for help. Otherwise, buy a basic fare ticket and pay the excess amount when you leave the train. Look for the fare adjustment window, which is usually somewhere near the exit gate, and present the ticket you've traveled with. The official will take it, indicate how much more you have to pay, and give you a receipt that you surrender at the exit. Journey accomplished.

Another above-surface JNR line is the *Chuo*. Its coaches are orange, and its trains begin from Tokyo Station and travel west out to Shinjuku and beyond. The *Sobu* line, with yellow coaches, also runs between Shinjuku and Ochanomizu, but then goes off on a different route.

By subway. Tokyo's subway system has 10 lines that cover the city underground. Some are private lines, some are run by Tokyo City Government. With the use of a subway map, you should be able to get around with a minimum of difficulty and a maximum of speed. Again, we recommend your coping with the ticket machines in the manner described above.

By bus. Buses crisscross the city. Fares begin at ¥140. Buses are not easy to use unless you have familiarity with both language and routes.

By taxi. Taxi basic fare is ¥470 for the first two kilometers, and ¥80 for each additional 405 meters. There is also a time charge, when traffic holds you up, registered automatically on the meter. After 11:00 P.M., the total fare increases by 20 percent. You can flag down a cruising taxi in the street, or go to a taxi stand. In Tokyo's central district, between 10:00 P.M. and 1:00 A.M., cabs stop at only eleven designated taxi stands.

By car. More expensive and more comfortable than taxis are the big *haiya cars*. The word "haiya" is how the Japanese say "hire." Cost is about ¥5,000 per hour within Tokyo. They will call for you if summoned by phone. Their drivers are especially careful and polite.

By special arrangement you can hire chauffeured cars for longer trips (ask at any hotel) or self-drive cars. You'll need an operator's permit for the latter. International licenses are valid in Japan. If you do not have one, take your own national licence to the Samezu Test Center, and after a sight test you can get a Japanese license. Otherwise, you have to take the same practical and theoretical tests as the Japanese.

Hire taxis: *Anzen,* 404–6361; *Daiwa,* 201–7007; *Eastern Motors;* 503–0171; *Fuji,* 571–6411; *Green Cab,* 585–4625; *Hato Bus,* 761–8111; *Hinomaru,* 583–8146 and 591–1371; *Kokusai,* 585–5931 and 583–7161; *Nihon,* 231–4871; *Oda-kyu Kotsu,* 453–6711 and 453–3911; *Seibu,* 432–7581; *Taiyo,* 583–8756 and 541–2141; *Takara,* 403–7931/2; *Teito,* 214–2021.

Rent-a-car: *ACU Co.,* 364–2211; *Isuzu,* 452–3097; *Japaren,* 352–7635; *Mit-subishi,* 213–8071; *Nippon,* 463–8881/8; *Nissan,* 586–2301; *Nissan Kanko,* 584–2341; *Tokyo,* 407–4431; *Toyota,* 263–6321.

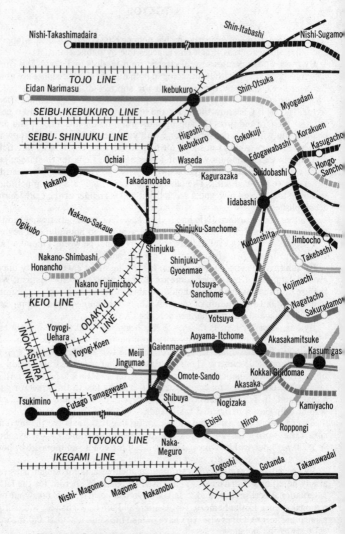

Nishi-Takashimadaira
Shin-Itabashi
Nishi-Sugamo

TOJO LINE
Eidan Narimasu
Ikebukuro
Shin-Otsuka
Myogadani
Korakuen
Kasugacho
SEIBU-IKEBUKURO LINE

SEIBU-SHINJUKU LINE
Higashi-Ikebukuro
Gokokuji
Edogawabashi
Hongo-Sancho
Ochiai
Waseda
Suidobashi
Nakano
Takadanobaba
Kagurazaka
Iidabashi
Nakano-Sakaue
Shinjuku-Sanchome
Kudanshita
Jimbocho
Ogikubo
Takebashi
Nakano-Shimbashi
Honancho
Shinjuku
Shinjuku-Gyoenmae
Kojimachi
Nakano Fujimicho
Yotsuya-Sanchome
Nagatacho
KEIO LINE
Sakuradamo
Yotsuya
Yoyogi-Uehara
ODAKYU LINE
Aoyama-Itchome
Akasakamitsuke
INOKASHIRA LINE
Yoyogi-Koen
Meiji Jingumae
Gaienmae
Kasumigas
Omote-Sando
Kokkai-Gijidomae
Tsukimino
Futago Tamagawaen
Shibuya
Akasaka
Kamiyacho
Nogizaka
Ebisu
Hiroo
Roppongi
TOYOKO LINE
Naka-Meguro
IKEGAMI LINE
Togoshi
Gotanda
Takanawadai
Nishi-Magome
Magome
Nakanobu

TOKYO SUBWAYS

TOKYO 147

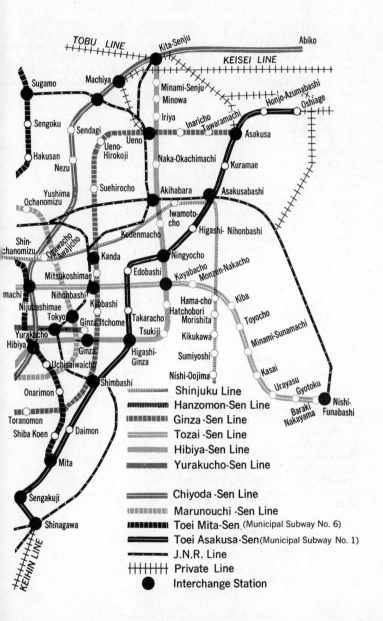

Shinjuku Line
Hanzomon-Sen Line
Ginza -Sen Line
Tozai -Sen Line
Hibiya-Sen Line
Yurakucho-Sen Line

Chiyoda -Sen Line
Marunouchi -Sen Line
Toei Mita-Sen (Municipal Subway No. 6)
Toei Asakusa-Sen (Municipal Subway No. 1)
J.N.R. Line
Private Line
● Interchange Station

TOURIST INFORMATION. Most major hotels in Tokyo have information corners where pamphlets can be picked up and the weekly *Tour Companion* obtained, so it's worth popping in to the nearest one even if you're not staying there. The other essential place to know about is the *Tourist Information Center,* at Kotani Building, 1–6–6 Yurakucho, Chiyoda-ku. It is operated by the Japan National Tourist Organization and located near Yurakucho Station. The TIC is open from 9:00 A.M. until 5:00 P.M. on weekdays and from 9:00 A.M. until noon on Saturdays. It is closed on Sundays. The center also operates a telephone information service, and can be reached at 502–1461. Outside Tokyo, use the toll-free Travel-Phone. Dial 106 from a yellow or blue phone, and say, "Collect Call T.I.C." 9:00 A.M. to 5:00 P.M. An *airport office* is located in the New Tokyo International Airport, Narita.

Japan Travel Bureau will also be glad to help you. Some of their offices: Narita (0476–32–8805); *Foreign Tourist Department,* Nittetsu-Nihonbashi Bldg., 1–13–1, Nihonbashi, Chuo-ku, 276–7777; and in several hotels. JTB's headquarters are next to the Hotel Marunouchi, Otemachi.

Japan National Tourist Organization, 10th floor, Tokyo Kotsu Kaikan in Yurakucho, 216–1901, will assist you with any particular problems. If you dial Tokyo 503–2911 between 7:00 A.M. and midnight, a 90-second tape-recorded message in English will give information on current exhibitions, entertainment, and events in and around Tokyo.

JAL also have an information service, dial 747–1200 for the answer to any tourist problem.

 RECOMMENDED READING. There are five daily English-language newspapers in Japan, all of them available at hotels and newsstands around Tokyo. The *Japan Times,* the *Mainichi Daily News,* the *Daily Yomiuri,* and the *Shipping and Trade News* are morning papers, and the *Asahi Evening News* comes out in the afternoons. Other journals include the *Japan Times Weekly,* which appears every Saturday, and *Tokyo Journal,* which is a monthly information paper. *Tour Companion* is an information weekly for tourists which can be obtained free of charge at most major hotels. *Time* and *Newsweek* publish weekly English editions in Tokyo. All hotels catering to foreigners have them on sale each Wednesday.

The larger hotels all have stands and bookstores where English-language magazines and books can be purchased. The main bookstores in Tokyo are **Kinokuniya** in Shinjuku and Shibuya, **Biblos** in Takadanobaba (opposite Takadanobaba Station), **Kitazawa** and **Sanseido** in the Kanda-Jimbocho district, **Maruzen** (also in the Kanda-Jimbocho district and opposite Takashimaya Department Store on Chuo-dori Ave.) and **Jena** (near Yurakucho Station) in Ginza.

 MONEY. Banks, and most well-equipped hotels have licensed money-changing facilities. Our advice is to use traveler's checks. Your yen is reconvertible into dollars at official counters. Tokyo's foreign banks can give you direct service and further information. They are:

American Express, Toranomon-Mitsui Bldg., 3–8–1 Kasumigaseki, Chiyoda-ku. *Bank of America,* Tokyo Kaijo Bldg., 1–2–1 Marunouchi, Chiyoda-ku. *Bank of India,* Mitsubishi Denki Building, 2–2–3 Marunouchi, Chiyoda-ku. *Banque de l'Indochine,* French Bank Bldg., 1–1–2 Akasaka, Minato-ku. *Barclays Bank International,* Mitsubishi Bldg., 2–5–2 Marunouchi, Chiyoda-ku. *Chartered*

Bank, Fuji Bldg., 3–2–3 Marunouchi. *Chase Manhattan Bank,* AIU Bldg., 1–1–3 Marunouchi, Chiyoda-ku. *First National Bank of Chicago,* Time-Life Bldg., 2–3–6 Ote-machi, Chiyoda-ku. *Grindlays Bank Ltd.,* 303 Palace Bldg., 1–1–1 Marunouchi. *Hongkong & Shanghai Banking Corp.,* Chiyoda Building, 2–1–2 Marunouchi, Chiyoda-Ku. *Manufacturer's Trust,* 21st Floor, Asahi Tokai Bldg., 2–6–1 Otemachi Chiyoda-ku. *Algemene Bank Nederland,* Fuji Bldg., 3–2–3 Marunouchi, Chiyoda-ku. *Bank Negara Indonesia,* Kokusai Bldg., 3–1–1 Marunouchi, Chiyoda-ku. *Bangkok Bank,* 2–8–11 Nihombashi, Muromachi, Chuo-ku. *Lloyds Bank International,* Yurakucho Denki Bldg., 1–7–1 Yurakucho. Chiyoda-ku. Chiyoda-ku. *Mellon Bank, N.A.,* 242 Shin-Yurakucho Bldg., 1–12–1 Yurakucho, *Midland Bank,* Togin Bldg., 1–4–2 Marunouchi, Chiyoda-ku. *Morgan Guaranty Trust Co. of New York,* New Yurakucho Building, 1–12–1 Yurakucho, Chiyoda-ku. *Wells Fargo Bank,* N.A., Fuji Building, 3–2–3 Marunouchi, Chiyoda-ku. *National Westminster Bank,* Mitsubishi Building, 2–2–5 Marunouchi, Chiyoda-ku. Many foreign banks have representative offices in Tokyo, but do not carry out banking transactions.

BUSINESS AND COMMERCIAL INFORMATION. The *Tokyo Trade Center* can give the foreign businessperson any information concerning Japanese industry and trading affairs. The Trade Center has a showroom where you can see almost any kind of product made in the country. Open 9:00 A.M. to 5:00 P.M., daily except Sundays. 3F. World Trade Center Bldg. Annex, Hamamatsucho; 435–5394.

The *Japan Export General Merchandise Show Center* is located at the *Tokyo International Trade Center,* Harumi Pier, the site of Tokyo's international trade fairs. The address of the Trade Center is 2, 6-chome Harumicho, Chuo-ku. The Merchandise Center is open from 10:00 A.M. to 5:00 P.M. daily, except Sunday.

Machines and machine tools are on display at the *Ota Trade Center,* 5, 4-chome Nakakamata, Ota-ku. Open daily except Sundays and holidays, 9:00 A.M. to 5:00 P.M. The permanent exhibition hall of the Japan plastic industry is the *Plastic Centre,* 8, 2-chome Ginza-Higashi (3rd Floor, Chushokigyo Kaikan). *Japan Industrial Design Promotion Organization* has an office and an exhibition hall on the Annex 4th floor World Trade Center Bldg., 2–4–1 Hamamatsu-cho; 435–5633. The *Tokyo Chamber of Commerce and Industry* has offices in Marunouchi; 283–7867. The *American Chamber of Commerce* is at 4–1–21 Toranomon, Minato-ku; 433–5381.

Useful Hints. For name cards, English one side Japanese the other, you can get quick printing at *Iwanaga Inc.* (209–3381); and at *Wakabayashi,* (255–7909). Hotel newsstands have business directories in English. Ask your hotel for document copy service, or call *Fuji Xerox Co.,* (585–3211). Interpreters and secretaries are supplied by *I.S.S.* (265–7101), and *E.S.S.* (251–5755). *JAL* also has an "Executive Service," from 747–3191.

COMMUNICATIONS. All good hotels will handle your communications problems for you. Tokyo's *Central Post Office* is on Tokyo Station Plaza, but there are branch post offices all over the city. The Central Post Office is open around the clock daily.

The overseas telegraph office foreign visitors will be most likely to use is: *K. D. D. (International Telegraph & Telephone Center),* 3–2–5 Kasumigaseki, Chiyoda-ku. It issues credit cards for "credit-card calls."

Book your overseas calls at your hotel through the operator. For the international operator, dial 0051. Major hotels operate a direct dialing system.

USEFUL ADDRESSES. Embassies and Consulates. *American Embassy and Consulate,* 1–10–5 Akasaka, Minato-ku. The Consular hours (Passport and Citizenship branch); 8:00 A.M. to 4:00 P.M.; closed Saturdays (583–7141).

British Embassy and Consulate, 1 Ichiban-cho, Chiyoda-ku. Consular hours; 9:00 A.M. to noon, 2:00 to 4:00 P.M.; closed Saturdays and holidays (265–5511).

Canadian Embassy, 7–3–38 Akasaka, Minato-ku. Hours: 9:00 A.M. to 12:30 P.M., 2:30 to 4:30 P.M.; closed Saturdays and holidays (408–2101).

New Zealand Embassy. 20 Kamiyama-cho, Shibuya-ku. Consular hours: 9:00 A.M. to 12:30 P.M., 2:00 to 5:00 P.M.; closed Saturdays and holidays (460–8711).

Australian Embassy, 2–1–14 Mita, Minato-ku. Consular hours: 9:00 A.M. to noon, 2:00 to 4:00 P.M. Closed Saturdays and holidays (453–0251).

Imperial Household. If you have any business with the Imperial Household agency (for example, if you wish to view part of the palace grounds normally not open to the public), you may telephone them at 213–1111, ext. 485. The office of the Imperial Household Agency Visitors' Department is at the Saka-shitamon across from the Palace Hotel. If you wish to write, the address is 1–1 Chiyoda-ku, Tokyo.

MEETING PLACES. The following coffee shops serve as English conversation lounges where Japanese students of English and native speakers can meet and chat together: **English Inn.** 470–0213. One minute from Meiji-Jingumae subway station in Harajuku. **International Pacific Club.** 358–1681. Seven minutes from Yotsuya Station on the Chuo line. **E.S.S.** 498–2056. Five minutes from Shibuya Station. **Com'inn.** 793–3371. Three minutes from Ebisu Station on the Yamanote line.

ESCORT SERVICE. The following offer English-speaking female companions for dining, dancing, shopping, and sightseeing. Tokyo Escort Service, 358–7322; International Escort Service, 451–5515; Aloha Escort Service, 444–5449; Sunpole International Escorts, 814–0777 and 941–7166; and Escort Service Club, 645–2741.

MEDICAL SERVICE. The following hospitals are accustomed to dealing with foreigners, and many of their staff members are foreign-trained. *Tokyo Eisei Byoin Hospital* in Suginami Ward; 392–6151. *International Catholic Hospital* (Seibo Byoin) in Naka-Ochiai, Shinjuku Ward; 951–1111. *St. Luke's International Hospital* in Akashicho, Chuo Ward; 541–5151. *Tokyo Medical and Surgical Clinic* in Shiba-Koen; 436–3028.

EMERGENCIES. If you wish to report a fire or accident, and if you speak Japanese or if you want to take a chance that somebody at the other end will understand you, you can dial the following numbers from any telephone: *Fire,* 119; *Ambulance,* 119; *Police,* 110. There may be someone at the other end who understands English if you speak slowly.

TELL, Tokyo English Life Line. A telephone service for anyone in distress needing a listener and counselor. TELL-a-phone, 264–4347.

LOST AND FOUND. The Central Lost and Found Office of the Metropolitan Police is at 1–9–12 Koraku, Bunkyo-ku; 814–4151. If you leave something on a train, report to the Lost and Found Office at any station. If you leave anything

TOKYO 151

in a taxi, report to *Tokyo Taxi Kindaika Center,* 33 Shinanomachi, Shinjuku-ku; 355–0300.

 ELECTRIC CURRENT. The electric current in Tokyo is 100 volts and 50 cycles, AC (American current is 110 volts and 60 cycles and British is 220 volts). You can use most American appliances, such as electric shavers, radios, irons, etc., on this current, but delicate machines such as record players require adjustment because of the difference in cycles.

 CHURCHES. There are many churches of all denominations in Tokyo, although very few of them are English-speaking. The main ones where services are held in English are as follows:

Catholic. *Franciscan Chapel Center* in Roppongi; 401–2141. *St. Mary's Cathedral* in Bunkyo Ward; 941–3029. *St. Ignatius Church* near Yotsuya Station; 263–4584. *German-Speaking Catholic Church* in Meguro Ward; 712–0775. *French-Speaking Catholic Church* in Chiyoda Ward; 446–9594.

Christian (other). *Church of Jesus Christ of Latter-Day Saints* in Shinjuku; 952–6802. *Keio Plaza Chapel Service* in Shinjuku; 344–0111. *New Otani Garden Chapel* in Chiyoda Ward; 265–1111. *Ochanomizu Church of Christ* in Chiyoda Ward; 291–0478. *Tokyo International Church* in Ebisu, Shibuya Ward; 464–4512. *Tokyo Union Church* near Omotesando Subway Station; 400–0047.

Christian Science Church in Shibuya; 499–3951. *Church of Christ* in Ochanomizu; 291–0478. *German-Speaking Protestant Church* in Shinagawa; 441–0673. *Tokyo Lutheran Center* near Iidabashi Station; 261–3740. *Tokyo Baptists Church* in Shibuya Ward; 467–7829. *St. Alban's* in Shiba-Koen; 431–8534.

Muslim. *Tokyo Mosque* in Shibuya Ward; 469–0284. *Japan Muslim Association* in Yoyogi; 370–3476.

Russian Orthodox. *Russian Orthodox Church* in Shinjuku Ward; 341–2281. *Nicolai Cathedral* in Kanda; 291–1885.

Others. *Bahai Center* in Shinjuku; 209–7521. *Jewish Community* of Japan in Hiroo, Shibuya Ward; 400–2559. **Buddhist.** English lectures on Buddhism are given every Sunday at 10:30 A.M. at the *Tsukiji Honganji Temple,* on Harumi Avenue, by Japanese missionaries. This is not a Zen temple.

Regular meetings in English are scheduled by the *International Transcendental Meditation Society;* 0425–92–2744.

Zen Buddhist. Regularly scheduled services are not part of Zen, but instruction in English may be obtained at the following temples, a short distance from downtown Tokyo (from 25 to 45 minutes by train); *Sojiji Temple,* 128 Tsurumi, Tsurumi-ku, Yokohama; *Enkakuji Temple,* 478 Yamanouchi, Kamakura; or *Kenchoji Temple,* 8 Yamanouchi, Kamakura. You should telephone and make arrangements to visit these places well in advance so that they can have English-speaking preceptors on hand.

 BEAUTY PARLORS AND BARBERS. All the leading hotels have good beauty salons, in which imported beauty preparations are widely used. Also excellent, the shops run by Japan's leading cosmetic maker, Shiseido. *André Bernard of London* is on the 4th floor, Horaiya Bldg., Roppongi (404–0616). Other beauty salons where English is spoken include: *Maroze,* above the National Abazu Supermarket at Hiroo (444–4225); *Sweden Center House of Beauty* at Roppongi (404–9730); *Hollywood* at Roppongi (408–1293); and

Yamano with shops in ten locations (main one in the Ginza; 561–1200). Cosmetic plastic surgery is performed by highly skilled doctors at *Jujin Hospital,* 1–12–5 Shimbashi, Minato-ku, Tokyo (571–2111).

The barbershops in the major hotels usually are best for the foreign visitor, as they have had experience cutting non-Japanese hair, and you can get your instructions across to them in the English language. Haircuts and shampoo will cost you about ¥4,000 in these places, and all of the side services, such as manicure, scalp massage, shoeshine, and facial treatment are available. In addition to the shops in the hotels, *Nisshin Barbers* in Yurakucho's Sanshin Building (591–1839) and *Yonekura* in the Asahi Building, 6–6–7 Ginza (571–1538), Tokyo's most expensive, are recommended. *Andre Bernard* at Roppongi (address above) accepts men as well as women customers, as indeed do many others.

 CLOSING DAYS AND HOURS. To the casual observer, it seems that the shops and restaurants of Tokyo never close. Generally, establishments in the Ginza area open around 10:00 A.M. and close about 7:00 P.M. Department stores are usually open on Sundays, but close on Mondays, Wednesdays, or Thursdays. (Each store has its own closing day.) Smaller shops remain open seven days a week, as do restaurants. Dining out can be a problem sometimes, because many fine restaurants close at 8:00 or 9:00 P.M. A special law seems to govern the restaurants in the Roppongi and Akasaka areas, however, where you can eat Chinese, Italian, or American food until 2:00 or 3:00 A.M. Some hotel arcade shops close on Sundays. It is a 5½-day week for banks, business houses, and government offices. From Monday to Friday banks are open from 9:00 A.M. to 3:00 P.M., and on Saturday until noon. They do not open on the second Saturday of each month. From Monday to Friday business and government offices are open from 9:00 A.M. to 5:00 P.M., and on Saturday until noon. Some business houses enjoy a five-day week. In liaison with the banks, post offices are not handling money nor insurance transactions on the second Saturday of each month.

 SEASONAL EVENTS AND FESTIVALS. Most festivals and fairs are held in honor of local deities and are religious in nature. Often portable shrines and decorated floats, in which dancers and musicians entertain, are carried around the districts. Often people of the neighborhood join in street parades. These are occasions especially for children to wear their brightest kimono, helping to make festivals and fairs colorful and convivial. Usually shopkeepers sell trinkets, flowers, and snacks at streetside stalls along the approaches to temples and shrines.

Although we try to be as up-to-date as possible, dates of festivals are subject to change and should be verified through the local press or the Tokyo Tourist Information Center.

The following are markets and fairs that can be enjoyed every month:

Every morning except Sundays and national holidays. Fish market at Tsukiji, held in the Tokyo Central Wholesale Market from early morning until about 11:00 A.M. From Tsukiji station on the Hibiya subway line.

First Sunday. Antique market at Araiyakushi Temple in Nakano Ward. From Araiyakushimae station on the Seibu-Shinjuku line.

Second Sunday. Antique market at Nogi Shrine in Akasaka. From Nogizaka station on the Chiyoda subway line.

Third Saturday and Sunday. Antique market on 1st floor of Sunshine 60 building in Ikebukuro. From Ikebukuro station on the Yamanote line or Higashi-Ikebukuro subway station on the Yurakucho line.

Fourth Thursday and Friday. Antique market at the Roi Building in Roppongi. From Roppongi Station on the Hibiya subway line.

Fourth Saturday. Antique market at Yushima Shrine. From Yushima Station on the Chiyoda subway line.

Fourth Sunday. Antique market at Togo Shrine in Shibuya Ward. From Shibuya Station on the Yamanote line.

On the 1st and 21st. Local fair at Nishiarai Daishi Temple in Adachi Ward. From Daishimae Station on the Tobu line from Asakusa, changing onto a branch line for the temple at Nishiarai.

On the 4th, 14th, and 24th. Local fair held by the Togenuki Jizo Temple in Sugamo, Toshima Ward. From Sugamo Station on the Yamanote line.

January. Daruma doll festival at Kitain Temple in Kawagoe on the 3rd, on the western outskirts of Tokyo. This is a red, legless doll that, because its bottom is weighted and rounded, always returns to the upright position no matter how much it is pushed around. The doll symbolizes buoyancy and resilience. At New Year, Japanese people like to buy new daruma dolls to ensure their good fortune for the coming year. The Kitain Temple festival, which sells daruma dolls, is well known for its huge stock of dolls of all sizes.

Demonstrations of traditional skills and acrobatics by firemen along Chuo-dori Ave. in Harumi district, from 10:00 A.M. until noon on the 6th.

From the 15th to 16th is the famous flea market called the Setagaya Boro Ichi. Held along Daikan Yashikimae Ave. in Kamimachi, Setagaya Ward. Take bus 1, 3, or 34 from the south exit of Shibuya Station and get off at Kamimachi bus stop.

February is the month for plum blossoms in Tokyo. Good places to view them are *Shinjuku Gyoen* park in Shinjuku, from Shinjuku Gyoenmae Station on the Marunouchi subway line or from Sendagaya Station on the Sobu line; *Ume Yashiki Park* in Ota Ward, from Keihin-Kyuko Line Ume Yashiki Station; *Koishikawa Korakuen Garden,* from Iidabashi Station on the Sobu line; *Koishikawa Botanical Garden,* from Shireyama Station on the Mita subway line; and *Yushima Tenjin Shrine* in Bunkyo Ward, from Yushima Station on the Chiyoda subway line. Yushima Tenjin Shrine holds a plum blossom festival from mid-February until mid-March.

Annual bean-throwing festival is held on the 3rd at shrines and temples across the country to herald the coming of spring. In Tokyo, the most popular (but also most crowded) places are Asakusa Kannon Temple in Asakusa and Zojoji Temple in Shiba.

March is the month of tulips, and while most parks have at least some in their collections, the most colorful spot is *Hibiya Park,* reached from Yurakucho Station on the Yamanote line or Hibiya Station on the Hibiya subway line.

Daruma doll fair is held from the 3rd to 4th at Jindaiji Temple, reached by bus from Chofu Station on the Keio line.

On the second Sunday in March a fire-walking ceremony is held at Mount Takao. Priests, and anyone else who wants to, walk barefoot over burning ashes.

April is the month for cherry blossom viewing, accompanied by much song, drink, and dance, in parks across the capital. Perhaps the most popular spot, especially for cherry blossom parties in the evenings, is *Ueno Park,* but others include *Shinjuku Gyoen; Yasukuni Shrine,* from Kudanshita Station on the Tozai subway line; *Ikegami Honmonji Temple,* from Ikegami Station on the Ikegami line from Gotanda; *Kinuta Park,* from Yoga Station on the Shin-Tamagawa subway line from Shibuya; *Yoyogi Park;* the *Outer Garden of Meiji*

Shrine in Harajuku; and *Senzoku Park,* from Senzoku-ike Station on the Ikegami line.

April is also the month for peonies, and *Nishiarai Daishi Temple* (from Daishimae Station on the Tobu line) has an excellent peony garden in its grounds.

The best azalea festival of April is held at *Nezu Shrine* (Nezu Station is on the Chiyoda Line). Besides the banks of flowers, scheduled events include drum performances and open-air tea ceremonies.

Annual spring festival of Yasukuni Shrine is held on the 22nd.

From April 25–May 5 is the annual plant fair, said to be the biggest in Kanto, at Ikegami Honmonji Temple in Ota Ward. Also held during this period is the wisteria festival, at Kameido Tenjin Shrine in Koto Ward (from Kameido Station on the Sobu line).

Late April–early May is the annual spring festival at Meiji Shrine in Harajuku.

May is the month of camellias, and good places to view them include *Komazawa Olympic Park,* from Komazawa Daigaku Station on the Shin-Tamagawa subway line from Shibuya; *Yoyogi Park; Shinjuku Central Park,* located near the Shinjuku skyscrapers; and *Nezu Shrine,* from Nezu Station on the Chiyoda subway line.

May 12–15. Kanda Festival, a huge affair with many local shrines taking part in street processions in the Kanda area.

May 16–18. Sanja Festival, the annual festival of Asakusa Shrine in Asakusa, located near the Asakusa Kannon Temple.

June brings the irises, and fine displays can be seen at several places in Tokyo, including *Meiji Shrine's Iris Garden, Jindai Botanical Garden* in Chofu, *Yasukuni Shrine,* and *Horikiri Iris Garden,* near Horikiri Shobuen Station on the Keisei line from Ueno.

In mid-June is the annual Sanno Festival of Hie Shrine in Akasaka, a few minutes' walk from Akasaka-Mitsuke Station.

The Fuji Festival from June 30–July 2, marking the opening of Mount Fuji for the climbing season, takes place at Fuji Shrine near Komagome Station on the Yamanote line. Snakes made of scrolls are sold. These are believed to protect people from evil. Many open-air stalls selling potted plants, trinkets, and food are set up around the shrine.

July. A morning glory fair is held from the 6th–8th in the grounds of *Kishibojin Temple* near Iriya Station on the Hibiya subway line.

A ground cherry fair is held in the grounds of *Asakusa Kannon Temple* in Asakusa from the 9th–10th.

From the 13th–16th is the *Mitama* (spirit of the dead) *Festival of Yasukuni Shrine.* Memorial service for the enshrined deities. Demonstrations of the martial arts and ancient Imperial Court music and dances.

Plum fair of *Okunitama Shrine* in Fuchu, near Fuchu Station on the Keio line from Shinjuku. Takes place on the 20th.

At the end of July is the grand evening fireworks display on the Sumida River. This fireworks display originated in the 18th century, when a Buddhist mass was held for the souls of famine victims. It also marked the opening of the river for sweet trout fishing.

From July 11-Aug. 11 is the summer evening festival by Shinobazu Pond in Ueno Park. Stalls are set up and various forms of entertainment held to help people forget the heat of the day.

September. Annual festival of *Nogi Shrine* is held on the 12th–13th in Akasaka.

October. From the 11th–13th is Oeshiki Festival at *Ikegami Honmonji Temple,* commemorating the anniversary of the death of Priest Nichiren in 1282. Annual autumn festival of *Yasukuni Shrine* runs from the 17th–19th.

From October 30–November 4 is the annual autumn festival of *Meiji Shrine.*

From mid-October–mid-November chrysanthemum displays can be seen at *Meiji Shrine, Shinjuku Gyoen, Yasukuni Shrine, Tsukiji Honganji Temple,* and other places around the city.

November. Ornamental rakes said to bring good luck and prosperity are sold at Otori (cock) fairs. The fairs take place two or three times during the month at Otori Shrine in Asakusa, from Minowa Station on the Hibiya subway line; Otori Shrine in Meguro, from Meguro Station on the Yamanote line; and Hanazono Shrine in Shinjuku, from the east exit of Shinjuku Station on the Yamanote line. The dates of these fairs vary from year to year.

December. Year-end fair at Suitengu Shrine on the 5th. Near Ningyocho Station on the Hibiya subway line.

The 14th is the festival at Sengakuji Temple in memory of the 47 loyal retainers, who, in the feudal past, took their own lives after avenging the death of their master. From Sengakuji Station on the Toei Asakusa subway line.

Boro Ichi flea market is held from the 15th-16th along Daikan Yashikimae Av. in Kamimachi, Setagaya Ward. Also held on **Jan. 15–16.**

From the 17th-19th the annual hagoita (battledore, an early form of badminton) fair is held at Asakusa Kannon Temple in Asakusa. Very ornate battledores are sold. They are used in New Year displays in the home.

From Dec. 31st-Jan. 1st people make New Year visits to shrines and temples to pray for health, happiness, and fortune in the coming 12 months. Meiji Shrine is the biggest crowd-puller.

TOURS. All the travel agents listed in the *Facts at Your Fingertips* section earlier in this book have Tokyo offices and can arrange private tours to your specifications. In addition, there are regularly scheduled bus tours with English-speaking guides offered by **JTB** (276–7777) and private agencies such as **Fujita Travel Service** (573–1011); **Tobu Travel** (272–1421), **Hankyu Express** (508–0129), and **Japan Gray Line** (436–6881). Their precise itineraries change somewhat from year to year, according to what proves popular, but the main places of interest are well established. A recent and typical JTB listing included 10 different tours: *Tokyo Morning, Tokyo Afternoon,* different full-day *Tokyo* tours and *Night Life* tours. Prices range from ¥3,500 to ¥12,000, times from 3 to 8 or 9 hours. The *Tokyo Bright Night* course, for example, starts with a sukiyaki dinner at a top-class restaurant, then goes to see part of a kabuki performance at the Kabuki Theater, and finishes with geisha entertainment at a restaurant in Asakusa. The cost is ¥12,000. The *Tokyo Morning Tour* takes about 4 hours and includes Tokyo Tower, Keio University, Happo-en Garden, the National Diet Building, Imperial Palace and Ginza. The price is ¥4,000 for adults, ¥2,500 for children.

JTB is now offering three full-day tours of *Industrial Tokyo.* Each one visits various industrial plants, with the most popular proving to be the Japan Air Lines maintenance center at Tokyo's Haneda Airport. Visitors are shown the B747 hangar and the airline's power plant overhaul center, where jet engines are stripped and repaired. Industrial Tokyo tours cost ¥9,000 for adults and ¥7,000 for children, including lunch. The tour is made on Tuesday, Thursday, and Friday, and occupies about 9 hours. The Tuesday tour is the one that takes in the airline maintenance base.

DO-IT-YOURSELF TOURS. The independent-minded can see a lot of Tokyo on their own and at minimal cost. Here are some suggestions:

The Diet Building and the Parliamentary Museum. At Kasumigaseki, near Kokkai-Gijidomae Station, which is on both the Marunouchi and the Chiyoda subway lines. To enter the Diet Building and see the chambers where the governing of this country goes on, applications have to be made to your embassy and permission awaited. The Parliamentary Museum, that is directly opposite the Diet Building at Kasumigaseki, is the next best thing. Admission is free. The Museum is open from 9:30 A.M. to 3:30 P.M. every day except Sundays, National Holidays, and the last day of each month. On the second floor is a large model of the Diet Building. The model is equipped with an audio/color-slide system, operated by push-button, and giving pictures on a screen and a narration in English. Here you can learn about the development of Parliamentary conduct in Japan and its survival through earthquakes and war. Next to the Museum is the Ozaki Memorial Hall, revering Yukio Ozaki, who was a member of the Diet for more than 60 years.

Japan Broadcasting Corporation (NHK) Center. Follow the map (your first purchase in Tokyo) from either Shibuya or Harajuku stations on the Yamanote line. NHK's broadcasting center was built over a period of several years, is thought to be the "world's best," and at a total cost of ¥31,700 million is also probably the world's costliest.

The center is open for public inspection any weekday, between 8:30 A.M. and 6:00 P.M. There's no need to make a reservation for a tour, as you go right in and proceed unescorted. If you would prefer to have an English-speaking guide, call 465–1111. You walk past control rooms, see what is going on under the lights in the studios, inspect elaborate sets that are the actual ones used in screening long-running serial dramas. Studio 101 is NHK's famed and largest studio. If you want to probe deeper into NHK's complexities, call 464–0114 or 464–0115 to make special arrangements.

Through the **Japan National Tourist Organization,** you may receive names, addresses, telephone numbers and details of several enterprises willing to receive individual tourists. Usually no charge is made. Often English-speaking guides are available. Sometimes just to see, without explanations, is enough. These enterprises include car manufacturers; makers of optical instruments (cameras, lenses); producers of beer and whiskey; makers of electrical goods; makers of musical instruments, of cloisonné, chinaware; a slaughterhouse; a dyeing factory; the stock exchange; makers of confectionery and glassware. In most cases, the head offices are in Tokyo, but the factories in different parts of the country. Those factories in Tokyo, or within reasonable distance from Tokyo, include Honda Motor Co.; Nikon, Asahi Pentax and Konica; Suntory and Sapporo Beer; Sony and Toshiba; Mashiko ware; the slaughterhouse; the stock exchange; Morinaga Confectionery; Hoya Crystal. JNTO is also able to introduce tourists interested in gardens to some of Japan's most outstanding garden designers.

Newspaper Plants. For an example of an immense and complex operation, go on a tour of one of the newspaper plants in Tokyo. The Asahi Shimbun (545–0131) and the Mainichi Shimbun (212–0321) arrange guided tours daily, without charge. Reservations should be made in advance, as each group is limited in size.

These Japanese enterprises manufacture daily papers, weeklies, monthlies, quarterlies, and annuals. English-language dailies, special publications, and books. They have thousands of employees, airplanes and helicopters, affiliated radio and television stations, and other companies handling clipping services, sound recording and real estate. Their daily editions roll off presses simultaneously in different major cities. English-speaking guides are available, if you make your arrangements well in advance.

State Guest House. Formerly the Akasaka Detached Palace, the State Guest House has been renovated and splendidly decorated. It is not open to the public, but can be seen from the road near Yotsuya station and the Hotel New Otani.

The Sumida River. Walk, or take a short taxi ride, from Shimbashi Station to the waterfront gardens of Hamarikyu. There is no admission charge to this beautiful city park where there was once a detached palace. Take the path that runs parallel to the canal until you reach a ramshackle landing stage. A "water bus" is timed to leave the landing stage every day except Tuesday. The boat is comfortable with an enclosed cabin and an outside deck. For ¥480, you cruise along the Sumida River as far as Asakusa, getting a different view of the city. Near Azuma-bashi are tilting wooden waterfront houses with washing hanging outside. Logs float on the river. Bobbing pink lanterns decorate the landing stage. From Azuma-bashi, famed Asakusa Kannon Temple is only a block away, and downtown Tokyo is all around you. Your return route can be underground, on the Ginza subway line back to Shimbashi.

Tokyo Bay. In summer, the *Tokai Steamship Co.*, (432–4551) operates a 2-hour evening cruise on a ship that puts on variety shows and that has a beerhall. Departures nightly from Takeshiba Pier, fares from ¥500 to ¥2,500.

Walkaholics International. For the foot-loose in Tokyo. You are invited to join half-day walking tours that make use of both JNR and subway trains. Call Mr. Oka, 0422–51–7673.

HOME VISIT PROGRAM. In 1968, the Tokyo government in cooperation with the Japan National Tourist Organization inaugurated a Home Visit program. To apply, go in person to the JNTO Tourist Information Center at 1–6–6 Yurakucho, Chiyoda Ward (502–1461) at least one day before the visit, to get your instructions. (No mail or telephone applications.) You usually visit the family after dinner, stay for an hour or two. No charge, but it's gracious to take a small gift, such as flowers or cakes.

TEA CEREMONY. Several places in Tokyo welcome visitors from abroad to see and take part in Japan's traditional tea ceremony. These include: *Sakura-kai.* 3–2–25 Shimo-Ochiai, Shinjuku-ku; 951–9043. Near Mejiro Station, on the Yamanote line. Fee ¥600. For a lesson, lasting 40 mins., ¥1,200. A lesson in flower arrangement may be added: one hour, with tea: ¥2,500. From 11:00 A.M. TO 4:00 P.M. Thursdays and Fridays. Reservations necessary.

Toko-an. Imperial Hotel 4th floor; 504–1111. Fee ¥1,100. From 10:00 A.M. to 4:00 P.M., except Sundays and national holidays.

Chosho-an. Hotel Okura 7th floor; 582–0111. Fee ¥1,000. From 11:00 A.M. to 5:00 P.M., with a noon lunch break.

Seisei-an. Hotel New Otani Tower 7th floor; 265–1111, ext. 2567. Fee ¥1,000. From 11:00 A.M. to 4:00 P.M. Open Thursdays, Fridays, and Saturdays.

LESSONS. Flower Arranging. If you have time for lessons, try the following: *Ikenobo Gakuen* in Kanda Surugadai, Chiyoda Ward; 292–3071; lessons for tourists on Wednesday mornings. *Ohara School of Ikebana*

in Minami Aoyama, Minato Ward; 499–1200; lessons every morning (¥ 2,000). *Sogetsu School of Ikebana* in Akasaka, Minato Ward; 408–1126; Tuesday mornings (¥ 3,000). Reservations are necessary.

Yoga. Contact the *Ghosh Yoga Institute* in Shinjuku (352–1307), the *Yoga College of India* in Shibuya (461–7805), or the *Tokyo Yoga Center* in Shinjuku (354–4701). The *Tomonaga Yoga School* in Ogikubo (393–5481) offers classes in both yoga and Zen.

Japanese Cooking. *Akabori Cooking School* in Mejiro (953–2251) offers two-hour lessons for foreigners three times a month on Mondays. ¥ 3,500. Reservations necessary.

There are schools in Tokyo for just about everything you could imagine. If you want to try your hand at something other than those mentioned above, such as doll making, weaving and other handicrafts, how to wear a kimono, and, of course, Japanese language, ask for up-to-date information on classes and prices at the Tokyo Information Center in Yurakucho (see the *Tourist Information* section).

 PARKS AND GARDENS. Nearly all the parks mentioned below are open from 8:30 A.M. to 4:00 P.M. daily, including holidays. **Hibiya Park.** Across from the Imperial Hotel. A small but pleasant spot in the heart of the city. About 40 acres. Hibiya Hall features frequent concerts and there are shows and exhibitions in the park from time to time. In November, Japan's biggest chrysanthemum show is held here. Among the trees are dogwoods sent by the United States in return for the famous Washington cherry trees.

Ueno Park. A moderate distance directly north of the center of Tokyo (the Yurakucho-Ginza districts). This is a huge park, full of attractions; you can easily spend a day exploring the area. It contains a popular zoo; various museums of art, science and natural history, temples, pagodas, shrines, and a monument to Ulysses S. Grant. A tree he planted on his visit to Japan still stands. In Ueno Park you can also take a short ride on Japan's first monorail train.

Hamarikyu Park. Just south of the center of Tokyo and on the harbor. 60 acres with lovely walks, lawns, foliage, and a pond with an island. There is a beachlike stretch along the harbor, and there are traditional cottagelike structures here and there; plus a Japanese archery club and range.

Oi Bird Park. For birds and bird watchers. On Tokyo Bay, and a 15-minute walk from Ryutsu Center Station on the monorail line from Hamamatsu-cho to Hareda.

Imperial Palace East Garden. At the east end of the Imperial Palace grounds. Opened in 1968 to commemorate construction of the new palace. One of the best examples of modern Japanese gardening.

Kiyosumi Garden. Just east of the center of Tokyo, and everything you've imagined an exquisite Japanese garden ought to be. Ponds, rock stepping stones, stone lanterns and winding walks. Highly photogenic.

Tama Zoological Park. On the southwest edge of Tokyo, in the Tama district. Large, sylvan grounds and displays of animals behind moats and in naturalistic habitats. Amusement facilities nearby: merry-go-rounds, roller coasters, etc.

Shinjuku Gyoen. Certainly one of Japan's loveliest gardens. Huge grounds, exquisitely landscaped. Botanical displays from all over the world. In west central Tokyo, not far from Shinjuku Station. Cherry blossoms in April and chrysanthemum displays throughout October.

Rikugien Garden, perhaps the most beautiful and most typical Japanese garden in Tokyo, is located near the Komagome Station on the Yamanote Line (the loop around central Tokyo). A favorite resort of the *shogun* and other officials, it includes a large pond, a teahouse, and some magnificent, twisted trees. Dates back to early 18th century.

Meiji Shrine Inner Gardens are particularly beautiful during the last two weeks of June when the iris are at their best. An amazing display of varieties in a lovely setting. The gardens are inside the shrine, which is at Harajuku Station on the Yamanote loop. Open from 8:30 A.M. to 4:30 P.M. daily. In the fall, usually the entire month of October, displays of chrysanthemums are held here.

National Park for Nature Study is just what it says it is, and is an oasis in Shirogane. An insectarium is open from April to November.

Yoyogi Park, near Harajuku station, is the site of Olympic Village in 1964, and of an American housing area before that. It has now reverted to nature, a delightful green area close to Tokyo's beating heart.

Tokyo Metropolitan Medicinal Plants Garden, Kodaira City, Tokyo, is a representative herb garden. Open daily, 9:00 A.M. to 5:00 P.M. No entrance fee. On the Seibu Shinjuku line from Shinjuku to Omebashi.

Hoshi Pharmaceutical College, Ebara, Shinagawa-ku. Visits by appointment. Tel. 786–1011.

Tokyo Shobu-en (Iris Garden) is also a fine place for viewing the gorgeous violet flowers in June. Located near Tamagawa Station on the Keio Teito private railway line from Shinjuku Station.

A littoral park built on reclaimed land in Tokyo Bay is near an oceanographic museum that has the shape of a 60,000-ton passenger liner. The *Soya,* a former Antarctic expedition ship, is now moored there.

 ZOOS. Ueno Zoo, which is in Ueno Park, stars two very popular pandas, gifts from China. In the Children's Zoo, small children may ride ponies. Open 9:00 A.M.– 4:30 P.M., Closed Mondays, Dec. 29–31. **Tama Zoo** allows its animals to live in as natural a setting as possible. A Lion Bus drives visitors through the area where lions roam freely. Take a Keio line express train from Shinjuku Station to Takahata-fudo Station, and change there for a local train to Tama Dobutsu-koen. Open 9:00 A.M.–4:30 P.M.; closed Mondays.

 BATH HOUSES. Tokyo Onsen. 6 Ginza; 541–3021. This is a five-story emporium dedicated to hedonistic cleanliness. You can spend about ¥3,000 here and enter the large public baths (segregated), or you can hire a private room, where you will find a steam cabinet, small pool, and a massage team of two women, one of whom will probably walk up and down your spine as the high point of your massage. The top floor boasts a "human dock" where battered wrecks are presumably repaired. The fee up here is about ¥7,000 for which you can enjoy (or suffer) a Finnish sauna, a whirlpool bath, a massage by the usual light-fingered women or the bone-breaking masseurs, and end your experience with a fast shakedown on the torture rack known as the Swedish electrical massage machine. (The masseurs are alleged to be apprentice sumo wrestlers, and presumably they are building their muscles at the expense of yours.) Sauna baths are being installed for tired executives in many business buildings and hotels. No hanky panky in these high-priced establishments. Neighborhood public bathhouses are a vanishing institution, but there are still 2,700 of them left in Tokyo. ¥220 per adult, all the hot water you want and no time limit. Americans Hatch and Wilson run a Fitness Center in **Azabu Towers,** next to the Soviet Embassy. The **Swedish Health Center for Ladies,** in the Sweden Center Building, Roppongi, has sauna baths and massage. In the **New Shimbashi Building** at Shimbashi is a sauna bath for women only. It is billed as "North European Mood" and costs ¥3,000. Another ladies-only is the **Tarner,** at Myogadani, ¥2,500 with sauna. **Ginza Steam Bath,** at 1 chome, has a 70-minute service for ¥3,500, daily from noon to midnight.

THEME PARKS AND AMUSEMENT CENTERS. There can be only one leader among Tokyo's many amusement centers. That is **Tokyo Disneyland,** far and away the winner in its field, the first Disney theme park outside the United States. Some folks who have been to all three say that Tokyo Disneyland is better than Disneyland in California and Walt Disney World in Florida. In every way, Tokyo Disneyland is faithful to the original concepts, with that little bit extra: the Japanese touch.

JTB runs a daily *Sunrise Tokyo Disneyland and City Tour,* except on the days when Tokyo Disneyland is closed. The tour lasts about 8½ hours. It costs ¥8,000 for adults, ¥7,500 for the 12–17 year olds, and ¥5,000 for ages 4–11. These prices include Tokyo Disneyland and individual attraction tickets. The tour also takes in the Imperial Palace plaza and the Asakusa Kannon Temple and district.

The Hato Bus Company also offers a visit to Tokyo Disneyland. Its 4½-hour tour costs ¥6,300 for adults. Its 4-hour tour includes Tokyo Tower together with Tokyo Disneyland, and costs ¥7,400 for adults.

Admission tickets to Tokyo Disneyland are sold by reservation. They are available in two categories:

1. Passport—usable on weekdays except for holidays, Golden Week, and summer. Admission Passport includes unlimited use of all attractions except the Shooting Gallery. Adults, ¥3,900; 12–17 years old, ¥3,500; 4–12 years old ¥2,800.

2. Big 10—usable on all days. A Big 10 ticket book is made up of an admission ticket and 10 attraction tickets. Adults, ¥3,700; 12–17 years old, ¥3,300; 4–11 years old, ¥2,500.

Gate tickets are also available at the Tokyo Disneyland Main Entrance on a space available basis, however, foreigners showing their passport will be allowed to buy a ticket even if the day is sold out. General admission day tickets cost: Adults, ¥2,500; 12–17 years old, ¥2,100; 4–11 years old, ¥1,400.

Starlight tickets, at the same prices as general admission day tickets, are good for summer evenings when the park is open until 10:00 P.M. Starlight tickets are made up of an admission ticket and five attractions tickets.

Reservations for individual visitors and groups may be made through major travel agents in Japan, and directly from the Tokyo Disneyland Reservation Center, (0473) 51–1171. Tokyo Disneyland Information Center is (0473) 54–0001, or, within Tokyo, 366–5600.

Adjustments in the park's hours are continuously being made, and vary from month to month, so it is advised that you call for information concerning the time you wish to visit.

From either Nihonbashi or Otemachi Stations, the train to Urayasu, Tozai subway line, takes 15 minutes. A nonstop shuttle bus from Tokyo Disneyland bus terminal (5-minute walk from Urayasu Station) takes 20 minutes. ¥200 for adults, ¥100 for children, one way. On peak days, a bus leaves the terminal every minute.

UNESCO Village and Murayama Reservoir. Almost directly west of Tokyo and about 25 miles from the center is a huge reservoir with several lakes. It is surrounded by picnic grounds, has a nearby amusement park, and adjoins a village of cottages in the styles of all nations, built as a United Nations project. A quaint narrow gauge train runs from the park to the village. Official name of the reservoir is Lake Tama.

The area may be easily reached by automobile, though in this case you'll need a guide of some sort. By train, from Tokyo Station, take a subway to Ikebukuro (about 15 minutes), change to the Seibu-Ikebukuro line and go to Nishi-Tokorozawa (about 40 minutes), then change to the Seibu-Sayama line and ride to the terminal—Seibu Kyujomae Station. The terminal is but a few hundred feet away from UNESCO Village.

Toshimaen Amusement Park. This is a large, well-equipped amusement park in the northwest corner of Tokyo proper. It is about 45 minutes from the center by automobile. You can also ride there by subway from Tokyo Station to Ikenbukuro, where you change to a special train, that runs often, from Seibu-Ikebukuro Station to Toshima-en, the end of the line.

Yomiuriland. This is a huge recreation center on the outskirts of Tokyo, and is billed as "the world's first religious, cultural, sports, and recreation center." Golf courses, aquariums, artificial ski runs, a parachute tower and other amusement facilities, plus a pagoda housing relics of Buddha. On Tamagawa River near Kawasaki.

Toyama Traffic Park. Located at Nishi-okubo, Shinjuku-ku, this park is designed to teach children traffic safety. Those between the ages of eight and 16 may drive go-carts along roads that simulate real ones, and must obey regular rules of the road. Outdoor play equipment is available, too.

CHILDREN'S ACTIVITIES. Tokyo, with its busy air of make-believe, can be one vast toyland for children. There are, of course, the parks, zoos, and gardens. In the city itself there are toy shops on all the main shopping streets and in many out-of-the-way areas. Tokyo's fabulous department stores also have huge toy sections, guaranteed to provide several hours' diversion for any youngster.

Some big department stores have miniature amusement rinks on their roofs. Sometimes these include small zoos of birds and monkeys. There are slides and rides of various kinds for the smaller youngsters.

Surprisingly, many children enjoy eating out with the grown-ups at Tokyo's restaurants. Eating places are often interestingly decorated, especially Japanese or Chinese restaurants, where there may be gardens with rocks and pools and where there are enough colorful shapes and gadgets such as miniature waterfalls to keep interest at a high level. Restaurant people are apt to be fond of children and anxious to help keep them amused. High chairs are nearly always available.

Baby sitting can be a problem if you're on a short visit. Most of the better hotels can arrange for a maid or someone to take care of children.

If the youngsters can stand movies all day you might take them to the **Tokyu Kaikan Building** across from the Shibuya Station, in a large shopping section about 20 minutes west by southwest of the center. There are five motion picture theaters in this one building.

Bicycling. Try the Yoyogi Park Cycling Course, where free bicycles are provided for children 15 years and younger, between the hours of 9:00 A.M. and 4:00 P.M. daily. Near Harajuku station. Other possibilities: Ichinohashi Traffic Park (taxi from Roppongi;) Kitanomaru Cycling Course, near Takebashi station. Palace Cycling Course, on Sundays and holidays.

Fishing. No standing around in the cold with never a bite, but waters full of rainbow trout that you catch as fast as you can cast your line. Artificial, but fun. Attendants clean your fish for you, and you can cook and eat them on the spot. For Akikawa River, go to Tachikawa on the Chuo line and change for Musashi Itsukaichi on the Itsukaichi line; ask for the fishing pond. For Ohtaba-gawa International Trout Fishing Ground, go from Tachikawa on the Ome line, get off at Kawai and ask for the fishing ground.

Planetarium. Easy to reach, in Tokyu Bunka Kaikan on the seventh floor at Shibuya. The performance lasts one hour, with narration in Japanese except for large groups making arrangements in advance.

Rowboating. Several sites in Tokyo have rowboats for rent. Some of the most central are: Ueno Park; the Imperial Moat at Chidorigafuchi; Akasakamitsuke.

Tokyo Tower. The Waxworks Museum on the third floor has tableaux appealing to children, as well as horror scenes better avoided. Adventure World, a Disney-type animation show on the ground floor, can keep children entertained for half a day. Taxi there from Kamiyacho subway station; or from Hamamatsu-cho station on the Yamanote line.

 PARTICIPANT SPORTS. Don't expect a lot of opportunities to indulge in your favorite sport. Facilities in Tokyo are cramped, and often limited to club membership.

Several of the super deluxe hotels—but by no means all of them—have pools, outdoor for summer swimming, indoor for year-round use. Several have gymnasia. If your concern is to keep fit, take advantage of the jogging courses that exist. Again, the super deluxe hotels will help, with jogging outfits and joggers' maps.

Japan Gray Line offers a **golf** tour, daily from Tuesday to Friday. It means a full day's outing, but you do play on one of Japan's finest private golf courses, the Fuji Ace Golf Club. The cost is ¥24,000. Contact a travel agent, a hotel information desk, or telephone 433–5745 or 433–5746.

Quite satisfactory **skiing** can be enjoyed on a man-made run about an hour by train west of Tokyo, at the *Seibuen Park* adjacent to Yamaguchi and Murayama reservoirs. In winter, spring, and fall, the three major **ice skating rinks** are: *Ikebukuro Skating Center* (Ikebukuro, northwest part of Tokyo); *Korakuen Ice Palace* (near Suidobashi Station on Chuo Line) (north-center); *Tokyo Skating Rink* (near west entrance of Shinjuku Station). The Gold Rink at Shinagawa Sports Land is the nation's first exclusively for figure skating.

Bowling is available at the *Korakuen Bowling Arena,* near the Ice Palace and the baseball stadium. There are 62 AMF lanes and you can bowl from 7:00 A.M. to midnight in air-conditioned comfort. Shoes and balls can be rented here, as well as at the other lanes listed below. One game will cost you ¥300. You can try to make a reservation. The *Tokyo Bowling Centre,* in Meiji Park, now has 46 Brunswick automatic alleys, and a few of Japanese manufacture. ¥300 per game. Snack bar and restaurant. Open daily 7:00 A.M. to 11:30 P.M. The *Tower Bowl,* located in Shiba Park under the Tokyo Tower, charges ¥300 per game. It has 78 automatic alleys.

For **cyclists,** there is good news. Rent-a-bike facilities are increasing. Consult the *Japan Cycling Association* in Tokyo (582–3311), or the *Tokyo Cycling Association* (832–6895). 500 cycles are available free of charge for Sunday cyclists at Tokyo's 4.6-mile-long course round the Imperial Palace; closed to cars 10:00 A.M.–5:00 P.M. Inquiries on cycling or bicycles are handled in English at the *Bicycle PR Center* (586–0404), between 10:00 A.M. and 4:00 P.M. (2:00 P.M. on Saturdays) except on Sundays and national holidays.

For **field athletics** such as running and jumping (over a simple obstacle course setup), approach the Japan Field Athletics Ass., YH Bldg., 1–36–1 Higashi Ikebukuro, Toshima-ku.

The Tourist Information Center will give you a complete rundown on **fishing** facilities near Tokyo. About 150 species of fish are available.

The *YMCA* in Kanda, 293–1911, provides a variety of sports and games for members who pay a registration fee of ¥5,000 and a monthly fee of ¥3,000. Other sports facilities, including those for T'ai Chi, are available at reasonable rates at the *Tokyo Taiikukan,* opposite Sendagaya station (408–6191); in the bleacher basement of the *Kokuritsu Kyogijo* (National Stadium), left from Sendagaya station (403–1151); in the *Do Sports Plaza,* Sumitomo Building Annex, Nishi-Shinjuku (344–1971); and at *Tokyo Athletic Club* in Nakano (384–2131).

SPECTATOR SPORTS. Japanese **sumo** tournaments are held in Tokyo at New Year's time, in May and in September. They last 15 days. Two sides, or leagues, called *East* and *West,* compete with each other. Sumo takes place in a huge arena just beyond central Tokyo; the *New Kokugikan,* by Ryogoku Station on the Sobu line. With a taxi driver you need no other address than its name-Kokugikan.

Tickets are hard to come by, since blocks are bought up in advance by firms and organizations. Your Japanese friends will have to help you here. It is possible, sometimes, to buy tickets at the box office, but they'll be fairly distant from the ring. Complete television coverage is given.

Rabid fans attend the long daily sessions from late morning till 6:00 P.M. Food boxes and baskets are served, along with beer and sake. The lesser wrestlers start the day; the grand champions come later.

Tokyo is dotted with smaller **judo** halls and clubs, but the big center-almost the shrine of judo-is the *Kodokan* in north-central Tokyo. (1–16 Kasugacho, Bunkyo-ku—tel. 811–7151—near the Suidobashi Station on the Chuo Line.) Best hours for watching are from 5:00 to 7:00 P.M. on Tuesdays and Wednesdays, when the more advanced foreigners practice. Regular practice hours are 3:00 to 7:30 P.M. weekdays; 9:00 to 12:00 noon on Sundays.

You may be interested too in **Aikido:** at Wakamatsucho, Shinjuku (203–9236); in **Karate:** at 1–6 Ebisu, Shibuya-ku (462–1415); and in *Nippon Budokan,* the martial arts hall where judo events were held in the Olympic Games, and where many martial arts are now practiced: 2–3 Kitanomaru Koen, Chiyoda-ku, 216–0781). The nearest station is Kudanshita on the Tokyo Municipal Subway Shinjuku line and the Tozai subway line. For **T'ai-Chi Ch'uan,** Chinese exercises, approach Asahi Culture Center in the Shinjuku Sumitomo Building; or the Tokyo YMCA Athletic Gymnasium in Kanda.

If you are a **baseball** fan you'll find Tokyo a paradise. The long season breaks only for year's end and the dead of winter. There are often two major games in town and the brand of ball played is first rate. The big baseball center is at *Korakuen Stadium* in Bunkyo-ku, an amusement area that includes several arenas; a few minutes from the center of Tokyo. About once a year a major league American team visits Japan and plays a series with a Japanese all-star team. Five or six of these games will be in Tokyo. Consult your English-language newspapers for daily baseball schedules.

There are two major **racetracks** in the Tokyo area: *Tokyo Race Course,* Fuchu (about 20 miles west); and *Oi Race Course,* Samezu-machi, Ota-ku (about 6 miles south). Meets are held year-round. Excellent thoroughbreds are raced clockwise around the track. There is government controlled betting but the system is complicated, involving multiple bets something like the daily double, and you have to work with immensely long odds.

HISTORICAL SITES. Twice destroyed in modern times—once by the 1923 earthquake, once by wartime bombing during the 1940s—Tokyo doesn't have a lot to offer along the lines of ancient monuments. The **Emperor's Palace** is a new building, built in 1968, although the grounds were also the site of Edo Castle (also known as Chiyoda Castle) built by Dokan Ota (1432–1486). The Tokugawa shoguns lived in the castle for 265 years, but the palace was destroyed during World War II. The present Imperial Palace is on the site of the old western keep. It is Japanese in style, but of ferro-concrete, one story. The grounds are encircled by moats and high stone walls.

As the seat of government, the **National Diet Building** warrants attention. Visitors are admitted to the gallery when the Diet (legislature) is in session. The building was 18 years in construction, and was opened in 1936. It is at Kasumigaseki near Kokkai-Gijidomae Station, which is on both the Marunouchi and Chiyoda subway lines. **Asakusa Kannon Temple** has to be on everyone's itinerary, with its traditional architecture, enormous temple gate, and giant paper lanterns. It represents feudal times in today's modern city. The main hall is a replica of the one built in 1651 and destroyed in World War II. Asakusa is the name of the nearest station on the Ginza subway line.

Honganji Temple is at Tsukiji, south of the Ginza district in Chuo Ward. The nearest station is Higashi Ginza on the Hibiya subway line. The temple is on an historical site, though the present building dates from only 1935. Honganji Temple was founded in 1630 and destroyed repeatedly by fires. It is a branch of Nishi-Honganji, headquarters of the Jodo-Shinshu sect of Buddhism in Kyoto. **Zojoji Temple** was founded in 1393 and is the headquarters of the Jodo sect of Buddhism. Main Hall was destroyed in World War II, but a new ferro-concrete building was completed in 1974. The Main Gate, an "Important Cultural Property," was built in 1605.

Yasukuni Shrine honors the memory of the war dead, and comes the closest to being a national monument. Shrine buildings, in themselves, are usually quiet, austere, dignified places, not always striking in appearance. Shrine grounds, however, with trees and stone lanterns, conjure a special atmosphere. Yasukuni is on Kudan Hill, a few minutes walk from Kudanshita station on both the Tozai subway line and the Tokyo Municipal Shinjuku line.

Meiji Shrine, dedicated to Emperor Meiji, who died in 1912, and to his consort, was completed in 1920. It's a holy pilgrimage center. Main shrine, oratory, and some other buildings were destroyed in 1945, restored in 1958. The nearest station is Harajuku on the Yamanote line. **Hie Shrine** is another that has a sense of grandeur and nobility. Dedicated to Oyamakui-no-Mikoto, an ancient Shinto deity, the shrine was very popular during the Edo Period (1603–1867). Main shrine and other structures were burned during the war; the new main shrine was constructed in 1959 and the gate in 1962. Hie Shrine is on a hilltop in Akasaka, near the Capitol Tokyu Hotel. The nearest station is Akasaka-Mitsuke on both the Ginza and the Marunouchi subway lines.

LIBRARIES. There are several libraries in Tokyo that have English-languages books available. The following are the main ones: **American Center.** ABC Kaikan, 6–3 Shiba-Koen 2-chome, Minato Ward; 436–0901. **British Council.** Iwanami Hall, 1 Kanda Jinbocho 2-chome Chiyoda Ward; 264–3721. **The Japan Foundation.** Park Bldg., 3–6 Kioicho, Chiyoda Ward; 263–4504.

National Diet Library. 10–1 Nagatacho 1-chome, Chiyoda Ward; 581–2331.
Tokyo Metropolitan Central Library. 7–13 Minami-Azabu 5-chome, Minato
Ward; 442–8451.

MUSEUMS. Of course, museum riches emphasize Orientalia, but Tokyo has astonishing wealth in Western treasures also. Insatiable curiosity has long been a characteristic of Tokyo citizens. Those who haven't been able to travel to America or Europe have wanted to see all they can of other countries at home. Those museums that put on shows brought in from abroad are assured of record crowds.

As well as the establishments that show their own collections, department stores and galleries often stage special exhibitions. Several department stores also have sections where they have antiques on sale.

Please note that **Ueno Park** is the center for Tokyo's principal museums. The *Tokyo National Museum* is there, with the finest and most extensive collection of Japanese art and architecture. The *Tokyo Metropolitan Art Museum* is there, with permanent displays including many familiar masterpieces. The *National Museum of Western Art* is there, featuring the famous Matsukata colection of masterpieces with original pieces by Rodin and works of Matisse, Cézanne, and Picasso. And the *National Science Museum* is there, with displays of unfamiliar Japanese flora and fauna.

Other museums and galleries are to be found all over this vast, spreading city of Tokyo. For what is on each week, see Tokyo's English-language newspapers and, especially, *Tour Companion*.

CULTURE AND HISTORY

Calligraphy Museum. Materials related to the art of calligraphy. From Uguisudani Station on the Yamanote line; 872–2645. Closed Mondays.

Communications Museum. Everything from early postal services to the next generation of telephones. Also a good stamp display. From Otemachi Station on the Marunouchi subway line; 270–3841. Closed Mondays.

Constitution Museum. Materials on constitutional government, the Diet, and so on. From Kokkai-Gijidomae Station on the Marunouchi subway line; 581–1651. Closed Sundays and holidays.

Daimyo Clock Museum. Private collection of old Japanese-style clocks. From Nezu Station on the Chiyoda subway line; 821–6913. Closed Mondays.

Earthquake Museum. Materials on the Great Kanto Earthquake of 1923. From Ryogoku Station on the Sobu line; 622–1208. Closed Mondays.

Furniture Museum. Display of old Japanese furniture. Take bus from Tokyo Station to Harumi, alighting at Harumi Post Office bus stop; 533–0098. Closed Sundays and holidays.

Haiku Museum. Materials on haiku poetry and poets. From Okubo Station on the Sobu line; 367–6621. Closed Thursdays.

Iwasaki Chihiro Picture Book Museum. Gallery and reading room of children's books, including some English ones. From Kami-Igusa Station on the Seibu-Shinjuku line from Seibu-Shinjuku Station; 995–0612. Closed Mondays.

Japan Calligraphy Museum. Materials on the art of calligraphy. From Tokiwadai Station on the Tobu-Tojo line from Ikebukuro; 965–2611. Closed Mondays and Tuesdays.

Japan Toy Museum. Toys of the postwar period on display. From Minami-Senju Station on the Hibiya subway line; 871–3171. Closed Mondays, Tuesdays, and Wednesdays.

Kite Museum. Exhibition of kites from around Japan and around the world. From Nihonbashi Station on the Ginza subway line; 275–2704. Closed Sundays, holidays.

Meiji University Penal Museum. Materials on the history of crime and punishment; From Ochanomizu Station on the Chuo line. Closed Sundays. 296–4431.

Museum of Industrial Safety Techniques. How to prevent accidents at work. From Tamachi Station on the Yamanote line; 453–8441. Closed Sundays and holidays.

Musical Instruments Museum. Belonging to Musashino University of Music. Instruments from around the world on display. From Ekoda Station on the Seibu-Ikebukuro line from Ikebukuro; 992–1121. Open on Wednesdays only, from 10:00–3:00 P.M. Closed during vacation.

NHK Broadcasting Museum. Materials related to the history of broadcasting. From Kamiyacho Station on the Hibiya subway line; 433–5211. Closed Mondays.

Paper Museum. Materials related to Japanese-style and Western-style paper. From Oji Station on the Keihin-Tohoku line; 911–3545. Closed Mondays and holidays.

Printing Museum. Take a look at how stamps and banknotes get made. From Ichigaya Station on the Sobu line; 268–3271. Closed Mondays.

Shitamachi Museum. A museum about the life of the common people in the Edo Period, including homes, lifestyles, and games. From Ueno Station on the Yamanote line; near Shinobazu Pond; 823–7451. Closed Mondays, holidays.

Sugino Gakuen Costume Museum. Materials on women's fashion both old and new, national and international. From Meguro Station on the Yamanote line; 491–8151. Closed Sundays, holidays and in August.

Sword Museum. Collection of Japanese swords. From Sangubashi Station on the Odakyu line from Shinjuku; 379–1386. Closed Mondays.

Tobacco and Salt Museum. Standing displays on these two items, plus special exhibitions of ukiyoe prints. From Shibuya Station on the Yamanote line; 476–2041. Closed Mondays.

Tokyo Modern Literature Museum. Materials on modern Japanese literature. From Komaba Todaimae Station on the Inokashira line from Shibuya; 466–5150. Closed Mondays.

Transportation Museum. Materials on the history of transport. Children will love it. From Akihabara Station on the Sobu line; 251–8481. Closed Mondays.

Waseda University Theatrical Museum. Materials on national and international theater. From Waseda Station on the Tozai subway line; 203–4141. Closed Sundays and holidays.

World Bag Museum. Over 300 bags on display from 28 countries. From Asakusa Station on the Toei-Asakusa or Ginza subway line; 843–8141. Open the 1st–15th of every month; closed Saturdays, Sundays, and holidays.

SCIENCE

Goto Planetarium. If there's too much smog in the air outside, view the stars from inside. From Shibuya Station on the Yamanote line; 407–7409. Closed Mondays.

Kokugakuin University Archeological Museum. A look at what Japan's Stone Age was like. From Shibuya Station; 409–0111.

Meguro Parasitological Museum. Plenty of fascinating specimens here. From Meguro Station on the Yamanote line; 716–1264. Closed Mondays and holidays.

Museum of Maritime Science. Housed in a building shaped like a ship. Good for children. Located in Tokyo Bay. Take bus from Monzennakacho Station on Tozai subway line, or boat from Takeshiba Wharf in Hamamatsucho; 528–1111. No holidays.

National Science Museum. All the sciences under one roof. In Ueno Park; 822–0111. Closed Mondays.

Science and Technology Museum. Keeps up to date with all the latest inventions. From Takebashi Station on the Tozai subway line; 212–8471. No holidays.

Sunshine Planetarium. In Ikebukuro's Sunshine 60 skyscraper. 989–3466. No holidays.

Telecommunications Museum. For the latest in computers. From Tokyo Station; 241–8080. Closed Mondays.

Toshimaen Insect Museum. Inside Toshimaen amusement ground. From Toshimaen Station on the Seibu-Ikebukuro line; 990–3131. No holidays.

ART MUSEUMS

All have changing exhibitions and are closed Mondays. Museums also sometimes close on national holidays, sometimes on the day following.

Ancient Orient Museum. On the 7th floor of Sunshine City Culture Center at Ikebukuro; 989–3491. Prehistoric items excavated in Syria by a research team from Tokyo University. Nearest station: Ikebukuro on JNR Yamanote line and Marunouchi subway line. Open 10:00 A.M. to 4:30 P.M.

Bridgestone Art Museum. 1–1 Kyobashi, on the main Chuo-dori, Ginza district; 563–0241. Traditional and modern paintings, both Japanese and Western, and some Greek and modern sculpture. Nearest station: Kyobashi on the Ginza subway line. Open 10:00 A.M. to 5:00 P.M.

Crafts Gallery, National Museum of Modern Art. 3 Kitanomaru Koen, Chiyoda-ku; 211–7781. Exhibits dyed cloths, porcelain, lacquerware, metal works. Nearest station: Takebashi on the Tozai subway line. Open 10:00 A.M. to 5:00 P.M.

Goto Art Museum. 3–9–25 Kaminoge, Setagaya-ku; 703–0661. Features stone Buddhas in the hillside garden, many old mirrors, paintings, Buddhist sutras and books, ceramics. Scrolls illustrating the Heian Period story *Genji Monogatari* are exhibited for only one week in May. Nearest station: Kaminoge on the Denen Toshi line. Open 10:00 A.M. to 4:00 P.M.

Hara Museum of Contemporary Art. 4–7–11 Kita Shinagawa, Shinagawa-ku; 445–0651. Concentrates on the very modern, and often holds temporary exhibitions. Nearest station: Shinagawa on JNR Yamanote line and Keihin line. Open 10:00 A.M. to 4:00 P.M.

Hatakeyama Collection. 2–10–12 Shiroganedai, Minato-ku; 447–5787. A very select collection that emphasises tea ceremony ceramics, some of them having belonged to the original tea master Sen Rikyu. Nearest station: Takanawadai on the Tokyo Municipal Subway Asakusa line. Open 10 A.M. to 4 P.M. Closed Mondays, and the last two weeks of March, June, September, and December, and the first week of January.

Idemitsu Art Museum. 9th floor, Imperial Theater Building, 3–1–1 Marunouchi, Chiyoda-ku; 213–3111. The private collection of a Japanese oil king comprises Chinese and Japanese pottery, prints, and screens. Nearest station: Hibiya on the Hibiya subway line, the Tokyo Municipal subway Asakusa line, and the Chiyoda subway line. Open 10:00 A.M. to 5:00 P.M.

Matsuoka Museum of Art. 5–22–10 Shimbashi, Minato-ku; 431–8284. Houses 20,000 international items of a family collection. Nearest station: Onari-mon, on the Tokyo Municipal subway Mita line. Open 10:00 A.M. to 5:00 P.M.

National Museum of Modern Art. 3 Kitanomaru Koen, Chiyoda-ku; 214–2561. A mixed collection reflecting what has been going on in Japanese arts since the Meiji Period. Nearest station: Takebashi on the Tozai subway line. Open 10:00 A.M. to 5:00 P.M.

National Museum of Western Art. Ueno Park; 828–5131. Le Corbusier designed the main building, which was opened in 1959. See Museums introduc-tion. Open 9:00 A.M.–4:00 P.M.

Nezu Art Museum. 6–5–36 Minami Aoyama, Minato-ku; 400–2536. Fea-tures Chinese bronzes, lacquerware, ceramics, and some really exquisite scrolls, the latter being displayed only by appointment. The garden here is also a work of art. Nearest station: Omote-sando on the Chiyoda subway line, the Hanzo-mon subway line, and the Ginza subway line. Open 9:30 A.M. to 4:30 P.M., except September to November when it opens and closes 30 minutes earlier.

Nippon Mingeikan. (Museum of Folk Crafts), 4–3–33 Komaba, Meguro-ku; 467–4527. A fine display of many Japanese handicrafts, mostly of wood, pottery, and straw, in a rustic old building. Special folkcraft sales during November, in time for Christmas shopping. Nearest station: Komaba on the Inogashira line from Shibuya. Open 10:00 A.M. to 4:00 P.M. Closed throughout January and February.

Okura Shukokan Museum. 3 Aoi-cho, Akasaka, Minato-ku; 583–0781. In the garden of the Hotel Okura, this museum contains a wide range of items, both European and ancient Oriental. Nearest station: Toranomon on the Ginza subway line. Open 10:00 A.M. to 4:00 P.M.

Ota Memorial Ukiyoe Museum. Harajuku; 403–0880. Collection of ukiyoe woodblock prints. Open 10:30 A.M. to 5:30 P.M. Closed Mon. and from 25th to end of each month.

Riccar Museum. 2–3–6, Ginza; 571–3254. Specializes in ukiyoe prints. Near-est station: Ginza on the Ginza subway line, the Marunouchi subway line, and the Hibiya subway line. Open 10:00 A.M. to 6:00 P.M.

Seibu Art Museum. Seibu Department Store, 12th fl., Ikebukuro; 981–0111.

Seiji Togo Museum. Nishi Shinjuku; 349–3080.

Striped House Museum. Roppongi; 405–8108.

Suntory Art Museum. 1–2–3 Moto Akasaka, Minato-ku; 470–1073. In the Suntory Building, this museum features articles from the Edo and Muromachi periods. Nearest station: Akasaka-Mitsuke, on the Ginza subway line, the Marunouchi subway line, and the Hanzomon subway line. Open 10:00 A.M. to 5:00 P.M.

Tokyo Central Museum of Arts. Ginza, Boeki Bldg., 5th fl.; 564–0711.

Tokyo Metropolitan Art Museum. Ueno Park; 823–6921. The museum often stages temporary exhibitions of contemporary art. See also Museums introduc-tion. Open 9:00 A.M. to 4:00 P.M.

Tokyo Metropolitan Teien Museum. Meguro-dori, Meguro-ku; 265–2111. Opened as a museum in 1983, the building used to be the mansion of a prince. Designed by a French architect, it is in art-deco style and still has many original fittings. Since the war it has been used as a guest house for foreign dignitaries. Now it features changing exhibitions, many of them brought for limited periods from overseas. Sculptures in the garden. Nearest station: Meguro on JNR Yamanote line. Hours and closing dates are irregular. Call for information.

Tokyo National Museum. Ueno Park; 822–1111. Houses more than 86,000 items, many of them designated National Treasures. It is the largest museum in Japan. See also Museums introduction. Open 9:00 A.M. to 4:00 P.M.

Ueno Royal Museum. (Ueno no Mori Bijutsukan) Ueno Park; 833–4191.

Yamatane Art Museum. 2–30 Kabuto-cho, Nihonbashi, Chuo-ku; The only museum in the world dedicated specially to Japanese paintings, including pastel-type Nihon-ga, of the last 100 years. Art Academy member Architect Taniguchi designed the interior. Nearest station: Kayabacho, on the Hibiya subway line and the Tozai subway line. Open 11:00 A.M. to 5:00 P.M.

PHOTO GALLERIES

Canon Salon. Ginza; 571–7358. Closed Sunday.

Contax Salon. Harajuku; 400–2651. Closed Sunday.

Fuji Photo Salon. Sukiyabashi; 571–9411. Closed Sunday.

Konishiroku Photo Gallery. Shinjuku, 320–4460. Closed Sunday.

Nikon Salon Ginza. Closed Monday.

Nikon Salon Shinjuku. 344–0565. Closed Monday.

Pentax Forum. Shinjuku; 348–2941. Open daily.

Photo Gallery International. Toranomon; 501–9123. Closed Sunday and holidays.

Polaroid Gallery. Toranomon; 434–5201. Closed Saturday, Sunday, and holidays.

Zeit Foto Salon. Nihonbashi; 246–1370. Closed Sunday.

DEPARTMENT STORE GALLERIES

Daimaru. Tokyo Sta.; 212–8011. Closed Wednesdays.

Isetan. Shinjuku; 352–1111. Closed Wednesdays.

Keio. Shinjuku; 341–2111. Closed Thursdays.

Matsuya. Ginza; 567–1211. Closed Thursdays.

Matsuzakaya. Ginza; 572–1111. Closed Thursdays.

Matsuzakaya. Ueno; 832–1111. Closed Wednesdays.

Mitsukoshi. Nihonbashi; 241–3311. Closed Mondays.

Odakyu. Shinjuku; 342–8416. Close Thursdays.

Seibu. Ikebururo; 981–0111. Closed Thursdays.

Shibuya Seibu. Shibuya; 462–0111.

Takashimaya. Nihonbashi; 211–4111. Closed Wednesdays.

Tobu. Ikebukuro; 981–2111. Closed Wednesdays.

Tokyo Nihonbashi. 211–0511. Closed Thursdays.

Tokyu Toyoko. Shibuya; 477–3111. Closed Thursdays.

STAGE. The following are Tokyo's principal theaters for traditional shows: **Ginza Nohgakudo.** 6–5–15 Ginza, Chuo-ku; 571–3872 or 571–0197. Noh and Kyogen. **Hosho Suidobashi Nohgakudo.** 1–5–9 Hongo, Bunkyo-ku; 811–4843. Noh and Kyogen. **Kabuki-za.** 4–12–15 Ginza, Chuo-ku; 541–3131. Usually stages Kabuki. **Kanze Kaikan.** 1–16–4 Shoto, Shibuya-ku; 469–5241. Stages Noh and Kyogen. **Kita Nohgakudo.** 4–6–9 Kami-osaki, Shinaga-wa-ku. 491–7773. Noh and Kyogen. **Kokuritsu Gekijo.** The National Theater, 4–1 Hayabusa, Chiyoda-ku; 265–7411. Stages shows of different types, including dances and Bunraku. **Umewaka Nohgakudo.** 2–16–14 Higashi-Nakano, Naka-no-ku; 363–7748. Noh and Kyogen. **Yarai Nohgakudo.** 60 Yarai-cho, Shinjuku-ku; 268–7311. Noh and Kyogen. The new *National Noh Theater* is at 4–18–1 Sendagaya, Shibuya-ku; 423–1313. Reached from Sendagaya Station on the Sobu line.

MUSIC. Scarcely a night passes in Tokyo without a concert somewhere, and nearly all are well attended. Japan's own soloists and ensembles vie for attention with visiting foreign performers. There are several symphony orchestras of varying degrees of excellence in Tokyo. Best known are the following. Give them a call if you wish to have a seasonal program mailed to you, or to reserve seats for a single concert or a series. Usually someone at the other end of the phone speaks English. The **Japan Philharmonic Orchestra,** 354–9011, the **New Japan Philharmonic,** 501–5639; the **Tokyo Metropolitan Symphony,** 822–0726; the **Tokyo Philharmonic,** 591–6742; the **Yomiuri Nippon Symphony,** 270–6191; the **NHK Symphony Orchestra,** 443–0271. Individual tickets cost from ¥2,000 to ¥5,000. Prices will be very much higher in the case of distinguished visiting foreign artists.

Foreign orchestras, opera companies, ballet troups, ensembles, and solo artists are constantly coming to Tokyo, usually in the fall and winter seasons. Leading American and European organizations, including Soviet groups, make frequent tours. There are also famed jazz, popular, and novelty performers from time to time. Occasionally, foreign artists work as guest performers or conductors with Japanese musical groups.

Tickets to the best concerts are quickly sold out. The best method is to get them about two weeks in advance at any of Tokyo's several *Play Guides*—ticket offices that handle reservations for every imaginable sort of event. Many of the major department stores have *Play Guides* on the first floor or in the basement.

Tokyo's best concert halls are the following: **Bunka Kaikan.** Tokyo Festival Hall, 5–45 Ueno Park, Daito-ku; 828–2111. There is a small hall on the second floor of the same building. It has the same telephone number. **Hibiya Kokaido.** Hibiya Public Hall, 1–3 Hibiya-Park, Chiyoda-ku; 591–6388. **Iino Hall.** 7th floor Iino Building, 2–1–1 Uchisaiwai-cho, Chiyoda-ku; 506–3251. **Koseinenkin Kaikan.** 19 Banshu-cho, Shinjuku-ku; 356–1111. The small hall, with the same telephone number, is in the basement. **NHK Hall.** 2–2–1 Jinnan, Shibuya-ku; 465–1111. **Nihon Seinenkan.** 15 Kasumigaoka-machi, Shinjuku-ku; 401–0101. **Toranomon Hall.** 3–2–3 Kasumigaseki, Chiyoda-ku; 580–1251. **Yubinchokin Hall.** 13, Shiba Park, Minato-ku; 433–7211.

TOKYO SHOPPING. Shopping in Tokyo can be either delightful and fruitful or bewildering to the tourist. The trick is to know about yourself—what you want to buy and how much time you have at your disposal. Does your shopping list contain the names of specific items or does it just have names of persons for whom you want to buy "something" as a gift? Does your schedule allow for shopping only a couple of hours on just one day or do you have two or three days or a week? And, how much confidence do you have in moving around Tokyo? Plan your shopping foray in accordance with your answers to these questions and you can be sure of a successful expedition.

The person who has little time should stick to the hotel arcades or department stores and one-stop shopping centers. These are easy to locate, so you won't waste hours finding them. And, they stock a fair variety of items, ranging from folkcraft items and tourist souvenirs to the latest electronic products. If you don't have anything specific on your mind, these are the places to browse around to look for something that would be suitable as a gift for any person on your list.

If you have little time but you have one or two specific items you want to buy, such as lacquerware or a camera, you should head straight for one of the many specialty shops mentioned below, where the range of choice is wide.

If you have plenty of time and want to make the best buy possible, whether you are looking for a specific article or just something suitable, it might be a good idea to spend the first couple of hours browsing through a department store or a one-stop shopping center, noting the choices, quality, and prices. Then, go to a specialty store or one of the many centers where store after store specializes in the same product and where some bargaining is possible, such as *Akihabara* for electric appliances and electronic gadgets, *Asakusabashi* for dolls, *Harajuku* for boutiques and fashion goods, *Kanda* for books, or *Asakusa* for a slice of old Japan and articles that are out-and-out Japanese.

To go to stores outside your hotel, the most efficient and least time-consuming means of transport is generally the subway or the Japanese National Railways (JNR) trains. Taxis could be frustrating because roads are congested and sometimes traffic crawls slower than you can walk. (For information on Tokyo's transport system, pick up "Tour Companion," a giveaway weekly, at the counter of your hotel or airline.)

One final note: Most of the small stores do not have anyone who can speak English. If you need to call for information, have someone who can speak Japanese do it for you.

HOTEL ARCADES

Most of the hotels have shopping arcades, which have a number of obvious advantages. For one, the stores offer the range of articles that tourists usually purchase. You don't have to worry about transportation and waste time walking around the streets with a map in hand. The clerks speak English and the shops are branches of reputable and well-established stores, not only of Tokyo but also of Kyoto and other places. The prices in an arcade shop are the same as in its main store.

The **Imperial Hotel Arcade,** for example, in the basement of the Imperial Hotel, has *Mikimoto* and *Uyeda,* both big names in pearls, *Hanae Mori* boutique, and *Suga Camera,* in addition to stores dealing in antiques, ceramics, toys, ukiyo-e woodblock prints, watches, electronic products, and stationery, including Japanese-style greeting cards. The latest addition to the hotel is the **Imperial Plaza,** which houses 64 world-famous shops and boutiques, not only of Japan but also of France, Britain, Switzerland, Italy, and West Germany, including *Tasaki Pearls, Lanvin, Gucci, Celine,* and *Cartier.*

Hotel arcades invariably have a bookstore where foreign magazines and books on Japan are available. Many hotel arcade shops are open throughout the year, including Sundays.

ONE-STOP SHOPPING

International Arcade (501–5774), one of Tokyo's biggest bargain centers, is only a few steps from the Imperial Hotel. It houses a number of tax-free shops, most of which are stores of well-established Tokyo companies and all of which specialize in Japanese products that are proven favorites of tourists. They deal in quality name brands.

Tax-free prices and, in some cases, additional discounts are available. Clerks are multilingual and communication is no problem. A great variety of items from pearls and cameras to sophisticated electronic gear, kimono, and small souvenirs for the youngsters is available. The International Arcade is open from 9:30 A.M. to 7:00 P.M. daily. Two of the shops are:

Hayashi Kimono (501–4014). Has a huge stock of kimono, both for men and women, plus obi and items such as happi coats and tablecloths made of kimono and obi fabric to suit the Western taste. Used, but clean and good-as-new, high quality obi and gorgeous wedding kimono can be had at a fraction of what they cost new.

Sun-Dry Camera (501–5774). Specializes in electronic goods, cameras, Canon and Nikon lenses, filters, tripods, and other camera equipment as well as pocket calculators. Overseas shipping service is available from 9:30 A.M. to 7:00 P.M. daily.

Japan Taxfree Center, 5-8-6 Toranomo, Minato-ku (432–4341), is conveniently located—within walking distance of Hotel Okura and about 50 meters from the Kamiya-cho Station on the Hibiya subway line. Its eight-story building catches the eye as soon as you surface from the subway. It has pearls and accessories on the 1st floor, kimono and dolls on the 2nd, watches and china-ware on the 3rd, handicrafts and gift items on the 4th, electric appliances and toys on the 5th, and cameras and a one-hour photo printing service on the 6th. There is also a cozy cafeteria on the 7th floor to rest your tired feet. Open 9:30 A.M.–5:30 P.M. daily throughout the year except on Wednesdays between December 1 to February 28.

Sukiyabashi Shopping Center (571–8027/8), across the road from the International Arcade, houses many stores selling apparel, fabrics, sporting goods, cameras, jewelry, pearls, Japanese sweets, books, etc. The center also has coffee shops, restaurants, and snack stands under its roof. Patronized almost entirely by ordinary Japanese consumers. Open 10:00 A.M.–8:30 P.M. daily throughout the year.

Nikkatsu Shopping Arcade, in Hibiya Park Building at a corner of the Hibiya intersection, is small but has a number of attractive stores selling popular tourist items. Most store hours in the arcade are 9:00 A.M. to 7:00 P.M., although some stores close at 6:00 P.M.

TOC (Tokyo Oroshiuri Center) is about 10 minutes walk from Gotanda Station of JNR Yamanote Loop Line or of the Toei Asakusa-sen subway line. Surfacing from the subway station you will come out on wide Sakurada Dori. Take that wide road, crossing the overhead railway tracks and crossing Meguro River. You will soon find a giant sign "TOC" on top of a big building ahead on the right-hand side. TOC is a consumer's heaven, housing what seems like hundreds of wholesale dealers, many of whom sell directly to individuals. There is not much glamour in the merchandise available, but TOC is one of the few places in Tokyo where you can drive a hard bargain on already discounted merchandise. Shops here sell furniture, furs, accessories, watches, jewelry, Chinese fans, ready-to-wear apparel for men, women, and children, and a lot more.

DEPARTMENT STORES

If your shopping time is limited and if your shopping list contains a variety of items or if you are undecided about what to buy, the most convenient place to go is a department store. Big department stores are found in all the subcenters of Tokyo.

Ginza-Nihonbashi Area

Ginza is Japan's most celebrated quality shopping district. There are almost a dozen big department stores in this area, all fronting Chuo-dori Ave., popularly called Ginza Street.

Mitsukoshi in Nihonbashi (241–3311), the oldest in Japan, is at Mitsukoshimae Station of the Ginza subway line. It is *the* prestige store. A number of big-name boutiques are located here, such as *Balenciaga, Givenchy, Celine, Chanel, Bartolo Bartolomei, Oscar de la Renta,* and *Dunhill.* The store is noted for its stock of kimono and obi materials and fine selection of ceramics, lacquerware, and chinaware. Open 10:00 A.M.–6:00 P.M. Closed on Mondays.

Takashimaya (211–4111), a short distance from the Ginza-side exit of Nihonbashi Station on the Ginza subway line, is modern and one of the largest in Japan, famous for its high quality merchandise, especially its excellent kimono section. It boasts a floor layout that makes shopping very easy. The folkcraft section on the 7th floor offers both Japanese and imported articles and is a must for tourists. Its fashion section features *Chanel, Laroche, Courreges, Givency, Lanvin, Celine, Boucheron, Dunhill, Louis Vuitton, Gucci,* and *Salvadore Ferrogamo.* It also features famous Japanese fashion designers such as Jun Ashida, Yuki Torii, Issey Miyake, Kansai Yamamoto and Kenzo Takada. The curio section in the 1st basement is one of the most popular haunts of Tokyo's foreign residents. There is a special corner devoted to old textiles. This is the only department store in Japan that sells Rosenthal chinaware. Open 10:00 A.M.–6:00 P.M. daily; 10:00 A.M.–6:30 P.M. on Fridays and Saturdays. Closed on Wednesdays.

Tokyu (211–0511), located between Takashimaya and Mitsukoshi and closer to Nihombashi Station, has a popular image and is preferred by the ordinary housewife. Prices are moderate. Its furniture section has a good stock of Swedish furniture of Ikeya brand. Open 10:00 A.M.–6:00 P.M.; 6:30 P.M. on Saturdays, Sundays, and national holidays. Closed on Thursdays.

Mitsukoshi (562–1111), at a corner of the Ginza 4-chome intersection of Chuo-dori and Harumi-dori. One of the branches of Mitsukoshi, this one is oriented to young people. Open 10:00 A.M.–6:00 P.M. Closed on Mondays.

Matsuzakaya (572–1111), located one block toward Shimbashi from Ginza 4-chome intersection, is one of the oldest department stores in Japan and has a good kimono fabric section. Open 10:00 A.M.–6:00 P.M. daily; 6:30 P.M. on Sundays. Closed on Wednesdays.

Matsuya (567–1211), located one block toward Nihonbashi from Ginza 4-chome intersection and just above Ginza Station of the Ginza subway line. A very popular store among male and female salaried workers. Prices are moderate and store layout makes shopping easy. It is known for its good stock of household accessories as well as folkcraft items and play things native to various parts of Japan. Open 10:00 A.M.–6:00 P.M. daily, but until 6:30 P.M. on Saturdays and Sundays. Closed on Thursdays.

Wako (562–2111), at a corner of Ginza 4-chome intersection opposite Mitsukoshi. Strictly speaking this does not fall in the category of either department store or specialty store. It has a high-class image like Saks Fifth Avenue in New York. Specializes in quality, high-priced, luxurious fashion items and accessories, including clothing. The glassware section is famous. It has what is probably the widest selection of Seiko-brand timepieces. Open 10:00 A.M.–5:30 P.M. Closed on Sundays and national holidays.

Yurakucho-Tokyo Station Area

Hankyu (573–2231), at the Sukiyabashi intersection over the Ginza Station of the Marunouchi subway line and opposite the Sony Building, is popular with young office girls working in the Ginza area. Large stock of medium-priced fashion goods and accessories. Open 10:00 A.M.–6:00 P.M. Closed on Thursdays.

Sogo (284–6711), adjacent to JNR Yurakucho Station, is the Tokyo branch of Sogo Department Store of Osaka. Popular with salaried men and women. Open 10:00 A.M.–6:00 P.M. daily, but until 6:30 P.M. on Fridays and Saturdays. Closed on Thursdays.

Daimaru (212–8011), in JNR Tokyo Station Building, is the Tokyo branch of the famous chain originating in the Kansai region surrounding Osaka. Popular with men because it has a good men's wear section. Open 10:00 A.M.–6:00 P.M. Closed on Wednesdays.

Printemps Ginza (433–9300/9301), two minutes from Yurakucho Station, specializes in French products. Open 10:00 A.M. to 6:00 P.M. daily except Wednesday.

Seibu and **Hankyu,** one minute from Yurakucho Station opens in fall 1984.

Shinjuku Area

Shinjuku is one of Tokyo's many subcenters and is a city in itself. It is the terminal of three interurban private railways lines—Odakyu, Keio, and Seibu.

Isetan (352–1111), less than 5 minutes walk from JNR Shinjuku Station and just above Shinjuku Sanchome Station of the Marunouchi subway line, is contemporary and Western-oriented, which makes it popular with the young people. Its atmosphere is more casual than that of the dignified Mitsukoshi or the sophisticated Takashimaya. It has one building exclusively for men's goods and a very good furniture and interior section. Open 10:00 A.M.–6:00 P.M. daily, but until 6:30 P.M. on Saturdays, Sundays, and national holidays. Closed on Wednesdays.

Mitsukoshi (354–1111), across the street from Isetan, is a branch of Mitsukoshi in Nihonbashi and is good for casual shopping. Open 10:00 A.M.–6:00 P.M. Closed on Mondays.

Odakyu (342–1111) is conveniently located in the Shinjuku Station building and a short distance from Shinjuku Station of the Marunouchi subway line. It is known for its cosmetics section on the 1st floor where special cosmetics for delicate and sensitive skin are available. A separate building known as Odakyu Halc building specializes in furniture and interior goods. Open 10:00 A.M.–6:00 P.M. daily, but until 6:30 P.M. on Saturdays, Sundays, and national holidays. Closed on Thursdays.

Keio (342–2111) is conveniently located in the Shinjuku Terminal Bldg. Its policy is "simple life," and it sells only the essentials of life. Open 10:00 A.M.–6:00 P.M. daily, but until 6:30 P.M. on Fridays, Saturdays, and national holidays. Closed on Thursdays.

Shibuya Area

Considered a notch above Shinjuku in class, the Shibuya area is accessible by JNR Yamanote loop line, and the Ginza and Hanzomon subway lines.

Tokyu (477–3111) is about 10 minutes walk from the JNR Shibuya Station and Shibuya terminal of the Ginza subway line. This is an elegant store selling high-class merchandise. Spaciously laid out, the store makes shopping a leisurely pleasure. It offers attractive imported goods. Open 10:00 A.M.–6:00 P.M. daily, but until 6:30 P.M. on Saturdays, Sundays, and national holidays. Closed on Thursdays.

Toyoko (477–3111), in the Shibuya Terminal Building, is the sister store of Tokyu, and caters to the masses. Open 10:00 A.M.–6:00 P.M. daily, but until 6:30 P.M. on Saturdays, Sundays, and national holidays. Closed on Thursdays.

Seibu (462–0111), several minutes walk from JNR Shibuya Station, has a good stock of fashion apparel. Open 10:00 A.M.–6:00 P.M. daily, but until 6:30 P.M. on Saturdays, Sundays, and national holidays. Closed on Thursdays.

Parco (464–5111), several minutes walk from JNR Shibuya Station and near Seibu Department Store, is a department store housing fashionable specialty shops very popular with the young and Western-oriented. Open 10:00 A.M.–8:30 P.M. daily throughout the year.

Tokyu Hands (476–5461), near Parco, about 10 minutes walk from JNR Shibuya Station, is a specialty store and a paradise for do-it-yourself enthusiasts. It has a complete stock of handicraft, needlework, and sewing tools, gadgets, and materials as well as of paints, and carpentry tools and materials. The electronics parts section, the audio workshop, and the video center are musts for audiophiles. The store is known for its wide stock of scale models of trains, planes, ships, etc. Its fabric section is a must for those looking for fabrics, particularly indigo Chinese cotton fabric. Open 10:00 A.M.–8:00 P.M. Closed on the second and third Wednesdays of each month.

Ikebukuro Area

Seibu (981–0111), conveniently located in the Ikebukuro Terminal Building, has the largest floor space among all the department stores in Tokyo. Each floor is so long that a section has been set up in the middle of each floor where chairs are available for a short rest. Seibu has very good furniture and interior sections besides a good collection of chinaware, pottery, and lacquerware. Its Sports Center satisfies the equipment needs of enthusiasts of any sport. Open 10:00 A.M.–6:00 P.M. daily, but until 6:30 P.M. on Saturdays, Sundays, and national holidays. Closed on Thursdays.

Tobu (981–2211), located on the opposite side of Seibu in the Ikebukuro Terminal. It has a large stock of merchandise like a supermarket. Open 10:00 A.M.–6:00 P.M. daily, but until 6:30 P.M. on Saturdays and Sundays. Closed on Wednesdays.

Mitsukoshi (987–1111), a short distance from JNR Ikebukuro Station facing Seibu Department Store, is a branch of Mitsukoshi in Nihonbashi. Open 10:00 A.M.–6:00 P.M. Closed on Mondays.

Parco (981–2111), located next to Seibu Department Store, houses boutiques, apparel shops, accessory shops, and many other attractive stores. Open 10:00 A.M.–8:30 P.M. daily throughout the year.

Kichijoji Area

Kichijoji on the JNR Chuo Line is a newly emerging shopping and entertainment town very popular with young people. Many department stores have set up branches here: **Isetan** (0422–21–1111; closed on Wednesdays), Tokyu (0422–21–5111; closed on Thursdays), **Kintetsu** (0422–21–3331; closed on Tuesdays), and **Parco** (0422–21–8111, open 10:00 A.M.–8:00 P.M., may be closed on some Thursdays).

ELECTRONICS CENTERS—AKIHABARA, NISHI-GINZA

Akihabara is unexcelled for electronic goods. Store after store is packed to the ceiling with every imaginable article connected with electrical appliances. Here you get a panoramic glimpse of the entire range of Japanese electronics products—at greatly discounted prices. When you get off at Akihabara Station of the JNR Yamanote loop line or the Sobu line, you get the feeling of being in the middle of an electronics jungle.

In most of the smaller shops, very little, if any, English is spoken but that is not much of a problem because all the goods are there before your eyes, the prices are listed, and you can bargain with the aid of pencil and paper. The bigger shops housed in buildings several stories high are authorized to sell duty free and have clerks to attend to tourists. These include *Yamagiwa, X-One,*

LAOX, Onoden, Nishikawa Musen, and *Hirose Musen.* You can't miss them because they are big and display their names prominently.

Wholesalers and retailers deal in anything from the tiniest screws and bolts for electrical appliances to audio components and completely assembled stereo tape and phonograph consoles at prices that are apt to make the hungry addict from abroad lose his head.

Although it is probable that some items of Japanese audio gear can be bought in Hong Kong at somewhat lower prices, that colony has nothing like Akihabara's selection. Many of the items you'll find in Akihabara are sold in America under their importer's brand name, at much higher prices. Some of the equipment on sale in Akihabara may need adjustment for frequencies, voltage, and cycles in other countries. If you shop at a store offering duty-free goods, they will be able to tell you.

Nishi Ginza Electric Center (501–5905/5910), located across the road from the International Arcade, which is near the Imperial Hotel, houses a number of tax-free shops that specialize in audio/video equipment as well as electric and electronic appliances.

If you are a fan of a particular maker, you can go straight to the service shop or showroom maintained by the manufacturer. At most of these places, you can audition equipment in relative calm. *Matsushita Showroom,* Technics Ginza, Ginza Core Bldg., 7th Floor, 572–3871; *Sony Showroom Tokyo,* Sony Bldg., Sukiyabashi intersection, Ginza, 573–2371; *Sharp Showroom* 8-8 Ichigaya, Shinjuku-ku (near JNR Ichigaya Station), 260–1161; *Hitachi Showroom,* Hotel New Otani, 261–1701; *Toshiba Showroom,* Toshiba Tourist Corner, Dowa Bldg., 2–22 Ginza, Chuo-ku, 572–2331.

TOYS

Japan is one of the great toy manufacturing nations of the world, and you'll have no trouble finding gifts for the young. Mechanical toys are an especially good buy. The department stores all have large toy departments. *Kiddy Land,* on Omote Sando between Aoyama-dori and Meiji-dori, is a wonderland of toys, paper kites, Christmas and party decorations of all sorts. Electric trains are another good buy. Kiddy Land is open 10:00 A.M.–7:00 P.M. on weekdays, 10:00 A.M.–8:00 P.M. on Saturdays, Sundays, and national holidays. Closed on third Tuesday of each month. Address: 6–1–9 Jingumae; Shibuya-ku; 409–3431/5.

Tenshodo, on Harumi-dori between Chuo-dori and Sotobori-dori Ave., is famous for its HO gauge equipment. You can buy O gauge sets (same as the Lionel O gauge) as well as HO at department stores. Tenshodo is open 10:30 A.M.–7:00 P.M. and closed on Thursdays. Address: 4–3–9 Ginza; Chuo-ku; 561–0021/3.

Japanese folk toys are more popular with the old than the young these days, and make wonderful small, inexpensive presents to bring back home. At department stores or the shops listed under "Folkcrafts."

DOLLS CENTER—ASAKUSABASHI

You'll find doll shops in all the arcades and shopping centers, but for a much bigger selection try the department stores or, best of all, the area near Asakusabashi Station of the JNR Sobu Line where there are numerous stores specializing in dolls of a great variety. Among the biggest are Kyugetsu and Shugetsu at 1 Yanagibashi, Taito-ku, practically in front of Asakusabashi railway station. *Kyugetsu* (861–5511) is open from 9:00 A.M. to 5:00 P.M. throughout the year, while *Shugetsu* (861–8801), is open daily from 10:00 A.M. to 6:30 P.M. all the year-round.

A small but charming doll shop in the Ginza area is *Kabuki-ya,* just next to the Kabuki-za theater (543–4297). This shop specializes in Ichimatsu-ningyo—little-boy and little-girl dolls. The store is open every day, Sundays and national holidays included, from 10:30 A.M. to 7:00 P.M.

HARAJUKU FOR YOUTHFUL FASHION

Harajuku is the classy district centering around the intersection of Meiji-dori and Omote-sando avenues near JNR Harajuku Station. The district has a tradition of being Western-oriented because of the close proximity of what was once a huge family housing complex of the American occupation forces and later the Olympic Village during the Tokyo Olympic Games. Thus, there are many shops here designed to satisfy foreign tastes in souvenirs, chinaware, brass, lamps, lanterns, furniture, toys, and silverware. Always keeping a step ahead of the times, Harajuku today caters to the most progressive sector of Japanese youth. Numerous boutiques in this section include *Hanae Mori Boutique* (400–3301), which occupies the 1st and 2nd floors of Hanae Mori Building at 3–1–6 Kita-Aoyama. The boutique is open 11:00 A.M.–7:00 P.M. daily throughout the year.

BOOKS—KANDA-JIMBOCHO

No book lover should leave Tokyo without taking a stroll along Yasukuni-dori, the famous street in the Kanda-Jimbocho district of Chiyoda ward, where close to 100 secondhand bookstores are packed eave to eave. You'll find books from all over the world here, and the determined bibliophile will often unearth a real find.

Many of the secondhand bookstores specialize in a particular discipline ranging from art and history to technology and medicine. Below is a listing of some of the notable stores:

Sanseido, 1–1 Kanda-Jimbocho, Chiyoda-ku; 233–3312. This store does not sell secondhand books, but it is the centerpiece of this district. On its seven floors, Sanseido has Japan's largest stock of current books and magazines, both Japanese and foreign. Located on Yasukuni-dori Ave. near the Surugadai-shita intersection, it is 2 minutes walk from Jimbocho Station of the Toei (municipal) Mita and Shinjuku subway lines. Open 10:00 A.M.–6 P.M. daily from December to end of May. Closed on Tuesdays from June to November.

Isseido, 1–7 Kanda-Jimbocho, Chiyoda-ku; 292–0071/6. This store has art books new and old, and out-of-print Orientalia. Open 9 A.M.–6:30 P.M. Closed on Sundays.

Kitazawa, 2–5 Kanda-Jimbocho, Chiyoda-ku; 263–0011. This store has new foreign books, old books, and rare books. Open 10:00 A.M.–6:00 P.M. Closed on Sundays.

Matsumara, 1–7 Kanda Jimbocho, Chiyoda-ku; 291–2410. This store has many secondhand foreign books on Japan. Open 10:00 A.M.–6:00 P.M. daily. Closed on Sundays and on rainy national holidays.

Ohya Shobo, 1–1 Kanda-Jimbocho, Chiyoda-ku; near Sanseido bookstore; 291–0062. This is a reputable store dealing in old Japanese illustrated books, Ukiyo-e prints, Nagasaki-e prints, Yokohama-e prints, old maps, and Japanese graphic art books. The store has its name written in English and has a large Kabuki picture board above its entrance. Can't be missed. Open 10:00 A.M.–6:30 P.M., closed on Sundays and national holidays.

Shogakudo Shoten, at the far end of the secondhand bookstore row from Sanseido; 262–0908. You can buy foreign language books published in Japan in this store. Open 10:00 A.M.–7:00 P.M. on weekdays. Closed on Sundays.

Major bookstores selling new books, besides Sanseido, are:

Charles E. Tuttle, 1–3 Kanda Jimbocho, Chiyoda-ku; 291–7071/2. An old Vermont firm that runs a publishing house in Tokyo. Current books on Japan at their shop near Sanseido. Open 10 A.M.–6 P.M. Closed on Sundays and national holidays.

Shosen Grande, a multistory bookstore, a few steps from Sanseido, sells only current volumes; 295–0011. Open 10:30 A.M.–6:50 P.M. on weekdays and 10:30 A.M.–6:20 P.M. on Sundays and weekdays. Closed on some Mondays depending on the month. About 50 meters away is its sister store, Shosen Book Mart (294–0011), whose business hours are the same as Shosen Grande, but it may be closed on some Wednesdays.

For new foreign-language books and magazines, Maruzen in Nihonbashi 2-chome across Chuo-dori from Takashimaya Department Store in the Ginza district; 272–7211. Open 10:00 A.M.–6:00 P.M., closed on Sundays. Maruzen has a branch near JNR Ochanomizu Station in Chiyoda district; 295–5581. Open 10:00 A.M.–6:00 P.M., closed on Sundays. Jena is on Harumi-dori near the Ginza 4-chome intersection; 571–2980. Open 10:30 A.M.–7:50 P.M.; closed on national holidays. Yosho Biblos, 4th floor, F.I. Bldg., in front of Takadanobaba Station; 200–4531. Open 10:30 A.M.–7:30 P.M. on weekdays; 11:00 A.M.–6:30 P.M. on Sundays and national holidays; closed on the third Sunday of each month. and Kinokuniya in Shinjuku, between JNR Shinjuku Station and Isetan Department Store. (10:00 A.M.–7:00 P.M. Tel: 354–0131, closed 1st and 3rd Wednesdays).

CAMERAS AND OPTICAL GOODS

Camera shops are all over the city. The best places to buy are the tax-free shops and the huge discount stores that specialize in cameras, including the products of the top names in the industry.

Camera manufacturers' showrooms are *Asahi Kogaku (Pentax), Service Center,* 8 Ginza Nishi, Chuo-ku; 571–5621. *Canon,* behind Matsuzakaya Department Store, 5 Ginza Chuo-ku; 571–7388, open 9:00 A.M.–5:30 P.M. *Minolta,* Kawase Bldg., 3rd Floor, Shinjuku-ku; 356–6281, open 10:00 A.M.–6:00 P.M. *Nihon Kogaku (Nikon),* Mitsubishi Bldg. opposite Central Post Office, 2 Marunouchi Chiyoda-ku; 215–0561, open 9:00 A.M.–5:00 P.M. *Olympus Kogaku,* Ryumeikan Bldg., 6th Floor, Kanda-Ogawacho, Chiyoda-ku; 255–2425, open 9:00 A.M.–6:00 P.M.

Convenient and representative camera shops that are accustomed to dealing with tourists are, in the Ginza district, *Sundry Camera* in International Arcade (501–5774), *Igarashi Camera* in Sanshin Building not far from Imperial Hotel (591–4919), *Hero Camera* inside Sony Building at Sukiyabashi intersection (561–8361), and *Ginza Orient Camera Center* in Ginza 8-chome (574–6121). *Ohba Camera* is in Shimbashi 1-chome (591–0070).

Yodobashi Camera and Doi are huge discount stores on Nishiguchi (west entrance) side of JNR Shinjuku Station.

Yodobashi Camera, Nishi-Shinjuku, Shinjuku-ku; 346–1010. The biggest discount store in Japan, it has a stock of about 30,000 kinds of camera and accessories, representing about 100 leading makers. It sells 500 to 600 cameras daily on weekdays and about 1,000 on Sundays and national holidays. It has small cameras on the 1st floor, medium and large-sized cameras on the 2nd floor, and films on the 3rd floor. Open 10:00 A.M.–8:00 P.M. daily throughout the year.

Doi, Dai-ni Seiko Bldg., Nishi-Shinjuku, Shinjuku-ku; 344–2310. Near Keio Plaza Hotel, this store has compact cameras, exchangeable lenses, strobes on the 1st floor and darkroom equipment, medium-sized and large cameras on the 2nd floor. Open 9:00 A.M.–8:30 P.M. daily throughout the year.

Contact lenses figure among Japan's bargains. A specialist who makes appointments with foreigners by telephone (241–6166) is *Hoya Contact Lens Clinic,* 1–6 Nihonbashi-Muromachi, Chuo-ku; Amano Shika (dental clinic) Bldg., 9th floor, which is open 10:00 A.M.–7:00 P.M. on weekdays, 10:00 A.M.–6:00 P.M. on national holidays. Closed on second and third Sundays. Another such specialist is *International Vision Center,* 3 Kita-Aoyama, Minato-ku; 497–1491. Open 10:00 A.M.–7:00 P.M. on weekdays and closed on Sundays and some national holidays.

WATCHES

Wako, Ginza 4-chome intersection of Chuo-dori and Harumidori and nearby Nippondo; 562–2111. This store carries a selection of the best watches of both Japanese and foreign makes, and most of the hotels have a *Seiko* store in their shopping arcades. Wako is open 10:00 A.M.–5:30 P.M. on weekdays and closes on Sundays and national holidays. Tel: 562–2111. *Nippondo,* 5–7 Ginza, Chuo-ku; 571–5511. Open 10:00 A.M.–9:00 P.M. daily throughout the year.

PEARLS

The list below is by no means exhaustive, and there are many other fine pearl dealers in Tokyo.

K. Uyeda is one of Tokyo's leading jewelry and silver dealers. Japanese and South Sea pearls. In the Imperial Hotel Arcade and in his own shop opposite the Imperial Hotel; 503–2587/9. In business since 1884, and absolutely reliable, as are the other shops in our very selective list. The Imperial Hotel Arcade shop is open from 10:00 A.M. to 7:00 P.M. on weekdays, but from 10:30 A.M. to 5:30 P.M. on Sundays and national holidays.

Mayuyama, noted jeweler. Some of the finest pearls find their way to Mayuyama, then to distinguished customers throughout the world. Very elegant. In the Imperial Hotel Arcade; 591–6655. Open 10:00 A.M.–7:00 P.M. on weekdays but 10:00 A.M.–5:00 P.M. on Sundays and national holidays.

Kuki, owned by Mr. Kuki, former New York manager of Mikimoto, is one of Tokyo's reliable pearl jewelers. In the International Arcade; 501–5675. Open 10:00 A.M.–7:00 P.M. daily, but 10:00 A.M.–6:00 P.M. on Sundays and national holidays.

Mikimoto 4–5–5 Ginza, Chuo-ku; 535–4611. The great Mikimoto Kokichi is the "Pearl King" who discovered the secret of making cultured pearls. The main Mikimoto store, the first in the world to deal exclusively in pearls, is on the Chuo-dori several buildings away from Wako at Ginza 4-chome intersection and diagonally opposite Matsuya Department Store. Open 10:30 A.M.–6:00 P.M. Closed on Wednesdays.

Takashima Shinju specializes in giant South Sea pearls cultivated in the tropical waters of Southeast Asia. Opposite Atago police station near Shiba Park. 432–1601. Open 9:30 A.M.–5:30 P.M. on weekdays; closed on Sundays and national holidays.

Okubo, in Imperial Hotel Arcade; 504–0088. One of the oldest dealers in Japan. Open 9:30 A.M.–7:00 P.M. daily, but 9:30 A.M.–5:00 P.M. on national holidays.

H. Ono, 6–5–10 Ginza, Chuo-ku; 571–6788. Within walking distance from the Imperial Hotel, this store keeps a selection of unusually designed brooches and bracelets.

Matoba and Co., main store in the Nikkatsu Arcade; 271–2170. Has a good variety and will accept mail orders. Shop here for tins of oysters with cultured pearls inside—fun souvenirs. Open 9:30 A.M.–6:00 P.M. on weekdays but 9:30 A.M.–5:00 P.M. on national holidays. Closed on Sundays.

Tasaki Shinju, 1–3–3 Akasaka, Minato-ku; 584–0904/5. Halfway between NCR Building and Tameike intersection in Akasaka, this store has a large selection of cultured pearls, freshwater pearls, etc. Open 9:00 A.M.–6:00 P.M. daily throughout the year.

SILVER

K. Uyeda in the Imperial Hotel Arcade, and Uyeda's own shop, opposite Imperial Hotel Annex; 591–8501. The oldest and best known silver dealer in Tokyo. A reliable firm, all work guaranteed. (See also Pearls.) *Miyamoto Shoko* is another old, well-established firm. Located in Asahi Building at Ginza 6-chome on Namiki-dori street near Mikasa Kaikan restaurant complex; 573–3011. Open 9:30 A.M.–5:30 P.M. on weekdays; closed on Sundays and national holidays.

CLOISONNÉ AND DAMASCENE

Ando, 5–6–2 Ginza, Chuo-ku; 572–2261. The largest and best known cloisonné dealer in Tokyo in Ginza 5-chome on Harumi-dori, one block west of Chuo-dori from Ginza 4-chome intersection. Open 9:00 A.M.–5:30 P.M. daily except Sundays and national holidays.

Inaba Kogei Katsura, branch shop of the noted Kyoto manufacturer Inaba Kogei, is on the second floor of Sukiyabashi Shopping Center; 571–8071. Open 10:00 A.M.–7:30 P.M. daily throughout the year, but it may be closed on some Sundays.

Amita is Japan's leading damascene maker on the second floor of the Sukiyabashi Shopping Center; 571–3274. Cigarette lighters, compacts, jewelry, and a fine selection of pearls. Open 10:00 A.M.–6:00 P.M. daily throughout the year.

IVORY

Hodota in the Imperial Hotel Arcade; 580–6056. *Kitagawa,* on Omote-sando opposite the entrance to Meiji Park; 504–1111. Open 9:30 A.M.–7:00 P.M. weekdays; 10:00 A.M.–5:00 P.M. Sundays and national holidays. *Sunamoto,* opposite the Imperial Hotel's newly opened Imperial Tower; 591–5610. Sunamoto is open 9:45 A.M.–6 P.M. on weekdays and 10:30 A.M.–6:00 P.M. on Sundays and national holidays.

LACQUER

Yamada Heiando, 3–10–11 Nihonbashi, Chuo-ku; 272–2871. Makes lacquer by appointment to the Imperial Household, and ranks as tops in the field. Their work is exquisite, and prices are high. On street behind Takashimaya, a block north of Yaesu-dori Ave., and about five minutes walk from Nihonbashi Station on Ginza subway line. Open 9:00 A.M.–6:00 P.M.; closed on Sundays and national holidays.

Kuroeya, 1–2 Nihonbashi, Chuo-ku; 271–3356. An old Ginza firm where discerning Japanese have shopped for years. It sells everything from lacquer furniture to chopsticks. On Chuo-dori between Eitai-dori Ave. and Nihonbashi bridge.

Inachu Japan, 1–5–2 Akasaka, Minato-Ru; 582–4451. A newly opened store specializing in Wajima-nuri lacquerware. On sale is a vast range of high-quality lacquerware from such decorative items as jewelry boxes and flower stands to kitchenware and tableware. At Tameike intersection on Sotobori-dori St. on the same side as NCR Bldg. Open daily from 10:00 A.M. to 7:00 P.M. throughout the year.

BAMBOO

Department stores are a good place to find bamboo products, both in the household tableware department (trays, baskets, etc.) and in the flower-arranging sections (bamboo vases). *Nippon Craft Corner* on the 7th floor of Takashimaya Department Store in Nihonbashi is recommended.

PAPER AND PAPER PRODUCTS

Haibara, 2–7 Nihonbashi, Chuo-ku; 272–3801. In Nihonbashi opposite Tokyu Department Store is a venerable old firm dating back to 1803. Sells all kinds of handmade papers, wall paper, Christmas cards, fans. Open 9:30 A.M.–5:30 P.M. on weekdays, but closes at 5:00 P.M. on Saturdays. Closed on Sundays and national holidays.

Isetatsu. 2–18–9 Yanaka, Taito-ku; Top shop for lovely, reasonable paper things. (Sendagi stop on the Chiyoda subway line; walk up hill opposite the exit. Isetasu is 200 yards up on the right.)

Takumi for wonderful folkcraft papers, in sheets or made up into all sorts of fetching boxes, calendars, and placemats. Shimbashi, near Hotel Nikko; 571–2017.

Matsuya is a small tatami-floored shop that hides a wealth of glorious papers, both for Western walls and Japanese *fusuma* (sliding paper doors). Located on the willow-lined street one block west of Chuo-dori.

Washikobo, Roppongi, On the first floor of Yoshikawa Bldg., 1–8–10 Nishiazabu, Minato-ku; 405–1841. Paper craft in all its diversity. Open 10:00 A.M.–6:00 P.M. Closed on Sundays and national holidays. About 7–8 minutes walk from Roppongi Station on Hibiya subway line or about 10 minutes from Nogizaka Station on Chiyoda subway line.

The Gifu lanterns, handpainted with summery pastoral scenes, are daintier than other Japanese paper lanterns. If you have time to explore, a fun way to lantern shop is to make a trek out to the lantern and paper decoration wholesale shops in the Asakusa area. The shops below are easier to get to than those in Asakusa, and all specialize in lanterns and other typically Japanese products popular with foreigners.

Kiddy Land, 6–1–9 Jingumae, Shibuya-ku; 409–3431/5. On Omote Sando between Meiji and Aoyama streets, store is well stocked with paper lanterns as well as toys. Open 10:00 A.M.–7:00 P.M. on weekdays, 10:00 A.M.–8:30 P.M. on Saturdays, Sundays, and national holidays. Closed on third Tuesday of every month.

Shimura is on the same street as Kiddy Land. 6–3–9 Jingumae, Shibuya-ku; 400–6322. They have kites, big fireplace fans, butterfly paper, bamboo and shoji screens, other household accessories. Paper umbrellas for the hand and the giant processional umbrellas, about 7 feet in diameter, ideal for garden or beach. Open 9:30 A.M.–8:00 P.M. Closed on Thursdays.

Wafudo, first floor of the Marubiru Arcade. (See Folkcraft.)

Wataroku, 2–5–9 Shinjuku, Shinjuku-ku; 354–3658. Store has been in business since 1918, specializing in writing family names and store names on *chochin* paper lanterns, and making small flags. It sells a great variety of paper lanterns, flags, and *tenugui* cotton towels. Open 8:30 A.M.–6:30 P.M. every day except

Sunday and national holidays. One traffic signal toward Yotsuya from Isetan Department Store in Shinjuku.

FANS

There are many small fan shops along the Ginza and in the arcades. One of the leading Ginza fan shops is *Haibara,* 2–7 Nihonbashi, Chuo-ku; 272–3801. Noted for its fine paper products, it's located on Eitai-dori, opposite Tokyu Department Store. Haibara is open from 9:30 A.M. to 5:30 P.M. on weekdays, but from 9:30 A.M. to 5:00 P.M. on Saturdays. It is closed on Sundays and national holidays. Another shop is *Eiraido* 1–3 Nihonbashi, Chuo-ku; 271–8884. On Chuo-dori opposite Tokyu Department Store, it specializes in dance and Noh fans. It is open from 10:00 A.M. to 5:30 P.M. on weekdays but from around 1:00 P.M. to 5:30 P.M. on Sundays and national holidays.

STATIONERY

If you need a writing pad and envelopes to write letters to your friends at home, the best place to go is the stationery counter of any department store or to a stationery shop in your hotel arcade. For a great variety of stationery goods, both domestic and imported, go to *Ito-ya* in Ginza 2-chome near Matsuya Department Store; 2–7–15 Ginza, Chuo-ku; 561–8311. The multistory store on Chuo-dori opens from 9:30 P.M. to 6:00 P.M. on weekdays but from 10:00 A.M. to 6:00 P.M. on Sundays and national holidays.

Maruzen 2–3–10 Nihonbashi, Chuo-ku; 272–7211. Famous for its comprehensive book section, it has a good stationery section, too. Open 10:00 A.M.–5:30 P.M. on weekdays; closed on Sundays.

Bunshodo, 3–4–12 Ginza, Chuo-ku; 563–1511. Established in 1912, store deals principally in office supplies and business equipment. Bunshodo is behind Sumitomo Bank, which is diagonally across the Chuo-dori (Ginza Street) from Matsuya Department Store. Open 10:00 A.M.–5:00 P.M. from Monday through Friday, closes earlier at 4:00 P.M. on Saturdays. Closed on Sundays, national holidays, and first and third Saturdays.

Kyukyodo, next to the circular San-Ai Building at Ginza 4-chome intersection; 571–4429. A very old stationery shop doing business for more than 300 years. It sells Mt. Fuji picture postcards, writing implements, washi handmade paper and folkcrafts (inexpensive and packable), fans, ukiyo-e woodblock prints, prints by contemporary artists, miniature folding screens, photo albums, and much more. Open 10:00 A.M.–8:00 P.M. from Monday through Saturday and 11:00 A.M.–7:00 P.M. on Sundays and national holidays.

MASKS

Old Noh masks, and other dance masks dating further back into Japan's history, are prized works of art. The mask still plays an important role in Japanese theater, dance, and shrine festivals. Craftsmen have discovered that masks are also popular as decorative items in the home, and now turn them out in all sizes as well as in bizarre shapes. A shop that specializes in masks is *Ichy's,* 11–14, Minami-Aoyama 2-chome, Minato-ku; 401–2247. Open 10:30 A.M.–5:00 P.M., closed on Sundays and national holidays. In front of Meiji Memorial Hall wedding hall, Halfway between Aoyama-Itchome Station and Gaien-mae Station on Ginza subway line.

FURNITURE AND HOME FURNISHINGS

Department stores are the best place to shop for new tables and rattan furniture; antique and curio shops for old pieces.

Oriental Bazaar, 5–9–3 Jingumae, Shibuya-ku; 400–3933. A large establishment catering to Westerners. The taste level is considerably lower here, but the selection of lamps and shades is good. On Omote-Sando, between Aoyama-dori Ave. and Meiji-dori Ave. About 10 minutes walk from JNR Harajuku Station. Oriental-style building painted in vermilion. Open 9:30 A.M.–6:30 P.M. Closed on Thursdays.

An appealing shop is *Onoya* at 5–12–3 Ginza, diagonally across the road from Kabuki-za.

Fujiya, 2–2–15 Asakusa, Taito-ku; 841–2283. One of the very few shops specializing in *tenugui* Japanese-style cotton towels and *noren* divided curtains of varying lengths. Stocks more than 100 varieties of decorative towels of its own creation and design. Open 10:00 A.M.–8:00 P.M. every day except Thursday. One street to the right of the famous Nakamise shopping alley.

Bamboo window blinds, called *sudare,* are another interesting item of strictly Japanese home furnishing. They come in a wide range of styles, and ingenious decorators can often find a use for them in the Western home. Visit the department stores for *zabuton* and *sudare* shopping.

The shops and design centers listed in the Good Design section below, are also good places to shop for the latest in up-to-date home furnishings.

STONE LANTERNS

If you're feeling ambitious enough to cart one home, the best place to go is *Ishikatsu,* 3–4 Minami-Aoyama, Minato-ku; 401–1677. Stone lanterns and other garden ornaments. They will handle packing and shipping. Open 9:30 A.M.–5:00 P.M. except Sundays.

GOOD DESIGN, MODERN CRAFTS

Japan Industrial Design Center, a showroom for products of good design. On the 4th floor of Boeki (trade) Center Building at Hamamatsucho railway station; 435–5633. Open 10:00 A.M.–5:00 P.M. on weekdays, 10:00 A.M.–12 noon on Saturdays. Closed on Sundays and national holidays.

Also *Craft Center Japan,* third floor of Maruzen bookstore, on the Ginza. *Living Arts,* on Aoyama-dori Ave. between Omote-sando and Gaien-Higashi-dori Ave. *Matsuya Department Store,* the Good Design Corner on the 7th floor and the New Crafts Section on the 6th floor. (See Ginza-Nihonbashi Department Stores.) *Takashimaya Department Store.* Rosier Corner on the 7th floor. (See Ginza-Nihonbashi Department Store.)

TEXTILES

The most convenient may be the *Tokyo Kanebo* store, on the 5th floor of the Ginza Cygnas Bldg., at 3–5–2 Ginza; 562–2751. Open 11:00 A.M.–7:30 P.M.; closed third Wednesday of every month. Also *Toa,* at Udagawacho 23 in Shibuya-ku. They seem to have just about everything.

Tokyu Hands in Shibuya (see "Department Stores") has an excellent textile section on the fourth floor-A, with stress on cotton fabrics, including indigo dyed cotton from China.

Kyoto Silk in International Arcade; 501–4757. Store has one of the richest stocks of silk material in Tokyo. The fabrics on display are brought from its main store in Kyoto (established in 1895) and are less expensive than at other stores in Tokyo. Open 10:00 A.M.–6:00 P.M., year-round.

Teoriya, 2–8 Kanda-Ogawacho, Chiyoda-ku; 294–3903. Hand-dyed, hand-spinned, and handwoven fabrics made from natural materials are sold here. Open 11:00 A.M.–6:00 P.M. every day except Sunday, Monday, and national holidays. On the 2nd floor of Ogi Building close to Ogawacho Station of Shinjuku subway line and Shin-Ochanomizu Station of Chiyoda subway line.

SILK

A department store kimono department is a dazzling place, counter after counter piled high with rolls of material, no two alike. *Mitsukoshi Nihonbashi* and *Takashimaya* have the best kimono and obi materials.

The shops listed below all sell material in standard Western widths.

Kanebo is the Tokyo outlet for Japan's leading silk manufacturer where you can find almost any kind of silk in your mind. Kanebo has the Japan license for Dior. Also has branch shops in Okura, Palace, Capitol Tokyu, Imperial. See above for hours and address.

Moh Long, Imperial Hotel Arcade; 591–4012. Open 10:00 A.M.–7:00 P.M. on weekdays, 10:00 A.M.–5:00 P.M. on Sundays and national holidays.

Kawamura, 8–9–7 Ginza, on Chuo-dori, opposite Shiseido Parlor. Open 10:00 A.M.–7:30 P.M. daily throughout the year.

Yamatoya on the first floor of the Sukiyabashi Shopping Center. Open 10:00 A.M.–8:30 P.M. daily throughout the year.

Kogei Sotobori-dori Ave., same block as Hotel Nikko. One of the most interesting little shops in Tokyo. It sells cottons and wools as well as silk, and all its fabrics are hand-woven and hand-dyed. The atmosphere is definitely *shibui* (refined). Materials come in both Western and narrow kimono widths, and there is a large selection of upholstery and curtain fabrics.

Kyoto Silk has a branch in the International Arcade, Ginza; 501–4757. Yuzen prints, scarves, and everything else. Open 10:00 A.M.–6:00 P.M. daily throughout the year.

If you like bargain hunting and have the time to spare, the Asakusa wholesale textile district is fun. Best to have a guide, as the district is confusing. *Fujikake* is one of the biggest and best of the Asakusa shops. Fujikake is at 1–21 Kotobuki Taito-ku. 843–0021, 0026, 841–0217. On the street just off Kikuyabashi on Asakusa-dori Ave.

KIMONO AND OTHER JAPANESE WEAR

You'll find for-tourist-only kimono for sale in the arcade shops, particularly at *Nikko Shokai* (Palace Hotel) and in *Ichi-Fuji* on Ginza, opposite Theater Tokyo.

The best place to do real kimono-viewing is the department stores. Silk kimono prices start at about ¥ 100,000 and, unlike the tourist-only kimono, are made to order. Elaborate hand-dyed and embroidered kimono begin about ¥ 180,000 and go way up. Prices for first-rate *obi* are even more expensive.

If you want something fairly spectacular but aren't prepared to pay too much for it, the best thing is to buy a secondhand kimono. Takashimaya's second basement has a good selection of secondhand kimono and obi. Ingenious foreign women, incidentally, long ago discovered that obi, which are made of heavy silk or brocade, can be turned into handsome evening jackets, sheath dresses, or even used to upholster chairs.

Another popular place for secondhand kimono and obi shopping is the International Arcade, behind the Imperial Hotel. Several shops in the arcade sell both new and secondhand kimono, etc. The best is *K. Hayashi* (open 9:30 A.M.–7:00 P.M. daily throughout the year. 501–4014), which also has a branch shop in the Capitol Tokyu (open 9:00 A.M.–7:00 P.M. on weekdays but 9:30 A.M.–6:00 P.M. on Sundays and national holidays. 581–5015). Hayashi has a good collection of secondhand obi, and also of men's black silk formal kimono (discreet *mon*—family crests—on the shoulder and sleeves add to the elegance), which make handsome dressing gowns for men of distinction. Prices are reasonable.

Happi coats are standard tourist items, but it's not always so easy to get the genuine article. The International Arcade has them, and it also has heavy dark blue workmen's aprons.

Blue and White, at Juban in the Azabu district, makes the most attractive goodies out of *yukata* material.

To top your new kimono in proper style, maybe you'd like to buy a geisha wig, made up into a traditional Japanese hairdo. If so, the place to go is *Komachi,* at 2–6 Ginza, Chuo-ku; 561–1586. There you can splurge on a genuine geisha wig or be content with paper models. Either kind is grand for costume parties. Samurai wigs are available for gentlemen. Fans and traditional Japanese hair ornaments also sold here. Some of the combs and pins adapt beautifully to a Western chignon. Komachi is open from 9:30 A.M.–7:00 P.M.; closed Sundays.

To hold over yourself in the rain you need a *bangasa,* a Japanese umbrella made of oiled paper and bamboo. Two Asakusa shops specialize in bangasa, *mingeigasa* (traditional paper umbrellas), and umbrellas for Japanese dancing; *Inami Shoten* (open 8:00 A.M.–6:00 P.M., closed ono Sundays and national holidays. 10–14 Hanakawado, Taito-ku; 841–9524), and *Sekiguchi* (open 9:00 A.M.–5:30 P.M. Closed on Sundays and national holidays. Two minutes from Asakusa Station on Ginza subway line. near Matsuya Department Store in Asakusa. 1–10–13 Hanakawado, Taito-ku; 843–4647). Prices from ¥2,500.

KNITWEAR AND OTHER APPAREL FOR LADIES

The Japanese are making excellent knitwear these days, and it's becoming easier to find large foreign sizes in the shops. The *Mitsukoshi* and *Takashimaya* department stores (both in Nihonbashi) have a wide variety. *Isetan* at Shinjuku excels in summer fashions.

Ladies' fashion floors of big department stores in Tokyo are good places to have a dress or suit made to order. Each department store is affiliated to an haute couturier of Paris. The price is lower than you would pay in Europe or America. Two or three fittings, minimum of three weeks required. The affiliated haute couturiers are *Isetan* (Balmain); *Daimaru* (Givenchy); *Takashimaya* (Pierre Cardin); *Mitsukoshi* (Guy Laroche); *Matsuzakaya* (Nina Ricci).

Kiyomizu in Shibuya sells Western-style dresses made up from Kyoto kimono fabrics. Most of the dresses are of much the same style. English is not spoken in this store but everything is clearly labeled and priced. Near Miyamasuzaka-shita intersection and a few yards short of the big Shibuya Post Office; 409–1886. Open 10:30 A.M.–7:00 P.M. on weekdays but closed earlier at 6:00 P.M. on Sundays.

Recently, many cozy boutiques have sprung up in Tokyo as in other big cities around the world. They are scattered along the valleys of Nishi-Ginza running parallel with Chuo-dori. You will find some good boutiques in the Roppongi and Aoyama areas, also. In the Palais France Bldg. at Harajuku, is the Irish fashion house of *Donald Davies.*

Mme. Mori Hanae, probably the most noted Japanese designer in America, has her own building in Harajuku. She has other fashion rooms in the Hotel Okura's South Wing, in the Imperial Hotel's arcade, and in many department stores. *Mori Hanae,* 3–1–6 Kita-Aoyama, Minato-ku; 400–3301. Open 11:00 A.M. to 7:00 P.M. daily throughout the year.

Jun Ashida, designer to Crown Princess Michiko, has his own building above the subway station at Akasaka-Mitsuke; 588–5030/5084. Open 11:00 A.M.–8:30 P.M.

Issey Miyake, a designer of international fame, has his boutique on the first floor of From 1st building at 5 Minami-Aoyama; 499–6476. Open 12 noon–8:00 P.M. Closed on Sundays.

Kansai Yamamoto, still another Japanese designer of world renown, has his boutique, *Kansai International Harajuku* in Harajuku fashion town; 3–28–7 Jingumae, Shibuya-ku; 478–1958. Open 11:00 A.M.–8:00 P.M. throughout the year.

Japanese sweaters are a good buy, particularly the embroidered models. The beaded sweaters sold in Tokyo are imported from Hong Kong; therefore, you will find a wider range of choice in the place of origin.

SHIRTS

Many Tokyo shops make handmade shirts in a wide range of materials. On the whole, tailored shirts are a fair bargain, but it's best not to go shirt-buying unless you have ample time for at least one fitting and a bit more time for final adjustments. Collar styles are sometimes a bit difficult and it is best to have a model to copy from. Also insist that any material used be preshrunk before cutting. *Moh Long* in the Imperial Hotel Arcade, *Kanebo* at Gallery Center Bldg., Miyuki-dori, and *Tani Shirt Company* in the arcades of Hotel Okura and Imperial Hotel, are all good shops with a wide assortment of materials. The Tani shirt people will come to your hotel with samples and for measuring and fittings.

HANDBAGS

Beaded bags are a wonderful bargain in Japan, but you should also have a look at the handsome hand-stenciled cottons, brocades, and fancifully designed leather handbags. *M. Yamamoto* in Sukiyabashi Shopping Center, Ginza, has many lovely items. Handbag sections in Wako and Mitsukoshi Nihonbashi are also good. Shops in the hotel arcades specialize in beaded and brocade bags. For something more Oriental, try any of the dozens of small kimono accessory shops around the Ginza. One of the best is *Izumiya* (sign in English), a tiny shop with an old-fashioned traditional air and a chic clientele of Tokyo's upper-class ladies and higher-class geisha. Two blocks west of Chuo-dori, in the first block south of Harumi-dori.

FURS

An expert on the subject says that Japan's furs now equal those of an American "top second-class furrier." While the quality of the furs themselves is equal, Japanese styling and workmanship aren't up to the high standards of leading foreign furriers. On the other hand, furs here are cheaper than in the United States. Ranch mink is bred in Japan from stock imported from Canada, Norway, and the United States, and is cured by processes adapted from those used elsewhere. The difference comes in the workmanship—cutting, matching skins, sewing, etc. Ranch mink is available in several grades, a wide variety of mutation colors, and in a fairly good range of styling—nothing spectacular, but good basic styles.

Japan also produces so-called mink items that really come from the lowly weasel. This fur is exported to the United States for trimmings on children's and cheaper garments, but in Japan it turns up in full-length "mink" coats, at, naturally, bargain prices. You're not likely to mistake it for the real thing, but it is simpler to make it clear from the beginning that it's "ranch" mink you're after.

Nutria, marten, fox, and sable are also available in Japan. Among the top Tokyo furriers is *Futaba*, 1–10 Ginza, Chuo-ku; 571–0518. Main store is on the street beside the Imperial Hotel towards Ginza. Open 10:00 A.M.–7:00 P.M. daily throughout the year. Futaba has a branch in the Imperial Hotel. *Nakamura* 4–3–15 Ginza, Chuo-ku; 563–3451. At Ginza 4-chome on Namiki-dori St. is also this well-known furrier.

POTTERY AND CHINA

The china section in any of the department stores is fun, but *Takashimaya* and *Mitsukoshi* (at Nihonbashi) have the best selections of both Japanese and Western-style ware.

Koyanagi, 1–7–5 Ginza, Chuo-ku; 561–3601. 100 years old, this shop carries first-class Kiyomizu, Kutani, Imari ware. One of the most attractive little shops on the Ginza across the Chuo-dori street from Melsa department store. Open 10:00 A.M.–7:00 P.M. on weekdays, 12:00 noon–6:00 P.M. on Sundays and national holidays. Closed on third Sunday of every month.

Noritake is sold all over town, but the easiest place to inspect the products of this most famous Japanese manufacturer of Western-style dinnerware is the *Noritake*, 1–1–28 Toranomon, Minato-ku; 591–3241. Also on sale here is Okura china, a higher quality porcelain manufactured by Noritake. On the first floor of TOTO Bldg. at Toranomon intersection. Open 10:00 A.M.–6:00 P.M. Closed on Sundays and national holidays.

Takumi (see Paper and Paper Products), one of Tokyo's best-known shops, specializes in Japanese folkcraft. Here you will find pottery from the many small country kilns still operated by farmer-craftsmen. Thanks to the crusading work done by leaders of Japan's folkcraft revival movement, many of the kilns are now turning out pottery in shapes and sizes adapted to the Western table.

Tachikichi, 5–6–13 Ginza, Chuo-ku; 571–2924. The Tokyo outlet of an old (over 200 years) and renowned Kyoto porcelain manufacturer. A small shop, unfortunately with no signboard in English, located two blocks west of Chuo-dori, near Komatsu Store. On Nishi-Gobangai-dori street about 70 meters from Harumi-dori towards Shimbashi. Open 11:00 A.M.–7:00 P.M. Closed on Sundays. On the other side of the street it has Adam & Eve chinaware, and specializes in Western-style dinner sets and glassware.

Kuroda Toen, near Ginza 4-chome intersection (571–3223), sells both crockery for everyday use as well as "works of art" and tea ceremony utensils. It has an unbelievably profuse array of ceramics of all kinds, from inexpensive teacups to a tea bowl of beautiful perfection from Aichi Prefecture, priced at a whopping ¥9,000,000. Kuroda Touen is in the middle of the block past Matsuzakaya Department Store towards Shimbashi, but on the opposite side of Matsuzakaya. Open 10:00 A.M.–7:00 P.M. every day.

Nippon Kogei, Sanshin Building Arcade near Hibiya intersection. A minute shop but worth a visit. Designers of their own "Mikado China," Western-style dinner sets with tasteful Japanese patterns. You can have a set made with your own name painted on in Japanese *kana* or Chinese *kanji* characters. Also small pottery collection. Open 10:00 A.M.–7:00 P.M. throughout the year.

Odawara Shoten, old Kutani and Imari ware. In Imperial Hotel Arcade; 591–0052. Open 9:00 A.M.–7:15 P.M. on weekdays and 9:00 A.M.–6:15 P.M. on Sundays and national holidays.

Though a bit garish for some tastes, the heavily decorated gold Satsuma ware has been a popular tourist item for years, and Satsuma manufacturers long ago learned to turn out coffee cups, tea sets, and the like for the Western table. You can find Satsuma at *Bon Tokyo* in the Nikkatsu Arcade, *Toyo* and *Okubo* in the Imperial Hotel Arcade, and *Koshida Satsumaya* on the second floor of the Sukiyabashi Shopping Center. (See Hotel Arcades and One-Stop Shopping for addresses.)

FOLKCRAFT

Several Tokyo shops specialize in folkcraft, or *mingei* products. They are good places to go for original and inexpensive gifts.

Takumi Craft Shop, 8–4–2 Ginza, Chuo-ku; 571–2017. Still the acknowledged leader in the field. Specializes in Mashiko ware, the most famous folk pottery. On Sotobori-dori corner opposite the Hotel Nikko. Open 11:00 A.M.–7:00 P.M. on weekdays and 11:00 A.M.–5:30 P.M. on national holidays. Closed on Sundays.

Wafudo, 1st floor of the Marubiru Arcade, in the Marubiru Building in front of Tokyo Station (201–3639), is a tiny shop packed to the rafters with folkcraft goodies. Open 9:00 A.M.–6:00 P.M. on weekdays and 9:00 A.M.–3:00 P.M. on Saturdays. Closed on Sundays and national holidays.

Kacho-do, 2nd floor of the Marubiru Arcade, (201–3809), has an interesting, but less extensive mingei collection. Open 10:00 A.M.–6:00 P.M. on weekdays. Closed on Saturdays, Sundays and national holidays.

Izumi, 5–26 Ogibuko, Suginami-ku; 391–3645. This shop is a far trek from the center of town, and only recommended for those who will be in Tokyo for some time. Outside JNR Ogikubo Station in Suginami-ku. It has a big collection of Mashiko pottery, Nanbu cast iron kettles, pans and ashtrays, bamboo ware, straw mats and many other folkcraft items. The shop has Izumi written in English alphabet. Open 10:00 A.M.–7:00 P.M. Closed on Wednesdays.

Tsukamoto, 4–1–19 Mikawadaimachi, Minato-ku; 403–3747. Another shop specializing in Mashiko ware, few blocks north from Roppongi intersection, on the left going towards Tameike. Prices here are a little lower than Takumi's. Open 10:00 A.M.–7:00 P.M. daily throughout the year. *Liberty House,* (467–5558) in Tomigaya, 4th stop on Shibuya-Hatagaya bus, sells mashiko ware.

Bingoya at Wakamatsucho in Shinjuku-ku near Tokyo Joshi Idai (Tokyo Women's Medical University) and in front of Kawadacho bus stop, resembles a traditional storehouse and has six floors brimming with folk toys, baskets, pottery, hand-dyed fabrics, lacquerware and country furniture. All are simple, strong, and practical things. Open 10:00 A.M.–7:00 P.M. Closed on Mondays.

WOODBLOCK PRINTS

Old prints by the great masters are hard to come by, but good reproductions abound, and late 19th-century prints are plentiful. The postwar years have brought a renaissance in the print-making art, and a whole crop of new artists is creating exciting prints in a contemporary style.

Watanabe, 8–6–19 Ginza, Chuo-ku; 571–4684. Sells originals and reproductions. In the early years of the 20th century, the head of this old Tokyo firm became famous for his crusade to revive the then-disappearing art of print making. The shop has continued its fine tradition of craftsmanship. A block east of Sotobori-dori Ave., behind the Hotel Nikko. Open 9:30 A.M.–8:00 P.M. on weekdays, 9:30 A.M.–4:30 P.M. on national holidays. Closed on Sundays.

Shobisha for old and modern prints and reproductions, 5–2 Sotokanda, Chiyoda-ku; 831–4669. On Chuo-dori, about 7 minutes from Akihabara Station.

Ohya Shobo, 1–1 Kanda-Jimbocho, Chiyoda-ku; 291–0062. Near Sanseido Bookstore, this shop has a large collection of unusual old prints. Open 10:00 A.M.–6:30 P.M. on weekdays and closed on Sundays and national holidays.

Yoseido, 5–5–15 Ginza, Chuo-ku; 571–1312/2471. One of the first galleries in Tokyo to take up the cause of the new school of modern print artists. Abe Yuji, the owner, speaks English and will be happy to answer your questions on what's going on in the Tokyo art world. The upstairs gallery has shows of modern artists in all media. Framing and *kakemono* (hanging scroll) mounting. On Namiki-dori, behind the Sony Bldg. and two stores from Mikasa Kaikan restaurant complex. Open 10:00 A.M.–6:30 P.M. Closed on Sundays and national holidays.

Kaigado for reproductions and modern prints, greeting cards, art supplies, and framing. The gallery on the second floor is devoted solely to the works of Saito Kiyoshi, one of the best known of the modern print artists. On Aoyama-dori Ave. near entrance to Meiji Park.

Munakata Gallery, on the 6th floor of the Tokyu Department Store at Nihonbashi, is devoted exclusively to the creations of the late Munakata Shiko, Venice Beinnale first prize winner.

Also three old shops—*Nakazawa, Sakai,* and *Takamizawa*—on the street across from the Imperial Hotel and running towards Ginza. The *Franell Gallery* in the Hotel Okura specializes in the moderns. Franell Gallery opens 10:00 A.M.–6:30 P.M. all the year-round.

ANTIQUES, CURIOS, FINE ARTS

There are two places in Tokyo where you can find a concentration of antique and curio shops.

At the Shibuya end of the fashionable Aoyama district is a street that could be called Antique Row because of the couple of dozen antique shops located on both sides of it. It is several minutes walk towards Shibuya from Omote-sando Station of the Ginza, Chiyoda, and Hanzomon subway lines. The road runs off at right angles from Aoyama-dori Ave. at the place where Kinokuniya, the famous supermarket patronized by foreign residents, stands. The antiques you find in these shops are substantial ones.

A well-stocked shop popular with visiting decorators and buyers on this street is *Toraya,* 5–13–1 Minami-Aoyama, Minato-ku; 400–8121/5. Open 11:00 A.M.–5:30 P.M. Closed on Sundays and national holidays. Completely closed down for summer holidays throughout August.

Tokyo Antique Hall (Tokyo Komingu Kotto-kan), 1–23–1 Kanda-Jimbocho, Chiyoda-ku; 295–7112/5. In Kanda near Sanseido Book Store (few minutes from Jimbocho Station of Mita and Shinjuku subway lines), this complex houses 55 small antique and curio shops on four floors. They sell a huge variety of curios and antiques, including *netsuke, ukiyo-e* woodblock prints, old clocks and watches, medicine boxes, ancient Korean *tansu* (wardrobe) and old ceramics. Here you can find something to fit your budget, whether it is just ¥1,000 or a million yen—from three-for-¥100 old coins to a *tsubo* pot costing several million yen. The emphasis, however, is on the inexpensive curios and trinkets, so the whole building is like a giant flea market. Open 10 A.M.–7:00 P.M. daily throughout the year.

Otsuka Kogeisha in Nihonbashi next door to Takashimaya Department Store is an old, established store dealing in *kakemono* scrolls, *gaku* framed pictures, and excellent reproductions of Japanese art, mostly *sumie* India ink-brush paintings. The store is on the 3rd floor of Shin-Nihonbashi Bldg. next to Takashimaya on its Kyobashi side (to the right as you face the department store). The ground floor is a bank. The store is open from 9:00 A.M. to 5:00 P.M. daily on weekdays, but from 9:00 A.M. to 2:00 P.M. on Saturdays except the first and third Saturdays of the month, when it is closed. Closed on Sundays and national holidays. 271–3587.

Scattered around the city are many shops for the very serious collector who is searching for objects of museum quality and is prepared to pay accordingly.

Mayuyama, 2–5–9 Kyobashi, Chuo-ku; 561–5146. The most famous name among Tokyo's fine art dealers, and a must stop for every visiting museum curator. It specializes in Japanese and Chinese ceramics. A handsome modern building, on the corner one block west of Showa-dori and north of Takara-cho. Open 9:30 A.M.–6:00 P.M. Closed on Sundays and national holidays. Mayuyama has branches in the Imperial and Nikkatsu arcades, but these deal only in jewelry, handbags, ivory, etc.

Kochuko Art Gallery is another shop that handles only the best. Noted for its excellent collection of Oriental ceramics. Opposite Takashimaya department store, south side entrance. In this same block are several other small, discreet shops patronized by connoisseurs.

Heisando, 1–2–4 Shiba Koen, Minato-ku; 434–0588/9. An old Tokyo firm that deals in collector's items but also handles more popularly priced things. Good for screens, lacquer, and *kakemono* (hanging scroll pictures). Near Shiba Park Hotel in Shiba Park. Open 10:00 A.M.–5:00 P.M. Closed on Sundays and national holidays.

Yushima-Seido, 1–4–25 Yushima, Bunkyo-ku; 811–4606. is sometimes known as the Confucian Temple, for it is located in the compound of the only shrine in Tokyo dedicated to the Chinese sage. Many of the pieces here are on consignment, and it's another fascinating hodgepodge—everything from English trout flies to 12-panel screens. You can browse for hours among the hundreds of books, *kakemono,* and old woodblock prints. Near JNR Ochanomizu Station. Open 10:00 A.M.–4:00 P.M.

Yokoyama, Inc., the famed Kyoto store, has a branch on the 2nd floor of the Sukiyabashi Shopping Center (572–5066), where modern arts and crafts can be had in addition to a sampling of the Kyoto treasury of antiques. Open 10:00 A.M.–6:00 P.M. Its branch in Hotel Okura Arcade (582–0979) is open 9:00 A.M.–7:00 P.M. on weekdays, 10:00 A.M.–5:00 P.M. on Sundays.

Edo Antiques, 2–21–12 Akasaka, Minato-ku; 584–5280. Between Roppongi and Tameike, it has an impressive stock of restored country furniture, and of ceramics and bamboo baskets. Near Tokyu Kanko Hotel and five minutes walk from Akasaka Station on the Chiyoda subway line. Open 10:00 A.M.–6:00 P.M. Closed on Sundays.

Uchida, a branch of the Kyoto firm, has in addition to a few antiques, many woodblock prints, painted screens, and scrolls. In Sukiyabashi Shopping Center; 571–8077. Open 10:00 A.M.–6:00 P.M. daily throughout the year.

Fuso, 7–6–47 Akasaka, Akasaka New Plaza, 1st fl., Minato-ku; 583–5945. Long established, it has curios in a new shop near Nogi Shrine, about 7 minutes' walk from Nogizaka Station on Chiyoda subway line. Open 10:00 A.M.–6:00 P.M. Closed on Sundays.

Art Plaza Magatani, 5–10–13 Toranomon, Minato-ku; 433–6321. Near Japan Taxfree Center, this is actually two shops, one dealing in antiques and the other selling new Japanese ceramics and folkcraft items. Open 9:30 A.M.–6:30 P.M. daily except Sundays and national holidays.

Nihon Netsuke Society in Prosper House, Hiroo district, has netsuke and ivory carvings.

Ohno, 2–31–23 Yushima, Bunkyo-ku; 811–4365. A popular shop noted for its screen collection. Also good ceramics, bronzes. Be sure to go up to the 2nd floor. Near Yushima Tenjin Shrine and on Kasuga-dori Ave., at Yushima. About three minutes walk from Yushima Station on Chiyoda subway line. Open 10:00 A.M.–6:30 P.M. Closed on Sundays and national holidays. There are several other curio shops nearby, and a shop called *Suzuka,* the only pewter manufacturing company in Tokyo. Beautifully made sake sets, tea pots, and canisters.

Seigado Shimizu Honten (842–3777) is located in the Asakusa amusement area, just behind the famed Kannon Temple. Easily reached by subway from the Ginza. The temple is a tourist attraction, so you can easily combine temple and antique viewing. Open 9:00 A.M.–9:00 P.M. Closed second and fourth Wednesdays of each month.

Two long-established shops run by American women connoisseurs are *Mildred Warder,* in the South Wing of the Okura Hotel (open 10:00 A.M.–6:30 P.M., closed on Sundays and national holidays; 585–8274), and *The Gallery* (open 10:00 A.M.–6:00 P.M. on weekdays, 11:00 A.M.–4:00 P.M. on national holidays, closed on Sundays; 585–4816/5019), located on the narrow street at the back of the American Embassy. Both shops have unusual and valuable stock.

Senpudo, behind the Mitsukoshi Department Store at Shinjuku, has the town's best collection of high-quality Japanese swords and sword guards, as well as a wide variety of other objects.

Fujiya, in the Nikkatsu Arcade (211–6996), deals in curios, ancient samurai armors, old paintings. Open 10:00 A.M.–7:00 P.M. on weekdays, closed on Sundays and national holidays.

Kurofune, Roppongi, is run by American John Adair, and *Harumi Antiques,* near the Defense Agency, by American David Rose.

Japan Art Center, Tokyo Green Heights, 1–22–10 Takadanobaba, Shinjuku-ku; 200–5387. though small, it is crammed with furniture of an earlier Japanese era. You'll find items such as *tansu, hibachi, andon* (graceful lamps from the days before electricity), teapots and lacquered picnic boxes. About 5 minutes walk from Takadanobaba Station on JNR Yamanote loop line. Open 10:30 A.M.–4:30 P.M. every day except Monday, including Sundays and national holidays.

MUSICAL INSTRUMENTS

There are many musical instrument stores near JNR Ochanomizu Station. They sell a great variety of instruments for light and classical music—electric guitars, electronic keyboards, drums, strings, woodwinds, and percussions. *Ishibashi* is open from 10:00 A.M. to 7:00 P.M. every day throughout the year, but until 6:00 P.M. on Sundays and national holidays. 291–0541. *Crosawa* is open from 10:00 A.M. to 7:30 P.M. daily throughout the year. 291–9791.

SWORDS

Japan Sword, 3–8–1 Toranomon, Minato-ku; 434–4321/3. If you are a complete novice, this is the place to start. Near Hotel Okura, they handle all the paraphernalia and speak English. Japan Sword also deals in less archaic items of cutlery for daily use. About 4–5 minutes walk either from Toranomon Station on Ginza subway line or from Kamiyacho Station on Hibiya subway line. Open 9:30 A.M.–6:00 P.M. Closed on Sundays and national holidays.

FLOWER-ARRANGING EQUIPMENT

For information and guidance on all flower-arranging topics, including current exhibits in Tokyo, *Ikebana International,* an organization devoted to worldwide promotion of Japanese flower arrangement, has its office at Room 301, Tokiwa Bldg., Shibuya. Address is 4–5–6 Shibuya, Shibuya-ku; 400–8108/9.

Shops selling vases and other ikebana equipment are found in most neighborhoods. The department stores also have large sections devoted to vases and ikebana supplies. The Japanese don't go in much these days for the small tray garden figurines, but you can find a large selection of these in the *Hibiya Kadan* flower shop in the Imperial Hotel Arcade; 503–8781.

You can also buy flower arranging equipment at any of the flower-arrangement schools, such as the *Sogetsu School* on Aoyama-dori near the Canadian Embassy (7–2 Akasaka, Minato-ku; 408–1126), *Ikenobo College* near JNR Ochanomizu Station, and *Ohara Center* at Minami-Aoyama near the Aoyama-dori intersection. (5–7 Minami-Aoyama, Minato-ku; 499–1200.)

FISHING EQUIPMENT

The shop patronized by Japanese experts are *Tosaku* in Ginza 2-chome on Sotobori-dori, three blocks north of Harumi Dori. Tosaku carries a good line of Western-style equipment, but the emphasis is on the local brand. Tosaku is open from 10:00 A.M. to 7:30 P.M. daily except Sundays and national holidays. Address is 2–2–17 Ginza, Chuo-ku; 567–6950. A very good shop with a complete line of Western equipment is *Tsuruya* in Kyobashi on the east side of Chuo-dori. It is open from 10:00 A.M. to 7:00 P.M. daily, but from 11:00 A.M. to 5:00 P.M. on Sundays and national holidays. It is closed on the third Monday of every month. Address is 2–6–20 Kyobashi, Chuo-ku; 563–4071.

PROVINCIAL SPECIALTIES

In the Kokusai Kanko Building, close to the northern entrance, or Yaesu side, of Tokyo Station (that's the side with the Daimaru Department Store above the exits), there are showrooms on the 2nd, 3rd, and 4th floors, where the products of 27 Japanese prefectures are displayed. The display rooms of an additional 12 prefectures are located on the 9th floor of Daimaru. If you do not have time to visit the provinces, you might go here to see what kind of handicrafts you are missing. Some items can be purchased in Tokyo and the officials on duty can tell you where. If your itinerary includes trips to the provinces, it is all the more reason you should visit this center to gain advance knowledge of the specialties available in the places you will visit.

SUPERMARKETS

Tokyo's international "soopers" are excellent. Shop for food, for picnics, or "box lunch" ideas, at *Kinokuniya* and *Peacock* both in Aoyama district), Todoroki district in Setagaya Ward, and west of Tokyo in the town of Kunitachi); *National Azabu* (Hiroo); *Meidi-Ya* (The head store is in Kyobashi 2-chome (271–1111), and its branch stores are in Ginza 2-chome (563–0221) and Marubiru (201–6611) in front of Tokyo Station.) *Olympia* (Harajuku). All open every day. There are *7-Eleven* shops all over.

ART GALLERIES

If you want to view traditional prints showing you the Japan you wish you were seeing, almost any hotel arcade will have a gallery just right for your needs. But don't flinch when you see the price tags. The galleries listed below tend to deal in more contemporary artworks. Typically a show will last only six days, opening on a Monday and closing at about 4:00 P.M. on Saturday.

In addition, almost every major department store has a craft or ceramic salon, where weekly shows are staged. Some are very prestige-oriented and the prices of the works displayed reflect that. Others give new craftspeople the exposure they need to begin moving up the ladder of success.

Tokyo is a goldmine of galleries, but those listed below have proven their staying power.

Akasaka Green Gallery, at 4–8–8 Akasaka, 03–401–5255, has a varied schedule of events, leaning heavily toward ceramics. Kiyotsugu Sawa has shown his Shigaraki wares here in the past.

Galeria Grafica Tokio operates out of the Kato Building at 7–8–9 Ginza; 03–573–7731. Specializes in prints, rotating between antique Western (18th- and 19th-century works) and those of contemporary Japanese. Owner, Ms. Reiko Kurita speaks flawless English and has a respected knowledge of the contemporary art scene.

Gallery Inoui is on the 4th floor of the Narihiro Building at 3–9–3 Akasaka; 03–582–9660. Their varied collections are usually ceramics. Prices tend to be moderate on the Japanese scale and many new talents have been introduced here.

Galerie Laranne is in the basement of the Nishi Building at 2–8–2 Ginza; 03–567–5596. Owner Setsuko Sumi's small space is generally hung with printed artworks that herald the outer edge of print making in Japan. Shows include the lithography of Mineo Gotoh and the extremely limited edition woodblock artistry of Toshiharu Maekawa.

Galerie Mukai can be found on the 6th floor of the Tsukamoto Fudosan Building at 5–5–11 Ginza; 03–571–3292. Fine prints include those of Mayumi Oda and a number of rising stars from the United States. Madame Mukai has championed a number of fine artists, including Marion Korn, the late Kenzo Okada, and Morkazu Kumagai. Both the latter two were respected masters before their deaths.

Gallery Seiho is located on the 3rd floor of the Daiichi Iwatsuki Building at 6–7–16 Ginza; 03–573–5678. A sculpture-oriented gallery whose shows include the works of Shiro Hayami from Shikoku.

Gallery Te is found on the 4th floor of the Tojo Building at 8–10–7 Ginza; 03–574–6730. Artists shown here include minimalist Insik Quac and painter/ printmaker Shingo Honda.

Gallery Yamaguchi is two blocks behind Matsuya Department Store at 3–8– 12 Ginza, on the 3rd floor of the brick-faced Yamato Building; 03–564–0633. The wide range of shows here includes sculpture, prints, and paintings.

Ginzado Gallery is located on the 2nd floor of the Kyohana Building at 3–2–12 Ginza. 03–567–0648. The graphics and drawings of both Ryoji Ikeda and Masuo Ikeda art shown here.

Kakiden Gallery is found just outside the east exit of Shinjuku's JNR Station, on the 7th floor of the Oyasu Building at 3–36–6 Shinjuku; 03–352–5118. Tea ceremony items are the type of ceramic ware most often shown here.

Maki Gallery is at 4–9 Nihombashi Honcho, Chuo-ku; 03–241–1310. The list of new talents emanating out of Nobuo Yamagishi's galleries reads like a who's who of Japanese contemporary art. The other galleries are *Tamura* and *Komai.* Open daily.

Minami Aoyama Green Gallery is adjacent to the Aoyama Gakushuin University campus off Aoyama-dori, at 5–10–12 Minami Aoyama; 03–407–0050. Shows are almost exclusively ceramics, with such luminaries as Hideto Satonaka and Rikichi Miyanaga regularly displaying their latest kiln efforts.

Miyuki Gallery, located directly above Mune Craft (one of Tokyo's better craft and ceramic galleries) in the Ginza Chushajo Building at 6–4–4; 03–571–1771. Displays an ever-changing array of painting, print, and sculpture collections.

Nichido Garo (Gallery), is on Sotobori-dori Ave., near the Sony Bldg., at 5 Ginza, Chuo-ku; 571–2553. The most influential gallery of the Japanese academic school. There is an annex on the same street.

Q is located on the 4th floor of the Tojo Building at 8–10–7 Ginza (as is Gallery Te, mentioned above); 03–573–1696. Q tends toward experimental, oversize canvas works and arranged constructions of steel beams and rough quarried rock.

Tokyo Gallery is on the street three blocks west of Ginza and three blocks south of Harumi-dori, toward the Shimbashi entertainment district.

PACKING AND SHIPPING

Department stores will pack and ship your purchases overseas. Major hotels have a counter of a shipping agent. Best known worldwide for excellent work is *Odawara Shoten* in the Imperial Hotel Arcade (591–0052). Equally reliable, and more experienced for larger shipments, is *Nippon Express (Nittsu* in Japanese), which guarantees safe arrival of any shipment, including objets d'art and other precious items. If you ask, the shop where you purchase something can telephone Nippon Express, and the latter will pick up the item directly from the shop for shipment to your destination.

DINING OUT. If you stir outside your hotel restaurants, eating in Tokyo becomes an adventure.

Finding a given restaurant among the thousands in the sprawling metropolis is in itself a task of some magnitude, as Japan does not aid the visitor by having a recognizable address system. Having arrived at your restaurant you will frequently find (if in a Western-style one) that familiar dishes somehow taste quite unlike what you expected or (if it is a Japanese-style one) that there are gastronomic touches of such delicacy and beauty that a whole new world of cuisine opens up before you.

If you are at all in the mood for adventure, you will probably be pleasantly surprised to find that delicacies such as octopus, raw prawns, sea urchin eggs, or eel liver are quite palatable.

Apart from the modestly priced chair-and-table lunch places, which are similar to their counterparts all over the world, Japanese restaurants may be divided into two broad categories: the *o-zashiki* (private room) restaurant, where the meal is served in your own Japanese-style room, and the counter restaurant, where you sit up at a long counter of scrubbed white wood. Generally (although not invariably) the former is more expensive than the latter.

Indeed, the best Japanese restaurants (known as *ryoriya*) charge prices comparable to those leading Parisian restaurants. In general Japanese restaurants specialize in one or two dishes, which are served on a *table d'hôte* basis. Thus you must go to a special *sukiyaki* restaurant, or a special eel restaurant, or a special snapturtle restaurant if your fancy takes you in the direction of those dishes.

At most Japanese-style restaurants the only choice of drinks you will have will be beer, *sake,* or whisky (*Suntory,* the best Japanese brand of whisky, is a good, smooth whisky with a Scotch-like character). Expensive *ryoriya,* however, may have imported liquors.

Japanese tend to eat early and, with only a few exceptions, you must be prepared to arrive at any Japanese-style restaurant before 8:00 P.M.

You should have your hotel front desk phone ahead to any high-class restaurant to make sure that a room is available. Reservations are becoming necessary at higher-priced Western-style restaurants.

Bills and tipping are tricky in Japan.

Japanese who can afford to go to the best *ryoriya* (mostly on expense accounts) generally have charge accounts and the bill is sent to their offices. For those who wish to pay cash, a small slip of paper with the total charge is discreetly handed to them at the end of the meal. There is no itemized bill. This is supposed to include a service charge, but since the patrons of such restaurants are expected to have great *face,* they are expected to add a generous tip as well. This should not be less than 1,000 yen, no matter what your bill is. If the bill is over 10,000 yen, you should make the tip at least 2,000 yen.

These subtleties, however, are best left to those lucky (and wealthy) enough to be regular patrons of such places. For most ordinary mortals, including most Japanese, the situation is much simpler—and blessedly easy on the wallet. Routine tipping of the Western variety is a custom alien to the Japanese. Nine times out of ten there is not the slightest need to pay more than the sum at the bottom of your bill. There will be no churlish looks when you pocket your change, and if you leave money on the table, more often than not the waitress will assume you did so by mistake and will hurry after you to return it.

A word about locating the restaurants listed below. The only sure way of finding them on your own, given Tokyo's idiosyncratic address system, is to have a detailed map leading from the nearest landmark, usually a railway station, to the restaurant's door. Obviously this was impossible to provide, given the concise nature of this book, but there are two practical alternatives: (1) Have the front desk at your hotel phone ahead and draw you a map according to the instructions he/she receives; or (2) give the restaurant's phone number to your taxi driver and have him phone ahead for directions—assuming he doesn't know the place to begin with, which, in Tokyo, is more than likely. Only those bent on proving something would try to find a Tokyo restaurant unaided. Old hands who have been here for many years, not to mention the Japanese themselves, would not dream of doing such a thing.

Note: The rate of mortality among new restaurants in Tokyo is extremely high. There are restaurants which have stood on the same site for 200 years—but many more last less than one year, and some have gone into bankruptcy even before they opened their doors! This means that it would take a weekly publication to keep an up-to-date list of operating restaurants—and there are estimated to be about 500,000 of them in metropolitan Tokyo! It would therefore be advisable to consult with your hotel desk or read local English-language publications before setting out for any of the restaurants listed below.

Our price categories for the listings below are per person as follows: *Super Deluxe,* ¥20,000 and up; *Deluxe,* ¥10,000–20,000; *Expensive,* ¥5,000–10,-000; *Moderate,* ¥2,000–5,000; and *Inexpensive,* up to ¥2,000. "All major credit cards" means that establishment takes American Express (AE), Billion, Diamond, Diner's Club (DC), Japan Carte Blanche (JCB), MasterCard (MC), UC, and Visa (V).

JAPANESE STYLE

When American and European diners pay astronomical prices for dining out they are in part paying to become celebrities for the evening, "the observed of all observers"; the pleasure is almost as much social as gastronomical. Japanese diners, on the other hand, pay the highest prices for the privilege of withdrawing from society altogether, into a private, cocoonlike room where they are treated like emperors or sultans. The entrance of the restaurant is almost certain to be small, dark, and hidden down a narrow back street. As everything about restaurants of this type is unfamiliar to the visitor from abroad, much the best way to experience them is to be taken by a sympathetic and bilingual Japanese companion. Indeed, without one it will be difficult even to make a reservation—it may even be impossible.

This is particularly true of Tokyo's *kaisekiryori* (tray cuisine) restaurants, but any of those little hole-in-the-wall joints that look at first glance as if they'd be likely to serve you instant coffee in a cracked cup need to be approached warily. Smallness denotes intimacy; the Japanese language does not distinguish between "customer" and "guest" so walking in off the street is like gate crashing someone's kitchen. Grit your teeth and brazen it out and you'll probably get served, but the experience may be a bizarrely chilly one.

In all such places a Japanese companion, or competence in speaking Japanese, is the prerequisite of an enjoyable evening. But the many larger, cheaper, or more internationally minded Japanese restaurants pose no such problems. The word "accessible" below denotes restaurants that are not likely to prove difficult for the casual foreign customer.

Super Deluxe

Hamadaya. 13–5, Nihonbashi, Ningyo-cho 3-chome, Chuo-ku; 661–2648. Hamadaya is one of a number of central Tokyo *kaisekiryori* restaurants that must rank among the most expensive places to eat in the world. Your meal here will be a full-blown introduction to Japanese aesthetics; every aspect of the decor, the service, the tableware, and the foot itself will reflect the Japanese preoccupation with delicacy, harmony, and attention to detail. The food will be served on trays in a private tatami-matted room. No credit cards.

Ichinao. 8–6, Asakusa 3-chome, Taito-ku; 874–3032. Another super-pricey kaiseki restaurant, this one located in Asakusa, the legendary old entertainment quarter on the east side of town. No credit cards.

Deluxe

Goeimon. 1–1–26 Hon-Komagome, Bunkyo-ku; 811–2015. Where it has gained entry at all, tofu remains a second-class citizen in the Western kitchen, but in this exquisite, Kyoto-like restaurant it attains its apotheosis. Goeimon is a gourmet Japanese restaurant of the highest caliber, which just happens to use tofu as a basic ingredient in many of the dishes. A pretty garden and running water enhance the experience. Open 5:00 to 11:00 P.M. Tuesdays through Saturdays; 3:00 P.M. to 8:00 P.M. Sundays and holidays. Closed Mondays and holidays. No credit cards.

Holytan. 2–30–10 Kabuki-cho, Shinjuku-ku; 208–8000.. Located behind Koma Stadium in the heart of Kabuki-cho, Tokyo's naughtiest square mile, Holytan is an impressive teppanyaki steak restaurant with a variety of other dishes on the menu, including seafood. The Hibiya branch (2nd basement, Fukoku Seimei Bldg., Hibiya City) has *kaiseki ryori* in addition to steak. Both shops are open 5:00 P.M. to 2:00 A.M. weekdays and 4:30 to 10:00 P.M. on Sundays and holidays. Accessible. All major credit cards.

Inagiku. 9–8 Nihonbashi, Kayaba-cho 2-chome, Chuo-ku; 669–5501. A venerable (80-year-old) *tempura* shop that cooks some of the lightest, freshest tempura in town at its old headquarters near Nihonbashi, heart of the Edo-Period merchant's quarter. A small branch on the 7th floor of Shinjuku's Keio Plaza Hotel maintains comparable standards but with lower prices (344–0111). All major credit cards.

Jisaku. 14–19 Akashi-cho, Chuo-ku; 541–2391. A large old restaurant on the bank of the Sumida River, behind St. Luke's Hospital. The specialty is *mizutaki*, country-style sukiyaki using fish or poultry in place of beef. Other dishes are served too. Reservations preferred. Open noon to 10:00 P.M. All major credit cards.

Kissho. 8–7, Akasaka 4-chome, Minato-ku; 403–2621. Located near Aoyama Dori. Kissho has three different restaurants, one on each floor, with the most expensive at the top. Specialties of the house are sukiyaki, shabu-shabu, and tempura, and the atmosphere is quiet and elegant. Accessible. All major credit cards.

Le Vert. Ginza Sanwa Building, 6–1, Ginza 4-chome, Chuo-ku; 535–3232. Close to Ginza subway station, opposite Matsuya Dept. Store. East meets west at Le Vert, where the specialty is European-style kaiseki-ryori and teppanyaki. The meeting of classical Japanese cuisine and France's nouvelle cuisine is one of the most interesting things to have happened in the restaurant world for years; in places like Le Vert the implications of the marriage are explored. The Kobe beef is said to be the most popular item. Open daily 11:00 A.M. to 2:00 P.M. and 5:00 P.M. to 9:30 P.M. All credit cards honored.

Shiruyoshi. 6–2–12 Akasaka, Minato-ku; 587–1876. Located in front of Shin Kokusai Bldg., West Annex. An authentic and classy Japanese restaurant where the tempura is prpepared before your eyes. The full course dinner is about ¥12,000 but they do reasonable lunches for less than ¥3000. Open daily, noon to 11:00 P.M.; closed Sundays and holidays. All major credit cards.

Expensive

Ashibe. Tsukiji; 543–3540. One of the many fine fish restaurants strategically located near Tsukiji fish market, Ashibe's speciality is *fugu,* the blowfish whose liver and ovaries contain tetrodotoxin, .024 of an ounce of which can kill a grown man in hours. Ashibe, like all fugu shops, is government-licensed, and they've never lost a customer! Most fugu eaten in Japan is frozen, but Ashibe's is fresh and therefore only available between October and March. The rest of the year console yourself with the shop's delicious *suppon* (snapping turtle) dishes. No credit cards.

Chinzanso. 10–8, Sekiguichi 2-chome, Bunkyo-ku; 943–1111. A gigantic restaurant set in a magnificent garden. A speciality is Genghis Khan lamb and vegetable barbecue, a splendid feast. The enjoyment is increased by the entertainment—Hawaiian bands, *Son et Lumière* presentations. Fireflies are released in the garden during the summer months. Open daily until 9:00 P.M. Accessible. All major credit cards.

Edo Gin. 5–1, Tsukiji 4-chome, Chuo-ku; 543–4401. Reputed to be one of the best sushi shops in Japan, Edo Gin is not only on the doorstep of Tsukiji fish market, but the restaurant's interior is dominated by a huge tank in which the evening's ingredients swim blithely about. Raw fish doesn't come any fresher. Edo Gin is big, too, which helps to make it more accessible than other places in the vicinity. Open daily till 9:30 P.M. closed Sunday. All major credit cards.

Five Farmers. Square Building, 10–3 Roppongi 3-chome, Minato-ku; 470–1675. Traditional food served in a rustic, snow country ambience. Reservations are preferred. All major credit cards.

Fuku Sushi. 9–22, Roppongi 5-chome, Minato-ku; 402–4116. Another famous sushi shop, this one is in the fashionable and international Roppongi section. Reservations are preferred. Open till 11:00 P.M. closed Sundays. All major credit cards.

Furusato. 4–1 Aobadai 3-chome, Meguro-ku; 463–2310. At the top of Dogenzaka Street in Shibuya, near Osaka-ue bus stop. A 300-year-old farmhouse dismantled, brought to Tokyo and re-erected, Furusato (Old country home) offers a wide range of local Japanese dishes. Folk dancers perform nightly. Definitely accessible and full of charm—though perhaps a bit of a tourist trap; there is a "foreign tourist course" priced ¥6000 to ¥10,000. Lunch 11:00 A.M. to 2:00 P.M., dinner 5:00 P.M. to 10:00 P.M. Showtime 7:00 P.M. and 8:30 P.M. Closed Mondays. All major credit cards.

Happo-en. 1–1, Shiroganedai 1-chome, Minato-ku; 443–3111. Two restaurants in one: the barbecue garden restaurant Rokumeikan; and Saji, a country-style place where the food is cooked on a charcoal fire in the traditional *irori* (hearth). Open 11:00 A.M. to 10:00 P.M., reservations preferred. AE, DC.

Kiraku. 12–1, Tsukiji 4-chome, Chuo-ku; 541–0908. Another highly recommended Tsukiji sushi shop. Open daily until the supply of fresh fish runs out, usually about 8:30 P.M. Visa.

Kushihachi. 10–9 Roppongi 3-chome, Minato-ku. 403–3060. When Jimmy Carter paid a return visit to Kushihachi, his favorite Tokyo yakitoria, in 1983, the news magazine *Focus* captioned the photo "only the yakitori hasn't changed." Most yakitoria are bright and garish, but this classy specimen is decorated with antiques and has a cozy atmosphere. The prices are less than presidential. AE, DC, JCB.

Kyubei. 5–23 Ginza 8-chome, Chuo-ku; 571–6523. The famous Ginza sushi shop, with branches in the Hotel Okura, Hotel New Otani, and Keio Plaza Hotel. All major credit cards.

Neo Japonesque. Blf. (1st-floor basement), Izumiya Building, 8–17, Akasaka 3-chome, Minato-ku; 583–0080. A highly fashionable Akasaka restaurant, another marriage of European cuisine with such Japanese favorites as sashimi and tempura. Open 6:00 P.M. to 11:00 P.M.; closed on Sundays and holidays. All major credit cards.

Okahan. Ginza Kanetanaka Bldg, 6–16 Ginza 7-chome, Chuo-ku; 571–1417. Okahan's speciality is *sukiyaki,* served in classically Japanese surroundings. There's another branch at the New Otani. Open noon to 10:00 P.M. except Sundays. Reservations preferred. Accessible. No credit cards.

Sasanoyuki. 15–10, Negishi 2-chome, Taito-ku; 873–1145. A pioneer of *tofu* cuisine, Sasanoyuki is a large restaurant that has managed to keep a friendly, solicitous atmosphere typical of the proletarian eastern quarter in which it is located. *Every* dish has tofu in it—which may seem too much of a good thing, though the variety of preparations amazes. Accessible: there's an English menu. Open 11:00 A.M. to 9:00 P.M., closed Mondays. Diamond.

Seryna. 12–2, Roppongi 3-chome, Minato-ku; 403–6211. A famous restaurant with French and Chinese as well as Japanese menus. Seryna is renowned for its shabu-shabu and sukiyaki as well its *Kani Seryna,* made with fresh crab daily. Accessible. All major credit cards.

Ten-Ichi. 6–5, Ginza 6-chome, Chuo-ku; 571–1949. Ten-Ichi's well-intentioned local advertising, which shows a row of aproned *gaijin* (foreigners) tucking in to the tempura, might be counterproductive if it leaves the impression that the place is a tourist trap. True, it welcomes foreign guests, but there is no need to fear you are being taken for a ride—Ten-Ichi's reputation is solid. All major credit cards accepted. Open 11:30 A.M. to 9:30 P.M. Branches at the Imperial

Hotel's Imperial Tower, Akasaka Plaza of Akasaka Tokyu Hotel, and 1st basement of West Shinjuku's highrise Mitsui Building. All major credit cards.

Zakuro. TBS Kaikan, 3–3, Akasaka 5-chome, Minato-ku; 582–6841. A famous chain of shabu-shabu restaurants with branches in central Akasaka, Kyobashi, Marunouchi, and Nihonbashi besides the main restaurant in Akasaka. Open daily 11:00 A.M. to 10:00 P.M. Reservations preferred.

Moderate

Aoi Marushin. 4–4, Asakusa 1-chome, Taito-ku; 841–0110, 841–5439. In the old east side entertainment quarter, Aoi Marushin has shows to accompany the varied menu, which includes yakitori, tempura, and sukiyaki. Open daily 11:00 A.M. to 10:00 P.M.

Chikuyotei. 14–7, Ginza 8-chome, Chuo-ku; 542–0787. Very conveniently located next to the Lion Beer Hall at the main Ginza intersection with Harumi-dori Avenue, Chikuyotei specializes in *unagi* (broiled eel) dishes. Reservations are preferred. There are three other branches in the city center.

5-Chome Tsubo-Han. 3–9, Ginza 5-chome, Chuo-ku; 571–3467. An island of elegant antiquity in racy, high-rising Ginza, with interior walls of dark wood, dimly lighted from behind *shoji* paper and dotted with folkcraft tableware, Tsubo-Han is the place to come for an authentic and undiluted image of Japan which is so strong that afterwards it is almost impossible to shake from the memory. The cuisine is far removed from the sukiyaki and tempura standards: *zosui,* a rice stew with fish, chicken, or vegetables, and *o-chazuke,* rice with green tea, *nori* seaweed and, in the case of *sake chazuke,* salmon. It's the sort of food the Japanese eat every day, but in marvelous surroundings. Open noon to 3:00 P.M., 4:00 P.M. to midnight. Closed Sundays and holidays.

Hassan. Blf, Denki Building, Roppongi, Minato-ku; 403–9112. Hassan's interior is designed in the style of a *sukiya-zukuri* tea house—rustic-looking, a little gloomy, but full of subtle refinement. Reasonable prices, tremendous portions: all the shabu-shabu you can eat for ¥4000, for example. Also sukiyaki, tempura, sashimi (raw fish), tea ceremony cuisine. Accessible. Open daily 11:30 A.M. to 11:30 P.M.

Ichioku. 4–4–5 Roppongi, Minato-ku; 405–9891. Small restaurant in back-street Roppongi that transcends categories. Menu includes mussels, spring rolls, tofu steak, dumplings, garlic toast . . . gasp at the eclectic imagination of the modern Japanese chef. Located behind the Self-Defence Agency.

Inagiku. Roppongi Branch: Hotel Ibis, 14–4, Roppongi 7-chome, Minato-ku; 403–5507; Shinjuku Branch: Keio Plaza Hotel, 2–1, Nishi-Shinjuku 2-chome, Shinjuku-ku; 344–0592. Shibuya Branch: 15–1, Udagawa-cho, Shibuya-ku; 464–6887; Tokyo Stn. Branch: Tokyo Station Building, 9–1, Marunouchi 1-chome, Chiyoda-ku; 212–7777. Inagiku is the fine tempura specialist whose Nihonbashi headquarters appeared in the *Deluxe* section. The word is that the branches are almost as good—and a lot cheaper.

Inakaya. Nishiyama Social Building, 12–7, Akasaka 3-chome, Minato-ku; 586–3054. In a robatayaki restaurant a wide variety of ingredients—various kinds of fish, vegetables, tofu, meat—are grilled by the chef, put on the end of a long paddle, and passed to the customers sitting at the semicircular counter. Ordering-by-pointing is effective, the atmosphere is friendly and informal, and the food is generally cheap. *Inaka* means "the country," *inakaya* "country house" and that's the best description of the ambience. Definitely accessible.

Noboritei. 1–12–6 Shimbashi, Minato-ku; 571–0482. You shouldn't leave Japan without investigating what the Japanese do to eel—*unagi,* as it's called. It's art. They bone, steam, and broil it until it is rich and succulent, a deep amber in color, then serve it, often on a bed of rice, in lacquered boxes. Noboritei is a fine place to sample this dish at its best.

Minokichi. Roi Roppongi, 5–1, Roppongi 5-chome, Minato-ku; 404–0767. Kaiseki ryori and shabu shabu served in an ambience of old Kyoto. Open until 2:00 A.M. on weekdays, 11:00 P.M. on Sundays. All major credit cards.

Tenmi. 10–6, Jinnan 1-chome, Shibuya-ku; 496–7100. The leading natural food restaurant in Tokyo, Tenmi serves a good variety of excellently cooked vegetarian Japanese dishes, notably *o-fukuro no aji*, "flavors of mother," a plate of up to a dozen different exquisite tastes in small portions, served with steamed brown rice, miso shiru (soup), and pickles. Downstairs is a natural food super-market that sells organically grown vegetables and much else besides. Open 11:30 A.M. to 2:30 A.M., 4:30 P.M. to 7:30 P.M.; Sundays and holidays 11:30 A.M. to 6:00 P.M. Closed 3rd Thursday of the month. Highly accessible.

Inexpensive

There is a great deal of inexpensive food available in Tokyo, much of it approximately Japanese. A lot of it, however, is not terribly wholesome. Sometimes it seems that the Japanese have learned their Western lessons a good deal too thoroughly, for the cheap restaurant food is laden with preservatives, artificial coloring, and monosodium glutamate. It's probably much healthier to eat cheap in a relatively poor country like neighboring Korea, where the chefs are less sophisticated and the ingredients relatively pure.

If you can ignore that aspect of it, however, you will find that every miniscule shopping street has its array of restaurants. Among the tastiest Japanese-style dishes offered almost everywhere are *soba* (buckwheat noodles), *oden* (see below), *donburi* style (scrambled egg with meat or chicken on a bed of rice) and *udon* (thick, white, wheat-based noodles in broth). There are also many cheap *sushi* shops, including some where the sushi travels around on a little conveyor belt and the diners pick the dishes they fancy, but we strongly recommend that you save up your pennies for the more expensive version. There's a world of difference.

The handful of restaurants listed below combine superb food with really cheap prices. It's not surprising that they are few and far between. In their own way they are as distinguished, and as Japanese, as the ¥20,000 plus kaiseki ryori places.

Carrot. 10–8, Jingumae 6-chome, Shibuya-ku (near Harajuku Stn); 406–6309. Natural Japanese food with a base of brown rice and rich miso soup, marvelous salads prepared by a qualified nutritionist, and beautiful *sashimi* (raw fish). This is health food without the sackcloth and ashes—and at terrifically low prices. Open 11:30 to 2:00 P.M., 5:00 P.M. to 11:00P.M., closed Saturdays and Sundays.

Musashino Sobadokoro. 55–11, Nakano 5-chome, Nakano-ku; 389–4751. *Soba*, buckwheat noodles usually served in broth, is a Japanese favorite that foreign visitors are apt to overlook because it is so cheap and humble-seeming. When it is made by hand and only the purest ingredients are used, however, it can be a real treat. Tucked away among the nightclubs of Nakano, west of Shinjuku on the Chuo line, this little shop serves some of the best soba in town. Open 6:00 P.M. to 2:00 A.M., closed Sundays.

Otako Honten. 4–16 Ginza 5-chome, Chuo-ku; 571–0057/3203. *Oden* is a mystifying and little-known Japanese dish consisting of bits of *kamoboko* (fish sausage), vegetables, fried and stuffed tofu, and many other puzzling bits and pieces kept bubbling in a great vat of stock and eaten with hot mustard. It is most enjoyable on a cold winter's night, washed down with tumblers of hot, cheap sake in one of those tent-like bars that litter the fringes of Tokyo's railway stations. Otako in the Ginza is one of the two classiest oden places in town. The other is Yasuko, described below. Otako is Kanto, i.e., Tokyo-style, which means the stock is fish- (not chicken-) based, and the flavor is saltier. Open noon to 2:00 P.M. and 5:00 P.M. to 10:30 P.M. Closed Sundays and holidays.

Yabu Soba. 10, Kanda Awaji-cho 2-chome, Chiyoda-ku; 251–0287. A really high quality *soba* shop located in Kanda, conveniently close to the center of town. They also serve Ebisu beer—Japan's best and purest.

Yasuko. 4–6 Ginza 5-chome, Chuo-ku; 571–0621. Not far from Otako (above) in Ginza 5-chome, *Yasuko* means "cheap" and "happy"; the quality of the food and the size of the bill should explain why. This is Ginza's other *oden* shop; the stock is chicken-based and the flavor (and decor) are somewhat lighter than Otako's. Open 4:00 P.M. to 11:00 P.M. daily.

AMERICAN

Deluxe

Fisherman's Wharf. Dobashi Bldg., B1, 17–8, Akasaka 3-chome, Minato-ku; 583–0659. Tokyo branch of San Francisco's famous seafood restaurant. Chef Fujita worked in San Francisco for ten years. Reservations preferred. Open 11:00 A.M. to 3:00 P.M., 5:00 P.M. to 11:30 P.M. All major credit cards.

Lobster Inn. Roppongi, Minato-ku; 478–1261. Across from Stars and Stripes Bldg. Tokyo's Main lobster specialists—they have them flown in from New England. Open 11:30 A.M. to 2:00 P.M., 5:30 P.M. to 10:00 P.M.

Expensive

Spago. 7–8, Roppongi 5-chome, Minato-ku; 423–4025. First Japanese branch of Austrian-born chef Wolfgang Puck's creation, Spago is the place for California cuisine. "Spago" is actually Italian slang for pasta, but there's a lot more to the menu than that. Open 5:00 P.M. to 11:00 P.M. daily. Spago may be the only restaurant in Tokyo that encourages tipping! AE, DC, JCB, Visa.

BRAZILIAN

Moderate

Saci Perere. PL Yotsuya Bldg., 9 Honshio-cho, Shinjuku-ku; 353–7521. Authentic Brazilian food with samba and bossa nova performances. Open 6:00 P.M. to 2:00 A.M.; closed Sundays and holidays.

BRITISH

Moderate

Berni Inn. Ginza branch: Yayoi Bldg., 6–19, Ginza 7-chome, Chuo-ku; 571–8210. Roppongi branch: No 3 Goto Building, 13–14, Roppongi 3-chome, Minato-ku; 405–4928. Shinjuku branch: New Sun Park Building, 20–5, Shinjuku 3-chome, Shinjuku-ku; 341–5982. Pub restaurants with Victorian decor, branches of the large British chain. Japanese beer. 11:30 A.M. to midnight.

CAMBODIAN

Inexpensive

Angkor Wat. 44–12, Yoyogi 1-chome, Shibuya-ku; 370–3019. Near Yoyogi Station. The first Cambodian restaurant in town, opened by Cambodian refugees. Very simple and inexpensive, with a menu of traditional rice-based dishes. Not spectacular.

CHINESE

There are plenty of moderately priced Chinese restaurants in Tokyo, and innumerable extremely cheap ones. Most of them use too much monosodium glutamate (*aji-no-moto,* as it's known in Japan, the country in which it was invented), which is the problem with cheap Chinese food all over the world. In the cheap places, the food has also undergone substantial adaptations to suit it to the Japanese palate, so true aficionados may get a shock. Undoubtedly the most popular Chinese dish locally—perhaps the single most popular food—is *ramen,* Chinese-style noodles swimming in broth. About ¥500 will buy you a basic bowl of ramen, hot, nourishing, and tasty (if you can forget about the additives).

Below we have listed some of the more expensive Chinese restaurants, where you are more likely to be served authentic Chinese food.

Expensive

Bodaiju. 2nd fl., Bukyo Dendo Center Bldg., 3–14, Shiba 4-chome, Minato-ku; 456–3257. "Unique" is an overworked word, but it applies to Bodaiju, which is the first and only restaurant in Japan to specialize in Chinese vegetarian dishes. Many visitors to Hong Kong will have seen the incredibly crafty imitations of meat dishes produced by vegetarian restaurants in the Colony, and now they're available here too. The owner, Mr. Numata, is the man responsible for putting Buddhist bibles alongside the Christian ones in many of Japan's hotels. Open 11:30 A.M. to 2:00 P.M., 5:30 to 9:00 P.M.; closed Sundays. Closest subway stations are Mita (on the Tori No. 6 Mita line) and Tamachi on the Yamanote line. AE, Diamond, DC.

China Doll. 27–19, Minami-Aoyama 2-chome, Minato-ku; 479–0201. Next to Orange House in Aoyama. A famous restaurant with a wide range of dishes. All major credit cards.

Fu-Ling. 8–4, Roppongi 4-chome, Minato-ku; 401–9769. A Cantonese-style restaurant that is open from morning to late at night—as late as 3:00 A.M. All major credit cards.

Heichinrou. 28th fl. Fukoku Seimei Bldg., 2–2, Uchisaiwaicho 2-chome, Chiyoda-ku; 508–0555. A branch of the oldest restaurant in Yokohama's China-town, Heichinrou has an elaborately Chinese interior and a great view of the Imperial Palace moat. The Cantonese cuisine is prepared by a chef sent from one of Hong Kong's leading hotels. Open 11:00 A.M. TO 9:30 P.M.; closed on Sundays and national holidays. All major credit cards.

Heichinrou. Shibuya Branch, 2nd fl., Shibuya Hillside, 19–3, Jinnan 1-chome, Shibuya-ku; 464–7888. The Shibuya branch of the famous restaurant, near Parco II Department Store, specializes in Cantonese-style fresh seafood. Open daily 11:00 A.M. to 10:30 P.M. All major credit cards.

Hoa Hoa. Roppongi, Minato-ku; 402–8787. Five minutes walk from Roppongi intersection towards Shibuya. Another example of the East-West marriages that have been cropping up in *haute cuisine* lately, Hoa Hoa's chefs provide Cantonese cuisine cooked in a French manner. Open 11:30 A.M. to 3:00 A.M. (last orders 2:30 A.M.). Open 5:00 P.M. to 11:00 P.M. on Sundays and holidays. All major credit cards.

Hokkai-En. 12, 1, Nishi-Azabu 2-chome, Minato-ku; 407–8507. Located close to the Almond coffee shop at Roppongi intersection. A large restaurant that is widely believed to be one of the best Peking-style places in town. It's also expensive. Quiet decor, English menu. All major credit cards.

New Asia Restaurant. 3–2, Shiba Daimon 2-chome, Minato-ku; 434–0005. Shanghai cuisine, with a menu that changes daily. Open lunchtime and 5:00 P.M.

to 11:30 P.M. Reservations are preferred. Hamamatsu-cho is the nearest Yama-note line station.

South China. 35, Jingumae 6-chome, Shibuya-ku; 400–0031. Also at 14–10, Sakuragaoka-cho, Shibuya-ku; 461–7592. Two Cantonese restaurants with high reputations. All major credit cards.

Tokyo Daihanten. JC Bldg., 17–3, Shinjuku 5-chome, Shinjuku-ku; 202–0121. With over 200 dishes on the menu and reportedly over 60 chefs to prepare them, this is a very special Szechuan-style restaurant. Open daily from 10:00 A.M. to 10:00 P.M. AE, Diamond, DC, UC, Visa.

CZECHOSLOVAKIAN
Moderate

Castle Praha. Tonichi Bldg., 2–31, Roppongi 6-chome, Minato-ku; 405–2831. Czechoslovakian cuisine with Bohemian music. Open lunchtimes and 5:00 P.M. to 10:00 P.M. Reservations preferred.

FRENCH
Deluxe

Chardonnay. 16–15, Roppongi 3-chome, Minato-ku; 584–0954. Cooking supervised by a French chef in this thirteen-year-old restaurant. Reservations preferred, room for private parties available. Open lunchtime and 6:00 P.M. to 11:00 P.M.; Sundays 5:00 P.M. to 11:00 P.M. All major credit cards.

Crescent. 8–20, Shiba-Koen 1-chome, Minato-ku; 436–3211. Rebuilt in late-Victorian style; live musical entertainment accompanies the food. Open daily 11:30 A.M. to 11:00 P.M.; closed on Sundays in the summer. All major credit cards.

L'ecrin Ginza. Ginza Mikimoto Pearl Bldg., 5–5, Ginza 4-chome, Chuo-ku; 561–9706. The chef de cuisine is a member of France's prestigious Academie Culinaire. Open lunch, tea, and dinner; closed on Sundays. Reservations preferred. Live musical entertainment. All major credit cards.

John Kanaya Azabu Restaurant. Kanaya Hotel Mansion, 1–25, Nishi-Azabu 3-chome, Minato-ku; 402–4744. A sleek spot, fashionable with diplomats and fast-lane locals. Open 5:30 P.M. to 11:00 P.M. All major credit cards.

Maxim's de Paris. Sony Bldg., 3–1, Ginza 5-chome, Chuo-ku; 572–3621. A clone of the famous Parisian original with French chef and manager direct from Paris, Maxim's is in the basement of the Sony Bldg. in the heart of the Ginza. Lunchtime set menu a hefty ¥5,400; dinner set menu ¥18,000. Open 11:30 A.M. to 2:30 P.M.; 5:30 P.M. to 11:00 P.M.; bar open 11:30 A.M. to 11:00 P.M.; closed on Sundays. AE, DC, V.

Prunier. Imperial Hotel, 1–1, Uchsaiwai 1-chome, Chiyoda-ku; 504–1111. Tokyo's branch of the famous Parisian establishment, in the capital's oldest five-star hotel. All major credit cards.

Rengaya. Daikanyama branch: 29–18, Sarugaku-cho, Shibuya-ku; 496–8991. The cuisine of Lyon in the famous "brick house." Daikanyama shop (1st stop on Toyoko Line from Shibuya) open noon to midnight. All major credit cards.

Virgo. Hotel New Otani, 4, Kioi-cho, Chiyoda-ku; 262–1127. La nouvelle cuisine prepared by a Parisian chef. Terrific views of Tokyo from the top floor of the New Otani Tower. All major credit cards.

Expensive

Bistro Lotus. JBP Bldg., 8–17, Roppongi 6-chome, Minato-ku; 403–7666. Changing menu, respectable cellar of French wines. Reservations preferred. All major credit cards.

Chez Figaro. 4–1, Nishi-Azabu 4-chome, Minato-ku; 400–8718. Tokyo's best bistro, wildly popular with French residents. The ¥2,000 lunch served Tuesday through Saturday is an especially outstanding bargain. Private parties (4 to 30 persons) catered. Reservations preferred. Open for lunch and from 6:00 P.M. to 10:00 P.M. All major credit cards.

Isolde. Hokushin Bldg., 2–1, Nishi-Azabu 3-chome, Minato-ku; 478–1055. Impressively authentic-seeming French cuisine in an elegant Parisian ambience. Live music, reservations preferred. Open every day 11:30 A.M. to midnight. All major credit cards.

Le Poisson Rouge. 3–10, Minami-Aoyama 5-chome, Minato-ku; 499–3391. Reservations preferred. All major credit cards.

La Promenade. Sanshin Bldg., 4–1, Yuraku-cho 1-chome, Chiyoda-ku; 504–3668. Very popular restaurant, menu changes daily. Reservations preferred. All major credit cards.

Regence. 32nd fl., Toho Seimei Bldg., 15–1, Shibuya 2-chome, Shibuya-ku; 406–5291. Authentic French cuisine at the top of Shibuya's tallest building. Open daily 11:30 A.M. to 2:00 P.M., 5:30 P.M. to 9:30 P.M., 8:30 P.M. on Sundays and holidays. All major credit cards.

Shido. TBS Kaikan Bldg., 3–3, Akasaka 5-chome, Minato-ku; 582–5891. Daily specials and a mid-afternoon 9-course set. Reservations preferred. All major credit cards.

GERMAN

Expensive

Alte Liebe. 29–8 Minami Aoyama 2-chome, Minato-ku; 405–8312. Ginza branch: 8, Ginza 7-chome, Chuo-ku; 573–4025. Live music at the Ginza shop. Reservations preferred.

Bei Rudi. 11–45, Akasaka 1-chome, Minato-ku (Dai-san Kowa Building B1); 583–2519, 586–4572. Said to serve the best German food in town, Bei Rudi has a cheerful, beer hall atmosphere, with live music. Open 5:00 P.M. to 2:00 A.M.; closed Mondays. Nearest stations Toranomon and Akasaka.

Ketel's. 5–14, Ginza 5-chome, Chuo-ku; 571–4642. German dishes from the firm that pioneered brown bread and pumpernickel in Japan. 11:30 A.M. to 9:30 P.M.

Lohmeyer's. Igami Bldg., 3–14, Ginza 5-chome, Chuo-ku; 571–5024. A well-established restaurant in Ginza, near the Sony Bldg. Open daily 11:00 A.M. to 10:00 P.M.

GREEK

Moderate

Double Ax. Koshi Bldg., 10–4, Roppongi 3-chome, Minato-ku; 401–7384. Tokyo's only Greek chef prepares a wide variety of dishes, in a carefree Greek atmosphere. Dinner course: ¥7,000 for two. Open 5:30 P.M. to 11:30 P.M. daily.

INDIAN

Moderate

Ajanta. 15–14, Kudan Kita 1-chome, Chiyoda-ku; 264–4255. Classiest Indian restaurant in town, located near Indian Embassy. Saris for sale. Open 11:30 A.M. to 9:00 P.M.

Ashoka. Pearl Bldg., 9–18, Ginza 7-chome, Chuo-ku. Sitar music, incense. Many delicious specialities, bland or hot. Open from 11:30 A.M. to 9:30 P.M. Reservations preferred.

Maharaja. Takanao Bldg., 26–11, Shinjuku 3-chome, Shinjuku-ku; 354–0222. Located in the "World Snack," a floor of international restaurants in the Takano Fruits Parlour Bldg., which stands on what is alleged to be the most expensive land in the world, near Shiyuku Station. Fortunately this is not reflected in Maharaja's prices. Nan and tandoori cooked before your eyes by Indian chefs. Other branches near Ginza's Mitsukoshi Bldg. and in basement of Odakaya Department Store in Yokohama Station Bldg.

· **Maharao.** Hibiya Mitsui Bldg., 1–2, Yurakucho 1-chome, Chiyoda-ku; 580–6423. Very popular, always crowded. A sister shop to Maharaja, above.

Moti. Roppongi branch: Roppongi Hama Bldg. 3rd fl., 2–35 Roppongi 6-chome, Minato-ku; 479–1939, 479–1955. Akasaka branch: Akasaka Floral Plaza 2nd fl., 8–8, Akasaka 3-chome, Minato-ku; 582–3620, 584–3760. Also at Akasaka 2-chome: 584–6640. The best Indian food in Japan, many say. Piping hot, balloon-like *nan,* delicious *sagh.*

Nair's. 10–7, Ginza 4-chome, Chuo-ku; 541–8246. A little piece of India, friendly, informal and sometimes delicious. Open noon to 9:30 P.M.

The Taj. Pagoda Bldg., 2–7 Akasaka 3-chome, Minato-ku; 586–6606. Next to Moti's in Akasaka. A stylish, international interior, sophisticated service, unusual and delicious dishes. Lunchtime menu is a bargain.

INDONESIAN

Moderate

Bengawan Solo. 18–13, Roppongi 7-chome, Minato-ku; 408–5698. National dishes, strongly spiced. Open 11:30 A.M. to 2:30 P.M., 5:30 P.M. to 10:30 P.M.

Indonesia Raya. 4–3, Shinbashi 4-chome, Minato-ku; 433–7005. Exotic decor with Indonesian folk art objects; waitresses in traditional attire. Open 11:30 A.M. to 10:30 P.M.; closed Sundays and holidays.

Sederhana. 5–4, Kami-Osaki 3-chome, Shinagawa-ku; 473–0354/5. Meguro is the nearest station; the restaurant is upstairs in the Tanaka Bldg. on the corner of No. 2 Expressway. A rarity in Japan, a totally un-phony neighborhood-style ethnic restaurant, run by an Indonesian family, with the wife taking the orders and her husband doing the cooking. The food is entirely authentic and there's an English language menu. Open noon to 2:00 P.M., 5:00 P.M. to 10:00 P.M. daily.

ITALIAN

Expensive

La Cometa. 1–7 Azabu Juban, Minato-ku; 470–5105. A cozy and authentic little restaurant serving Italian fish and meat dishes. Dinner menu hovers around ¥7,000; lunch menu is more in the moderate category. Open 11:45 A.M. to 2:00 P.M. and 6:00 P.M. to 10:30 P.M.

Moderate

Antonio's. 1–20, Nishi-Azabu 3-chome, Minato-ku; 408–1971. Daikanyama Branch: Hillside Terrace D, 29–9, Sarugacho, Shibuya-ku; 464–6041. Jiyugaoka Branch, Kawazu Bldg., 9–20, Jiyugaoka 2-chome, Meguro-ku; 717–2085. Long established, with a high reputation. Open noon to 2:30 P.M., 5:00 P.M. to 10:30 P.M.

Borsalino. S. K. Heim Bldg., 8–2, Roppongi 6-chome, Minato-ku; 401–7751. Authentic dishes in a relaxing black-and-white interior. Open noon to 2:00 A.M., Sun. 6:00 P.M. to 11:00 P.M., Closed on Mondays.

Nicola's. Roppongi Plaza, 12–6, Roppongi 3-chome, Minato-ku; 401–6936. Owned by Nicola V. Zapetti, this restaurant is famous for its 50 varieties of pizza. Also spare ribs and New York-cut steaks. Open daily noon to 3:00 A.M.

Roma Sabatini. Center Bldg., 29–8, Dogenzaka 2-chome, Shibuya-ku; 461–0495. Italian chef; the menu is a copy of the original in Rome. The restaurant is Japan's only recipient of the Diploma di Benemerenza, awarded by Turismo di Roma. Open noon to 2:30 P.M., 5:30 P.M. to 10:30 P.M.

Sabatini di Firenze. 7th fl., Sony Bldg., 3–1, Ginza 5-chome, Chuo-ku; 573–0013. The first overseas branch of this famous restaurant, superbly appointed. Open noon to 2:30 P.M. and 5:30 P.M. to 11:30 P.M.

KOREAN
Moderate

JuJu. 1F Kotsu Anzen Kyoiku Bldg., 3–24–20 Nishi Azabu, Minato-ku; 405–9911. *Yakiniku* in cool surroundings in Roppongi. Open 6:00 P.M. to 5:00 A.M.

Sankoen. Asami Bldg., 11–16 Azabu Juban 1-chome, Minato-ku; 585–6306. Open 11:30 A.M. to 2:00 A.M.; Sundays 11:30 A.M. to 1:00 A.M.; closed Wednesdays.

Seikoen. 6–6, Ginza 1-chome, Chuo-ku; 561–5883. Open 11:30 A.M. to 11:00 P.M.; Sundays and holidays 3:00 P.M. to 10:00 P.M.

LATIN AMERICAN
Moderate

Restaurante Gaucho. Nomura Bldg., 4–8, Yonban-cho, Chiyoda-ku; 262–8621. Live Latin music, a relaxed, carefree, and cheerful atmosphere. A popular item on the menu is Churrasco Libre, barbecued chicken, pork, and beef. Open 11:00 A.M. to 11:00 P.M.; closed Sundays and holidays.

MIDDLE EASTERN
Moderate

Laila. Roppingi Forum, 2nd fl., 16–52, Roppongi 5-chome, Minato-ku; 582–8491. Probably the first Middle-Eastern restaurant in Japan. Belly dancing and a real Afghan-cum-Middle-Eastern atmosphere. Open daily from 11:00 A.M. to 2:00 A.M.

PAKISTANI
Moderate

Gandhara. Ginza Five Star Bldg., 8–13, Ginza 5-chome, Chuo-ku; 574–9289. Tokyo's only authentic Pakistani restaurant. Open 11:30 A.M. to 2:00 P.M.; 5:00 P.M. to 9:30 P.M.; closed Sundays.

RUSSIAN
Moderate

Volga. 3–5–14 Shibakoen, Minato-ku; 433–1766. Onion domes outside, pre-Revolutionary gloom within. Open 11:00 A.M. to 11:30 P.M.

SPANISH
Expensive

Patio Flamenco. 10–12, Dogenzaka 2-chome, Shibuya-ku; 464–8476. Open 11:00 A.M. to 3:00 A.M. daily. Live flamenco. Paella, seafood dishes.

Los Platos. Terrace Akasaka Bldg., 13–11, Akasaka 6-chome, Minato-ku; 583–4262. Flamenco guitarist. Open 2:00 P.M. to 10:30 P.M.; closed Sundays.

SWEDISH

Expensive

Stockholm. Sweden Center, 11–9, Roppongi 6-chome, Minato-ku; 403–9046. Swedish smorgasbord and other Scandinavian delicacies in a large restaurant with live music. Open throughout the year, 11:00 A.M. to 11:00 P.M.

SWISS

Moderate

Movenpick. Shinjuku Center Bldg., Annex, 25–1, Nishi Shinjuku 1-chome, Shinjuku-ku; 344–5361. A handsome, low-rising, polygonal building among the skyscrapers of West Shinjuku, houses the very best place in town for quiche Lorraine and other pie dishes, as well as a number of hard-to-come-by European delicacies. Open daily, from breakfast to dinner. Ginza branch: Ginza Sanwa Bldg. B2, 6–1, Ginza 4-chome, Chuo-ku; 561–0351.

Tokyo Swiss Inn. Tokyo Bed Bldg., 1–16, Roppongi 4-chome, Minato-ku; 584–0911. Swiss-managed, this intimate restaurant features good veal dishes. Open 5:00 P.M. to 11:00 P.M.

THAI

Moderate

Chiang Mai. Kaitei Building 6–10, Yuraku-cho 1-chome, Chiyoda-ku; 580–0456. Friendly, intimate, Thai-managed restaurant with fiendishly hot items on the menu. Open 11:00 A.M. to 11:00 P.M.; closed Saturdays.

VIETNAMESE

Moderate

Aodai. Akasaka Trade Bldg., 4–14, Akasaka 5-chome, Minato-ku; 583–0234. Open 5:30 P.M. to 11:00 P.M.; closed Sundays.

Hi Lac Nam. 9–16, Kita Shinjuku 3-chome, Shinjuku-ku; 369–5431. Open 10:00 A.M. to 10:00 P.M.; closed first and third Mondays.

NATURAL FOOD RESTAURANTS

Inexpensive to Moderate

Ashun. Shimo-Kitazawa Credit Bldg., 2nd fl., 26–2, Kitazawa 3-chome, Setagaya-ku; 465–7653. Believe it or not, curry rice is one of the most popular of all dishes, Japanese or foreign, in Japan. This is a brown rice-based vegetarian curry house with a number of highly original dishes—like fried *natto* (fermented soybeans). Open noon to 1:00 A.M., 2:00 P.M. to 1:00 A.M. on Saturdays; closed on Mondays. Shimokitazawa Station on the Odakyu Line is five minutes away on foot.

Carrot. This Harajuku restaurant is also listed in the Japanese section.

Fure-ai no Mura. 2–45–6 Kabuki-cho, Shinjuku-ku; 209–8622. Located in Tokyo's naughtiest square mile, Fure-ai is said by some to have the finest menu of natural foods in the capital. Open 11:00 A.M. to 11:00 P.M.

Manna. 16–5, Shinjuku 1-chome, Shinjuku-ku; 344–6606, 342–2659. Long-established, somewhat severe, vegetarian restaurant run by Seventh Day Adventists. Open 11:00 A.M. to 9:00 P.M.; 11:00 A.M. to 3:00 P.M. on Fridays; closed Saturdays, holidays, and some Sundays.

Shinbashi Kenko Shizenshoku Centre, 26–3, Shinbashi 3-chome, Minato-ku; 573–4181. Old-established health food restaurant and shop. Open 9:30 A.M. to 6:00 P.M., dining room open 11:30 A.M. to 2:00 P.M.; closed Sundays and holidays.

Tenmi. This famous Shibuya natural food center is listed in the Japanese section.

Tofuya. 1st fl., Sanyo Akasaka Bldg., 5–2, Akasaka 3-chome, Minato-ku; 582–1028. Classic Japanese tofu dishes plus rice dishes. Open 11:30 A.M. to 1:30 P.M.; 5:00 P.M. to 10:00 P.M.; closed Saturdays, Sundays, and holidays.

Tojinbo. B1, New Shinbashi Bldg., 16–2, Shinbashi 2-chome, Minato-ku; 580–7307. Very near Shinbashi Station. Wild vegetables, delicious Japan Sea fish specialities, no MSG. Open 5:00 P.M. to 11:00 P.M., closed on first and third Saturday and Sunday of the month and holidays.

STEAK AND PRIME RIBS

Due to the artificially high price of beef in Japan, eating steak is an expensive business. This doesn't deter the serious steak man, and a number of fine Tokyo restaurants serve this dish.

Deluxe

Aragawa. Hankyu Kotsusha Bldg., 3–9, Shinbashi 3-chome, Minato-ku; 591 –8765. Open from 11:00 A.M. to 11:00 P.M. Painstakingly reared beef, lovingly prepared for the table. All major credit cards.

Hama. No. 5 Polestar Bldg., 7th fl., 6–12. Ginza 7-chome, Chuo-ku; 573–0915. Roppongi shop: 2–10 Roppongi 7-chome, Minato-ku; 403–1717. Teppanyaki and seafood as well as steak are specialities of Hama, noted for its elegance. Open 11:00 A.M. to 2:00 P.M.; 5:00 P.M. to 2:00 A.M.; closed 1st and 3rd Sundays. All major credit cards.

Expensive

Benihana of New York. 3–7, Ginza 6-chome, Chuo-ku; 571–0700. Hibachi and Teppanyaki steak are specialties of the house, though the New York-cut steak is said to be more popular. There are 50 Benihana restaurants in the United States now. Open 11:00 A.M. to 10:00 P.M. All major credit cards.

Colza. Clover Bldg., 15–10, Roppongi 7-chome, Minato-ku; 405–5631. Next to Meiji-ya in Roppongi. Colza specializes in teppanyaki, steak, and seafood. Open 11:30 A.M. to 2:00 P.M.; 5:00 P.M. to 2:00 A.M.; Sundays and holidays 5:00 P.M. to 11:00 P.M. All major credit cards.

Moderate

Chaco Atago Ten. MY Bldg., 4–1, Nishi Shinbashi 3-chome, Minato-ku; 432–4850.

Suehiro. Ginza branch: Kintetsu Bldg., 4–10, Ginza 4-chome, Chuo-ku; 562–0591. Others at Ginza 6-chome: 571–9271; Harajuku: 401–4101; Ikebukuro: 985–6232; and Shinjuku: 356–4656. A chain famous for the quality of its Kobe steak.

OTHERS

American fast food is very well established in Tokyo, and nobody nostalgic for the taste of a Big Mac need remain nostalgic for long. **McDonald's**—"Makudonurarudo" it comes out in Japanese—far and away leads the field, but **Kentucky Fried Chicken, Wendy's Hamburgers, Barby's Beef Sandwiches, Mister Donut,** and **Baskin-Robbins** are all hanging in there. Local imitations have sprung up, among them **Morinaga** and **First Kitchen.**

Japanese chain restaurants that sell reasonable and inexpensive food include **Fujiya, Morinaga,** and **Coq d'Or.** Most big buildings in central Tokyo have concentrations of cheaper restaurants in their basements. The Yuraku Food Center, under the elevated expressway at Sukiyabashi, between Ginza and Hibiya, also has numerous small restaurants of various kinds. Other good bets are the city's numerous German-style beer halls, including **New Tokyo** at Sukiyabashi, between Ginza and Hibiya subway stations. **Kirin Beer Hall** near Sukiyabashi; **Munchin Beer Hall,** and **Lion Beer Hall,** Shinbashi both accessible from Ginza and Shinbashi subway stations,; the **World Service Snack Bar** in the Sanshi Bldg., Ginza; and the dining rooms of department stores.

British-style pubs with fish and chips or tidbits and darts include **Eri's Cabin, Uncle Michael,** and the **Bull and Bear** (no darts), all at Roppongi station on the Hibiya line, and the **Rising Sun** at Yotsuya station on the Marunouchi and Chuo lines.

In locating these bars you will find the area maps printed in *Tokyo Journal* (monthly ¥300) and *Tour Companion* (weekly, free) an invaluable aid.

The visitor who seriously needs to cut his everyday expenditure will find that many small coffee shops offer "morning service." During the morning hours only, these shops include something extra—a boiled egg and toast, perhaps, or a sandwich—for the price of a cup of coffee or tea. "Morning service" is almost the same in Japanese—*moningu sabisu.*

Heading out of the center of town and into the suburbs, visitors may be amazed to see how American-style roadside restaurants have caught on. **Denny's,** for example, has more than 150 family restaurants in the Tokyo region.

HOTEL DINING

Expect hotel dining rooms to be *Deluxe* and *Expensive;* snack bars, tea lounges and coffee shops fall in the *Moderate* and *Inexpensive* ratings.

Akasaka Prince Hotel. 1–2, Kioi-cho, Chiyoda-ku. Near Akasaka-Mitsuke subway station; 234–1111. Tokyo's striking new landmark offers terrific views from the *Blue Gardenia* on 40th floor. Other restaurants in the tower are: *Potomac* Western cuisine, 3rd fl.; *Kioi,* Japanese cuisine; *Tachibana,* sushi; *Kiri,* tempura; and *Riou,* Cantonese—all in the basement. *Ohmi* steak house is in the diminutive annex, while the original building, constructed before the war as the palace of a Korean prince (hence the hotel's name), houses the French restaurant *Torianon.*

Capitol Tokyu, formerly Tokyo Hilton. 2–10–3 Nagato-cho, Chiyoda-ku. A taxi ride from Akasaka-Mitsuke subway station; 581–4511. The Tokyo Hilton became the Capital Tokyu when the lease reverted to the owner (the Tokyu Corporation) in January 1984. On September 1, 1984, the Tokyo Hilton International relocated to West Shinjuku, near the Century Hyatt. The Capital Tokyu retains the old Hilton's reputation for excellent food. The *Keyaki Grill* features gourmet food and a well-stocked cellar of select wines. Noon to 3:00 P.M., 5:30 P.M. to 10:30 P.M. *Genji-no-ma* features Japanese specialties in Japanese atmosphere and has a *Teppan-yaki* counter and a *Sushi* counter. Cocktail and tea lounge serves breakfast buffet, 7:00 A.M. to 10:30 A.M.; luncheon buffet, noon to 2:30 P.M. (except Sundays and holidays). The *Star Hill Chinese Restaurant* has 177 dishes on the menu, on Sundays and National Holidays all-you-can-eat for ¥4,200. *Coffee Shop,* informal and versatile, has a view over the Japanese garden.

Century Hyatt. 2–7–2 Nishi-Shinjuku, Shinjuku-ku. A taxi ride from Shinjuku subway and national railway stations; 349–0111. From the simple to the sumptuous, in 10 restaurants and lounges. Japanese food is Kansai-style, Chinese food is Beijing and Shanghai-styles. The Italian restaurant *Caterina* is the only one in Japan operated by a hotel itself. *Chenonceaux* is a French restaurant on the 27th floor—super-elegant.

Ginza Dai Ichi 1–2 Shinbashi, Monato-ku. Near Shinbashi subway and national railway station; 542–5311. *Restaurant Carnaval:* A large room offering quick service and moderate prices. Features excellent roast beef every Wednesday. *Pai Lo-tien:* A Chinese buffet. *Olympia:* A buffet restaurant featuring food from all round the world.

Ginza Tokyu. 5–15–9 Ginza, (huo-ku. Near Ginza subway station; 541–2411. *Grill:* Good food. The roast beef is particularly worthwhile. Trout in season is also a specialty. *Kung Chiao Ting:* Chinese buffet with an elaborate selection of dishes and plenty of room. Lunchtime, and for dinner from 5:30–9:30 P.M. Moderately expensive.

Hilton International. 344–5111. Second floor restaurants in the new Shinjuku Hilton include *Musashino,* for sushi, tempura and teppan-yaki, and *Dynasty* for Chinese dishes.

Hotel Okura. 2–10–4 Toranoman, Minato-ku. A taxi ride from Toranomon and Kasumigaseki subway stations. Right behind the U.S. Embassy; 582–0111. As befits Tokyo's most luxurious hotel, the Okura is swarming with restaurants. *Continental Room,* open for lunch and dinner, serves European food and overlooks downtown Tokyo. *Orchid Room* (French Restaurant), open for breakfast, lunch and dinner, has band music at night. *Yamazato:* An attractive Japanese restaurant serving yakitori, suki-yaki, and the like. *Toh-ka-lin:* An excellent Cantonese restaurant. *Starlight Lounge:* piano and combo music, 6:00 P.M. to 11:00 P.M. *Terrace Restaurant,* informal and pretty, is open from 7:00 A.M. to 9:00 P.M., and serves Chinese food. *La Belle Epoque* in the South Wing, 19th-century in style, serves European cuisine and has room for dancing.

Imperial. 1–1–1 Uchisaiwai-cho, Chiyoda-ku. Near Hibiya subway station; 504–1111. The top-floor *Fontainebleau* French restaurant, open for lunch and dinner, is outstanding any time, often memorable. The last Friday of each month is the *Diner Gastronomique,* for which you will want to schedule long in advance. *Rainbow Room,* 17th fl., open 6:00 P.M. to 11:00 P.M. except Sun. & holidays, gives a superb night view of Tokyo. Organ music in *Rainbow Lounge,* 17th fl., 6:30 P.M. to 11:00 P.M. *Prunier* is now part of the Main Dining Room. Excellent fish dishes. The new *Coffee Shop, "Pedals,"* facing street specializes in pancakes. The Imperial's mighty new Imperial Tower has a number of new restaurants in the basement: *La Brasserie,* French; *Peking, Sushi Gen, Ten-Ichi* (tempura) and *Kiccho,* Japanese. The 1st floor has a *Salon de Thè.*

Keio Plaza Hotel. 2–2–1 Nishi-Shinjuku, Shinjuku-ku. Near Shinjuku subway and national railway station; 344–0111. Full complement of restaurants from basement to 45th floor. *Aurora Lounge* at the highest level is open from 10:00 A.M. to midnight. On clear days, Mt. Fuji can be seen in the distance.

Marunouchi. 1–6–3 Marunouchi, Chiyoda-ku. Near Tokyo Station; 215–2151. *Bamboo Room:* an attractive grill that serves fine food.

Miyako Hotel. 1–1–50 Shirogane-dai, Minato-ku. By taxi from Meguro or Shinagawa national railway stations; 447–3111. *La Cle d'Or* dining room specializes in beef. Periodically, the menu of a state dinner party from the original Miyako, in Kyoto, is re-planned. Szechuan-style food served in Chinese restaurant. *Silver Hill* coffee shop has a buffet breakfast; chef's special at lunchtime—bouillabaisse.

The New Otani. 4 Kioi-cho, Chiyoda-ku. Near Akasaka-Mitsuke subway station; 265–1111. *Rose Room:* large and attractive grill. *Top of the Tower,* buffet restaurant, breakfast, lunch, and dinner. *Trader Vic's,* the first in the Orient. Chinese snack-style buffet, lunch and dinner, in the revolving *Blue Sky Lounge.*

Taikan-En: Chinese food, atmosphere. *Kioi:* Japanese restaurant. *Belle Vue:* a continental restaurant on the 16th floor with good food and a smashing view of Tokyo by night. *Rib Room* in the basement offers good steak and is well worth a visit. *Barbecue* in ten-acre Japanese garden. Open year-round.

Pacific Meridien. 3–13 Takanawa, Minato-ku. Near Shinagawa national and private railway station; 445–6711. *Garden Restaurant Ukidono,* and music 5:00 P.M. to 11:00 P.M. *Sky Lounge Blue Pacific,* 5:00 P.M. to 11:00 P.M., for drinking and dancing. Cellar bar *El Vencedor,* 5:00 P.M. to 11:00 P.M. Koto music in the *Tea and Cocktail Lounge,* 5:00 P.M. to 7:00 P.M.

Palace Hotel. 1–1–1, Marunouchi, Chiyoda-ku. Near Otemachi subway station; 211–5211. The 10th-floor *Crown Room* overlooks the Imperial Palace moat and grounds. Elegant dining, menu, and wine-list supervised by Paris-trained head-chef Tokusaburo Tanaka. Food is also good in the moat-side *Swan Room,* the hotel's main dining room. The basement houses the *Grill and Prunier* and a pub-restaurant *Ivy House.* The *Viking Room* offers a vast buffet that doesn't try too hard to pretend it's Scandinavian.

Takanawa Prince. 3–13–1 Takanawa, Minato-ku. Near Shinagawa national and private railway station; 447–1111. A French chef imported from France prepares his own specialities for royalty in *Le Irianon,* open from 7:00 A.M. to 11:00 P.M.

Tokyo Prince. 3–3–1 Shiba Koen, Minato-ku. Near Shiba Keon subway station; 432–1111. *Blue Gardenia* on the 11th floor offers continental cuisine in a very pleasant setting with a panoramic view of Tokyo. Music for dancing. A circular bar in the restaurant. *Grill Princess* for Western menu. *Gotoku* for sushi and *Fukusa* room for tempura. The garden-view *Prince Villa* is a simple, cheerful (somewhat Japanized) European restaurant open till 10:00 P.M. with chicken, seafood, steak, good pilaffs, and a young clientèle. Prices unbelievably low for Tokyo, prompt, efficient service.

NIGHT LIFE. Japanese cultural tradition is conducive to a flourishing night life, much of which is geared to the male Japanese. In a country where a sort of marital division of labor exists and the home is conceded to be the wife's castle, husbands do their entertaining on the outside. To accommodate them, countless bars, cabarets, and other kinds of nightspots have sprung up, making the entertainment areas of Japan among the most active in the world.

As night starts to fall in Tokyo, varicolored neons begin to blaze along the major streets. Behind the brilliantly lighted main drags, in dark little alleys and byways that twist and crisscross in mazelike patterns, are a multitude of nightspots, where women, as gorgeous as beauty parlors can make them, sit primly in kimono and Western dress and wait for business. Starting as early as 6:00 P.M., for the sidewalks are rolled up early in Japan, business comes—in the form of men who buy them drinks, complain about their wives and bosses, and air their troubles in general to sympathetic ears, while avid eyes watch the bill run up. This keeps up until about midnight, when a silence suddenly overtakes most areas (except where after-hours joints abound) as closing time arrives.

Night life in some variation on this theme has had a long history in Japan's traditionally male-dominated society. Ladies of the night reached their peak in the mid-18th century when the *oiran* reigned as queen of the Yoshiwara entertainment district, during the Tokugawa Shogunate. *Geishas* then were entertainers who sang and danced as a preliminary to an evening with an oiran, who was specially trained for her part. If some of the glowing reports of her accomplishments are correct, she surpassed even the fabulous *hetaerae* of ancient Greece in the knowledge and practice of the art of love.

The Yoshiwara, called Tokyo's Gay Quarters in the days before "gay" took on its current meaning, began to decline at the end of the 18th century and finally lost all claim to its so-called gaiety in 1958, when the Diet, under pressure from female members, outlawed prostitution. In so doing, it also removed the area from Tokyo's tourist attractions. It is now a far cry from what it was, even from what it had been in the postwar years before its legal demise. It is dotted with cheap bars and "massage" parlors where one can get a sort of massage if he insists.

As the oiran declined, the geisha rose in importance and, in the 19th century, took over as the main source of after-dark entertainment. But the geisha was a different sort of entertainer. Her forte was and still is singing, dancing, and playing the *samisen.* Geisha are very much in evidence today, and a geisha party is still the place where important business and political deals are sealed. Few foreigners, though, will have an opportunity to attend one, except as a guest. Proper standing in Japanese society along with a proper introduction is necessary.

Night life for foreigners centers around bars, cabarets, those restaurants that provide stage shows, discos, and nightspots of questionable character. In general, few places close their doors to foreigners. Those that do are not xenophobic. They are, instead, fearful of the language barrier. They are also worried about the foreigner's reaction to the bill, which may strike him as a figure taken from Japan's GNP. From past experience they know that the non-Japanese, especially the Caucasian, does not hesitate to make his views known. Since loud voices and threatening gestures are foreign to the Japanese way of life, a bar can lose regular customers when such an altercation arises.

The main night life areas of Tokyo include the **Ginza,** the heart of the city, with plenty of places for both foreigners and Japanese; **Shibuya,** about half an hour west of the Ginza, with a number of bars and clubs operating on a nonsegregated basis (its night life continues rather later than that of the Ginza area); **Shinjuku,** also about half an hour west of the Ginza, a large entertainment quarter that once included one of Japan's biggest red light districts, and now contains numerous theaters, bars, and nightclubs; and **Roppongi,** which has burgeoned recently as a competitor to the Ginza. In addition to its bars and clubs, many of which cater to foreigners, Roppongi is the center of the popular discos. Whereas the other districts tend to shut down at about 11:30 P.M., the night prowler in Roppongi can always find something going on.

Akasaka, ten minutes west of the Ginza, has geisha and a number of nightclubs catering to foreigners and to Japanese on the expense-account circuit. **Asakusa,** a center of night life for the ordinary working-class Japanese, lies to the north about half an hour from the Ginza. It is a fascinating place to visit at night but its small bars and clubs should not be visited unless you are with a Japanese who knows his way around.

Foreign women are accepted where Japanese women don't go, for example, at geisha parties, bars, and nightclubs. However, this is still not commonplace. Women accompanying their husbands, male friends, or associates to such places tend to be regarded (especially by the hostesses) with the curiosity reserved for visitors from Mars. And, in general, although the streets of Tokyo are safe at any time, a woman alone at night is looked at askance. Women can expect to feel comfortable at discos, kabuki theater, the movies, and restaurants with stage shows, but even in these cases, it is still the practice to go with a friend or with a male companion.

One other Japanese phenomenon should be mentioned here, and that is escort clubs for women only. Theses are places where women go and have young men dance and talk with them for a fee, just as hostesses entertain the men at the male-oriented clubs. Many of the customers are neglected Japanese wives. Three such establishments are: *Aoi Tori* (Blue Bird), at 7–17–12 Roppongi (486–4059), reservations from 4:00 P.M. to 3:00 A.M.; *Club Taboo* in Shibuya (464–4438), two hours for ¥10,000; and *Mr. Blue* in Roppongi (582–6887), two hours for ¥25,000.

The pleasure-seeking foreign male will find himself welcome in most places in Tokyo's entertainment areas. Throughout the narrow byways he will find a wide variety of nightspots. There are the bars without hostesses, often called "stand-up bars" because they formerly had no seats. In such places a knowledge of Japanese will help. As one goes up the scale to those spots where hostesses are provided, the price rises. Not only are the drinks subject to payment, but so are the women, in terms of hostess charge and tip, the latter being negotiable. Then there are the nightclubs, which provide some type of stage show along with hostesses, drinks, food, and dancing. Prices sometimes vary with the show, where higher cover charges are exacted relative to the fame of the entertainer. Prices at nightclubs cost from ¥20,000 on up per person. Finally, there are the high-class bars, which are the most expensive of all despite the fact that they provide no floor show. In such bars one might run across a prominent politician, a giant of industry, or a star entertainer on any given night. At the high-class bars the tab can run as high as ¥100,000 each.

In the tempestuous struggle for existence in the entertainment areas, where Darwin's rule of the survival of the fittest prevails, some interesting types of bars have sprung up. One is reported to dress up its hostesses as nuns to appeal to some people's subconscious quirk. Another provides a wall with a photograph holder in which customers are invited to place a picture of their boss or wife or someone else who has caused them frustration and throw glasses and bottles at it. Relieved of their frustrations, they do not complain about the bill for the glassware. Another, to appeal to the shortness of elderly Japanese, hires women under five feet as hostesses and calls itself a "transistor" bar.

Tokyo is also filled with hundreds of *karaoke* bars, the majority of which are in the Shinjuku area. Karaoke equipment consists of tape machine and microphone for the frustrated singers among the guests. Though foreigners are welcome at such bars, they should remember that the songs are generally popular Japanese songs with which they may not be familiar.

Discos have brought something new to Tokyo night life, another type of female companion, the foreign model, who is given free entrance and a free meal, because "she brings in the customers," just by being there. In this way, she is very much like her Japanese colleagues, whose function is exactly the same.

Tokyo discos can be, and often are, selective as to whom they allow in. Proper attire, though flexible in definition, is required. Discos have taken over with the younger generation and with those who would like to be or believe they are members of that age group. Foreign celebrities are found in many of them, as the discos undoubtedly remind them of home.

There is nothing wrong with Tokyo's night life that a well-filled wallet cannot cure. Without that wallet, though, it is not necessarily dull. Tokyo's nightspots have developed over the years in such a way as to suit almost every budget, and no person need feel left out because of lack of cash.

Here are charges that will be tacked on to a bill in addition to what one eats and drinks:

Service charge. Rate is dependent upon the type of service. Where only drinks and food are involved, it is about 10 to 15 percent. Where a hostess serves the client and sits at the table with him, acting as an absorbent for the story of his life, its trials and tribulations, it could be as much as 85 percent of the bill. In addition to this, there is a **hostess charge,** which is itemized separately from the service charge.

Tax. In pubs and restaurants where there are no hostesses, bills up to ¥2,500 are not charged a tax. Where a hostess is involved, as little as a ¥1,000 charge is taxable.

In the following list of nightclubs and bars, *Expensive* is anything over ¥20,000 a person; *Moderate* are those where one can expect a bill of from ¥10,000 to ¥20,000; *Inexpensive* are nightspots where a normal bill will be under ¥10,000.

Note. Nightspots of any sort are high-risk businesses in Tokyo as in any place else. By the time this book is published, some may have gone out of business, changed their name, or changed ownership. The list below is current at press time. For additional information on many of the places mentioned, or for more listings of places used to catering to foreign visitors, you might also consult the English-language *Tour Companion.*

Each entry below gives the name of the establishment, the district it's in, and the phone number. The simplest and most practical thing for visitors to do is to have someone, perhaps the hotel doorman, phone for directions and give them to the cab driver.

We have listed nightclubs and high-class bars together. To the Japanese mind, the difference is vague, except for the extremes like Copacabana on the one hand and Hime on the other. As one progresses toward the center, though, the differences disappear, and the names can stand for one or the other.

NIGHTCLUBS AND BARS

Expensive

Club Casanova. Roppongi; 583–8841. Open 8:00 P.M. to 3:00 A.M., with hostesses available until midnight. Drinks, food, hostesses. Bill will run from ¥25,000 a person, all inclusive. AE, DC.

Copacabana. Akasaka; 585–5811. Open from 6:00 P.M. to 2:00 A.M., except Sundays. Two shows nightly at 9:45 P.M. and 11:30 P.M. Cover charge ¥6,000 and hostess charge ¥3,000 an hour. Club service charge of 20 percent added to the bill as is a tax of 10 percent. Food is available, but the *Little Copa* above the nightclub has some of the best roast beef in Japan, as well as other food. At the Little Copa a 15 percent service charge and 10 percent tax is tacked on to the bill. At the nightclub a cost of ¥30,000 to ¥40,000 a person is considered reasonable. AE, DC.

Gres. Ginza; 573–0777. Open 7:00 P.M. to midnight. Live piano music, with drinks, food, hostesses. Bill will run to ¥40,000 per person, all inclusive. AE, DC.

Hime. Ginza; 572–2423. Open from 7:30 P.M. to midnight. Live music for entertainment, with drinks, food, hostesses. Bill will run from ¥50,000 to ¥100,000, including hostess, service charge, and tax. Price also depends on whether one is on the company expense account or is paying it out of one's own pocket and whether the customer is a regular or a first-time visitor. AE, DC.

El Morocco. Tameike; 585–5141. Open from 7:00 P.M. to 1:30 A.M. Live band with drinks, food, and hostesses. Bill will run to ¥22,000 per person, all inclusive. AE, DC.

The New Latin Quarter. Akasaka; 581–1326. Open 7:00 P.M. to 1:30 A.M., except Sundays. Floor shows at 8:30 P.M. and 10:30 P.M. Hostess charge is ¥4,000 an hour; cover charge is ¥6,000; drinks from ¥1,700. Special steak dinner at ¥12,000 if reserved a day in advance. Price includes food, cover charge, drinks, service charge, and tax. Chinese cuisine also available. Otherwise service charge is 20 percent and tax is 10 percent. With a hostess, the bill will come to ¥30,000 or more. AE, DC.

Le Rat Mort. Ginza; 571–9296. Open 7:00 P.M. to midnight. Live piano music, with drinks, food, hostesses. Bill will run from ¥35,000 to ¥60,000 a person depending on number of guests. Alone, the bill can come to almost ¥60,000, all inclusive. With two or more it could come to ¥35,000 a person. AE, DC.

Moderate

Club Fontana. Roppongi; 479–2358. Open 7:00 P.M. to 1:00 A.M., except Sundays. Cover charge of ¥3,000, hostess charge of ¥3,000 an hour, drinks at ¥1,000 each. No shows but piano and vocalist. AE, DC.

Club Maiko. Ginza; 574–7745. Open from 6:00 P.M. to midnight, except Sundays and holidays. Four shows nightly at 7:30 P.M., 8:40 P.M., 9:50 P.M. and 10:45 P.M., featuring geisha and maiko (apprentice geishas) dances. Performers wait on customers before and after shows. Table d'hôte menu at ¥8,000 a person with two drinks. Additional drinks at ¥1,000 each, plus tax and service charge. Japanese food available on request at ¥15,000 to ¥20,000 a person. Japanese credit cards accepted; otherwise, cash only.

Club Morena. Roppongi; 402–9337. Open from 7:30 P.M. to 1:00 A.M. Cover charge of ¥1,500 per person. Hostess charge ¥4,000 an hour and a compulsory plate of peanuts and other tidbits called "charm" at ¥800 a person. Drinks from ¥1,000 each. English-speaking hostesses. AE, DC.

Club Penthouse. Akasaka; 582–1803, 586–5929. Open 8:00 P.M. to 2:00 A.M. except Sundays. No shows but live band. Hostess charge at ¥7,000 a person for two hours. Cover charge at ¥4,000. Also, a 30 percent charge and 10 percent tax is added. About ¥25,000 a person will be sufficient. AE, DC.

Cordon Bleu. Akasaka; 582–7800. Open from 7:00 P.M. to 3:00 A.M., except Sundays. Nightly topless shows at 8:00 P.M., 10:00 P.M. and 12:30 A.M. French cuisine with table d'hote menu at ¥15,000 plus 10 percent tax, or hors d'oeuvres only at ¥12,000 plus 10 percent tax. Hostess charge at ¥8,000 for two hours. Count on ¥20,000 a person as reasonable to budget for an evening. AE, DC.

May Flower. Ginza; 563–2426. Open from 6:00 P.M. to 11:30 P.M. except Sundays and holidays. Live band but no shows. Hostesses available. About ¥20,000 a person will take care of an evening, inclusive of service charge and tax. AE.

Mikado. Akasaka; 583–1101. Open from 6:00 P.M. to 11:30 P.M., except Sundays. Nightly shows featuring Japanese and Western dances at 8:10 P.M. and 10:10 P.M. Count on ¥20,000 a person which includes cover charge of ¥3,500, hostess charge of ¥3,000 per hour, and ¥1,000 a drink. No cover charge for foreigners. Mikada claims to be the largest cabaret with hostesses in the world, boasting of 600 women and a capacity for 1,300 customers. It has its own dancing team and four regular bands. Food such as spareribs and sandwiches served. AE, DC.

Monte Carlo. Ginza; 571–5671. Open from 6:00 P.M. to 11:30 P.M., except Sundays and holidays. Japanese and foreign show nightly at 9:00 P.M. and 10:30 P.M. Special price of ¥15,000 to foreigners, which includes five drinks, a hostess to serve, cover charge, and tax. Additional drinks at ¥1,000 each. English-speaking hostesses available. AE, DC.

Play Boy Club. Roppongi; 478–4100. Open from 6:00 P.M. to 2:00 A.M. except Sundays and holidays. Nightly shows at 7:30 P.M., 9:00 P.M., and 10:30 P.M. Drinks at ¥750 for scotch, ¥550 for beer. Play Boy Club cardholders only. AE, DC.

Inexpensive

Bag Pipe. Shibuya, 499–1097; and Roppongi, 401–0580. Open from 5:00 P.M. to 5:00 A.M. daily. English-style pub. About ¥5,000 per person will cover two kinds of snacks, drinks, service charge, and tax. Drinks from ¥500. Japanese credit cards. DC.

Berni Inn. Roppongi; 405–4928. Open daily from 4:00 P.M. to 11:30 P.M.; on Fridays and Saturdays to 2:00 A.M. English-style pub. Beer at ¥500, food available at reasonable price. AE, DC.

Club Charon. Akasaka; 586–4480. Open from 7:30 P.M. to 1:00 A.M., except Saturdays, Sundays, and holidays. Piano and singer. Scotch at ¥900 or more, depending on brand. Small bottle of beer at ¥800. Hostess charge at ¥4,000 an hour. Table charge at ¥1,000 a person. Service charge and tax at 10 percent each. AE, DC.

Club Lee. Shinjuku; 209–2291. Open from 6:00 P.M. to midnight. Two shows nightly at 8:30 P.M. and 10:30 P.M., featuring Japanese singers. Between 6:00 P.M. and 8:00 P.M., about ¥12,000 will cover drink, service, hostess charge, and tax. After 8:00 P.M. budget ¥15,000 for the evening. AE, DC.

Crystal Room. Akasaka; 265–8000. Open from 6:00 P.M. to 11:30 P.M. Two top-class Parisian shows nightly at 7:30 P.M. and 10:00 P.M. Table d'hote menus at ¥16,500 and ¥22,000. Hors d'oeuvres only at ¥11,000. A la carte menu also available. No hostesses. AE, DC.

El Cupid. Roppongi; 405–6339. Open from 7:30 P.M. to 2:30 A.M., except Sundays and holidays. Filipino trio from 8:30 P.M. Drinks from ¥1,000. Cover charge ¥1,500. English-speaking hostesses at ¥3,000 an hour. Cover charge at bar only ¥500. Sandwiches at ¥1,000 and steak at ¥5,000 available. AE, DC.

The Glasshopper (sic). Akasaka; 586–3579. Open from 11:30 A.M. to 2:30 A.M. Drinks from ¥400, beer at ¥600, mixed drinks from ¥600, food from ¥450 but steak is ¥1,800. Popular with young Japanese. AE, DC.

High Grade Pub My Place. Roppongi; 401–3112. Open from 6:00 P.M. to 4:00 A.M., except Sundays and holidays. Table charge at ¥4,000 including two drinks. Food and drink from ¥1,000. AE, DC.

Lamp Light. Aoyama; 409–9594. Open from 5:30 P.M. to 2:00 A.M., except Sundays and holidays. Piano music. No hostesses. Will run about ¥8,000 to ¥10,000 a person. AE, DC.

My Scotch. Roppongi; 402–6649. Open daily from 6:00 P.M. to 2:00 A.M. Live music from 8:00 P.M., except Sundays and holidays. Drinks from ¥700, food from ¥700. Cover charge of ¥500 per person, which includes "charm." Service charge and tax at 10 percent each.

Nawanoren. Uchisaiwaicho, behind the Imperial Hotel; 508–9660. Open from 4:00 P.M. to 4:00 A.M. Japanese sake from ¥350, beer at ¥400, whiskey at ¥400, food from ¥500. Cash.

Peter and the Rabbits. Akasaka; 263–0400. Run by a television personality. Open from 7:00 P.M. to 4:00 A.M. This is a bottle club where the customer must buy his own bottle from ¥6,000 to ¥12,000. Table charge at ¥1,000 and "charm" at ¥500. Service charge and tax at 10 percent each. Chinese food available. Ice and water at ¥500. DC.

Potato Club. Akasaka; 585–3907. Open from 6:30 P.M. to 3:00 A.M., except Sundays. Live band music. No hostesses. About ¥10,000 will be enough. AE, DC.

Pub Central. Shinjuku; 356–0073. Open from 5:00 P.M. to 11:30 P.M. Drinks from ¥400. Table charge of ¥300. About ¥5,000 a person should be sufficient and would include some snack. DC.

Pub Grazie. Shinjuku; 209–8989. Open from 6:00 P.M. to 1:30 A.M., except Sundays. About ¥5,000 a person should be enough. Drinks from ¥500 and table charge at ¥1,000. DC, V.

Pub Happy Box. Shibuya; 476–2734. Open from 2:00 P.M. to midnight, except Sundays and holidays. Drinks from ¥450. Table charge at ¥500. About ¥4,000 per person should be enough. Cash only.

Pub House Cross. Roppongi; 402–8553. Open from 6:00 P.M. to 4:00 A.M., except Sundays and holidays. Table charge at ¥1,300 including one drink. Live band. Food available from ¥800 and drink from ¥800. AE, DC.

Pub House Royal Kan. Akasaka; 584–9426. Open 5:00 P.M. to 5:00 A.M. Drinks from ¥500, food from ¥600, table charge at ¥700. Before 7:00 P.M. all food is half the menu price. About ¥5,000 a person should be enough. Japanese credit cards.

Pub Passport. Ginza; 574–7576. Open from 6:00 P.M. to 11:30 P.M., except Sundays and holidays. About ¥5,000 per person will cover reasonable number of drinks, service charge, and tax. Snacks available. Drink starts at ¥500. Japanese credit cards or cash.

Pub Yagurachaya. Ginza; 571–3494. Open from 5:00 P.M. to midnight. Old Japanese country-style bar. Beer at ¥380, sake at ¥240, whiskey from ¥440, food from ¥180 to ¥880. Menu in English with colored pictures for better understanding. Guests must remove shoes on entering but chairs and stools available. Can accommodate 260 customers. Cash.

La Siesta. Ginza; 573–1021. Open from 5:00 P.M. Table charge of ¥500, whiskey from ¥450, draft beer at ¥350, food from ¥450. Tax, 10 percent. No service charge. Cash.

Suntory the Cellar. Akasaka; 470–1071. Quaintly named pub run by a whiskey manufacturer. Open from 5:00 P.M. to 11:00 P.M., daily. Suntory whiskey from ¥400. Graciously offers scotch at ¥500. Suntory beer from ¥500. Food available. Service charge and tax at 10 percent each. For bills over ¥2,500 there is a consumption tax. AE.

RESTAURANTS WITH STAGE SHOWS
The restaurants listed here require prior reservations.

Furusato. Shibuya; 463–2310. Open from 5:00 P.M. to 9:30 P.M. Open daily. Two shows a night at 7:00 P.M. and 8:30 P.M., featuring traditional Japanese dances. Set menu, including only Japanese food, available to foreigners at ¥6,000 to ¥10,000 inclusive of service charge and tax. AE, DC.

Matsubaya. Yoshiwara; 874–9401. Open from 6:00 P.M. to 10:00 P.M. Two shows nightly at 7:00 P.M. and 9:20 P.M. Table d'hôte menu from ¥6,000 plus 15 percent service charge and 10 percent tax. Private room available at ¥60,000, excluding food. Show features 18th-century courtesan, the *oiran*, dressed in kimono of that period and other authentic items of clothing. Food is Japanese *kaiseki-ryori*. DC, but cash preferred.

Miyarabi. Kudan; 261–3453. Open from 5:00 P.M. to 11:00 P.M., except Sundays and holidays. Okinawan restaurant with nightly show featuring Okinawan traditional dances at 8:00 P.M. Table d'hote menu of Okinawan food from ¥7,000 to ¥12,000 plus 20 percent service charge and 10 percent tax. Cash only.

DO-IT-YOURSELF BARS
The two bars listed below are high class yet not so expensive. There are other piano bars, but the ones listed here are representative, refined, and usually patronized by customers who speak English.

Little Manuela. Akasaka; 582–0469. Open from 7:00 P.M. to 1:00 A.M., except Sundays and holidays. Jet setters and top Japanese entertainers meet here. Its unique attraction is a jazz combo of piano, bass, and drum plus a saxophone, steel guitar, trumpet, and clarinet that are available for the clients to try their hand at with the combo accompanying them. Standard jazz is the fare. Table charge including "charm" is ¥2,500 for women; ¥3,000 for men. AE, DC.

Reverie. Akasaka; 582–8017. Open 7:00 P.M. to 1:00 A.M., except Sundays. Tokyo Jet Setters frequent this one and the one below. Hiroyuki Nishtoka, the very able pianist, is the drawing card. Vocalist sings from 9:00 P.M. Table charge of ¥800. Drinks from ¥900. No service charge but 10 percent tax. About ¥5,000 will produce a pleasant evening, where one can even check out his voice quality on songs he is familiar with, as pianist Nishioka knows almost all of them. What he does not know, he will pick up from a few hummed bars. AE, DC.

KARAOKE BARS

The Best Ten. Roppongi; 405–9934. Open from 6:30 A.M. to 3:30 A.M. Table charge is ¥1,000 with "charm" (tidbits) compulsory at ¥500. Drinks start from ¥600. A bottle of Suntory Black Label is ¥4,800. Ice and mineral water available at ¥500. Service charge and tax are 10 percent each. One bottle with two guests would come to ¥5,000 per person for the three. AE.

Karatto. Shibuya; 464–7073. Open from 6:30 P.M. to 2:00 A.M., except Sundays and holidays. Cover charge ¥1,000. Music to charge to ¥1,000. toDrinks from ¥800. Table d'hôte menu, including cover and music charge, "charm," and drinks at ¥4,400. Otherwise about ¥7,000 will insure a good evening. Japanese credit cards or cash.

Sharps and Flats Nodojiman Dojo. Roppongi; 405–7929. Open from 6:00 P.M. to 4:00 A.M., except Sundays and holidays. ¥3,500 will cover all drinks, tax and service charge. Cash.

DISCOS

Chakras Mandala. Roppongi; 479–5600. Open from 5:00 P.M. to 11:30 P.M. It is a favorite with the gilded youth, many of whom promenade on Sundays along the notorious or noted Harajuku Pedestrian's Paradise. Entrance fee of ¥3,500 for men and ¥2,500 for women includes all drinks and food. Three shows nightly, at 8:30 P.M., 10:00 P.M. and 11:00 P.M. AE, DC.

The Giza. Roppongi; 403–6538. Loud music, Egyptian decor and topless dancers make it a favorite among those whose eyes force the eardrums to take it. Entrance fee after 8:00 P.M., ¥3,000 for men and ¥2,500 for women, includes drinks and sushi. AE, DC, Visa.

The Lexington Queen. Roppongi; 401–1661. Reputedly the best disco in Tokyo, attracting local and visiting fashion personalities, musicians, film stars, and other celebrities. Entrance fee of ¥3,000 covers the cost of most drinks and also includes ¥1,000 worth of sushi at the club's sushi bar. Most of the staff speak some English. The club also employs American and European waiters. Among foreign celebrities visiting the club have been Sylvester Stallone, Stevie Wonder, Rod Stewart. AE, DC, Visa.

Make Up. Roppongi; 479–1511. Open from 5:00 P.M. to midnight. Admission charge ¥3,000 for men and ¥2,000 for women, ¥500 less for those who come before 8:00 P.M. Price includes all drinks and all the salad and noodles desired.

Mugen. Akasaka; 584–4481. Claims to be the very first disco in Tokyo. Open from 6:30 P.M. to 1:00 A.M. Table d'hôte menu of ¥3,000 for men and ¥2,000 for women, including one drink. Additional drinks are ¥300 for soft drinks, ¥400 for beer and ¥500 or more for whiskey. Food from ¥500. Cash only.

Nepenta. Roppongi; 470–0751. Open from 5:00 P.M. to midnight. Weekday admission charges are ¥2,500 for men and ¥2,000 for women. On Saturdays and Sundays the charge is ¥2,500 for men, but remains the same for women. After 8:00 P.M. it is ¥3,000 for men and ¥2,000 for women. Price includes all drinks and all the noodles one may want. AE, DC.

The Pacha. Roppongi; 479–0522. Another favorite oasis for the fashion crowd. Entrance fee of ¥4,000 includes two drinks. AE, DC, Visa.

Samba Club. Roppongi; 470–6391. Dark-is-elegant is apparently the theme of this lively nightspot. Its decor combines black velvet with mirrored walls and it is popular with the older disco crowd. Open from 6:00 P.M. to midnight. Entrance charge is ¥4,000, which includes three drinks, food, service charge, and tax. Additional drinks are from ¥800. French cuisine, as the club describes it, is available. AE, DC.

Tsubaki Ball. Roppongi; 478–0087. Attracts a younger crowd, lots of punk fashion and new-wave music. Chic lounge area upstairs. Dynamic dance area downstairs. Entrance fee is ¥3,000 for women and ¥3,500 for men and includes drinks and the club's buffet. AE, DC, Visa.

HOTEL DANCING

Hotel Century Hyatt. Shinjuku; 349–0111. A lively disco, the *Samba Club Regency,* provides loud music for guests. All international credit cards accepted.

Hotel Keio Plaza. Shinjuku; 344–0111. Visitors can dine, drink and dance until 11:30 P.M. in the 2nd floor *Consort Room.* Shows at 8:00 P.M. and 10:00 P.M. All international credit cards accepted.

Hotel New Otani. Akasaka; 234–2321 or 265–1111. *Tap Chips,* a restaurant on the 1st floor of the new wing, provides dancing until 2:00 A.M. in addition to food and drinks. All international credit cards accepted.

Hotel Pacific. Shinagawa; 445–6711. Dancing at the romantically named *Blue Pacific* Restaurant on the 30th floor to live music, from 7:00 P.M. to midnight. All international credit cards accepted.

Imperial Hotel. Hibiya; 504–1111. Dancing at the *Rainbow Room* Restaurant on the 17th floor, overlooking the bustling Ginza on one side and the Imperial Palace grounds on the other. A pleasant evening for those who still enjoy the old-fashioned way of dancing. All international cards accepted.

Takanawa Prince Hotel. Shinagawa; 447–1111. Dancing to live music at the 1st floor *Night Spot* until midnight. All international credit cards accepted.

CHIBA-KANTO

by
John Turrent

Most visitors to Japan start off in Tokyo, and after brief trips to Kamakura and Nikko head south for the well-known tourist centers of Kyoto and Nara. Unfortunately, the region immediately surrounding Tokyo to the north and east, called the Chiba-Kanto area, is still off the beaten track to most tourists. This is surprising for three reasons. One is that the vast majority of people who come to Japan by air arrive, not in Tokyo, but in Narita, which is in Chiba Prefecture. The second reason is that the Chiba-Kanto region offers a great variety of tourist spots, from mountains to beaches to traditional crafts, and these can be reached (the third reason) very easily from Tokyo.

The name Chiba-Kanto refers to Chiba Prefecture, lying to the east of Tokyo and including Boso Peninsula to the southeast, and the area called Kanto, which includes the Kanto Plain to the north and the Chichibu hills to the west and northwest, and which covers the prefectures of Tochigi and Ibaraki to the north and Saitama and Gunma to the northwest and west. There are very few organized tours to places in the Chiba-Kanto region, but the adventure that goes with making your own way there should be considered part of the experience. Certainly, traveling alone or with friends or family members will mean that you meet many more local Japanese than you would by going on a bus excursion tour.

Chiba

Let's start with Chiba, to the immediate east of Tokyo. Within Chiba our starting point should be Narita, which is more than just the home of the New Tokyo International Airport. It is also a temple town in which is located the well-known Shinshoji Temple, said to have been originally founded in the 10th century. The temple, which adjoins an extensive park, can be reached in about 15 minutes by foot from either the Japan National Railways' Narita Station or Keisei-Narita Station of the Keisei Railway, which runs from Keisei-Ueno Station. Shinshoji's present main hall is a newly built structure, but behind it is located a former main hall building; other structures of interest in the temple's precincts include the Niomon gateway, the bell tower, and the three-storied pagoda.

From Narita, trains can be taken to the Pacific Ocean coast. If you have time, it is possible to plan a course that takes in Kashima Shrine, the Itako and Suigo districts, and Choshi, which is Chiba's easternmost point. The Narita line connects Narita and Choshi, with a branch line running from Katori through Itako to Kashima-jingu Station, from where it is a 10-minute walk to Kashima Shrine. This shrine is dedicated to a deity of martial valor, and is famous for its Saito-sai festival in March, during which people dressed up in armor hold colorful parades. Kashima Shrine also has a Treasure House with displays of swords and old armor.

It is possible to return directly to Tokyo from Kashima by special express trains, which cover the distance in just less than 2 hours. If you are touring the area, however, you might want to make Itako your next stop. The town is famous for its iris blossoms and for the Twelve Bridges boat ride in which visitors are punted in traditional style along the rivers in the vicinity. The journey takes about 30 minutes, and you arrive back at Itako.

From Itako, return to Katori Station, and from there change to the Narita line, which goes to the fishing port of Choshi. There are plenty of accommodations available in this town, and a couple of information offices at the station where reservations can be made if you haven't booked a place beforehand. The main sites to be seen in Choshi are Cape Inubozaki, which can be reached by taking the local Choshi Railway line from Choshi Station, and the nearby cliffs of Byobugaura, which are called the "Japanese Dover" because of their resemblance to the Dover cliffs in southern England. There is a lighthouse on Cape Inubozaki, and a walking course along the seafront offering fine views of the ocean.

Boso Peninsula

The southern part of Chiba Prefecture is called the Boso Peninsula. The Sobu main line connects Tokyo Station with the town of Chiba, at the western entrance to the peninsula, and there the line branches into the Uchibo line, which goes down the peninsula's west coast, and the Sotobo line, which goes across to and down the east coast.

Going down the east coast of the Boso Peninsula, there is a 66-km-long stretch of sandy beaches called the Kujukuri Coastal Park, and then the seaside resorts of Ohara, Onjuku, and Katsuura. The latter is famous for its morning market of vegetables and seafood, held along a street near Katsuura Station every day except Wednesdays. Also located near Katsuura—a 15-minute bus ride from the station—is the Katsuura Ocean Park, with an observation tower that extends below the sea to let visitors view the sea bottom with its many fish and marine plants.

Farther down the coastline there are similar tourist spots, the main ones being Namegawa Island with its flamingo and peacock shows, and Kamogawa Sea World with its huge aquarium. At the southernmost tip of the peninsula there is the seaside town of Shirahama, which is famous for its spectacular sea views and its female shell divers. It is about 40 minutes by bus to Shirahama from Tateyama, the main town in the Boso southwest and the terminus of the Uchibo line. Also located in this southern part of the peninsula are the Tateyama Bird Forest, Awa Natural Park, and Nambo Paradise, which boasts a 300-meter-long greenhouse and an extensive botanical garden of tropical plants.

Going up the west coast from Tateyama, the main stations to note are Hamakanaya, Sanukimachi, and Kisarazu. Hamakanaya is the terminus for the 40-minute ferry trip across Tokyo Bay from Kurihama. A short walk from the station lies Mount Nokogiri, which can be ascended by ropeway. The summit of the mountain offers splendid views of Tokyo Bay, with the Miura Peninsula visible on the opposite side. On the slopes of the mountain are Nihonji Temple and a 31.5-meter-tall statue of Buddha, said to be the largest in Asia.

From Sanukimachi Station, a 25-minute bus ride can be taken to a tourist farm called Mother Bokujo, where you can try your hand at milking cows and take part in pig races, among other things. Although these are probably not activities you expected to participate in during your stay in Japan, a visit to the farm makes for a very enjoyable outing and a good chance to meet Japanese people at leisure. Kisarazu, meanwhile, is the terminus for boat services, including a car ferry, across Tokyo Bay to Kawasaki and Yokohama.

Kanto

Visitors to Japan who head north from Tokyo usually go straight to Nikko without seeing the attractions that lie in between. If time is available, there are many sights in the Kanto region worth seeing. Starting in Ibaraki Prefecture in the east, there is Mito, which is famous for Kairakuen, said to be one of the three most beautiful landscape gardens in the country (the others being Korakuen in Okayama and Kenrokuen in Kanazawa).

Express trains reach Mito in about 90 minutes from Ueno Station in Tokyo. Kairakuen is situated about 1 mile west of Mito Station. The best time of the year to go is in February when the plum trees are in blossom and Kairakuen takes on a festive atmosphere. The garden,

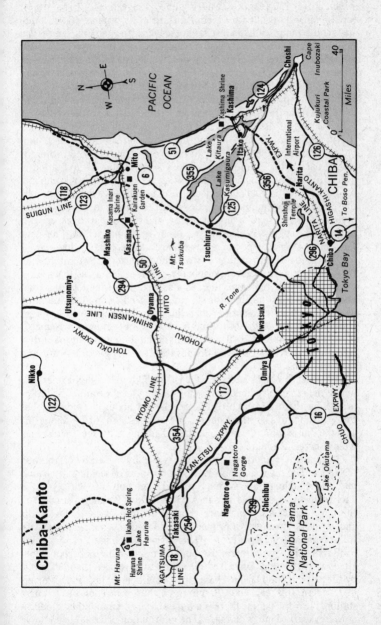

Chiba-Kanto

which is over 130 years old, was originally designed as a private retreat for the ninth lord of Mito. About a third of its original 10,000 plum trees still remain. Unlike most Japanese landscape gardens, Kairakuen does not have a lake as its central feature, nor does it have the usual waterfalls and stones. It does, however, have much splendid garden scenery, as well as the Kobuntei Building, a reproduction of the original pavilion used by the lord of Mito for his poetry parties. It is a classic example of Japanese architecture, with highly polished wooden corridors and beautifully painted fusuma doors separating the rooms. A high balcony in the building commands a view of the whole park.

Another popular tourist spot in Ibaraki Prefecture is Mount Tsukuba, an 876-meter-high peak which stands out as one of the few summits in this part of the Kanto Plain. Take the train from Ueno Station in Tokyo to Tsuchiura, which is on the western shore of Lake Kasumigaura, and from there take the local Tsukuba line as far as Tsukuba Station. It is a 15-minute bus ride from the station to the foot of the mountain, with Tsukuba Shrine nearby, and then a short cable car ride to the top. Tsukuba is also the site of an academic city and the stage for a large science exposition from March to September this year.

One of the Kanto region's two famous pottery towns is also in Ibaraki Prefecture. Kasama originally developed as a castle town (of which little trace remains), then as a shrine town with Kasama Inari Shrine located just north of the station, and is now famous as a pottery center. To reach it, take the Joban line from Ueno as far as Tomobe, and then change to the Mito line for a 10-minute ride to Kasama. It is possible to rent bicycles from in front of the station to visit the shrine, the Sambutsu Kaikan with its displays and sales of Kasama-ware, and the local kilns.

The other famous pottery center is Mashiko in Tochigi Prefecture, where the streets are lined with shops selling local ceramics and kilns producing them. Mashiko can be reached in about one hour by bus from Utsunomiya on the Tohoku line out of Ueno, or by taking the Tohoku line as far as Oyama, and then changing to the local Moka line, which serves Mashiko.

Utsunomiya is another station that is usually passed by on the way to Nikko. The town has, however, several spots of scenic and historic interest, including Futarayama Shrine, Hachimanyama Park, where a cherry blossom festival is held in April, the Ohya Kannon Temple, and the Nagaoka caves, which are thought to have been tombs in the ancient past. Utsunomiya originally developed as a shrine town, with Futarayama Shrine at its center. This shrine, which has a history going back more than 1,600 years, is about 10 minutes on foot from Tobu-Utsunomiya Station. Ohya Temple is said to have been founded in 808 by the priest Kobo Daishi. The temple is built partly inside a 50-meter-high cavern. It is reached in 20 minutes by bus from Tobu-Utsunomiya station. Near the temple there is a huge statue of Kannon, the Goddess of Mercy, carved into a cliff face. The information office at Utsunomiya Station has English-language maps available for foreign tourists.

Northwest Kanto

The area to the immediate northwest of Tokyo is dominated by the Chichibu hills, which make up part of the wider Chichibu-Tama National Park. The mountains in this district are neither as high nor as rugged nor as beautiful as the central Japan Alps, but the rivers flowing through them have cut away several scenic gorges which make pleasant day-trip or overnight destinations for people in the capital. One such place is Nagatoro, where it is possible to walk along the cliffs by the river for a few kilometers, and then return by traditional boat service over the rapids. Nagatoro is a particularly popular place in spring when the cherry blossoms bloom, and in autumn when the foliage turns many shades of red, yellow, and golden. Nearby is the Chichibu Natural Science Museum, and Mount Hodo, whose 497 meters can be climbed by ropeway. If you're planning to stay overnight, you might be interested in the SL Hotel, which provides accommodation in old railway carriages. To reach Nagatoro, take the super express Red Arrow from Seibu-Ikebukuro Station (located under the same roof as the Japanese National Railway's Ikebukuro Station in Tokyo) to Seibu-Chichibu, and there go to the nearby Ohanabatake Station and change to the local Chichibu line for Nagatoro.

About 12 kilometers to the south of Nagatoro lies the town of Chichibu, the site of Chichibu Shrine, where the truly spectacular Chichibu Yo Matsuri, or Chichibu Night Festival is held every year on the night of December 3. Special trains are run from Tokyo for the occasion and the festival, one of the oldest and largest in Japan, consists of huge floats being hauled around the streets accompanied by much drumbeating, singing, dancing, and shouting. Fireworks set alight from the mountainside add even more color to the scene. Chichibu used to be a prosperous silk center, and the festival began as a harvest thanksgiving ceremony.

Saitama Prefecture, within whose borders Chichibu lies, is also the center of several traditional crafts, the most noted ones being papermaking, dollmaking, and bonsai. For papermaking, visit the small town of Ogawamachi, which can be reached by taking the Tobu-Tojo line from Ikebukuro Station. The journey takes about 75 minutes. Ogawamachi has been a center of Japanese-style papermaking for many centuries, and there are still many households in the district carrying on the craft. As you walk through the streets, you'll be able to see the paper hung outside to dry, and visitors are welcome to enter the workshops and observe the craftsmen at work, making a difficult task look so easy. There are several places where souvenirs of this Japanese paper, called *washi,* can be purchased.

The doll-making center is at Iwatsuki, reached in 14 minutes by the Tobu-Noda line, which leaves from Omiya Station in northern Tokyo, while *bonsai* (dwarf tree culture) can be seen in Omiya itself. Omiya Bonsai Village is a short walk from Omiya Park, which can be reached from Omiya Koen Station on the Tobu-Noda line. If you have time, it is worth visiting Hikawa Shrine as well. The shrine was built in 1180, and is located inside the park.

The Bonsai Village consists of Japanese-style cottages fronted by rows and rows of the small potted plants set out on benches. Visitors can walk freely through the village and enter gardens as they please. Dwarfed trees have all the characteristics of normal trees while being only inches tall. They may be gnarled and knotty oaks, colorful maples, or blossoming cherries. Their prices can be astronomical, and their ages staggering.

Going a little farther afield, the town of Takasaki, just across the border from Saitama Prefecture in Gumma Prefecture, is a center of daruma doll making. Like many of the crafts in this region, daruma doll making developed as winter work for farmers, and then became a deeply rooted tradition. The red daruma dolls come in many sizes. When you buy one, paint in the left eye of the face and, while doing so, make a wish. When the wish comes true, you can paint in the right eye, too.

The place to go is Daruma Temple, a 25-minute bus ride from Takasaki Station, where a daruma fair is held in January every year, but where the dolls can be bought at any time. On the main road nearby, you'll see homes where the dolls are made, and you'll probably see rows of them drying outside. Takasaki, which is also well known for its large statue of the goddess of mercy (Kannon), can be reached in about 90 minutes by express train from Ueno Station in Tokyo, via the Takasaki line.

PRACTICAL INFORMATION FOR CHIBA-KANTO

HOW TO GET THERE. Public transportation east of Tokyo to Chiba and west to the Chichibu-Tama National Park region is highly developed. **By train.** The *Red Arrow* express from Ikebukuro on the Seibu line takes 83 mins. to reach Chichibu. Twelve semi-expresses of the *Japanese National Railways* depart daily from Tokyo Station (platform 2 or 3 underground) for Chiba and thence down the west coast of the Boso Peninsula to Tateyama, with local train link to Awa-Kamogawa. Time: 2 hours. Twelve similar trains go to the east coast passing through Oami and Ohara for Awa-Kamogawa. Time: 2 hrs. 20 min. There are also four semi-express trains daily for Choshi. The *Skyliner* is a super-express connecting Tokyo and the new Tokyo International Airport, operating non-stop between Keisei-Ueno and Narita Airport Station. 60 minutes. **By boat.** There are vehicular ferry services across the mouth of Tokyo Bay from Kurihama to Kanaya and from Yokohama to Kisarazu. Reservations through *Tokyo Bay Ferry Co.* (03–272–1641). In summer, hydrofoils of the *Tokai Kisen Co.* (03–432–4551) leave Tokyo's Takeshiba Pier several times daily for Katsuyama and Tateyama. Reservations suggested.

HOTELS AND INNS. The following is a list of convenient hotels and Japanese-style inns in the Chiba-Kanto area. Charges vary according to season, but in general you can expect to pay between ¥7,000 and ¥12,000 per person per night in hotels, and a little more for Japanese inns, although the latter usually include two meals. All the accommodation is western-style, except where "Japanese-style" is stated. The Japan Pension Center (407–2333) will provide information on cheap pension accommodations in the area.

KANTO

Itako

Fujiya Hotel. 02996–2–2000. 5 min. by foot from Itako Station.
Itako Hotel. 02996–2–3130. 2 min. by foot from Itako Station.

Tsuchiura

Kasumigaura Kanko Hotel. 0298–21–5110. 5 min. by foot from Tsuchiura Station.
Sun Route Tsukaba. 0298–52–1151. 15 min. by car from Tsuchiura Station.
Tsuchiura Keisei Hotel. 0298–21–5225. 5 min. by car from Tsuchiura Station.
Tsuchiura City Hotel. 0298–24–8111. 5 min. by car from Tsuchiura Station.
Tsuchiura Daiichi Hotel. 0298–22–4111. 10 min. by foot from Tsuchiura Station.

Mito

Chuo Hotel. 0292–21–3101. 10 min. by foot from Mito Station.
Hotel Kameya. 0292–27–2611. 8 min. by foot from Mito Station.
Hotel Izumi. 0292–31–2295. 10 min. by bus from Mito Station.
Kikuya Hotel. 0292–24–2417. 5 min. by car from Mito Station.
Mito City Hotel. 0292–25–4511. 16 min. by foot from Mito Station.
Mito Daiichi Hotel. 0292–21–8855. 10 min. by foot from Mito Station.
Mito Grand Hotel 0292–25–8111. 5 min. by car from Mito Station.
Mito Kanko Hotel. 0292–25–3611. 6 min. by car from Mito Station.
Mito Keisei Hotel. 0292–26–3111. 2 min. by foot from Mito Station.
Mito Park Hotel. 0292–41–1671. 15 min. by bus from Mito Station.

Tsukuba

Tsukuba-san Edo-ya. 02986–6–0321. 10 min. by bus from Tsukuba Station. Japanese style.
Tsukuba Grand Hotel. 02986–6–1111. 10 min. by bus from Tsukuba Station.
Tsukuba-san Keisei Hotel. 02986–6–0831. 30 min. by bus from Tsukuba Station.

Utsunomiya

Hotel New Asahi. 0286–34–4070. 5 min. by bus from Utsunomiya Station.
Palace Hotel. 0286–33–3321. 10 min. by bus from Utsunomiya Station.
Riverside Hotel. 0286–33–7151. 2 min. by foot from Utsunomiya Station.
Station Hotel. 0286–37–0111. 2 min. by foot from Utsunomiya Station.
Sun Route Utsunomiya. 0286–21–3355. 1 min. by foot from Utsunomiya Station.
Tobu Hotel. 0286–36–3063. Above Utsunomiya Station.
Utsunomiya Central Hotel. 0286–25–1717. 5 min. by car from Utsunomiya Station.
Utsunomiya Royal Hotel. 0286–34–2401. 5 min. by car from Utsunomiya Station.

Tochigi City

Fujimi. 0282–22–0618. 3 min. by foot from Tochigi Station. Japanese style.
Hotel Yamaguchi. 0282–22–0017. 1 min. by foot from Tochigi Station.

Ashikaga

Ashikaga Town Hotel. 0284–21–4114. 5 min. by car from Ashikaga Station.
New Miyako Hotel. 0284–72–3333. 3 min. by foot from Ashikaga-shi Station.
Ryokan Miyako. 0284–71–1151. 3 min. by foot from Ashikaga Station.

Takasaki

Takasaki Business Hotel. 0273–26–2828. 5 min. by car from Takasaki Station.
Takasaki Plaza Hotel. 0273–26–1211. 5 min. by foot from Takasaki Station.

Haruna-ko

Haruna Lake Hotel. 02737–4–9021. 90 min. by bus from Takasaki Station.
Haruna Agatsuma-so. 02737–4–9106. 100 min. by bus from Takasaka Station.
Kohan-tei. 02737–4–9511. 90 min. by bus from Takasaki Station. Japanese style.

Ikaho Spa

Ikaho Grand Hotel. 027972–3131. 30 min. by bus from Shibukawa Station.
Ikaho Kanko Hotel. 027972–3266. 40 min. by bus from Shibukawa Station.
Ikaho Plaza Hotel. 027972–2281. 30 min. by bus from Shibukawa Station.
Ikaho View Hotel. 027972–2772. 30 min. by bus from Shibukawa Station.

Nagatoro

Hodosan-tei. 0494–66–0013. 1 min. by foot from Nagatoro Station. Japanese style.
SL Hotel. 0494–66–3011. 8 min. by foot from Nagatoro Station. Accommodation is in converted railway carriages. Very popular, so reservations essential.

Chichibu

Chichibu Kaikan. 0494–22–1280. 8 min. by foot from Chichibu Station. Japanese style.
Chikuju-kan. 0494–22–1230. 13 min. by foot from Chichibu Station. Japanese style.
Ohtsuki Ryokan. 0494–22–0310. 7 min. by foot from Chichibu Station. Japanese style.

CHIBA

Kisarazu

Fujiya Hotel. 0438–22–2117. 5 min. by car from Kisarazu Station.
Kisarazu Daiichi Hotel. 0438–25–1151. 7 min. by foot from Kisarazu Station.
Kisarazu Park Hotel. 0438–23–3491. 10 min. by foot from Kisarazu Station.

Kisarazu Spa

Kisarazu Onsen Hotel. 0438–22–2171. 7 min. by foot from Kisarazu Station.

Hamakanaya

Nokogiri-yama Kanko Hotel. 04396–9–2211. 3 min. by car from Hamakanaya Station.

Katsuyama

Katsuyama Minshuku. 04705–5–0115. 5 min. by foot from Awa-Katsuyama Station. Japanese style.

Katsuyama-tei. 04705–5–0306. 7 min. by foot from Awa-Katsuyama Station. Japanese style.

Tateyama

New Kikuya Hotel. 0470–22–2810. 7 min. by foot from Tateyama Station.
Seaside Hotel. 0470–22–0151. 3 min. by car from Tateyama Station.

Awa Shirahama

Grand Hotel Taiyo. 047038–3331. 40 min. by bus from Tateyama Station.
Hotel Kuroiwa. 047038–3321. 45 min. by bus from Tateyama Station.
Shirahama Keisei Hotel. 047038–2511. 45 min. by bus from Tateyama Station.

Awa Kamogawa

Kamogawa Chisan Hotel. 04709–2–1341. 5 min. by foot from Futomi Station.
Kamogawa Royal Hotel. 04709–2–3111. 5 min. by car from Awa-Kamogawa Station.
Sotobo Kanko Hotel. 04709–2–1143. 5 min. by car from Futomi Station.
Universe Hotel. 04709–2–1361. 5 min. by bus from Awa-Kamogawa Station.

Katsuura

Katsuura Hotel Mikazuki. 04707–3–1111. 5 min. by foot from Katsuura Station.
Mikazuki Ryokan. 04707–3–1331. 1 min. by foot from Katsuura Station. Japanese style.
Shoei-kan. 04707–3–1321. 8 min. by foot from Katsuura Station. Japanese style.

Katsuura Spa

Katsuura Onsen. 04707–7–0311. 15 min. by car from Katsuura Station. Japanese style.

Onjuku

Hotel New Hawaii. 047068–2121. 3 min. by car from Onjuku Station.
New Onjuku. 047068–4121. 2 min. by car from Onjuku Station.

Ohara

Nishiki-ya Ryokan. 04706–2–0005. 7 min. by foot from Ohara Station. Japanese style.
Unagi-ya Ryokan. 04706–2–1323. 7 min. by foot from Ohara Station. Japanese style.

Choshi

Business Hotel Izu-ya. 0479–22–1282. 1 min. by foot from Choshi Station.
Hotel Riverside. 0479–24–7772. 3 min. by car from Choshi Station.

Inubosaki

Grand Hotel Iso-ya. 0479–24–1111. 20 min. by bus from Choshi Station.
Inubo Hotel. 0479–22–3205. 25 min. by bus from Choshi Station. Japanese style.
Inubosaki Kanko Hotel. 0479–23–5111. 20 min. by bus from Choshi Station.
Inubosaki Royal Hotel. 0479–25–1331. 15 min. by bus from Choshi Station.

Narita

Holiday Inn Narita. 0476–32–1234. 10 min. by car from Narita Station.
International. 0476–93–1234. 15 min. by bus from Narita Terminal.
Narita Airport. 0476–32–1212. 3 min. by foot from Narita Terminal.

Narita Nikko Hotel. 0476–32–0032. 5 min. by bus from Narita Terminal.
Narita Prince Hotel. 0476–33–1111. 2 min. by car from Narita Terminal.
Narita View Hotel. 0476–32–1111. 10 min. by car from Narita Station.

HOSTELS. These cost about ¥2,700 per person with two meals.

Ibaraki Prefecture. *Mito Tokuda Youth Hostel.* 02967–7–3113. 20 min. by bus from Tomobe Station, then 7 min. on foot. *Tsukubasan Youth Hostel.* 02965–4–1200. 15 min. by bus from Tsukuba Station, then 8 min. on foot, 8 min. cable car ride, and 20-min. walk. *Youth Hostel Tsukuba-Sanso.* 0298–66–0022. 15 min. from Tsukuba Station, then 5 min. on foot.

Tochigi Prefecture. *Nasu-Kogen Youth Hostel.* 02877–8–1615. 35 min. by bus from Kuroiso Station, then 10 min. on foot. *Youth Hostel Nishinoda Kannon.* 02824–2401. 10 min. by bus from Tochigi Station, then 2 min. on foot.

Gunma Prefecture. *Haruna Kogen Youth Hostel.* 02737–4–9300. 80 min. by bus from Takasaki Station, then 15 min. on foot.

Saitama Prefecture. *Chichibu Youth Hostel.* 04945–5–0056. 35 min. by bus from Mitsumineguchi Station on the Chichibu line, then 15 min. on foot. *Hanno Youth Hostel.* 04297–2–4018. 10 min. by bus from Hanno Station, then 7 min. on foot.

Chiba Prefecture. *Inage Kaihin Youth Hostel.* 0472–43–9505. 10 min. by bus from Inage Station. *Tateyama Youth Hostel.* 0470–28–0073. 30 min. by bus from Tateyama Station, then 3 min. on foot. *Youth Hostel Inubo-so.* 0479–22–1252. 3 min. on foot from Inubo Station in Choshi.

HOT SPRINGS AND RESORTS. Although there are some spas in the Chiba and Chichibu areas, the most popular spa resort in northern Kanto is the town of Ikaho Onsen, which can be reached in about 1 hour by bus from Takasaki, and in 40 minutes by bus from Shibukawa Station. The extra attraction of this spa resort is its location near Mount Haruna, often called Fuji-Haruna, because it resembles Mount Fuji in shape. Mount Haruna can be scaled by ropeway, and Lake Haruna, which lies at its base, provides boating fun in summer and skating in winter. For hotels in the Ikaho spa area, refer to the hotel information given above.

As for seaside resorts, the place to head for is Chiba, and especially the east coast of the Boso Peninsula at such places as Onjuku, Ohara, and Katsuura.

HOW TO GET AROUND. Train services from Tokyo to the Chiba-Kanto area are quite sufficient enough to enable you to get around the region. Once you have reached your destination, you will find that buses going to local places of interest operate from the main railway stations. Tourist information centers at the main railway stations such as Narita, Choshi, Chichibu, and Takasaki will help with hotel reservations, and sometimes they stock English-language literature and maps on the district.

SEASONAL EVENTS. January. Daruma fair on the 3rd in Kawagoe, Saitama Prefecture. Daruma fair on the 6th–7th at Daruma Temple in Takasaki, Gunma Prefecture. Otariya-sai, or early spring festival of Futarayama Shrine in Utsunomiya, Tochigi Prefecture, on the 15th.

February. Setsubun bean-throwing ceremonies are held at temples and shrines across the country, and in this region, Shinsoji Temple in Narita is a particularly popular place on the 3rd of the month. Many prominent personalities usually take part in these ceremonies, in which handfuls of beans are thrown in the belief that evil spirits will be frightened away.

The Doronko Matsuri is held on the 25th at Ubusuna Shrine in Yotsukaidomachi, Chiba Prefecture, involving much splashing about in muddy water. The throwing of people into muddy rice fields is said to induce a bumper crop. From Yotsukaido on the Sobu main line from Chiba.

From Mid-February to mid-March, the Plum Blossom Festival takes place at Kairakuen Garden in Mito. Blossom viewing is accompanied by open-air tea ceremonies and koto music.

March. The Saito-sai Festival of Kashima Shrine in Kashima is held on the 9th, with parades of people dressed as armed warriors of the past.

April. Another Doronko Matsuri is held at Katori Shrine in Noda, Chiba Prefecture on the 3rd. From the end of April–early May, pottery fairs are held at the pottery centers of Mashiko in Tochigi Prefecture and Kasama in Ibaraki Prefecture. The former can be reached in one hour by bus from Utsunomiya on the JNR Tohoku line, and the site of the latter fair can be reached in 10 minutes by bus from Kasama Station on the JNR Mito line.

June. An Iris Festival is held in Itako, Ibaraki Prefecture, throughout the month, the main site being the Maekawa Iris Garden, near Itako Station on the JNR Kashima line.

July. The Gion-e Festival of Shinshoji Temple in Narita is held from the 7th–9th, with colorful float and mikoshi (portable) shrine parades throughout the streets.

From the 19th to 20th the Kawase-sai Festival of Chichibu Shrine in Chichibu is held, with float and mikoshi shrine parades.

The Uchiwa Matsuri, or paper fan festival, of Yasaka Shrine in Kumagaya, Saitama Prefecture, is held from the 20th–22nd, featuring float and mikoshi shrine processions and much drumbeating.

The Tanabata Matsuri is held across the country from the 26th–27th, and one of the most popular places is Ogawa-machi in Saitama Prefecture. Streamers made with local Japanese paper decorate the town.

August. The summer festival of Lake Sagami is held on the 1st, with drumming contests and the floating of lighted lanterns on the lake. From Sagamiko Station on the JNR Chuo line.

The Funatama Matsuri of Nagatoro Gorge in Chichibu features a splendid fireworks display and the floating of lighted lanterns on the river. The festival takes place from about 6:00 P.M. on the 15th.

Traditional lion dances can be seen throughout the 26th at Mitsumine Shrine in Chichibu, reached by bus and ropeway from Mitsumineguchi Station on the Chichibu Railway line.

October. From late October–early November, autumn pottery fairs are held at Mashiko and Kasama (see April entry).

December. Night Festival of Chichibu Shrine is held on the 3rd, featuring floats, dancing, and fireworks. The Daito-sai festival of Hikawa Shrine in Omiya Park, Saitama Prefecture, takes place on the 10th. Lots of open-air stalls selling lucky rakes, daruma dolls, and so on. On the 15th is the Otariya-sai, or late autumn festival of Futarayama Shrine in Utsunomiya, Tochigi Prefecture.

PARKS AND GARDENS. (See also "Theme parks and Amusement Centers," following.) **Ashigakubo Village.** In Saitama Prefecture. Has orchards where fruit can be picked in season. Reached from Ashigakubo Station on the Seibu-Ikebukuro line from Ikebukuro.

Awa Natural Park. Southern Boso Peninsula. Zoo and park looking out to sea. Reached in 30 minutes by bus from Tateyama Station.

Ayame Garden. In Ibaraki Prefecture. Has fine iris blossoms in June. Reached in 5 minutes on foot from Itako Station.

Chiyoda Village. In Ibaraki Prefecture. Features orchards where you can pick fruit yourself. Pay-as-you-pick system. Reached in 30 minutes by bus from Tsuchiura Station.

Kairakuen Garden. In Ibaraki Prefecture. This is one of Japan's three most spectacular landscape gardens. Reached in 10 minutes by bus from Mito Station.

Mount Nokogiri Park. Western Boso Peninsula. Includes a large statue of Buddha and Nihonji Temple. Short walk from Hamakanaya Station, then a cable car climb.

Nambo Paradise. Southern Boso Peninsula. More flowers and a collection of butterflies. Reached in 40 minutes from Tateyama Station.

Shinrin Park. In Saitama Prefecture. A large park with cycling facilities. Reached from Shinrinkoen Station on Tobu-Tojo line from Tokyo's Ikebukuro.

Shirahama Flower Park. Southern Boso Peninsula. Includes a fine banana hothouse. Reached in 35 minutes by bus from Tateyama Station.

Tateyama Family Park. Southern Boso Peninsula. A great variety of flowers is displayed here. Reached in 33 minutes by bus from Tateyama Station.

 THEME PARKS AND AMUSEMENT CENTERS. **Kamogawa Sea World.** Eastern Boso Peninsula. Spectacular dolphin shows. Reached in 5 min. by bus from Awa-Kamogawa Station. 9:00 A.M.–5:00 P.M.

Katsuura Monkey Park. Eastern Boso Peninsula. Overlooking the sea, with monkeys following you around everywhere. Reached in 30 min. on foot from Katsuura Station. 8:30 A.M.–5:00 P.M.

Katsuura Ocean Park. Eastern Boso Peninsula. Has an observation tower going down into the sea. Reached in 15 min. by bus from Katsuura Station. 9:00 A.M.–5:00 P.M.; 8:30 A.M.–6:00 P.M. in summer.

Mother Farm. Western Boso Peninsula. A large rambling park on a farm site where you can milk cows and race with pigs. Reached in 25 min. by bus from Sanukimachi Station on the west coast of the Boso Peninsula. 8:00 A.M.–5:00 P.M.; 8:00 A.M.–9:00 P.M. in summer.

Namegawa Island. Eastern Boso Peninsula. Lots and lots of birds and a popular flamingo show. Reached from Namegawa Island Station. 9:00 A.M.–5:00 P.M.; 9:00 A.M.–10:00 P.M. in summer.

Tateyama Bird Forest. Southwestern Boso Peninsula. Located behind Awa Shrine. Good for observing wild birds. Reached in 30 min. by bus from Tateyama Station. 9:00 A.M.–4:00 P.M.

Tokyo Disneyland. Opened in 1982 at Urayasu in Chiba Prefecture (see this section in the *Tokyo* chapter).

SPORTS. *Bathing* on two of Chiba's three coastlines is magnificent but watch for posted warning signs. Riptides are killers and swimming after typhoons is out. There is good *golfing* at a dozen suburban places—Oami, Oarai, Abiko, Koganei, Tokyo Country Club, Kasumigaseki, Ome, to name a few. The whole outdoors is to do with as you will—fishing, boating, surfing, yachting, skindiving, sunbathing, hiking, biking, horseback riding, motoring, mountain climbing, and tennis. Skiing on artificial snow is possible from Oct. through Feb. at the Sayama Ski Ground, near Seibu Kyujomae Station on the Seibu-Shinjuku line in western Tokyo.

HISTORICAL SITES. Chichibu Shrine. 5 min. walk from Chichibu Station on the Seibu-Ikebukuro Line. One hour from Ikebukuro. Site of a splendid night festival every December 3. **Futarayama Shrine.** 10-min. walk from Tobu-Utsunomiya or Utsunomiya stations in Tochigi Prefecture. **Kasama Inari Shrine.** Near Kasama Station on the local Mito line, which runs from Tomobe (on the Joban Line from Ueno). **Kashima Shrine.** 10-min. walk from Kashima-jingu Station on the Narita Line. **Ohya Temple and Ohya Kannon statue.** 20-min. bus ride from Tobu-Utsunomiya or Utsunomiya stations. **Shinshoji Temple.** 15-min. walk from Keisei-Narita or Narita stations. **Tsukuba Shrine.** 15-min. bus ride from Tsukuba Station on the local Tsukuba Line which runs from Tsuchiura.

MUSEUMS. Most of Chiba's attractions are connected with the sea, and so although there are many aquariums and "ocean worlds" in the area, there are not that many museums of interest. The main ones in the Chiba-Kanto region as a whole are as listed below.

Awa Museum. Displays materials on fishing and coastal lifestyles and folklore. A 10-min. walk from Tateyama Station. Open 9:00 A.M.–4:30 P.M.; closed Mon.

Chichibu Natural Science Museum. Displays on the geography and geology of the area. Located 5 min. from Kami-Nagatoro on the Chichibu railway line. Open 9:00 A.M.–4:00 P.M.

Mashiko Kiln Museum and **Mashiko Sankokan Pottery Museum.** Both have displays of Mashiko-ware pottery, and both are reached from Mashiko Station by foot.

Nagatoro Museum. Houses materials on local history and geology, and is located near Nogami Station on the Chichibu line. Open 9:00 A.M.–4:30 P.M.; closed Mon., and all of January and February.

National Museum of Japanese History. Opened in March 1983 in Sakura, Chiba Prefecture. Has displays on Japanese history, archaeology, and folklore. Reached in 15 min. by bus from Sakura Station on the Japan National Railways' Sobu main line, or in 15 min. on foot from the Keisei-Sakura Station on the private Keisei line, which starts at Ueno Station in Tokyo. It takes 60 min. to get from Tokyo or Ueno to Sakura. Open 9:30 A.M. until 4:30 P.M. Closed on Mondays (except when Sunday or Monday is a national holiday, in which case it closes instead on Tuesday) and from December 27 until January 4.

Shirahama Ocean Art Museum. Has materials on fishing, whaling, etc. Reached in 5 min. on foot from Shirahama. Open 9:00 A.M.–5:30 P.M.

The **Tsukada Memorial Museum, Tochigi Mingeikan, Yokoyama Local History Museum,** and **Okada Memorial Museum** are all located in Tochigi, and display exhibitions on the town's past as an important post-town and distribution center. They are all situated by the Uzuma River, which flows through Tochigi, and all can be reached by means of a walking course from Tochigi Station. Open 9:30 A.M.–5:00 P.M.

 SHOPPING. Little villages often have their specialties, and every festival overflows with inexpensive and attractive souvenirs. The trouble with acquiring more valuable items, such as *bonsai* trees or heavy *Mashiko* pots, is carrying them back with you. A good packing and mailing service operates in Mashiko, however.

There are several factories and plants in the area that welcome visitors, including *Mashiko-ware Pottery* and *Asahi Pentax* plants. Reservations are necessary. Ask for information Center in Yurakucho.

 DINING OUT. Anywhere you go in the entire region, you will find good, cheap restaurants where you can order what you want by pointing to it in the shop window. Don't be afraid of trying anything that looks good to you. You will never be far, either, from greengrocers and fruiterers—and at every season of the year some excellent fruit is on the market in abundance. In the cities you may want to take advantage of hotel dining rooms.

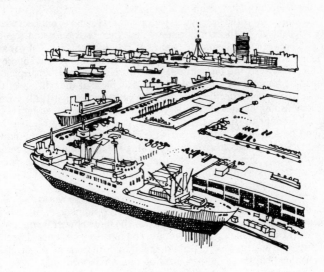

YOKOHAMA

by
K.V. NARAIN

K.V. Narain has written for publications in India, Sri Lanka, and the United States. A long-time resident of Tokyo, since 1960 he has been Far East Correspondent for The Hindu, *one of India's leading English-language newspapers.*

Yokohama is known the world over as a major port, bustling mercantile center, a city with international flavor, and as home for nearly three million Japanese who pride themselves in being "hamakko" (denizens of the port city). Just a little over a century ago, however, Yokohama was on no map, not even on the Japanese map; it was a sleepy fishing village off the then-important port of Kanagawa, one of the 53 stages on the busy Tokaido Highway, which has been immortalized in the paintings of the great Japanese painter, Hiroshige. Yokohama perhaps would have remained no more than a fishing village but for the new developments that were taking place as Japan opened up to the outside world.

Students of Japan-America relations will recall that the reluctant and suspicious shoguns were forced to open the doors of Japan after Commodore Perry's Black Ships pounded on the shore of nearby Uraga in 1853. After a treaty was signed three years later, the American Consul, Townsend Harris, lost no time in establishing his consulate in the temple of Hangakuji in Kanagawa.

Kanagawa was the designated port for the foreigners, but because of its importance on the Tokaido, on which there was busy and regular traffic between the shogunate capital of Edo (present-day Tokyo) and the imperial capital of Kyoto, it was a potentially dangerous source of conflict between the big white-skinned foreigners and the suspicious Japanese samurai. It was to avert such trouble that the officials of the shogunate quietly decided to shift the port for foreign trade to the nearby fishing hamlet of Yokohama. This action was taken by Harris as an attempt to isolate the foreigners and he angrily protested, but found he had little choice. Harris decided to comply with the move, re-establishing his consulate in the fishing village. If he were to return to life today, there is no doubt that the whole of Yokohama would shower Harris with bounty and honors for having contributed to the birth of this great port.

In the years just after Japan had been opened to the world, Yokohama's foreign community consisted of a large number of Britishers. Britain, like Japan, was an island, it was the most powerful country in the world, commanding a vast empire, and it had a royal house like that of Japan. Thus, it was to Britain that Japan turned for much of its determined efforts at industrialization and modernization.

Although they were 10,000 miles away from home, the Britons of Yokohama, like Britons everywhere in those times, doggedly maintained their own style of life in Yokohama. After the day's work was over in their offices on the seafront, they retired home to their bungalows on the Bund (the waterfront) for their scotch or gin or beer. They even imported cricket and soccer and had built a spacious club where they could indulge in these favorite pastimes of theirs on weekends. The Yokohama Country and Athletic Club (YCAC) with its cricket pitch of turf and its vast grounds continues to thrive to this day, but its membership is now as international as the port city itself.

The Years as a Major Port

For many years Yokohama reigned as the prima donna of all major Japanese international ports. It was the center through which the bulk of Japan's foreign trade flowed in and out. In fact, Japan's only foreign exchange bank, Yokohama Specie Bank, was headquartered in the port city until the end of World War II. It had to be situated here because of the large number of foreign businessmen who lived in the city, mostly Americans and Britishers, but also Germans, Indians, and many others who handled the bulk of Japan's foreign trade in those days. For long years silk was Japan's main export and virtually all the silk was shipped out of the port of Yokohama, as were many of the other products exported by Japan like textiles, tea, and other miscellaneous items. The major imports were cotton and woolen goods.

In political importance, Yokohama suffered by its proximity to Tokyo, but it maintained a position as a fashionable destination for Japanese, American, British, and French passenger ships. Tourists from abroad arrived regularly by the thousands, and sailors brought prosperity to the many bars and cabarets that thrived near the various piers.

Yokohama became Japan's doorway to Western civilization, and it was not unusual for a resident of Tokyo to travel all the way to Yokohama just to see how the foreigners lived and behaved, and to sniff and imbibe the cosmopolitan atmosphere that the foreign community exuded. Western manners and customs demonstrated by foreign residents of this city exerted a great influence on the living styles and mannerisms of the Japanese people. It was also through Yokohama that merchandise and technological advances arrived in Japan from abroad—railways, telegraphy, photographic equipment, gaslight, and so on. The first railway to be built in Japan linked Shimbashi in Tokyo with Yokohama in 1872.

Disaster and Recovery

In the 20th century, Yokohama suffered two crushing blows to its existence as a major port. The great Kanto earthquake that hit the Tokyo-Yokohama area on September 1, 1923, was disastrous. Sixty thousand houses of wood and paper were razed to the ground and 20,000 human lives taken. It took over six years for the city to build itself back up, but in the interim many of the resident foreign businessmen, who had contributed much to the prosperity of Yokohama, had left it for good, moving over to Kobe or Osaka and other places.

Nevertheless, Yokohama continued to prosper reasonably well. By 1943, two decades after the earthquake, a large industrial zone emerged in the area where much reclamation work had been done. However, on May 29, 1945, Yokohama suffered the second disastrous blow in a morning air raid by some 700 American B-29s, which flattened 42 percent of its urban area in a mere four hours. The damage was far heavier than that caused by the 1923 earthquake. Together with the other cities of Japan after the war, Yokohama had its share of problems in regaining prosperity, however, during the rapid economic growth of the sixties and early seventies, the city made phenomenal progress as an industrial town, building a large factory zone along the shoreline and bringing more prosperity to its residents.

Airplanes today have virtually replaced the passenger ship as the mode of transport across the oceans, so ships no longer arrive at the port of Yokohama week after week to disgorge streams of tourists and businessmen as they used to. Today there are no regular passenger liners touching Yokohama the year round, and the big luxury vessels like the *Queen Elizabeth* only visit Japan once or twice a year at most. The only regular passenger ship touching Yokohama nowadays is a Soviet vessel, which plies to this port from Nakhodka in the Soviet Far East once a week between May and December. The service is suspended from January to April.

What to See

Yokohama is not exactly a prime sightseeing destination for foreign tourists. Since the port city has no history extending into the ancient past, it does not have indigenous Buddhist temples and Shinto shrines noted for their architectural grandeur, as can be found in the older cities of Kyoto, Nara, Nikko, or Tokyo. Nor are there numerous beautiful Japanese-style gardens as can be seen in many an old castle town. Whatever sightseeing there is to do is limited to what has sprung up in the last 120 years or so.

Life in the city revolved primarily around the foreign community, particularly during the Meiji, Taisho, and early Showa years, so many of the points of interest are associated to a considerable extent with the foreign residents. The Bluff, located on a gentle hillock, where the houses of the foreigners were concentrated in the early years, and the large International Cemetery on the Bluff are regular stops for the city's sightseeing buses.

Some of the old Meiji-era (19th century) buildings withstood the great earthquake as well as wartime air raids. Two of these structures remain to this day, well preserved and still in use. The Customs House, about a 10-minute walk from Sakuragicho Station (of the Japan National Railways and the private Toyoko line), the Prefectural Government Building next door, and the Yokohama Archives of History Building adjacent to it are all old buildings known for their architectural beauty.

The Yokohama Archives of History Building housed the British Consulate General for many years, up until the 1970s. It is open daily 9:30 A.M. to 4:30 P.M., except on Mondays and days after national holidays. An entrance fee of ¥200 for adults and ¥100 for children is charged. The building not only houses historical material relating to the opening of Japan and of the port of Yokohama, but is itself a place of historical interest, having been the site of the signing of the Treaty of Kanagawa.

Next to this graceful and majestic old-style building, you'll find the Silk Center, built in 1959 to commemorate the centenary of the opening of Yokohama Port. On the second and third floors is a silk museum illustrating the history of silk making and the evolution of silk manufacture from its old origins as a cottage industry. A variety of pretty silk products are on display and any questions on Japanese silk can be answered by the attendants. In addition, the Yokohama Foreign Trade Advisory Institute, several foreign consulates, travel agencies, steamship offices, a shopping arcade, and the Yokohama Municipal Tourist Information Office can be found here.

Just a stone's throw away is the waterfront and Yamashita Park. Completed in 1930, Yamashita Park is the first seaside park to be created in Japan. Sea breezes add to the enjoyment of the exotic surroundings, the view over the port, the extensive lawn, and the flower gardens, which are in bloom in all seasons. Occupying an area of 17 acres, this park contains a fountain in the center in which stands a statue called the "Guardian of Water" presented by San Diego, California, U.S.A., a sister city of Yokohama. Yokohama also has sister-city relationships with the cities of Lyons (France), Odessa (Union of Soviet Socialist Republics), Bombay (India), Manila (the Philippines), Vancouver (Canada), Shanghai (the Peoples' Republic of China), and Constanta (Romania). Sister-port relations exist with Vancouver, Oak-

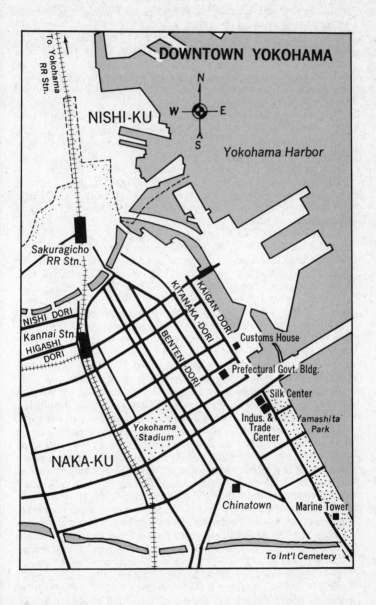

DOWNTOWN YOKOHAMA

N
W E
S

NISHI-KU

Yokohama Harbor

To Yokohama RR Stn.

Sakuragicho RR Stn.

KITANAKA-DORI
KAIGAN DORI
BENTEN DORI

NISHI DORI

Kannai Stn.
HIGASHI DORI

Customs House

Prefectural Govt. Bldg.

Silk Center

Indus. & Trade Center

Yamashita Park

Yokohama Stadium

NAKA-KU

Chinatown

Marine Tower

To Int'l Cemetery

land (U.S.A.), and Shanghai. While enjoying the park, you may see vessels leaving port, announcing their departure with a ship's whistle or the beating of gongs.

Continuing from north to southeast, you'll come to the Marine Tower, a decagonal building 106 meters high, with navigational light beacons and television antennas at the top. At a height of 100 meters, there are an observation lounge (open from 10:00 A.M. to 7:00 P.M. daily), an aviary which houses many exotic birds from all over the world, a restaurant, and a marine science museum.

To the tower's immediate southwest is the city's famous Chinatown, known for its brightly decorated Chinese restaurants, bars, cabarets, teahouses, and souvenir shops. Restaurants number well over seventy, and there are some twenty shops selling Chinese foodstuffs and spices.

Proceeding farther to the southeast will bring you to the Bluff, with its Harbour View Park (Minato No Miero Oka). The park is famous for its picturesque view of Yamashita Park and the port of Yokohama, particularly at night when the lights of the harbor flower gardens add to the beauty of the scene.

A 2- to 3-minute walk west from the park will lead you to the International Cemetery, also located on the Bluff. Many foreigners, particularly Englishmen, who came to Japan to help the country in the process of modernization on which it had embarked, are buried here. Among them are Edmund Morell (d. 1871), an English railway engineer who contributed much to the construction of the first railway in Japan between Tokyo and Yokohama. Morell's bronze bust in relief was inlaid in 1958 in the wall of Sakuragicho Station. Another Englishman whose grave is in the International Cemetery is Charles Wirgman (1834–1891), an English journalist and cartoonist, who came over to Japan as a correspondent for the *Illustrated London News.* Around 1862, Wirgman launched *Japan Punch,* a comic magazine.

Bordering the southwestern edge of the International Cemetery is Motomachi Park, a beautiful area of greenery created on the hillside. A swimming pool and archery grounds are located within the park.

The city is proud of Sankeien, a purely Japanese-style garden on Honmoku Point by Negishi Bay. Wandering through the garden you can feast your eyes on the green of the rolling hills. The garden, which covers an area of 170,000 square meters, was originally built by a noted millionaire silk merchant by the name of Tomitaro Hara (Sankei), and opened to the public in 1906. Several ancient buildings were moved from nearby Kamakura and from the Kansai area in western Honshu, and have been skillfully arranged among the hills, valleys, and ponds in the garden. Nine of them have been designated as important cultural assets. The garden was destroyed during the bombings of the second world war, but in 1958 it was restored and reopened to the public.

The Sankeien can be reached by bus in 5 minutes from the Negishi Station of the Japan National Railways or by bus from Sakuragicho Station in about 20 minutes. The bus to take from Negishi Station is No. 54, while the bus from Sakuragicho is No. 8. The Sankeien Garden is attractive all the year round, with flowers blooming in profusion during the spring, the summer marked by cool breezes, and the autumn offering a vista of scarlet leaves that is transformed to a beautiful snowscape in winter.

Yokohama, like most other Japanese communities, has its share of shrines and ancient Buddhist temples. The biggest of these is the Sojiji Temple, which is located near the Tsurumi Station between Yokohama and Tokyo on the JNR line. Sojoji was transported to this site in 1911 from Ishikawa Prefecture, where it was founded in 1321. Second in size is Iseyama Shrine within 10 minutes walk west of Sakuragicho Station. The shrine is considered to be the guardian of Yokohama. Another attractive temple is the Shomyoji, which is located in the southern part of Yokohama in the direction of Kanazawa-ku.

PRACTICAL INFORMATION FOR YOKOHAMA

 HOW TO GET THERE. See also "To and From the Airport" under *How to Get Around,* below. **By train.** If you are coming from Tokyo, the quickest way to reach Yokohama is by one of the Japanese Railways' Shonan expresses, which leave Tokyo Station every 30 minutes and take less than 30 minutes to reach Yokohama. You can also take the Yokosuka express leaving every 15 minutes, which also takes about the same time. For those who want to take a train in Tokyo from stations other than the Tokyo main, Shimbashi, or Shinagawa stations, there is also the local commuter train (the blue Keihin Tohoku line) which will take you to Yokohama or Sakuragicho stations in a slightly longer time.

The super fast bullet trains (Shinkansen) also pass through Yokohama, but the station for the Kodama trains that stop in Yokohama is at a different location and is called Shin (New) Yokohama. Shin Yokohama Station is approximately 5 miles from Yokohama Station and it can be reached from Yokohama Station by the JNR's Yokohama Line via Higashi Kanagawa. The faster Hikari bullet trains, however, do not stop in Yokohama. Thus, for people traveling from Osaka or Kyoto to Yokohama, the Kodama is fast, convenient, and comfortable.

By boat. If you happen to arrive by ship, the South Pier is the usual disembarkation point and you will be setting foot right in the heart of the city.

TELEPHONES. The area code for Yokohama is 045. For emergencies, dial 110 for *Police;* 119 for *Fire* or *Ambulance.*

 HOTELS. Since Yokohama is located close to the capital city, it does not have the posh and glamorous hotels that one finds in Tokyo, but there are quite a number of comfortable ones. Major hotels accept American Express, JCB, Union, and Visa credit cards. MasterCard is also accepted at some hotels.

Naka-ku is Yokohama's primary business district, and Nishi-ku is the area surrounding the main Yokohama railway station.

WESTERN STYLE

Expensive

Bund Hotel. 1-2-14 Shin Yamashita-cho, Naka-ku. 621–1101. 45 rooms. Near Marine Tower. Five minutes walk from Motomachi shopping street. ¥11,000–16,400 for two, including tax and service charge.

Holiday Inn Yokohama. 77 Yamashita-cho, Naka-ku. 681–3311. Rooftop restaurant and bar, health club. Close to Chinatown. 200 rooms. ¥18,700–21,100 for two, including tax and service charge.

Hotel Aster. 87 Yamashita-cho, Naka-ku. 651–0141. Chinese restaurant, cocktail lounges, nightclub. Near Chinatown. 70 rooms. ¥11,100–15,200 for two, including tax and service charge.

Hotel New Grand. 10 Yamashita-cho, Naka-ku. 681–1841. The prewar and aging Hotel New Grand which used to be the pride of Yokohama is still there, a bit jaded but with comfortable rooms. Located just on the seafront opposite Yamashita Park. 200 rooms. ¥11,000–16,900 for two, including tax and service charge.

Hotel Rich. 1-11-3 Kitasaiwai Nishi-ku. Near west side of Yokohama Station. 312–2111. 216 rooms. ¥15,200–29,500 for two, including tax and service charge.

The Hotel Yokohama. 6-1 Yamashita-cho, Naka-ku. 662–1321. Just in front of Yamashita Park and next to Hotel New Grand. Close to Chinatown. Well appointed, clean rooms. 170 rooms. ¥16,900–19,900 for two, including tax and service charge.

Yokohama Prince Hotel. 3-13-1 Isogo-cho, Isogo-ku. 753–2211. Five minutes by taxi from Isogo Station of the JNR and Keihin Tohoku lines. Located on a hill with a nice view. Swimming pool, golf course, bowling green. 23 rooms. ¥14,000–33,200 for two, including tax and service charge.

Yokohama Tokyu Hotel. 1-1-12 Minamisaiwai, Nishi-ku. 311–1682. Located conveniently near the west exit of Yokohama Station. 219 rooms. ¥17,500–19,900 for two, including tax and service charge.

Moderate

Hotel Sun Route Yokohama. 2-9-1 Kitasaiwai, Nishi-ku. Fifteen minutes walk from west exit of Yokohama Station. 314–3111. 150 rooms. ¥12,700 for two, including tax and service charge.

Satellite Hotel. 76 Yamashita-cho, Naka-ku. 641–8571. Close to Chinatown. 108 rooms. ¥11,000 for two, including tax and service charge.

Shin Yokohama Hotel. 3-8-17 Shin Yokohama, Kohoku-ku. In front of Shin-Yokohama Station of the bullet line. 471–6011. 50 rooms. ¥9,800 for two, including tax and service charge.

JAPANESE STYLE

Azuma Ryokan. 2-10-18 Takashima, Nishi-ku. 453–1155. Located very close to Yokohama Station. 12 rooms. ¥5,500–7,500 per person per day, including dinner and breakfast.

Echigoya Ryokan. 1-14 Ishikawa-cho, Naka-ku. 641–5960. Located two minutes by foot from Ishikawa Station of the JNR Line. 14 rooms. ¥3,500 per person per day, without meals.

Matsuo-so. 2-95-1 Asama-cho, Nishi-ku. 311–5325. Located about 700 yards from Yokohama Station. 18 rooms. ¥7,000–10,000 per person per day, including dinner and breakfast.

Negishi-en Ryokan. 1-1 Negishi-machi, Naka-ku. 621–3741. Located five minutes by bus from Negishi Station, the Negishi-en is perhaps the most typical Japanese-style hotel in the city. Offers traditional Japanese style food and service. ¥6,000 per person per day, without meals.

Nishikigawa. 2-7-12 Takashima, Nishi-ku. 441–4809. Located close to Yokohama Station. 8 rooms. ¥7,000–8,500 per person per day, including dinner and breakfast.

Yamashiroya Ryokan. 2-159 Hinode-cho, Naka-ku. 231–1146. The Yamashiroya is located near Hinode Station on the Keihin Kyuko line. It is ten minutes walk from the Isezaki shopping center. Offers traditional Japanese-style food and service. 13 rooms. ¥3,500 per person per day, without meals.

YOUTH HOSTELS. Kanagawa Youth Hostel. 1 Momijigaoka, Nishi-ku. 241–6503. Located close to Sakuragicho Station. The daily rates are ¥1,700 for bed, ¥600 for dinner, and ¥400 for breakfast, but meals are optional. Those who wish to stay, however, must be members of the Youth Hostel Association.

HOW TO GET AROUND. Subways. Yokohama has one subway line which runs from Yokohama Station to Kaminagaya Station passing through Takashimacho, Sakuragicho, Kannai, Isezaki-Chojamachi, Bandobashi, Yoshinocho, Maita, Gumyoji, Kamiooka, and Konanchuo. The first subway train starts at 5:20 A.M. from Yokohama Station and the last train leaves from there at 11:53 P.M.

The suburban local trains of the JNR and the private Keihin Kyuko line operate every few minutes from about 5:00 A.M. till past midnight.

Car rental. Many rent-a-car companies operate in Japan. Reservations can be made either through a travel agent, a hotel, or directly. The average rental charge is ¥6,000 to ¥15,000 per day. Weekly and monthly rates are also available. The two rent-a-car companies in Yokohama are: Japaren Company Limited, 3-32-1 Furuya-cho, Kanagawa-ku, 311–4201; and Nippon Rent-A-Car Service Inc., 64 Yoshidamachi, Naka-ku, 261–2751.

Would-be rented car users should keep in mind that road traffic in Japan is on the left side of the road. There are many parking lots in the city, the charge being about ¥300 an hour.

To and from the airport. A direct bus service to Yokohama is available for visitors arriving at the New Tokyo International Airport at Narita. The buses leave the airport at intervals of 20 to 30 minutes, depending on the time of the day, and take approximately 120 minutes to reach the Yokohama City Air Terminal (YCAT) located near the east exit of the Japan National Railways' Yokohama Station. There are 30 trips daily in each direction, 12 by deluxe *Sea Gull* buses operated by Keihin Kyuko Company. The remaining 18 runs are by the *Tokyo Airport Transport Service Company*. The deluxe Sea Gull buses, equipped with a washroom, go direct to Narita, while those operated by the Tokyo Airport Transport Service Company travel via Haneda Domestic Airport. The Sea Gull buses also have emergency cards placed by each seat. When a passenger shows a card to the driver in case of sudden illness, the driver will arrange for an ambulance. The one-way bus fare at the present time is ¥3,100 (for children ¥1,550). The first bus leaves the airport for YCAT at 7:00 A.M., and the last bus leaves at 11:00 P.M. For passengers going to Narita Airport from the YCAT, the first bus leaves at 5:30 A.M. and the last bus at 7:30 P.M.

Those who have booked domestic flights out of Haneda Airport—as well as international flights by the only two international air carrier flying out of Haneda, namely, China Air Lines (CAL)—can catch Haneda-bound buses at the Yokohama Station east exit (higashiguchi) bus terminal. The buses run quite frequently with some of them also stopping at YCAT. The fare for the 30-minute ride from Yokohama to Haneda is ¥370 for adults and ¥190 for children. There is also a shuttle bus service from Yokohama Station to YCAT.

TOURIST INFORMATION. *Yokohama Municipal Tourist Association,* Silk Center, 1 Yamashita-cho, Naka-ku (641–5824 or 651–2668); *Tourist Bureau Kanagawa Prefectural Office,* 1 Nihon-odori, Naka-ku (201–1111); *Japan Travel Bureau,* 1-6 Onoe-cho, Naka-ku (662–7811). Located in front of City Hall.

USEFUL ADDRESSES. *Immigration Office.* 37-9 Yamashita-cho, Naka-ku (681–6801); *United Seamen's Service.* 84 Yamashita-cho, Naka-ku (623–2236); *Y.M.C.A.* 1-6 Tokiwa-cho, Naka-ku (662–3721); *Y.W.C.A.* 225 Yamashita-cho, Naka-ku (681–2903). *Missions to Seamen* have a new club at 194 Yamashita-cho, Naka-ku (662–1871).

MEDICAL TREATMENT. There are many doctors and dentists who understand English or German. Protestant and Catholic affiliated hospitals are accustomed to treating patients from abroad. In case of emergency, the hospital to contact in Yokohama is: *Washinzaka Hospital,* 169 Yamate-cho, Naka-ku, 623–7688.

SEASONAL EVENTS AND FESTIVALS. May. The International Masquerade Parade, also commonly known as the Port Festival, takes place on the 3rd or 5th (depending on the weather) in commemoration of the opening of Yokohama Port. It is undoubtedly Yokohama's biggest and most cosmopolitan festival because the afternoon parade through the streets is joined by a large number of resident foreigners. The Port Festival attracts a crowd of well over 200,000 persons from the city and its vicinity. It's a bonanza for the local merchants, who cash in by setting up large numbers of stalls on the main pier and along the route of the parade. The festival lasts until July 20, with fireworks marking the grand finale on the last day.

From the 14th to 16th the annual festival of the Iseyama Shrine is celebrated in the usual and boisterous way of all Japanese festivals, with the usual ceremonies and the procession featuring the portable shrine. This shrine, which is a branch of the grand shrine of Ise, is located on a hill near Sakuragicho Station in Nishi Ward.

June. Anniversary of the opening of Yokohama Port, June 2nd. Yokohama Dontaku Festival is held around Yamashita Park in the beginning of the month. Dontaku comes from the Dutch word for Sunday, Zondag. On this day, people parade in the costumes, both Western and Japanese, that were the fashion when the port of Yokohama opened in 1859.

July. The International Fireworks Festival on the 20th, marked by a display of eye-pleasing fireworks, is the grand finale of the events of the Port Festival, which begins in early May.

TOURS. For those who want to see the city, there are sightseeing coach tours which start at 10:00 A.M. every day from the east exit (higashiguchi) of Yokohama Station. The itinerary includes the Sankeien Gardens, Chinatown, Minato No Mieru Oka Park (Harbor View Park) with its view of the port, and Yamashita Park. Only Japanese spoken by the guides. For further information, telephone (045) 441–3360 or ask the porter at your hotel.

HOME VISITS. Visitors who have an interest in how the Japanese people live and who wish to see their homes and talk with them firsthand can avail themselves of the Yokohama home visit system. Foreigners can learn about the Japanese way of life by visiting participating homes and chatting in English for a few hours with the families. Some 28 families, most of them living within the city district of Yokohama, are registered with the Yokohama Municipal Tourist Association for this purpose. Contact Yokohama Municipal Tourist Information Office for details (641–5824 or 651–2668). Applications will be accepted by this office and visits arranged.

SPORTS. Participant. Every year on a Sunday during the middle of November, Yokohama holds its own men's international marathon. This event, which began in 1981, is open to anyone who wishes to participate. The race starts from Marathon Park. Anyone wishing to participate can telephone the education section of Yokohama City Office (671–3286).

Spectator. The city now boasts a full-fledged baseball stadium, which is the home ground for the Yokohama Taiyo Whales, one of the six professional baseball teams in the Central League, but apart from the pro baseball matches they play against other teams in the league during the season, there are no other important sporting events in the city.

MUSEUMS. The **Kanagawa Prefectural Museum** located near Sakuragicho Station contains many items related to the history of Kanagawa Prefecture. The museum is open daily from 9:00 A.M. to 4:30 P.M. on weekdays. Closed Mondays and last Friday of each month.

The **Yokohama Marine Science Museum** is located inside the Marine Tower. It is open from 10:00 A.M. to 5:00 P.M. daily. The **Silk Museum** in the Silk Center Building is open from 9:00 A.M. to 4:30 P.M. every day.

SHOPPING. Yokohama has a number of fine shopping areas in close proximity to the waterfront where many of the hotels are located. The Isezaki Mall, just a few minutes walk from Kannai Station of the JNR line, is the main shopping street, and it is particularly popular with overseas visitors. In addition to the Yokohama Matsuzakaya Department Store (261–2121), there are any number of souvenir shops, restaurants, coffee shops, tax-free shops, and others.

Motomachi Street, located below the Bluff, has an international flavor and featurs shops and boutiques containing the latest in fashion.

Near Yokohama Station, about a mile away from Motomachi Street, one can find the city's biggest and busiest shopping area both to the west and east of the station and immediately adjacent to it. There are branches of three major department stores (Mitsukoshi, 312–1111; Okadaya, 311–1471; and Takashimaya, 311–1251), in addition to a large selection of smaller shops offering just about anything a visitor could want. Purchases are usually on a cash basis, and very few stores accept credit cards.

 DINING OUT. With its growing prosperity, Yokohama is more and more assuming the character of a gourmet's paradise. Yokohama's Chinatown has always been known for its large number of restaurants serving rich fare in all styles of cooking that characterize Chinese food.

However, in the past two decades, a large number of restaurants serving foods in various styles of European cooking have made their debut one after another, joining the very good dining rooms, grills, and coffee shops that already exist in some of the department stores and better hotels in the city. The Mitsukoshi Department Store in Yokohama alone has 32 tearooms and restaurants. There are also now a large number of restaurants scattered in and near the Bund (the waterfront).

JAPANESE STYLE

Sukiyaki and Shabu-Shabu

Araiya. 2 Akebono-cho, Naka-ku; 251–5001. 11:30 A.M.–10:00 P.M. ¥5,000 and up. Sukiyaki, shabu-shabu (tatami floor for over three people).

Janomeya. 5-126 Isezaki-cho, Nakan-ku; 251–0832. 11:30 A.M.–9:30 P.M. ¥5,000 and up. Sukiyaki (tatami floor for over three people).

Seryna. Shin-Kannai Building B1, Sumiyoshi-cho, Naka-ku; 681–2727. Lunch 11:30 A.M.–4:00 P.M. (¥2,000 and up); dinner 4:00–9:00 P.M. (¥5,200 and up). Shabu-shabu, Ishiyaki steak (fried on a hot stone).

Shabusen. Sotetsu Joinus B1, 1-5-12 Minamisaiwai, Nishi-ku; 321–6731. West exit of Yokohama Station. 11:00 A.M.–11:00 P.M. ¥1,500 and up. Shabu-shabu.

Suehiro. 3-33 Masago-cho, Naka-ku; 681–6054. 11:00 A.M.–10:00 P.M. ¥1,000 and up. Steak, shabu-shabu. Closed third Tuesdays.

Takeuchi. 5-75 Onoe-cho, Naka-ku; 681–3725. 11:00 A.M.–9:00 P.M. ¥5,000 and up. Sukiyaki, shabu-shabu. Closed second and third Sundays.

Tempura

Tenkichi. 2-9 Minato-cho, Naka-ku; 681–2220. Lunch 11:00 A.M.–2:30 P.M.; dinner 5:00–9:00 P.M. ¥3,000 and up. Closed second and fourth Thursdays.

Tenshichi. 1-4 Sumiyoshi-cho, Naka-ku; 681–3376. Lunch 11:30 A.M.–2:00 P.M. (¥5,000 and up); dinner 5:00–9:00 P.M. (¥6,500 and up). Closed Sundays, holidays.

Tsunahachi. Lumine, 7th Floor, 2-16-1 Takashima, Nishi-ku; 453–6795. East exit of Yokohama Station. 11:00 A.M.–10:00 P.M. ¥1,000 and up.

Sushi

Igetazushi. 5-79 Aioi-cho, Naka-ku; 681–4101. 11:00 A.M.–9:00 P.M. ¥1,000 and up. Closed Sundays and holidays.

Sasagozushi. 2-33 Aioi-cho, Naka-ku; 681–1510. 11:30 A.M.–3:00 P.M. and 5:00–11:30 P.M. ¥1,000 and up. Closed Sundays and holidays.

Tamazushi. Center Building, 5th Floor, 3-33 Masago-cho, Naka-ku; 651–1431, ext. 286. 11:00 A.M.–10:00 P.M. ¥1,000 and up. Closed third Tuesday.

Yakitori

Konosu. 3-10 Yoshidamachi, Naka-ku; 251–8110. 5:00–10:00 P.M. ¥1,500 and up.

Toriise. 2-9 Minato-cho, Naka-ku; 662-9236. 5:00–11:00 P.M. ¥2,000–¥3,500.

Torishin. 5-63 Ohtamachi, Naka-ku; 662-9051. 4:30–11:00 P.M. ¥2,000 and up. Closed Sundays and holidays.

Crab

Kani Doraku. 2-84 Isezaki-cho, Naka-ku; 252-5511. 11:30 A.M.–10:30 P.M. ¥2,500 and up.

Tofu (Bean Curd)

Sannin Byakusho. 6-79 Benten-dori, Naka-ku; 212-1714. 5:00–11:30 P.M. ¥3,000 and up. Closed Sundays and holidays.

Eel

Wakana. 5-20 Minato-cho, Naka-ku; 681-1404. 11:00 A.M.–9:00 P.M. ¥2,200 and up. Closed first and third Wednesdays.

Yasohachi. 5-63 Sumiyoshi-cho, Naka-ku; 681-3788. 5:00–9:00 P.M. ¥1,500 and up. Closed Sundays and holidays.

Oden

Noge Oden. 4 Yoshidamachi, Naka-ku; 251-3234. 11:30 A.M.–9:00 P.M. ¥1,000 and up. Closed Sundays.

WESTERN STYLE

American Roast Beef

Victoria Station. 5-56 Tokiwa-cho, Naka-ku; 681-0393. Lunch 11:00 A.M.–5:00 P.M. (¥1,000–1,200); dinner 5:00–11:00 P.M. (¥3,000–4,000). Prime rib (hot roast beef), ¥2,280 for 200 grams.

Danish

Scandia. 1-1 Kaigandori, Naka-ku; 201-2262. Monday to Saturday 11:00 A.M.–midnight; Sunday 5:00 P.M.–midnight. ¥6,000 and up.

French

Kaori. 70 Yamashita-cho, Naka-ku; 681-4401. 11:30 A.M.–10:00 P.M. ¥3,500 and up.

Pet de Nonne. 3-5 Bandai-cho, Naka-ku; 662-2696. Lunch 12:00–2:00 P.M. (¥1,000); dinner 5:30–10:00 P.M. (¥4,000 and up). Crepe de crab, Poulep de bresse bucherom. Closed Mondays.

German

Alte Liebe. 11 Nihon Odori, Naka-ku; 201-2231. Lunch 11:30 A.M.–2:00 P.M. (¥2,000 and up); dinner 5:00–11:00 P.M. (¥7,000 and up). Raw steak.

Hof Brau. 25 Yamashita-cho, Naka-ku; 662-1106. 7:00 A.M.–10:00 P.M. ¥2,000 and up. Potato salad, pizza. Closed Sundays.

Italian

Italian House. 38 Fukutomi-cho Higashidori, Naka-ku; 251-5651. 11:30 A.M.–3:00 A.M. ¥1,100 and up. Lasagna, cannelloni.

Original Joe's. 3-60 Aioi-cho, Naka-ku; 651-2315. Monday to Saturday 11:30 A.M.–midnight; Sundays and national holidays 5:00–midnight. Steak, pizza.

Rome Station. 26 Yamashita-cho, Naka-ku; 681-1818. Monday to Saturday 11:30 A.M.–11:00 P.M.; Sundays and national holidays 12:00–10:00 P.M. ¥3,000. Chichukai-nabe (bouillabaisse).

Russian

Baikal. Chushokigyo Kaikan B1, 5-80 Onoe-cho, Naka-ku; 681–5561. Monday to Friday 1:00–9:00 P.M. Saturday 1:00–8:00 P.M. ¥2,000 and up. Borscht (Russian stew), piroshki (Russian meat pie). Closed Sundays and holidays.

Spanish

Casa de Fujimore. 1-25 Aioi-cho, Naka-ku; 662–9474. Monday to Saturday 11:00 A.M.–11:00 P.M.; Sundays and national holidays 12:00–9:00 P.M. ¥2,000 and up. Zarzueia (bouillabaisse).

OTHERS
Chinese

Dohatsu. 148 Yamashita-cho, Naka-ku; 681–7273. 10:30 A.M.–9:00 P.M. ¥2,000–10,000.

Kaseiro. 186 Yamashita-cho, Naka-ku; 681–2918. 11:30 A.M.–9:30 P.M. ¥4,000–15,000.

Indian

Kashmir. 2-13 Tokiwa-cho, Naka-ku; 681–2431. 9:00 A.M.–8:00 P.M. ¥500 and up. Variety of Indian curries. Closed Sundays and holidays.

Maharaja. Okadaya Department Store B2, 1-3-1 Minamisaiwai, Naka-ku; 311–1221, ext. 526. West exit of Yokohama Station. 11:00 A.M.–10:00 P.M. ¥2,000 and up. Tandoori chicken and Indian curries.

 NIGHT LIFE. Yokohama has its share of nightclubs, some posh and expensive and others garish and expensive. In some of the better places, one can find English-speaking hostesses, but the facility of the English language does not come cheap. Tips are on the higher side. There are a large number of bars in the area from Sakuragicho and Isezaki-cho all the way up to the Kannai district and, being the busy port Yokohama is, one often runs into sailors speaking various foreign languages. For the quiet drinker the bars in the hotels are recommended. Some of the smaller watering places are just as quiet but they are rather tucked away deep inside narrow lanes. Two places that can be recommended for the tourist, one expensive and the other reasonable, are:

Cliff Side. 2-114 Motomachi, Naka-ku; 641–1244. 6:00–11:45 P.M. ¥7,000 and up. Specializes in Afro-Cuban music. English-speaking hostesses available.

Cowbell. Center Building, 3-33 Masago-cho, Naka-ku; 641–9804. Cowbell, located at Kannai, is a 12th floor disco pub from which one can enjoy a view of the port of Yokohama. The pub boasts a cosmopolitan atmosphere with many foreigners patronizing it. ¥4,000–5,000 per person.

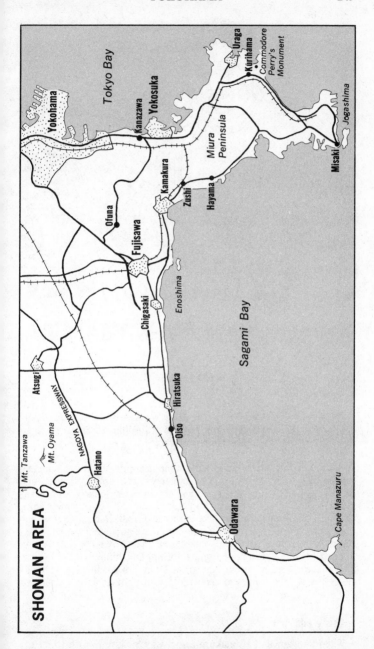

KAMAKURA, KITA-KAMAKURA

by
MICHAEL COOPER

Dr. Cooper is the author of numerous books and articles on Japan, including a guide to Kamakura. He also is a frequent lecturer on Japanese history and modern Japanese society.

Although Kamakura admittedly cannot compare with the ancient capital city of Kyoto for the grandeur of its temples, shrines, and historical monuments, the place has an endearing charm and merits more than one visit. For most people, Japanese and non-Japanese alike, the city is primarily associated with the Great Buddha statue and Hachiman Shrine, but in fact Kamakura has a good deal more to offer. Its proximity to Tokyo and Yokohama makes it an ideal place of interest for one-day sightseeing, exploring, and hiking. And not only is Kamakura easily reached by train from Tokyo, but its relatively small size allows visitors to view a lot of interesting places within one day.

Early History

The importance of Kamakura began way back in the 12th century. Up to that time the emperor and his aristocratic court in Kyoto had ruled Japan, but the increasing social unrest in the 12th century obliged the government to call upon the tough military families to keep law and order. One of these warrior houses was the Minamoto, and taking advantage of the central administration's weakness, the family set about seizing military and political power for itself. The scion of the family, Yoritomo, was captured as a young boy after his father's defeat in battle in 1159 by a rival clan. Mercifully (unusual for those times) the boy's life was spared and he was packed off to a monastery in Izu peninsula.

But Yoritomo was not cut out for the monastic life, so he rallied his late father's supporters, and with the help of his half-brother Yoshitsune, he eventually won military control of Japan. In theory the emperor in Kyoto still ruled the land, but in practice Yoritomo, while showing due deference to the throne, was very much in charge of governing the country. Thus began military rule, which continued down to 1868, when the Emperor Meiji came to the throne and political power was restored to civilian hands.

Yoritomo chose the small fishing village of Kamakura as his base of operations and set up his headquarters there in 1180. The place is surrounded by hills on three sides and by the sea on the fourth. The seven entrances to the city lay through narrow defiles set between cliffs and these could be easily blocked in time of attack. As a result the place was considered so impregnable from the military point of view that, when Kamakura finally fell to an enemy assault in 1333, records suggest divine intervention to explain the defeat. It is worth noting that Kamakura was never actually the capital of Japan (as is often asserted), but for one and a half centuries it served as the military and political center of the country.

The clan deity of the Minamoto family was Hachiman, the Shinto god of war, and so Yoritomo lost no time in transferring the deity's shrine from an obscure site near the seashore to a prominent position in the middle of his city. Even today Hachiman Shrine is the religious and cultural focus of Kamakura. After the birth of his first son Yoriie in 1182, Yoritomo ordered the construction of a broad avenue from the seashore to Hachiman Shrine so that the baby could be carried in solemn procession to the shrine and there dedicated to his family's tutelary deity. To this day Wakamiya (Young Prince) Avenue, spanned by three Shinto archways, or *torii*, cuts through the middle of the city and forms an impressive landmark.

A host of legends and stories are associated with the colorful personalities who played a role in the early history of the city. Becoming jealous of his half-brother Yoshitsune's growing popularity, Yoritomo had the young man hounded to death. Yoshitsune's lover, the dancing girl Shizuka, was captured and ordered to dance before Yoritomo at Hachiman Shrine. Instead of acting submissively and begging for her life, Shizuka enraged Yoritomo by performing an exultant dance, singing the praises of her lover Yoshitsune. This is probably the most famous dance in Japanese history, and it is re-enacted every year at the shrine's spring festival.

Yoritomo died in 1199 and was succeeded first by Yoriie, who was assassinated five years later, and then by his second son, the poet

Sanetomo. Sanetomo suffered the same fate as his elder brother. In a famous episode of Japanese history he was killed in 1219 as he walked down the steps of Hachiman Shrine during a New Year visit. It is said that his assassin (who, incidentally, was his nephew, Yoriie's son) jumped out from behind the giant ginko tree that still towers over the steps on the left-hand side.

Political power then passed to the Hojo, the family of Yoritomo's widow Masako, who is reputed to have been the strongest-willed woman in Japanese history, a claim that is not lightly made, as she enjoyed a great deal of political influence during her sons' administrations. The Hojo family ruled Japan from Kamakura for more than a century, and some of their rulers, especially Tokiyori and Tokimune, were greatly devoted to Zen Buddhism. With its stress on ascetical living and mental discipline, the sect's teachings were considered eminently suitable for tough warriors. At that time many Chinese monks fled to Japan to escape persecution in their own country. They found it difficult to be accepted in conservative and traditional Kyoto, but they were warmly welcomed in the new and innovative Kamakura. With the encouragement and support of the Hojo rulers, large Zen monasteries were founded in the city, and two of these, Kencho-ji and Engaku-ji, are still flourishing today.

A prominent religious figure in the 13th century was the monk Nichiren, who lived in Kamakura for many years. He founded the only purely Japanese sect of Buddhism, for all the other sects were imported to Japan from China. Owing to his strong language and outspoken criticism of the government and other Buddhist sects, Nichiren often found himself in trouble with the authorities. On one occasion he was saved from execution when a bolt of lightning broke the executioner's sword in two, and this divine intervention persuaded the authorities to commute his sentence to banishment.

As a result of these two religious influences in its history, most of Kamakura's sixty-five Buddhist temples belong either to the Zen sect or to the Nichiren sect. As a general rule, the temples to the left of Wakamiya Avenue (as you look toward Hachiman Shrine) belong to the Zen sect, while those to the right (where Nichiren used to live) are affiliated with the Nichiren sect.

The Statue of the Great Buddha

Kamakura's chief religious monument, the Great Buddha, or *daibutsu,* was erected in 1252. In 1182 Yoritomo visited the Kyoto region and took part in the rededication service of the enormous Nara *daibutsu,* which had been severely damaged in the fighting between rival military families.

It is quite possible that Yoritomo then conceived the idea of raising a similarly imposing statue in Kamakura to add to the prestige of his headquarters. But the project was not completed in his lifetime, and it wasn't until a large wooden statue had been constructed and then wrecked soon after in a violent storm that the present bronze image of the compassionate Amida Buddha was successfully cast and assembled. Some 11 meters in height, the statue was originally enclosed

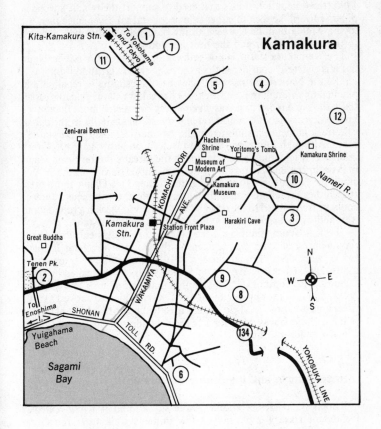

Temples

1) Engaku-ji
2) Hase
3) Hokoku-ji
4) Kakuon-ji
5) Kencho-ji
6) Komyo-ji
7) Meigetsuin
8) Myoho-ji
9) Myohon-ji
10) Sugimoto-ji
11) Tokei-ji
12) Zuisen-ji

within a wooden building, but this was swept away by a tidal wave in 1495 (the foundation stones that used to support the temple's wooden pillars can still be seen to either side of the statue). Ever since then the loving Amida Buddha has been sitting peacefully in the open, exposed to the cold of winter and the heat of summer.

The Kamakura statue is not so large or as old as the one in Nara, but it is generally considered to be the finer artistic creation. Moreover, unlike the Nara *daibutsu,* which has been substantially repaired and patched up through the centuries, the Kamakura statue remains essentially the same today as it was when it was completed more than seven hundred years ago. Of considerable interest, incidentally, is the classical Greek influence manifested in the symmetrical folds of the statue's robes. Although Europeans did not reach Japan until the 1540s, Greek influence, originating from Alexander the Great's military campaigns in Asia in the 2nd century B.C., was transmitted across northern Asia along the famous Silk Route and entered Japan via China and Korea. It is rather remarkable that the cultural influence of ancient Greece could be transmitted to the other side of the world in such a roundabout way and be incorporated in this enormous Buddhist statue.

The Kamakura statue has been described many times, but perhaps the quaintest account was written by the English merchant Richard Cocks, who passed through the city in 1616. Recording his impressions in his diary, Cocks referred to "a mighty idoll of bras, called by them Dibotes." He continued, "This idoll is made siting cros legged (telor lyke) and yet in my opinion it is above 20 yardes hie and above 12 yards from knee to knee. . . . I do esteem it to be bigger then that at Roads [Rhodes], which was taken for 1 of the 7 wonders of the world. In fine, it is a wonderfull thinge."

Hase Temple and the Statue of Kannon

Kamakura possesses another large statue, and it is conveniently located in Hase Temple only a few minutes walk from the Great Buddha. The gilt-covered wooden statue of the merciful Buddhist deity Kannon is 9 meters in height. Smaller heads emerge from the main head to symbolize Kannon's quest to search in all directions for suffering humans in need of her help. The statue is said to date back to the 8th century, when the pious monk Tokudo carved two images of Kannon from the trunk of an enormous camphor tree. The other statue is preserved in the village of Hase, near Nara, while the Kamakura statue was cast into the sea to be washed up wherever fate decreed. It eventually floated into Kamakura Bay, and so the area in which it is now housed is also called Hase after the village that preserves its twin.

The tall, enigmatically smiling statue now stands in a well-lighted hall, but was formerly hidden in obscure darkness. The author Lafcadio Hearn has left a dramatic account of the first time he saw the statue in 1891. The only illumination in the otherwise dark temple was a lantern attached to a rope suspended from the ceiling. As a monk pulled on this rope and slowly raised the lantern, the statue was revealed portion by portion until finally the face came into view.

The small garden of the temple is attractive, and in recent years thousands of little statues of Jizo, the guardian deity of children, have been placed by the steps leading up to the main shrine. Many of these miniature statues are clad in knitted shawls and bonnets, and some of them clutch a child's toy in their hands. Some of the Jizo have been put here in supplication for a sick child or for an easy childbirth, but many of them are intended to placate the spirits of aborted children, or *mizuko*.

Temples in Other Areas

It is obviously impossible even to begin to describe all of Kamakura's many temples; some of them are in such a ruined state that they hold little interest to the casual tourist. A number of temples take advantage of Kamakura's hilly terrain and nestle peacefully in small valleys, the natural surroundings thus adding to their attraction. Myohon-ji Temple, for example, is within only a few minutes walk from Kamakura Station, and yet its peaceful and lovely setting gives the impression of being miles away from the busy city center. But the place was not always so quiet and tranquil. After Yoritomo died, there was a succession dispute and the small child Ichiman was put forward as a possible candidate for power. His family's mansion, located at the present site of Myohon-ji, was attacked by a rival clique in 1203 and Ichiman's family was wiped out in the fighting. All that survived was the sleeve of the baby's robe, and so you can still see the so-called Sleeve Tomb commemorating the poor child, caught up unawares in the political struggle for power. It is difficult to reconcile this violent history of intrigue and slaughter when you look on the ancient and mossy tombs of Ichiman's family beneath the tall trees.

Nearby is Myoho-ji Temple with its moss-covered steps running up the hillside in the quiet and usually deserted garden. Nichiren lived in this vicinity for many years, and the temple is especially sacred to the members of his sect. Although Kamakura is a seaside city, the only temple within sight of the sea is said to be Komyo-ji, an impressive structure dating back to the 13th century. Particularly worthy of notice are its lotus-covered pond and the small graveyard on the hillside to the rear of the temple, where the abbots of Komyo-ji over the past six centuries are buried. The temple grounds usually present a deserted and empty appearance, but all this is abruptly changed at its September festival when the precincts and surrounding streets are crowded with devotees and sightseers alike.

Kita-Kamakura

Kita-Kamakura, or North Kamakura, is particularly rich in cultural and religious monuments. The great Zen temple of Engaku-ji, founded in 1282, is located next to Kita-Kamakura Station and is easily accessible. Although much damaged by the great earthquake of 1923, Engaku-ji still preserves some buildings of impressive grandeur, especially the ancient Shariden, which is reputed to house a relic of the historical Buddha. Here again it is instructive to take note of how the monastery complex utilizes to the full its natural surroundings and fits so harmoniously into the little valley.

A few minutes walk along the road from this Zen monastery is Tokei-ji Temple, noted for its plum blossoms in March and its beautiful graveyard set among towering cryptomeria trees. But the temple has another claim to fame—it is known throughout the region as the Divorce Temple. In olden times men could easily dismiss their wives and send them packing back to their families by issuing a short writ of divorce. Wives, on the other hand, had no such rights and were not able to free themselves from undesirable husbands. But the government mercifully decreed that "women desirous of ending the thrall of conubial woes," as an English woman author delicately expressed it back in 1918, could take refuge with the nuns at Tokei-ji, and after two years of residence in the temple they would be considered legally divorced. Not surprisingly there are a number of legends attached to this unusual temple, with accounts of distracted wives, hotly pursued by their irate husbands, just making it to Tokei-ji in time.

Kencho-ji, Kamakura's other still-active Zen monastery, is also located in Kita-Kamakura. Its impressive ceremonial gate is a marvel of technology and beauty. The timbers of the mighty structure are held together by wooden wedges, and somehow or other the massive gate looks light and airy, belying its many tons of weight.

In both Kencho-ji and Engaku-ji, communities of Zen monks lead an austere and ascetical life in quest of spiritual enlightenment. Usually the monks are not much in evidence because the interior of the monasteries is closed to visitors, but occasionally a line of straw-hatted monks may be seen marching out of the grounds on an expedition to beg for alms at houses in the vicinity. Sessions of Zen meditation are organized for lay people at both temples, and sometimes it is possible to glimpse a group of people squatting bolt upright in the lotus position in one of the public halls, their eyes half-closed as they strive to reach enlightenment. A custodian monk, suitably armed with a hefty wooden stick, prowls up and down through the seated ranks and heartily chastises anybody who may appear to be dozing off.

Two small temples in the area are worth visiting. The first is Meige-tsuin, a sleepy little place with considerable charm. Throughout the year it slumbers on, undisturbed and unfrequented, but in June the calm is rudely shattered as thousands of visitors descend on the temple to admire the fine display of hydrangeas in its extensive grounds. In contrast, Emmado Temple consists of only one dark and gloomy hall. Around the walls of its dim interior are seated statues of King Emma and his assistants, who judge people after death and punish them for their sins and misdeeds. One look at the glowering and horrifying features of King Emma should be enough to keep most people on the strait and narrow path of virtue.

Hachiman Shrine

Like most Shinto shrines, Hachiman Shrine possesses few statues and relies on its buildings and natural surroundings to create an impression of religious awe and veneration. The great *torii* arches spanning Wakamiya Avenue are intended to put visitors in a religious frame of mind even before they enter the sacred precincts. A steep Drum Bridge at the entrance tests the stamina of hardy souls who try to cross over and provides considerable mirth to the less venturesome onlookers; ascent up the precipitous slope is arduous and slippery, while descent down the other side is usually hurried and undignified. On either side of the shrine's main avenue is a large pond. The bigger one to the right possesses three islands and is dedicated to Yoritomo's victorious family; the one on the left has four islands and recalls his vanquished enemies. The significance of these numbers lies in the fact that "three" in Japanese is *san*, which can also mean "birth, life," and "four" is *shi*, also meaning "death."

Within the precincts of the shrine, to the left of the Wakamiya Avenue, is the modern building housing the Kanazawa Prefectural Museum of Modern Art, which organizes periodic exhibitions of modern and contemporary paintings. In contrast, to the right of the avenue is the Kamakura Museum, with its permanent, representative collection of ancient statues selected from the temples and shrines within the city, plus a rotating exhibition of paintings and scrolls relating to Kamakura's history. For the tourist with limited time to visit many of the local temples, an hour or so spent in this museum will provide a good idea of typical Kamakura art. Notice, for example, that most of the religious statues of Kamakura, a military city governed by warriors, portray powerful, muscular figures, unlike those of civilian, artistocratic Kyoto, where the statuary tends to be decidedly more ethereal and other-worldly.

At the bottom of the broad flight of steps leading up to Hachiman's main shrine buildings is a roofed dance stage, and here Shizuka's famous dance is re-enacted every year in the spring festival. During the autumn festival in September the city organizes a long historical procession, featuring well-known personalities from Kamakura's past, such as Yoritomo, Yoshitsune, Masako, and Shizuka. During these festivals visitors may watch the exciting spectacle of *yabusame*, when mounted archers, clad in ancient hunting costume, gallop one by one down a shrine avenue shooting arrows at three targets.

The red-painted shrine buildings at the top of the steps may not be entered by the casual visitor, although it is possible to look in and watch as young babies are dedicated in services similar to that in which Yoriie was dedicated at this shrine some 800 years ago. Wooden votive tablets, or *ema*, hang from racks in front of the building. Messages written on the tablets ask for a variety of favors—good health, a kind husband, and, especially in the spring of each year, success in the entrance examinations for high schools and universities.

Quite near to the shrine is the tomb of Yoritomo, a modest monument, considering that for all intents and purposes it was he who founded the city and put it on the political map. The lack of a suitable memorial has been remedied in recent years by the construction of a fine seated statue of the founding father, clad in full armor, in Genji Park overlooking the city. Here Yoritomo gazes broodingly on the city that he founded so many centuries ago after much fighting and bloodshed.

Kamakura Shrine and Nearby Temples

One of the few modern shrines in the city is Kamakura Shrine, inaugurated in the last century to commemorate Prince Morinaga. The cave where he was imprisoned and put to death in 1335 can still be seen on the site. It was only after the young prince's death that his father, Emperor Go-Daigo, realized that his son had been falsely accused and had in fact been loyally striving to further the imperial cause. Soon after political power was restored to the throne in 1868, this shrine was built in an effort to boost popular devotion to the imperial institution. Kamakura Shrine is particularly crowded at New Year, and at the Seven-Five-Three celebration in November when brightly dressed children of those three ages visit the precincts. But the most noteworthy event in the calendar of Kamakura Shrine takes place on two evenings in September when *noh* plays are performed in the open air. Illumination is provided by the flickering light of wooden torches, and the resulting effect on the actors' masks is both fascinating and eerie.

A mile or so behind Kamakura Shrine is the delightful temple of Zuisen-ji. This was founded by the versatile monk Muso, who managed to stay on good terms with both the military government of Kamakura and the imperial court of Kyoto. Muso is renowned for his theological writings and artistic talent, and the garden of this temple (as well as a garden in Kencho-ji) was laid out by him. Roosters strut around the attractive grounds famed for their plum blossoms, while in the rear is the rock-and-sand garden planned by Muso and adjoining a cave where he is said to have practiced Zen meditation. The temple possesses a fine wooden statue that realistically portrays the founder, but unfortunately this is not usually on display.

Situated a little way to the left of Kamakura Shrine is the quiet and isolated temple of Kakuon-ji, whose peaceful surroundings offer a startling contrast to the bustle of the nearby shrine. The temple guards its privacy jealously and it is not always possible to enter. But it is well worth the effort, especially in late autumn when its extensive grounds are carpeted with yellow leaves. Also in the same area is Sugimoto-ji, reputedly the oldest temple in Kamakura and said to date from the 8th century. This friendly and homey temple displays three ancient statues of Kannon; such are their sanctity that, according to legend, anyone riding his horse past the temple entrance and not bothering to dismount out of respect was thrown to the ground as a punishment for his impiety. Nearby is Hokoku-ji, or the Bamboo Temple, a pleasant cluster of well-kept buildings with a lovely bamboo grove in the rear.

Harakiri Cave and the Fall of Kamakura

There is one out-of-the-way spot of historical interest quite near Wakamiya Avenue. This is the famous Harakiri Cave, and it represents the abrupt end of Kamakura's role as the political and military center of Japan. The Hojo rulers gradually declined in quality and leadership, and in 1333 the emperor in Kyoto saw his chance to seize back military power. An imperial army attacked Kamakura, but was held up for several days by the well-guarded hills surrounding the fortified city. Finally the imperial commander, one Nitta Yoshisada, climbed the cliff jutting into the sea at Inamuragasaki, prayed to the goods to support his cause, and then hurled his sword into the ocean. His prayers were answered in dramatic fashion, for the sea rolled back allowing Nitta's troops to rush around the bluff and storm into the city.

After some desperate fighting the Kamakura soldiers could offer no further resistance and the senior officers retired to the Hojo family temple of Tosho-ji. There in July 1333 some eight hundred men committed harakiri, or ritual disembowelment, rather than suffer the disgrace of falling alive into the hands of the enemy. As the only thing left on the temple site is one small cave, this has become known as the Harakiri Cave, and seldom will there not be fresh flowers and burning incense there to honor the memory of the defeated warriors. As you walk up the narrow, peaceful lane leading to the cave, it is difficult to imagine the dreadful scene of carnage that took place on this site back in 1333. Interestingly enough, although the temple itself has long ceased to exist, the nearby stream is spanned by a small bridge still called Tosho-ji Bridge. Memories are long in Kamakura.

After this defeat, political power reverted to Kyoto and the importance of Kamakura dramatically waned. In fact, when the English merchants passed through in 1616, the place was scarcely more than a small fishing village, with only some temples and monuments as reminders of its once glorious past. The much traveled Tokaido Highway, linking Kyoto and Edo (present-day Tokyo), bypassed Kamakura to the north, and as Cocks observed, "At present, it is no cittie, but scattared howses seated heare and theare." This state of decline continued until the end of the last century. The railroad running from Yokosuka to Tokyo, via Kamakura, was completed in 1889, and as a result of this transport link, the fortunes of Kamakura began to revive.

Kamakura Today

With its mild climate, ancient past, and proximity to Tokyo, Kamakura has become a bedroom city with a population of 174,000. It asccessibility has also made the city a popular tourist attraction. Visitors are most numerous at the New Year, when Hachiman Shrine attracts well over two million people in the first three days of the year. Other crowded occasions are cherry blossom time (the first week of April), summer weekends, and the autumn festival of Hachiman Shrine. It is worth bearing in mind that the public transport system is strained to its limit during these periods, and the streets are clogged with traffic and crowds. While it is true that there is a good-humored and friendly atmosphere at such times, non-Japanese might well consider visiting the city on another day. The Japanese people are well used to crowding and take it in their stride, but visitors from abroad may not regard the crowded conditions with such equanimity.

Although not part of the ancient city, the area to the west toward the island of Enoshima has now been absorbed into modern Kamakura. Part of the pleasure of visiting here is the ride on the little Enoshima Railway, running from the rear exit of Kamakura Station along the seacoast to Enoshima, and then inland to Fujisawa. A cross between a glorified streetcar and a miniature train, the train winds its tortuous way around people's backyards and then importantly rattles along the shore to Enoshima. Even lovers of Kamakura have to admit that this shore is something of a disaster area. The enormous crowds that flock to swim and surf here during the summer have to be seen to be believed. The beach of unattractive, gray sand becomes littered and dirty, and the narrow beach road is jammed with bumper-to-bumper traffic that moves, when at all, in infrequent fits and starts. Only the most gregarious visitor will find any pleasure on or near Kamakura Beach on a summer weekend.

Two places in the area are worth visiting. The first is Ryuko-ji Temple, with its fine pagoda nestling among the trees and blending in perfectly with its natural background. Before the temple was built, this used to be an execution site, and it was here that Nichiren was miraculously saved from beheading in 1271. In the following century the temple was founded to commemorate the happy event. Each year on September 12, the day of the patriarch's delivery, thousands upon thousands of faithful converge on the temple bearing lanterns and beating drums, and the festival continues well into the night.

Nearby Enoshima is a small hilly island joined to the mainland by a long bridge. The steel climb to the top of the island is now made easy by a series of escalators gliding up the hillside. A jumble of souvenir shops, all selling apparently identical wares, line the street leading to an impressive Shinto shrine, and at the top of the hill is a small botanical garden. On the far side of the island there is a large cave reputedly linked to the crater of Mt. Fuji (some 50 miles away) by an underground passage, but the danger of falling rock has forced the local authorities to close off the tunnel's entrance in recent years. A number of modestly priced restaurants are dotted around the island. Several have lofty balconies jutting from the cliff facing east, and so it is possible to enjoy a fine view of the yachting marina and Kamakura Bay far below while having some light refreshment.

As a tourist center, Kamakura is amply provided with restaurants serving both Japanese and Western food. Restaurants are especially plentiful along Wakamiya Avenue and the parallel Komachi-dori that begins under a red *torii* gate in the far left-hand corner of the plaza in front of the station. The latter road is closed to traffic on holidays and weekends, and has become something of an enjoyable tourist attraction with its coffee shops, tea shops, restaurants, boutiques ("Kickapoo, Super Duper, Natural Roots and Hearts" is the mystifying announcement outside one of them), and folk-art stores ("Fine Prints for Beautiful Communications," etc.). Much pleasure can be had by browsing inside the antique stores, while several shops display an amazing assortment of the lovely, soft Japanese *washi* paper.

The local speciality is Kamakura-bori, or Kamakura Carving. These are wooden utensils or ornaments such as trays, salvers, small boxes, backs of mirrors, and clogs, delicately carved and then covered with as many as eight layers of dark red lacquer. They make appreciated and easily transportable gifts, but such hand-crafted wares do not come cheaply. A medium-sized salver costs at least ¥12,000, and so visitors with limited resources may care to settle for a pair of lacquered chopsticks at ¥1,000. Kamakura-bori shops are scattered throughout the city, but a cluster of them are conveniently located just in front of the main entrance to Hachiman Shrine.

A word about hikes in and around Kamakura. The hilly terrain surrounding the city is crisscrossed with ancient paths dating back many centuries, and it is possible to walk from one end of the city to the other without crossing a single congested road. The hills behind Hachiman Shrine make up Tenen Park and are sometimes rather grandiloquently called the Kamakura Alps, although the loftiest hill does not reach 500 feet in height. Many of the hill paths serve as rain courses, and so walks through the hills should not be attempted during or immediately after heavy rain.

The neighboring city of Zushi has few historical landmarks to attract tourists, but in recent years it has become a popular resort place in the summer. Its beaches tend to be a little less crowded than those of Kamakura, while the town itself has a pleasant, laid-back atmosphere.

To sum up: A visit to Kamakura is a worthwhile experience, especially if you are prepared to depart from the well-beaten track and explore some of the less-known temples, historical sites, and hill paths. Not only is Kamakura relatively close to Tokyo, but the surrounding hills make it small in area and as a result a good deal can be seen in one day. Lacking the stately monuments of aristocratic and sprawling Kyoto, the city is a homey place, and although proud of its colorful history, it is without the slightly self-conscious atmosphere of Kyoto. The pity is that most visitors are satisfied with viewing the Great Buddha, Hachiman Shrine, and a Zen temple. There is a lot more to see and enjoy if you only have the energy and imagination to seek it out.

PRACTICAL INFORMATION FOR
KAMAKURA-KITAKAMAKURA

WHEN TO GO. Kamakura can be visited at any time of the year, but the spring and autumn seasons are most enjoyable. The summer tends to be rather hot, and in addition the city becomes crowded with tourists, especially during the weekend.

HOW TO GET THERE. Trains run punctually and frequently from Tokyo on the Japan National Railways Yokosuka line. The journey takes 62 minutes from Tokyo Station (Track #1 underground. *Beware!* Track #1 on the surface is the Chuo line and will *not* take you to Kamakura). The same train may be caught at Shinagawa Station, Track #10 (51 minutes), and Yokohama Station, Track #9 (28 minutes). On a busy summer weekend it is a good idea to buy your return ticket immediately after leaving Kamakura Station on your arrival; this will save a lengthy wait in line at the end of the expedition.

262   **JAPAN**

 HOTELS AND INNS. As Kamakura is so near Tokyo and Yokohama, with their large and numerous hotels, there is not a great deal of comfortable accommodation easily available.

Kamakura Hotel. 2-22-29 Hase, Kamakura-shi 248; (0467) 22–0029. Western and Japanese rooms, from ¥6,000 to ¥10,000. An old-fashioned establishment halfway between the Great Buddha and the beach. Credit cards: American Express, J.C.B., Million, Diners, Diamond, Suruga B.K.

Ryokan Kaihinso. 4-8-14, Yuigahama, Kamakura; (0467) 22–0960. An updated Japanese inn near the sea. Comfortable and elegant. ¥12,000 to ¥20,000 per person per night, including dinner and breakfast. American Express.

Shinto-Tei. 2-10-3, Zushi; (0468) 71–2012. Near Zushi Station. In season, the inn serves wild boar hunted by the master. Credit Cards: J.C.B.

Tsurugaoka Kaikan. 2-12-27 Komachi, Kamakura-shi 248; (0467) 24–1111. An attractive modern building in the center of the city, near Kamakura Station and Hachiman Shrine. Japanese-style, with 22 rooms, from ¥18,000 to ¥22,000 for two people. No credit cards.

Zushi-Nagisa Hotel. 2-10-18 Shinjuku, Zushi-shi 249; (0468) 71–4260. 26 rooms from ¥9,900 to ¥16,500 for two people (higher prices in July and August). Founded back in 1926 and proud of its long tradition, the Nagisa is a favorite with foreign residents and visitors. As it faces the beach, it is an ideal place for families with children. Credit cards: J.C.B., Diners, and Diamond.

 HOW TO GET AROUND. By bus. All buses conveniently leave from Kamakura Station and serve outlying districts. **By train.** The Enoshima Railway also starts from the station, although new tickets have to be bought before boarding. JNR connects Kamakura with Zushi. Station stops are Kita-Kamakura, Kamakura, Higashi-Zushi, and Zushi. **By taxi.** Kamakura is a small city, so taxi fares are relatively cheap, especially in the case of three or four passengers.

 TOURIST INFORMATION. Lamentably Kamakura is not well equipped to handle non-Japanese visitors. A tourist information bureau in the station will supply an illustrated pamphlet and map in English, but this does not provide information on how to reach the various places of interest. However, a reassuring smile and a question in slow and simple English can produce miracles in Kamakura and elsewhere. Starting from 9:40 A.M. daily, six tourist buses leave Kamakura Station and visit places of interest, but no English explanation is provided. Reservations may be made at the bus office to the right of the station.

Help for the non-Japanese visitor comes in two forms. On Sunday mornings between 10:00 and 11:00 A.M. in spring and autumn, a group of students from local universities waits outside Kamakura Station and will guide non-Japanese visitors around the city in return for English-language practice. In addition, there is an English-language guidebook which will provide practical information and tell you more than you ever wanted to know about Kamakura and its temples: Michael Cooper, *Exploring Kamakura: A Guide for the Curious Traveler* (Weatherhill, Tokyo, and New York, 160 pages).

SEASONAL EVENTS AND FESTIVALS. January. New Year visits to Hachiman Shrine and Kamakura Shrine from the 1st–3rd. Archery at Hachiman Shrine on the 5th.

February. Bean throwing at spring equinox festival on the 3rd at Hachiman Shrine and Kamakura Shrine.

April. Spring Festival of Hachiman Shrine from the 7th–14th. This includes Shizuka's dance and the historical procession (the two events are usually held on the second Sunday of the month).

June. From the 1st–14th is the hydrangea display at Meigetsuin Temple.

July. From about the 7th–14th is the Enoshima Festival, during which portable shrines, or *mikoshi,* are carried into the sea.

August. Lantern festival at Hachiman Shrine from the 7th–9th. Lanterns are strung around the shrine and food, toys, plants and the like are sold. The Festival of Kamakura Shrine takes place on the 20th. Stalls with knickknacks for sale. Religious services are held in the morning, and you can see a long line of gorgeously robed monks processing through the grounds en route to one of the temple buildings. From the 23rd–24th the foundation ceremonies take place at Kencho-ji Temple.

September. Foundation ceremonies take place at Engaku-ji Temple from the 2nd–3rd. The festival at Ryuko-ji Temple, from the 11th–13th, involves religious services throughout most of the day, stalls in neighboring streets, and processions of the faithful beating drums and chanting. The autumn festival at Hachiman Shrine, from the 14th–16th, includes mounted archery on the last day. Torchlight *noh* can be seen at Kamakura Shrine from the 21st–22nd.

October. Festival of Komyo-ji Temple runs from the 10th–15th.

November. Seven-Five-Three Festival at Hachiman Shrine and Kamakura Shrine on the 15th.

December. Festival of Hase Temple is held on the 17th and 18th. On the 31st is the ceremonial ringing of temple bells throughout the city.

TEMPLES AND SHRINES. See the introductory essay for more information on the temples and shrines mentioned below. They are listed in order of their appearance in the text, and can be visited any day during daylight hours.

Great Buddha. Kamakura's chief religious monument, erected in 1252. Buses leave from stands #3 & #7 outside Kamakura Station. Alternatively, a 10-minute walk from Hase Station on the Enoshima Railway.

Hase Temple. Houses the 9-meter-high statue of the Buddhist diety Kannon. Same buses as above, or 5-minute walk from Hase Station.

Myohon-ji. Situated in a tranquil and lovely setting. A 10-minute walk from Kamakura Station.

Myoho-ji. Especially sacred to members of the Nichiren sect. Within 5 minutes walk of Myohonji.

Komyo-ji. A 13th-century structure with a small graveyard and a view of the sea. Buses leave from stand #1 at Kamakura Station.

Engaku-ji. A late 13th-century Zen temple reputed to house a relic of the historical Buddha. Next to Kita-Kamakura Station, the stop before Kamakura Station.

Tokei-ji. Also known as the Divorce Temple where wives could take refuge from their husbands. Noted for its plum blossoms and beautiful graveyard. A 5 minute walk from Engaku-ji in the direction of Kamakura.

Meigetsuin. A small temple, noted for its hydrangeas in June. Walking from Kita-Kamakura Station in the direction of Kamakura, cross the level crossing and turn left.

Kencho-ji. A still-active Zen monastery, with an impressive ceremonial gate. A 15-minute walk from Kita-Kamakura Station. Alternatively, bus from stand #9 outside Kamakura Station.

Emmado. A small temple with a statue of King Emma, who judges people after their death. A 10-minute walk from Hachiman Shrine, or bus from stand #9.

Hachiman Shrine. The religious and cultural focus of Kamakura, built in honor of the Shinto god of war. A 10-minute walk from Kamakura Station along Wakamiya Avenue. Alternatively, buses from stands #5 & #9.

Kamakura Shrine. Built around 1870, in an effort to promote popular devotion to imperial rule. Bus from stand #5.

Zuisen-ji. Has beautiful gardens renowned for their plum blossoms. A 15-minute walk from behind Kamakura Shrine.

Kakuon-ji. A quiet temple in peaceful surroundings. A 10-minute walk to the left of Kamakura Shrine.

Sugimoto-ji. Dates from the 8th century and houses three ancient statues of Kannon. A 15-minute walk from Kamakura Station, on the far side of Wakamiya Avenue.

Harakiri Cave. Site where 800 Kamakura warriors took their own lives after defeat in 1333.

Ryuko-ji. A fine pagoda, situated on the spot where Nichiren is said to have been miraculously saved from execution in 1271. Near Enoshima Station on the Enoshima Railway.

WALKS & HIKES. There are a number of most enjoyable hikes that can be made in and around Kamakura. The **Asahina Pass** was once the busy eastern exit of Kamakura but is now a quiet path leading to the town of Kanazawa Hakkei. Take a bus from stand #5 and get off at Juniso Shrine.

Tenen Hiking Course may be entered either at Juniso Shrine or (for a shorter trip) by Kakuon-ji Temple. It offers a splendid view of the city. The path leads down behind Kencho-ji Temple.

The **Daibutsu Hiking Trail** starts from Genji park, a 20-minute walk from the rear of Kamakura Station, and leads over the hills, coming down behind the Great Buddha.

MUSEUMS. Modern Museum of Art (Kanazawa Kenritsu Kindai Bijutsukan), Hachiman Shrine. 10:00 A.M. to 5:00 P.M. Closed Mondays. ¥500. **Kamakura Museum** (Kamakura Kokuhokan), Hachiman Shrine. Ancient statues, as well as a rotating exhibit of paintings and scrolls relating to the city's history. 9:00 A.M. to 4:00 P.M. Closed Mondays. ¥100.

SHOPPING. Kamakura has no good large stores and most non-Japanese visitors will prefer to do their shopping in Tokyo. Even the local specialty, Kamakura-bori, is available in Tokyo department stores as well as in Kamakura shops. There are four or five Kamakura-bori shops located in front of Hachiman Shrine. Souvenirs, folk-art items, and antiques can be obtained at a number of stores in Wakamiya Avenue and Komachi-dori. *Mr. Takeshita's House of Antiques* displays art and antique objects for sale; reservation needed to view, (0467) 43–1441. Pictorial maps can be bought at many shops; although they are usually printed in Japanese, their pictures and clearly indicated routes will help in finding your way around.

DINING OUT. There is almost a limitless choice of restaurants in and around the city. Private homes converted into traditional eating places have a special charm and are to be recommended. Restaurants along Wakamiya Ave. and Komachi-dori, and on the narrow roads joining these two thoroughfares, are particularly numerous, especially near the large *torii* arching over Wakamiya Ave., halfway between Kamakura Station and Hachiman Shrine. Among the traditional Japanese menus there is a choice of *tempura, sashimi, soba, tonkatsu, sushi,* and other less-known dishes. Or you can fall back on Western food in a variety of places. McDonald's, on Wakamiya Ave., is a popular spot, and regularly breaks sales records for the chain in Japan by remaining open on January 1 and catering to the enormous crowds flocking to Hachiman Shrine.

The following four restaurants can be recommended for special occasions. Be advised that, however simple it may appear, traditional Japanese food can be very expensive. Lunchtime prices at the more expensive places run around ¥3,000 to ¥5,000 per person. Prices in the less expensive category range between ¥1,000 to ¥3,000 per person. Of course if you order just a bowl of noodles you can pay around ¥800 or so.

Hikage Chaya. 16 Horiuchi, Hayama-machi 240-01; (0468) 75–0014. Traditional Japanese seafood. Despite the dainty portions, the final bill can be very high. 12:00 noon to 2:30 P.M., 5:00 P.M. to 9:30 P.M. Open all week. Reservations required. Credit cards: J.C.B., Diners, Diamond, AE, Sumitomo, and U.C.

Raitei. Takasago, Kamakurayama, Kamakura-shi 248; (0467) 32–5656. Traditional Japanese food (*kaiseki,* etc.). Reservations required. Lunch and dinner. Closed Wednesdays in some months. Credit card: Diamond.

Roast Beef no Mise (Roast Beef Shop). Fueda 894, Kamakura-shi 248; (0467) 31–5454. Set in spacious surroundings with large garden. 12:00 noon to 2:00 P.M., 5:00 P.M. to 8:00 P.M. Closed Tuesdays. Reservations needed. All credit cards.

Tori-ichi. 1-4-16 Ogiyazu, Kamakura-shi 248; (0467) 22–1818. Japanese food (*yakitori, obento, kaiseki,* etc.) served in delightful, peaceful surroundings. Reservations required. To get there, take a taxi at the rear exit of Kamakura Station and just ask for "Tori-ichi." Lunch and dinner. Closed Tuesdays. Credit cards: D.C., U.C., Sumitomo, and J.C.B.

The following less expensive establishments can be recommended.

Asabaya. 2-15-5 Komachi; (0467) 22–1222. Traditional eel dishes. Located near the *torii* over the Wakamiya Avenue, halfway between the station and Hachiman Shrine. 11:00 A.M. to 8:00 P.M. Closed Thursdays. No credit cards.

Kaseiro. 3-1-14 Hase, Kamakura-shi 248; (0467) 22–0280. Chinese food. Conveniently located near the Great Buddha and Hase Temple. 11:00 A.M. to 9:00 P.M. Open all week. Credit cards: Diners, U.C., D.C., Amex, and J.C.B.

Kayagi-ya. 2-11-16 Komachi, Kamakura-shi 248; (0467) 22–1460. Traditional restaurant on Wakamiya Ave. serving moderately priced meals to aficionados of eels. 12:00 noon to 7:30 P.M. Closed on Fridays. No credit cards.

La Marée de Chaya. 24-2 Abuzuri Dori, Hayama 249; (0468) 75–6683. Chic French restaurant located in Hayama Marina; easily reached by taxi from Zushi Station. Pleasant atmosphere, wonderful view of the ocean. 12:00 noon to 2:00 P.M., 5:00 P.M. to 9:00 P.M. Closed on Thursdays. Credit cards: American Express, J.C.B., Sumitomo, U.C. Reservations advised.

Maruyama-tei. 14-1 Onaricho, Kamakura-shi 248; (0467) 24–2452. A new restaurant conveniently located close to the rear exit of Kamakura Station and serving French food. 11:30 A.M. to 2:00 P.M., 5:00 P.M. to 9:00 P.M. Closed on Mondays. Credit cards: Diners, AE, U.C., Diamond, Sumitomo, J.C.B.

Monte Costa. 1-5-7 Yukinoshita, Kamakura-shi 248; (0467) 23–0808. A new restaurant overlooking small, pleasant garden. Italian food with Japanese flavor. English menu is said to be under preparation. 11:30 A.M. to 9:00 P.M. Closed on Mondays. Credit cards: Diners, Diamond.

Nakamura-tei. 1-7-6 Komachi-dori, Kamakura-shi 248; (0467) 25–3500. Traditional restaurant where you can watch your *soba* being made and cooked. 11:30 A.M. to 6:00 P.M. Closed on Thursdays. No credit cards.

O-ebi. 4-12-25 Yuigahama, Kamakura-shi 248; (0467) 22–0540. As its name implies ("ebi" means shrimp), the beach-side restaurant specializes in shellfish. Open all week, 11:30 A.M. to 9:00 P.M. Credit cards: American Express, J.C.B., U.C., Sumitomo, Diners, Million.

Saison. 5-419-2 Kotsubo, Zushi-shi 249; (0467) 25–0480. Modern seafood establishment in Zushi Marina; take taxi from Zushi Station. 11:30 A.M. to 2:30 P.M., 5:00 P.M. to 9:30 P.M. Credit cards: American Express, Diamond, Diners, J.C.B., Sumitomo. Reservations advised.

Tonkatsu Komachi. 1-6-11 Komachi, Kamakura-shi 248; (0467) 22–2025. Conveniently located on Kamochi-dori and serving tasty *tonkatsu* (pork cutlet). 11:30 A.M. to 8:00 P.M. Closed on Tuesdays. Credit cards: J.C.B., Sumitomo, Million.

FUJI-HAKONE-IZU

by
JOHN TURRENT

By far the most popular tourist district in the immediate vicinity of Tokyo is the Fuji-Hakone-Izu National Park area, located in the southern part of the Kanto region around the capital. Every type of entertainment imaginable is available here. There are camping sites, lakes for boating, skating resorts, riding and hiking courses, hunting, fishing, and water-skiing facilities, as well as a wealth of hot springs where visitors take the waters for relaxation or for their health. Transportation from Tokyo is also very convenient, and accommodation facilities can be found almost everywhere.

The area, which was designated as a national park in 1936 with the Izu peninsula being added later, is dominated by Mount Fuji, which, at 3,776 meters (12,365 feet), is Japan's tallest mountain. The Hakone district lies on the southern side of the mountain. On a clear day, Mount Fuji can be seen from the observation floors of Tokyo's skyscraper buildings, and sometimes it can be glimpsed from pedestrian crossovers in Harajuku, near Yoyogi Park. Scaling the peak is a must for anyone who has the time and stamina to do it, but even more than that, catching a view of Mount Fuji at its best can be a thrilling and awe-inspiring experience, for it really is an impressive monument of nature. Fuji-san, as it is called in Japanese, can also be seen sometimes from trains running along the Chuo line westward from Tokyo, and from the Shinkansen line running down toward Nagoya. Indeed, such is the importance of viewing the giant mountain, Shinkansen trains have been known to slow down on a good day to allow passengers to take in the view.

Mount Fuji's spectacular shape is the result of volcanic eruptions in the past. The volcano has been dormant for a long time now, the last major eruption having been in 1707, when ash was carried as far as Tokyo (then called Edo). It is not known when or whether there will be another eruption, but the possibility that the shape of Fuji-san might change again dramatically sometime in the future only seems to add to the romanticism that surrounds the mountain.

Climbing Mount Fuji

Mount Fuji is open to climbers for only two months during the year—the rest of the time its peak is snowcapped, although there are still people up there working at the meteorological station on the peak. In July and August, however, vast numbers of people hike their way up the mountainside to stand at the top, some for the first time, some for the "nth" time, some of them as old as 80 or even 90, some of them still young elementary schoolchildren.

Despite the fact that so many people make the ascent, however, it should not be treated lightly. Temperatures during the climb can vary from extremely hot to extremely cold. It is now possible to reach the fifth station, about halfway up the mountain, by car or by bus. Most climbers aim to leave the fifth station on the climb by early afternoon, reaching stone huts at the seventh or eighth station before darkness falls. After spending the early part of the night in a hut, climbers then set off in hopes of reaching the summit in time to see the sunrise. Other climbers start out from the fifth station late in the afternoon and keep going through the night, again reaching the top in time for the sunrise. Whichever course you decide on, make sure you have plenty of food and drink with you (although snacks are sold on the way), a warm sweater, a raincoat, a stick for the difficult stretches, and be certain to wear a pair of strong shoes.

There is a total of six paths up to the summit of Mount Fuji, each of them known by the name of the starting place: Gotemba, Subashiri, Yoshida, Funatsu, Shoji, and Fujinomiya. Each of the routes is divided into ten sections, with each section having a "station" at which there is a signpost, shops, and, at the higher stages, hut accommodation. The total climbing time is about seven to nine hours if you begin at the beginning, and four to five hours if you start from the fifth station. Buses leave for the fifth station from the west exit of Shinjuku railway station in Tokyo, the journey taking about 3 hours, and also from Kawaguchiko, Gotemba, and Fujinomiya stations.

After reaching the summit of Mount Fuji, most climbers explore the crater in the morning and then start the descent in the afternoon. Helped by a sand-slide stretch, the descent to the foot of the mountain should take only about 3 to 5 hours.

The Fuji Lakes

A 2-hour train ride from Shinjuku brings travelers to the Fuji Five Lakes area. The five lakes in question are Lake Yamanaka, Lake Kawaguchi, Lake Saiko, Lake Shoji, and Lake Motosu. The area can be toured in one day from Tokyo, but if you have time a 2- to 3-day trip makes for an enjoyable stay and gives you the chance to see the many attractions of the area, including the splendid Otodome and Shiraito waterfalls, and to take in the relaxing alpine atmosphere. This is also one of the best vantage points from which to observe Mount Fuji, which towers over the district. On a good day, you might even be able to enjoy a double view of the mountain, its reflection being visible on the surface of Lake Kawaguchi. All of these lakes on Fuji-san's northern side are over 830 meters above sea level. Lake Yamanaka is the largest, and Lake Shoji the smallest.

"Fujikyuko" express trains leave from Shinjuku Station and arrive at Fuji-Yoshida Station, where a bus can be taken to Lake Yamanaka. Many people visit the area in summer to escape the heat of the city, while skating and fishing are enjoyed on the frozen surface in the winter months. A 20-minute walk from Fuji-Yoshida Station, by the way, will bring you to Fuji Sengen Shrine, starting point for the Yoshida path up the mountain. Cycling and hiking around the lake, and sightseeing boats on the water can be enjoyed at Lake Yamanaka.

Lake Kawaguchi can be reached in 10 minutes by foot from Kawaguchiko Station and is, like Lake Yamanaka, a very popular summer resort. As well as all the usual lakeside attractions, Lake Kawaguchi also has a local mountain of its own—Mount Tenjo—which can be ascended by ropeway. Splendid views of Mount Fuji and the lake can be had from the summit of the 1,080-meter-high Mount Tenjo. A 10-minute walk from Lake Kawaguchi is the Fuji Museum, which on its first floor offers a display of local history and folklore, and on its second floor houses a display of sex-related exhibits which only people over the age of 18 are permitted to see.

Other attractions in this area include the Fujikyu Highland Amusement Park, the Gotemba Family Land Recreation Park, Fuji Safari Park, and the Nihon Land Amusement Park (for details, see the *Practical Information* section under "Parks, Gardens, and Amusement Centers"). Returning to more scenic features, the aforementioned Shiraito Falls, said to resemble countless white threads hanging over a cliff, are located 30 minutes by bus from Fujinomiya Station. These falls, over 20 meters high and over 100 meters across, are called the feminine counterpart of the more masculine-looking Otodome Falls located nearby. Another place not to be forgotten is the main Sengen Shrine, reached in 10 minutes on foot from Fujinomiya Station. It is the parent shrine of the other Sengen shrines in the area, all of which are dedicated to the goddess of Mount Fuji. There is also a shrine on the summit of the mountain itself.

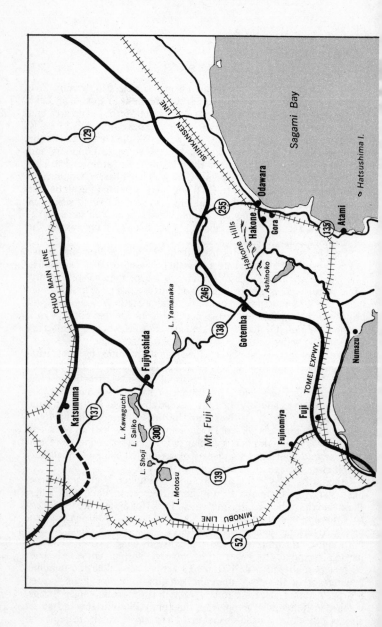

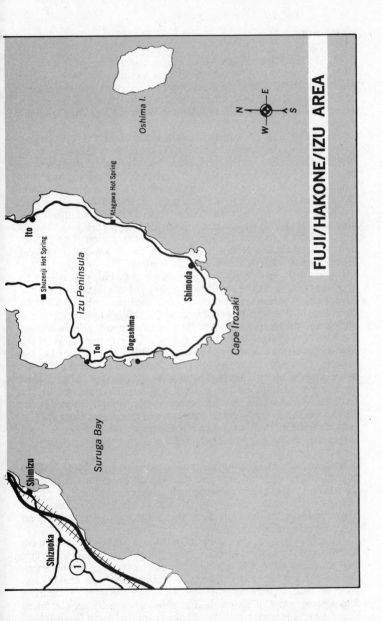

FUJI/HAKONE/IZU AREA

Hakone

While the northern side of Mount Fuji is taken up by the famous five lakes, the southeast side is occupied by the mountainous district called Hakone, a popular day-trip destination from Tokyo, but also a good place at which to spend either a leisurely few days soaking up the waters of the spas or a busy few days covering the area's many hiking courses.

The Hakone district can be reached easily from Tokyo by taking either the Japanese National Railways' Tokaido line to Odawara, or the private Odakyu line, which starts from Shinjuku and reaches the same destination. From Odawara, the local Hakone Tozan railway line hauls you up into the hills, or a bus can be taken to Lake Ashinoko (sometimes called Lake Hakone), the focal point of the area. If you have time available, however, you might like to begin your Hakone trip with a visit to Odawara itself, the main point of interest being the town's castle, which is located a short walk from the station. The present four-story castle was rebuilt in 1960, and houses a museum of local historic items, such as armor and old weapons.

If you opt to go directly to Lake Ashinoko by bus, you will arrive at Moto-Hakone on the southeastern shore of the lake in about one hour. Excursion boats can be taken across the lake. A short walk from the bus stop are several places of interest, including a museum, Hakone Shrine, and the remains of the old Hakone Checkpoint. The checkpoint has been rebuilt in its original form. It was an important place in the past because it was located on the main road linking the capital of the country (Edo, now Tokyo) with Kyoto, the former capital and the seat of the imperial court. The checkpoint was established in 1618 at a time when movement around the country was strictly controlled by the central government. The museum contains many exhibits related to the checkpoint and to the feudal lord processions that passed along the Old Hakone Road on their way to and from the capital. Such a procession is recreated every year in early November during the annual Daimyo Gyoretsu Festival.

Hakone Shrine lies about 500 meters away from the Moto-Hakone bus stop, from where a large *torii* gateway of the shrine can be seen. The shrine is said to have been originally founded in 757, and its symbol is the *torii* gateway standing in the waters of the lake. There is a Treasure House in the grounds of the shrine with paper scrolls and other historic items on display.

The other course to take from Odawara is to catch a Hakone Tozan Railway train from the station and head straight into the hills. The first stop is usually Gora, where a cable car can be taken up Mount Sounzan, and then a ropeway can be taken across the Owakudani Valley. Here volcanic activity can still be observed in the form of sulfurous fumes pouring out of the earth. The ropeway actually goes as far as Togendai on the northern shore of Lake Ashinoko, but it is possible to alight at Owakudani to observe the "boiling valley" at close hand. From the northern shore of the lake, you can take a boat across to the southeastern shore, and thereby link up with the aforementioned course.

There is one other popular attraction to be mentioned here, however, and that is the Chokoku no Mori open-air sculpture museum, which can be reached from Chokoku no Mori Station on the Hakone Tozan Railway line. Man-made monuments and mountain scenery blend together at this museum, which contains works by many foreign sculptors, including Henry Moore. Another modern attraction to note is Hakone-en, a recreation center that includes a large aquarium and folk houses from around the world. It can be reached by boat or by bus from Moto-Hakone.

Izu Peninsula

After the lakes and mountains comes the sea, and the great attraction of the Izu Peninsula, located to the southeast of Hakone, is its splendid coastline and port cities. The entrance to the peninsula is usually said to be Atami, a seaside and spa resort which can be reached in less than an hour by train from Tokyo Station.

Atami has developed something of a reputation as a "red-light" resort city where most of the fun occurs at night, on short trips from Tokyo. The streets are lined with Japanese-style ryokan inns, Western-style hotels, souvenir shops, restaurants, and other amusement centers. One positive result is that the night view of the illuminated city is quite spectacular when viewed from the surrounding hills or from Hatsushima Island, floating in the ocean a 25-minute boat ride away.

Other than the purely entertainment side, the main tourist attractions of Atami are the Atami Baien plum garden, where splendid plum blossoms can be observed in January and February, and the MOA Art Museum, located a short bus ride from Atami Station. Situated on top of a hill, the extravagant museum offers wonderful views of the port and bay below, as well as a rich collection of art exhibits. The initials of the museum come from the name of its founder, Mokichi Okada, who was the leader of one of Japan's "new religions," the World Church of Messianity. Until his death in 1955, Okada collected over 3,000 works of art, including ukiyoe prints and ceramics, and three Japanese national treasures, and it is his private collection that forms the museum's exhibition. The three-story, ultra-modern museum building is also the center of much attention in itself.

Also worth noting in the Atami area are Atami Korakuen, a comprehensive recreation center reached in 10 minutes by bus from Atami Station; Atami Cactus Park, reached in 25 minutes from the station by bus; the aforementioned island of Hatsushima, which makes for a nice day trip if you're staying in Atami; and Nishikigaura cove, which can be reached in 15 minutes by bus from the station and which offers excellent night views of Atami.

Atami is also one starting point for boats going to the island of Oshima, the nearest of the seven isles of Izu, which stretch out into the ocean. It takes about 1 hour 40 minutes to reach the island from Atami by boat, although a fast service is also operated covering the distance in just 1 hour. Oshima can also be reached from Tokyo in 7 hours by overnight boat leaving from Takeshiba Wharf near Hamamatsucho Station on the Yamanote line. There are plenty of accommodation facilities on the island—mainly Japanese-style ryokan inns—and the major tourist attraction (in addition to the coastal scenery and the tropical vegetation to be seen in the botanical garden) is the volcanic Mount Mihara, rising to 758 meters in the center of the island. In the second half of January every year the island holds a large camellia festival.

A boat service also operates between Oshima and Ito, just down the eastern coast of the Izu Peninsula from Atami. Like Shimoda on the peninsula's southern shore, Ito has strong historic connections with America and the West. Its shops and arcades are much less lavish than Atami's. The port offers plenty of sunshine, warmth, and hot springs, as well as good fresh fish, potted cacti, and various novel souvenirs made from shell and coral.

Ito's historic connections with the West go back to the 17th century. William Adams arrived in Japan in 1600, and after running into difficulties down in Kyushu, eventually settled in Ito for a few years, where he helped to build Japan's first European-style ships. He also instructed the Shogun Ieyasu Tokugawa on navigational affairs. Adams, who is said to have been the first Englishman ever to set foot in Japan, lived in Ito from 1605–10, and a monument to him can be seen on the seafront.

Ito is a good place to stay for a couple of nights. It is a quiet town, and yet an excellent base from which to visit the many tourist attractions in the area such as Lake Ippeki, the Izu Cactus Garden, Ito Aquarium, and Mount Omuro Park, which rises to 581 meters and can be ascended by means of a lift. There is bus service from Ito Station to all of these places.

A train can be taken down the east coast of Izu Peninsula from Atami and Ito as far as Shimoda, which is where the Black Ship Squadron of Commodore Perry anchored in 1854. This is also where the first American consulate in Japan was located, headed by Townsend Harris, whose relationship with his maid Okichi has become part of Shimoda folklore. Harris lived at Gyokusenji Temple before moving to a new consulate in Edo (Tokyo) in 1857.

In a quick spin around Shimoda, you can visit the temple, with its Townsend Harris Memorial Museum and graves of sailors who died during the Black Ships' expedition to this country. You can also visit Hofukuji Temple, where you'll find a small memorial museum dedicated to Okichi. Just behind the museum is her grave. Okichi eventually committed suicide after Harris returned to America, and today there are various versions of her story. One has Okichi separating from her lover in order to become Harris' mistress on the orders of the authorities who wanted the new consul to feel as much at home as possible. Another has Harris picking her from among a number of local prostitutes. After Harris left the country, Okichi tried a reunion with her former lover, failed, and was driven to drink and then to the river, where she drowned herself. These days Okichi is usually considered to have been a victim of tragic circumstances. The fresh incense sticks always burning at her grave are witness to the continuing romantic interest in her story.

There is history around every corner in Shimoda. After Hofukuji, you can visit Ryosenji Temple, where the Treaty for American-Japanese Amity was concluded in 1857. Ryosenji also houses a small museum of phallic symbols into which crowd all the busloads of tourists, old and young alike, going around the port city's sites. It is also possible to take a sightseeing boat around the bay where the Black Ships originally arrived, and a ropeway can be taken up Mount Nesugata, a hill overlooking the city and offering good views of the bay. On the top of the mountain is a museum that displays many exhibits related to the American and Russian expeditions that arrived in the 1850s.

From Shimoda, it is a 40-minute bus ride to Cape Irozaki on the very southernmost tip of the Izu Peninsula. As well as its spectacular cliffs and coastal scenery, this spot is also well known for its daffodils, which bloom in January, and for the Irozaki Jungle Park with its hothouses full of varied and colorful tropical plants.

Many people end their visit to the Izu Peninsula at Cape Irozaki, and return to Tokyo by train via Shimoda and the east coast. However, if your appetite for coastal scenery has not yet been satisfied, you might try taking a bus up the west coast to Dogashima, a small seaside town famous for its rock formations caused by sea erosion. Boats can be taken to get a closer view of the cliffs and caves. Excursions last a choppy 20 minutes. Note that boat services also operate between Shimoda and Cape Irozaki, and between Matsuzaki, Dogashima, Toi, and Numazu on the west coast.

Izu Peninsula is also famous for its spas. In addition to the many spa hotels located in Shimoda, Ito, and Atami, spa resorts of fame can be found at Nagaoka and Shuzenji in the north, and at Atagawa on the east coast, just north of Shimoda. Atagawa uses the local spa water to run a unique Banana and Alligator Park, where both banana trees and alligators are raised. The park can be reached from Atagawa Station on the Izu Kyuko line from Tokyo.

When returning to Tokyo via the west coast of Izu Peninsula, take a bus north as far as Mishima, and then catch a Kodama Express Shinkansen train to Tokyo Station.

Shizuoka

Located on the opposite side of Suruga Bay from Izu Peninsula, and just to the south of the Mount Fuji area, are the towns of Shizuoka and Shimizu. This district is famous for its groves of tangerine orchards and rows of tea bushes. About 45 minutes by bus from either of the two stations, Shizuoka or Shimizu, lies Nippon-daira, a high plateau near the coast, from which fine views can be had of Mount Fuji. It is possible to take a ropeway ride across the valley to Mount Kunozan, on which is located Toshogu Shrine, where Ieyasu Tokugawa, the first shogun in the 17th century, was buried before being moved to Nikko. Midway between Kunozan and Shizuoka is Toro, where the remains of a 2,000-year-old village were accidentally discovered in 1943. In Shimizu, you can visit the birthplace and grave of Jirocho, a popular 19th-century local hero who was a philanthropic "Robin Hood" character. You can also take an excursion boat round Shimizu Bay.

PRACTICAL INFORMATION FOR

FUJI, HAKONE, IZU

WHEN TO GO. Any time of the year, but autumn is best, when there's a crispness in the air, clear skies for better long-distance viewing, and the trees are displaying their most vivid colors. Spring is the next best time to visit, when the white, pink, and red plum blossoms are out, followed by cherry blossoms. Summer is crowded, but fun, with plenty of local festivals and the sense of joining in the crowd of Japanese vacationers. Winter is a bit cold, but the Western-style hotels can take the chill from the atmosphere, and you can enjoy skating. Winter also boasts clear weather for those vistalike views. The average temperature in Izu is a full 10 degrees higher than in Tokyo during the winter.

HOW TO GET THERE. Access to the **Five Lakes and Mt. Fuji district** from Tokyo is best by bus from downtown Tokyo via the Chuo Expressway to Lake Kawaguchi. *Fuji Kyuko* and *Keio Teito* run buses every hour from Shinjuku to Lake Kawaguchi. Fare ¥1,250, time 1 hr. 45 mins. Lake Yamanaka can be reached from Tokyo via the Tomei Expressway. About 3 hours. *Japanese National Railway* trains are another good way. Leaving Shinjuku Station in Tokyo, an 85-minute semi-express ride on the Chuo Line takes the traveler to Otsuki Station, where it is necessary to change to the privately owned *Fuji Express Company's* rail line. This takes you to the lake via Fuji-Yoshida in another hour. Several trains daily from Shinjuku go directly to Kawaguchi without the necessity of changing. The *Odakyu Private Railway* line to Gotemba from Shinjuku Station connects with a bus at the former city, the motorized portion of the journey being a one-hour trip from Gotemba to Lake Yamanaka. (The Odakyu rail section takes 1 hour 40 minutes.)

To **Lake Ashinoko** and its area, a comfortable way is by the *Odakyu Railway's* route from Shinjuku Station in Tokyo to Yumoto, taking 80 minutes by the line's modern Romance Cars, all-reserved limited expresses. More complicated, but going via Yokohama and Odawara, giving you a glimpse of the sea, is the *Japanese National Railway's* route from Tokyo Station to Odawara. At Odawara, you change to the *Hakone-Tozan Railway* line which goes up the Hayakawa River valley through Yumoto, Miyanoshita, and Kowakidani, to Gora (45 minutes). From Gora, you can go even farther by cable car (9 minutes) to Sounzan. A ropeway connects with the high-altitude lake directly. From Yumoto and/or Gora-Sounzan, you can take a taxi or bus to the lake. From Yumoto to Hakone town itself is about 45 minutes, and from Miyanoshita, about 30 minutes. From Hakone to Sengokuhara is another 40 minutes, and from the latter through the highlands to Miyanoshita, 20 minutes by car. A direct highway from Hakone to Atami via Ten Countries Pass (Jikkoku-toge) is a 75-minute drive, and a different route, the Taikanyama road, leading to Yugawara, takes 90 minutes.

An automobile trip from Tokyo will require about four hours, traffic conditions permitting. Regular motorbus service from Tokyo to Hakone via Yokohama and Odawara is supposed to take 3 hrs. 45 min. to Miyanoshita, 4 hours 10 min. to Hakone town. One excellent bus is the 40-passenger Golden Deluxe service, air-conditioned in summer and heated in winter, operated by the *Kokusai Kanko Company* between Tokyo and the town of Hakone daily via Yokohama and Enoshima. About 4 hrs. 30 min.

To the **Izu area.** Regular *Japanese National Railway* Tokaido line expresses reach Atami in about 90 minutes, and on the Shinkansen line in 50 minutes. The comfortable Izu Express takes about 1 hour from Ito to Shimoda. Through service from Tokyo to Shimoda is also provided by JNR daily in cooperation with the Izu Electric Railway Co. Automobile travel to Atami takes up to four hours if traffic is bad. The highway from Tokyo to Atami is excellent, and affords many beautiful views along the sea coast between Odawara and Atami, the area around Manazuru being especially lovely.

Driving beyond Atami will take you over one hour to Kawana, at least 1 hour from there to Imaihama and at least another hour to Shimoda. From Imaihama up the central mountain range in the middle of the peninsula will take you 40 minutes to Yugashima, and another 35 minutes to Shuzenji. The quiet lovely mountain town of Shuzenji itself can be reached directly from Tokyo by *JNR* express in two hours and 20 minutes. Such trains depart Tokyo every day with extra trains provided on weekends and holidays.

Other forms of transportation in the region include ropeways and cable cars, many of which provide spectacular views. One of the routes runs first from Gora by cable car up towering Mount Sounzan, and then by ropeway from the mountain to Lake Ashinoko. The ropeway is said to be the longest in Asia, taking 30 minutes to descend a distance slightly over two miles. A fabulous view. From Yunohanazawa, where there is a hot spring, another cable car rises to the top of Mount Komagatake, where you'll find a lovely view and an ice-skating rink. From this peak, another cable car, billed as the "biggest in the world" (cap. 101 per car), descends to Lake Ashinoko. The Ten Countries Pass on the highway between Hakone and Atami is the site of a short cable car ride at the top of which you can see 10 "countries" as the Japanese used to call their ancient provinces. In Atami itself is a short ropeway from the shore to a platform near the town's so-called castle.

Oshima and Hachijojima can be reached by air daily, flights leaving Tokyo for Oshima twice and for Hachijojima six times. The *Tokai Kisen Company* provides scheduled steamer service from Tokyo's Takeshiba pier six times a week to Oshima (7 hours), and Hachijojima (10 hours). The ships average about 1,800 tons, and leave at 10:00 P.M. and 10:10 P.M., respectively. You can reach Oshima on TKK ships from Atami in 1 hour and from Inatori in 1 hour 30 mins.

To **Shizuoka.** There are nearly 30 express trains from Tokyo to Shizuoka daily, taking about 90 minutes to make the trip on *JNR's* Shinkansen line. From the Fuji-Hakone area the traveler should catch the *Kodama Express* of the Shinkansen line at Odawara or at Atami.

HOTELS. The following is a list of the most convenient hotels and Japanese-style inns in the area. In general, hotels charge from ¥ 7,000–12,000 per person per night, and Japanese-style ryokan inns charge a little more, although the latter usually includes two meals. Youth hostels, which in general cost about ¥ 3,000–4,000 per person per night, are given in a separate list after the hotel information. Prices of hotels and inns will vary a little according to season, being more expensive in the New Year and summer holiday periods.

All accommodation below is Western style, except where "Japanese style" is stated.

FUJI FIVE LAKES

Lake Kawaguchi

Daiichi Hotel. 05557–2–1162. 3 min. by bus from Kawaguchiko Station.

Fuji Lake Hotel. 05557–2–2209. 5 min. by bus from Fujikyu-Fuji-Yoshida Station.

Fuji View Hotel. 05558–3–2211. 10 min. by bus from Fujikyu-Fuji-Yoshida Station.

Hotel New Fuji. 05557–2–0297. 5 min. by bus from Kawaguchiko Station.

Kawaguchiko Grand Hotel. 05557–2–2111. 5 min. by bus from Kawaguchiko Station.

Kawaguchiko Hotel. 05557–2–1313. 5 min. by bus from Fujikyu-Fuji-Yoshida Station.

Lakeland Hotel. 05557–2–1831. 10 min. by bus from Kawaguchiko Station.

Lake Yamanaka

Hotel Mount Fuji. 05556–2–2111. 40 min. by bus from Fujikyu-Fuji-Yoshida Station.

Keio Yamanakako Hotel. 05556–2–2221. 20 min. by bus from Fujikyu-Fuji-Yoshida Station.

New Yamanakako Hotel. 05556–2–2311. 20 min. by bus from Fujikyu-Fuji-Yoshida Station.

HAKONE

Moto-Hakone

Ashinoko-en. 0460–3–6341. 60 min. by bus from Odawara Station. Japanese style.

Hakone Lake Hotel. 0460–4–7611. 60 min. by bus from Odawara Station.

Hakone Prince Hotel. 0460—3–7111. 80 min. by bus from Odawara Station.

Hakone-machi

Hakone Hotel. 0460–3–6311. 60 min. by bus from Odawara Station.

Hakone-Kojiri

Hakone Ashinoko Hotel. 0460–4–7811. 60 min. by bus from Odawara Station.

Hakone Kogen Hotel. 0460–4–8595. 60 min. by bus from Odawara Station.

Kowakidani Spa

Hakone Kowaki-en. 0460–2–4111. 35 min. by bus from Odawara Station. Japanese style.

Hotel Kowaki-en. 0460–2–4111. 25 min. by bus from Hakone-Yumoto Station.

Gora Spa

Chokoku-no-mori Hotel. 0460–2–3375. 3 min. by foot from Chokoku-no-mori Station.

Gora Hotel. 0460–2–3111. 30 min. by bus from Gora Station.

Miyanoshita

Fujiya Hotel. 0460–2–2211. 5 min. walk from Miyanoshita Station.

Hakone-Yumoto Spa

Hotel Okada. 0460-5-7161. 5 min. by bus from Hakone-Yumoto Station.
Kisen-so. 0460-5-5701. 2 min. by bus from Hakone-Yumoto Station.
Tsuiki. 0460-5-5791. 5 min. by foot from Hakone-Yumoto Station. Japanese style.
Yoshiike Ryokan. 0460-5-5711. 3 min. by car from Hakone-Yumoto Sta.

Yugawara Spa

Amano-ya. 0465-62-2121. 15 min. by bus from Yugawara Station.
Ohizu Hotel. 0465-62-2111. 10 min. by bus from Yugawara Station.

IZU

Ito Spa

Business Hotel Itoh. 0557-36-1515. 5 min. by foot from Ito Station.
Ito Fujiya Hotel. 0557-37-4174. 3 min. by car from Ito Station.
Palace Hotel. 0557-37-2681. 3 min. by foot from Ito Station.
Young Villa Ito. 0557-37-1710. 10 min. by foot from Ito Station.

Atagawa Spa

Atagawa Daiichi Hotel. 0557-23-2200. 7 min. by foot from Izu-Atagawa Station.
Atagawa Grand Hotel. 0557-23-2121. 5 min. by foot from Izu-Atagawa Station.
Atagawa Onsen Hotel. 0557-23-2217. 4 min. by foot from Izu-Atagawa Station.
Atagawa Prince Hotel. 0557-23-1234. 2 min. by car from Izu-Atagawa Station.

Shimoda

New Shimoda. 05582-3-0222. 3 min. by foot from Izu-Shimoda Station.

Shimoda Spa

Kurofune Hotel. 05583-2-1234. 3 min. by bus from Izu-Shimoda Station.
Shimoda Grand Hotel. 05582-2-1011. 5 min. by bus from Izu-Shimoda Station.
Shimoda Onsen Hotel. 05582-2-3111. 2 min. by bus from Izu-Shimoda Station.
Shimoda Tokyu Hotel. 05582-2-2411. 5 min. by car from Izu-Shimoda Station.

Shirahama Kaigan

Shimoda Prince Hotel. 05582-2-7575. 15 min. by bus from Izu-Shimoda Station.

Atami Spa

Atami Kanko Hotel. 0557-81-6266. 5 min. by foot from Atami Station.
Atami Sanno Hotel. 0557-81-3664. 15 min. by bus from Atami Station.
Chuo Hotel. 0557-81-6251. 3 min. by car from Atami Station.
Kokusai Ryokan. 0557-81-0518. 10 min. by foot from Atami Station. Japanese style.
New Fujiya Hotel. 0557-81-0111. 5 min. by car from Atami Station.

Izu-Nagaoka Spa

Izu Hotel. 05594-8-0678. 6 min. by bus from Izu-Nagaoka Station.

Izu Prince Hotel. 05594–8–1788. 5 min. by bus from Izu-Nagaoka Station.
Nagaoka Hotel. 05594–8–0801. 10 min. by bus from Izu-Nagaoka Station.

Shizuoka City

Central Hotel. 0542–54–0308. 10 min. by foot from Shizuoka Station.
Hotel New Shizuoka. 0542–83–8811. 1 min. by foot from Shizuoka Station.
Shizuoka Green Hotel. 0542–52–2101. 5 min. by foot from Shizuoka Station.
Shizuoka Park Hotel. 0542–83–6855. 2 min. by foot from Shizuoka Station.
Shizuoka Business Hotel. 0542–52–5118. 10 min. by foot from Shizuoka Station.

 YOUTH HOSTELS. Fumoto-no-Ie Youth Hostel; 0544 –27–4314. 25 minutes by bus from **Fuji** Station, then 10 minutes by foot.

Onshoji Youth Hostel; 0544–52–0024. 45 minutes by bus from **Fujinomiya** Station, then 3 minutes on foot.

Hakone Sounzan Youth Hostel; 0460–2–3827. 10 minutes by cable car from **Gora** Station, then 2 minutes on foot.

Gotemba Youth Hostel; 0550–2–3045. 20 minutes by bus from **Gotemba** Station, then 15 minutes on foot.

Ito Youth Hostel; 0557–45–0224. 15 minutes by bus from **Ito** Station, then 8 minutes on foot. Totaru Youth Hostel; 0557–45–2591. 30 minutes by bus from Ito Station, then 5 minutes on foot.

Miho Youth Hostel; 0543–34–0826. 25 minutes by bus from **Shimizu** Station, then 5 minutes on foot. Youth Hostel Nihondaira Lodge; 0543–34–2738. 30 minutes by bus from Shimizu Station, then 10 minutes on foot.

Gensu Youth Hostel; 05586–2–0035. 25 minutes by bus from **Shimoda** Station.

Omaezaki Youth Hostel; 05486–3–4518. 1 hour by bus from **Shizuoka** Station.

Irori-so Youth Hostel; 05588–5–0108. 30 minutes by bus from **Shuzenji** Station, then 2 minutes on foot. Shuzenji Youth Hostel; 0558–72–1222. 15 minutes by bus from Shuzenji Station, then 10 minutes on foot.

 PENSIONS. The Japan Pension Information Counter, Tokyo, (03) 407–2333, Osaka, (06) 375–1601, can give you information about cheap accommodation at such pensions as Christie at Lake Yamanaka, Weekend Shuffle at Lake Kawaguchi, Saturday Closet and Sea Moon in Izu, and many more.

 HOT SPRINGS. The reason for the popularity of this entire region, aside from the beauty of Mount Fuji, lies in the existence of the many hot springs. In fact the name *Izu* comes from the old Japanese words meaning "hot water gushing." In the Hakone area, there are 12 excellent hot-spring resorts, known as Yumoto, Tonosawa, Miyanoshita, Dogashima, Sokokura, Kiga, Gora, Ubako, Sengokuhara, Kowakidani, Ashinoyu, and Yunohanazawa. Yumoto's water has the lowest mineral content, and the temperature is about 130 degrees Fahrenheit. Slightly hotter waters are available at Tonosawa (152 degrees). Miyanoshita's springs are liberally dosed with common salt, the temperature being 172 degrees. Kowakidani tends toward sulfur, and the water is supposed to be good for nervous trouble and skin diseases (180 degrees). Gora spring, at a 2,600-foot level, is supposed to help rheumatism with its salty and sulfurous water of 160 degrees temperature. Sengokuhara has the same kind of water but the thermometer reads only 149 degrees. Of course, the water in all these places is considerably reduced in temperature before reaching the actual bathing pools.

Down on the Izu peninsula, the most popular spas are at Yugawara, Atami, Ito, Shuzenji Atagawa, and Nagaoka. Of course every other town has its own spring, and you will never lack for variety of mineral content, temperature, or decor. In many spas there are *roten-buro,* or open air baths.

The easiest way to enjoy the hot springs *(onsen)* is to check in at one of the hotels that has its own private baths. Public bathhouses are available, but the pools are usually not as clean as those in the hotels. If you want to visit a variety of public baths ask your hotel to guide you.

 HOW TO GET AROUND. The main method of transport around the Fuji-Hakone-Izu area is bus. Once you have reached a main place like Odawara, Hakone-Yumoto, Atami, Ito, Shimoda, or Kawaguchiko by train from Tokyo, the next step will be to find the bus going to your destination from outside these railway stations. All the main railway stations have tourist information offices where you can ask for directions and bus times. If you are going on a day's trip from one of these places by bus, it's a good idea to check on the times of returning buses as well so that you don't miss the last one. Another possibility not to be overlooked are the Japanese tourist buses that have regular trips around the main sites. One example is the tourist bus that leaves Shimoda every morning and makes its way up the west coast of the Izu Peninsula via Cape Irozaki and Dogashima, depositing participants at Mishima from where the Shinkansen line can be caught for the journey back to Tokyo. All the explanations on such a bus tour will be in Japanese, but more than likely there will be one or two people willing to help out with translations—most of the time the scenery speaks for itself anyway.

 TOURIST INFORMATION. Before setting out on a tour of this area, it's wise to pick up as much information as you can from the tourist information center in Tokyo and through reading this book. If, however, you happen to arrive in the area without having made the necessary plans and reservations, head for the tourist information office at the station where you arrive. The staff there will provide you with English-language pamphlets if they have them, and will help you make accommodation arrangements. And don't forget that if you're really in trouble, the tourist information center's telephone service is toll-free when used outside Tokyo. All you have to do is insert a ¥10 coin in a public phone and dial 106. Then tell the operator, in English, "Collect call, T.I.C." The ¥10 coin will be returned after your call.

Japan Travel Bureau maintains offices at Odawara (0465–22–1101), Shizuoka Station (0542–53–2218), and Atami (0557–81–7157).

 SEASONAL EVENTS. January–mid February. Plum festival at Atami Baien Plum Garden in Atami begins on the 15th and runs through the 15th of February. The nearest station is Kinomiya on the Japan National Railways' Ito line.

February. Plum blossom festivals are held through the month at Odawara Joshi Koen Park in Odawara and at the Soga Bairin Plum Garden, which is near Shimo-Soga Station on the Gotemba line.

The Setsubun festival is held throughout the country, and in this region it can be seen at Hakone Shrine in Hakone on the 3rd. The festival includes the traditional bean-throwing ceremony carried out on this day.

March. A traditional lion dance, called Yudate Shishimai, takes place on the 27th in the precincts of Suwa Shrine in Sengokubara, a 50-minute ride by bus from Odawara Station. The dance usually takes place in the morning.

A camellia festival is held in Yugawara City in late March.

May. Kite demonstrations and contests, including the flying of giant kites, take place in Zama and Hamamatsu from the 3rd–5th. The former takes place on the dry riverbed near Zakkaibashi Bridge, which can be reached from Zama Station on the Odakyu line from Shinjuku. The latter takes place as port of the Hamamatsu town festival. Buses leave for the site at Nakatajima-Sakyu from Hamamatsu Station.

From the 3rd–5th, the Castle Festival of Odawara is held on the castle grounds, and is highlighted by a procession of people dressed up as feudal lords. The procession is usually held on the 3rd.

The Black Ship Festival, or Kurofune Matsuri, is held in Shimoda in mid-May, usually for three days around the 17th. The festival commemorates the arrival of Commodore Perry and his Black Ship Squadron in the small port in the 19th century.

An umbrella-burning ceremony, called Kasa-yaki, is held on the 28th at Jozenji Temple in Odawara. The origins of this ceremony go back to 1193, when two brothers avenged the death of their father by killing his murderer. They found their way to the enemy's camp at night by burning paper umbrellas. The ceremony is usually accompanied by various festive events for children.

July. Ceremonies take place at Fuji Sengen Shrine in Fuji-Yoshida on the 1st to mark the opening of Mount Fuji for the climbing season. Similar ceremonies also take place on the 5th stage of the mountain.

An iris festival, called Ayame Matsuri, is held from the 1st–3rd in Nagaoka Spa in Shizuoka, with folk dancing, mikoshi shrine processions, and firework displays.

The Black Ship Festival of Kurihama is held on the 14th, commemorating the first landing in Kurihama of Commodore Perry. In the evening, a fireworks display is held on the beach and folk dancing takes place in Perry Park.

A lion dance, called Yudate Shishimai, takes place on the 15th at Suwa Shrine in Hakone Miyagino, usually in the afternoon.

On the 31st, the annual festival of Lake Ashinoko in Hakone takes place, with lighted lanterns being floated on the water and a fireworks display held in the evening.

August. Torii-yaki Matsuri, or *torii* gate-burning festival, is held on Lake Ashinoko in Hakone on the 5th. Torii gates standing in the lake are burned in the evening.

The Anjin Matsuri, a festival in memory of William Adams, the first Englishman to set foot in Japan, is held in Ito City in early August.

A Daimonji Okuribi festival, with a large fire in the shape of the Chinese character for "great," is held on Mount Myojo in Gora, Hakone on the 16th. Fireworks and dancing accompany the event.

At the end of August a festival is held in Fuji-Yoshida to mark the close of the Mount Fuji climbing season. Ten-foot-high bonfires are lit along the streets at 7:00 P.M.

November. The annual Daimyo Gyoretsu, or feudal lord's procession, festival is held at Hakone-Yumoto in Hakone on the 3rd, with people dressed in 17th-century costumes walking along part of the old Hakone Road from Sounji Temple.

Also on the 3rd, horseback archery can be seen at Muro-o Shrine, 25-minute walk from Yamakita Station on the Gotemba line.

TOURS. Many travel agents operate bus or auto tours to the Hakone area. Among the most popular are the two-day tours that swing through the Kamakura and Hakone region, operated by *Fujita Travel Service.* A ¥35,000 tour, for example, includes a stop at Kamakura's Great Buddha on the way out, and an overnight stay in the Lake Hakone resort area, with a trip on the lake itself. Departs Tokyo daily. *JTB* operates a one-day excursion to Kamakura and Hakone for ¥16,000 and a two-day trip for ¥24,000. *Hankyu Express* tours are similar. *Odakyu Express* has a guideless one-day Hakone tour for ¥12,000.

PARKS, GARDENS, AND AMUSEMENT CENTERS. There is a whole range of fascinating parks and gardens to be found in this area. Included in the list below are amusement centers, which children in particular will enjoy.

Atagawa Banana and Alligator Park. Uses the local spa water to keep the former growing and the latter smiling. Located near **Atagawa** Station. *Atami Baien.* A plum garden, with over 1,300 trees. Reached by bus from **Atami** Station. *Atami Cactus Park.* Over 600 types of cactus and tropical plants. By bus from Atami Station. *Atami Korakuen.* A leisure park reached by bus from Atami Station.

Gora Park. A French-style garden located 5 minutes from **Gora** Station.

Fuji Safari Park. Watch the lions from inside special buses. Reached in 40 minutes by bus from **Gotemba** Station. *Nihon Land.* This is another large amusement park complete with golf course and pony rides. Reached in 55 minutes by bus from Gotemba Station. *Gotemba Family Land.* Has everything from roller coasters to sports facilities to a meadow. Open 9:00 A.M.–5:00 P.M. Reached in 15 minutes by bus from Gotemba Station. *Otainai Botanical Garden.* Good display of highland plants. Reached in 20 minutes by bus from Gotemba Station.

Fujikyu Highland. Has lots of mechanical delights for kids, a pool, skating facilities and so on. Open 9:00 A.M.–5:30 P.M. Reached in 5 minutes from **Highland** Station.

Izu Cactus Park. Large display of cactus plants and a small zoo, reached in 40 minutes by bus from **Ito** Station. *Mount Omuro Park.* Well-known for its azaleas, which blossom in April. Reached by bus from Ito Station.

Hakone-en. A large park displaying folk houses from around the world, located on shore of **Lake Ashinoko.** You can reach it by boat or bus from Moto-Hakone. *Hakone Picnic Garden.* Located a 15-minute walk from Hakone-en, with fine displays of alpine plants and good views of Lake Ashinoko.

Izu Oshima Hawaii Botanical Garden. Six greenhouses and a rich variety of plants. Reached in 5 minutes by bus from **Motomachi Port** on Oshima Island. *Oshima Nature Park.* Includes a small zoo and a walking path by the coast. Reached in 45 minutes by bus from Motomachi Port.

Kowakien. A large leisure center with tropical plant garden. Reached in 35 minutes by bus from **Odawara** Station. *Odawara Castle Park.* Consists of a small zoo and the castle building itself. Short walk from Odawara Station.

Irozaki Jungle Park. Offers yet more tropical plants, and is located near the splendid cliffs of Cape Irozaki. Reached by bus or boat from **Shimoda.**

SPORTS. This area being the example *par excellence* of the great outdoors in Japan, sports are impossible to ignore. Any Western-style hotel can provide you with facilities, or lead you to the proper place, for engaging in every kind of athletic venture.

Perhaps the best **hiking** area is around Fuji Lakes. Ocean **fishing** is easiest at Numazu, and on the offshore islands of Oshima and Hachijojima. Besides fishing in the Five Lakes, **sailing** is also possible. At Numazu Marina, yachts and boats are available for rent. The *Suruga Bay Diving Center* offers 4-day diving courses. Tel: (0559) 31–5252, Numazu city. Interesting **boating** trips may be had to the island of Hatsushima near Atami and everywhere else in the region. Fresh water **swimming** in the lakes and ocean plunging on the east coast of Izu, except at Atami, where the water is too dirty. Best **skin diving** and underwater fishing is had at Manazuru, the little peninsula north of Atami. **Bicycling** is easiest in the Five Lakes district where there are good roads, less traffic, and not so many hills. A "Cycle Sports Center," the first of its kind in Japan, stretches its facilities over a scenic corner or Izu peninsula at Shuzenji-cho. **Water skiing** should be confined to offshore, because of the huge crowds on the beaches.

Tennis can be played at any large Western-style hotel, public courts being quite scarce. Slazenger Tennis Club members may play at the Fuji Wimbledon Tennis Club every day. The entire area is a **golfers'** paradise, the two best spots being Kawana and Sengokuhara, the former having two 18-hole links and the latter, three. Again the best way to take advantage of these courses is to stay at the hotels connected to them.

Skating and **skiing** are obviously confined to the winter season and your headquarters should be the Five Lakes district, from where the slopes of Mount Fuji can easily be reached. (There is rarely any snow in the Izu area.) An open-air ice skating rink at Sengokuhara provides rented skates, and claims it can accommodate 7,000 skaters a day. Located near Hakone Kanko Hotel. Open November through March. The company operating the rink also provides some cottages and skaters' beds for overnight skaters. From ¥4,000 per person including two meals. For details call *Tokyo Korakuen.* Other skating rinks in Hakone are: *Kojiri Skate Rink* near Lake Ashinoko; *Hakone-en Skate Rink* in Hakone-en Park on east shore of the lake; *Komagatake Skate Center,* atop Mt. Komagatake. (Here are both indoor and outdoor rinks; the former open around the year.) All rinks provide rental skates.

Mountain climbing is for those who enjoy walking uphill rather than scaling local cliffs, and the most obvious destination is Mount Fuji itself. The season opens on July 1 and closes about August 25. During this time you will see a continuous line of people climbing the lovely mountain, many of them old men and women to whom the symbol of Japan is still sacred. It is not as easy as it looks, and do not be embarrassed if a 75-year-old lady passes you at a fast pace ringing a bell and reciting prayers while you stop to catch your breath. She has probably been in training for this trip all her life, and has a better motive for getting to the top than you do. Do not take the mountain's gracious appearance lightly, as every winter several people die trying to reach the top. In season it is absolutely safe unless you try very hard to get hurt. If you hire a guide on the mountain for a full day with a night's lodging, expect to pay ¥30,000. Overnight stay in a mountain hut costs ¥6,000 with two meals. Beer on the mountain costs about ¥600 a bottle, and Chinese noodles ¥800 a bowl.

Yoga. Masahiro Oki runs an ashram at 450, Sawachi, Mishima; 0559–86–5655. Macrobiotic food. Tuition ¥6,000 per day, but discounts for foreigners "because they come a long way to study."

MUSEUMS. The main museums of note in this area are the **Chokoku no Mori** sculpture museum in Hakone and the **MOA Art Museum** in Atami. The former, an open-air museum, can be reached in a 2-minute walk from Chokoku no Mori Station on the Hakone Tozan Railway line, and the latter, with its rich collection of Japanese paintings, prints, and ceramics, can be reached in 5 minutes by bus from Atami Station. The sculpture museum is open every day from 9:00 A.M. to 4:00 P.M., and until 6:00 P.M. in summer; the MOA Art Museum is closed on Thursdays. Other museums in the area include:

Fuji Museum, with folklore and sex-related exhibits; 10-minute walk from Kawaguchiko Station. Closed Tuesdays and December-February. Open 8:30 A.M.–4:00 P.M.

Hakone Art Museum with displays of Japanese and Chinese ceramics; 10-minute walk from Gora Station. Open 9:30 A.M.–4:00 P.M. Closed on Thursdays.

Hakone Checkpoint Museum, with items related to the history of the checkpoint and the Old Hakone Road; located near Hakone Checkpoint. Open 9:00 A.M.–4:30 P.M.

Hakone Museum, with displays on 17th and 18th century Hakone; near the Hakone-machi bus stop. Open 9 A.M.–5 P.M.

Ikeda Museum of 20th Century Art, located by Lake Ippeki in Ito, reached by bus from Ito Station. Open 10:00 A.M.–5:00 P.M.

Owakudani Science Museum, with displays on the geography and nature of the Hakone area; near the Owakudani ropeway station.

Hofukuji, Ryosenji and **Gyokusenji** temples in Shimoda all have small museums related to the history of the port and the arrival of Perry's black ships and the American Consulate.

 DINING OUT. You are always safe in dining at your hotel, as these well-known establishments usually provide the best food and service anyhow. Individual restaurants are scarce, and frequently are in out-of-the-way locations, catering to select clientèle with their specialties. Generally speaking, the hotels and restaurants in the Fuji-Five Lakes and Hakone region serve food more customary to the Western diet, such as sukiyaki and tempura. On the Izu peninsula you will find several specialties, including the open-air *okaribayaki,* a barbecue featuring wild boar, chicken, vegetables, and such game as pheasant. Wild boar sukiyaki is also a winter specialty in the central mountainous part of the peninsula. At Shimoda, fish is of course the specialty, and the lobsters in season are highly recommended. Always, though, wherever you go, you'll find simple, cheap Japanese dishes in unpretentious cafés. Don't forget: chopstick eating is budget eating in ordinary places. Look for *miso-shiru* soup and *tofu* dishes for good nutrition.

Among the better hotel dining rooms are those in the following establishments: New Fujiya Hotel, Hotel Kowakien, Atami Kanko Hotel, and Shimoda Tokyu Hotel. Local spots you might try are *Fuji-ichimaru Isohama Shokudo* in Ito (0557–37–4705) for seafood, and *Hakone Highland Hotel* (0460–4–8541) for its special Japanese-style fondue. JTB tours of Mount Fuji and Hakone include lunch at the *Fuji View Hotel.*

 NIGHT LIFE in this area is limited to that provided by the hotels, plus festival activities, unless you can count the dubious pleasures of Atami. The cabarets in Atami are presently shabby affairs, and finding an English-speaking hostess is next to impossible. The *Suntory bars* in any of these towns are recommended because of their moderate prices and lack of high-pressure techniques. In the summertime many of the hotels organize lavish programs of entertainment in the evening.

If you decide to have a massage after your bath, a common thing in Atami, you should expect to pay about ¥ 5,000 per hour. (Apparently, some people want a massage lasting over an hour.)

NIKKO

by
SIR HUGH CORTAZZI

Hugh Cortazzi was British Ambassador to Japan from 1980 to 1984. A former president of the Asiatic Society of Japan, Sir Hugh is also a translator, author, and editor.

Nikko, which literally means sunlight, has become almost as well known internationally as the old capitals of Kyoto and Nara and is on almost everyone's list of top priorities on an initial visit to Japan. I deliberately say *almost* because a few may have read in advance some disparaging remarks by scholars and earlier visitors suggesting that Nikko's shrines are gaudy and rather vulgar. I do not agree. Nikko is very well worth a visit.

Nikko is usually taken to mean the shrines containing the mausolea of the Tokugawa shoguns, who were the feudal rulers of Japan between 1603 and 1868, and who for some two and a half centuries kept Japan closed to the outside world. In fact Nikko is really the name of the mountainous area around the shrines, although it is now also the name of the town district in which they are situated. The two villages of Hachiishi and Irimachi, which stood above and below the shrines, have been absorbed by the new town.

Nikko may not be the favorite place of Japanese poets and artists, but it has been a popular spot to visit for many centuries. The Japanese saying "Do not use the word magnificent until you have seen Nikko" or "Nikko wa minai uchi wa, kekko to iu na" is no modern phrase. The great Japanese poet Basho, in his most famous poetical journey, sensitively translated by Dorothy Britton under the title *A Haiku Journey— Basho's Narrow Road to a Far Province,* tells of how, on the first day of the fourth moon (May 20 in the modern calendar) in 1689 he paid his respects at Mount Nikko. His comments, brief though they are, show no signs of the contempt that might have been expected by those who claim to disdain the bright colors of the shrines or who know that with Basho originated the concepts of "wabi" and "sabi" (which can only be very approximately translated by "solitude" and "elegant simplicity"). Basho wrote: "In olden times, the name of this mountain was written Ni-ko, using the Chinese characters for 'two' and 'wild,' but when Saint Kukai [774 to 835, the founder of the Shingon (or esoteric) sect of Buddhism and better known by his posthumous name of Kobo-Daishi] built a temple here, he changed the characters to 'Nikko' meaning 'sun' and 'light.' He must have forseen what was to come a thousand years later [a slight poetic exaggeration], for now the august light of the Tokugawa rule illumines the whole firmament, and its beneficient rays reach into every corner of the land so that all the people may live in security and peace."

Was this last phrase just flattery, used simply to avoid persecution? I don't think so. Basho was not writing for the Tokugawa, but for other literati. And after the turbulent years of earlier centuries, the settled rule of the Tokugawa had indeed brought a welcome peace and relative prosperity.

Basho was filled with such awe of the place that he "hesitated to write a poem" but nevertheless did so. This brief haiku has been translated by Dorothy Britton as:

> O holy, hallowed shrine!
> How green all the fresh young leaves
> In thy bright sun shine.

In the late 19th century, after Japan reopened its doors to the Western world, enthusiasm for Nikko reached a high point. That intrepid traveler Isabella Bird, whose adventures in Colorado are recorded in her *A Lady's Life in the Rocky Mountains,* reached Nikko in June 1878. The description of Nikko in her book *Unbeaten Tracks in Japan* is full of Victorian superlatives: "Mountains for a great part of the year clothed or patched in snow, piled in great ranges round Nantaizan, their monarch, worshipped as a God; forests of magnificent timber; ravines and passes scarcely explored; dark green lakes sleeping in endless serenity." She was equally enthusiastic about the shrines: "The Yomei gate whose splendour I contemplated day after day with increasing astonishment. . . . To pass from court to court is to pass from splendour to splendour; one is almost glad to feel that this is the last, and that the strain on one's capacity for admiration is nearly over."

Mrs. Hugh Fraser, the wife of the British Minister to Japan in the early 1890s, whose letters were republished in 1982 under the title *A Diplomat's Wife in Japan—Sketches at the Turn of the Century,* was also captivated, referring to Nikko as, "the most beautiful, the most solemn place in Japan." She, like other early travelers, was particularly impressed by the setting and the magnificent avenues of cryptomeria trees.

"But that which pleases me most are the finely carved panels of the splendid halls. . . . Every bird and beast seems to have been pressed into the service of decoration, every device which unlimited treasure and redundant imagination could produce has been lavished on these temple rooms, each more beautiful than the last."

She found the mountains in their autumn colours breathtakingly beautiful: "Beyond the sombre mantle of the pines, the mountain-sides were clothed in a curtain of scarlet and gold, a curtain of star-shaped leaves of innumerable maple trees, hanging to the cliffs as children hang to the skirts of their mother."

Some may argue (I think wrongly) that Isabella Bird and Mary Fraser were just Victorian gushers. But then we have Basil Hall Chamberlain, the great 19th-century scholar of Japan and the Japanese, who was not normally sparing in his criticisms (indeed these were often quite acerbic) and W. B. Mason, another Westerner with a wide knowledge of Japan. In the fourth edition of *A Handbook for Travellers in Japan* published in 1894, they wrote: "Nikko is a double glory—a glory of nature and a glory of art."

They describe Nikko as " . . . the most perfect assemblage of shrines in the whole land. But though there is gorgeousness, there is no gaudiness. That sobriety, which is the key-note of Japanese taste, gives to all the gay designs and bright colours its own chaste character."

Up to the 20th century there seems to have been no disagreement. But then we have a relatively mild note of dissent from the great British scholar, Diplomat Sir George Sanson, in his *Japan—A Short Cultural History.* He says of the shrines: "Though gorgeous in colour and marvellous in detail, they are fiddling and aesthetically ill conceived; but they are saved from vulgarity by a noble setting among giant trees and a certain impressive profusion."

Others have gone much further in their criticism. Fosco Maraini, in his *Meeting with Japan* in 1959, is almost vituperative: "At the Yomei gate . . . nature is unable to swallow up the horror. True you are put on your guard in advance by various structures of dubious taste . . . Nevertheless you are taken aback; you ask yourself whether it is a joke, or a nightmare, or a huge wedding cake, a masterpiece of sugar icing made for some extravagant prince with a perverse, rococo taste, who wished to alarm and entertain his guests."

The same kind of sentiments were recently expressed by Sir Laurens van der Post in his book *Yet Being Someone Other* published in 1982. He writes that the shoguns " . . . exploited without taste or shame almost every vantage point, confusing the grandiloquent and pompous, the magnificent and bombastic, with art in a way that is typical of imaginations obsessed with power."

While I too prefer the more restrained charm, beauty and grace of the best of Kyoto and Nara, I do not share the extreme sentiments of these visitors about the shrines. I wonder whether they are not being more Japanese than the Japanese, or perhaps I should say what they think Japanese culture is or should be? Color and vitality flowered in 17th-century Japanese art and culture, culminating in the Genroku period (1688 to 1703). The new bourgeoisie, encouraged by the growing demands of an aristocracy able to enjoy the settled peace brought to the country by the Tokugawa shoguns, delighted in the spectacle and splendor of art forms such as the Kabuki drama and the Bunraku puppet plays. The wise observer will allow room in a culture for both the gorgeous and the restrained.

What to See

Against this background let us take a brief look at the Nikko area. It is important not to miss the long avenues of cryptomerias (cedar trees), along the roads to Nikko until the recent past when the effect of the fumes of motor vehicles on the trees and the narrowness of the avenues made bypasses necessary. Arriving in the town of Nikko, one finds essentially a long, gently rising street—a mixture of modern and old houses (unfortunately, due to earthquakes and wars, "old" in Japan often only means some 50 or 60 years). At the top of the street a steep slope up to the left leads to the Kanaya Hotel. It is still owned and managed by the Kanaya family and has been patronized by royalty and other important personages for over 100 years, as can be seen from a perusal of the visitors' book. The road then crosses a fast flowing river, the Daiya, and on the left is the famous red bridge, or Shinkyo, built in 1636. Visitors are allowed onto the bridge on payment of a fee, but normally are not allowed to cross it. For more than 300 years, only the shoguns and emissaries of the emperor were allowed to walk on the bridge.

Across the road bridge you will enter the area of the shrines. In fact these are a mixture of Shinto shrines and Buddhist temples, representing the period when the two religions were joined, though never merged, and underlining the eclectic nature of Japanese traditional religious beliefs.

But before entering the area, you will see a monument to Masatane Matsudaira, one of the two commissioners charged with the construction of the Toshogu, the shrine and mausoleum of the first Tokugawa shogun, Ieyasu Tokugawa (1542 to 1616). Matsudaira's great contribution was the planting of the magnificent crypotomerias surrounding the shrine and on the avenue leading to it. Despite the ravages of time, some 16,000 trees still stand.

Nikko's Shrines and Temples

Across the road beyond the sacred bridge the visitor can either climb a ramp or a stone stairway. At the top by a car park the main hall of the Rinnoji temple can be seen. Here a ticket for Toshogu shrine, Futaarasan shrine, the Daiyuin (part of Rinnoji), and a temporary treasurehouse can be purchased, but this does not give admittance to inner sanctuaries or other structures for which additional charges are made.

Buddhism (in Japan this is of the Mahayana or "greater vehicle" school) and Shinto (literally the "way of the Gods"), which was the indigenous religion of the Japanese, are totally different in origin and teaching. Nevertheless, the two religions became fused from early times until the Meiji restoration in 1868, when they were forcibly separated. However, here in Nikko they remain very closely connected—Buddhist elements can be found in the Toshogu, which is essentially a Shinto shrine, and Shinto elements can be found in the Daiyuin, which is part of the Rinnoji, a Buddhist temple. The Toshogu commemorates the first Tokugawa shogun, while the Daiyuin commemorates the third shogun, Iemitsu. The other shoguns of the Tokugawa Period were commemorated in Edo, now Tokyo.

The Rinnoji

The Rinnoji is a temple of the Tendai sect of Buddhism, whose headquarters in Japan were at Enryakuji on Mount Hiei near Kyoto. The Hombo, or abbot's quarters, where General Ulysses S. Grant stayed in 1879, enshrines the votive tablets of the priests. There is an attractive small Japanese garden behind, called the Shoyoen (or strolling garden). It was completed in 1815 and is particularly lovely in the spring and autumn. An extra charge is made to enter the garden and the adjacent museum, which contains some fine lacquer, paintings, and Buddhist statues. The main hall, the Sambutsudo, built in 1648, is the largest building in Nikko and enshrines statues of Amida Nyorai, the Buddha of the Western paradise, flanked on the right by a Senju Kannon (thousand-armed Boddhisatta of mercy) and on the left by a Bato-Kannon (or horse-headed Kannon, regarded as a protector of animals). The original hall is said to have been built in 848 by the famous priest Ennin (794 to 864), also known by his posthumous title of Jikaku-Daishi, on the model of the Komponchudo, the main building of the most important temple on Mt. Hiei. An extra charge is made for entry to the Sambutsudo. If you go around to the right and descend some steps to a stone-paved floor you'll find on the right a small shrine to Daikokuten, a deity said to bring wealth and protection from burglary. The three main images are lacquered in gold and date from the early part of the 17th century. At the top of the stairs there is another set of Buddhist images and a stall where charms can be bought. There are twelve different charms for the twelve years of the Zodiac.

The Gohotendo on the north side of the Sambutsudo enshrines the three popular Buddhist deities of Daikokuten, Bishamonten, and Benzaiten. Close by is a bronze pillar, called Sorinto, built in 1643 to repel evil influences.

Toshogu

On leaving Rinnoji temple it is only a short walk through tall cryptomerias to the entrance of the Toshogu, completed in 1636, the most important complex among Nikko's shrines and temples. To the left of the *torii* (archway in stone) stands a five-story pagoda (32 meters high) reconstructed in 1818. The first story is decorated with the twelve signs of the zodiac and there are black-lacquered doors on each of the other stories with the Tokugawa crest (of three hollyhock leaves) emblazoned on them.

Entry to the Toshogu is through the Omotemon (front gate) or Niomon (gate of the two guardians, or Deva Kings, carved by Hogan Ko-on in the early 17th century and painted red) at the top of some stone steps. Within the gate the path turns to the left. Note the wealth of painted carved lintels. In front and to the left stands the Sanjinko (literally the storehouse of the three gods). This was modeled after the Shosoin (the imperial treasurehouse) at Nara, although the Shosoin, which dates from the 8th century, was unadorned. Note the carving of two elephants. These were based on drawings by the famous painter Kano Tanyu in the early part of the 17th century. The elephants, with their ears opening outwards and their peculiar tails, were clearly of imaginary origin. One of the first buildings on the left is the stable, which is in natural wood, housing the sacred white horse found in other Shinto shrines (sometimes a real animal, sometimes a model). The latest occupant of the Toshogu stable is a white horse, supplied as a gift from New Zealand. The stable is decorated with carvings of pine trees and monkeys. The second panel from the left is the famous trinity of monkeys representing the three Buddhist precepts of "Hear no evil, speak no evil, see no evil" as one monkey covers his ears, another his mouth, and the third his eyes.

Nearby stands the Omizuya, or cistern of water for purification. In accordance with Shinto rites, you should wash out your mouth and wash your hands here before entering the inner precincts. Next on the left is the Rinzo or sutra library. In front, at the top of some stone steps, stands what is generally regarded as the centerpiece and outstanding marvel of the Toshogu, namely the Yomeimon—the Sunlight Gate.

Before passing through the Yomeimon, note to the right the ornate belfry and the bell under a bronze canopy. On the left there is first a revolving lantern under another bronze canopy (with the Tokugawa crest accidently inscribed on it upside down). The lantern was presented by the Dutch in 1643. Secondly, farther to the left and behind, stands an octagonal gold-decorated pavilion containing a bronze chandelier also presented by the Dutch in 1636. (During the 220 or so years of Japan's seclusion from the rest of the world under the rule of the Tokugawa shoguns, only the Dutch, confined to the closely guarded island of Deshima in Nagasaki, kept a toehold in Japan. They sent regular embassies to the Tokugawa capital of Edo with various gifts to ensure continuing trade.)

Farther on the left is an ornate drum tower and beyond it is the Yakushido (or hall of the Yakushi Nyorai, a manifestation of the Buddha devoted to healing). An extra charge is made to enter the hall and shoes must be removed. On the ceiling there is a famous painting entitled the Nakiryu or "roaring dragon." If you clap your hands hard at the spot marked on the floor, the echoes are supposed to give the impression that the dragon has roared.

The Yomeimon is also called the Higurashimon (Twilight Gate)—the implication being that there is so much to look at that one needs all day to do so. The gate has twelve columns and two stories. It is

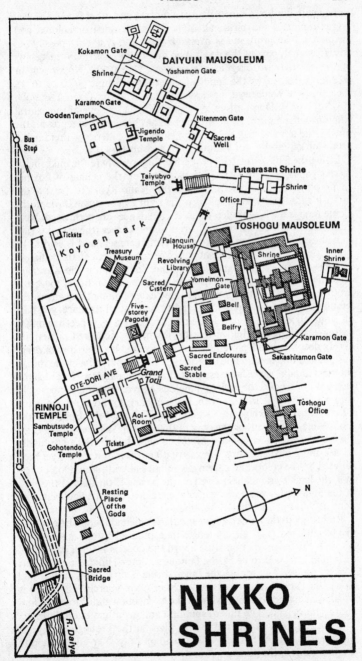

Kokamon Gate

DAIYUIN MAUSOLEUM

Shrine

Yashamon Gate

Karamon Gate

Go-oden Temple

Nitenmon Gate

Jigendo Temple

Sacred Well

Bus Stop

Taiyubyo Temple

Futaarasan Shrine

Shrine

Office

Tickets

Koyoen Park

Palanquin House

TOSHOGU MAUSOLEUM

Treasury Museum

Revolving Library

Shrine

Inner Shrine

Sacred Cistern

Yomeimon Gate

Five-storey Pagoda

Bell

Belfry

Karamon Gate

Sacred Enclosures

Sakashitamon Gate

OTE-DORI AVE

Grand Torii

Sacred Stable

RINNOJI TEMPLE

Aoi-Room

Toshogu Office

Sambutsudo Temple

Gohotendo Temple

Tickets

Resting Place of the Gods

N

Sacred Bridge

R. Daiya

NIKKO SHRINES

carved with flowers, Chinese figures, dragons, and other fanciful as well as real animals and birds, all of which are golden or colored and lacquered. The profusion is overwhelming and it is only possible to absorb a small part of the decoration on any one visit. On the ceiling of the portico two dragons are painted. One is the Noboriryu, or ascending dragon, by the famous painter Kano Tanyu (1602 to 1674), the other the Kudariryu, or descending dragon, by Kano Yasunobu (1613 to 1685). Don't miss the two lions carved on one of the central columns—the natural grain of the wood has been used to represent the fur. To the left and right of the Yomeimon are galleries with a further profusion of carvings of various trees and birds.

Inside the gate to the left is the Mikoshigura, where the mikoshi, or sacred palanquin, are kept. The paintings on the ceiling of floating angels playing musical instruments are by Kano Ryokaku. Next to the Mikoshigura, holy sake is sold. To the right as you come through the Yomeimon is the Kaguraden where sacred dances are performed. Note the basket of flowers carved in the right-hand corner (the basket is said to be based on one used by the early Dutch traders and is said to be the only carving in the shrine showing Western influence). Immediately in front of you as you come through the Yomeimon is the Karamon or Chinese gate, the official entrance to the inner shrine. It too has a profusion of colored carvings, and these extend along the walls to the left and the right. Go along to the right where, at an entrance, you take off your shoes (these may be left in lockers) and proceed along a passageway into the Haiden (oratory), with its lacquered pillars and highly decorated and carved friezes. The ceiling is covered with dragons painted in panels, while over the lintels, the portraits of the thirty-six most famous early Japanese poets have been painted. Note also the paintings of a *baku,* or tapir (a fabulous animal which is supposed to eat up bad dreams) and of a *kirin,* or imaginary giraffe. Both are by the famous 17th-century painter Kano Tanyu. Behind the Haiden is the Ishi-no-ma, or stone room leading to the Heiden (sanctuary). An extra charge is made to enter the Ishi-no-ma and Heiden. Both are highly ornate and gilded and very impressive if your senses have not yet been satiated by the colors and carvings you have already seen. Don't overlook the female attendants carved on the panels of the door at the back of the building as you come out of the Heiden, and the fine lacquered door as you re-enter the Ishi-no-ma.

Returning to the courtyard behind the Yomeimon, note the passages in red cinnabar (220 meters long), then proceed to the inner shrine through the Sakashitamon. Just above the door is a small carving of a sleeping cat, said to be by the famous sculptor Hidari Jingoro. This is easy to miss. The way to the inner shrine is up a flight of over 200 stone steps and through a cluster of huge cryptomerias. The climb is worth making if only for the view of the Yomeimon and Karamon from above and behind. The inner sanctum contains a fine old holy tree.

Some 120 festivals are said to take place at the Toshogu each year, the largest being the Spring Festival held on May 17 to commemorate the founding of the shrine.

Futaarasan Shrine

On returning to the exit for the Toshogu, turn left and go on to the Futaarasan shrine. It dates from from 767, predating the Toshogu by nearly 1,000 years. Futaarasan shrine is in three parts: the main shrine, or Honsha, next to the Toshogu; the Chugushi, or middle shrine, by Lake Chuzenji; and the Okumiya, or inner shrine, on the top of Mount Nantai. The latter is said to have been founded by the Buddhist priest Shodo in 784 (at the same time as the temple at Chuzenji, discussed below). It is dedicated to three Shinto deities, Okuni-nushi-no-mikoto, his wife, and their son. Okuni-nushi-no-mikoto, who is also worshipped at Izumo on the Japan Sea coast of Shimane Prefecture, is regarded as the god of the rice fields and hence prosperity.

The red-lacquered Honden (main hall) was built in 1619 on the orders of Hidetada, the second Tokugawa shogun. Beyond the Honden is an entrance (extra charge) to a garden with a number of other shrine buildings and the holy spring, including the spring of sake (rice wine) and the waters of wisdom and youth. Note also the bronze lantern under a red canopy. This is called the bake-doro, said to look like a goblin at night. Opposite the Honden stand some particularly fine cryptomeria trees, sanctified by the holy rope stretching round their trunks. The visitor with time to spare and plenty of energy may also walk to another sub-shrine, some distance behind Futaarasan. This is the Takio-jinja (or waterfall tail shrine). Its main attraction is its fine setting.

Daiyuin

Leaving Futaarasan shrine by the main steps, turn right at the bottom and enter the Daiyuin, which is the mausoleum of the third Tokugawa shogun Iemitsu (1603 to 1651), and which is part of the Rinnoji temple. First you will pass through another Niomon (gate of the two guardians, as at the Toshogu shrine) with a dragon painted on the ceiling by Kano Yasunobu (1613 to 1685). Twenty-one stone steps lead on to a second gate, the Nitenmon, with two carved and painted images of guardians in the outside niches and two images of the gods of wind and thunder in the inside niches. Another two flights of steps with a bell tower on the right and drum tower on the left lead to the third gate, the Yashamon, with four figures of Yasha (a demon, originally a tree spirit). This is also called the Botanmon, or the peony gate, because of the carvings of peonies that decorate it. The fourth and last gate is another Karamon (Chinese gate), which is highly ornate, with two white panels on either side depicting baskets of flowers. Beyond this is the Haiden, or oratory (an extra charge is made for entry and shoes must be removed). The ceiling of the Haiden is decorated with dragons; Chinese lions are painted on the panels at the rear. Passing through some curtains, you will enter the Ai-no-ma, or anteroom, which is decorated with phoenixes. Beyond is the Honden, which is not open, but can be viewed from the Ai-no-ma. After leaving the Haiden, turn to the left and view the extremely ornate exterior of the Honden.

At the end on the right, through a small gateway, is the so-called Kokamon, a gate built in the Chinese style of the late Ming dynasty.

The Daiyuin is rarely crowded and the setting among magnificent trees is very fine. After the Toshogu, it is the finest collection of buildings in Nikko.

The treasurehouse contains objects from the shrines and temples, but not many visitors can absorb much more after viewing the main parts of the complex.

The Nikko Mountains, Including Lake Chuzenji

Beyond Nikko town you will find what is still one of the most beautiful parts of the Japanese countryside—the new roads, the new ugly hotels, and the cable cars have fortunately not so far been allowed to destroy, except marginally, the wonders of the environment.

Before leaving Nikko consider a call at the Nikko Museum. This is in a former Imperial Villa used by the Emperor Taisho, the present Emperor's father. It is located on the left-hand side just off the road leading toward Lake Chuzenji from the shrines. There is not much in the museum, but the house is a pleasant example of the period, complete with the Imperial "toilet."

From the villa it is only a short walk to the Kanman-ga-fuchi, or Ganman-ga-fuchi, an attractive row of stone Buddhas (Jizo Bosatsu) set by the side of a rushing torrent. On leaving the Imperial villa carry on down the side road; after an unavoidable left turn, turn right at the next crossing, then straight down the hill to a T junction, turn right, then sharp left over a bridge, then right by the river to a small car park by a playground, pass behind the playground and through a small gate to a tiny temple (Jiunji). Beyond this are the statues, in two groups, covered in moss and with little piles of stones set before them by previous visitors. They date from the mid-17th century and originally numbered one hundred, but as a result of storms and floods, many are now missing. Of those remaining, some are old, but others are replacements dating from the late 19th century. They are sometimes called the ghostly statues, because if you count them more than once, the numbers seem to vary. There is a small pavilion overlooking the torrent.

The road from Nikko toward Chuzenji offers a look at the Jakko-no-taki and the Urami-no-taki waterfalls. The Jakko-no-taki (or waterfall of the lonely light) lies some two or three kilometers off the Chuzenji road. Turn right about one kilometer from the shrines along a narrow road with 30 km speed limit signs. The turning is beside a wood and just before the road divides into two. At the top of this narrow road there is a rough parking spot by some ugly construction work. The walk to the falls is up some steep steps to a small shrine. The Falls of Seven Steps (a series of seven waterfalls, one after the other) are some 60 meters high and are quite striking, but this is not a visit to be undertaken by the aged or by women in high-heeled shoes.

The great poet Basho described the Urami-no-taki as follows: "A mile or so [a rather long mile!] up the mountain was a waterfall. The water seemed to take a flying leap and drop a hundred feet from the top of a cave into a green pool surrounded by a thousand rocks. One was supposed to sidle into the cave and enjoy the falls from behind, hence its name 'The waterfall viewed from behind'."

The Urami-no-taki is reached by continuing on the road toward Chuzenji for about another kilometer after the lane leading to the Jakko-no-taki, then turning right at a gasoline stand just before a bridge. The road is somewhat better than that to the Jakko-no-taki. There is also a better parking lot and path, but although this is only 460 meters long, it is steep and rough. The gorge is fine and the falls striking, but only the intrepid with strong shoes and the willingness to get wet should attempt to go behind the falls.

Another fine waterfall is that of the Kirifuri falls, which is reached via the toll road to the Kirifuri Kogen (heights). This is reached by taking the road to the north from the center of Nikko town below the bridge.

The real climb to Lake Chuzenji (the lake of the Middle Zen temple) begins at Umagaeshi (literally, horse return) where, in the old days, the rider had to leave his horse and set out on foot. The lake is 1,270 meters above sea level. Today there is a new one-way toll road up the pass; the old road has been widened and paved, and is used for down traffic. The two roads are called the Irohasaka (or slope of the Japanese syllabary) because of the large number of steep hairpin bends. On clear days the views from the road down the valley are magnificent, and a lucky visitor may even catch sight of a wild monkey. From the top of Akechidaira, note the view of Mount Nantai, the extinct volcano that dominates Lake Chuzenji. Mount Nantai also can be seen from Chanokidaira, reached by cable car from Chuzenji village or by another cable car from Akechidaira.

Despite the motor boats and the crowds of visitors in the summer, Lake Chuzenji seems to have a magical quality. The surrounding mountains, with their varying trees and shapes, provide a superb setting. The water remains sparklingly clear and cold, even in summer, though the hardy can swim in it on a hot day. Colors change constantly as the sun moves and the mists rise. A totally sunny day is a rarity, but the clouds actually give the lake its variety and much of its charm. One moment it is still and clear, another the waves are rising as the wind begins to blow, then just as suddenly mists descend in one part or spread right across the lake as small boats pass in and out of them.

The fishing season begins on the first of May and some good trout can be caught by the expert. Boats and tackle can be hired, a license is needed, and patience and care are called for.

Chuzenji temple, which was founded in 784 and is part of Rinnoji in Nikko, is reached by turning left from the village and going about a mile along the shore. The temple has a fine bell, but its chief attraction is the statue of a Senju-Kannon (thousand-handed Kannon), known as the Tachiki-Kannon, said to have been carved over 1,000 years ago from a single Judas tree by the famous priest Shodo—who saw a reflection of Kannon in the lake. In front of the temple was the Uta-ga-hama, or "singing beach," named after the angel who is said to have come down from heaven to sing and dance to Shodo. Alas, the beach has now disappeared into a parking lot and steamer pier.

Futaarasan shrine's Chugushi, or middle shrine, lies just outside the village of Chuzenji on the road that skirts the foot of Mount Nantai towards Shobugahama and Yumoto. Its setting by the lake is attractive and its red-lacquered buildings give it color. The treasurehouse, entry to which is included in the admission ticket, contains some interesting historical objects including some medieval long swords, some lacquer, and medieval mikoshi, or shrine palanquins. The main festival here is the lantern festival between July 31 and August 8.

A visit to the top of the Kegon Falls, where the water gushes 250 feet into the valley, is "a must." The falls lie just on the outskirts of the village before the road starts to descend into the valley. It is also well worth going down in the lift to see the falls from below, but there is little chance of doing this except with a crowd of others. The flow of water is carefully regulated, but is most impressive after the summer rain or a typhoon. In winter the falls do not freeze completely, but the icicles that form give them a special beauty.

Above Chuzenji there are a number of places from which panoramic views of the lake and mountains can be obtained. One possibility is to take the toll road that runs from beyond the temple up the side of the mountains at the bottom end of the lake. There are parking lots at the top from which a short but steep climb can be made to another very fine view. The toll is expensive and the road comes to a dead end at the top.

If you have the time and the energy, consider the possibility of walking round the lake, but allow a day for this. The road covers barely a third of the distance of 28 kilometers and the rest must be done on foot. The path is well marked, but it is steep and very rough in places, with many fallen trees as a result of typhoons. Refreshments are only available at Shobugahama on the road to Yumoto and by the Ryuzu Falls, and in the summer at Senjugahama at the foot of the lake. From the village of Chuzenji take the road beyond the temple, keeping right down an unpaved road that you'll come to before the main road becomes the toll road up the mountain. Then follow what is little more than a track going behind the British and Italian villas and past two minshuku (visitor hostels). From just beyond the minshuku a rough path to the left takes you on a hard climb of about an hour to an hour and a half, up to the Hangetsu (halfmoon pass) from which it is possible to continue on to the viewing points served by the toll road or to other passes above the lake. But if you walk on for about three quarters of an hour (3.5 kilometers) from the temple, you will reach the campsite at Asegata. From Asegata to Senjugahama at the top of the lake, the path is narrow and rough. The distance is some 9 kilometers, but three hours should be allowed, as the path winds up and down and there are many inlets.

Senjugahama can also be reached by an unpaved road from above the Ryuzu Falls (see below). There are other good walks in this area. From Senjugahama to Shobugahama is 4.5 kilometers on a steep path, for which an additional one and a half hours should be allowed. From Shobugahama it is possible to get a boat or a bus back to the village of Chuzenji. There is a path off the road most of the way, but this is the least attractive part of the walk.

In any case whether you walk or go by road from the village, it is worth stopping at Shobugahama to see the Ryuzu Falls, which enter the lake here. They are especially fine in the spring when the wild azaleas are out (spring does not come until May in the mountains) and in the autumn when the reds and yellows of the October leaves add to the attractions of the rushing water. There is also a trout hatchery here that can be visited.

From Shobugahama the road rises to Senjogahara or the moor of the battlefield, so called because of a battle fought there in 1389. It looks rather like a battlefield, with its swamps, reeds, and volcanic remains. Crossing the plain, you can walk into the hills via the Sano pass over a woodman's route or continue on until you reach Yu-no-taki, another famous and impressive waterfall. Yu-no-taki flows from the Yunoko, or lake of hot water, which is a small lake that can be circuited in an easy walk of not more than an hour. At one corner near the hot spring village of Yumoto, hot water bubbles into the lake and the smell of sulfur can be overpowering. Yumoto is now a rather ugly collection of Japanese-style hot-spring hotels, most of the old Japanese inns having been converted into brash hotels for the busloads of group travelers.

A toll road beyond to Numata in Gunma prefecture over the Konsei Pass provides access for those who wish to climb Mount Shirane, the mountain that can be seen at the foot of the lake. But the most important mountain to climb is Nantai (2,484 meters). This is still the objective of some pilgrims. Access from May 5 to October 25 each year is via Futaarasan shrine in Chuzenji village; the shrine takes a hefty fee to allow the visitor the privilege of making what is a tough and steep climb.

PRACTICAL INFORMATION FOR NIKKO

WHEN TO GO. Nikko is popular the year-round and worth visiting in every season, especially May, when the wild azaleas are in flower, and October for the autumn colors. However, visitors should beware of coming on a Sunday or a public holiday, especially in spring, the middle of the summer, or autumn, when roads may be paralyzed with traffic (it once took us three and a half hours to come down from Chuzenji to Nikko, a journey that should take little more than half an hour). The shrines, the Kegon Falls, and the temple at Chuzenji will also be inundated with groups led by flag-waving guides, making it difficult if not impossible to see properly or take photographs.

HOW TO GET THERE. By car. You can reach Nikko from Tokyo in about 2½ to 3 hours, depending on traffic. The main problem is to get onto the Tohoku Expressway and this is likely to take up to an hour or more. The exit for Nikko is exit 10 and it is marked in roman script. The exit leads onto the toll road to Nikko, but take care to follow the green toll road signs or you may find yourself on the ordinary road, which can be crowded.

By train. You can go very easily by train from Tobu Asakusa Station, a 7 minutes' walk from Asakusa Station on the Ginza subway line. The journey

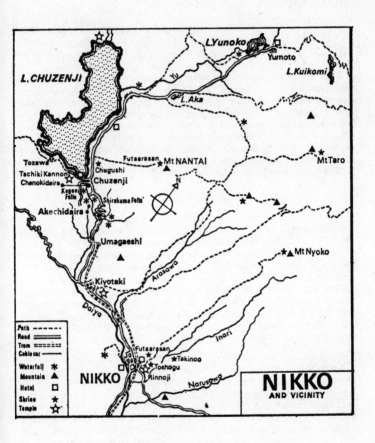

JAPAN

takes 1 hour 45 minutes by limited express, and 2 hours by slower trains. It is sensible to book seats in advance, on either a limited express train or an express. Seats on the rapid service trains are not reservable. There are many trains from which to choose.

TELEPHONES. The area code is 0288.

**HOTELS AND INNS.** Although Nikko can be visited in a day from Tokyo, it is much better to spend a few days in the area in order to enjoy fully the splendors of the shrines and the wonders of the natural scenery.

There are many semi-Western hotels as well as numerous Japanese inns and minshuku in Nikko, Chuzenji, and Yumoto, where it is possible to stay in moderate comfort, depending on your taste. In semi-Western hotels your meals may be served in a dining room, rather than the room in which you're staying; there may be bedrooms as well as tatami rooms where you sleep on the floor; and they may have Western-style lavatories. Inquire at hotels and inns that display signs showing vacancies. Rooms may, however, be scarce at peak periods, especially if finding a room is left until late in the day. If you wish to book in advance, it's best to do so through an agent.

WESTERN STYLE

Nikko

Nikko Kanaya. 1300 Kami-Hatsuishi, Nikko 321–14, Tochigi Pref.; 0288–54 –0001. This is the best Western-style hotel in Nikko. Near the shrines. Although of course it has been developed and modernized since the 19th century, it still has an atmosphere, as some would say, of old-world charm. The rooms (82 of them) are spacious, if old fashioned, and the decor has nothing of the slick modern hotel. Some of the furnishings may seem shabby, but it is warm and there is always plenty of hot water. From Mon.–Fri. you can get a twin with bath for ¥13,000; twin with shower for ¥9,000, and single with bath for ¥11,000. From Sat.–Sun. the same accommodations will cost you ¥16,000; ¥12,000; and ¥14,000, respectively.

Shobugahama

Nikko Prince. Shobugahama Chugushi, Nikko 321–16, Tochigi Pref.; 0288–55–0661. If you don't want to pay an early visit to the shrines to avoid the crowds and want to enjoy the beautiful lake and mountain scenery, then stay by Lake Chuzenji. The Nikko Prince Hotel is a modern luxury hotel at Shobugahama by the lake and near the Ryuzu Falls. It has two tennis courts, a swimming pool and all modern facilities. There are 44 twin rooms and 16 split-level "maisonette" rooms with views of the lake and Mount Nantai. From Nov. 1 to Dec. 29 a twin with bath will cost you ¥17,000; during the rest of the year, the cost is ¥22,000.

Chuzenji

Lakeside Chuzenji. 2482 Chugushi, Nikko 321–16, Tochigi Prefecture; 0288–55–0321. This is a newly built 100-room hotel in the village of Chuzenji. At the foot of the lake, with good views, it also has the use of tennis courts and is very convenient for transport, both buses and steamers. A twin with bath costs ¥13,000.

Chuzenji Kanaya. 2482 Chugushi, Nikko 321–16, Tochigi Pref.; 0288–55–0356. On the road from the village to Shobugahama and the Ryuzu Falls, this hotel has its own boat house and restaurant on the lake. Somewhat old fashioned but comfortable and relaxed. Mon.–Fri., twin with bath is ¥ 10,000; single with bath ¥ 9,000. Sat.–Sun., ¥ 13,000 and ¥ 12,000, respectively.

JAPANESE AND SEMI-WESTERN

Chuzenji

Chuzenji Hashimoto Hotel. By the lake in the village near the bridge; 0288–55–0310. All rooms Japanese tatami. Weekdays, ¥ 11,000–13,000 with two meals; Sat.–Sun. ¥ 12,000–14,000.

Chuzenji Hotel. By the lake, in the village, near the pier; 0288–55–0333. All Japanese-style—tatami. ¥ 9,000–12,000 with two meals.

Misaku Kurata. 2482 Chuzenji, Nikko; 0288–55–0072. Japanese style—tatami. ¥ 5,000 with two meals.

Nikko Katsuragikan. Maruyama Chuzenjikohan, Nikko; 0288–55–0252. All Japanese style—tatami. Suitable for students. ¥ 4,130 with two meals.

Nikko

Nikko Green Lodge. Honcho 9, Nikko 321-14, Tochigi Pref.; 0288–54–1756, 1839, or 3487. Twin with bath ¥ 7,000–8,000; Japanese style, ¥ 8,000–12,000 with two meals.

 YOUTH HOSTELS, PEOPLE'S LODGES, AND PENSIONS. Nikko YH. 2854, Tokorono, Nikko City; 0288–54–1013. 25 min. walk from Nikko Station. Bed Charge: ¥ 1,600 (¥ 150 additional for a bed sheet), ¥ 2,800 with two meals. **Nikko Daiyagawa YH.** 1075, Nakahatsuishi-machi, Nikko City; 0288–54–1974. 20 min. on foot from Nikko Station. Charge with two meals: ¥ 2,850.

Yumoto Lake Lodge. Yumoto, Nikko City; 0288–62–2421. 10 min. walk from Yumoto Bus Stop, which is 80 min. by bus from Nikko Station. **People's Lodge Ogurayama Sanso.** 2823, Tokorono, Nikko City; 0288–54–2487. 30 min. walk from Shinkyo Bus Stop, which is 5 min. by bus from Nikko Station.

Japan Pension Bellwood. 1829 Hanaishi-cho, Nikko; 0288–53–3332. ¥ 6,000 for bed and breakfast. Apply to the Japan Pension Center for reservations: Tokyo 407–2333, and Osaka 375–1601. Bellwood is an 8-minute bus ride from Tobu Nikko Station, in a scenic location. Get off the bus at Hanaishi-cho stop.

 TOURIST INFORMATION. Nikko. The *Nikko Tourist Association* is located inside the Nikko City Office; 0288–54–2496. *Tobu Travel* has a branch office within the Tobu Nikko Station; 0288–54–0864, through which local accommodation and tours can be booked.

Chuzenji. Accommodation can be booked through the local association of Japanese inns (Ryokan Kumiai Annai) near the entrance to Chuzenji village; 0288–55–0067.

The front desks of the Western-style hotels can also provide information and help in arranging tours in the Nikko area.

 SEASONAL EVENTS AND FESTIVALS. April. *Yayoi Festival,* the annual celebration of Futaarasan Shrine, runs from the 13th–17th. Protective shrine of the Nikko area. Palanquin processions, with musicians and dancers, are on the 14th and 17th.

304 JAPAN

May. *Gohan-shiki,* a rice-eating ceremony, is held at Sambutsudo, Rinnoji Temple on the 2nd. A popular event.

Toshogu Shrine Grand Festival, from the 17th–18th, is one of the most elaborate in all Japan, featuring an afternoon procession of three portable shrines from the main building to Futaarasan Shrine. They remain there overnight, and on the 18th, from 11:00 A.M. are carried to the Otabisho (Sojourn Hall), arriving at noon. There are about 1,000 marchers in dress of the Tokugawa period, as well as people costumed as sacred lions, soldiers, child monkeys, falconers, samurai, fairies, etc. From noon there are ceremonies at the Otabisho (just above the Sacred Bridge) with offerings, shrine dances, and priests' dances. Then the entire procession returns to the main shrine while Buddhist priests perform the Ennen-no-mai dances at Rinnoji. At 2:00 P.M. there is a demonstration of mounted archery at the Treasure Museum. This festival commemorates the death of Tokugawa Ieyasu in 1616.

July. From the 31st–Aug. 2nd is the *Lantern Floating Festival* (Kojo Matsuri). The people of the town of Chuzenji on the lake, float thousands of lighted paper lanterns on the waters from dusk to midnight, and enjoy folkdances.

August. *Pilgrims' Festival,* takes place from the 1st–7th on Mt. Nantai. A ritual ascent to the Three Shrines of 8,197-ft. Mt. Nantai. Pilgrims purify themselves by bathing in the lake, then set out at midnight dressed in white, carrying sticks and lanterns. The climb is about 5 miles, taking 2–5 hours, to arrive in time for the sunrise. Thousands participate, anyone is welcome. Also held Sept. 20–22.

Waraku Dance, from the 6th–7th, is apparently related to the O-bon Odori, but is more elaborate. Anyone may join in, evening of both days in the Kiyotaki section of Nikko.

October. On the 17th is the *Toshogu Shrine Grand Festival,* similar to the one in May, but slightly smaller. At 10:00 A.M. ceremonies in the shrine, and procession to the Otabisho at 11:00. The rest of the schedule is as in May, but without the archery. In case of rain, postponed one day.

 TOURS. There is no need to take a tour. Even if you cannot speak or read Japanese you can get a bus easily or walk from the station to the shrines and there are frequent buses from the shrines to Lake Chuzenji. However, if you are in a hurry or have a well-loaded wallet and prefer to make your visit with your fellow countrymen and a babbling guide, then you will find plenty of regular tours. The Japan Tourist Bureau will gladly provide details.

 HOT SPRINGS. There are numerous hot springs in the area. The most popular are Yumoto above Lake Chuzenji, and Kawaji and Shiobara on the way north from Nikko to Nasu. All the hot spring resorts in the area tend to be frequented by Japanese groups traveling in hired buses, and are only recommended to those who enjoy happy throngs of merry locals in their yukata or bath robes singing choruses after enjoyable evenings drinking sake and beer.

 SPORTS. Golfers will enjoy the Nikko Country Club, 15 minutes by car from Nikko Station. Staying at the Kanaya Hotel gives you access to its 18-hole, 7,000-yard course. You can hire paddle boats, row boats or speedboats on Lake Chuzenji from one of the many boatmen by the lake. It may also be possible to do water-skiing. Sailing is not advisable because of the speedboats. A fishing license is needed whether you go out in a boat or fish from the shore.

In season (May–September) there are hundreds of fishermen on and by the lake. Many go out very early in the morning, before daylight. Fishing at the top end of the lake is forbidden. Lake Chuzenji has excellent small salmon trout.

Winter sports center around lakes Chuzenji and Yunoko where there are ski slopes for every degree of ability. Best snow, from three to 6 feet deep, is January through March. Skating is at the rinks of the Kanaya and Chuzenji Kanaya hotels and the Toshogu Shrine, open all day and lighted at night, January through February. The Hosoo Rink in Nikko has ice hockey, and a 400-yd. racing course.

 MUSEUMS. The best gallery in the neighborhood is the **Tochigi Prefectural Art Gallery** in Utsunomiya. The gallery shows modern art in changing exhibitions, and the fine new building is worth visiting if you are passing through the town by car. Utsonomiya is also on the main National Railway line to the northeast (Tohoku). A branch line runs between it and Nikko, about 30 kilometers away. But anyone with time to spare should visit **Mashiko,** about three quarters of an hour by road southeast of Utsunomiya. This was the home of one of the greatest of modern Japanese potters, the late Shoji Hamada, friend of the world-famous British potter, Bernard Leach, and co-developer with Kanjiro Kawai and Soetsu Yanagi of the modern Japanese folk craft (or Mingei) movement. His old houses have now been turned into a museum and represent some of the first country architecture in Japan. Anyone in Mashiko should be able to give you directions to the museum. There are innumerable kilns and pottery shops in the town. The greatest living Mashiko potter and disciple of Hamada is Tatsuzo Shimaoka.

Kurita Museum. 1542, Komabacho, Ashikaga-shi; 0284–91–1026. A mecca for those interested in the 17th- and 18th-century pottery of Arita in Kyushu. The building is elegant, the collection attractively displayed. In the garden are a teahouse and a temple. Open from 10:00 A.M. to 5:00 P.M. daily except over the New Year holidays. Admission ¥1,000, students ¥800. A branch museum is in Ningyo-cho, Tokyo. From Ashikaga-shi Station take a Kanto bus going to Sano and get off at Kurita Bijutsukan-mae. The museum is a 20-minute taxi ride from Ashikaga-shi Station.

 SHOPPING. There are a few antique shops in the town of Nikko, but there are no bargains left. The local specialty is wood carving, especially in cherry, pine, cypress, and birch. Salad bowls and servers, as well as other wooden items, including walking sticks and door signs (they will carve your name and address for you in a few minutes) can be bought in Nikko and Chuzenji. Prices are no longer cheap but are competitive with prices of similar products elsewhere. Some shops also sell attractive rustic pottery from Mashiko, the traditional pottery village on the southeast side of Utsunomiya.

 DINING OUT. There is no shortage of restaurants in Nikko or Chuzenji. The popular places show their menus, with the usual plastic displays marking their costs. Anyone with some flexibility about what he or she eats and willingness to try Japanese cooking should have no difficulty in getting a reasonable meal. For the unadventurous there is even a Wimpy hamburger house in Chuzenji village, and at the corner of the road at the foot of the slope to the Kanaya Hotel is a modern bakery where you can buy doughnuts, but beware of those filled with *an* (beancurd) unless you have become used to this

Japanese specialty. If you insist on a solid Western meal, the Western hotels listed above will all provide you (at a cost) with the usual steak or trout. Picnic food is available at the local shops, but in Chuzenji village there is not much choice. Bread is likely to consist only of thick white sliced, which has the texture of cotton wool, and Japanese salami and sausages, with their flavor of fish, are not to everyone's taste. Cheese will be processed. The fruit is better and cheaper in the valley below.

THE JAPAN ALPS, SNOW
COUNTRY AND BEYOND

by
PETER POPHAM

*Peter Popham is a free-lance writer who has lived in Japan for over
six years. His work has appeared in the* Times, *the* Sunday Times, *and
many other leading papers and magazines around the world. He writes
regularly on cultural topics for the* Mainichi Daily News, *the English-
language Tokyo daily.*

For much of its length the narrow main island of Japan is divided
roughly down the middle by a spine of steep mountains, the most
central of which are known as the Japan Alps. The south side, cold but
dry and practically snowless for most of the winter, has been the center
of population and economic activity throughout the nation's history.
Here is where all the major cities and much of the modern industry is
located.

The area northwest of the mountains languishes for much of the
winter under a thick blanket of snow, as deep in places as anywhere
in the world. This is the snow country, setting for Yasunari Kawabata's
famous novel of that name, where large towns are few and far between

307

and solitary figures pick their way precariously across whitened slopes, where time moves slowly, and the trades are still traditional.

At least, that's the image. Central Japan's snow country is no longer as remote and lonely as it once was. Geographically it's right in the middle of the country, just a few hours by train from Tokyo and Kyoto. There are still large areas where the solitude of the mountains can be found, but more and more foreign visitors are discovering that there is far more to "the back of Japan" than solitude.

Except on the highest peaks the snow is, after all, a wintertime phenomenon. In other parts of the area and in other seasons there is a rich variety of things to do and places to see. Two of the region's cities, Takayama and Kanazawa, are prosperous and elegant "little Kyotos," which have done a remarkable job of preserving their traditional characteristics while keeping up economically with the rest of the nation. Elsewhere there are long expanses of coastline, both rugged and gentle, villages with huge old thatched houses, sophisticated summer resorts, and innumerable centers of hot spring bathing. Far to the north, though now barely more than a two-hour ride from Tokyo thanks to the new Shinkansen (bullet train) line, is the tranquil island of Sado with its fishing boats and puppet plays.

Chubu, meaning "central part," is the Japanese name for that relatively fat section of Japan's main island that is bracketed by Tokyo on the east and Kyoto on the west. All the places described in this chapter, with the exception of Sado Island, are in the northern half of Chubu.

If we move north and west into the region from Tokyo, the first place of importance we hit is Karuizawa, a fashionable resort town a couple of hours by train out of the capital and nearly 1,000 meters above sea level. Karuizawa's value as a cool and accessible retreat from Tokyo's muggy summers was first appreciated by a foreign prelate, Archdeacon A. C. Shaw, who built a villa here in 1888. Other foreigners quickly followed his example and before long the idea began to catch on with the wealthier natives too. Though its winter population remains small, in summer Karuizawa is a very busy town indeed, and tens of thousands of visitors, the majority now Japanese, fill the streets, pools, tennis courts, and the many branches of trendy Tokyo stores that do business here for the season.

As this description probably suggests, Karuizawa is of more interest to the resident of Japan than the visitor, unless he or she is curious to observe the affluent natives at play. The major natural attraction nearby is Mt. Asama, a volcano that erupted with enormous power two hundred years ago and is still active. On its quieter days it makes a relatively easy climb, and its crater is an awesome sight. When eruption threatens, climbing is forbidden.

Karuizawa is located just inside the border of Nagano Prefecture, the largest province in this part of the country and the most mountainous —"the Roof of Japan" as it is known. Nagano City, capital of the prefecture, is another hour up the tracks. Zenkoji Temple is Nagano's main attraction, a vast and ancient establishment, a visit to which, according to one sect of believers, is a prerequisite for entering Paradise.

Nagano is the gateway to some of the best skiing grounds in central Japan, notably Shiga Heights, a plateau 1,500 meters above sea level, in the heart of the Joshin-Etsu Kogen National Park. With its many lakes and ponds, its white birch forests and its hot springs, Shiga is a strikingly beautiful spot, drawing visitors all the year round. It's in a hot spring resort in this area that the novel *Snow Country* is set.

Matsumoto and Journeys Beyond

Equally prominent as a gateway to the mountains is the city of Matsumoto, due west of Karuizawa, which has rather more than Nagano in the way of intrinsic interest. In particular it has a fine and authentic castle, called *Karasujo,* "Crow Castle," because of its black protective walls. As befits a castle town, Matsumoto has its share of picturesquely winding streets; it also has a folkcraft museum and a brand-new museum of *ukiyoe* prints and, from the footbridge above the station, a noted panoramic view of the Northern Japan Alps.

Matsumoto is on the southeastern side of the Northern Japan Alps. It used to snow a bit in the old days, the locals will tell you, but hardly at all now. But a 30-minute train ride west is Kamikochi, center of the Japan Alps National Park and one of the most scenic places in Japan. It's the starting point for numerous exhilarating hikes, notably the one that leads over the little suspension bridge, Kappa Bridge, which has become a symbol of the area, past a bust of the Reverend Walter Weston, the British missionary who first called these mountains "alps" and who introduced mountaineering into Japan. Before Weston arrived in 1888, the natives believed the mountains to be full of gods and goblins, and shunned them.

Above the gentle hiking trails soar the truly Alpine peaks of the mountains: Mt. Yari (Japan's "Matterhorn"), 3,180 meters; Mt. Hotaka, 3,190 meters; Mt. Yake, 2,458 meters; and others. These great buttresses are not to be trifled with; they take many lives every year.

If you cannot resist the call of the mountains and yet are no climber, there is one route through them that is safe and stunningly beautiful— though rather complicated, and pricey for those on a budget. This is the Tateyama-Kurobe Alpine Route, and it offers a wide sampling of transportation modes, as well as the grandest of views. Starting from Shinano-Omachi Station, an hour by train from Matsumoto, the route involves transport by bus, cable car, trolley bus, and train, and takes the traveler right through the heart of the Alps, ending finally in Toyama City near the Japan Sea coast. The trip can be done in a day but it's a rush, and the many hotels and *minshuku* along the way tempt one to break it in half.

This transportation network has only been in existence since 1971. The route offers the closest thing to an experience of virgin nature that one can hope to find in Japan without risking life and limb.

The route southwest from Matsumoto along the Kiso River, in the direction of Nagoya, brings an encounter with a different sort of unspoiled territory, though one which is equally rare in construction-crazy Japan, the villages of Narai, Tsumago, and Magome. In a European country, finding a trio of villages that time seems to have passed

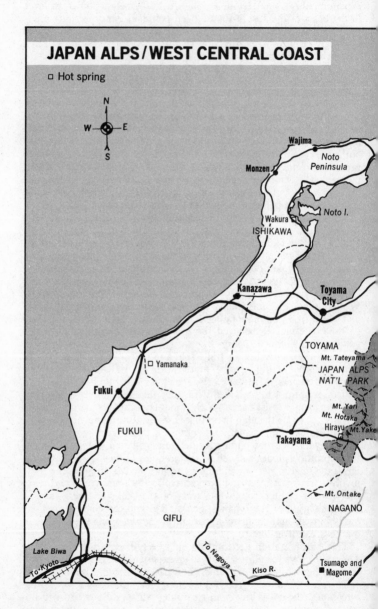

JAPAN ALPS/WEST CENTRAL COAST

□ Hot spring

N
W   E
S

Wajima
Noto
Peninsula
Monzen
Noto I.
Wakura
ISHIKAWA
Kanazawa
Toyama
City
TOYAMA
Mt. Tateyama
□ Yamanaka
JAPAN ALPS
NAT'L PARK
Mt. Yari
Mt. Hotaka
Fukui
Hirayu Mt. Yake
FUKUI
Takayama
Mt. Ontake
NAGANO
GIFU
Lake Biwa
To Kyoto
To Nagoya
Tsumago and
Kiso R.
Magome

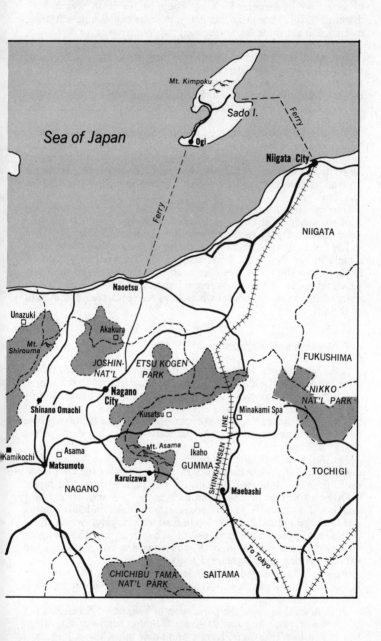

by would not be a matter for much comment; in Japan, where every thatched cottage seems to be set off by an array of gleaming soft drink machines, it's a cause for amazement.

In the feudal period there were two routes between Edo (Tokyo) and Kyoto. One, the Tokaido, which runs parallel to the Pacific coast, remains the nation's greatest artery. But the other, the Nakasendo, is virtually forgotten. It's along this old highway that many of the Chubu region's attractions are located: Karuizawa and Matsumoto, Takayama, and Kanazawa (described below), as well as the villages of Narai, Tsumago, and Magome.

All three were posting villages, and as visitors included *daimyo* with large retinues, some of the many *ryokan* in each village were very classy. With the end of the feudal period the villages lost their reason for being and sank into obscurity. They were rediscovered by a younger generation casting around for evidence of the way their grandfathers had lived.

Interspersed with the *ryokan* and *minshuku* are old tea shops and craft workshops. All the houses are of wood, deep and narrow, and some have courtyard gardens. Some are hundreds of years old.

The best way to appreciate the charm of these villages is to spend a night in one. Narai has fewer visitors, but Tsumago and Magome, farther down the valley, are connected by a footpath, and the walk, which takes 2½ to 3 hours, is recommended. Each village also has its share of *shiryokan,* old houses which have been preserved as museums of the old way of life.

Takayama and Kanazawa

Some 60 kms west of Matsumoto, in the midst of the Hida mountains, is the elegant old city of Takayama. Laid out on a grid pattern like Kyoto, it's renowned for its magnificent old townhouses and its traditional craft products. One street of venerable shops near the center, Kami-san-no-machi, has sake breweries and miso factories where the freshly made products can be purchased, and other shops selling textiles and antiques.

Not far from the town center is the Hida-no-Sato Village, final resting place for a fascinating assortment of old houses and craft workshops from the Hida area, perhaps the best park of its type in Japan.

Other attractions of Takayama include the two open-air morning markets, Takayama Jinya (the administrative office in feudal times), and the large and richly decorated festival wagons, *yatai,* which are on permanent display in the grounds of Hachiman Shrine. These wagons and many more roll through the town twice a year, in April and October, during two magnificent festivals.

Another 60 km jump over the mountains, this time to the northwest, brings us to the Japan Sea coast and another and much larger island of culture: Kanazawa.

With more than twice the population of Takayama, Kanazawa is a much busier place and has its share of traffic snarl-ups and urban blight. But like Takayama, Kyoto, and a few other towns, it escaped bombing during the war, and much of its historic fabric remains intact.

The city's single biggest draw, for native and foreigner alike, is Kenrokuen, the large landscaped garden near the center. Laid out in 1819 by a member of the Maeda clan, which ruled the city with an enlightened hand during the feudal period, Japanese regard it as one of the three most beautiful gardens in the country. "Kenroku" means "combining six features"; these are vastness, solemnity, careful arrangement, venerability, coolness (thanks to the streams), and scenic charm. In these democratic times a seventh must regretfully be added to the list: congestion. Kenrokuen is a mite too popular. Still, its beauty survives.

Kanazawa has an abundance of other charms. Little survives of the old castle, but not far away is a great rarity, a tightly contained quarter of old samurai mansions, bordered by heavy, sloping earthen walls. One of them contains a silk dyeing workshop that is open to the public.

Silk dyeing is one of several old trades that continues to flourish alongside the city's modern textile, machinery, and metal-working industries. Others include Kutani pottery, gold and silver leaf work, and paulownia wood carving. Several other workshops around the city welcome visitors.

There is also an ancient Noh theater, a number of good museums (see the Museums section, below), and a temple, colloquially known as Ninjadera (Ninja or "Secret Agent" Temple), which is riddled with secret stairways, concealed entrances, and other tricky devices.

The Noto Peninsula and Sado Island

Kanazawa is the gateway to the Noto Peninsula, a crooked finger of land jutting into the Japan Sea. Here much of the scenery is softer than elsewhere in the back of Japan, and in places the hills almost roll. Transport around the peninsula is by bus or car, and for long stretches the road hugs the spectacularly jagged and rocky western coastline.

Just in from the coast, on the northwestern portion of the peninsula, is the town of Monzen, which is dominated by Sojoji Temple, a beautiful and expansive structure that still houses a small community of monks. Sojoji is the former headquarters of the Soto school of Zen Buddhism. Farther north is the town of Wajima, famous for its lacquerware products.

The peninsula's east coast has a milder charm than the west coast, with many indentations, some offering sea-bathing possibilities, and a deep bay with an island, Notojima, that was recently connected to the mainland by a bridge at Wakura Onsen. The island boasts an elaborate new marine park.

Toyama City, at the base of the Noto Peninsula on the east side, has little to interest the tourist, and the same is true of the long stretch of flat, rice-producing country of Niigata Prefecture, which stretches farther to the east, bordering the Japan Sea. Niigata City, constituency of Kakuei Tanaka, the former prime minister indicted in the Lockheed bribery scandal, is astonishing in its elephantine modernity, but an hour away by hydrofoil on a fine day is one of the quaintest corners of Japan: Sado-ga-shima (Sado Island).

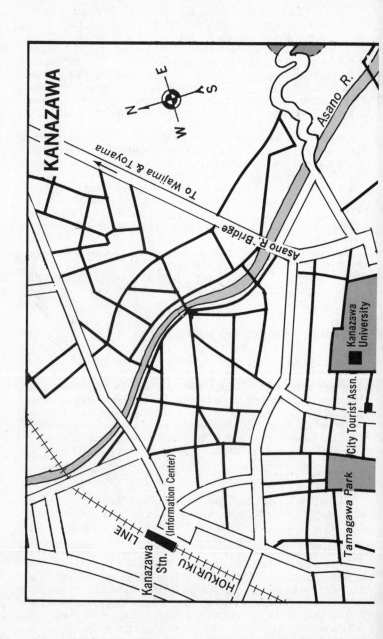

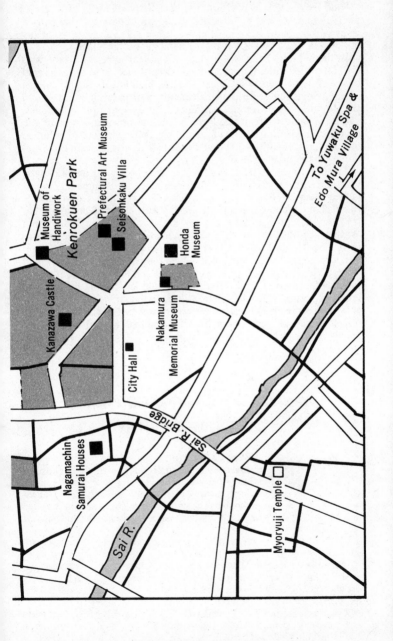

Sado feels a long way from anywhere. It plods along at a gentle, premodern pace, severely depopulated but still up to sustaining a rich array of folk traditions: puppet plays, festivals, and a theater company of "demon drummers" that makes its home on the island.

In the old days Sado was a place of exile for men in disfavor with the authorities. Later the government sent prisoners to work in the gold mines of Aikawa on Sado Island, Japan's sixth largest island. Golden Mountain has suffered complete depletion of its natural resources, and the old mine is now a tourist attraction. In the underground tunnels, figures in tableaux realistically represent the prisoners at their toil, chiseling and hammering. At festival time, Sada women clad in indigo blue kimonos chant the plaintive Okesa ballads and perform the traditional dances of the island.

The first travelers to Sado are said to have been a fox and a badger, who turned themselves into a parasol and a pair of slippers and attached themselves to a human traveler to make the crossing to the island. Contemporary visitors are greeted with shoals of flying fish that lend a tropical appearance to the island. Sado also has the Sekizaki and Washizaki waterfalls, the "Palace of Unhewn Timber" where an Emperor once languished in exile, a type of red porcelain called *mumyoiyaki*, and a hut on Mt. Kimpoku, where the great Buddhist priest and patriot Nichiren played the role of prophet and foretold the coming of the *Kami-kaze*, or Divine Wind, that would shatter the fleets of the invading hordes of Kublai Khan. It is advisable to visit Sado between May and September, because the waters between the island and the mainland can be very rough in other months, and often boats are unable to put out.

PRACTICAL INFORMATION FOR
THE SNOW COUNTRY

WHEN TO GO. Winters in the Snow Country are long and severe, and snowfall is a daily occurrence. The snow is heavy and wet and has given rise to a proverb popular in the Kanazawa area: "Even if you forget your lunchbox, never forget your umbrella." The contrast with Tokyo and other points east, which enjoy dry weather and crystalline skies for much of the winter, could hardly be more striking.

Weather in the Japan Alps is truly Alpine, and travelers should pack accordingly.

While the weather in the mountains remains chilly until the summer, the most comfortable seasons in the low-lying areas are spring and autumn. As elsewhere in Japan, autumn can be relied on for successive perfect days, and the spectacle of the reddening foliage makes this a popular time to travel.

Residents of Japan flee to the mountains to escape the sticky heat of summer. The August temperature in the resort town of Karuizawa, for example, is 20.5°C, but the winds can be chilly, so travelers are advised to pack cardigans or jackets.

HOW TO GET THERE. By train. The area described in this chapter is a large one, and is served by three separate train routes from Tokyo to and through the mountains. Another useful line follows the shoreline of the Japan Sea coast.

The first line that should be mentioned is the new Shinkansen Joetsu Line, which links Omiya, half an hour north of Tokyo, with Niigata. Bullet trains cover the distance in about two hours. Shuttle trains take passengers from Ueno, the Tokyo station at which the line is eventually intended to terminate, to Omiya in about half an hour, then there is usually a wait of about 20 minutes before the bullet train leaves. Much of the Joetsu line bores through mountains, and includes the longest tunnel in the world.

Three other lines link Tokyo and other cities in the east with "the back of Japan." The Joetsu Honsen (trunk line) runs north from Tokyo's Ueno through Takasaki, up to Iwappara and on to Niigata. Regular expresses cover the distance in about 5 hours, but there are no longer many through trains, because Japan National Railways are keen to encourage passengers to use the faster (and more expensive) Shinkansen service.

The second line, the Shinetsu, also runs from Ueno to Takasaki but then branches off to the west through Karuizawa and Nagano, terminating at Naoetsu. Ueno to Karuizawa takes just over 2 hours, to Nagano takes 3 hours 10 minutes. A couple of trains per day go on through Toyama to terminate at Kanazawa, covering the distance in a little under 7 hours.

The third and most southerly of the lines is the Chuo line, which leaves from Tokyo's Shinjuku Station. Several expresses shuttle between Shinjuku and Matsumoto every day, some leaving late at night. They take between 3–4½ hours over the journey.

Takayama is most directly accessible from Nagoya via the Takayama line, which goes on to terminate at Toyama. Some trains continue on to Kanazawa. The fastest service from Nagoya to Takayama takes about 2½ hours.

By air. All Nippon Airways (*Zenniku* in Japanese) operates daily flights from Tokyo to Kanazawa, and there are also direct flights to Niigata scheduled by Zenniku and Toa Domestic Airlines.

By bus. The Tokyu Electric Railway Co. has one bus daily from Tokyo's Shibuya Station in July and August only. Call 03–477–6111 for information (in Japanese).

TELEPHONES. Area Codes: Karuizawa, 02674; Matsumoto, 0263; Kamikochi, 026395; Takayama, 0577; Kanazawa, 0762; Niigata, 0252.

HOTELS AND INNS. This region is full of hotels and ryokan, and even if the traveler gets stuck for the night in the middle of nowhere (provided he or she is not at the top of a mountain) there is likely to be a minshuku not far away that offers bed-and-breakfast-style accommodation.

The Western-style hotel listings are divided as follows: *Expensive,* above ¥7000 per night for a single room. *Moderate,* ¥4000 to ¥7000 per night for a single. *Inexpensive,* under ¥4000.

Expensive ryokan are ¥15,000 and upwards, per night per person; *Moderate,* between ¥4,000 and ¥15,000. These prices include two meals.

Please note: For details about what to expect for your money, see "Hotels and Inns" in the *Nagoya* chapter.

WESTERN-STYLE

Kamikochi

All Kamikochi hotels are closed from mid-November to late April.
Hotel Shirakaba-so. *Expensive.* 026395–2131.
Kamikochi Imperial Hotel. *Expensive.* 026395–2001.
Taishoike Hotel. *Expensive.* 026395–2301.

Kanazawa

Business Hotel Ishiya. *Moderate.* 2-8-3 Hikosocho, Kanazawa, Ishikawa Pref.; 0762–64–0161. 10 min. walk from Kanazawa Stn.
Castle Inn Kanazawa. *Moderate.* 10-17 Konohanamachi, Kanazawa, Ishikawa Pref.; 0762–23–6300. 4 min. walk from Kanazawa Stn.
Holiday Inn Kanazawa. *Expensive.* 0762–23–1111. Tokyo office, 03–553–6631.
Kanazawa Miyako Hotel. *Expensive.* 6-10 Konohanacho, Kanazawa, Ishikawa Pref.; 0762–31–2202. Tokyo office, 03–572–8301.
Kanazawa New Grand Hotel. *Expensive.* 1-50 Takaoka-machi, Kanazawa, Ishikawa Pref. 920; 0762–33–1311. Tokyo office: 03–663–4921.

Karuizawa

Karuizawa Prince Hotel. *Expensive.* 1016-75 Karuizawa, Karuizawa-machi, Nagano Pref. 389-01; 02674–2–8111. One of a famous chain. Facilities include golf, swimming, and skiing.
Mampei Hotel. *Expensive.* 925 Sakuranosawa, Karuizawa-machi, Nagano Pref. 389-01; 02674–2–2771. Tennis, golf and horseback riding among other facilities.

Matsumoto

Matsumoto Tokyu Inn. *Expensive.* 0263–36–0109. Tokyo office, 03–406–0109.
Hotel Shirokiya. *Expensive.* 0263–33–1311.
Matsumoto City Hotel. *Moderate.* 0263–32–5025.
Hotel New Station. *Moderate.* 0263–35–3850.
Matsumoto Green Hotel. *Moderate.* 0263–35–1277.
Matsumoto Town Hotel. *Moderate.* 0263–32–3339.

Takayama

Hida Hotel. *Moderate.* Tel. 0577–33–4600. 3 min. walk from Takayama Stn.
Takayama Green Hotel. *Moderate.* 2-180 Nishino-issikicho, Takayama, Gifu Pref. 506; 0577–33–5500. 7 min. walk from Takayama Stn.

JAPANESE-STYLE

Kanazawa

Asadaya. *Expensive.* 23 Jukken Machi, Kanazawa; 0762–31–2228. This new inn is expensive, but worth the price.
Chaya Ryokan. *Expensive.* 2-17-21 Hommachi, Kanazawa, Ishikawa Pref.; 0762–31–2225. 3 min. on foot from Kanazawa Stn.
Kincharyo. *Expensive.* 1 Teramachi, Kanazawa; 0762–43–2121. A lovely inn, located on a hillside.
Kinjoro. *Expensive.* Hashiba-cho; 0762–21–8188. A 100-year-old inn, noted for its food.
Miyabo. *Expensive.* Shimo Kakinokibatake; 0762–31–4228. Set in one of the oldest private gardens in Kanazawa.

Hikoso Shinboya Hotel. *Moderate.* 1-12-3 Hikosocho, Kanazawa, Ishikawa Pref.; 0762–21–6650. 5 min. by taxi from Kanazawa Stn.

Ryumeikan. *Moderate.* 39-2 Nishicho-Yabunouchi, Kanazawa, Ishikawa Pref.; 0762–63–8444. 5 min. by bus from Kanazawa Stn.

Kamikochi

All Kamikochi ryokan are closed from mid-November to late April.
Gosenjaku Ryokan. *Expensive.* 026395–2111.

Karuizawa

Hoshino Onsen Hotel. *Expensive.* 2148 Oaza Nagakura, Karuizawa-machi, Kitasaku-gun 389-01; 02674–5–5121. 5 min. by bus from Naka-Karuizawa Stn. Hot spring bathing.

Shiotsubo Onsen Hotel. *Expensive.* Address as ryokan above; 02674–5–5441.

Takayama

Ryokan Hishuya. *Expensive.* 2581 Kamioka-moto-machi, Takayama City 506; 0577–33–4001. 10 min. by bus from Takayama Stn.

Ryokan Seiryu. *Expensive.* 6 Hanakawa-machi, Takayama City 506; 0577–32–0448. 3 min. by taxi from Takayama Stn.

KOKUMIN SHUKUSA

Takayama: **People's Lodge.** 0577–32–2400. 20 min. walk from Takayama Stn.

YOUTH HOSTELS. *Kanazawa:* **Izuminodai Youth Hostel.** 0762–41–2802. **Kanazawa Youth Hostel.** 0762–52–3414. **Matsuiya Youth Hostel.** 0762–21–0275.

Karuizawa: **Karuizawa Youth Hostel.** 1362 Kyu-karuizawa, Karuizawa-machi, Kita-saku-gun, Nagano Pref. 389-01; 02674–2–2325. 4 min. by bus from Karuizawa Stn.; 18 min. on foot. 50 beds.

Matsumoto: **Asama-onsen Youth Hostel.** 302-1 Asama-onsen, Matsumoto City 390-03; 0263–46–1335. 5 min. by bus from Matsumoto Stn.; 20 min. on foot. 150 beds. Closed before and during New Year holiday.

Sado Island: **Hosen kan Youth Hostel.** 1111 Katagami, Niibo-mura, Sado-gun, Niigata Pref.; 025942–3125. 10 min. by bus from Ryotsu Port, then 6 min. on foot. **Sotokaifu Youth Hostel.** 131 Iwayaguchi, Aikawa-machi, Sado-gun, Niigata Pref.; 025979–3815. 2 hr. 40 min. by bus from Ryotsu Port.

Takayama: **Tenshoji Temple Youth Hostel.** 0577–32–6345. 15 min. walk from Takayama Stn.

HEALTH SPAS AND RESORTS. Hot-spring bathing is a national passion for the Japanese. The visitor will almost certainly appreciate the occasional hot dip and may enjoy the novelty of being buried in hot sand, but it takes years of conscious effort before one can simulate the sort of intense emotions the Japanese feel about the whole thing.

By all means take the opportunity to sample a hot spring. There are a great many fine ones in this area. But if you find the pleasure paling, don't suppose there's anything wrong with you.

You will find good hot springs in several of the leading ski resorts, and many hotels have their own pools in the basement. Recommended spots are: Shiga Heights, Akakura, and Sekiyama. Other good spas in the area (though not necessarily good for skiing) are: Ikaho (nearest Tokyo), Minakami (near Iwappara), Kusatsu (near Karuizawa), Tateshina (near Suwa), Asama (near Matsumoto), Shirahone, Nakanoyu, and Hirayu (all near Kamikochi), Unazuki (in the Kurobe Gorge), Yuwaku (near Kanazawa), Yamanaka (near Fukui), and Wakura (near Nanao on the Noto Peninsula).

For accommodations, ask at the Kanko Annaisho (Tourist Information Center) at the station upon your arrival.

HOW TO GET AROUND. You will have to rely upon the rail lines that brought you here, plus buses or hired automobiles. **By bus.** One cheap and convenient way to see this region is by the increasingly numerous half-day and full-day excursion buses that take advantage of the new toll roads and scenic parkways. Fares are in the region of ¥1000 to ¥2000 and you obviously cannot get lost or confused if, for example, you ride out from Chino City on the new Tateshina Plateau Toll Road, spend several hours enjoying the sweeping views, then return to your point of origin.

By train. Rail transportation through the region is adequate if not speedy, and there are a number of private lines in addition to the JNR services.

The rail links between the major towns in the region are described under "How to Get There," above. In addition, the Hokuriku Honsen (Hokuriku trunk line) provides the best link between the cities of Kanazawa, Toyama, and Niigata. From Kanazawa to Niigata takes a little over 4 hours.

By car. Automobiles may be hired in major centers such as Kanazawa and Niigata, and also in Karuizawa.

By boat. The channel between Niigata and Sado Island is crossed by Boeing jetfoils, which take 55 minutes. The ferry, however, which takes 2½ hours, perhaps puts one in a better frame of mind to appreciate the island's slow-paced charm. In the depth of winter, between January and March, the channel is very rough and the island is often cut off.

The most varied menu of transportation is provided by the spectacular **Tateyama-Kurobe Alpine Route.** This is reached by traveling from Matsumoto to Shinano-Omachi by JNR's Oito Line (journey time: 1 hour). From there the trip involves the following modes of transport: Bus (x 2), cable car (x 2), trolley bus, bus, cable car, and finally train to Toyama. The whole route is described in detail in a Tourist Information Center leaflet.

The **Noto Peninsula** is best explored by bus, though there is also a limited train service.

TOURIST INFORMATION. Before you set off. The foreigner-oriented Tourist Information Center, which has branches at Narita Airport, near Yurakucho Station in central Tokyo, and Kyoto, is the best source of English language information about the area. In particular, they stock a number of useful "mini-guides," prepared by TIC staff, which treat places of special interest reliably and in some detail. Mini-guides of relevance to this area are: *Karuizawa Kogen, Matsumoto and Kamikochi, Takayama and Vicinity, Kanazawa and Noto Peninsula.*

The TIC people are always careful to point out that they are not travel agents and that it is not their job to help with hotel bookings, etc., but if they are not too busy they are often good enough to lend a hand, if solicited politely (or desperately).

The other source of information in Tokyo is the building close to Tokyo Station that houses the tourist offices of many of the nation's prefectures. Little used by foreign tourists, these offices often contain elaborate displays of characteristic craft and industrial products of the prefecture in question, as well as a great deal of information. Most of the information is of course in Japanese, but almost invariably there turns out to be at least one colorful pamphlet in English (of a sort).

The area covered in this chapter is divided into Nagano, Gifu, Ishikawa, Toyama, and Niigata prefectures, and the offices of all these prefectures are located in a building just outside the north exit of Tokyo Station, on the Yaesu side. Leaving the station building, it's the first building on the left: Kokusai Kanko Kaikan, by name.

These are the phone numbers of the prefectural offices: Nagano Prefecture: 03–214–5651. Gifu Prefecture: 03–231–1775. Ishikawa Prefecture: 03–231–4030. Toyama Prefecture: 03–231–5032. Niigata Prefecture: 03–215–4618.

When You Get There. All large towns and other places of interest to tourists (in particular Japanese tourists) that are served by rail have their own *Kanko Annaijo* or Tourist Information Office, which is usually very close to the main exit of the station. Staff at the larger offices, and at those where foreign tourists are relatively numerous, make an effort to speak English, and may well have maps and other literature in English too. But even if their linguistic skills are limited they can often offer invaluable help with booking hotel rooms and the other problems associated with orienting yourself in your destination.

One last tip: If you plan to spend time in Kanazawa, Ruth Stevens, an American who lived in the city for several years, has written an invaluable guide that tells you everything you could possibly want to know. It's entitled *Kanazawa: the Other Side of Japan* and is published by the Society to Introduce Kanazawa to the World, at the Kanazawa Chamber of Commerce, 9-13 Oyamacho, Kanazawa; 0762–63–1151. The book is available at major hotel bookstores and English-language book chains.

 SEASONAL EVENTS AND FESTIVALS. Japanese festivals do not invariably take place on the same date year after year. Some are scheduled according to the old lunar calendar. Some occur on a particular Saturday or Sunday of a particular month. Always check, either with the TIC or with the relevant prefectural association, before making a special expedition to see a festival.

January. On the 14th is the *Snow Festival of Niino*, Niino, Anan-cho, Shimoina-gun, Nagano Pref. A sacred ritual at the town's Izu Shrine in honor of the snow, which is considered, curiously, the symbol of a year of good harvest. Purification rites, a procession, and dances, culminating at 1:00 A.M. in the lighting of great torches and the performance of other rituals, which go until early morning. Access: JNR Iida line to Nukuta Stn., then bus.

The *Fire Festival of Nozawa Spa* takes place on the 15th at Nozawa-onsenmura, Shimotakai-gun, Nagano Pref. Nozawa is known for its abundant hot springs, its ski slopes, its local specialty (pickled *nozawa* greens)—and this spectacular fire festival. It is a traditional ritual for warding off evil spirits. Men born under the year's symbol and aged either 25 or 42 (both ages that are considered unlucky) build a scaffold some 15 meters high. New Year's decorations and lanterns are stacked on it, then, at about 8:00 P.M., a large crowd of villagers throws lighted torches toward the scaffold, while the Men of the Year try to defend it. Not as dangerous as it sounds. The fire from the burning scaffold lights up the winter sky. Access: JNR Liyama line to Togari Stn., then bus.

March. On the Sunday nearest the 15th is the *Nenbutsu Odori Dance*, Saku City, Nagano Pref. A Buddhist dance reputedly over 700 years old. Access: JNR Koumi line to Nakagomi Stn.

JAPAN

April. On the second Saturday and Sunday is the *Toyama Spring Festival,* Toyama City, Toyama Pref. A cheerful modern-sounding festival, which mingles a grabbag of fun events under the city's blossoming cherry trees. There's a masquerade contest, a brass band parade, and, most intriguing of the lot, the "All-Japan Chindonya Contest," in which professional musical sandwichmen from all over the country compete with each other. The sandwichmen, a hold-over from the Meiji Period, dress in garish costumes or semitraditional garb and play trumpets, drums, etc., while publicizing local businesses. Access: JNR Hokuriku trunk line to Toyama Stn.

The *Takayama Festival,* Takayama City, Gifu Pref., takes place on the 14th–15th. This is the first of two grand annual festivals in Takayama (the second is in October). This spring event is the *Sanno Festival,* featuring a street procession of 12 of the city's magnificent, gorgeously decorated and ancient festival floats. Lion dancers, drummers, and parishioners dressed in old ceremonial dress and headgear add atmosphere. Access: JNR Takayama trunk line to Takayama.

From the 19th–20th is *Okoshi Daiko,* Furukawa-cho, Yoshiki-gun, Gifu Pref. Furukawa is a mountain village not far from Takayama, and sharing some of that city's antique charm.The dramatic Okoshi Daiko event takes place on the eve of the Furukawa Festival proper, which marks the coming of spring to the village. A scaffold of logs latticed together is constructed. A large drum is placed on top of it and two young men sit on the drum, straddling it, and beat it with drumsticks more than a meter long. The great scaffold is then lifted by more than a hundred young men. Preceded by a bearer holding a large paper lantern, the procession parades through the streets carrying the drum scaffold till another group of young men, carrying drums, charges at the scaffold. The struggle between the two sides continues till daybreak. When the sun rises, gorgeous floats are brought out, and the main festival begins. Access: JNR Takayama trunk line to Hida-Furukawa Stn.

From late April–May 5 is the *Tonami Tulip Fair,* Tonami City, Toyama Pref. Tulips are produced in great number in Toyama Pref. and this festival celebrates them with a Miss Tulip contest and other bright modern events. Access: JNR Johana line to Tonami.

In April and May once every 7 years (1987, 1994 . . .) is the *Gokaicho Ceremony,* Zenkoji Temple, Nagano City, Nagano Pref. Zenkoji, Nagano's massive temple, some 1,300 years old, permits worshippers to see the temple's sacred image only once every 7 years. And even then it's not the real thing but a substitute. This does not deter the many thousands of worshippers who pour into the city. Access: JNR Shinetsu line to Nagano Stn.

May. The *Yotaka Festival,* Fukuno-machi, Higashi-Tonami-gun, Toyama Pref. takes place from the 1st–2nd. When the Fukuno Shimmei Shrine building was completed in 1652, a duplicate of the image of the Sun Goddess enshrined in the Grand Ise Shrine, the most important in Japan, was brought to the town. Because the sacred spirit arrived at the town very late at night, the townspeople welcomed it with lanterns in their hands. That's the origin of the Yotaka Festival. During the festival, giant paper-covered floats, illuminated inside and shaped like portable shrines, boats, castles, flowers, and birds, are pulled through the streets by the local youth singing the gallant Yotaka Bushi tune to the accompaniment of bamboo flutes and drums. This is a gorgeous and gallant festival, which is often compared to the Nebuta Matsuri in Aomori, northern Japan. Access: JNR Johana line to Fukuno Stn.

On the 1st is *Takaoka Mikurumayama Festival,* Takaoka City, Toyama Pref. Seven beautiful floats, reputedly well over 300 years old, are the focus of Takaoka's spring festival. Access: JNR Hokuriku trunk line to Takaoka Stn.

From the 13th–15th is *Seihaku-sai Festival,* Nanao City, Ishikawa Pref. Originally a rice-planting festival in which prayers were offered for a good crop, this has developed into a lavish demonstration of floats. The three that provide the climax to the festival are over 15 meters high, weigh 20 tons, and move on wheels 2 meters in diameter. The floats are as tall as a two-story house. Nearly lifesize dolls stand in kabuki-like tableaux on the upper story, while the floats move slowly forward, swaying from side to side, to the accompaniment of gongs, drums, and firemen's chants. Something to see! Access: JNR Nanao line to Nanao.

Otabi Matsuri Festival, Komatsu City, Ishikawa Pref. takes place from the 13th–16th. This is the "traveling" festival, and true to its name it wanders through the whole city, involving everyone. Houses of prominent parishioners become a temporary lodging of the god by turns, and prayers are offered to the god at each of these homes. The festival is also famous for the Kabuki dramas performed by children on an exquisitely lacquered and decorated portable shrine-like stage set up in the middle of the street. Access: JNR Hokuriku trunk line to Komatsu Stn.

June. At the beginning of June, the *Weston Festival,* takes place at Kamiko-chi, Northern Alps. Observed in memory of the Rev. W. Weston, who introduced mountaineering into Japan and named these peaks the Japan Alps, it marks the official opening of the climbing season. Access: Matsumoto Electric Railway from Matsumoto to Shin-Simashima, then bus.

Hyakuman-goku Festival, Kanazawa City, Ishikawa Pref., runs from the 13th–15th. Kanazawa was ruled for centuries by the Maeda clan, and this festival commemorates the beginning of that epoch. Hyakuman-goku means "a million *koku* of rice," and as rice was the currency as well as the staple food, a loose translation might be the Billion Dollar Festival; under the Maedas, Kanazawa prospered. Main feature of the festival is a costume procession of the feudal lord, vassals, firemen, lion dancers, and footmen through the city's streets. Access: JNR Hokuriku trunk line to Kanazawa Stn.

July. On the Sunday nearest the 15th is the *Bessho-no-take no Nobori,* in Ueda City, Nagano Pref. In 1504 farmers suffering from a long drought raised banners to petition the deity of Mt. Ogami to bring them rain. In commemoration of the event, people of the town still carry gorgeous banners to the top of the mountain before dawn on this day. Access: JNR Shinetsu line to Ueda Stn.

Yabusame takes place on the 17th at Nyakuichioji Shrine, Omachi City, Nagano Pref. Yabusame is archery on horseback. Young boys ride through the town in traditional samurai costume, complete with swords, then fire off their arrows in the shrine precincts. Access: JNR Oito line to Shinano-Omachi Stn.

From July 31–August 1 is the *Gojinjo Drums Festival,* Wajima City, Ishikawa City. Wearing the grotesque masks of old men and specters, and shaking their shaggy seaweed wigs, the local fishermen beat great drums to commemorate the successful defense of their region by their ancestors against the depredations of a powerful warlord. There are also demonstrations from early spring to late fall, every Sat. night. Access: JNR Nanao line to Wajima Stn.

August. On the 1st is the *Suwa Shrine Festival,* Suwa, Nagano Pref. Hundreds of young men tow a portable shrine installed in a gaily decorated and garlanded boat from shrine to shrine along Lake Suwa. Access: JNR Chuo line to Kami-Suwa Stn.

Tatemon Festival, Uozu City, Toyama Pref., runs from the 7th–8th. The Tatemon are great poles, about 15 meters high, from each of which hang more than 80 lanterns in the shape of a sail. The festival is to pray for a big catch and the safety of the fishermen at sea. Young men lug the great poles around the streets to the music of bamboo flutes and drums. Access: JNR Hokuriku trunk line to Uozu Stn.

Kiso Bon Odori, Kiso-Fukushima, Nagano Pref. On the 15th a typical August *bon* dance is performed in every village in the Kiso valley, the center of which is Kiso-Fukushima. Access: JNR Chuo line to Kiso-Fukushima.

Sado Okesa, Aikawa, Sado Island, Niigata Pref. The townspeople turn out on the 15th to sing and dance the famously melancholy ballads and folk dances unique to Sado Island, place of exile in the old days. Access: ferry or jetfoil from Niigata City.

September. *Owara Kaze-no-bon Festival* at Yatsuo, Yatsuo-machi, Nei-gun, Toyama Pref. Yatsuo, town of slopes, is immersed in Owara Dance frenzy for 3 days from September 1, around which time a typhoon is usually expected. Etchu Owara Bushi is a folk tune sung by spinning girls generation after generation for 300 years. Day in and day out, men in happi coats, vests, and tight-fitting trousers, and women in colorful crude silk crepe kimono dance through the streets to the music of Chinese fiddle, drum, and shamisen. Access: JNR Takayama line to Etchu Yatsuo Stn.

From the 15th–16th is the *Mugiya Festival,* Johana-machi, Higashi-tonami-gun, Toyama Pref. It is said that remnants of the Taira Clan, defeated by the rival Minamoto Clan in the late 12th century, took up residence deep in the Gokayama mountains where they sang and danced as they tilled the land, a totally new activity for these former samurai. On the festival day, the whole town, centering on Zentoku-ji Temple, is engulfed by wave on wave of people executing this stylish and dignified dance in the formal costume of the Taira. Access: JNR Johana line to Johana Stn.

Yamanaka Bushi Festival, Yamanaka-machi, Enuma-gun, Ishikawa Pref., from the 22nd–24th. Lines of dancers and musicians weave through the town, dressed in summer kimono. Access: Hokutetsu Bus to Yamanaka Onsen. Take the bus from Kaga Onsen Stn. on Hokuriku trunk line.

October. *Torch Festival of Asama Spa,* Asama Onsen, Matsumoto City, Nagano Pref. On the 3rd many torches, gigantic ones among them, are lit at Misa Shrine's sacred flame and paraded round the streets. The streets of the spa are bright with the fire, shrouded in smoke, At dawn the torches are thrown into the river and the festival comes to an end. The festival is an offertory ritual to the guardian deity of Asama Spa. Access: JNR Shinoi line to Matsumoto Stn., then bus.

Autumn festival (*Hachiman Matsuri*) in Takayama City, Gifu Pref., from the 9th–10th. See description of Sanno Festival (April).

TOURS. Kanazawa and other places in "the back of Japan" were included in foreigner-oriented package tours for the first time in 1982. Japan Travel Bureau's 5-day tour, which is guided in English, starts from Tokyo every Tuesday between April and November and visits Matsumoto, Takayama, Kanazawa, and the Noto Peninsula on the way to Kyoto. A leaflet is available from offices of JTB or from a Tourist Information Center.

Scheduled daily conducted bus tours operate from the major towns in the area and details are available at the Tourist Information Office located in or near the station. This offers a cheap and rapid way of becoming familiar with a given area, but the guiding will always be in Japanese, which is frustrating.

PARKS. Kenrokuen, in the center of Kanazawa City, is one of the three most beautiful landscaped gardens in Japan. See essay above for further details. The park is open 6:30 A.M. to 6:00 P.M. except from November to March, when it is open 8:00 A.M. to 4:30 P.M. Entrance fee is ¥150.

AMUSEMENT CENTER. Notojima Marine Park on Notojima Island just off the Noto Peninsula. The park incorporates large aquaria, a dolphin pool, fishing facilities, a monorail, tennis courts, and a race track for kids. Notojima can be reached by the great bridge from Wakura Onsen. Open 9:00 A.M.–5:00 P.M., April–Oct.; 9:00 A.M.–4:00 P.M., Nov.–March. Admission: Summer—Adults, ¥800; children ¥200. Winter—Adults ¥600; children ¥100. Separate admission for fishing center: Adults ¥700; children ¥50.

PARTICIPANT SPORTS. **Skiing** is probably the most popular sport in this region. Japan is the major winter sports vacationland of Asia. Many major skiing resorts are well equipped with hotels, *ryokan,* and all the usual skiing apparatus, plus hot spring baths to relax in at the end of the day. The majority of Japan's best resorts are in the Japan Alps, with others in the Tohoku district (extreme north of the main island) and Hokkaido. Depending on how you want to lodge, the resorts can be impressively cheap or startlingly expensive. Cheapest accommodation is a bunk bed in a ski lodge, which can cost less than ¥3,000 per night. Village *minshuku*—the Japanese bed and breakfast—are a little more expensive. Rental equipment is available everywhere, but sizes are Japanese, so it may be difficult to find boots to fit. The length of the season varies from place to place. It is usually December through March but in some places it goes on to May.

Among the most popular resorts are Shiga Heights and its sister slopes at Sun Valley; and Ishiuchi and Yuzawa, which are nicknamed "Skiing Ginza" to convey their fashionable and expensive appeal. Ishiuchi claims to be Japan's biggest ski resort. Naeba is where the World Ski Championships of 1973 were held, and where the Japanese Crown Prince takes his family every year.

The Tourist Information Center in Yurakucho, Tokyo (1st. floor Kotari Building, Hibiya; 03–502–1461), issues up-to-date listings every year in late November, giving details of transportation, season, facilities, accommodation, and special local events. At weekends and holidays, resorts are very crowded and people spend a great deal more time standing in line than skiing. In particular the New Year holiday period is to be avoided at all costs. The Japanese passion for skiing increases year by year. JNR operates hundreds of special trains, which are always packed. The best chance of getting a seat on one is to book through an agency.

There are five **skating** rinks in Karuizawa: Karuizawa Skate Center (open late Nov.–late Mar.); Karuizawa Ekimae Rink (late Dec.–early Mar.); Lake Shiozawa Rink (late Dec.–early Mar.); Hoshino Spa Rink (late Dec.–late Feb.); and Shiotsubo Spa Rink (mid Dec.–early Mar.).

Japan is great for **golf**—at least, for the wealthy. Karuizawa is the best place in the Alps region to play. Among the better public courses are: Minami-Karuizawa Golf Course, 9 holes and 18 holes, 6,545 yards; Asama Golf Course, 18 holes in a beautiful course opened in 1962; and the Saian Golf Course, 18 holes, 7,100 yards.

Mountaineers will like several of the higher peaks, especially Shirouma, Tateyama, and Ontake. You can also walk up the 8,389-foot Mt. Asama outside

Karuizawa (a live volcano), or climb the rather difficult Mt. Shirane (10,472 feet and also active).

Cycles may be rented, usually by the train stations, at Karuizawa, Takayama, and Kanazawa.

 SPECTATOR SPORTS. The region's multitudinous festivals are without doubt the best spectator sports on offer. One festival, not listed above, which comes closer to the Western idea of a spectator sport is the outdoor **sumo** performed once a year at Hakui, Noto Peninsula, Ishikawa Prefecture. Judges and spectators alike sit crosslegged around the improvised circular ring while the local heavyweights test their skills. The bouts begin at 8:00 P.M. when a brazier is lighted. Date: September 25. Access: 10 min. on foot from JNR Hakui Stn.

 HISTORICAL SITES. Nagano City. *Zenkoji Temple.* In the old days Zenkoji was the name of the city as well as the temple. This gives some idea of the temple's central importance in the city's life. It occupies a huge site (56,000 square meters) at the north end of the city, about 2 kms from Nagano Stn, 10 min. by bus. The temple is administered by two groups of priests and priestesses. The regular morning service, held about half an hour after dawn and attended by hundreds of worshippers, is quite an experience. The temple was founded in 642. The present main hall dates from 1707.

Matsumoto. *Matsumoto Jo* (Matsumoto Castle). Built in 1504, this is one of the best-preserved castles in the country; the donjon is a National Treasure. Fine Alpine views to be had from the upper floors, but nothing but the old timbers to be seen inside. 10–15 min. walk from Matsumoto Stn. Open daily 8:30 A.M. to 5:00 P.M. Admission ¥200. The *Folklore Museum* opposite makes up for the emptiness of the donjon. On display are farming tools, Star Festival dolls, and about 50,000 other items pertaining to the history and folklore of the region. Open daily 9:00 A.M. to 6:30 P.M., admission ¥150.

Takayama. *Takayama Jinya Manor House.* 1816 reconstruction of the manor house from which Takayama was ruled throughout the feudal period. A great rarity, for although many earlier temples and shrines survive in Japan, there are few buildings that bear witness, as this does, to the way the country was administered. There's a beautiful old garden at the back and the morning market is held at the front. Open from 8:45 A.M. to 5:00 P.M. (Apr. to Oct.) and 8:45 A.M. to 4:30 P.M. (Nov. to Mar.). Closed Wednesdays and Dec. 27 to Jan. 4. Admission ¥250 for adults. 10 min. from Takayama Stn. by taxi.

Yoshijima Family Home. Built in 1908, this is one of the most magnificent surviving traditional townhouses in the country. The house of a wealthy merchant. Fifteen minutes' walk from the station. Open daily from 9:00 A.M. to 5:00 P.M. (Mar.–Nov.), and from 9:00 A.M. to 4:30 P.M. (Dec. to Feb.); admission ¥200 for adults.

Hida-no-Sato Village. One of Japan's largest and best reservations of old buildings, with well over a dozen old country cottages, including several of the huge multistory thatched *gassho-zukuri* (A-frame) farmhouses for which the mountain villages around Takayama are renowned. Demonstrations of wood carving and lacquerwork take place in craft workshops. 10 min. from Takayama Stn. by taxi. Open 8:30 A.M. to 5:00 P.M. throughout the year, except Dec. 30 to Jan. 2. Admission ¥300 for adults.

Kanazawa. *Seisonkaku Villa.* In the southeast corner of Kenrokuen Park, this lovely villa was built for the mother of one of the ruling Maedas in 1863. Fine collection of art objects, amazingly bold interior design upstairs, serene garden. Open 8:30 to 4:30 except Wednesdays. 10 min. by taxi from Kanazawa Stn. Admission ¥400—and well worth it.

Kanazawa Castle. The donjon was destroyed by fire in 1881 but a long dwelling house, previously home for the castle's samurai, and a famous gate survive. 10 min. by taxi from Kanazawa Stn.

Nagamachi Samurai Houses. A fascinating and unique section of authentic samurai houses with their heavy mud outer walls. This is one of the few such concentration of samurai houses that survives in Japan. 5 min. on foot from Korimbo bus stop, which is 10 min. by taxi from Kanazawa Stn.

Ninja-dera ("Temple of the Secret Agents"; real name: *Myoryuji Temple*). Famous for its incredible number and variety of assailant-foiling tricks and devices. Open 9:00 A.M. to 4:00 P.M., but reservations necessary; 0762–41–2877. Closed on 1st and 13th of every month. Admission ¥400. 15 min. by taxi.

Edo Mura Village. A reservation of old houses outside the city, including a samurai mansion, farmhouses, merchant's shops, and post-town inns. Open 8:00 A.M. to 6:00 P.M., 8:00 A.M. to 5:00 P.M. from November to March. Admission ¥800. 5 min. walk from Yuwaku Spa, 10 kms southeast of the city.

Monzen, Noto Peninsula. *Sojiji Temple.* Former headquarters of the Soto sect of Zen Buddhism. This is an urbane and spacious temple close to Noto's wild west coast.

Sado Island. *Sodayu-ko Gold Mine, Aikawa.* Formerly one of the most productive gold mines in the Orient, the mining was done by the many prisoners exiled to the island. Visitors can tour this mine, which is about 360 years old. Mechanized figures demonstrate how the work was done. Aikawa is in the extreme west of Sado, and is linked to the principle town, Ryotsu, by bus.

 MUSEUMS. Museums of folklore abound in rural Japan, and this area is no exception. But there are a number of more unusual museums as well. **Matsumoto area.** *Matsumoto Folkcraft Museum.* Shimo-Kanai, 15 min. by bus or taxi from Matsumoto Stn. Built 20 years ago by a renowned local folk artist. Collection of local folk products. Open 9 A.M. to 5 P.M., Apr. 1–Nov. 30; closed on Mondays. ¥200 adults; ¥100 children.

Rokuzan Bijutsukan. Rokuzan Ogiwara was one of the first and most accomplished Western-style Japanese sculptors and it so happens that he was born in the town of Hotaka, 30 min. by train from Matsumoto. They call him "the Rodin of the Orient." This art museum, which commemorates him, is a red brick, churchlike structure—very exotic in the heart of Nagano Prefecture. 7 min. walk from Hotake Stn. Open from 9:00 A.M. to 5:00 P.M. (Apr. to Oct.) and 9:00 A.M. to 4:00 P.M. (Nov. to Mar.). Closed on Mondays and the days after national holidays. Admission: ¥300.

Utsukushigahara Plateau Museum. An open-air sculpture museum commanding panoramic views of the Northern Alps. One hour 40 min. by bus from Matsumoto Stn. Open 9 A.M. to 5 P.M. Admission ¥600.

Ukiyo-e Art Museum. Designed by celebrated architect Kazuo Shinohara, it houses the Sakai collection of Edo Period woodblock prints. A taxi ride from Matsumoto Stn. Open 10 A.M. to 5 P.M. Admission ¥500.

Takayama. *Folk Toy Museum.* Over 2,000 Japanese toys, dating from the Edo Period to the present. Open 8:30 A.M. to 5:00 P.M., except Dec. 31–Jan. 1. Admission ¥200 for adults.

Takayama Yatai Kaikan Hall. Takayama's spring and autumn festivals are famous for their magnificent floats, and 11 of them are on display in this hall, along with figures representing people in the festival. If you can't be in Takaya-

328 JAPAN

ma for the festival, this is the next best thing. Open from 8:30 A.M. to 5:00 P.M. (Mar. to Nov.) and from 9:00 A.M. to 4:30 P.M. (Dec. to Feb.). Admission: ¥ 380 for adults.

Kanazawa. *Ishikawa Prefectural Art Museum.* 0762-31-7580. The best permanent collection of Kutani pottery, dyed fabrics, old Japanese-style paintings, and other artistic products of Kanazawa. Open 9:00 A.M. to 4:30 P.M. daily, except Dec. 29 to Jan. 3, and when exhibitions are changing. Admission: ¥ 300 to ¥ 1000. Near Seisonkaku Villa at Kenrokuen Park.

Honda Museum. The Honda family were chief retainers of the Maedas, Kanazawa's enlightened feudal rulers. This museum has art objects, armor, and household objects of the Hondas. Open 9:00 A.M. to 5:00 P.M., closed on Thursdays. Admission: ¥ 500. 20 min. by taxi from Kanazawa Stn.

Ishikawa Prefectural Museum of Handiwork. On the third floor craftspeople demonstrate local skills: the making of Kaga-yuzen silk fabrics, Kutani pottery, Wajima lacquer ware, and gold and silver leaf work. Open 9:00 A.M. to 6:00 P.M. (10:00 A.M. to 5:00 P.M., Nov. 21 to Mar. 20), closed on Thursdays. Admission to the craft center: ¥ 200. Located beside Kenrokuen Park.

 PERFORMING ARTS. This region is strong on festivals, weak on more literary dramatic forms. For kabuki, for example, you must re-cross the mountains. Kanazawa, however, undoubtedly the most cultured corner of the region, has a fine Noh theater. The modern (1972) building put up by the prefecture contains an entirely traditional Noh stage facing a plush modern auditorium. A full-scale professional production of a Noh play is given on the first Sunday of every month, but classical dance and music, either in rehearsal or in actual performance, can be enjoyed here almost every day. The theater is south of Kenrokuen Park. For information: Ishikawa Kenritsu Nohgaku Bunkakaiken, 18-3, 4-chome, Ishibiki, Kanazawa-shi 920; 0762-64-2598.

 SHOPPING. Don't come to this region for the department stores. Concentrate your shopping on the various local specialties—craft products. To list shops would be redundant, as the crafts products of a given area are always stocked by a number of shops in the vicinity. The following are among the products to look out for on your travels in this region:

Nagano Prefecture. *Wasabi,* so-called "Japanese horseradish," delicious with all sorts of unlikely things; *Shinshu soba,* locally produced buckwheat noodles.

Takayama. Local sake (*jizake*); local miso; textiles, wallets, purses, etc., covered with local textiles, antiques, not very old but often fun.

Kanazawa. *Kutani* pottery, items carved from paulownia wood, gold and silver leaf products, dolls, Wajima lacquerware, Kaga-yuzen silk fabrics.

 DINING OUT. There is only one major international hotel in this region (Kanazawa Holiday Inn), so dining out usually means either going native or going the native idea of Western—and the former is usually much the best bet. For the cautious, the many thriving local hotels provide meals that are dependable. Restaurant eating is best in the major towns such as Matsumoto, Takayama, and Kanazawa—especially Kanazawa.

Kanazawa is noted for its local *kaga* cuisine, which includes the usual delicate array of little dishes containing, among other things, raw shrimp and baked sea bream. A recommended place for kaga cuisine is *Zeniya;* (0762) 33-3331. Dinner costs from ¥ 5,000 up. Another restaurant serving kaga ryori is *Otomo-*

ro, one of the most charmingly traditional restaurants in the city. Dinner from ¥4,000 up, reservations a must; (0762) 21–0305.

Wherever you go in the region, though, the surest way to sample the best of the local cuisine is simply to put up at a high-quality *ryokan.* Unless you are unlucky the food will be fresh, full of local treats, and fabulous. This is a far simpler and more fruitful way to sample the local food than traipsing the streets with a list of restaurants in hand. Use the guide to *ryokan* and hotels above.

 NIGHT LIFE. A thriving nightlife exists in towns such as Takayama and Kanazawa, and in some cases it has been going on for centuries. But for the foreign visitor, it is virgin territory. We can offer no clear advice other than to take your courage in both hands. A world of bizarre experiences awaits the traveler bold enough to brush his way through the *noren* curtains—tiny hostess bars with deafeningly loud live rock music and pneumatic hostesses, *karaoke* palaces where the customers take turns crooning into a microphone on a small stage to prerecorded backing, traditional little *nomiya* (bars) where the local politicians gather after hours and the hot sake is accompanied by little dishes of raw fish intestine. It's all good material for a novel, or at least a few lively postcards.

NAGOYA AND ISE-SHIMA

by
PETER POPHAM

Nagoya, almost midway between Tokyo and Kyoto, is a huge city of huge importance that compensates for its only modest charms by giving visitors a warm and eager welcome. And as the focus of a highly developed transportation network, it offers convenient access to a number of the traditional and historical attractions that must be high on any visitor's list of places to see.

Look at a map of Japan and you will notice that Nagoya is almost slap bang in the middle. Nagoya is central in another sense, too. The heart of economic activity of Japan is the *Tokaido,* the "Eastern Sea Road," which runs from Tokyo in the northeast to Hiroshima in the southwest. Though formally divided into cities, this entire length of coast, nearly 900 kilometers from end to end, forms virtually a single, extraordinarily elongated megalopolis—one of the most formidable concentrations of human, industrial, and economic energy in the world. In the middle of it is Nagoya, situated at the center of the vast Nobi Plain, home for 6 million people.

Yet within an hour or two of the city center by train or bus are a number of places that remind one, in very different ways, of the age and richness of Japan's culture: serene and noble shrines; rivers where birds are used to catch fish for men to eat; and centers of religious training and sword-smithing.

EXPLORING NAGOYA AND ISE-SHIMA

But let's start in the city itself. Nagoya, with a population of more than 2 million people, is a great deal older than it looks, and though as a destination it ranks quite a ways behind Tokyo and Kyoto, it has pleasures and distinctions of its own.

All three of the great feudal warlords who worked toward the unification of Japan in the 16th century came from this area. The third, Shogun Ieyasu Tokugawa, established Nagoya Castle in 1610 for his ninth son, and this date is accepted as the beginning of the city's history. As elsewhere in Japan, craft industries and pleasure quarters grew up in the shadow of the castle walls. It wasn't until the beginning of the present century, however, with the construction of the Port of Nagoya, that the city really began to expand with a vengeance. During the thirties Nagoya became a center of the aircraft and munitions industries, and as a consequence, it was almost completely flattened by bombs in 1945.

The city's postwar development has been rather special, in that it is one of the very few examples in Japan of systematic and successful city planning. The new city was built on wide, straight roads that intersect roughly at right angles. The fast, remarkably comfortable subway (very likely the only one in the world with curtains) takes the course of the major roads, and buses thread the city like the stitching on a patchwork quilt. It's almost boringly easy to find your way about.

The centerpiece of the city's plan is 100 meter-wide Hisaya-Odori Boulevard, known locally as "Park Way," which runs broad and straight from the Prefectural Government Building in the north to Yabacho in the south, a distance of more than 1.5 kilometers. Nagoya's 180-meter-high Television Tower is located on the boulevard, and from the observation platform some two thirds of the way up, there are grand views of the city itself, of the Japan Alps to the north, and Ise Bay to the southwest.

Sakae, plum in the middle of the boulevard, is the section of town where it all happens, such as it is. Here are all the city's major department stores, restaurants, cabaret bars, and cinemas.

North of Hisaya-Odori Boulevard and slightly to the west is Nagoya Castle, originally built more than three centuries ago by Ieyasu Tokugawa. Destroyed in the war, it was rebuilt in 1959 in ferroconcrete, and unlike, say, Osaka Castle, which is apparently much smaller than it should be, Nagoya Castle is as faithful to the original as a retainer to his feudal lord. Its concrete construction is perhaps a little more obvious than we might wish, but the lifts will be used gratefully by anyone who has toiled up the endless steps of more authentic donjons, and the displays of weapons and works of art that fill the rooms are worth lingering over. The explanatory booklet that comes with your ticket of admission is an excellent read.

On the fourth floor of the castle are several glass cases full of exquisite paper dolls. They represent the people who take part in the city's colorful October festival, highlighted by a historical procession. In the same month, the castle grounds are the site of a chrysanthemum show, the chief feature of which is a series of tableaux with lifesize dolls dressed in costumes made of chrysanthemums.

As large billboards inform those who arrive in the city by train, Nagoya is the home of Noritake china. Porcelain was an Oriental invention but its manufacture was modernized by the industrializing Europeans. After the Meiji Restoration of 1868 set Japan racing off toward the 20th century, Noritake's founders adopted the new technology. They are now the world's largest manufacturers of porcelain.

Five minutes from Nagoya Station is Noritake's model factory, where the pick of the company's artisans make the top-of-the-line "Diamond Collection" chinaware. Small, quiet, humane, the factory shows capitalism wearing its most avuncular smile. It makes an interesting tour. The tourist information people in the station can help arrange it for you.

Way over to the east of downtown is the Tokugawa Art Museum, which was built on the site of an ancient mansion of the Tokugawas, the family that ruled Japan, at least in name, during the 250-plus years preceding the Meiji Restoration. The museum contains some 7,000 works of art, historical relics, and heirlooms belonging to the family. Overlooking this part of the city is Kakuozan hill, on which stands Nittaiji Temple, built in 1904 as a present from the King of Siam.

Atsuta Shrine, south of the city center, halfway to the port, is said to have been founded in the 3rd century. It's one of the oldest and most sacred shinto shrines in Japan, though the buildings were rebuilt in 1955, and it is the repository of the sacred sword, which is one of the three emblems of the emperor. The other two are the mirror (kept in the inner shrine at Ise, see below) and jewels (in the Imperial Palace in Tokyo).

A trip a little farther south to Nagoya Port (Nagoya-ko) will bring you back to earth. It's the third largest port in Japan, after Yokohama and Kobe, and sees more than 5,000 billion yen's worth of goods flow in and out in the course of a year. In 1983, for example, 1,487,776 automobiles floated *out*.

But traditional Japan calls. Two directions offer the most interesting opportunities for exploring, north and southwest. Let's go north first.

Parasols and Cormorants

Gifu is an old but not terribly scenic city (blame the bombs), forty minutes to the north of Nagoya by train. It does, however, boast two interesting traditional industries: paper lanterns (*chochin*) and paper umbrellas (*kasa*). While the latter are mostly made in small workshops, lanterns are made in factories, and at least one factory, Ozeki, allows visitors to watch this intriguing process. Ozeki's factory is located in Oguma-cho, not far from Kinkazan ("Silver Mountain"), the peak that looms over the city. The old castle that stood on Kinkazan was destroyed in an earthquake in 1891, but a new one, which houses a

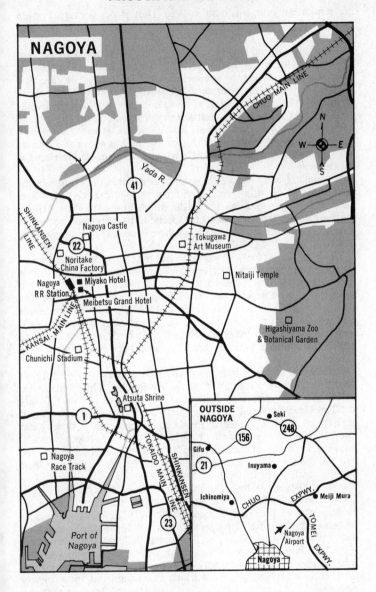

NAGOYA

CHUO MAIN LINE

Yada R.

41

Nagoya Castle

22

Tokugawa
Art Museum

Noritake
China Factory

Miyako Hotel

Nagoya
RR Station

Nitaiji Temple

Meibetsu Grand Hotel

SHINKANSEN LINE

KANSAI MAIN LINE

Higashiyama Zoo
& Botanical Garden

Chunichi Stadium

Atsuta Shrine

1

Nagoya
Race Track

TOKAIDO MAIN LINE

SHINKANSEN LINE

23

Port of
Nagoya

OUTSIDE
NAGOYA

Seki

248

156

Gifu

21

Inuyama

Ichinomiya

CHUO

EXPWY.

Meiji Mura

TOMEI EXPWY.

Nagoya
Airport

Nagoya

prefectural museum, was built in 1956. Though not perhaps worth a special visit, Kinkazan looks beautiful at night when it is illuminated by floodllights.

But what Gifu and nearby Inuyama ("Dog Mountain") are perhaps most famous for is the curious sport of cormorant fishing (*ukai*), which takes place here during the summer months. The beaky birds are used to catch delicious *ayu* (river smelt or sweetfish) from the local rivers on moonless summer nights. It's a spectator sport in which the spectators, too, take to the water—suitably supplied with strong drink. Like so many of those Japanese rituals that sound poetic and ethereal at a distance of several thousand miles, *ukai,* we find, is above all a pretext for a picturesque booze-up—and what could be nicer? Here's what happens:

A couple of hours before the fishing commences the visitors board their craft and eat, drink, and set off fireworks. During this time a boat filled with singing and dancing geisha drifts among the throng (there are more than 130 covered boats for spectators). Other small boats pass to and fro selling food and drink, so there is no fear of running short of anything.

Spectators have plenty of warning when the cormorant boats appear, for the word runs ahead of them downstream and soon their bright flares are visible. The flares are lit to attract fish, and consist of wood set alight in wire baskets suspended from poles over the water. The birds, several to a boat, are on leads, and the ring around their necks prevents them from swallowing all but the smallest fish. With deft, swift movements the fishermen control their birds, pulling each one inboard as it makes a catch, then slipping it back overboard to dive again.

Cormorant fishing at Inuyama (about 30 minutes by Meitetsu railway from Nagoya) takes place on the River Kiso. The 12-kilometer stretch of the river between Imawatari and Inuyama is known fondly as "The Japanese Rhine"—though natives of the real Rhine are not likely to buy this. The general area is pretty, however. It's rocky and forested, and it's one of the best places in Japan for shooting rapids. Imawatari is the most accessible spot to start from, and summer is the best time to do it. Inuyama is also noted as the site of Japan's oldest existing castle, built in 1440.

A short distance to the east of Inuyama is Meiji Mura (Meiji Village). Located on a hillside overlooking a lake, this is a museum of more than 50 buildings of the Meiji Period (1868 to 1912), bearing eloquent witness to the incredible changes that overtook Japan during that first, hectic phase of modernization. Traditional buildings—a kabuki theater, a bathhouse—can be seen alongside early churches and Western-style mansions. Like all such parks it lacks one vital ingredient: inhabitants. It does, however, have a working steam train. And in a country where the life of the average building is slightly shorter than that of a man, parks like this have an important place. Remember to half-close your eyes and people it with teeming, kimono-clad crowds.

A couple of stations south from Meiji Mura on the way back to Nagoya are two famous fertility shrines, one female and one male. Oagata-jinja, the female shrine, is accessible from Gakudan Station;

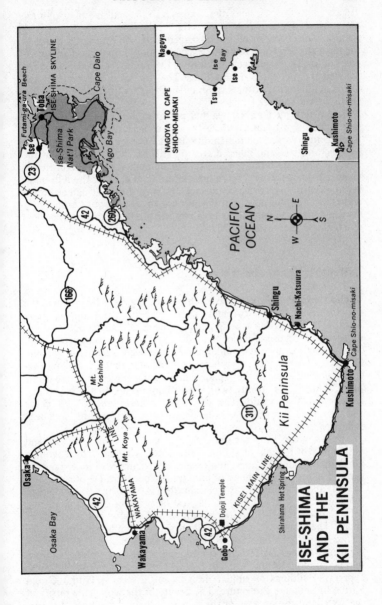

NAGOYA TO CAPE SHIO-NO-MISAKI

Nagoya
Ise Bay
Ise
Tsu
Shingu
Kushimoto
Cape Shio-no-misaki

Futami-ga-ura Beach
ISE-SHIMA SKYLINE
Cape Daio
Toba
Ise
Ise-Shima Nat'l Park
Ago Bay

PACIFIC OCEAN

N
E
W
S

Mt. Yoshino

Shingu
Nachi-Katsuura

Kii Peninsula

Cape Shio-no-misaki

Kushimoto

Mt. Koya

KISEI MAIN LINE

Osaka

WAKAYAMA LINE

Dojoji Temple

Shirahama Hot Spring

Osaka Bay

Wakayama

Gobo

ISE-SHIMA AND THE KII PENINSULA

Tagata-jinja is the name of the next stop to the south, and also of the male shrine, which is right next to the station door. Both shrines have remarkable collections of genital-shaped sacred objects, but the ones at the male shrine are, as might be expected, more imposing. The center-piece of the Tagata-jinja annual festival (March 15), indeed, is a carved wooden phallus three meters long. The festival is a very jolly and drunken affair that attracts thousands of visitors (including some for-eigners) every year.

Before returning to Nagoya and preparing for the trip south, let's take a final flying leap north to the city of Seki, about 15 kilometers from Gifu. It's one of the traditional centers for the production of swords, and this and allied crafts are still practiced by many of the citizens. Demonstrations of the traditional method of manufacture are given six times a year, on the first Saturday of each of the odd-num-bered months, in a corner of the city's Kasuga shrine. It's an elaborate and fascinating business, but if you want to take a sword home for a souvenir, come prepared: the type you will see being made costs some ¥6,000,000 each—about $25,000.

Shinto's Shady Heart

The Shima Peninsula to the southwest of Nagoya is the home of the two shrines of Ise, the two most sacred places of the Shinto religion. They are well worth a visit. When compared with cosmopolitan Bud-dhism, and because of its long-standing and intimate connection with Japanese nationalism and militarism via cults such as emperor worship, Shinto gives some foreign visitors the impression that it is the impene-trably private affair of the Japanese and the Japanese alone. Ise is one place, however (or strictly two), that communicates to all comers and to believers of every faith. The spirituality is almost tangible, and in the shrines' green and spacious grounds even the air seems to have been sanctified.

The two shrines are the Outer (Geku) and the Inner (Naiku), and both are worth your attention. The Outer is devoted to Toyouke-Omikami, goddess of grain and thence of agriculture, and it stands at the end of an avenue about 10 minutes on foot from Ise Station. The Inner is about 15 minutes away by shuttle bus. It enshrines Amaterasu-Omikami, the sun goddess, the highest deity in the Shinto pantheon, divine ancestress of the imperial family, and creator of the islands of Japan. The design of the shrine buildings, startlingly simple and unvar-nished (literally and metaphorically), follows an ancient and supposed-ly purely Japanese pattern, developed long before the arrival of Chinese temple-building techniques. The building material is *hinoki* (Japanese cypress). Buildings of similar design can be seen at Izumo Grand Shrine in Shimane Prefecture. The beauty of the wood, the purity of the style, and the majesty of the groves of huge cedar trees that sur-round them make the shrines of Ise one of the most deeply impressive and wholly Japanese experiences possible in this country. They are completely rebuilt every twenty years; for the 63rd time in 1973, at a cost of some ¥4,500 million.

From Yamada, which is part of the city of Ise, a 10-minute trip from Yamada Ueguchi Station by rail or tramcar will bring you to Futami-ga-ura, a pleasant beach with two rocks that rise out of the sea and are joined by a sacred straw rope. They are called the Wedded Rocks and are taken to represent the male and female creators of Japan. Japanese people like to see the sun rising behind them, a solemn scene replete with patriotic symbolism.

A train journey or a spectacular bus ride over the Ise-shima Skyline toll road from Ise brings you to Toba, a small seaside town famous above all for two things: pearls and pearl divers. Both are to be found on Pearl Island, which is a couple of hundred yards from the train station.

Diving for pearls has been a traditional occupation for the women of the Shima Peninsula for hundreds of years (women's lungs were thought to be stronger than men's). Pearls were, however, rare freaks of nature and consequently very expensive. Around the turn of the century Kokichi Mikimoto began his researches into the problem of how to cultivate pearls artificially, and Pearl Island is a monument to his amazing labors. The whole pearl-making process is painstakingly explained and demonstrated (in English, too), and you may find you'll learn more about pearls than you ever wished to know. However, the splendid diving ladies—*ama*—who demonstrate their skills near the island are a compensation. No longer hunting for pearls, they are still kept busy bringing up the sea vegetables of which the Japanese are so fond. Demonstrations are frequent.

The railway from Toba runs to Kashikojima on Ago Bay, which is now the center of the pearl industry. An alternative route, which will enable you to enjoy the magnificent scenery of this stretch of coast with its dark, jagged rocks and roaring surf, is to take a bus along the coast for at least part of the way. You can get off the train at Ugata and take a bus through Nakiri, where you can see the white lighthouse on Cape Daio and the rough waters that beat against the headland. The village of Wagu is unspoiled and full of the atmosphere of this fascinating coast. On the steep shore the fishing boats are ranged facing the tiny sheltered harbor. The coast between here and Goza is bright in summer with semitropical plants including the curious *hamayu,* which for some reason grows here in profusion. From Goza with its white breakwater reaching out across the green sea you can take a ferry to Kashikojima, across Ago Bay.

Ago Bay is crowded with wooden rafts from which oysters are suspended in the water. These are the big pearl farms where the cultured pearls are being formed in millions of oysters, a process that may take from five to seven years.

At Kashikojima on the shore of Ago Bay is the Cultured Pearl Institute, where visitors may see the process of making cultured pearl demonstrated. Two miles from Ugata on the road and railway linking Kashikojima with Toba is Yokoyama Park, with its observation post overlooking the entire southern part of the Ise-Shima National Park. This view is one of the best in the area.

On to the Kii Peninsula

To travel by rail to the Kii Peninsula you must go back to Taki, five stops up the tracks from Ise-shi in the direction of Nagoya, and transfer to the *Kisei* main line for Shingu and Kushimoto. The latter part of the route follows the coast and offers glorious views of the sea. Shingu lies at the mouth of the river Kumano, famed for the spectacular gorges in its upper reaches. The best way to see these is to take one of the excursion boats. A trip of just under 4 hours will bring you to the high gorge of Dorohatcho. This is the first of three fine gorges that extend for several miles. The tall cliffs are densely covered with vegetation and on a bright day the water is very clear. This is the heart of the Yoshino-Kumano National Park, which extends over the three prefectures of Wakayama, Mie, and Nara. From Shingu you may take a direct bus north through the mountain gorges of this park to Nara. The ride takes about 7 hours.

Nine miles from Shingu is Nachi, of which the chief claim to sight-seeing fame is Nachi-no-taki, the highest waterfall in Japan, with a drop of 430 feet. The falls can be reached in half an hour by bus from Nachi Station. Near the bus stop is a *torii* at the top of several flights of stone steps leading down to a paved clearing near the foot of the falls, which are more pretty than spectacular. On the mountainside some distance above the bus stop is the Kumano-Nachi shrine from which more views of the waterfall can be obtained.

A couple of miles south of Nachi is Katsuura, a fishing port and hot spring. It lies in a beautiful bay sheltered by a small peninsula and rocky islands. Sightseeing launches will take you for a cruise among the islands, which are somewhat fancifully compared with those of Matsu-shima near Sendai. Katsuura is equidistant by rail from Nagoya and Osaka, both of which can be reached in less than 6 hours.

The southernmost point of the Kii peninsula and indeed of the main island of Japan is the promontory of Shio-no-misaki, a lovely, verdant spot with a white lighthouse high above rocky cliffs and rough waves. But close by is Kushimoto, a small port and holiday resort which attracts many visitors from Osaka. There is a direct air route from Kushimoto to Osaka and also to Nagoya. Oshima is an attractive island a mile off the coast. In the sea between the island and the harbor of Kushimoto are many pillar-like rocks which have been named *Ha-shikui* ("bridge piers") on account of their appearance.

The greatest hot spring in the district is Shirahama. With its abundance of hot water, pleasant seashore, and extensive bay, it is very popular with tourists. It lies 34 miles to the north of Kushimoto on the *Kisei* line. The temple of Dojoji is another 30 miles. From there the railway turns northeast to Wakayama, but just before reaching that city it passes through Waka-no-ura, a resort that claims, not without justification, to have the most beautiful coastal scenery in Japan.

Sacred Mt. Koya

The two chief religious, historical, scenic, and artistic centers of the Kii region are Mt. Koya and Mt. Yoshino. Both may be reached from Wakayama; and Mt. Koya is three hours by direct train from Nanba Station, Osaka. This great complex of mountain temples, monasteries, schools, graves and a museum has been a pilgrimage site ever since Kobo Daishi, founder of the Shingon Sect of Buddhism, established it in 816. Its most remarkable feature is the mile-long avenue of mausolea where some of Japan's most illustrious families lie under moss-covered stone pagodas in a grove of magnificent cedar trees surrounding the Oku-no-in, tomb of the saint himself. The temples vary greatly in size and splendor; the most important are the Kompon Daito or Great Central Pagoda, and the Kongobuji, Temple of the Diamond Seat, headquarters of the sect. The museum is worth a visit, but, unfortunately, very badly lighted. October–November is the best time to visit Koya-san; for lodging details see the *Practical Information* section, following.

Mt. Yoshino, reached from Yoshino-guchi on the Wakayama-Nara line, is famous for its cherry trees, and during the month of April crowds of visitors fill the small town of Yoshino in order to see them. The mountain contains many temples and shrines with historical associations; most people combine visits to these with cherry viewing, that traditional spring custom in Japan. Many of the surrounding mountains were once climbed only by devout pilgrims but now they are the haunt of hikers and mountaineers. From Yoshino-guchi you can reach Osaka in less than 2 hours by way of Oji and the Kansai line.

PRACTICAL INFORMATION FOR NAGOYA AND ISE-SHIMA

WHEN TO GO. Like most other places in Japan, this region is best seen in spring and autumn. May is usually a pleasant month for weather and that's the month that the cormorant fishing season starts. Nagoya's historic procession takes place in October, a month which is often blessed with long stretches of crystal-clear weather. The lowlands tend to be hot and sticky in summer, though that is certainly the best season to climb Mt. Koya, while the slopes of neighboring Mt. Yoshino, with their thousands of cherry trees, are best seen in April. There are many different species of cherry on Mt. Yoshino, so on any given day in April at least some of them are bound to be in bloom. Winter is cold and exceedingly dry, and the coldest month is February. There is little snow on this side of the country.

HOW TO GET THERE. By air. Nagoya is served by an international airport, 45 to 55 min. by Meitetsu Bus from Meitetsu Bus Center, close to Nagoya Station. International airlines link the city with Manila, Hong Kong, Seoul, and Micronesia, while domestic operators connect with airports around Japan. Sample times: Nagoya–Tokyo: 45 min.; Nagoya–Sapporo: 1 hr. 30 min. Airline companies' phone numbers are as follows (prefix 052 when calling from outside city):

Domestic airlines. All-Nippon Airways (ANA or ZenNiKu): 971–0727; Toa Domestic Airlines: 201–8111

International Airlines. Air France: 551–4141; Air-India: 583–0747; Alitalia: 551–5411; British Airways: 971–0727; Cathay Pacific: 962–6931; Japan Air Lines: 561–2401; KLM Royal Dutch Airlines: 582–0811; Korean Air Lines: 583–1551; Lufthansa: 561–2428; Northwest-Orient: 562–0867; Pan Am: 571–5488; Qantas: 561–6061; Sabena Belgian: 251–1733; Scandinavian Airlines: 561–6913; Singapore Air Lines: 581–7571; Swissair: 582–0551; Thai Airways International: 561–6913; Varig Brazilian: 565–1641.

By train. Within the country the super-express "bullet" Shinkansen trains rival the planes for speed and convenience. The trains come in two speeds: the faster, *Hikari,* covers the distance from Tokyo nonstop in just over 2 hours; the *Kodama* in just over 2½ hours with stops. From Osaka, Hikari takes 1 hour (50 min. from Kyoto), while Kodama takes about 1½ hours. Nagoya Station's phone number is 551–8111.

Kinki-Nippon Railways, a private organization, has "nonstop" trains (actually they stop twice en route) that cover the distance between Kintetsu Namba (in central Osaka) and Kintetsu-Nagoya (in central Nagoya) in 2 hr. 14 min. The cost is ¥2,930 single, and there are 12 trains a day.

By bus. Those traveling on a budget may prefer to go to Nagoya by Japan National Railways' Highway Bus, the cheapest way of crossing the country except for hitchhiking. The fare from Nagoya to Tokyo, for example, is ¥4,500, compared with ¥9,200 for the Shinkansen. Buses leave between early morning and late afternoon for Tokyo (on the Tomei Highway) and Kyoto and Osaka (Meishin Highway). The time to Tokyo is just over 6 hr., to Kyoto 2 hr. 40 min., to Osaka 3 hr. 16 min.—though these times vary with traffic conditions. For Tomei and Meishin buses, phone (052)563–0489 in Nagoya, or (03)215–0489 in Tokyo.

TELEPHONES. Public telephones are, as in the rest of the country, ubiquitous and highly efficient. The Nagoya area code is 052.

HOTELS AND INNS. Nagoya has more hotels than it strictly needs, and there is said to be a price war in progress. The city lacks hotels of the very highest grade, but accommodation of every other type is plentiful. Outside the big city, Western-style accommodation is simpler, with one or two exceptions, and the *ryokan* alternative is often more attractive (and always more interesting).

One unusual feature of Japanese hotels is that a single room is barely more expensive per person than a twin, probably for the reason that a very large proportion of guests travel alone. Thus, in all price categories, you can expect to pay roughly twice as much for a twin as for a single.

The hotel listings are divided into the following categories:

Expensive. Above ¥7,000 per night for a single room. Nagoya's best hotels are only slightly less luxurious than Tokyo's best.

Moderate. ¥4,000 to ¥7,000 per night for a single. Most hotels in this category are "business" hotels. Their rooms are spotlessly clean (like almost all accommodation in Japan), marvelously well-equipped, with built-in bathroom units, refrigerators (sometimes), TV, etc.—but usually extremely small.

Inexpensive. Under ¥4,000. These hotels are like the "moderate" ones but smaller and more rudimentary; youth hostels are similarly priced.

Japanese-style accommodation—*ryokan* and *minshuku*—are listed in similar categories, but remember that even at the most expensive *ryokan* (the most expensive listed below has a maximum all-in fee of ¥30,000 per night) you are not paying for the privacy of your own room and will be expected to delight in sharing the opulence with a friend (or friends). Prices at *ryokan* are inclusive of two meals. *Expensive ryokan* are ¥15,000 upwards per night per person; *Moderate,* between ¥4,000 and ¥15,000.

WESTERN-STYLE

Gifu

Gifu Grand Hotel. *Moderate.* 648 Nagara, Gifu; (0582) 33–1111. This hotel has 82 Western-style and 75 Japanese-style rooms and also has a hot spring bath, a sauna, a swimming pool, and facilities for boating on the Nagara River (where the cormorant fishing takes place).

Nagaragawa Hotel. *Moderate.* 51 Ukaiya, Nagara, Gifu; (0582) 32–4111. With 50 Western-style and 47 Japanese-style rooms this hotel offers hot-spring water and boating.

Inuyama

Meitetsu Inuyama Hotel. *Moderate.* 107 Kita-Koken, Inuyama, Aichi Pref.; (0568) 61–2211. The hotel has 92 Western-style and 19 Japanese-style rooms. It also has a swimming pool.

Kashikojima

Shima Kanko Hotel. *Moderate.* 731 Shimmei Agocho, Shima-gun, Mie Pref.; (0599) 43–1211. A huge and famous hotel with 145 Western-style and 55 moderately priced Japanese-style rooms. The hotel has a swimming pool and facilities for golf, boating, and fishing.

Nagoya

Hotel Nagoya Castle. *Expensive.* 3–19 Hinokuchicho, Nishi-ku, Nagoya; 582–2121. 250 rooms. Just across from the real castle. Outdoor swimming pool.

International Hotel Nagoya. *Expensive.* 3–23–3 Nishiki, Naka-ku, Nagoya; 961–3111. 265 rooms. Choice of cuisine, sky saloon with live music.

Nagoya Kanko Hotel. *Expensive.* 1–19–30 Nishiki, Naka-ku, Nagoya; 231–7711. 505 rooms. A luxurious and stylish modern hotel, about 10 min. from Nagoya Station by taxi.

Nagoya Terminal Hotel. *Expensive.* 1–2–1 Meieki, Nakamura-ku, Nagoya; 561–3751. On the borderline between *Expensive* and *Moderate,* but conveniently close to Nagoya Station. 256 rooms.

Nagoya Plaza Hotel. *Moderate.* 3–8–21 Nishiki, Naka-ku, Nagoya; 951–6311. Three minutes walk from Sakae Station on Higashiyama subway line, two stops from Nagoya Station. 176 rooms.

Nagoya No. 2 Washington Hotel. *Moderate.* 3–12–22 Nishiki, Naka-ku, Nagoya; 052–962–7111. Same directions as for the Plaza. 320 rooms.

Nagoya Green Hotel. *Moderate.* 1–8–22 Nishiki, Naka-ku, Nagoya; 203–0211. Located close to Nagoya Kanko Hotel, this is a basic and unexceptionable business hotel. 10 min. by taxi from Nagoya Station. 105 rooms.

Lions Hotel Nagoya. *Moderate.* 1–2–22 Sakae, Naka-ku, Nagoya; 211–6511. 10 min. by taxi from Nagoya Station. Sakae is where Nagoya's big stores, restaurants, clubs, and cinemas are concentrated, so this hotel is well located. 117 rooms.

Hotel Kiyoshi. *Inexpensive.* 1–3–1 Heiwa, Naka-ku, Nagoya; 321–5663. One minute walk from Higashi-Betsuin Station on the subway's Meijo line, five stops (including one change) from Nagoya Station. 105 rooms.

Toba

Toba Hotel International. *Moderate.* 1–23–1 Toba, Mie Pref.; (0599) 25–3121. A large hotel—124 rooms—with facilities for golf, boating, fishing, and sea bathing. Also has a swimming pool. Famous for its French cuisine.

JAPANESE-STYLE
Gifu

Hotel Park Minatokan. *Expensive.* 397–2 Minato-machi, Gifu; (0582) 65–5211. 20 min. by bus from Gifu Station. Six Western-style rooms in addition to the 43 Japanese-style ones.

Juhachiro. *Expensive.* 10 Minato-machi, Gifu; (0582) 65–1551. 20 min. by bus from Gifu Station. 78 rooms.

Ryokan Sugiyama. *Expensive.* 73–1 Nagara, Gifu; (0582) 31–0161. Close to the Nagara River, 20 min. from Gifu Station. 49 rooms.

Nagarakan. *Moderaate.* 20–1 Nagara, Gifu; (0582) 32–7117. Location same as Ryokan Sugiyama, above. 52 rooms.

Inuyama

Meitetsu Inuyama Hotel Bekkan Hakuteikaku. *Expensive.* 107 Kita-Koken, Inuyama, Aichi Pref.; (0568) 61–2211. Annex to the Meitetsu Inuyama Hotel, with 19 Japanese-style rooms.

Geihanro. *Moderate.* 41–6 Aza Kitakoken, Inuyama; (0568) 61–2205. 3 min. by car from Inuyama-yuen Station.

Kashikojimaso

Daisan Kashikojimaso. *Expensive.* 718–3 Shimmei, Agocho, Shima-gun; (0599) 43–3111. 75 rooms, 3 min. by bus from Kashikojima Station.

Shima Kanko Hotel. (See Western-style, above.)

Nagoya

Maizurukan. *Expensive.* 1–18–24 Meiki-Minami, Nakamura-ku, Nagoya; 541–1346. 5 min. by taxi from Nagoya Station. All but two of Maizurukan's 23 rooms have their own bath.

Suihoen. *Expensive.* 4–1–20 Sakae, Naka-ku, Nagoya; 241–3521. 15 min. by taxi from Nagoya Station, Suihoen offers the most expensive accommodation in the area.

Satsuki Honten. *Moderate.* 1–18–30 Meieki-Minami, Nakamura-ku, Nagoya; 551–0052. A small ryokan—just 11 rooms—7 min. walk from Nagoya Station.

Toba

Toba Hotel International Wafu Bekkan. *Expensive.* 1–23–1 Toba, Mie Pref.; (0599) 25–3121. The International's Japanese-style annex.

Hotel Taiike. *Expensive.* 610 Ohamacho, Toba; (0599) 25–4111. 78 rooms. 10 min. by bus from Toba Station.

Pearl Palace Hotel Shoto. *Expensive.* 300–1 Ohamacho, Toba; (0599) 25–2200. Near Toba Station. 77 rooms.

Sempokaku. *Expensive.* 2–12–24 Toba; (0599) 25–3151. 66 rooms. 4 min. by car from Toba Station.

Kimpokan. *Moderate.* 1–10–38 Toba; (0599) 25–2001. 50 rooms. 3 min. on foot from Toba Station.

Kinkairo. *Moderate.* 1–13–1, Toba; (0599) 25–3191. 40 rooms. 3 min. on foot from Toba Station.

Kogaso. *Moderate.* 237–1 Ohamacho, Toba; (0599) 25–2170. 44 rooms, 5 min. by bus from Toba Station.

Yunoyama Spa

Kotobukitei. *Expensive.* 8585 Oaza Komono, Komono-cho, Mie-gun; (0593) 92–2131. 47 rooms. 10 min. from Yunoyama Station.

Grand Hotel Koyo. *Expensive.* 8497 Oaza Komono, Komono-cho, Mie-gun; (0593) 92–3135. Location as above. 35 rooms.

Hotel Yunomoto. *Moderate.* 8497 Oaza Komono, Komono-cho, Mie-gun; (0593) 92–2141. 32 rooms in this annex to the Grand Hotel Koyo.

YOUTH HOSTELS. Gifu Youth Hostel. 4716–17 Kami-kanoyama, Gifu; (0582) 63–6631. 15 min. by tram from Gifu Station then 20 min. on foot. 60 beds.

Youth Hostel Kodama-So. Kenei Ground, Nagara-fukumitsu, Gifu; (0582) 32–1922. 30 min. by bus from Gifu Station. 150 beds.

Inuyama Youth Hostel. 162–1 Himuro, Tsugao, Inuyama; (0568) 61–1111. 25 min. on foot from Inuyama-yuen Station. 92 beds.

Nagoya Youth Hostel. 1–50 Kameiri, Tashiro-cho, Chikusa-ku, Nagoya; 781–9845. 16 min. by subway to Hoshigaoka Station, then 8 min. on foot. 100 beds.

Youth Hostel Aichi Ken Seinen Kaikan. 1–18–8 Sakae, Naka-ku, Nagoya; 221–6001. 10 min. by bus from Nagoya bus terminal then 3 min. on foot. 50 beds.

YH Kontaiji. 3–24–1 Toba; (0599) 25–3035. 15 min. on foot from Toba Station. Only 7 beds, so be sure to book.

Iseshima YH. 1219–8 Anagawa, Isobe-cho, Shima-gun, Mie Pref.; (05995) 5–0226. 7 min. on foot from Anagawa Station. 120 beds.

STAYING ON MOUNT KOYA. On the summit of Koya-san is a "religious" city, headquarters of the Shingon sect of Buddhism, and within the precincts there are some 50 *shukubo* (temple lodgings). These are always comfortable and sometimes magnificent and unforgettable, set amidst art treasures, gardens, and massively timbered halls and kitchens. The food is vegetarian, tasty, and attractively served, and two meals are included in the ¥6,000 charge. Reservations must be made in advance. Apply to **Koyasan Kanko Kyokai** (Koyasan Tourist Association), Koya-san, Koya-machi, Itsu-gun, Wakayama Pref; (07365) 6–2616, or to the office of a travel agency such as *Japan Travel Bureau.*

There is also a youth hostel on Koya-san: **Henjoson-in Youth Hostel.** 303 Koya-san, Koya-machi, Itsu-gun, Wakayama Pref.; (07365) 6–2434. Reservations should be made in advance.

HEALTH SPAS AND RESORTS. Gifu City has a noted *onsen-gai* (hot spring quarter) near the castle and the Nagaragawa River. Both the hotels listed under Gifu, above, offer hot spring bathing, and the *ryokan* in the vicinity offer the same.

The coastal area to the southeast of Nagoya has a number of hot-spring seaside resorts that are very popular with Japanese holidaymakers, although little known to foreigners. Three of them are clustered around the seaside town of Gamagori on Atsumi Bay, which is 1 hr. 20 min. from Shin Nagoya Station by the special express of the private Meitetsu Line.

Miya is the farthest west, 22 min. from the industrial city of Toyohashi. The slopes of the town are dotted with large and ungainly looking concrete *ryokan* and it is in these that the bathing takes place. Miya also boasts a *Geisha Daigaku*, a "Geisha University," which is in fact a novelty nightclub. Here are three representative local ryokan: *Ikoiso,* (0533) 68–3838; *Musashi-ya,* (0533) 68–2933; *Iwamoto,* (0533)68–4566.

Katahara, a few miles west along Atsumi Bay, is an *onsen* with a history of 500 years. Ryokan include the following: *Akebono,* (0533) 57–3677; *Kataoka,* (0533) 57–2115; *Nopporo,* (0533)57–4567.

The third town, on the southern tip of Atsumi Bay, is **Nishiura.** Representative *ryokan* include: *Yumoto,* (0533) 57–3178; *Nishiura Grand Hotel,* (0533) 57–6111; *Hotel Tatsuki,* (0533) 57–5111.

HOW TO GET AROUND. Nagoya has a fast and impressive **subway** system with three lines traversing the city in several directions. Subway is the easiest and fastest way of getting about, except in morning and evening rush hours. A subway map with place names in Roman letters appears in "Your Guide to Nagoya," the invaluable booklet published by the city and available at the tourist information office in the station.

Nagoya also has a comprehensive **bus** service, but like buses all over Japan destinations and other details are only in Japanese so they are inordinately difficult to use for foreign tourists. Buses are one-man type, usually with a fixed fare: put the exact fare in the box beside the driver when you get on.

Taxis are readily available but expensive, and the fares are always rising; 871–0601.

Hire cars with guides, a few of whom may speak some English, are available from two firms in Nagoya: *Teisan Auto Company,* (052) 911–1351; and *Tokyu Shachi Bus,* (052) 913–1111. Cars are large size and the hourly rate is around ¥ 3,800.

For self-drive car hire, contact one of the following offices: *Nippon-Hertz Rent-a-Car,* (052) 551–1976; *Toyota Rent-a-Lease,* (052) 586–1318; *Nissan Rent-a-Car,* (052) 451–2300.

Outside Nagoya City, the Nagoya-Ise Shima area is well served by JNR lines, private railway lines and long-distance buses.

The fastest *JNR* express to Gifu takes 21 min. The JNR phone number is 541–7000. To go from Nagoya to Inuyama, take the private *Meitetsu Inuyama Line* from Shin Nagoya (New Nagoya) Station (not far from the JNR tracks). It takes about 33 min. Another Meitetsu line from Nagoya passes by the "Japanese Rhine" (River Kiso) and calls at Meiji Mura's museum of Victorian Orientalia (or Oriental Victoriana).

For trips to the scenic spots south of Nagoya, use the lines of the private *Kintetsu Railway.* Kintetsu is the biggest private railway in Japan and its trains link Nagoya with Osaka and Kyoto. To travel to Ise, Toba, and Kashikojima, take the Kintetsu from Nagoya via Yokkaichi. The express from Nagoya to Uji Yamada, one stop down the tracks from Ise-shi, takes 1 hr. 19 min. and is superbly comfortable. All over Japan private railways are both cheaper and more luxurious than their nationalized counterparts.

As elsewhere in Japan, railways are more developed than roads; as a result, services usually are quicker and more frequent. *Nagoya Airport,* however, is only accessible by road (Route 41). The buses from the bus terminal next door to Nagoya Station take 45–55 min.

TOURIST INFORMATION. Nagoya has no tourist office aimed specifically at foreigners, but the office at the East Exit of Nagoya Station is well-stocked with English language literature on the area and several of the staff speak English quite well enough to be helpful. There are maps, subway maps, and leaflets, all in flawless English. There is help with fixing up tours, finding a hotel and getting around. "Nagoya Calendar" is an invaluable monthly guide to what's on in the city—it's free but it's not on display, so you'll have to ask for it. It is better written than Tokyo's English language dailies.

Here are the phone numbers of offices which will provide you with information: *City Tourist Information* (at Nagoya Station): 541–4301; *Tourist and Trade Section, City of Nagoya:* 961–1111 (extension 2245–6); *Liaison and Protocol Division, City Hall:* 951–1814; Tourist Agencies: *Japan Travel Bureau:* 563–1501; *Kinki Nippon Tourist:* 586–4631; *Meitetsu World Travel:* 561–5217; *Nippon Travel Agency:* 961–7021.

Gifu City Tourist Association can be reached at (0582) 63–7291.

USEFUL ADDRESSES AND PHONE NUMBERS. Emergencies. Police: 110; Fire or other Emergency: 119. Overseas calls through the operator: 0051; Directory enquiries: 104; Nagoya Central Post Office (near station): 541–2271; Nagoya Overseas Telegraph and Telephone Office (KDD): 971–4222; Lost Property, City Bus/Subway: 961–1111; Nagoya Prefectural Hospital: Shiroyama Hospital, Tokugawa Yama-cho, Chikusaku 4–1–7; tel 052 –763–1511.

SEASONAL EVENTS AND FESTIVALS. The dates on which festivals take place change frequently, some festivals fade away, others are suddenly revived. The dates and details below, though up-to-date, can only be a rough guide. Always check with Tourist Information Center at Narita, Tokyo, or Kyoto before making a special trip to see a festival.

January. *Hatsumode,* on the 1st. At the New Year millions of Japanese all over the country visit major shrines to pray for a good year, and in Nagoya this takes place at Atsuta Shrine. Visits continue through the first week of January.

Demonstration by the city's fire fighters of their skills and equipment take place on the 8th.

March. *Fertility Festival* on the 15th at Tagata Shrine, 30 min. by Meitetsu train from Nagoya, two stops before Meiji Mura. Get off at Tagata Jinja. The festival consists of a procession in which the shrine's treasures, which include the biggest collection of erotic talismens in Japan, are borne through the town. For centuries the site of the shrine has been considered a lucky place, and it was believed that intercourse performed under a certain tree in the garden would assure the birth of a healthy, gifted child. This ancient custom is said to continue even today, and the collection of talismens has continued to accumulate through the years, all of them the gifts of grateful parents whose children were conceived under the influence of (even if not literally under) the sacred tree.

April. *Kagura-sai* at Ise Shrine, from the 5th–7th. *Kagura,* sacred Shinto music and dance, *Bugaku,* old court music (the oldest extant orchestral form in the world), and other entertainments are performed during the festival period.

Toshogu Matsuri, the grand festival of Toshogu Shrine in Nagoya takes place on the 16th and 17th. Gorgeous floats and palanquins wind through the streets of the city. The festival dates from 1618, the third anniversary of the death of city founder Ieyasu Tokugawa. It has had its ups and downs since then but is at present a splendid event.

May 11th–October 15th. *Ukai* (cormorant fishing) season at Nagara River in Gifu. The fishing takes place daily except when the water is excessively muddy or on nights of a full moon, for on those days the fish do not rise to the lanterns' light. Boat hire charge per person: ¥2,200 (May, Sept., Oct.), ¥2,400 (June, July, Aug.) exclusive of cost of food and drink. Reservations can be made through any office of Japan Travel Bureau or at the local ticketing office on the day.

June. *Idonozoki,* "Taking-a-look-into-the-well rite" at Takakura Shrine, Nagoya on the 1st. Parents with problem children bring them to the shrine on this day and have them stare into a particular well where a dragon is believed to live. By this means their troubles are believed exorcised.

Memorial Rites of Ancient Martial Arts at Atsuta Shrine, Nagoya on the 5th. Japanese martial arts such as judo, kendo, and archery are demonstrated. The purpose, we are told, is to pray for the stability of the nation and the continued happiness of the people.

Hamajima Lobster Festival is held on the 6th. At this seaside hamlet in Ise-shima folk dances are performed in front of a huge paper lobster.

June 1st–Sept 30th. *Ukai* (cormorant fishing) at Inuyama, 40 min. from Nagoya on Meitetsu Inuyama line. Charge ¥1,800 in June, Sept., ¥2,000 in July and Aug. Takes place on Kiso River, 2 min. walk from Inuyama-Yuen Station. Conditions as at Gifu, above. Book through JTB, or at Inuyama on the day.

August. On the 14th–15th (lunar calendar—date different every year). *Anori Bunraku* puppet show at Anori Hachimangu Shrine, Ago-cho, Ise-shima. 20 min. by Mie Kotsu bus from Ukata Station, which is one stop before Kashikojima.

On the 15th., the height of the O-bon season, gay dances for the dead are performed all over the country.

September. (Date changes annually) *Nakiri Waraji Matsuri.* At this seaside village a mammoth *waraji* (straw sandal) is set afloat in the sea during the typhoon season to scare off sea monsters and pray for safety at sea.

October. *Chrysanthemum Show* throughout the month. The chrysanthemum (*kiku*) is the emblematic flower of the imperial family. At Nagoya Castle there is an elaborate display of the flowers and of dolls made from them.

Nagoya Matsuri runs from the 10th. This is the city's biggest annual splash. Historic costume processions and elaborately decorated floats brighten the streets. Usually on a lavish scale, it lasts over a week. Nagoya Festival was established after World War II and is sponsored by local companies and commercial organizations. At present the lavish festivities involve the whole city and include various kinds of exhibitions, classical entertainments in the Japanese tradition, and folksongs and dances from all parts of Japan.

TOURS. There are four regular daily sightseeing bus tours in Nagoya, and all can be booked at Tourist Information in Nagoya Station. Though conducted in Japanese they are perhaps the most efficient way of getting to know what the city looks like. A, B, and C courses vary only slightly and all visit Atsuta Shrine and Nagoya Castle. B course also calls at Nagoya Port. The fourth is the Meiji Village course, which in addition calls at Nagoya Castle and Nagoya Airport. All tours leave in the morning and return between 3½ and 6 hours later. For information, phone *Nagoya Yuran Bus,* at 561–4036 (in precincts of Nagoya Station).

Japan Travel Bureau runs a two-day tour to Ise and Pearl Island. The tour originates and terminates in both Kyoto and Osaka, and costs ¥37,000 including one lunch.

Though the schedule varies—sometimes it's not available at all—an *Industrial Bus Tour,* which guides visitors round some local factories, is supposedly offered every Friday. Unconnected with this is the tour of *Noritake China's* model factory, located a few minutes from Nagoya Station on foot. Tourist Information should help set this tour up for you.

For details on industrial tours, phone *City Tourist Information,* 541–4301 (in Nagoya Station), or *City Tourist Center,* 262–2918 (1st floor of Chunichi Building).

 HOME VISIT SYSTEM. If you want to find out how a Japanese family lives at first hand, the city has a Home Visit System. This allows foreign visitors to call on a local family and chat for a couple of hours. There is no charge but visitors usually bring a small gift for the host families. As a rule visits take place for an hour or two after 7:00 P.M. You may be served tea and cake, but you will not be offered a meal or accommodation. To find out more, call the city's *Tourist and Trade Section* (961–1111, ext. 2245–6) at least one day before the day on which you hope to pay your visit.

 THEME PARKS AND AMUSEMENT CENTERS. Three attractive amusement centers are located close together near Inuyama, which is about 30 min. by Meitetsu railway from Nagoya. **Meiji Mura.** Meiji Village, in Inuyama on Nagoya's outskirts, is a large collection of 19th-century buildings and other memorabilia plus a few more recent items—part of Frank Lloyd Wright's original Imperial Hotel, for example. A real live steam train adds fun for the kids. Crowded on weekends. Open 10:00 A.M.–5:00 P.M. (March 1–Oct. 31); 10:00 A.M.–4:00 P.M. (Nov. 1–end Feb.). Admission: Adults, university students, ¥1,000; teenagers ¥900; younger children ¥500. Take the bus direct from Nagoya's Meitetsu Bus Center or Meitetsu train from Nagoya to Meiji Mura Guchi, then bus.

Nihon Monkey Centre. 1,000 monkeys of 100 different species, including some very funny-looking ones, are kept here (and observed by scholars) in circumstances similar to their natural habitats. One of the biggest parks of its type in the world. Open 9:30 A.M.–5:00 P.M. (Feb. 16–Nov. 30); 9:30 A.M.–4:00 P.M. (Dec. 1–Feb. 15). Admission: Adults ¥1,000; children ¥600; infants ¥400. Take the Meitetsu train from Nagoya to Inuyama Yuen Station, then 4 min. by monorail.

Little World. An outdoor ethnological museum, illustrating with real houses and other artifacts the ways of life of people from all over the world. The park covers an area of 1,230,000 square meters. Opened in 1983. Open 9:30 A.M.–6:00

P.M. (April 1–Oct. 31); 10:00 A.M.–4:30 P.M. (Nov. 1–March 31). Admission: Adults, university students, ￥1,000; teenagers ￥800; younger children ￥500. Take the Special Express (*Tokkyu*) bus from Meitetsu Bus Center or bus from Nishikani Station.

Shirahama has a wild animal park called **Adventure World.** There are three sections to the park: Marine Pavilion, Animal Pavilion, and Recreation Pavilion. Separate admission tickets are available, but admission to all three costs ￥2500 for adults, ￥1200 for children. Open 9 A.M.–5 P.M. (Mar.-Nov.); 9 A.M.–4:30 P.M. (Dec.-Feb.); closed Dec. 19–24.

SPORTS. Nagoya's *baseball* team is called The Dragons and you can see them at the Chunichi Stadium, which holds over 30,000 fans. *Athletic meetings* and amateur events take place in the Mizuho Stadium, which also has baseball, soccer, and rugby grounds. For *horse racing* you can go to the Nagoya Horse Race Track or the National Chukyo Track in Toyoaki Village. All sorts of indoor sports can be seen at the Kanayama Gymnasium, which is the venue for the mid-July *sumo* tournament. Nagoya Sports Center is open throughout the year for *ice skating.* The Shimo Pool in Showa-ku is open during July and August for *swimming. Tennis* can be played at the Sakae Tennis Courts in Higashi-ku.

For *golfers,* the Forest Park Course in Kasugai City, about 18 kilometers north of Nagoya, is open to the general public. An unusual golf course situated on a sandy beach surrounded by pines is the Shima Golf Course near Kashikojima in Ise-shima. This region is also good for *fishing.* Toba, Ago, and Ise Bays are all excellent fishing grounds and you can hire a boat for a reasonable charge.

HISTORICAL SITES. Most of this region's historical sites are, for one reason or another, not very historical, but this fact bugs the locals less than foreign visitors. Nagoya Castle, for example, dates from 1959. Toshogu Shrine, founded in 1619, was rebuilt in 1952, while the shrines at Ise, the holiest in the land, were reconstructed most recently in 1973 (they'll be doing it again in 1993). Don't bother with Nagoya's shrines and temples, unless you're just feeling in the mood for a good shrine—Kyoto is much more edifying. The Ise shrines are, however, a must. Meiji Mura (see Amusement Centers, above) is a unique collection of 19th-century buildings.

MUSEUMS AND ZOO. Gifu Prefectural Museum. Koyana, 15 min. by Meitetsu train from Gifu; 05752–8–3111. Natural and man-made treasures from the prefecture's history, housed in a modern building. Open 9:30 A.M.–4:30 P.M. Closed Mondays. Admission ￥150.

Higashiyama Zoological and Botanical Garden. Near Higashiyama Koen subway station; 052–782–2111. One of the finest collections of animals in the Orient. More than 1,000 animals from 260 species. Open 9:30 A.M.–4:30 P.M.; closed Mondays. Adults ￥300; children free.

Kuwayama Bijutsukan (museum). Near Yamanaka bus stop; 763–5188. Private collection of fine arts and crafts. Located on a hill with three tea ceremony cottages in a large Japanese garden. 10:00 A.M.–4:00 P.M., closed Mon. and some other days (phone to check). Adults ￥300; students ￥200.

The Museum of Fine Arts. Gifu. Near Gifu Station; (0582) 71–1313. This new museum has a large and varied collection of paintings and sculptures,

Japanese and otherwise, including famous works of Renoir and Miro. Open 9:30 A.M.–5:00 P.M., closed Mon. Entrance fee ¥200.

Museum Toba Marina. A maritime museum on Pearl Island in Toba. Features displays on the seabed, future marine development, and the history of men and the sea. Open 8:30 A.M.–5:00 P.M., April–Sept.; 9:00 A.M.–5:00 P.M., Oct.–March; closed June 28–June 30 and Dec. 20–Jan. 1. Admission ¥500 for adults, ¥200 for small children, ¥100 for tots. Close by is the *Brazil Maru,* a liner, which in the past served as an emigration vessel, taking Japanese farmers to start a new life in Brazil. The interior is open for inspection, at the same times as the Museum Toba Marina, but the admission fee is separate: ¥800 for adults; ¥400 for students; ¥200 for small children. Both museums are a short walk from Toba Station.

Nagoya Castle. Rebuilt version of the original, which was constructed in the early 17th century. 9:30 A.M.–4:30 P.M. Adults ¥300; children ¥50.

Nagoya City Hoseiniko Kensho Museum. Near Toyokuni Jinja bus stop; 411–0035. 10 min. walk from Nakamura subway stop. Historical properties of early shogun Hideyoshi. Open 9:30 A.M.–5:00 P.M.; closed Tuesdays. Free.

Nagoya City International Exhibition Hall. Kinjo Pier, near Kokusai Tenji-jo bus stop; 398–1771. Irregular exhibitions, often of a technological or scientific nature.

Nagoya City Museum. In Sakurayama area; 853–2655. Permanent interesting exhibition tracing history of the natives of this part of Japan down to the present. Open 9 A.M.–4:30 P.M.; closed Mondays. Adults ¥200; children ¥50. Extra for special shows.

Nagoya Municipal Science Museum. Near Fushimi subway station; 201–4486. Contains a planetarium. Open 9:30 A.M.–5:00 P.M., closed Mon. and third Fri. of month. Modest admission fee.

Shima Marineland. Kashikojima, one minute from Kintetsu Kashikojima Station, which is 55 min. from Toba on Kinki Nippon Railway's Shima line. Displays include a large number of fossils from more than 20 countries. Open 8:00 A.M.–5:00 P.M. year-round. No holidays. Adults ¥650; children ¥100–¥300, depending on age.

Toba Aquarium. Seven minutes' walk from Toba Station. Among the tanks of fish and other marine life are two tanks where Toba's diving ladies (*ama*) display their skills. Open 8:00 A.M.–5:00 P.M., Mar. 21–Nov. 20; 8:00 A.M.–5:30 P.M., July 20–Aug. 31; 8:30 A.M.–4:30 P.M., Nov. 21–Mar. 20. Admission: adults ¥1,200; children ¥600; ages 3–6, ¥300. No holidays.

Tokugawa Art Museum. Near Shindeki-machi; 935–6262. A huge collection of historical treasures, said to be the best museum in Nagoya. Open 10:00 A.M.–4:00 P.M.; closed Mon. Adults ¥300, children ¥250.

PERFORMING ARTS. This region has little to boast of in the way of traditional performing arts, and though there are three theaters in Nagoya, their modern Japanese fare is unlikely to be of much interest to foreign visitors. Major national and international performers sometimes come to Nagoya; details of their performances and others are printed in the monthly English language *Nagoya Calendar,* available on demand at Tourist Information.

SHOPPING. Nagoya has major department stores, specialty shops selling the region's noted products, and two bustling underground shopping arcades. Have your hotel front desk call and draw you a map. **Department stores:** *Mitsukoshi,* 251–2111. Subway to Sakae. Closed Thurs. *Mitsukoshi* (Hoshigaoka), 782–3111. Subway to Hoshigaoka. Closed Thurs. *Matsuzakaya,* 251–1111. Subway to Yaba-cho. Closed Wed. *Marui,* 251–1211. Subway to Sakae. Closed Fri. *Meitetsu,* 571–1111. Subway to Nagoya. Closed Thurs.

　　Specialty shops: *Ando* (cloisonne), 251–1371. *Mikimoto* (pearls), 261–1808. *Noritake* (chinaware), 961–6831. *Maruzen* (books, including English language publications), 261–2251.

　　Of the two **underground arcades,** one is under Nagoya Station, the other in Sakae, just beyond the ticket barrier of Sakae subway station.

DINING OUT. Unlike many cities in Japan, Nagoya cannot boast of any particular delicacies to tempt the foreign palate, though some travelers find *kishimen* noodles good. This is the Japanese version of *tagliatelli* and can be had at the noodle restaurants in the underground shopping arcades beneath Nagoya Station Plaza. There is no Chinatown, and not much of an old-style Japanese restaurant area as in Tokyo or Kyoto. Nagoya chicken is considered the best in Japan; many of the city's restaurants feature it in specialties. Several good places in Nagoya are listed below. Outside this city, you would be wise to eat at your hotel most of the time, as in every case, the hotel's dining room is the sole place for Western cuisine, and your Japanese inn is bound to be a combination restaurant and sleeping place, anyhow, and probably the best in town. The seafood of Ise is delicious, especially the fine Ise lobster.

　　The price range per person for a meal is *Moderate,* ¥2,000–¥5,000; *Expensive,* ¥5,000–¥10,000. The restaurants listed below are all *Moderate,* unless otherwise indicated. Most "Western" places are expensive.

NAGOYA

Western Cuisine

　　Hotel Okura's **Restaurant Nagoya.** On the top floor of Takihyo Marunouchi Building, the tallest structure in central Japan; 201–3201. Features continental and Chinese food. It also boasts a bar that has room for 24 at a time, six banquet rooms, and a wedding-ceremony room.

　　Alaska. Located on the second floor of the Toyota Building opposite Nagoya Station. Well up to the high standards of Western cuisine to be found in Asia. The roof beer garden is also run by Alaska and is the right place for a cool glass of beer in summer.

　　Pizza House Carina. North of Toyota Co. in Higashi-ku; 971–9034. Has Italian dishes, cozy surroundings.

　　Miami. Near the station in the Shin Nagoya Building; 541–0203. Has a beer garden on its roof. Specialty of the Miami is Genghis Khan (a Mongolian barbecue in which the mutton is broiled on a grill at your table) served in a separate roof garden, which is covered over and heated in winter. The first floor grill offers the usual Western menu. The vast building has so many places in which to eat that you are sure to find what you want somewhere.

　　Yachiyo. 3–20–12 Nishiki, Naka-ku. Main restaurant, 971–7596; Sakae branch, 262–7581. A steak house that has the art of charcoal broiling down to perfection. Moderately priced. Main restaurant, 971–7596; Sakae branch, 262–7581.

Suehiro. Minami-Gofu-kucho Building, Naka-ku. Another mecca for the steak lover. Other American-style dishes, including fried chicken.

Coq d'Or. 38 Aoi-cho, Higashi-ku. Looks like a small chateau, but has an interesting modern interior, a cocktail lounge, and a patio on which meals are served in the summer.

Laxsy. At Irinaka, near the subway station. Snack bar especially for non-Japanese, with notice boards, guitars, dancing. From 5:00 P.M.

Japanese and Chinese

Yaegaki. *Expensive.* Tsurushigecho, Naka-ku: 951–3250. One of the best *tempura* restaurants in Nagoya. First-class prices, but worth it.

Torikyu. 541–2747. Nayacho, Nakamura-ku. *Sukiyaki* and *yakitori* at reasonable prices.

Chugoku Dalhanten. Near Chunichi Bldg.; 261–6611. Authentic Chinese seafood.

Flamingo. *Expensive.* Near the side entrance of the Kanko Hotel. Will tempt you with a variety of dishes in the Shanghai style accompanied by not too obtrusive music.

Shinchukaku. *Expensive.* An excellent Chinese restaurant in the basement of the Kyowa Building, Sasajima; 586–2727. Good Cantonese cuisine and a little bit of everything else.

Gomitori. Sakae, Naka-ku; 241–0041. A *nomiya* (bar) that serves a great selection of exotic delicacies at reasonable prices in rooms decked out with charming Japanese antiques. Specialties include horsemeat sashimi, loaches, and frogs (in season) as well as spare ribs and kushiyaki. There is another branch close to Nagoya Kanko Hotel.

OUTSIDE NAGOYA

Visitors are well-advised to eat at their hotel or *ryokan.* It's probably the best place in town. **Gifu** has a steak and sukiyaki house, *Senryu,* in Nagaragawa Hotel.

Out on the Kii peninsula near Ise-Shima National Park, many farmers are engaged in raising the fine cattle for Matsuzaka beef, and if you want to go directly to the source, you can travel out to the town of **Matsuzaka,** 90 minutes by express from Nagoya en route to Ise. However, this is only for the intrepid, as most of Matsuzaka's best beef is shipped out to Tokyo, Osaka, and beyond.

At the *Shima Kanko Hotel* in **Kashikojima,** Ise-shima, there is a restaurant with a tremendous reputation for French cuisine and lobster dishes; (0599) 43–1211.

NIGHT LIFE. The biggest and by far the noisiest cabaret is the popular *Nagoya Mikado,* which puts on three shows nightly and has two bands, though of course they don't usually play at the same time. It can be found in Irie-cho, Naka-ku. Near the Mikado is *Monterrey,* a lounge where you may pay a high price for your highball but it includes the attentions of a hostess, who will give you reassuring pats if you buy her a drink or two. The *Club New York* is one of those madly modern places, or so it likes to think. There are the usual two bands but only two shows nightly. In Okeya-cho, a few blocks from the Nagoya Kanko Hotel, but any self-respecting taxi driver will get you there. In the basement of the Imaike Building is the *Three Aces.* Here the floor show is not emphasized, but of course the bands provide background music all the time. The lights are dim and the hostesses are bright. In Heidencho, is *Higashi-ku,*

the sort of place to which you can take your wife. The *Playboy Club* is at the top of Imaike Bldg., Chigusa-ku.

KYOTO

by
WALTER MILLER

Kyoto is one of those rare cities of the world that graciously and generously gives of itself to visitors—when they leave they know they have experienced something unique. Perhaps this is due to the fact that for more than 1,000 years Kyoto was the heart, soul, and mind of Japan. Much of what foreigners regard as Japanese culture and tradition was sown, took root, and flourished when Kyoto was the capital of Japan, from 794 until 1868. Even when the city of Edo became the effective seat of government under Ieyasu Tokugawa in 1603, and after Edo was renamed Tokyo ("eastern capital") and the emperor moved there in 1868, Kyoto remained the cultural heart of Japan.

Kyoto's more than 2,000 temples, shrines, and gardens are reason enough to make the 300-mile journey southwest from Tokyo for a visit. But also impressive are Kyoto's subtle gems offered unpretentiously: the generally refined politeness of the people, a daily pace that is directed but not hurried (a refreshing alternative to the frenetic sprint of Tokyo), the ease of walking without the fear of getting lost, made possible by founding fathers who had the good sense to lay the city out on a rectangular grid (an idea borrowed from Xian, the Chinese city that served as capital of ancient China for 11 dynasties), and much more—facts of life in Kyoto that often are so subtle the visitor sometimes fails to appreciate them until after leaving Japan. The Japanese have long recognized Kyoto's special quality, describing it as "Nihon no furusato" (the heart of Japan).

Most people arrive in Kyoto from Tokyo by the famed Tokaido Shinkansen or "Bullet Train," which covers the 300 miles in about three hours. If you are not traveling in a tourist group, one of the first stops you should make is at the government-operated tourist information center (TIC). To reach the TIC, go out the Chuo exit of Kyoto Station and walk straight across the street up Karasuma-dori, the throughfare that deadends at the station. The TIC is on the left side of this street, in the same building as the Tower Department Store and the Kyoto Tower across from the station. The staff speaks fluent English, and is helpful and friendly. There you can get maps and numerous brochures, train and airline schedules, information on special events, and make bookings for hotels or inns.

A word of warning—don't go to Kyoto expecting to find an antique utopia, a city isolated from modernity or devoid of ugly sections, construction noise, traffic jams, gaudy shopping and entertainment districts, or fast-food shops. This city of 1.5 million people has all those negative aspects. It is, after all, a modern city in an industrialized, developed nation. So these things should be accepted—and ignored. Also, don't be surprised when you discover that many of the temples and shrines aren't as old as you previously may have thought. Nearly all of these structures were built out of wood, making them susceptible to natural disasters like fires and typhoons, and man-induced conflagrations like wars. Much of the city, for example, was destroyed in the 15th century when Japan was engulfed in bloody civil wars. As a result, many of the historical buildings either were rebuilt completely or underwent extensive restoration. Nevertheless, if you stroll through one of the lush, aesthetically manicured gardens or visit one of the majestic temples or shrines, you can easily discover the tranquillity and beauty offered so freely by this remarkable city.

Kyoto is a marvelous cornucopia of Japanese history, culture, and tradition. You could, in fact, spend your entire time in Japan in Kyoto. When the capital was moved in 794 from Nara to a site 30 miles to the north, it was called Heian, which later became known as Kyoto. The period from 794 to 1192 is known as the Heian Period, a time of tremendous cultural growth when such rituals as the tea ceremony and flower arrangement, as well as landscape gardening in Zen monasteries —arts rooted in China's Sung dynasty (960–1279)—were developed in Japan.

Kyoto's sense of history and culture can be felt almost without conscious effort. Strolling along the city's Old Canal for example, you might stop at the Kanoh-Syojuan, a traditional teahouse where you can watch as a kimono-clad woman performs the tea ceremony. As you sip the bitter green tea you saw her make, you'll be served a traditional Japanese pastry with a sweet red bean filling. Afterward, refreshed and relaxed by the beauty of the ceremony, you can resume your walk along the cherry-tree shaded canal.

In most cases the attractions of Kyoto are in clusters and the best way to see them is to walk. To get from one group of sites to the next you can walk, too, or go by local transportation, which is very easy to do. The bus system is excellent and the city map you get from the TIC clearly marks the major routes. You also can travel by taxi, but cross-town fares can get expensive. There is also the city's new subway, which runs under the Karasuma thoroughfare, between Kyoto Station and Kitaoji. It presently has only one line, so you won't have to change trains, and since you'll be traveling in a straight line, it's nearly impossible to get lost or miss your stop. Like all the subway systems in Japan, the one in Kyoto is safe, spotlessly clean, and an easy way to cover long distances quickly. And the Kyoto system is rarely crowded—rarely will you be jammed into a car like sardines, as often happens in Tokyo.

In addition to its temples, shrines, and gardens, Kyoto is the site of modern industries such as electric appliance and precision machine manufacturing. It is also home to traditional industries, one of which is Nishijin silk weaving, which dates back to the founding of the city in 794. Other traditional items manufactured here include kimonos; Kiyomizuyaki ceramic ware, elegant pieces for use in the home or for the tea ceremony; Kyoto dolls, admired as the most graceful dolls made in Japan; and Kyoto lacquerware. The city's craftsmen also produce the largest number of hand-held fans in the country.

Shortly after you arrive in Kyoto is you will probably notice the huge number of Japanese tourists, especially schoolchildren, marching or running from temple to shrine to temple, all attired in sailor suit-style dresses for girls and military-style jacket and pants for boys. The Japanese love to travel in groups and they are the nation's number one tourists. If you go to Kyoto during the peak tourist seasons of spring and autumn, expect large crowds. And if you have permitted the charm of Kyoto to captivate you, your encounter with the Japanese tourists, particularly the schoolchildren, can only add to your overall enjoyment of this unique city.

If you ask a Japanese what it is that is so alluring about Kyoto, he or she is apt to reply that the main factors are the city's beautiful women and divine cuisine. When an eatery opens in Tokyo specializing in Kyoto-style cooking and the food prepared by the kitchen is authentic, the restaurant is usually assured of success.

Kyoto-style cuisine, or *Kyo ryori,* originated in three different styles: *Yusoku ryori*—dishes for the imperial court; *Kaiseki ryori*—dishes prepared especially for and served before the tea ceremony; and *Shojin ryori*—vegetarian dishes made for Buddhist priests. The city's cuisine is distinctive for its light seasoning, beautiful arrangement of food on serving dishes, and the varied use of vegetables. It is not, however, cheap. In fact, in the top restaurants, it is exorbitantly expensive. But the essence of this food can be savored in less expensive *Kyo bento,* or Kyoto-style box lunch—a lovely lacquered box containing rice, pickles, an assortment of vegetables, fish, meat, and eggs. Not to be missed. The city also is known for its high-quality tofu or bean curd. Restaurants in the Nanzenji and Sagano areas specialize in pot-boiled tofu.

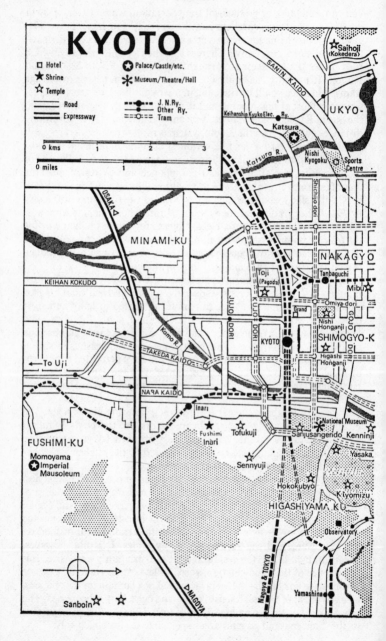

KYOTO

□ Hotel　　　　　　★ Palace/Castle/etc.
★ Shrine　　　　　　✳ Museum/Theatre/Hall
☆ Temple

——— Road
═══ Expressway
■━■━ J.N.Ry.
—○—○— Other Ry.
═○═○ Tram

0 kms　　1　　2　　3
0 miles　　1　　2

SANIN KAIDO

☆ Saihoji (Kokedera)

UKYO-

Keihanshin Kyuko Elec. Ry.

★ Katsura

Nishi Kyogoku

☆ Sports Centre

Katsura R.

Shichio dori

OSAKA △

MINAMI-KU

NAKAGYO

KEIHAN KOKUDO

Tanbaguchi ■

Mibu ☆

Toji (Pagoda) ☆

Omiya-dori

Grand ☆

JUJO DORI

KUJO DORI

Nishi Honganji ☆

SHIMOGYO-K

Kamo R.

KYOTO ●

TAKEDA KAIDO

Higashi Honganji ☆

← To Uji

NARA KAIDO

Inari ●

☆ Inari

National Museum ✳

Fushimi Inari ★

Tofukuji ☆

Sanjusangendo

Kenninji ☆

FUSHIMI-KU

Sennyuji ☆

Yasaka ★

Momoyama Imperial Mausoleum ★

Hokokubyo ☆

☆ Kiyomizu

HIGASHIYAMA KU

■ Observatory

Nagoya & TOKYO

Yamashina ●

Sanboin ☆　☆

△ NAGOYA

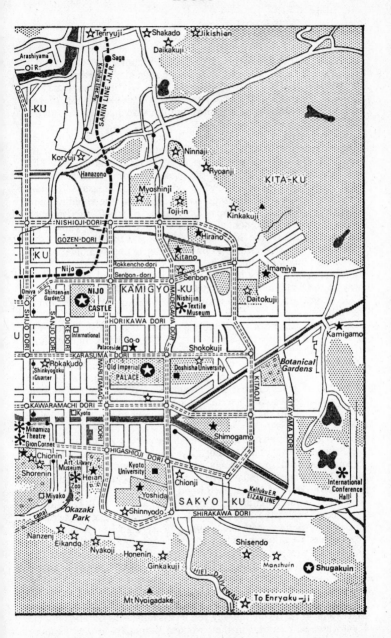

Kiyomizu Temple to Heian Shrine

Starting at the 17th-century Kiyomizu Temple, you can spend a delightful, leisurely morning or afternoon walking to Heian Shrine, constructed in 1895 to commemorate the 1,100th anniversary of Kyoto. If you walk really fast, you could probably finish this tour in an hour or two. But if you're pushed for time, save this walk for another day.

Before getting a bus at Kyoto Station for the ride to Kiyomizu Temple, take time to walk a few blocks east of the station to Sanjusan-gendo, the Hall of 33 Bays (the spaces between the front pillars). This was founded in 1132, although the present building, nearly 400 feet long, dates from 1266 and is designated a National Treasure. Its main attraction is a seated Thousand-Armed Kannon (the Buddhist personification of Mercy or Compassion), flanked by 1,000 other, smaller, standing images of Kannon, all gilded. This is the work of Tankei, the leading sculptor of the 13th century, who also did the remarkable statues of the "28 Faithful Followers," intriguing combinations of human and animal features. These are located in the corridor behind the Kannon figures. The building itself is the site of an annual *Toshiya* (way of the bow) archery demonstration held on January 15.

Upon returning to Kyoto Station, take bus No. 206 to Kiyomizu-michi bus stop.

Kiyomizu (Clear Spring) Temple is nestled on a hill rising above the city, an excellent spot to get a good view of the city's skyline. A short trek up a stone-paved winding road bordered on either side by souvenir and curio shops takes you to the gateway to the temple. As you head up to the temple, be sure to stop and take advantage of the free samples of traditional Kyoto sweets and Japanese tea, offered by enthusiastic shop employees who don't seem to mind if you sample without buying anything. Some of the shops have fine selections of pottery and other crafts.

The temple, designated as a National Treasure, was built in 1633 by the Tokugawa Shogunate, and displays the Momoyama Period's taste for spacious, bold, ornate design. Its wooden veranda is uniquely supported by 139 massive pillars. The Sanmon (front) Gate is of traditional Kyoto style. Built of dark stained wood, it has a multi-layered roof and is reached by climbing up stone steps. After a short walk beyond the gate one comes to the 3-story pagoda. The landscape of the temple's garden is attractive, particularly during the spring when the numerous cherry trees are in bloom. The waterfall is to be prayed under, preferably in mid-winter, a form of religious austerity popular in Japan, but authentically practised more in remote mountain valleys than in tourist centers like Kiyomizu.

After leaving the temple, backtrack downhill, turning right off Kiyomizuzaka Street down the steps on Sannen-zaka, and head for Maruyama Park. Along the way you'll pass numerous traditional-style Kyoto houses, beautiful in their wooden simplicity, as well as more antique and curio shops and pottery workshops. There are also several other temples and shrines on this route, as well as many cherry trees.

At the north end of Maruyama Park you'll pass Chion-in and Shor-en-in temples, both interesting and worth a stop if time permits.

Chion-in Temple is the headquarters of the Jodo sect. The enormous Sanmon gate at the south (main) entrance dates from 1619 and is the largest in Japan. The temple also has the country's largest bell, weighing 74 tons. Chion-in seems never to be overcrowded, making it both an excellent place to view many types of Buddhist symbols and a pleasant haven for relaxing.

Shoren-in Temple, north of the Chion-in, is a little off the beaten track, just below Sanjo Street, near Heian Shrine and the Miyako Hotel. Also called Awata Palace, it was built as a villa for retired emperors, and it housed a reigning empress for a period in the late 18th century. It was also the official residence of the head abbot of the Tendai sect, who was always a prince of the imperial family. The present buildings date from 1895 and the garden is one of Kyoto's finest. Both Shoren-in and Chion-in temples are still used and you'll probably be able to see priests chanting prayers.

Heian Shrine, also built in 1895, is relatively new for Kyoto. Here are enshrined the emperors Kammu, who established the city, and Komei, father of Emperor Meiji. The shrine's brilliant orange and green painted wooden outer frame and huge *torii* gate are impressive. There is a charming garden behind the main sanctuary, noted for cherry blossoms in spring, lotus flowers in summer, and maples in autumn.

Along the Old Canal

To reach the canal, take city bus No. 5 from Kyoto Station and get off at Eikando-mae stop. Cherry trees along the canal form a natural canopy, gorgeous in spring, summer, and autumn. The trail here is called "The Path of Philosophy" because a noted Japanese philosopher used to stroll this route while meditating.

This area has several temples and shrines of note. Following the old canal in first an eastwardly direction and then north you come to Nanzen-ji Temple, then Eikando, and finally Ginkakuji Temple. The walk takes about 50 minutes or so, depending on how much time is spent at each.

Nanzen-ji, the Temple of Enlightenment (founded 1293), lies in a lovely wooded area at the foot of the hills east of the city. There are beautiful paintings of angels and birds by artists of the Tosa and Kano schools and a number of colorful images in the chapel over the great Sanmon (1626), which is also worth going up in for the view and for the interest of the construction. It is famous as the hiding place of the outlaw Ishikawa Goemon. Captured, he and his son were boiled alive in an iron vat (1632?). Such was Ishikawa's courage that he held the boy above his head until he collapsed in death. The abbot's quarters have a well-known sand garden, and notable sliding screen paintings from the Imperial Palace and from Fushimi Castle. The subtemple of Konchi-in has an interesting garden with a large, black-lacquered shrine in it. Much of the charm of Nanzen-ji lies, however, not in specific works of art or architecture but in strolling at random through the grounds and the area around them, a quiet, relatively unmodernized part of Kyoto. Two of the subtemples serve traditional vegetarian lunches in their gardens, too.

First the bad news about Eikando Temple: it has loudspeakers that babble incessantly. But it also has beautiful gardens, one of which includes a graceful arching stone bridge. The temple's rock and sand garden is worth seeing too.

Perhaps the major sightseeing spot here is Ginkakuji, the Silver Pavilion. This was a shogun's retirement palace, built in 1479 by Ashikaga Yoshimasa and later turned into a Zen temple. The pavilion was never actually covered with silver. The intriguing sandpiles in the main courtyard are designed for moonlight viewing, and give the temple grounds a mysterious air. Some people say the sandpiles are supposed to represent famous lakes in China. A plaque at the entrance to the temple gives its history in English.

This entire area is made for the wanderer—don't map out an exact route. Just take your time and leave yourself open to discovery. In addition to other interesting temples such as Honenin and Shinyodo, and Yoshida Shrine, you will discover that nearly every street and alley contains something—a garden, antique shop, teahouse, charming restaurant, beautiful traditional Kyoto-style house, a bamboo grove.

Northwest Kyoto

To visit Kinkakuji, Ryoanji, and Ninnaji temples, take city bus No. 205 from Kyoto Station and get off at Kinkakuji-michi stop. Or try out the efficient city subway by going to the end of the line, Kitaoji, before catching the #205 bus. Across the street from the bus stop is Kinkakuji Temple. From here you can walk southwest for about 40 to 50 minutes to reach Ninna-ji, stopping along the way at Ryoanji Temple.

Kinkaku-ji, called the Golden Pavilion, is perhaps the best known temple in Kyoto, because it is covered in gold leaf. The original temple was built by Yoshimitsu, the third Ashikaga Shogun (1358–1408). He constructed it in 1397 for his retirement. The present pavilion is a replica, built in 1955, of the original, which was deliberately burned by one of its priests in 1950. The Japanese author Mishima based his *Kinkaku-ji* on the story of the student-monk who apparently was suffering from deranged notions when he set fire to the pavilion. The wooded grounds of the temple are lovely, as are the views around the pond within the temple area.

Located at Ryoanji-mae bus stop (bus #59 from Kinkakuji) or southwest on foot from Kinkakuji-mae bus stop is Ryoanji Temple, with what is arguably the most famous rock and sand garden in Japan, if not the world. A tile-topped earthen wall envelops the garden on three sides; a temple with a wooden veranda forms the fourth side where you can sit, relax, and contemplate this enigmatic arrangement of stones, created in the 1470s. Fifteen stones of various sizes have been placed together in separate groups on ash-white gravel that is raked daily into set patterns. Ryoan-ji is a popular spot, one often jammed with tourists, but try not to worry about others. Find a place to sit down and enjoy. Countless people have pondered the question of what the stones represent. It's like looking at clouds against the sky—your imagination will tell you what the rocks are, their meaning, if any. Perhaps you will simply find a rock and sand garden, or you may see mountains soaring above clouds. We are not even sure who the designer of the garden was or what the design meant to him.

But there is more to this temple than the famous rock garden. The grounds contain small groves of trees, a pond, a huge *moku-gyo* (a wooden gong that makes a "tonk" sound when struck by water), and a spacious plant garden that provides a marvelous place for a quiet stroll.

Next on your walk might be Ninnaji Temple with its two mammoth Nio-sama gods (excellent examples of their kind) guarding either side of the entrance gate. The temple is Chinese in its hierarchical series of courtyards, terraces, gates, and ceremonial halls, facing south behind an imposing entrance. But into this formal pomp the Japanese inserted their own style of living—low, rambling, irregularly placed wooden buildings with cedar roofs, open verandas, sliding panels and miniature gardens. To get the full flavor of the Ninna-ji compound, wander through the spacious grounds. The temple was built in 888 by the Emperor Uda, who then retired to become its first abbot; it now is a headquarters of the Shingon sect. Completely burned in the Onin Wars (15th century), it was rebuilt in the 17th century; the five-story pagoda (108 feet high) dates from 1637. The palace burned again in 1888; the present buildings were finished in 1915.

Just as the Kinkaku-ji is one of Kyoto's major attractions, so is Nijo Castle, built in 1603 by the Tokugawa shogunate. It is located in front of Nijojo-mae bus stop. You can also find it on a 10-minute walk northwest from Oike subway station. Despite its moat, turrets, and huge entrance, this actually was used as a luxurious residential palace. Ironically, it was from here that, on April 6, 1868, Emperor Meiji issued the edict that abolished the shogunate. Under the floorboards inside the palace, mechanisms were installed that emitted a chirping sound when a person was walking, a signal to warn of potential assassins. The garden is one of the finest in Japan. It was created by Kobori Enshu (1579–1647).

The Moss Temple

The Saiho-ji, or Moss Temple, is by tradition reputed to have 100 kinds of moss in its garden. The colors and textures of the garden are considered best during or just after a rain. The designer of the temple's pond was Muso Kokushi (1275–1351), an eminent Zen teacher. The pond is shaped like the Chinese character for "heart, mind." (In Zen Buddhism this designates consciousness and man's essential nature, which is enlightenment.)

This temple attracted so many visitors, the neighbors became irate over the noise and confusion—and fearful that the temple might suffer irreparable damage. Their protests induced authorities to close the temple to the general public in the summer of 1977. Entry is still possible, but you must write for an appointment and pay a ¥3,000 fee. If you want to visit the Saiho-ji, best to check with the TIC on the latest requirements for entry. You can reach the temple by taking a taxi from Arashiyama Station.

Headquarters of the Jodo Shin Sect

The Jodo Shin sect of Japanese Buddhism has two headquarters temples: Higashi (East) Hongan-ji and Nishi (West) Hongan-ji. The former is just north of Kyoto Station. Here, the ornate double-roofed Daishido (Founder's Hall), second largest wooden building in Japan and the largest in Kyoto, enshrines a wooden image of Shinran (1173–1262), founder of the sect. The Buddha sanctuary, to the south, enshrines Amida Nyorai, Buddha of the western Paradise, the particular personification of the Buddha principle worshipped in the Shin sect. About 10 minutes' walk west, Nishi Hongan-ji contains some of Kyoto's finest treasures. The two main halls are open to the general public. The Amida-do (1706) enshrines Amida Nyorai; to the south is the larger Founder's Hall (1636), which contains a sitting image of Saint Shinran, flanked by portraits of successive chief abbots of the sect.

At the temple office you can apply to view the inner buildings, which house some remarkable examples of Japanese Buddhist architecture. When the Fushimi Castle in southern Kyoto was dismantled around 1632, its parts were distributed among various temples; Nishi Hongan-ji received the best—the very colorful Karamon gate in the south wall, the Hiunkaku (Flying Cloud Pavilion) Villa, the Noh stage, and the hall of state. The latter two are divided into several rooms named after the dominant decoration motif—Stock Chamber, Sparrow Chamber, Wave Chamber, Hideyoshi's main Audience Hall; every room is lavishly decorated by the leading masters of the Kano school and by the wood sculptor Hidari Jingoro.

Down the Side Streets

Walking along Kyoto's seemingly endless number of side streets not only gives you a sense of adventure, but often you will discover that special tea shop, handmade silk kimono store, or a tiny establishment offering elegant pottery. Many tea shops, for example, also offer a wide variety of tea pots and cups, Japanese and Western style. You can browse at your own pace and usually the proprietor will offer you samples of freshly brewed tea.

As you stroll the side streets you may hear the hum of machines drifting from what appear to be houses. In many cases what you hear are sewing machines being operated by housewives who are sewing together kimonos to earn extra spending money. There are several small kimono manufacturers who can't afford to have their own factory, so they hire housewives to cut and sew kimono patterns.

A Matter of Zen

The seven administrative lines of the Zen ("meditation") sect of Japanese Buddhism all have their headquarters in Kyoto. East of Kinkaku-ji, about 5 minutes by streetcar, is Daitoku-ji, the Temple of

Great Virtue, a rambling, 27-acre, pine-shaded complex of headquarters, shrine halls, ceremonial gates, training monastery, and subtemples rich in art treasures, tea houses, and gardens. Daitoku-ji was founded in 1394; the present buildings are from 1479. The main ceremonial halls lie on a north-south axis along the east side. The first gate, Chokushimon, a special gate of the palace reserved for imperial messengers, was moved here in 1640. Next comes the two-story Sanmon, or "Mountain Gate" (1589), the symbolic main gate of Daitoku-ji (Zen temples are figuratively called "mountains"). To its right is a bath house, now unused. Next comes the Butsuden (1664), the main shrine hall, in T'ang Chinese style, enshrining an image of Shakyamuni, the historical Buddha (Siddhartha Gautama, c. 560–480 B.C.). Beyond it is the Hatto, or Lecture Hall (1636), also in Chinese style. To the right, a small building surrounded by a pond (for fire protection) is a storehouse for the Buddhist scriptures. Behind this is a belfry. The large walled complex beyond the Hatto is the Honbo, the abbot's quarters and administrative offices, containing notable painted screens by Kano Tanyu and two gardens by Kobori Enshu. The south, front garden, is an expanse of raked sand, representing water, with a few carefully shaped dwarf trees and a composition of stones. The east garden was designed to incorporate an open view across the city to Mt. Hiei. Modern construction has marred this. The Honbo's large collection of priceless paintings is aired once a year, the second Sunday of October.

Eight of Daitoku-ji's 22 subtemples are open for sightseeing. Each has its own characteristics; give yourself half to three-quarters of an hour for each of several, find one you particularly like, then linger there. Zen in other countries has produced very different results artistically, as five minutes in any Korean or Chinese monastery will show; but in Japan the interaction of a Buddhism based on a particularly unadorned type of meditation with the naturally puritanical Japanese temperament has produced an esthetic at once subtle and severe, a spare and disciplined tranquillity. It is nature refined by art to make it more natural than itself, to bring out the essence of each single one of the "ten thousand things." Some of these gardens, like Koto-in, are spacious; or, like Ho-shun-in, are elaborate; others, like Zui-ho-in, are small and simple. Some, using only rocks, moss and sand, are timeless. Others use maples and flowering bushes and are brilliant in autumn and lovely in spring. But the basic elements are few, so do not try to see too many or they will all blur together in your memory. And it is better to go where the crowds don't; these temples and their paintings, tea houses, and gardens are not built for mass traffic. Some of their best effects depend on empty spaces, long verandas, silent rooms. Try several and suit yourself. (One caution: Daisen-in, supposedly a temple, has become a commercial sideshow of unbelievably brassy vulgarity. Avoid it at all cost.) Just north of the east gate of Daitoku-ji is a wooded lot full of curious and beautiful stones, gnarled, veined, colored and oddly shaped. Japanese gardens do not just happen; they are painstakingly planned; and this is the storehouse of a dealer in garden stones. All of them have been carefully selected; many come from far away; some will bring astronomical prices.

Daitoku-ji is the best organized for sightseeing of Kyoto's Zen temples. Tenryu-ji, in Arashiyama, is noted mainly for its landscape garden by Muso Kokushi (who also did the Moss Temple garden) and for the tombs of the emperors Kameyama and Daigo II. Shokoku-ji, north of the Imperial Palace in the center of the city, has some remarkable and still little-known sliding panel paintings in the Hojo or abbot's quarters; these have just recently been opened to the public. The bamboos, by the Zen priest Gyokurin, are especially fine; and there are two interesting gardens, refreshingly uncrowded so far. Nanzenji, situated in a lovely area of the city, is discussed above, under "Along the Old Canal."

Myoshin-ji, largest of the Zen headquarters, is still not overrun by sightseers. The gardens and screen paintings of the Hojo are open to the public, and the dragon on the ceiling of the Hatto (Lecture Hall) by Kano Tanyu is considered the finest in Kyoto. Kennin-ji is located in the heart of the rather unmonastic Gion pleasure quarter. Tofuku-ji, in the southeast corner of the city, is largely unfrequented, a vast open hillside with an enormous meditation hall that suggests what the strength of Zen as a monastic discipline must have been 500 years ago. The grounds are popular for maple viewing in autumn.

Imperial Kyoto

Three places in Kyoto require permits from the Imperial Household Agency: the Imperial Palace (Kyoto Gosho) and the Katsura and Shugakuin villas. To see the Imperial Palace, apply at least 24 hours ahead of time through major hotels, JTB or the TIC. To see the Katsura and Shugakuin, call the Tokyo or Kyoto TIC as soon as you arrive, since applications must be made a week to a month in advance and they are not accepted from overseas. You must be over 20 years of age to receive permission to see them, which is free. For all three, you must be punctual, as these visits are privileges, restricted, and closely supervised.

The Gosho, surrounded by high walls, lies in a 200-acre park in the center of the city. The present location is from 1790; and the present buildings (1855) are in traditional style, characterized by careful proportions and great simplicity of line, ornament and materials. The effect is austere, but restful; this is one of Japan's very few examples of broad, open, monumental architecture, the style of the Heian period (794–1192). Not all the buildings may be entered, and specific works of art (carvings and paintings such as abound in Nijo Castle) are few, but the gardens (28 acres) are charming, and there is a scale and serenity, a feeling of clean, airy clarity about the Gosho that is very unusual in Japan. View it as a whole; this is a Chinese-inspired ceremonial ensemble, spacious, harmonious, symmetrical and dignified. (The Gosho is open to the general public for one week in early April and one week in early November each year.)

The Katsura Villa is widely admired as *the* crowning achievement of Japanese architecture. This is a narrow view—Katsura is the distillation of *one* of several distinct functional styles in traditional Japanese building. But it is both a distinguished achievement within its own style and important for the wide influence it has had on modern architecture everywhere in the last 50 years. Katsura is abstract art, a static work, silent, austere and perfectly balanced, with an almost inhuman restraint and discipline. This building with its garden is perhaps the ultimate expression of that peculiarly Japanese mentality in which iron discipline is so ingrained that art, artifice and nature become indistinguishable. No single thing is artificial; only the simplest of natural materials are used, but with the implacable logic, tight economy and icy precision of a geometry proof, to produce the timeless, distant, abstract beauty of clear water and utter silence. One cannot imagine Katsura lived in; not a pebble or a pine needle is out of place. No human passion or daily disorder could survive in this fragile, lucid work of art. Katsura is an experience in the mind, a cerebral esthetic of great subtlety, uniquely Japanese.

Begun in 1590, this became the masterpiece of Kobori Enshu (1579–1647), Japan's greatest garden designer, who imposed three conditions on his patron, the military dictator Hideyoshi: no limit on expense; no limit on time; no interference until completion. The villa itself is in three sections, each divided into several rooms, these decorated with priceless paintings by members of the Kano school and fittings of exquisite detail and craftsmanship. Yet the overall effect is of great simplicity and restraint. The garden is organized around a pond, with teahouses individually designed for each of the four seasons, a small temple, and various landscape features in miniature. It is planned so that wherever you stand seems to be the best place, the "main" view of the entire panorama including the villa. Katsura Villa has recently had a full-fledged renovation, the first in 370 years, that took six years to complete.

The Shugaku-in does not have Katsura's highly calculated, tightly organized unity; but Katsura has nothing of the Shugaku-in's superb position on a foothill of Mt. Hiei, overlooking the city. This is the most "western" of Kyoto's gardens, like a park, rather than a traditional Japanese garden with its shut-in, blocked feeling of small things carefully and cautiously crowded into small spaces. The Shugaku-in consists of three large gardens, each containing buildings, each on a different level. The grounds total 69 acres; the upper garden is the largest and is built around a lake with islands, bridges, waterfalls, long walking paths, and a fine view over Kyoto to the surrounding hills. Built in 1629 as a retirement villa for the Emperor Gomizuno-o, the buildings are in the same tradition as those of Katsura, the fragile, simple, airy summerhouse style used particularly for tea-ceremony rooms and garden pavilions, the aspect of Japanese architecture best known abroad. The Rakushiken pavilion in the middle garden has the best paintings in the Shugaku-in; and the gardens are best in autumn because of the skillful placing of maple trees among the pines; but there is a relaxed, open and peaceful quality about the Shugaku-in in any season.

Generally overlooked are three other former Imperial residences, now temples. Shoren-in, also called Awata Palace, is discussed above, under "Kiyomizu Temple & Heian Shrine."

Daikaku-ji, a few minutes' drive north of Arashiyama, in the western suburbs, was built as a retirement villa for the Emperor Saga; in 876 it became a temple of the Shingon sect, also with imperial princes as abbots. It resembles the Kyoto Gosho but on a less imposing, far more intimate and relaxed scale. The buildings themselves are Japanese; their arrangement is a pleasant combination of Chinese ceremonial symmetry and Japanese rambling, set in a garden that is noticeably less fussy than most Japanese gardens and unusually spacious, particularly to the east where it opens on to a small lake. The much touted unity of Japanese house and garden is particularly natural, unaffected, and hence successful at Daikaku-ji, for the garden really interpenetrates the palace, rather than being merely looked-at, as is often the case. The whole place meanders delightfully.

Ninnaji, the Omura Palace, is discussed above, under "Northwest Kyoto."

Off the Main Streets

Kyoto has been noted since earliest times for fine fabrics, and its people for their love of elegant dress. Nishijin is the textile-weaving area; during the Tokugawa Period (1603–1867) all the silks for the court and the nobility came from there. Most of the work is still done in the homes of the craftspeople themselves, or in small neighborhood workshops. Nishijin extends from around Daitoku-ji south to Imadegawa Street and from Kitano Shrine east to Horikawa Street. One way to see it is to start from Daitoku-ji and wander gradually south and east to the Horikawa-Imadegawa intersection. Or, begin at Kitano Shrine, visiting it first for its trees, shingled roofs and treasures. Its gates are designated "Important Cultural Properties," and its Main Hall and oratory are both "National Treasures." Then go east and somewhat north, then veer south to the same intersection, a bit west of which, at Imadegawa-Omiya, is the Nishijin Textile Museum (open 9:00 A.M. –5:00 P.M.) a good place to end such a tour.

Choose small quiet side streets rather than large ones full of shops and cars. Lanes and alleys are even better. Kyoto is built on the grid plan, so you cannot get lost. Five or ten minutes' walk in any direction leads to a street with taxis. And wherever you happen to be, there will be plenty of local color. Nishijin contains few cultural monuments, but the "real Japan" is made up of the daily lives of 115 million people, and they do not live in ancient palaces.

Nishijin houses (called "unaginedoko," eel sleeping places, by their inhabitants) are narrow and very deep. The fronts are covered by wooden grills, painted dark reddish-brown, one story high. The tiled roof rises gradually over a large attic; far in back is an inner garden and sometimes a smaller house beyond that. Everywhere you will hear the whirring rattle and click of weaving machinery; almost every house has at least one loom going. In warm weather, doors and windows are open, or even removed entirely, and you can see complex machinery in dim interiors. At the museum you will see the gorgeous and ingenious products of these hundreds of tiny workshops.

Another cross-section of traditional Kyoto is Nakagyo, the central
business district, a square between Marutamachi and Shijo, Horikawa
and Kawaramachi streets. On Shijo are great modern department
stores. Beside, between, behind, among them are little shops and workshops where traditional crafts are handed down in old family businesses
—fine papers, fans, dolls, lacquer work, bamboo, kimonos, tailoring,
tea utensils, scroll mounting, confectionery, traditional foods. Banks,
insurance offices, newspapers, public buildings overshadow temples
and public markets. A colorful walking street, Nishikidori, is devoted
to fresh foods of all kinds. The section east of Karasuma is rewarding
because it is so chaotic; there is no telling what you may find there.
Walk slowly, and watch out for traffic.

A systematic plan is to follow certain streets their full length. Try
Muromachi Street, just west of Karasuma, from Imadegawa down to
Shijo. A longer walk is Teramachi Street from its northern end at
Kuramaguchi, above Shokoku Temple, down past numerous temples,
a pleasant residential area, two universities, the Imperial Palace, an
interesting shopping area, an entertainment district, more shopping, to
its end, just above Gojo. This will be a long walk but an extremely
varied one; and it will give you a really full cross-section of all aspects
of life in Kyoto. The mixture of shops old and new is particularly
interesting from Marutamachi south.

These walks are all by day; but the entertainment districts are best
by night. The main ones are in a broad continuous belt from Teramachi
east to Higashioji, and from Sanjo south to Shijo, then irregularly down
to Matsubara. Within this area distinct variations occur.

On the west, Shinkyogoku Street runs parallel to Teramachi; both
streets and the lanes, alleys, passages, and corridors between and off
them are filled with restaurants, snack places, bars, movie theaters,
inns, short-time hotels, and baths, as well as the temples, shrines, craft
shops, clothing stores and other more sedate businesses that one sees
by day. It is all mixed up together; surrounded by bars is a dim shrine
where amateurs practice ancient Central Asian temple dances. Teramachi and Kyogoku streets are large, bright, noisy and garish; some of the
smaller side lanes are softly lit by paper lanterns.

East of this, many short, narrow alleys run east-west between
Kawaramachi and Kiyamachi streets. They are crammed with bars
and eating places. Most of these are raucously "modern" in their
plaster, glass, chrome and neon décor; the overall effect is crowded,
noisy, and delightfully colorful. Kiyamachi street itself is divided into
East and West sides by the Takase River, a shallow brook lined with
willow trees. East Kiyamachi is mostly small inns; south of Shijo it is
tiny, very exclusive inns and Japanese-style restaurants, many of which
require reservations. West Kiyamachi is bars, restaurants and night
clubs; south of Shijo it is in places shabby and dubious.

Pontocho is a tiny walking street from Sanjo to Shijo, no more than
a few feet wide, one row of houses away from the west bank of the
Kamo River. Though stucco, chrome, neon and plastic are creeping in,
this is still one of Kyoto's loveliest streets, with its freshly washed stone
pavement, soft lighting and the satiny textures of natural wood on
old-style houses. Walk slowly through Pontocho and look carefully

about you; it is rich in details that are the essence of Japanese taste, skill, and craftmanship. This street is the home of one of the two schools of Kyoto geisha; the other is in Gion, the area across the river up to Yasaka Shrine. North of Shijo it tends to run to flashily modernized bars, "nightclubs," and restaurants, though some quiet and attractive spots remain. Start at Yasaka Shrine and wander diagonally northwest to Sanjo Station. The part up to Shinmonzen Street and along the little river is best at night; Shinmonzen Street and north is better by day.

But for sheer atmosphere, the cream of Gion and of Kyoto by night is the area from Shijo south to Kennin-ji. It is only a few blocks each way, but nowhere else will you find, as here, a harmony of wood, stone, tile, water, and softly filtered light, a nocturnal magic that is totally, superlatively Japanese. Walk south on Hanamikoji, winding back and forth on the small east-west cross streets as far down as Yasaka Kaikan and Kennin-ji; after that it all degenerates into incredibly hideous short-time hotels. Some of these are worth looking at for the stupefying improbability of their décor; and it is well to realize that the myths about the universal artistic sensitivity of the Japanese are badly in need of an agonizing reappraisal. But save that for another time. Stop at Kennin-ji and keep intact the charm of what you have just seen. South Gion is unique; in Japan, or anywhere else in the world, there is no place quite like it.

Outside Kyoto

A pleasant suburb to visit is Arashiyama, 25 minutes by electric tram west of Shijo Omiya Station in central Kyoto. Steep wooded hills run from the Oi River, which is deep enough for swimming and boating. You can have tea or coffee or a meal at one of the many restaurants and cafes here, some of which have gardens and terraces overlooking the river. There is a pleasant park at the end of a famous footbridge across the river from Arashiyama Station. Throughout July and August there is cormorant fishing every night from around 7:30 to 9:30 P.M. on the river except during a full moon or after a heavy rain. This is a tourist attraction that demonstrates an old form of fishing and is exciting because of the flaming torches on the boats and the hundreds of lanterns lining the river.

Another attraction here is the Hozu River rapids boat trip. Go by train to Kameoka (on the San-in line), where you can descend by boat (6 miles in about 1½ hours) to Arashiyama. The journey down the river gorge is exciting but not dangerous—a great way to cool off on a hot summer afternoon. There are also a number of pretty temples in and north of Arashiyama, most of them within 20 minutes' walk of the tram station. At the station is a large, wall-size map that shows you how to walk to the temples. Tenryu-ji, Daikaku-ji, and Shaka-do are some of the best known.

About 15 kilometers southeast of Kyoto is the town of Uji, noted for its tea and two temples. The famous Phoenix Hall, built in 1053, of the Byodo-in Temple is a curious piece of sculpture. The three wings framing the building have no architectural function; they are there to create the image of a phoenix, a Chinese mythological bird.

Mampuku-ji, the Temple of Abundant Good Fortune, is the headquarters of the Obaku Sect, the smallest branch of Zen Buddhism in Japan. The temple was built in 1668, and the buildings are in modified Ming Chinese style. If you make an appointment at the temple's restaurant, you can enjoy a typical Kyoto-style vegetarian meal. To reach Byodo-in or Mampuku-ji temple, take the Uji line of the Keihan Railway from Sanjo Station; get off at Obakusan and walk east a short ways for Mampuku-ji. For Byodo-in get off at the Uji City terminus. The temple is within ten minutes' walk across the pink Uji bridge and to the left along the river.

Heading back into the city, you can stop off at Fushimi Inari Station for a short walk east to the Fushimi Inari Shrine. It is famous for its bright orange "tunnels" of torii (traditional gateways to Shinto shrines) that wind up a hillside.

Northeast of Kyoto is Enryaku-ji, a temple complex on Mount Hiei, the highest point in the ridge that separates Kyoto from Lake Biwa, the largest lake in Japan. Temples were first constructed here as early as 788, when Emperor Kammi (the one who moved the capital from nearby Nara to Kyoto) ordered some temples built to guard against what he believed to be evil spirits from the northeast. At one point there were 3,000 temples here, but all were destroyed by the army of Nobunaga Oda in 1571. Today there are about 130 temples on the mountain.

You can reach Enryaku-ji one of four ways, other than by car. The first two are either by Keifuku private railway from Demachi-Yanagi Station, or by bus from Kyoto Station to Yase-yuen and then cable railway to the top. The third route is by Keihan train from Sanjo-Keihan Station via Otsu along the shore of Lake Biwa to the terminus at Sakamoto. From there a cable car runs up the east side of the mountain. The fourth way is by bus from Kyoto; at least 10 buses a day depart from Kyoto Station to the temple.

PRACTICAL INFORMATION FOR KYOTO

WHEN TO GO? Kyoto is cold and often damp in winter, and hot and damp in summer. Spring is lovely but brief, with April the favorite month for cherry viewing. Best season of all is autumn-mid-September through late November (maples). Reservations are advisable, as Japanese tourists like Kyoto then, too. December is free of crowds but dress warmly. The entertainment and cultural season is October–May inclusive. July and August are hottest. Freedom from crowds commend both summer and winter for ease in seeing the real, old Kyoto.

HOW TO GET THERE. By air. There are daily flights from Tokyo to Osaka International Airport, as well as from other cities in Japan and abroad. From Tokyo, the flight takes about an hour. Buses leave the airport about every 20 minutes for Kyoto, a ride that takes about 75 minutes.

By bus. The most convenient service is the JNR "Dream" bus that runs at night. It leaves Tokyo around 11:00 P.M., arrives Kyoto Station at 7:45 A.M. The buses have reclining seats and are air conditioned. They are popular, so it is best to book in advance during the spring and autumn tourist seasons. Check with the tourist information center in Tokyo for current departure schedules and ticket bookings. There is also bus service from Tokyo to Nagoya, and from there to Kyoto during the day. But it's a long ride.

By car. The Tomei Expressway from Tokyo to Nagoya and the Meishin Expressway from Nagoya to Osaka are completed, and very good. Self-drive cars are available; but remember you drive on the left side of the road in Japan and traffic often is very heavy. Furthermore, rental cars, expressway tolls, and gasoline are expensive in Japan.

By train. This is the most relaxing, easiest way to get to Kyoto. Tokaido Shinkansen super express trains (the famed "Bullet Trains") take you right to the center of the city. There are about 90 Shinkansen trains daily from Tokyo. The fastest Shinkansen service is called *Hikari* and takes about 2¾ hours to reach Kyoto, making one stop. The other is the *Kodama,* which makes more stops, and takes about 4 hours to reach Kyoto. All Shinkansen trains have buffet cars, comfortable seats (reclining ones in the first class Green cars), and telephones. Unfortunately, there is only one nonsmoking car on each train and the seats are nonreserved. You are advised to purchase Shinkansen tickets in advance.

There is rapid train service from Kobe to Kyoto, taking about 1 hour. The trip from Osaka takes about 30 minutes.

TELEPHONES. The area code for Kyoto is 075. You do not need to dial the area code if it is the same as the one from which you are calling. International: Calls can be made to any country. Direct dialing is available for some calls but it is better to ask the operator. For information on overseas calls, telephone (03) 270–5111. Remember that noon in Kyoto is 10:00 in the evening of the previous day in New York and 3:00 in the morning of the same day in London.

HOTELS AND INNS. Accommodation is widely available in Kyoto but it is absolutely necessary to book well in advance during peak tourist seasons in spring, late summer, and autumn. There are super-deluxe, Western-style hotels as well as numerous Japanese inns, called *ryokans.* In either case the service is probably the best in Asia. The best ryokan will be more expensive than the usual Western-style hotels, but you will receive two banquet-like meals of traditional Kyoto cuisine served in your room and superb service. Less expensive ryokans offer varying qualities of service and food (you get what you pay for), but you can usually find a good ryokan at cheaper than Western-style prices.

The main points to remember about ryokans are these: you don't wear shoes inside, slippers will be provided; in your room you sleep on a tatami straw floor in futon quilts, all of which will be laid out for you. And remember, too, that when you enter your bedroom, take off the slippers beforehand. Your meals will probably be served to you in your room. When you're ready for your bath, which is taken in the evening, you soap yourself outside the tub and only enter *after* rinsing off all the suds. The tub is for soaking in. It's a terrific experience, but be forewarned, the water is often incredibly hot.

WESTERN-STYLE HOTELS

Deluxe

Hotel New Hankyu. Shiokoji-shinmachi, Shimogyo-ku; 343–5300. This hotel opened in early 1983 next to Kyoto Station. Excellent base for shopping, some walking tours, temples, and near to the tourist information center. There are 316 rooms. ¥ 6,800–18,000.

International. 284 Nijo Aburanokoji, Nakagyo-ku; 222–1111. Opposite Nijo Castle. Three times each summer evening, "Son et Lumiere" with Royal Shakespeare Theater Company members presents the Heian World of a thousand years ago. There are 332 rooms. ¥ 6,800–25,000.

Kyoto. Kawaramachi-Oike, Nakagyo-ku; 211–5111. Centrally located and a good base for walking tours. Next to the Kamo River, which is a good place for running. Also near some of the city's major shopping areas. Western and Japanese restaurants, bars, shops. There are 510 rooms. ¥ 7,000–27,000.

Kyoto Royal Hotel. Kawaramachi, Sanjo, Nakagyo-ku; 223–1234. Good location for shopping and walking tours. Not far from Kyoto Hotel. There are 395 rooms. ¥ 7,000–18,000.

Miyako. Sanjo Keage, Higashiyama-ku; 771–7111. Perhaps the most widely known hotel in Kyoto. Numerous facilities including pool, restaurants, bars, gardens, shops. There are 480 rooms. ¥ 7,000–50,000.

Expensive

Fujita. Nishizume, Nijo-Ohashi, Nakagyo-ku; 222–1511. Located along the Kamo River. Has a bowling alley among many other facilities. There are 198 rooms. ¥ 7,000–24,000.

Holiday Inn. 36 Nishihirakicho, Takano, Sakyo-ku; 721–3131. A typical Holiday Inn, no surprises. Near the Takano River. Not very convenient, but has all the facilities expected, including pool, tennis, bowling alley, bar, etc. There are 270 rooms. ¥ 7,900–15,400.

Kyoto Century Hotel. Higashi-no-Toin-dori, Shimogyo-ku; 351–0111. Near Kyoto Station. Located in the remodeled station plaza that has Kyoto's first underground shopping mall. There are 243 rooms. ¥ 7,500–19,000.

Kyoto Grand. Horikawa-Shiokoji, Shimogyo-ku; 341–2311. Near Kyoto Station and the business-shopping districts. Toji Temple is nearby. Has numerous facilities, including pool and sauna bath. There are 578 rooms. ¥ 7000–20,000.

New Mijako. Nishi-Kujoincho, Minami-ku; 661–7111. Sister hotel of the Miyako Hotel. In front of Kyoto Station. There are 714 rooms. ¥ 6,000–17,000.

Moderate and Inexpensive

Hotel Gimmond. Takakura Oike-dori, Nakagyo-ku; 221–4111. Central and convenient. There are 142 rooms. ¥ 6,800–19,000.

Hotel New Kyoto. Horikawa-Marutamachi, Kamigyo-ku; 801–2111. North of Nijo Castle and not too far from Old Imperial Palace grounds. There are 320 rooms. ¥ 6,000–12,000.

Kyoto Park Hotel. 644–2 Sanjusangendo, Mawari-machi, Higashiyama-ku; 525–3111. Located in center of old part of city; quiet. There are 307 rooms. ¥ 5,500–35,000.

Kyoto Prince Hotel. 43 Matsubaracho, Shimogamo, Sakyo-ku; 781–4141. Pleasant and comfortable. A regular with Japanese visitors. There are 100 rooms. ¥6,000–13,000.

Kyoto Station. Higashi-no-Toin-dori, Shiokoji, Shimogyo-ku; 361–7151. Good service. Diagonally in front of Kyoto Station. There are 117 rooms. ¥6,000–12,000.

Kyoto Tower. Karasuma-Shichijo-sagaru, Shimogyo-ku; 361–3211. Opposite station. There are 148 rooms. ¥5,600–17,000.

The Mount Hiei Hotel. Ipponsugi, Hiezan, Sakyo-ku; 701–2111. A mountain resort hotel with splendid views of Kyoto and Lake Biwa, but pretty far out of town. There are 73 rooms. ¥6,000–17,000.

JAPANESE INNS

Deluxe

Chigiriya. Takoyakushi-dori-Tominokoji-nishi-iru, Nakagyo-ku; 221–1281. 49 rooms (4 Western-style, others Japanese-style). Charges per person with two meals ¥20,000–30,000.

Hiiragiya Ryokan. Fuyacho-Aneyakoji-agaru, Nakagyo-ku; 221–1136. 33 Japanese-style rooms. Elegant and quiet. Charges per person with two meals ¥25,000–35,000.

Ikumatsu. Kiyamachi-dori-Oike-agaru, Nakagyo-ku; 231–4191. 24 Japanese-style rooms. Charges per person with two meals ¥12,000–20,000.

Kinta Ryokan. Yanaginobamba-dori-Shijosagaru, Shimogyo-ku; 351–1429. 29 Japanese-style rooms. Charges per person with two meals ¥18,000–20,000.

Ryokan Tsuruki. Kiyamachi-Gojo-agaru, Shimogyo-ku; 361–9261. 16 Japanese-style rooms. Charges per meals ¥12,000–20,000.

Tawaraya. Fuyacho-Aneyakoji-Agaru,Nakagyo-ku; 211–5566. 20 Japanese-style rooms. Charges per person with two meals ¥37,800–42,000.

Yachiyo. 34 Nanzenji-fukuchicho, Sakyo-ku; 771–4148. 26 Japanese-style rooms. Charges per person with two meals ¥25,000–30,000.

Moderate

Hatoya Zuihokaku. Aburanokoji-dori-Shiokojisagaru, Shimogyo-ku; 361–1231. 45 Japanese-style rooms; 15 Western-style rooms. Charges per person with two meals ¥10,000–15,000.

Matsukichi Ryokan. Goko-machi-Sanjo-agaru, Nakagyo-ku; 221–7016. 15 Japanese-style rooms. Charges per person with two meals ¥30,000–35,000.

Nabeshima Hizenya. Ayakoji-dori-Karasuyama-nishiiru, Shimogyo-ku; 361–8421. 38 Japanese-style rooms. Charges per person with two meals ¥15,000–25,000.

Ryokan Hotel Sanoya. Higashinotoin-dori-Shichijosagaru, Shimogyo-ku; 371–2185. 43 Japanese-style rooms. Charges per person with two meals ¥13,000–15,000.

Senryu. Toriimae, Gion, Shimokawa, Higashiyama-ku; 561–0381. 10 rooms. Charges per person with 2 meals ¥13,000–20,000. A lovely little inn near Yasaka Shrine.

Tozankaku. 431 Myohoin-maekawacho, Higashiyama-ku; 561–4981. 88 Japanese-style rooms; 44 Western-style rooms. Charges per person with two meals ¥15,000–18,000.

Inexpensive

Hokke Club Inn Kyoto. Nishideguchi Shomen, Kyoto-ekimae; 361–1251. Located in front of JNR Kyoto St. Charges ¥9,000–15,000.

KYOTO 373

Nashinoki Inn. Imadegawa-dori-Teramachi-nishi-iru, Futasujime-agaru, Kamigyo-ku; 241–1543. This is one of the best bargains in Kyoto. Located on a narrow, quiet street about a 5-minute walk from Kamo River and the Old Imperial Palace grounds. The owners, Mr. and Mrs. Yamamori, speak some English, are extremely helpful and friendly. Meals served here are ample and delicious. There are 8 rooms. ¥4,500–8,000.

New Ginkaku Inn. Nanajo-sagaru, Higashinotoin, Shimogyo-ku; 371–5252. 4 min walk from JNR Kyoto St. Charges ¥8,000–13,000.

Rokuharaya Inn. 147 Takemura-cho, Higashiyama-ku; 531–2776. Old-style inn in charming Gion quarter. ¥4,000–6,000.

Shichijo-so. 7, Ikkyo-Miyanouchicho, Higashiyama-ku; 541–7803. Take bus No. 206 or No. 208 to Nanajo-ohashi which is third stop from Kyoto St. Charges ¥3,000.

Tani House (or **Mrs. Tani's**). 8 Daitokujicho, Murasakino, Kita-ku; 492–5489. Take bus No. 206 to Funaoka Koen bus stop (about 20 mins). Well-known and popular. Charges ¥1,500.

Three Sisters Inn. Okazaki-michi, Kurodani-mae, Sakyo-ku; 761–6336. Mostly foreigners staying here. English-speaking staff. Nearby annex has bath in every room. ¥6,900–11,000.

Tokyu Inn. 35–1 Hananookacho, Kamihanayama, Yamashina-ku; 593–0109. Free bus service from Hachijoguchi Exit of Kyoto St. Departures at 8:30, 9:30, 10:30, 11:30 A.M., 4:00, 5:00, 6:00 P.M. Charges range from ¥12,000–16,000.

Traveller's Inn (Hotel Sunshine). 91 Enshojicho, Okazaki, Sakyo-ku; 771–0225. Take No. 5 bus to Heianjingu Bijutsukan-mae bus stop; takes about 25 mins. Charges ¥3,900–7,800. 42 western and 16 Japanese rooms.

KOKUMIN SHUKUSHA

These government-sponsored lodges offer low priced Japanese-style rooms with 2 meals. They are all located outside of the city.

Kojoso. 1436 Matsubaracho, Hikone-shi, Shiga Pref. 1 hr. by express train to Miabara Station.

Imazuso. 1 Minamishinpo, Imazucho, Takashima-gun, Shiga Pref. 1 hr. and 10 min. by express train to Omi-imazu Station.

Omi Maiko Lodge. 931 Kitahira, Shigacho, Shiga-gun, Shiga Pref. 44 min. to Omimaiko Station.

TEMPLES

This is very basic accommodation. Guests usually sleep in dorm-type rooms.

Myoken-ji. Shinmachi Nishi-hairu, Tera-no-uchi-dori, Kamigyo-ku; 414–0808. In the same cluster as Myoren-ji, and larger. Many rooms overlook the attractive gardens.

Myoren-ji. Tera-no-uchi-dori, Higashi-iru, Omiya, Kamigyo-ku; 451–3527. Several large wooden buildings, historic stone garden, in a cluster of old Nichiren-sect temples. Inexpensive and charming.

For both temples, take a bus No. 9 from Kyoto Station, get off at Horikawa Tera-no-uchi, and follow the English-language signpost.

 YOUTH HOSTELS. Higashiyama YH. 112, Shirakawabashi-goken-cho, Sanjo-dori, Higashiyama-ku, Kyoto City 605; 761–8135. 20 min. by bus from Kyoto Sta. and 5 min. on foot. 112 beds.

Kitayama YH. Hotori, Koetsuji, Takagamine, Kita-ku, Kyoto 603; 492–5345. 30 min. by bus from Kyoto Sta. and 4 min. on foot. 38 beds. Closed Jan. 17 thr. 26.

Ohara YH. 137, Ohara-todera-cho, Sakyo-ku, Kyoto City 601–12; 744–2721. 50 min. by bus from Kyoto Sta. 23 beds.

Utano YH. 29, Nakayama-cho, Uzumasa, Ukyo-ku, Kyoto 616; 462–2288. 50 min. by bus from Kyoto Sta. 172 beds.

YH Matsusan. 331, Ebiya-cho, Sanjo-sagaru, Goko-machi, Nakagyo-ku, Kyoto City 604; 221–5160. 15 min. by streetcar from Kyoto Sta. and 4 min. on foot. 40 beds.

HOW TO GET AROUND. By bus. City buses are the easiest way to get around. In rush hours, however, they are jammed. You pay as you get off at the front of the bus. Ask the tourist information center where you can buy a book of ¥140 tickets for the bus. Makes paying much easier. Most of the city buses are air conditioned. They run about every 7–20 minutes until is 9:30 P.M. Main terminals are Kyoto Station, Sanjo Keihan Station, Shijo Kawaramachi and Kitaoji Bus Terminal.

By subway. Opened in 1981. It is only one line, running from Kyoto Station north along Karasumma-dori to Kita-oji-dori. Easy to use, spotlessly clean, safe.

By automobile. Rent-a-cars available from Nissan or Nippon Rent-a-car. Check with your hotel or tourist information center.

From the airport. You'll be arriving in Kyoto from Osaka International Airport. Buses run every 20 minutes through the day in each direction, making the rounds of several of the better-known hotels and Kyoto Station.

By taxi. Numerous taxis; a fast way to get from point A to point B. The fare is about $2 for the first 2 kilometers, with a 30¢ increase for every 405 meters, and a time charge when going through slow traffic. After 11:00 P.M., the rate increases by 20 percent. Some drivers seem to delight in driving at a race driver's pace. Don't be afraid to tell them to slow down. Rarely will you encounter a dishonest taxi driver. But if they seem lost, it's not because they are trying to take you for a ride, it's usually because they are indeed lost or have no idea where it is you want to go. Many drivers have just arrived from the countryside and don't know the city. One final word: no tipping.

TOURIST INFORMATION. *Kyoto City Information Office:* In front of Kyoto Station; 371–2108. Open from 8:30 A.M. to 5:00 P.M. *Kyoto Station Information Office for Foreign Visitors:* Just to the left of the main entrance to Kyoto Station, open 9:00 A.M.–6:00 P.M. Railway information and ticketing, and some tourist information. *Japan Travel Bureau* (JTB): in front of Kyoto Station; 361–7241. Open 9:00 A.M.–5:00 P.M. *Nippon Ryoko Kai* (Japan Travel Association, or Japan Travel Agency): Kyoto Tower Building; 361–7371. Open 9:00 A.M.–6:00 P.M. *Tourist Information Center,* Kyoto Tower Building, opposite Kyoto Station, is operated by the Japan National Tourist Organization; 371–0480. Open 9:00 A.M.–5:00 P.M. *Japan Travel-Phone* operates to assist you every day of the year from 9:00 A.M. to 5:00 P.M. In Kyoto, call 371–5649. From outside, dial 106, from a yellow or blue public phone, and say slowly "Collect Call, T.I.C." Your ¥10 coin will be returned after the call. *Tourist Section, Kyoto City Government,* is in the Municipal Auditorium, (Kyoto Kaikan). Okazaki Park, Sakyo-ku; 761–6051. The City Information Office and the Tourist Section of the City Government (first and last listings above) are particularly helpful. In 1984 the Kyoto TIC began a 24-hour recorded information service, *Teletourist;* 361–2911.

Peter Pan is a center providing information on jobs and accommodations for foreigners: Top Hat Bldg., 7th fl., north of Lipton at Shijo.

 MEDICAL SERVICES. The *Japan Baptist Hospital* (47 Yamanomoto-cho, Kitashirakawa, Sakyo-ku) has American and American-trained staff. The *First Red Cross Hospital* (Hommachi Higashiyama) and the hospitals attached to *Kyoto University* (Yoshida Hommachi) and *Kyoto Prefectural Medical University* (Kawaramachi Hirokoji), all three employ skilled personnel. For home visits there are many English-speaking doctors, and you are advised to ask at your hotel.

EMERGENCIES. *Police* Headquarters, Shinmachi Shimodachiuri; 451–9111. *Fire* Department Headquarters is Teramachi Goshokoji; 231–5311. But in every public telephone booth you will see a little red box up to the right of the main phone and with quick emergency numbers indicated on it both in Japanese and by symbols. These are: Police: 110; Fire: 119; Ambulance: 119; General emergency: 110.

 MAIL. Kyoto Central Post Office (in front of Kyoto Station, west side) takes mail, parcel post, telegrams, and telephone calls domestic and foreign. Main post offices in each ward take foreign mail; small neighborhood post offices often do not. Easiest is to ask your hotel to handle it.

ELECTRIC CURRENT. Kyoto and Nara both have: 100 volts, 60 cycles, nearly the same as the U.S., which has 110 volts and 60 cycles.

 CLOSING DAYS AND HOURS. Most shops are open Sundays. Barbers and hairdressers close Mondays. Department stores have different individual closing days. Small shops often stay open until 9:00 or 10:00 P.M. Large shops close at 5:30, though some in the main shopping area along Karasuma stay open later. Most restaurants close by 9:30, many other places by 11:00, everyone by 11:30 (all P.M.). Nearly all museums in Kyoto (and elsewhere in Japan) are closed on Mondays.

 SEASONAL EVENTS. There is some type of festival or cultural event nearly every month. Many are held outside and are free of charge. They are famous all over Japan and attract tens of thousands of Japanese tourists. Don't let that stop you from going to watch. To make sure of current dates, check with T.I.C.

January. On the 1st–3rd *Yasaka Shrine* is visited by the women of Kyoto dressed in their finest kimono. Jan. 15, *Toshiya archery contest.* This is a traditional Japanese archery contest, dating from the 16th century. From 8:00 or 9:00 A.M. at Sanjusangen-do Temple.

February. On the 3rd or 4th the end of the coldest part of the winter is celebrated at *Setsubun* temples and shrines all over the city by throwing beans to drive out evil spirits. Evening bonfire at Yoshida Shrine. Demon-exorcising pantomimes at Mibudera, Rozan-ji.

JAPAN

Baika-sai. (Plum Blossom Festival), on February 25th at Kitano Temmangu Shrine. Outdoor tea ceremony and flea market.

March. *Otaimatsu* (Fire Festival) at Seiryoji Temple in Arashiyama at 8:00 P.M. on the 15th. This festival commemorates the death of Shakamuni, founder of Buddhism. The fertility of the crops in the coming year is predicted from the way in which three pine torches, 20 feet long, are consumed by fire.

April. Famous *cherry blossom festival,* usually in mid April. Check with tourist information center. The best cherry blossom viewing dates vary according to the weather. Kyoto has 20 noted cherry-viewing sites, including Nijo Castel, Heian Shrine, Maruyama Park, Kiyomizu Temple, Ninna-ji, and Arashiyama. To avoid masses of people, go on weekdays.

Mibu Kyogen, 21st–17th. Daily from 1:00 P.M. at Mibu Temple. Short pantomime farces on familiar themes, the popular counterpart to the *noh* drama. One of the city's most authentic traditions, dating back about 650 years. Temple parishioners play the characters.

The spring (and autumn) *geisha dances* are graceful and colorful. Performances are from early afternoons, between 2 and 5 times daily. Check with T.I.C. for exact dates, times, and places.

Fire-walking festival takes place from the 27th to the 29th at Shimei-in, Iwayayama, Kumogahata, Kita-ku.

May. On the 15th is *Aoi Matsuri* (Hollyhock Festival), one of Kyoto's three biggest festivals, dating back to the 6th century. An Imperial Messenger, his suite, and some 300 courtiers start from the Imperial Palace at 10:00 A.M., arrive at Shimogamo Jinja at 11:40 A.M. for ceremonies, leave around 2:00 P.M. and arrive at Kamigamo Jinja around 3:30 P.M. You must pay to have a seat at the palace.

Third Sunday, *Mifune Matsuri* (Three Boat Festival) at Arashiyama includes beautifully decorated boats carrying musicians, dancers, and guests who reenact the imperial boating parties of the Heian era (794–1192). Procession starts from Kurumazaki Shrine at 1:00 P.M., then members of the procession board boats at Nakanoshima Park and float down the Oi River.

June. On the 1st–3rd is the *Takigi-Noh.* 6:00 P.M. at Heian Shrine. The Noh Play in its traditional setting and atmosphere: outdoor by the light of flaming torches. Tickets (about ¥500) should be bought well in advance.

July. On the 16th–17th is *Gion Matsuri.* Begun in 876 for divine protection against an epidemic, this is now the biggest event of the Kyoto year. On July 17, from 9:00 to 11:00 A.M., 29 huge floats, carved, gilded, hung with rich tapestries, are conveyed through the downtown streets. There are two kinds: *yama,* weighing 1.2–1.6 tons, are carried; *hoko,* 4.8–12 tons, are pulled on wheels, some carrying orchestras of flutes, gongs and drums. The procession itself passes in about 30 minutes; highly rewarding is the evening of the 16th when the whole city is *en fête.* The floats themselves may then be visited at leisure; and the old houses and traditional shops in the area north and south of Shijo between Horikawa and Karasuma streets (especially Muromachi) are open and display their family treasures and heirlooms. This is a priceless chance to glimpse old Kyoto's usually closed inner life and hidden treasures in an atmosphere of gaiety and spontaneous friendliness. Reserve accommodations as far ahead as you can; this is one of the high spots of the year in Kyoto and worth careful planning.

Fire-walking festival takes place on the 28th at Tanuki-dani, Fudo-in, Ichijoji, Sakyo-ku.

August. *Rokusai Nembutsu* and *O-Bon.* The Rokusai Nembutsu were originally a form of danced prayer; by now they are largely folk dances. The most noted are at Kissho-in (Nishioji-Kujo) the evening of the 25th. Costumed teams,

KYOTO   377

accompanied by drums, flutes and bells, do tricky acrobatic dances. The grounds of the temple are lit by lanterns and filled with stalls and festivity.

O-Bon is the Buddhist festival for the souls of the dead; they return to earth in mid-August. People go back to their ancestral villages, families visit and care for their ancestors' graves; in towns, villages and neighborhoods there is dancing in the streets, and candle-lit vigils in temple graveyards. Large towns have fireworks. When the souls of the dead must return to Paradise they are lighted on their way by lanterns floated on rivers and by bonfires on hillsides. Notable observances in Kyoto are:

Aug. 8–10   Candle lighting at Rokuharamitsu Temple
Aug. 16   Floating paper lanterns at Arashiyama
Aug. 16   Daimonji Okuribi (see below)
Aug. 14–16 Candle lighting at Higashi Otani
Aug. 24   Candle lighting at Adashino Nembutsu Temple
Aug. 23–24 *Jizo Bon.* Jizo Bosatsu, the Buddhist guardian deity of children, is honored with a special children's festival. Lanterns, decorations, games, parties. Walk through any quiet, small, ordinary, old residential neighborhood (Nishijin is good for this); this is one of the year's loveliest and most charming and intimate festivals.

Toki Matsuri (Ceramics Festival) takes place between the 7th–10th, from early morning until midnight in Gojo Street. Ceramics from many parts of Japan are sold at astonishingly low prices from the booths lining the street. Be sure to bargain.

Daimonji-Okuribi. At 8:00 P.M. on the 16th, a bonfire in the shape of the Japanese ideograph for "big" is lighted on Mount Nyoigadake, and four other bonfires are subsequently lighted on other hills. The people of Kyoto watch from their roofs or the banks of the Kamo River.

Miyazu Toro Nagashi. (Miyazu Flowing Lanterns Festival.) On the day after the Feast of the Dead, the citizens of this city north of Kyoto on the Sea of Japan float thousands of colorful lanterns out to the deep to light the way of their ancestors back to Paradise. Accompanied by fireworks. From dusk until midnight. Miyazu is two hours from Kyoto by train.

October. *Kamogawa Odori* or Maple Dances run from the 10th to Nov. 6 at Pontocho Kaburenjo Theater. The autumn equivalent of the spring cherry dances (see above, for April).

Jidai Matsuri (Festival of the Eras) takes places Oct. 22nd. To the music of flutes and drums, a much-publicized but rather sedate costume procession, dating from 1895 and illustrating the 13 main periods of Kyoto's and Japan's history from the 8th to the 19th centuries, winds through the streets of the city from the Imperial Palace to Heian Shrine. About noon to 3:30 P.M., easily viewed from any point on the route.

Kurama Hi Matsuri (Kurama Fire Festival), also on the 22nd. A brilliant torch procession, roaring bonfire, and rowdy portable shrine procession through the single narrow street of a mountain village about 30 minutes (by car or electric tram) north of Kyoto. Spectacular, strenuous, extremely crowded, not sedate, 6:00–10:30 P.M. Go early to see the shrine, palanquins, and lovely old village houses which display their family treasures this night.

November. *Gion Odori,* geisha dances are performed between the 3rd and 11th, at Gion Kaikan, afternoons, admission ¥750–¥1,200.

Arashiyama Maple Festival, second Sunday. A boat festival similar to the Mifune Matsuri of May, with music, dances, processions, feasting, and enjoyment of the autumn colors. November is *momiji* (maples) month; choice viewing spots around Kyoto are: the suburban villages of Ohara and Yase, Kibune and Kurama, the valleys of Takao and Kiyotaki, and the temples of Eikan-do,

Nanzen-ji, Kiyomizu-dera and Tofuku-ji. Actually the entire eastern foothills area from the Shugakuin south is good and every temple garden will have at least one brilliant red tree skillfully placed amidst its greenery.

December. On the 31st is *Okera Mairi.* At night at the Yasaka Shrine. Throngs of people visit the shrine to bring home the sacred fire on a length of tarred string, to cook the first meal of the year.

On the same evening the famous bell of the Chion-in Temple is struck 108 times, once for each of the Buddhist sins which must be driven out before the New Year begins. This, like the evening of Gion Festival, is a chance to see Kyotoites in their warmest, happiest, most relaxed mood.

TOURS. Package tours of Kyoto and nearby Nara are offered by *JTB* (361–7241), *Fujita Travel Service* (222–0121), and *Kinki Nippon Tourist-Gray Line Tours* (222–1224), among others.

Industrial Tours. *Inaba Cloisonné* will show 50 visitors at a time its factory in Higashiyamaku. English-speaking guides available. The process of dyeing may be seen at the *Kyoto Yuzen Cultural Hall,* Ukyo-shi. Interpreters may not be available. Make arrangements through the Tourist Information Center (TIC) at the Tower Building, 1st floor, across from Kyoto Station; 371–5649.

HOME VISIT PROGRAM. Kyoto was the first city in Japan to arrange visits by foreign tourists to Japanese homes, generally upper-class. Visits last 1–2 hours, usually evenings after 7:30. Apply at least one, preferably two days in advance to: *Tourist Section,* Kyoto City Government; *Kyoto City Information Office; Kyoto Tourist Information Center; JTB,* or major hotels. No charge except for student-interpreter but to bring a small gift is the usual custom when you visit someone's home in Japan. Many kinds of cakes or fruit are sold just for this purpose.

CHILDREN'S ACTIVITIES. Visits to the following can be recommended in Kyoto: *Municipal Zoological Gardens,* Okazaki Hoshojicho (771–0210). Open: 9:00 A.M. –4:00 P.M.; *Iwatayama Monkey Park.* About 100 monkeys live on Iwatayama Hill, near Arashiyama, and come down in groups to the park. You can feed them apples, cookies, etc. Open: 9:00 A.M.–5:00 P.M. (10 minutes walk from Arashiyama Park).

Student baby-sitters can be obtained through Japan Travel Bureau at a moderate cost.

PARTICIPANT SPORTS. Golf. Can be played at the Kamigamo links on the northern edge of Kyoto, near Kamigamo Shrine. Tel. 791–2161. Equipment can be rented. Fees are high. Open 8:00 A.M. to sunset. Also, opposite the entrance to the Shimo-Gamo Shrine in the north of Kyoto, there is the Shimo-Gamo Golf Practice Course.

Jogging. If you like to jog or hike, then head for the banks of the Kamo River. You can reach the river easily if you're staying at the Kyoto Hotel, Kyoto Prince Hotel, Kyoto Royal Hotel, or the Holiday Inn. One of the best starting places for a run is at the Kyoto Imperial Park. From here it's just a short jog east over to the river; then bear to your left and head northwest and take the left fork of the river; the branch running to the right is the Takano River, which also provides good running territory farther out. The Kamo River is lined with cherry trees, and a path runs parallel to the river.

Tennis. Can be played on the courts of Nijo Castle. Modest charge. **Swimming.** Go to Lake Biwa, largest freshwater lake in Japan. Good beaches at the towns of Mano, Ohmi Maiko, and Kita-Komatsu. **Yachting** is available at either Otsu Harbor or Biwako Lodge, a resort in Otsu, both on the southwestern bank of Lake Biwa, 30 minutes by car from Kyoto. **Horses** can be hired from Otsu City Stable, within walking distance of Biwako Hotel.

SPECTATOR SPORTS. Horse racing. Held 5–6 times each year at Yodo Horse Track south of Kyoto. Each meeting lasts eight days. Check with T.I.C. or your hotel for more information.

HISTORICAL SITES. Around Kyoto Station. *Higashi-Honganji Temple.* 10-min. walk north of Kyoto Station. City's largest wooden structure; temple established in 1602 under Tokugawa Shogunate. Open daily 9:00 A.M. to 5:00 P.M.

Nishi-Honganji Temple. 10-min. walk west of Higashi-Honganji Temple. Present site dates from 1592; houses several national treasures. Open daily 9:00 A.M. to 5:00 P.M.

Toji Temple. 15-min. walk southwest of Kyoto St. Founded in 796. Most of buildings were destroyed by fires and reconstructed in later years. The five-story pagoda was rebuilt in 1641. Flea market held in temple grounds on 21st day of every month. Admission ¥300.

Around City Center. *Kyoto Imperial Palace.* Near Marutamachi subway station. Was residence of Imperial family from 1331 until 1868 when they moved to Tokyo. To visit you must have pass issued by the Kyoto Office, Imperial Household Agency at Kyoto Gyoen Nai, Kamigyo-ku; 211–1211. Apply with passport 20 min before 10:00 A.M. or 2:00 P.M. Admission free. (Apply here also for *Katsura* and *Shugakuin* villas.)

Nijo Castle. In front of Nijojo-mae bus stop or 10-min. walk from Oike subway station. Built in 1603. Tokugawa Shogun stayed here when he visited Kyoto. Closed Mondays. Admission ¥400.

Northwest Area. *Daitokuji Temple.* Get off at Kaitokuji-mae bus stop. Six of the subordinate temples are open, each requiring ¥300 admission fee. Noted for art objects and gardens.

Kinkajuji Temple or Golden Pavilion. 2-min. walk from Kinkakuji-michi bus stop. Originally a mountain resort for an Ashikaga shogun but on his death converted into a temple. The gold leaf-covered pavilion is a replica completed in 1955.

Ryoanji Temple. 5-min. walk from Ryoanji-mae bus stop. Zen temple famous for its rock and sand garden. Admission ¥300.

Ginkakuji (Silver) Temple. 10-min. walk from Ginkakuji-michi bus stop. Designated as a national treasure, the temple is so named because the Ashikaga Shogun originally wanted to cover the pavilion's outer walls with silver foil. Admission ¥200.

Heian Shrine. 3-min. walk from Bijutsukan-mae bus stop. Built in 1895 to commemorate 1,100 anniversary of founding of Kyoto. Back garden is noted for its cherry blossoms and iris flowers. Admission ¥300.

Kiyomizu Temple. 10-min. walk from Kiyomizu-michi bus stop. Main hall was built in 1633 and designated a national treasure. Wooden veranda is supported by 139 pillars at a height of 49 ft. and offers a panoramic view of the city. Admission ¥100.

Nanzenji Temple. 20-min. walk southeast of Heian Shrine. Noted for its paintings on the sliding screens in the main hall. Paintings date from 16th century, and were done by artists of the Kano school. Admission ¥300.

Sanjusangendo Temple. 15-min. walk east of Kyoto Station. This is well known for its Thousand Armed Goddess, made of wood during the Kamakura Period (1192–1333) and designated as a national treasure.

 MUSEUMS. All the museums listed are in Kyoto. Admission fees range between ¥250–500, more if there's a special exhibition. **Costume Museum.** Izutsu Bld., Horikawa. Has an exhibition of Japanese dress from ancient times to today. Open 9:00 A.M.–5:00 P.M. daily except Sundays.

Heian Hakubutsukan. Sanjo Takakura. Japanese and Kyoto history. Daily 9:00 A.M.–4:00 P.M. except Mondays.

Kawai Memorial Hall. Kaneimachi, Gojozaka, Higashiyama; 561–3585. The traditional house of the late potter Kanjiro Kawai, instrumental in reviving folk crafts in the 1930s, now houses his collection and displays his work. Open daily, 10:00 A.M.–5:00 P.M. except Mondays.

Kyoto Municipal Craft Center. In Okazaki Park, Sakyo-ku; 761–3421. Formal displays of today's versions of traditional Kyoto arts and crafts. Some demonstrations; replicated old geisha house. Open daily 9:00 A.M.–5:00 P.M. except Mondays. Free.

Municipal Art Museum. Okazaki Park; 771–4107. Houses permanent collection and temporary special exhibitions. Open daily 9:00 A.M.–5:00 P.M. except Mondays.

National Museum. 527, Chayamachi, Higashiyama-ku; 541–1151. Permanent collection and important temporary special exhibitions. Open 9:00 A.M. –4:30 P.M. except on Mondays.

National Museum of Modern Art. Okazaki Park; 761–4111. This has temporary special exhibitions of both Japanese and Western artists. Open daily 10:00 A.M.–5:00 P.M. except Mondays.

Ryozen Hakubutsukan. 1 Ryozen-cho, Seikanji, Higashiyama-ku. Presents the history of the Meiji Restoration. Daily 9:00 A.M.–5:00 P.M.

Yurinkan. Enshoji-cho, Okazaki. This is a small private collection of Chinese art open only on the 1st and 3rd Sundays of each month from 12:00–3:00 P.M.

MUSIC. Concerts are held at Kyoto Kaikan, the city auditorium near Heian Shrine. Programs available at most hotels and T.I.C. Concerts of light music are given at Maruyama Music Hall (outdoor, Maruyama Park) during the summer months.

 STAGE. Kyoto is one of the two chief centers in Japan for the Noh play. A performance lasts 4–5 hours, held usually on Saturdays and Sundays. The three theaters are the *Oe-Nogaku-do,* at Yanaginobamba Oshikoji; the *Kongo Nohgaku-kodo* at Shijo Muromachi (221–3049); and the *Kanze Kaikan* at Okazaki Enshojicho (771–6114).

During certain seasons Kabuki drama can be seen at *Minami-za,* near the Shijo Bridge (561–1155). Gala performances, with the best actors in Japan, are given in December.

At the *Yasaka Kaikan,* Shijo Hanamikoji, there is a changing repertoire of modern Japanese drama, ballet, etc.

Call the TIC (371–0480) for information on current performances.

SHOPPING. Kyoto is the place to shop for traditional arts and crafts, and for works of Oriental art. If in a hurry, try the shopping arcades in the Miyako, Kyoto, and International hotels. Traditional shops are found along both sides of Shijo from Yasaka Shrine west to Daimaru Dept. Store; and Teramachi street, from Marutamachi down to Gojo (this will take longer). Nawate Street and Shinmonzen and Furumonzen streets, south, then east from Sanjo Station, are good for curios and antiques. For expensive antiques, look around Shoren-in and the Miyako Hotel. Pottery and curios can be found in the area from Higashiyama street up to Kiyomizu Temple and north of this. For pottery only, try the north side of Gojo Street between Higashiyama and Kawaramachi.

For an excellent introduction to all of this go to the **Kyoto Handicraft Center,** Kumano Jinja Higashi, Sakyo-ku. Six leading handicraft shops have sales outlets and demonstrations of craftsmen at work.

Antiques. *R. Kita,* antiques, Imari and Kutani porcelains. 256 Shinmonzen Street.

Art and Curios. *Kaji's Antique* on Shinmonzen St. Original screens, scrolls, ceramics, *netsuke* and other works of art. *Kyobido,* 351 Ninenzaka Kodaiji, on a staircase street just down from Kiyomizu Temple, is just what you imagine a Kyoto art and curio shop to be. Atmosphere for everyone, art for the serious. *S. Okumura & Co.* Fine art curios, lacquerware, bronze, brass, ivory and woodcarvings. Shinmonzen St. *Y. Tsuruki & Co.* on Shinmonzen St. has extensive collections of screens and scrolls, but also noted for lacquers, porcelains, and other objets d'art. *Yagi Art Shop.* 200 Shinmonzen, Higashiyama-ku. A tiny shop crammed with Oriental art and curios. Wonderful browsing and real old Kyoto atmosphere. *Yamanaka & Co.* Japanese and Chinese works of art. Awata-guchi, Higashiyama-ku.

Art Galleries. Eleven small private galleries show modern Japanese art: *Azuma Gallery* (Teramachi Bukkoji, just down from the Kyoto Hotel); *Gallery Beni* (Nawate Street just above Shijo); *Gallery Coco* (Sanjo Jingumichi, just before the entrance to the Miyako Hotel); *Gallery 16* (Teramachi Sanjo-sagaru, east side); *Japan Art Center* (upstairs in JAL Building, Oike Fuyacho); *Gallery Oike* (just opposite JAL Building, Oike Fuyacho); *Gallery Ushio* (Shinmonzen Street near Higashiyama); *Yamada Art Gallery* (Shinmonzen, near Higashiyama); *Kiyamachi Gallery* (Kiyamachi Shijo-agaru); *Marronier Gallery* (Kawaramachi Takoyakushi); *Dobashi Gallery* (east of Karasuma Shijo).

Cloisonné. *Inaba Cloisonne Co.,* manufacturers and dealers, workroom demonstrations. Sanjo St. Shirakawa Bridge.

Dolls. *Nakayama Dolls.* Main shop: Dotemachi Shomen-sagaru, Shimogyo-ku; branch at Handicraft Center.

Flea Market. A flea-market is held at *Toji Temple* all day on the 21st of each month, and at *Kitano Shrine* on the 25th. Bargains, junk, and that one-in-a-million unrecognized art treasure. Excellent for local color.

Folk Craft. *Yamato Mingei.* Kawaramachi Sanjo-sagaru. Japanese folk craft, a great tradition too-little known in the West. Wide choice of items useful and handsome.

Handbags. *M. Yamamoto & Co.* Handbags and evening purses. Furumonzen St. Branch at Kyoto Handicraft Center.

Jewelry. *Amita Jewelry Corp.* Damascene & silver jewelry, cigarette cases, compacts, necklaces, bracelets, earrings, cufflink, pearl, etc. Kyoto Handicraft Center, Kumano Jinja Higashi, Sakyo-ku.

Lacquerware. *H. Nishimura Factory.* Demonstration work shop, Okazaki.

Novelties. *Yokoyama & Co.* Japanese souvenirs, novelties. Nawate Shinbashi-agaru.

Paper. *Kyukodo,* Teramachi St., corner of Anekoji, Kyoto's leading dealer in Japanese handmade papers, writing instruments, incense.

Pearls. *Komai Pearls.* Shinmonzen St. Courteous, low-pressure service, genuinely professional evaluations, and very fair, objective advice. Reliable, experienced, highly recommended. Good selection in excellent taste.

Porcelain. *H. Koshida Satsumaya.* Furumonzen St. at Kyoto Handicraft Center.

Silk. *Y. Murai & Co.* Kimonos, brocades, silk products. Shinmonzen St. *Kanebo Service Store.* Silk, silk, more silk. Every kind of design, ancient and modern, with a large variety of prices as well as textures. Kawaramachi Shijo. *Kyoto Silk Co.* Main shop in Kyoto Handicraft Center, Kumano Jinja Higashi, Sakyo-ku.

Stone. *Sawakichi Stone Co., Ltd.* Stone lanterns, stone arts and garden ornaments. Packing and shipping services. Gojozaka, Higashiyama.

Woodblock Prints. *Mikumo Wood-Block Print Co.* Modern prints. Shijo Naka-Shinmachinishi. *Uchida's Woodblock Prints.* Modern & old woodblock prints. Kyoto Handicraft Center, Kumano Jinja Higashi, Sakyo-ku.

Department Stores. *Daimaru* (Shijo Takakura, closed Wed.); *Takashimaya* (Shijo Kawaramachi, closed Wed.); *Fujii Daimaru* (Shijo Teramachi, closed Thurs.); *Marabutsu* (Karasuma Shichijo, closed Friday); *Kyoto Station Department Store* (upstairs in Kyoto Station, no closing); *Hankyu* (Shijo-Kawaramachi, closed Thurs.); *Kintetsu* (corner of Shichijodori and Karasumadori, closed Thursdays).

 DINING OUT. Those with time and a willingness to enjoy the unfamiliar will find that eating out in Kyoto can be as full of varied and pleasant surprises as the city itself. The English-language *Kyoto Restaurant Guide,* put out by the Kyoto Restaurant Association, and *Kyoto Gourmet Guide,* list a number of places offering different styles of cooking in varied price ranges, in addition to those listed below. Nearly all the places listed below are in central Kyoto. It's best to ask a staff member at your hotel to write directions in Japanese for the taxi driver. Few restaurants given require reservations, but it never hurts to make them. Most places honor major credit cards, especially American Express and MasterCard.

For good, inexpensive meals, Japanese and western, you'll have a wide selection on department store "restaurant floors," usually the upper floors, and at the restaurant row of Porta, Kyoto Station's underground shopping arcade.

WESTERN

Ajibil. 223–1431. Japanese cuisine and steak. ¥580–5,000.

Izutsu. 541–2121. French dishes. ¥4,000–20,000.

Java. 221–7851. Indonesian curry dishes and other Indonesian food. ¥3,000–8,000.

Kiev. 525–0860. Russian dishes. ¥2,000–7,000.

Le Relais D'Okazaki. 761–1326. French. ¥1,500–10,000.

Lyon. 223–2303. French. ¥2,500–10,000.

Steak House Nanzen. 771–1823. ¥1,800–15,000.

CHINESE

Hakuho. ¥3,000–8,000.
Karudan. 661–2464. ¥500–3,000.
Tower Chuka Hanten. 361–3211. ¥800–4,000.

JAPANESE

There are three different styles of Kyoto cuisine or *Kyo ryori: Yusoku ryori* —dishes for the Imperial Household; *Kaiseki ryori*—meals served before the tea ceremony; and *Shojin ryori,* vegetarian dishes for Buddhist priests. Kyoto cuisine traditionally, and today, stressed light seasoning in order not to mask the ingredients; many vegetables were used because in the past fresh fish was not as generally obtainable in Kyoto as it is today. The best, truest form of Kyoto-style cuisine is in numerous top-class restaurants and is not cheap, ranging in price per person between ¥4,000 to ¥8,000. There are numerous tofu eateries. Some of the best are located in the Nanzenji and Sagano areas. Inquire from your hotel or TIC. A branch of one of these, Izusen, is located just above the TIC in the Kyoto Tower Bldg.

Expensive

Gion Suehiro. 541–1337. Shabu Shabu (a kind of beef fondu but cooked in broth with several types of vegetables), sukiyaki, tempura (fish and vegetables quick-fried in light batter), grilled fish and chicken, Japanese soups, and vegetables. ¥4,000–15,000.
Gyozanen. 744–2321. Serves tofu lunch as well as traditional Japanese food. ¥2,000–15,000.
Inn Tamahan. 561–3188. Traditional Japanese food. Has a pretty Japanese garden. Reservations needed. Price: ¥10,000 and above.
Kikusui. 771–4101. Typical Japanese cuisine. ¥8,000–20,000.
Kyorinsen. 541–9111. Tempura, sukiyaki, and other traditional food. ¥2,000–12,000.
Minoko. 561–0328. Sukiyaki, shabu shabu, other Japanese food. ¥2,700–20,000.
Nanzen-ji Gimmond. 751–1320. Tempura lunch, typical Japanese food. ¥3,000–15,000.

Moderate

Daikokuya. 221–2818. Buckwheat noodles, Tempura, eel. ¥950–1,500.
Jubei Gion Shop. 561–2698. Sushi. ¥500–1,200.
Jubei Kitashirakawa Shop. 791–2131. Sushi lunch, other traditional Japanese food. ¥500–3,500.
Nishijin Uoshin. 441–0753. Tempura, sukiyaki, and other traditional food. ¥2,000–5,000.
Otowa. 221–2412. Sushi. ¥450–2,000.
Tamahan. 751–8285. Traditional food. ¥1,000–7,000.
Tivoli. 771–0075. Sukiyaki, steak. ¥3,000–5,000.
To riyasu. 771–2650. Yakitori (grilled chicken and vegetables) tempura, shabu shabu. ¥2,000–8,000.
Yasaka. 551–1121. Sukiyaki, other traditional dishes, grilled eel. ¥3,000–7,000.

NIGHT LIFE. Compared with Tokyo, Osaka and Kobe, Kyoto lacks glittering nightclubs with lavish revues for big spenders. And, undeniably, almost everything is over by the last trolley at 11:30 P.M.

Unless you are the guest of some Japanese firm or institution, or willing to spend a small fortune on yourself, there are two ways to get some idea of the traditional arts of the *geisha*. One is to attend the spring and autumn dances at various theaters (see above under *Local Festivals* for April). The other is to visit *Gion Corner* (in Yasaka Kaikan) where for about ¥ 1,800 you can see *geisha* dance, sing, and play the *samisen*. There are also brief excerpts from the *bunraku* puppet plays, *kyogen* farces, tea ceremony, flower arrangement, *gagaku* court and shrine music, and Japanese harp music. Admittedly this is for tourists; but it is a very convenient way to see in a short time Japanese traditional arts otherwise scattered, seasonal, and hard to locate. Two performances nightly, 8 and 9:10, March-November. You may see *geisha* and *maiko* (apprentice *geisha*) walking through Pontocho and the streets of Gion between 3:00 and 5:00 in the afternoon and after 7:00 in the evening.

Some night package tours include a "geisha party"; take it if you will, but don't fool yourself about it.

Bars. In Kyoto there are literally hundreds of bars, some the size of movie houses, some seating hardly six people at a time. Start with one beer and ask for the bill before you start the next round; that way you know how much padding has been packed into it and can continue or not accordingly. *Hors d'oeuvres* (called *tsukidashi*) may be pushed onto you rather aggressively, whether you order them or not, and they will be grossly overpriced. Reject them immediately or take the consequences of eating so much as one peanut. Be very wary of the attention of anything that looks like a "hostess"; such warmth of welcome is not for nothing, ever. The Kiyamachi area is particularly tricky to navigate for the novice; stroll, look, and leave.

NARA

Archeologists and historians differ about the origins of the Japanese people; the origins of the Japanese state are much clearer. From the High Plain of Heaven, Amaterasu Omikami, the Sun Goddess, sent her grandson, Ninigi-no-mikoto, down to earth, and he landed in Kyushu. From there, his grandson, Jimmu, led a band of followers up the coast of the Inland Sea until they came to the Land of the Reed Plains, where they settled, and where at 11:00 A.M. on February 11, 660 B.C., Jimmu was enthroned as the first ruler of Yamato, the Land of Great Peace. It is this district of Yamato, the present-day Nara Basin, that is still, despite miles of hideous and chaotic industrial slum, the sentimental as well as the historic heart of that Japan over which the 124th sovereign of the legendary Jimmu's line reigns today.

In other words, by the beginning of the Christian era, one of the small tribal-clan states of West Japan had gained control of most of the Kyoto-Nara-Osaka area. Life was simple in those days and when a ruler died the capital was moved, for reasons of ritual purity. By 710, this was no longer practical, and in that year the Empress-Regnant Genmei, 43rd ruler, settled the first permanent capital a bit west of the present city of Nara and called it Heijokyo. The 74 years that it remained there under seven rulers were a period of astonishing development. Japan's first written history, its first mythological chronicle, its first and greatest poetry anthology, and a geographical survey were all compiled. The chief characteristic of this era was the immense influence of China on every phase of Japanese life. Art, religion, architecture, city planning, political theory and government organization, dress, food, finance, literature, lacquer, metal-casting, all were profoundly changed by this contact; and from these borrowings what we now regard as the typical culture of Japan emerged. T'ang China was a brilliant and cosmopolitan society; and through it Indian, Persian, even Greek influences came to enrich the Yamato kingdom and to leave their mark on its Acropolis at Horyu-ji.

In 784 the capital moved again, to Nagaoka, then in 794 to Kyoto, where it stayed until 1868; and Nara became a backwater. Today finds it in uncertain flux. Although the chief business of the prefecture is still agriculture, the grain fields around Horyu-ji are fast being swallowed by factories and tract housing. Along with industrialization, the local authorities have welcomed mass commercial tourism. The horror of Dreamland, the landscape-marring Mikasa Spa Hotel, and the parking lots in front of Todai-ji bear witness to their success. Nara's most obvious enemy is the automobile, the trucks, buses and cars which here, as elsewhere, jam the streets and shake the buildings of an earlier and gentler age. Present-day Nara, a town of 312,000 people at the latest count, receives about 14 million tourists a year.

EXPLORING NARA

Standard treatment for Nara is a hurried one-day side-trip out of Kyoto. This is unfortunate. If you can, allow a full and leisurely day for the places of interest in the town, a quiet evening to stroll in the Deer Park, and a second day for Horyu-ji and other outlying temples. If you are an art buff, you will want that much time just for the museums.

The main street of the town is Sanjo-dori, running straight east from the National Railway Station to the entrance to Kasuga Shrine. About 400 yards up from the station is the mausoleum of the Emperor Kaika (set back, on the left); a bit farther, at a crossroads, two small shrines, Kango and Isakawa, date back to the 5th century. Along Sanjo itself and in the side streets off it are still a number of fine old town houses in traditional style; they are quite different in proportions, layout, and details from those of nearby Kyoto. As Sanjo-dori rises you come to Sarusawa Pond (on your right), and the Deer Park is ahead. On the east bank of the pond, the *Kinukakeyanagi* (Willow of Hanging Clothes) commemorates a court lady who is supposed to have drowned herself here.

The center, central landmark, and trademark of Nara is the great five-story pagoda of Kofuku-ji, the Temple of the Establishing of Happiness, headquarters of the Hosso Sect. Kofuku-ji was originally a tutelary temple of the Fujiwara family, the dominant political faction in Japan from the 9th to the beginning of the 11th century. Moved here in 710, the temple soon had about 175 buildings in its compound. As the Fujiwara family prospered, Kofuku-ji also increased in power and wealth. As the power of the Fujiwaras declined, Kofuku-ji suffered accordingly. During the civil wars of the 11th and 12th centuries its private army of soldier-monks fought with Enryaku-ji, the Tendai headquarters on Mt. Hiei (see Kyoto). In December of 1180, having backed a loser, it was burned flat. In succeeding centuries its fortunes rose and fell, but they never entirely regained the heights of the Nara and early Heian periods. In 1717 another huge fire destroyed almost everything then standing. The pagoda itself, 165 feet high and the second highest in Japan (after Kyoto's Toji), was rebuilt in 1426. Of the original structures of the Nara Period, nothing now remains. Five main buildings now exist and are of interest.

Chu-Kondo, the central hall, enshrines a wooden image of *Shaka-Nyorai,* the historical Buddha, flanked by his followers Bonten and Taishaku, all carved in the Kamakura Period (1185–1333) though in the style of the earlier Nara Period (710–794). The present hall was built in 1819.

Nan-en-do, southwest of the Chu-Kondo, was first built in 813; the present one dates from 1741. It is a large, well-proportioned, octagonal hall enshrining a gilded wooden image of Kannon, carved in 1181 by Kokei, a forerunner of the realistic school of artists of the Kamakura Period. At the four corners of the altar are notable statues of the Four Heavenly Guardians. As one of the 33 sacred pilgrimage stations of West Japan, Nan-en-do is generally crowded.

It is paired with the smaller, and usually unattended, Hoku-en-do, also octagonal, and enshrining a gilded wooden image of Miroku Bosatsu, the future incarnation of the Buddha. There are also two beautiful statues of Mujaku and Seshin, priests of the period; all of these images are the work of Unkei, the most noted sculptor of the Kamakura Period, and son of Kokei, who did the work in the Nan-en-do. Below and southwest of the Nan-en-do is a three-story pagoda dating from the Kamakura Period but in the graceful style of the earlier Heian era.

Just north of the five-story pagoda is the To-Kondo, first built in 726 by the Emperor Shomu, and rebuilt in the early 15th century. Intended as a hall of prayer for the well-being of the nation and the recovery of an empress from an illness, it enshrines *Yakushi Nyorai,* the Buddha in his aspect as a healer. He is flanked by two lovely statues called *Nikko* and *Gakko* (Sunlight and Moonlight), lacquered wood, dating from the Hakuho Period (645–701). These originally belonged to another temple, but were stolen by the monk-soldiers of Kofuku-ji to replace works that had burned in 1180. Flanking them are statues of Monju Bosatsu, the incarnation of Intuitive Wisdom, and of Yuima Bosatsu, the legendary Indian householder who is the Buddhist ideal of the lay follower. The statues of the *Shi-Tenno,* or Guardian Kings of the Four Directions, and those of the 12 Divine Generals are also noteworthy.

East of the Chu-Kondo is the *Kokuho-kan* (Hall of National Treasures), the museum of Kofuku-ji. All of the halls described above may be closed and their sculptures moved to the museum instead. Actually you can see them there under much better conditions and accurately labeled in English. The museum should on no account be missed; it is a remarkable concentration of masterpieces.

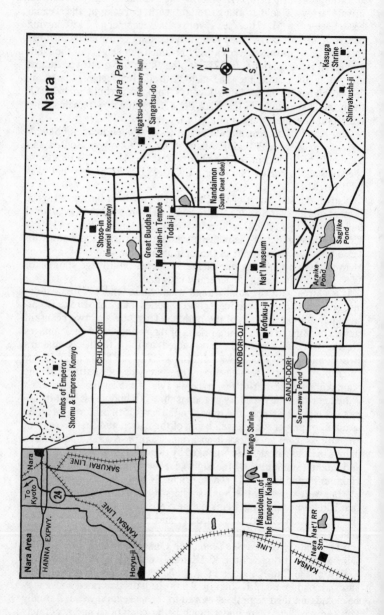

Nara

Nara Park

Nigatsu-do (February Hall)
Sangatsu-do

Shoso-in
(Imperial Repository)

Great Buddha
Kaidan-in Temple
Todai-ji

Nandaimon
(South Great Gate)

Kasuga Shrine

Shinyakushi-ji

Sagiike Pond

Araike Pond

Nat'l Museum

Kofuku-ji

ICHIJO-DORI

NOBORI-OJI

SANJO-DORI

Sarusawa Pond

Tombs of Emperor
Shomu & Empress Komyo

Kango Shrine

Mausoleum of
the Emperor Kaika

Nara Nat'l RR
Stn.

KANSAI LINE

LINE

Nara Area

To Nara

To Kyoto

24

HANNA EXPWY.

SAKURAI LINE

KANSAI LINE

Horyu-ji

N
W   E
S

The Largest Wooden Structure in the World

Continue east, then north at the next intersection; you will come to the Nandaimon (South Great Gate) of Todai-ji (East Great Temple). This temple, with its Great Buddha, is the foremost sight in Nara. It was founded in 745 by the Emperor Shomu, to be the headquarters of all the temples in the entire country. Nandaimon, the huge main gate, dates in its present form from 1195. Two-storied and painted vermilion, it is supported by 18 pillars each measuring 63 feet in height and 3.2 feet in diameter. The bracketing-and-structural work supporting the roof is unusually open and simple in its lines, reminiscent of Indian architecture, and the entire gate has an aspect of great simplicity, power and dignity. The outside niches contain wooden statues of *Kongo-rikishi* (thunderbolt-wielding protective deities) considered the best in Japan. They defend the Buddha from his enemies, and guard the sacred enclosure. *A-gyo*, on the left, has his mouth and left hand open; *Un-gyo*, on the right, has them closed. They are the work of Unkei and Kaikei, sculptors of the Kamakura Period. The inside niches of the gate contain guardian lions made in 1196 by a Chinese artist called Chin Nankei in the Sung Period style.

The *Daibutsu-den* (Great Buddha Hall) itself is surrounded by a pillared corridor. This is the largest wooden structure in the world, 161 feet high, 187 feet long, 164 feet wide. The original hall was at least a third again longer, but it was burned in a civil war, and the present building dates from 1708. It is by any standard a monumental and imposing structure, and an impressive engineering performance, given the weight of tile and the limitations of wood. The beautiful octagonal bronze lantern in front dates from the Tempyo Period (701–794) and is famous for the reliefs on its faces. The original gilding has long since disappeared. The gilded ornaments on the ends of the hall are called *shibi* (the tail of the *shi* bird, or black kite). As fire protection they have not been overly successful.

The World's Largest Bronze Statue

Enter the hall mindfully; the first shock of the tremendous, looming presence of the Great Buddha towering over you and filling this vast hall with its power can be a deeply impressive experience. This is *Dainichi-Nyorai*, the Great Sun Buddha, the central principle of Truth which is the basis of the entire universe. The totality of everything in the universe constitutes the body of the Great Sun Buddha, and everything, including all the other Buddhas and Bodhisattvas, emanates from Him as the origin. With or without a study of the philosophy of esoteric Buddhism, this statue is a powerful expression. The original casting, in the middle of the 8th century, took five years. Most of it has had to be recast since then to replace damage from successive fires. The (inevitable) statistics are:

Height, including pedestal	71 feet 6 inches
Length of face	16 feet

Width of face	9 feet 5 inches
Length of eye	3 feet 9 inches
Height of nose	1 foot 6 inches
Length of mouth	3 feet 7 inches
Length of ear	8 feet 5 inches
Length of palm	6 feet 5 inches
Length of thumb	5 feet 3 inches
Number of curls	966
Total weight	551 tons

To the west of the Daibutsu-den is the Kaidan-in, or ordainment platform, the oldest and most famous in Japan. It was first built in 754 by the Emperor Shomu for the Chinese priest Ganjin who had converted the emperor, the Empress Komyo, and many other important people to Buddhism. In a pine grove, it is largely overlooked by the visitors who crowd the Daibutsu-den itself. The present building is from 1731; but the four *Devas* at the corners of the altar are from the Tempyo Period; made of clay, they are famous for the solemn expressions with which they trample beneath their feet a host of squirming demons.

Behind the Daibutsu-den, in a fenced-in park, stands the *Shoso-in,* the Imperial Repository of the Emperor Shomu, containing a unique and priceless collection of ceramics, textiles, jewelry, musical instruments, glass, and metal work from as far afield as Persia and beyond, housed in a raised, three-compartmented, log-cabin style structure which, until the advent of automobile exhaust fumes, had kept them intact and under ideal conditions of temperature and humidity for over 1,200 years. The wedge-shaped log-cabin style of architecture is called *azekura,* and has been imitated in both the new National Theatre in Tokyo, and in the Kasuga Hotel in Nara. A genuine example may be seen close-up in front of the Sangatsu-do.

The Halls of February and March

From behind the Daibutsu-den, follow the dirt road north and bearing east until you come to a stone-paved staircase walking street that curves up the hillside. It is lined with the houses of Todai-ji priests and is one of the most charmingly atmospheric and photogenic spots in Nara. It will lead to the *Nigatsu-do* (February Hall), standing on a hillside with a fine view of the Yamato Plain and the roof of Todai-ji rising above the trees. It was founded in 752; the present building is from 1669. The interior consists of concentric zones around the main shrine; this is the site of the water-drawing ceremony (*Omizutori*) held annually in the second month of the lunar calendar, whence the hall's name.

Below this is the Sangatsu-do (March Hall), housing some of the most beautiful statues in Japan. This oldest surviving building in the Todai-ji complex was originally square; in 1199 an outer oratory was added. The name comes from the third-month *Hokke* ritual which is performed in this hall.

Inside, on a two-fold octagonal dais, the main object of worship is *Fukukenjaku Kannon,* a male incarnation of the Bodhisattva of Compassion, who carries a fishhook to pull men from the sea of Illusions to the shore of Enlightenment. Made of dry lacquer, the figure is surmounted by a crown of silver open work holding a nine-inch silver Buddha and more than 20,000 crystals, beads, and gems. The nimbus around the statue and the canopy above it are carved in an openwork design of lotus flowers. It is flanked by two clay statues, *Nikko* and *Gakko;* these were originally colored. There are many other notable statues in this hall; the best of them is probably the *Shu Kongo,* a guardian deity brandishing a thunderbolt with clenched fists. As it was generally kept hidden, the colors are those of the Tempyo Period, and prove the high level of color techniques of that era.

The Shrine of 3,000 Lanterns

You can reach Kasuga Shrine from the Sangatsu-do, but the more impressive approach is the main one, from Sanjo-dori through the two vermilion torii arches in the Deer Park and up the long avenue lined with stone lanterns that is the shrine's most famous feature. There are reported to be 1,780 stone lanterns and 1,012 of bronze. Anyway, they are all lighted on the nights of February 3 and August 15, a sight worth planning for. This, like Kofuku-ji, was originally a tutelary shrine of the Fujiwara family. The main sanctuary is composed of four substructures, each enshrining a different deity; this is the origin of the style of shrine architecture known as *Kasugazukuri.* The many rebuildings have always been in the original form, so these may be considered faithful examples of eighth-century Shinto shrine buildings. It is a particularly attractive place; the vermilion and white of the buildings, the dark shingled roofs, the long, sweeping lines of the corridors, the green of the trees, the lanterns, the moss, and the ever-present simplicity and cleanliness of Shinto precincts, all blend pleasingly together. Passing through the south gate, go down a long corridor whose eaves are lined with bronze lanterns, to the *Haiden,* a floorless building where offerings are made. Behind this is the *Utsushidono,* where the spirits of the deities are temporarily lodged when the main hall is under reconstruction. Close to it is a curious tree, a graft of wisteria, *nanten,* camellia, maple, cherry, *niwatoko* and *iso-no-ki.* Northwest of the main hall is the Treasure House, displaying armor, swords and other heirlooms of the Fujiwara family, including masks for Bugaku, a very ancient kind of shrine dance.

Temple in the Round

About 15 minutes' walk southwest of Kasuga Shrine is the temple of Shin-Yakushi-ji. The main hall, paved with tiles, has a circular dais of white clay in the center holding an image of Yakushi-Nyorai surrounded by the Twelve Divine Generals. In all other temples in Japan the images are enshrined at one end; the difference may be compared to theater-in-the-round vs. the ordinary proscenium stage. Shin-Yakushi-ji was built by the Empress Komyo for the recovery of the Emperor Shomu from an eye disease; the main hall is of the Tempyo Period, the other buildings of the Kamakura Period. The seated image of Yakushi-Nyorai, made from a single piece of wood, is flanked by two 11-faced

Kannons made of painted wood; all but one of the Twelve Generals are of clay.

Horyu-ji: Fountainhead of Japanese Culture

To visit Nara without seeing the Temple of the Noble Law would be like visiting Athens and not climbing the Acropolis. This was the center of art, architecture, scholarship, and teaching that illuminated an entire age and all that followed. It was founded in 607 by Shotoku Taishi (the Crown Prince of Holy Virtue), like Charlemagne an exceptionally able man whose court was a center of learning and a source of civilization for his country. Seven miles west of Nara, it can be reached by either train or bus. It was here, under Prince Shotoku, that Buddhism first began to thrive in Japan.

Horyu-ji is divided into two parts: the West Cathedral, in which are the *Kondo* (Main Hall) and the pagoda; and the East Cathedral, which contains the *Yume-dono* pavilion and the *Chugu-ji* nunnery. The proper approach is up an avenue of pine trees to the South Gate and into the West Cathedral. Here a road of white sand leads to the *Chu-mon* (Middle Gate), which dates from the year of the temple's construction. Its gently inclining roof and long eaves give it an air of stability and neatness, and a central pillar divides it into two entrances instead of the usual three. The Kongo-rikishi in the outside niches date from 711.

On your left stands the pagoda. On a double stone foundation, it is so constructed that the width of the pillars on each of its five stories becomes gradually smaller by mathematical progression until the top story is only half the width of the bottom one. This device gives the building airiness and grace. Inside the first story four Buddhist scenes are represented in clay—Exchanging of Questions and Answers between Yuima and Monju (east side); Cremation of Shakamuni's Bones (west side); Paradise of Miroku (south side); the Buddha's Entry into Nirvana (north side). The timbers are said to be the original ones of 607, and a vault under the central pillar may contain a bone of the historical Buddha.

The Kondo (Main Hall), on your right, is a two-storied building sharing many of the architectural features of the Chumon and the pagoda. Columns with *entasis* (a slight convexity just below the middle) separate the outside corridors and the ceiling is coffered. Unfortunately the superb frescoes that covered the walls were destroyed by fire in 1949; the present ones are faithful reproductions. The platform inside the columns holds the bronze Sakya Triad—a large central figure of Buddha Sakyamuni flanked by two smaller Bodhisattva images. These statues were cast in 623 in commemoration of Prince Shotoku. Sitting nearby is a statue of Yakushi, the "Healing Buddha," believed to have been cast sixteen years earlier in memory of the Prince's father—the Emperor Yomei. The Kondo once held Lady Tachibana's Miniature Shrine and the Golden Beetle Miniature Shrine, both of which are now in the Treasure Hall. All the images at Horyu-ji have certain features in common; they are in no sense realistic; the proportions of the body often lack balance, the mouths curve upwards in a faint smile reminiscent of archaic Greek sculpture, the eyes are shaped like gingko nuts, and the pleats of the robes are simple and sharp.

The back of this compound is the *Dai-Ko-do* or Great Lecture Hall, symmetrically flanked by two small buildings, *Kyozo* and *Shoro*, set into the corridors. Behind the Dai-Ko-do is the upper temple or *Kamino-Mido*, in a quiet setting and less visited. *Saiendo*, outside the enclosure and to the left, is an elegant octagonal hall built for the Lady Tachibana, mother of the Empress Komyo.

Todaimon is the eight-pillared gate which leads to the East Cathedral. The palace of Prince Shotoku once stood here, but after his death it was destroyed by his political enemies; and in 737 the East Cathedral was built on the ruins. Its main hall is the *Yume-dono* (Hall of Dreams) to which it is said that the prince would withdraw to meditate on difficult philosophical problems. A golden figure would appear and give him the answers he sought. The main image, of Kannon Saving the World, was found by the American scholar Ernest Fenollosa in 1884, after having been secluded for hundreds of years. It is (doubtfully) attributed to Prince Shotoku himself; the style is northern Chinese.

North of this is the *Dempo-do* (Preaching Hall), said once to have been part of the house of Lady Tachibana, and containing many beautiful images from the Tempyo and Heian eras. Northeast of this is Chugu-ji nunnery, originally built by Prince Shotoku for his mother. The present architecture is unremarkable, but visitors flock here to see the exquisite wooden statue of Miroku Bosatsu, which is also known as Nyoirin Kannon. Like the famous Kannon of Koryu-ji, in Kyoto, it is of basically Korean inspiration, and should not be missed. Another of the treasures here is a piece of embroidery, the oldest existing in Japan, called the *Tenjukoku-Mandala* (Tapestry of Heaven), said to have been worked by the prince's wife after his death.

Be sure to visit the new Treasure House, where priceless objects from many of the temples have been gathered for safety. It is impossible to list everything of note. Most frequently admired is the famous image of the Kudara Kannon, carved from a single piece of camphorwood. The shape is tall and slender, the arms unusually long. The garment flows and turns over as though the Kannon were standing in cool, crystal air. The two miniature shrines from the Kondo are also world-famous; and you will see photographs of the wall paintings pre the 1949 fire.

In March 1972 the village of Asuka near Nara excited the nation when richly colored murals were discovered inside its Takamatsuzuka Tumulus. The Tumulus, thought to have been built late in the 7th century, is a round barrow 18 meters in diameter and 5 meters high. The murals, covering the walls of an oblong stone chamber and showing the influence of Chinese and Korean cultures, depict human and animal figures. In the village of Asuka are tombs known to be those of emperors and powerful persons from ancient times. Since the discovery of the murals, it is wondered whether the Takamatsuzuka Tumulus is that of an Imperial Prince. The Tumulus is not open to the public, in the interests of preserving the 1,300-year-old murals.

PRACTICAL INFORMATION FOR NARA

 WHEN TO GO. As with most other tourist spots across Japan, spring (March–May) and autumn (September–November) are the best seasons to visit Nara. Winter and summer months are less comfortable, but the disadvantage is made up for by the freedom from crowds.

 HOW TO GET THERE? *From Kyoto;* Expresses of the Kintetsu Railway Co. leave hourly from separate platforms at the south end of Kyoto Station, and take 36 minutes into downtown Nara. The National Railway and the Kintetsu and Keihan bus lines also go to Nara, taking longer. *From Osaka* by the Kintetsu Railway takes 30 minutes.

TELEPHONES. The area code for the City of Nara is 0742.

 HOTELS AND INNS. Western-style hotels in Nara are limited in number although the so-called business hotels are mushrooming. In both expensive and moderate categories, all are generally well-kept. Japanese-style hotels are also quite clean. Their charges include supper and breakfast, both Japanese style. The bed is spread out on the straw-mat floor, which may make it rather uncomfortable for foreign visitors, except the adventurous types. For both Western and Japanese-style accommodations, reservations are recommended, except for some "business hotels."

What Will It Cost? Typical charges are as follows: For Western-style hotels in the *Expensive* category, single room, ¥7,600; twin room, ¥15,000. In the *Moderate* category (business hotels), ¥5,000.

For Japanese-style inns (all with breakfast and dinner included), *Expensive,* ¥25,000; *Moderate,* ¥13,000 and up.

Kokumin Shukusha (pensions), ¥3,000 (no meal) or ¥4,000–5,000 (2 meals).

WESTERN-STYLE

Hotel Fujita Nara. *Expensive.* 47–1 Shimo-Sanjo-Cho; 23–8111. Modern in this ancient city, this hotel is central, international in feeling and facilities, but with essential Japanese touches.

Nara Hotel. *Expensive.* 1096 Takabatakecho; 26–3300. Delightfully situated overlooking a small lake, the rambling, dowagerlike Nara Hotel is the oldest Western-style hotel in the city. 73 rooms, most with private bath. Red plush, polished brass, 12–15-foot coffered ceilings, spacious, opulent, leisured Edwardian dignity, with Momoyama roof lines—this place has character. Service is first class.

Hotel Sun Route. *Moderate.* 1110 Takabatake Bodaicho, near Sarusawa Pond; 22–5151. A modern hotel in this city of traditions. 95 rooms.

JAPANESE-STYLE

Hotel Yamatosanso. *Expensive.* 27 Kawakamicho; 26–1011. Westernized Japanese style, no single rooms. Invites honeymooners.

Kasuga. *Expensive.* 40 Noboriojicho; 22–4031. Western-style grill. 50 rooms.

Kikusuiro. *Expensive.* 1130 Bodaicho, Sanjodori; 23–2001. Rambling, elegant old mansion in a lovely garden on the edge of Nara Park. 13 rooms.

Miyako. *Expensive.* 1 Sanjo-dori; 23–5544. Comfortable with good service. 32 rooms.

Uosa Ryokan. *Expensive.* On the south side of Sarusawa Pond; 23–6035. Fine view of the Kofukuji pagoda. Spacious rooms, excellent Japanese food, and very courteous service. Has a rooftop "Gekko Bath." 34 rooms.

Nara Park Hotel. *Moderate.* 637 Horaicho; 44–5255. 20 rooms.

New Iroha. *Moderate.* 500 Sanjocho; 25–0168. 40 rooms.

KOKUMIN SHUKUSA

Ikoma Sanso. 8–7 Monzencho, Ikoma City; 07437–3–4801.

Katsuragi Kogen Lodge. 2568 Noborio, Kujira, Gose City; 07456–2–5083.

Shigi Sanso. 2150 Seya, Sangocho, Ikoma-gun, Nara Pref.; 07437–3–4801.

Yatadera Daimonbo. 3505 Yatacho, Koriyama City; 07435–3–1445.

YOUTH HOSTELS. *Nara.* 1716 Horencho; 22–1334. *Tonomine.* 487, Sakurai City, Nara Pref.; 07444–9–0105. *Okuyoshino Ike-no-Taira.* 764 Ikemine, Shimo-Kitayama-mura, Yoshino-gun, Nara Pref.

 TOURIST INFORMATION. Japan Travel Bureau (JTB) is in the Kitagawa Building, Nishi-Mikado-cho; 23–2525. Open 9:00 A.M.–5:00 P.M., closed Sundays and holidays. The **Nippon Travel Agency** Nara Office is at 511 Sanjo-cho; 26–7225. The **Kinki Nippon Tourist** Nara Office is in Higashimuki-Nakamachi; 24–0171. The **Nara City Tourist and Industry Department** is in the Nara City Office, 1–1–1 Minami, Nijo Oji; 34–1111. And the **Nara City Information** Office has windows in Nara National Railway Station and the Kintetsu Nara Station. The **Central Post Office** is at 5–3 Omiya-cho; 35–1611.

EMERGENCIES. As with all other communities throughout Japan, the *police* can be reached by dialing 110. Dial 119 for *fire* and *ambulance* services. The police headquarters is at 30 Nobori-oji (23–1101).

ELECTRIC CURRENT. The electric current in Nara is 100 volts and 60 cycles (hertz) A.C. This applies to all areas in Japan west of Shizuoka in the central part of Honshu (the main island).

PLACES OF WORSHIP. The Nara Catholic Church is at 36 Nobori-oji (26–2094). The Nara Anglican-Episcopal Church is at Higashimuki Minami (22–3818). The Seventh Day Adventist Church is at 829 Hiramatsu (44–9511).

LOCAL BUSINESS HOURS AND HOLIDAYS. Most offices and shops are open 9:00 A.M.–5:00 P.M.; closed on Sundays and a dozen or so annual public holidays.

SEASONAL EVENTS. January. *Wakakusa Yama Yaki* (Burning of Dead Grass on Wakakusa Hill). Takes place on the 15th. Hill climbing race 1:00 P.M. About 5:00, ceremonies and a procession of monks carrying torches. About 6:00, fireworks and grass-burning on the entire 60-acre hillside, silhouetting the monuments of Nara against a sheet of flame. Spectacular, and justly famous. The actual burning lasts about 40 minutes.

February. *Mandoro* (Lantern Festival) at Kasuga Shrine, takes place on the evening of the 3rd (4th in a leap year). The 3,000 stone and bronze lanterns on the shrine and in the park are all lighted at once, producing an atmosphere of unique charm and mystery. Also *bugaku,* stately shrine dances from Central Asia evening of the 3rd. *Tsuina-e.* Kofuku-ji temple, about 6:00 P.M. A demon-exorcising ritual to celebrate Setsubun (Seasons' Parting), the end of the coldest part of winter.

March. *Omizutori* in the Nigatsu-do hall of Todai-ji from the 1st–14th. A two-week ascetic training ritual combining elements of Shinto and of esoteric Buddhism culminates in the drawing of water from a sacred well and the brandishing of huge torches from the veranda of the temple. Best night to attend is the last, for the torch spectacle. Ritual dances are performed inside the temple in semi-darkness between 6:00 P.M. and dawn; no women are allowed in the inner areas, and both these and the grounds outside are unbelievably crowded.

Kasuga Matsuri, on the 13th. This is one of the three big festivals under imperial ordinance. A spectacular procession of people, clad in the costume of the Heian Period (794–1185), make their way through the streets. Afterwards *Okagura* (Sacred Dances) are performed in the garden of the Kasuga Shrine.

May. *Takigi Noh* from the 11th–12th. Beginning at twilight, Noh dramas are staged by torchlight on an outdoor stage at Kofuku-ji Temple.

June. *Saegusa Festival,* on the 17th. At Isakawa Shrine, one of the oldest in Nara. Sickness is expelled by the presentation to the shrine of white *sake,* black *sake,* and wild lilies from nearby Minayama Hill. A procession is then made through the city.

August. *Mandoro,* on the 15th. The 3,000 lanterns of Kasuga Shrine are lighted again, as part of the O-Bon Festival.

September. *Uneme* Festival (date variable according to the full moon, or August 15 of the old lunar calendar), from late afternoon at Uneme Shrine near Sarusawa Pond. An 8-foot Japanese fan is carried in costume parade through the city. When the full moon rises, the fan is carried across the pond in a boat full of musicians, then set afloat.

October. *Tsunokiri* or cutting of the antlers of the deer in Nara Park by priests from the Shinto shrines takes place in mid-month.

Treasures from the otherwise closed Shoso-in Imperial Repository are shown at the Nara Museum from mid-Oct. to early Nov.

November. 15 *Children's Festival* takes place on the 15th. All day at Kasuga Shrine and other shrines in the district. The children are dressed up with extreme lavishness, and prayers are offered for their health and happiness.

December. *On Matsuri* (Grand Festival) of Wakamiya Shrine. In honor of the God of Agriculture, an elaborate 3-day program runs from the 16th–18th, with sacrifices, torchlight procession, ancient shrine dances, Noh dramas, classical music, a costume procession, various folk dances, prayers, etc.

TOURS. Nara may be visited from Kyoto with JTB on a full-day tour for ¥8,500, lunch included. Places visited are confined to *Todaiji Temple, Kasuga Shrine,* the *Deer Park,* and *Byodoin* at Uji on the way. If you have more time go to Nara on your own. It is an easy place to get to know, and an unusually rewarding place to savor at leisure.

Student Guide Service. For a more flexible and intimate visit than package tours can offer, one may avail oneself of a free guide service staffed by English-speaking university students. Sarusawa Information Center, 4 Noborioji-cho, Nara 630; 26–4753 Hours 10:00 A.M.–4:00 P.M. daily, except Friday.

PARKS AND GARDENS. The **Deer Park,** also known as Nara Park, is a 260-acre natural park, located in the center of the city. **Isuien,** 5 minutes' walk west of Todai-ji Temple, is a spacious Japanese-style garden dotted with some 17-century arbors—a good specimen of traditional Japanese garden architecture.

HISTORICAL SITES. The major historical sites of the area are as follows: **Chogosonshi-ji.** Heguri-cho, Ikoma-gun. A hilltop temple, said to have been founded in 587 A.D.

Heijo Kyushi. Saki-cho. Site of Japan's capital in Nara Era (710–784 A.D.).

Hokke-ji Temple. Hokkeji-cho. A leading Buddhist nunnery.

Horyu-ji Temple. Ikaruga-cho, Ikoma-gun. The world's oldest wooden building.

Hozan-ji Temple. Monzen-cho, Ikoma City. Another hilltop temple known for a pair of hidden Buddhist statues.

Kasuga Shrine. Kasugano-cho. A Shinto shrine founded in 710 A.D.

Kofuku-ji Temple. Noborioji-cho. A prestigious Buddhist temple founded in 710 A.D.

Shin Yakushi-ji. Wariishi-cho. Founded in 747 A.D., the temple houses 12 statues rated as National Treasures.

Todai-ji Temple. Zoshi-cho. The world's largest wooden structure housing the Great Buddha.

Toshodai-ji Temple. Gojo-cho. Known for the statue representing Ganjin, an 8th-century Chinese priest who propagated Buddhism in Japan.

Yakushi-ji Temple. Nishi-no-kyo. Boasts an ancient pagoda and a beautiful Buddhist triad.

MUSEUMS. The **National Museum** (50 Noborioji-cho) is in Nara Park near Kofuku-ji. Open daily from 9:00–4:30 except Mondays and from Dec. 26–Jan. 3, it contains a valuable collection of Buddhist art objects. This museum has increased its space by opening a new *Shoso-in* style exhibition hall. **Nara Museum of Ethnology** has tableaux and old houses to show traditional Japan. At Koriyama, open 9:00 A.M.–5:00 P.M. except Mondays.

The **Yamato Bunka-kan** (1–11 Gakuen Minami) is in a pine grove overlooking a lake west of the city (15 minutes by car, or near the Kintetsu Gakuen-mae Station). It is noted for its Chinese ceramics in special exhibitions and houses the Enlarge-Jonas Netsuke Collection. 9:00 A.M.–4:00 P.M. daily except Mondays and Dec. 26–Jan. 3. **Neiraku Art Museum** in the Isuien Garden (74 Suimoncho 5 min. walk west from Todaiji) has an important collection of Chinese and Korean ceramics and also holds special shows of artistic and historical interest.

Open 10 A.M. to 4:30 P.M.; closed Tues. Located nearby is the **Nara Prefecture Art Museum,** with mostly contemporary works. A new room has been added to house 106 paintings of the Yura Collection. Open 10:00–4:30, ex. Tues. The **Kokuhokan** museum of Kofuku-ji houses mainly sculpture and is open daily year-round 9:00 A.M.–5:00 P.M. The **Nara-ken Bunka Kaikan** (Nara Prefecture Culture Hall), next to the Prefectural Office on Noborioji street, opposite Kofu-ku-ji, has halls for special exhibitions of historical, cultural and artistic materials. Open 9:00 A.M.–6:00 P.M. daily except Wednesdays. The **Daihozoden Treasure Hall** of Horyu-ji Temple exhibits works of Buddhist art connected with Prince Shotoku (573–621 A.D.) and of the Horyu-ji Temple.

About 8 km south of Nara, 20 min. by bus, is Tenri, headquarters of the Tenrikyo Shinto sect. Its great **Museum** (open 9:00 A.M.–4:00 P.M. daily except Mondays) contains some 20,000 pieces of classical art from China, Japan, Korea, Egypt, Greece, Rome, Persia and the Middle East; in addition to an equally large ethnological collection from all over the world. A major but little-known museum.

SHOPPING. Sanjo-dori, Higashimuki, and Mochidono, all in the central part of the city, are Nara's main shopping centers. For a quick look at souvenirs and local specialties, visit the showroom of the **Shoko Kanko Hall,** 38–1 Nobori-oji (22–4661), a minute's walk from the Kintetsu Station. On display and sale here are a variety of *sumi* (ink sticks), writing brushes, pottery, lacquerware, sculpture, fans, masks, and other traditional artifacts. Confectionery and *narazuke* (pickles seasoned in sake) are also available here and at other stores along the three shopping streets mentioned above. The Shoko Kanko showroom is publicly managed and foolproof pricewise.

DINING OUT. Western-style. The *Nara Hotel* is the only purely Western-style one, and, though the food is generally quite good, the old-fashioned dining room tends to be crowded at noon. Also recommended is the grill at the *Kasuga Hotel* (see "Hotels and Inns").

For budget eating, Higashi-muki-naka-machi (the arcade street to the right as you leave the Kintetsu Station) and Sanjo-dori itself have the usual large number of restaurants serving clean, plain, wholesome, semi-Western, semi-Chinese or semi-Japanese food which you can order from the price-marked models in the show windows.

Japanese-style. *Kikusuiro* (see "Hotels and Inns") and *Tsukihitei* are traditional gourmet restaurants. Price and service first class. Call for reservations; 26–2021. *Tsukihitei* is at 158 Kasugano-cho, 2 miles east of the Todai-ji Temple, deep in a primeval forest.

OSAKA

by
K.V. NARAIN

Osaka is the great financial, commercial, and industrial hub of western Japan. However, the city, now the third largest in the country, is also steeped in history, having played an important role in the early development of Japanese civilization.

At a time when Tokyo, the present Japanese capital, was unknown because it was nonexistent, Osaka played an important part as the entry point for cultural and material influences from China and Korea. It was through the gateway of Osaka Bay that art, science, and philosophy flowed into Japan, wielding a tremendous influence on Japanese society. Between the 5th and 8th centuries A.D., Osaka became the political center of the country as several emperors established their courts there.

Known in the early days as Naniwa (Rapid Waves), a name by which the city is known in a poetic sense even today, Osaka is conveniently located in the heart of the Japanese islands. There are abundant historical remains indicative of the prosperity and influence of Osaka since the 4th and 5th centuries. The cemetery of Emperor Nintoku, which can be seen in nearby Sakai City, is the biggest in the world covering 464,123 square meters. It was Emperor Nintoku who is recorded as having noticed that the village fires were burning low—a sign of hard

399

times—and who, accordingly, suspended tax collection for three years
to help his subjects regain their wealth.

For centuries, Osaka continued as the chief mercantile center for the
country. The merchant princes of the city had a sense of the esthetic,
and their patronage allowed great arts such as the Kabuki (which had
its origins in Kyoto) and Bunraku to grow and flourish. Osaka also
thrived as the gourmet's paradise, boasting literally thousands of restaurants known for their superb food. In fact, the people of Osaka today
are so fond of eating well that, according to a popular story, many a
well-to-do Osakan has gone bankrupt because of his passion for good
food.

Although between the 5th and 8th centuries several emperors established their courts in Osaka, it was in the latter part of the 16th century
that the city's heyday came, when the great soldier-statesman Toyotomi Hideyoshi (1536–1598) established his stronghold in Osaka. It was
Hideyoshi who was responsible for building the majestic Osaka Castle
in 1586, after three years of work. Hideyoshi, who managed to achieve
a degree of unification of the country torn by recurring civil wars,
ordered all the feudal lords loyal to him to help in the construction of
the gigantic castle. After power shifted to the Tokugawa family following the decisive battles of 1614 and 1615, some sixteen years after
Hideyoshi had died, the influence of the Toyotomis was completely
eliminated by the Tokugawas, who were to rule Japan for the next 250
years. Osaka Castle was reduced to ashes in the showdown battles.

Osaka shone at its cultural best during the brief Genroku Era (1688–
1704) when the affluent merchants of the city also gave encouragement
to such literary giants as the dramatist Chikamatsu Monzaemon (1653
–1724), often referred to as Japan's Shakespeare, and the novelist Ihara
Saikaku (1642–1693). The seat of political power of the Tokugawas
shifted to Edo (present-day Tokyo), but because of the distance, it was
not possible for the Tokugawas to maintain rigid control over the
merchant families of Osaka, who steadily laid the foundations for the
city's economic prosperity. Under these circumstances some of the
greatest business dynasties of Japan and the world had their beginnings,
including present-day names in the business and banking world such
as Sumitomo, Itochu, Marubeni, Sanwa, and Daiwa.

Today, Osaka is the nerve center of a vast megalopolis, which runs
from Kyoto on the north and Nara on the south, to Kobe on the west.
As the hub of Japan's textile and chemical industries, as well as certain
heavy industries, Osaka accounts for fully one fourth of the country's
industrial output and handles about 40 percent of its exports. At one
time, Osaka's foreign trade was conducted mainly through the port of
Kobe, but with the improvement of its own harbor facilities, Osaka's
direct foreign trade has grown tremendously. Among the city's manufacturing products are iron and steel, fabrics, ships, light machinery,
and chemicals, as well as textile, metal, and other goods. Between the
two world wars, Osaka was the production center for practically all
products (except for silk) on whose exports Japan depended heavily.

Osaka's appearance has changed over the years. The small wooden
buildings that crowded the congested narrow streets of the city's business center have been overtaken by modern multistoried high-rise

structures, giving Osaka all the characteristics of a concrete jungle. Nevertheless, despite the modernization, the city continues to perform its traditional function as a merchant town. Many streets concentrate on wholesale business activity as they have done for centuries. Do-buike, for example, is the wholesale district for clothing and accessories; although the stores look like ordinary retail shops, many of them do not deal with the general public. Medical and pharmaceutical companies are congregated in Doshomachi, where old-fashioned, open-fronted stores and modern office buildings stand side by side. One street of particular interest to foreign visitors to Osaka is, no doubt, Match-amachisuji, home of the toy, fireworks, and doll dealers who, unlike some of their counterparts in other lines of business, readily deal with the general public as well as with their wholesale and retail customers.

In the postwar years, Osaka also began to thrive as a center of heavy industry. Its metropolitan area and its vast suburban districts are criss-crossed by rivers and canals, making it easy to transport merchandise to the sea for shipment. This has contributed to the rapid growth of what is known as the Hanshin industrial zone, where industrial plants, textile factories, and chemical works are concentrated around Osaka Bay. Osaka's waterways have in this way played an important role in bringing about the city's commercial prosperity.

EXPLORING OSAKA

The nucleus of the city, leaving out the residential areas, is conveniently divided into two main districts—the Minami, or southern section, and the Kita, or northern section. The two are connected by Midosuji-dori (boulevard), Osaka's main street. It runs through the center of the city starting in front of Osaka Station and heading south to Namba for almost three miles.

Between Minami and Kita is Nakanoshima, the civic center of the city. Nakanoshima (middle island) is situated on a small delta island between the Dojima and Tosabori rivers, both effluents of the Yodo River. In this district are the City Office, the Asahi Shimbun (newspaper), Hotel Osaka Grand, Osaka Royal Hotel, Osaka Festival Hall, Osaka University (Faculties of Science and Medicine) as well as a number of banks, head offices of many businesses and international corporations, the Sogo and Daimaru department stores, and two large temples. The two temples are the Osaka branches of Kyoto's Nishi and Higashi Honganji temples, two of the most powerful Buddhist religious orders in the country. The Midosuji Boulevard is a broad road and is particularly pretty in the spring and summer when the four rows of gingko trees parallel to the tall buildings on both sides form a grand tunnel and provide city dwellers with a fresh touch of nature. The street, which is 47 yards wide and is the pride of the people of Osaka, is now one-way, serving southbound traffic.

The southern, Minami area of the city contains the chief entertainment centers, such as Shinsaibashi and Ebisubashi streets, known for their numerous department stores and specialty shops, and the Sennichimae and Dotonbori amusement centers famous for their innumerable theaters, restaurants, cabarets, and nightclubs.

The northern, Kita district also has many department stores, hotels, theaters, restaurants, cabarets, and nightclubs concentrated around the Japanese National Railways' Osaka Station. Kita is an interesting combination of the old and new, of order and disorder sometimes bordering on chaos. In this area, between the main Osaka Railway Station and the Dojima River, a maze of underground shopping arcades as well as several skyscraper buildings have sprung up. On the side streets countless small bars and snack joints can be found, as well as many fashionable nightclubs and other expensive drinking holes.

The tourist to Osaka would find it useful to note three other points of reference. North of Umeda, the area around the main Osaka Station for the JNR Tokaido Line, is Shin Osaka Station of the JNR's super express line from Tokyo. East of Nakanoshima is Temmabashi, where are found Osaka Castle, the Matsuzakaya Department Store, Temmangu Shrine and the Osaka Prefectural Office.

Southeast of Namba lies the Tennoji area, which includes the Tsutenkaku Tower, Tennoji Park, Zoo and Botanical Garden, Shitennoji Temple, and two railway stations.

Osaka Castle and Other Sights

Osaka Castle, the city's most famous sightseeing attraction, was built by the great Toyotomi Hideyoshi at the peak of his power. This majestic structure is in every way symbolic of Hideyoshi's great ambitions and prestige. Known as the "Golden Castle" or the "Brocade Castle," the original was about 1.7 miles long, 1.2 miles wide, and over seven miles around, a veritable fortified city, built between 1583 and 1586 with the labor of 630,000 men. This castle was besieged and burned in 1615 by Tokugawa Ieyasu, who took the shogunate from Hideyoshi's young son. Ieyasu's successors rebuilt the castle minus the outermost moats, but further fires, from lightning in 1665, and a brief civil war in 1867, burned everything except the front gate and a few turrets. The present donjon (five stories outside, eight inside), 189 feet high, was finished in 1931 in ferro-concrete and is a reproduction of Hideyoshi's original. The massive, imposing castle tower stands in the center of a huge park. Inside the castle tower is a historical museum containing materials and documents concerning the history of the castle and the Toyotomi family. The seventh floor commands a bird's eye view of the city.

To reach Osaka Castle, take the Tanimachi subway line from Minami-Morimachi Station to Tanimachi 4-chome Station, which is the second stop. The castle is a 10-minute walk from the station.

A 20-minute walk from the castle will bring you to the Temmangu Shrine, located 1.5 kilometers (about a mile) to the northwest. The shrine can also be reached in a 3-minute walk southeast from Minami-Morimachi Station, which is just one stop away from Higashi Umeda Station on the Tanimachi subway line. It is a slightly longer walk from the JNR Tennoji Station.

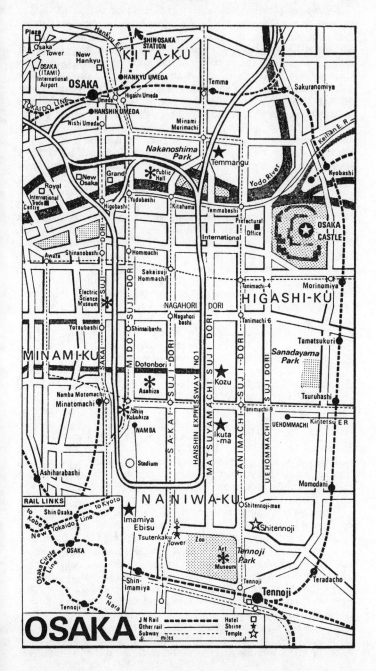

OSAKA

J N Rail ▬▬▬▬	Hotel	□
Other rail ▬▬▬▬	Shrine	★
Subway ▬ ▬ ▬	Temple	☆
miles		

Temmangu shrine is believed to have been founded in 949 A.D. Enshrined here is Sugawara Michizane, a great scholar of the 9th century and now admired as the God of Academics (Michizane is also enshrined at Kyoto's Kitano Tenmangu). Once much patronized by the military as well as the nobility and common people of Osaka, this shrine is now visited mainly by students praying for success in their entrance examinations. The shrine is nationally known for its "Tenjin Matsuri" festival on July 24 and 25, one of the three biggest festivals in Japan. The festival, attended by several hundred thousand people, features a beautifully decorated miniature shrine carried with much ado by worshipers. There is also the lion dance, a grand procession on the grounds, plus an evening parade of about 50 boats. The parade is accompanied by traditional Japanese festival music, and the whole event is climaxed by fabulous fireworks.

The Ohatsu Tenjin Shrine, located 1.5 kilometers west of Temmangu Shrine, is about a 10-minute walk from Osaka Station. It is known as the setting of the famous story, "Sonezaki Shinju" (Lovers' Suicide at Sonezaki), which has been dramatized by Chikamatsu Monzaemon, the very popular playwright of the Edo Period. Today the shrine is completely hidden away in the Sonezaki amusement district, surrounded by dozens of tiny eating and drinking places.

Shitennoji Temple, the oldest Buddhist temple in the country, was founded by Prince Shotoku in 593 A.D., 14 years before the world-famous Horyuji Temple of Nara City came into being. The temple can be reached in a 15-minute walk north of the JNR Tennoji Station, or a 5-minute walk south from the Shittenoji subway station of the Tanimachi line. The five-storied pagoda, the main hall, the Deva Gate, and the Gate of Happiness have been reconstructed to their original state in the majestic style of the Asuka Period. Over the inside wall of the pagoda is a large painted mural of the Four Deities. Another mural shows the dramatic scene of the Buddha's entrance into the priesthood. The third mural worth viewing is the pictorial description of the Buddha and his ten disciples.

The abbot's chamber of the main sanctuary building, Rokuji-do Hall, and the sacred stone arch (oldest in the country) are preserved and designated as important cultural assets. Housed in the treasury are the Senmen Hokkekyo (pictorial scriptures painted on fans), classed as important cultural assets, and more than 200 other paintings and sculptures.

Although the temple has burned down several times through wars or natural disasters, the entire architectural structure of the sacred buildings and the ground layout have been restored to their original state and are well preserved. Shitennoji Bugaku (sacred classical music and dance), which is performed in the court of the temple every April 22, recreates the elegant manners and customs of peers during the Heian Era. Although this court drama was introduced from the Asian continent and India, its exquisite nicety and refined elegance are not to be found in its continental prototype.

Tsutenkaku Tower, a 5-minute walk from Ebisucho subway station, is the best known landmark in the Tennoji area in southern Osaka. This 338-foot-high tower has an observation platform at the 299-foot level, commanding a view of Tennoji Park, Shinsekai amusement area, and the whole city. The tower, first constructed in 1912, was scrapped for war use in 1943 and the present one was rebuilt in 1957.

Jan-Jan Lane, running in the southeastern part of the Shinsekai downtown amusement quarter where the Tsutenkaku Tower is located, is jammed with pubs and taverns, game arcades, and cinemas. For the people of Osaka, this covered arcade is one of the most popular night spots.

Sumiyoshi Shrine (commonly known among the Japanese as "Sumiyoshi Taisha," Taisha indicating the second highest rank among Shinto shrines), is a popular shrine said to have been built in 202 A.D. It is located in the extreme southern part of the city, close to Sumiyoshi-Torii-mae Station on the Nankai Hankai line or Sumiyoshi-Taisha Station on the Nankai Railways' main line. Dedicated to the guardian deity of the sea as well as to the god of rich harvest, this shrine includes four main sanctuary buildings. The structure of the buildings is simple and refined, in what is called "Sumiyoshi style," which fully utilizes the beauty of nature with wooden pillars and back-thatched roofs. The arched bridge on the pond and row after row of stone lanterns along the pavement—about 600 in all, many of them donated by sailors and shipowners—add an extra loveliness to the tranquil atmosphere.

Theater in Osaka

Japan's puppet theater, known as Bunraku, is a unique kind of puppet show which has hardly any parallel elsewhere. It represents the acme of the great cultural refinement achieved in Osaka. Bunraku originated in the Heian Era (794–1192 A.D.) as a simple form of popular entertainment, but the great playwright Chikamatsu Monzaemon, with his masterful texts, elevated the puppet show to the level of dignified dramatic art in the late 17th and early 18th centuries. Long patronized by the great merchant classes of Osaka, the Bunraku continues to flourish to this day, representing one of the most important forms of the Japanese stage. The dramas that are performed are divided into love tragedies and stories dealing with historical events. One of Bunraku's memorable features is the chanted text, known as *Joruri,* which is accompanied by classical music played on the *shamisen,* the traditional three-stringed Japanese instrument. The Bunraku is performed by means of "three-man puppetry," in which three operators manipulate the principal puppet, which is about two thirds of human size. The puppets, in colorful costumes, are amazingly life-like.

Designated as an intangible important cultural asset in 1962, Bunraku is given special treatment by the government. It is performed seasonally, usually four times a year for two to three weeks at a time. If you are in Osaka during one of the seasons when Bunraku is on, it is well worth a visit. The performances are given at the Asahiza Theater which is located at 2–18 Dotombori 1-chome, Minami-ku. See the *Practical Information* section for details.

Osaka also has its own Kabuki theater, the Shin Kabukiza Theater, located at 3–25 Namba 4-chome, Minami-ku 5 minutes' walk from Namba Station. Unlike Tokyo, where Kabuki plays are performed throughout the year, in Osaka there is usually one performance a year lasting for 25 days during April.

The Kabuki plays presented in Osaka are no different from those that are presented at the Kabukiza, Shimbashi Embujo, or the National Theater in Tokyo. Although Noh drama, from which Kabuki evolved, was cultivated by the aristocracy of Kyoto, it was the soldiers, merchants, artisans, and commoners of Edo and Osaka who patronized Kabuki theater. Kabuki is characterized by swashbuckling melodrama, excruciating passion, tension and violence, as well as heavily, and often fiercely, made-up actors in gorgeous and extravagant kimonos. As in Tokyo, in the Kabuki plays presented in Osaka all the feminine roles are played by males. Some of the greatest actors in the history of the Kabuki theater have gained their fame because of their moving interpretations of female characters—somewhat ironical when it is considered that the beginnings of the Kabuki drama in Kyoto in the late 16th–early 17th century are credited to Izumo no Okuni, a woman.

The Kabuki plays are brilliant and spectacular to watch. Texts of the dialogue of the drama being performed usually are available in Japanese and, often, in English. Most of the ordinary Japanese also need to read the text to follow the play because even they have difficulty in understanding the highly stylized Kabuki form of speech. However, whether you can follow the story and appreciate Kabuki's finer points or not, it is a brilliant spectacle worth watching at least briefly for an hour or so.

The inside architecture of the Kabuki theater is designed to bring the artist close to the audience. A long corridor, known as the "hanami-chi," leads right across the theater to the stage, and there is at least one sequence in a Kabuki play where the hero or heroes make their entrance or exit by way of the hanamichi.

Osaka's Shin Kabukiza, located at the south end of Midosuji-dori in Namba, was built in 1958; its attractive façade is in the style of Momoyama Period architecture.

PRACTICAL INFORMATION FOR OSAKA

WHEN TO GO. In recent years, Japan has gotten its share of tourists in every season. Osaka, being neither too hot in summer nor too cold in winter, is all right to visit at just about any time, although the spring and autumn may be more pleasant. Osaka gets a little warmer than Tokyo in summer and a bit colder in winter. The mean temperatures are 41° F (5° C) in January and 75° F (24° C) in August.

HOW TO GET THERE. By train. From **Tokyo**, Osaka can be reached in 3 hours 10 minutes on the super express Hikari bullet train (fare: ¥ 12,200; the green (first) class fares are higher). There are 53 Hikari trains a day leaving Tokyo between 6:00 A.M. and 8:12 P.M. The slightly slower Kodama, which connects the two cities in 4 hours, has 31 trains daily between 6:04 A.M. and 7:28 P.M.

From **Nagoya,** Osaka can be reached either by Hikari bullet train or by many other ordinary express trains departing at frequent intervals. The Kintetsu Electric Railway, which takes a somewhat circuitous route by way of picturesque Toba (famous for its cultured pearls) in Mie Prefecture and parts of Nara Prefecture, has 27 trains a day and takes 2 hours and 13 minutes.

From **Kobe,** one can take the JNR's super expresses (the extra express fare makes the ticket for the half-hour ride rather expensive). More convenient are the JNR interurban expresses (kaisoku) which run from Kobe's Sannomiya Station to Osaka Station in 30 minutes. The same route by the Hankyu Electric Railways takes only 28 minutes.

From **Kyoto,** you can either take the JNR bullet train (again by paying high express ticket charges) or the JNR interurban fast trains (kaisoku), which take 36 minutes from Kyoto Station. The JNR interurban fast trains run at frequent intervals between Kyoto and Osaka, continuing onward to Sannomiya in Kobe.

The fast trains (tokkyu) by the Keihan Electric Railway from Kyoto's Sanjo Station to Osaka's Yodoyabashi Station take 45 minutes. The Hankyu Electric Railways also has fast trains from Kyoto's Kawaramachi Station to Osaka's Umeda in about 35 minutes by limited express (tokkyu) and in about 45 minutes by ordinary express (kyuko).

From **Nara,** the Kintetsu Line takes the passenger in half an hour to Uehonmachi (Ueroku) Station on the east side of downtown Osaka.

Generally speaking, the fares on the private railways are lower than those of the JNR. In many cases, the service also is superior, with attendants pampering passengers with comforts such as hot towels to wipe the face with.

By car. If you prefer to drive, the Meishin Express Highway links Nagoya, Kyoto, and Kobe with a branch that runs into and loops around downtown Osaka.

By air. The distance from Tokyo to Osaka is covered in 55 minutes (fare: ¥15,600). Osaka International Airport is conveniently linked with downtown Osaka in about 30 minutes.

Osaka is one of the two major aerial gateways to Japan, the other being Tokyo. It has now been decided to build a brand-new international airport on a manmade island in Osaka Bay at a cost of $3.9 billion. The airport, to have three runways, is scheduled to be completed by 1992. It will be the first international airport in Japan where planes can land 24 hours a day; at present, because the existing Osaka International Airport is built close to a congested residential area, no flights are permitted to land after 9:00 P.M. or before 6:00 A.M.

Ten international airlines now serve Osaka with flights from Europe (both direct from London or via Tokyo for the same fare). From North America, there are both direct flights as well as flights by way of Tokyo. Travelers can reach the city from Chicago, Cleveland, Los Angeles, New York, St. Louis, San Francisco, and Seattle without change of planes. From Asia, there are direct flights from Seoul, Taipei, Hong Kong, Singapore, Bangkok, and Bombay.

From Tokyo, there are over a dozen flights daily by two of the three domestic air carriers that link Osaka with the capital city—Japan Air Lines (JAL) and All Nippon Airways (ANA). Japan Air Lines is the only airline that connects Tokyo's Narita International Airport with Osaka.

 TELEPHONES. The area code for Osaka is 06. **Emergencies.** To call police, dial 110; for fire and emergency, 119. To make overseas calls, dial 0051. Taxicab Modernization Center (for possessions forgotten in taxis): 933–5610. *Travel-Phone:* If you have some difficulty in communicating with local people or need more detailed information on the places or attractions you want to see, the Japan Travel Phone will put you in touch with an English-speaking travel expert ready to help you solve a language problem or offer any travel information. The Travel Phone can be used in two ways—as a toll-free service anywhere in Japan outside Tokyo or Kyoto and by regular phone charge (¥10 per 3 minutes) within Tokyo and Kyoto. All you have to do is dial 106 and tell the operator, in English, "collect call, T.I.C." You are advised to speak slowly and clearly. When using a public phone, insert a ten-yen coin and dial 106. The coin will be returned to you after your call. The service hours of the Travel Phone are 9:00 A.M. to 5:00 P.M. daily.

HOTELS. Osaka's big hotels might not have the elegant surroundings of some in Kyoto nor the opulence of some in Tokyo but they are fitted out with the latest in international-style luxury gimmicks and are run with efficiency and thoroughness.

The big hotel boom that has swept Japan during the past two decades and more has caused a corresponding rapid decline in the number of traditional, Japanese-style *ryokan* (traveler's inns) in the big cities, including Osaka. However, most of the good hotels in Osaka do have limited numbers of Japanese-style rooms available.

WESTERN STYLE

Deluxe

The Plaza Hotel. 2–2–49 Oyodo-Minami, Oyodo-ku; 453–1111. Fifteen minutes by car from Shin Osaka Station. Tasteful decor; fast, efficient, polished service. 550 rooms. ¥9,800 and up for a single, ¥18,500 and up for two.

Royal Hotel. 5–3–68 Nakanoshima, Kita-ku; 448–1121. Fifteen minutes by car from Shin Osaka Station. 1500 comfortable, well-appointed rooms. ¥10,000 and up for a single, ¥20,000 and up for two.

Expensive

Holiday Inn Nankai. 28–1 Kyuzaemoncho, Minami-ku; 213–8281. Three minutes' walk from Namba Station. 229 rooms. ¥10,000 and up for a single, ¥18,000 and up for two.

Hotel Do Sports Plaza. 3–3–17 Minami Futaba, Shiomachi-dori, Minami-ku; 245–3311. Twenty minutes by car from Shin Osaka Station. 193 rooms. ¥7,800 and up for a single, ¥10,000 and up for two.

Hotel Osaka Grand. 2–3–18 Nakanoshima, Kita-ku; 202–1212. Five minutes by car from Osaka Station. 358 rooms. ¥8,000 and up for a single, ¥14,000 and up for two.

Toyo Hotel. 3–16–19 Toyosaki, Oyodo-ku; 372–8181. Five minutes by car from Osaka or Shin Osaka Stations. 641 rooms. ¥7,500 and up for a single, ¥13,000 and up for two.

Moderate

Hotel Echo Osaka. 1–4–7 Abenosuji, Abeno-ku; 633–1141. One minute walk from Osaka Station. 83 rooms. ¥5,800 and up for a single, ¥9,200 and up for two.

Hotel Hanshin. 2–3–30 Umeda, Kita-ku; 344–1661. One minute walk from Osaka Station. 243 rooms. ¥7,900 and up for a single, ¥13,000 and up for two.

Hotel New Hankyu. 1–1–35 Shibata, Kita-ku; 372–5101. Two minutes' walk from Osaka Station. 1029 rooms. ¥7,800 and up for a single, ¥13,500 and up for two.

Hotel Osaka Castle. 2–35 Kyobashi, Higashi-ku; 942–1401. Five minutes by car from Osaka Station. 90 rooms. ¥5,500 and up for a single, ¥9,000 and up for two.

International Hotel Osaka. 58 Hashizumecho, Uchihon-machi, Higashi-ku; 941–2661. Ten minutes by car from Osaka Station. 394 rooms. ¥7,500 and up for a single, ¥12,000 and up for two.

Osaka Dai-ichi Hotel. 1–9–20 Umeda, Kita-ku; 341–4411. One minute walk from Osaka Station. 478 rooms. ¥8000 and up for a single, ¥14,500 and up for two.

Osaka Miyako Hotel. 10–48 Hidenincho, Tennoji-ku; 779–1501. In Tennoji Station Building. 151 rooms. ¥7,000 and up for a single, ¥11,000 and up for two.

Osaka Riverside Hotel. 5–10–160 Nakanocho, Miyakojima-ku; 928–3251. Ten minutes by car from Osaka Station. 102 rooms. ¥5,000 and up for a single, ¥9,000 and up for two.

Osaka Tokyu Hotel. 7–20 Chayamachi, Kita-ku; 373–2411. Two minutes' walk from Umeda Station. 340 rooms. ¥7,500 and up for a single, ¥14,500 and up for two.

JAPANESE STYLE

Hotel Hishitomi. 1–23 Hommachi, Higashi-ku; 261–1112. Ten minutes by car from Osaka Station. 23 Japanese-style rooms with attached bath and 38 Western-style rooms with attached bath. ¥7,000 to ¥10,000 per person (inclusive of dinner and breakfast as well as tax and service charge).

BUSINESS HOTELS

These are mostly single rooms usually with attached bath and toilet, although some twin bedrooms are available.

Business Hotel Kikue. 3–6–4 Nihombashi, Naniwa-ku; 633–5656. Five minutes' walk from Nihombashi subway station. 58 rooms. ¥4,500 (including breakfast, service charge, and tax).

Hokke Club Hotel. 12–19 Toganocho, Kita-ku; 313–3171. Ten minutes by walk from Osaka Station. 257 rooms. ¥5,100 (without bath); ¥6,090 (with bath, inclusive of service and tax).

Hotel Nankai. 1–17–11 Namba Naka, Naniwa-ku; 649–1521. Two minutes' walk from Namba subway station. 214 rooms. ¥6,000 (including service charge and tax).

Hotel Osaka World. 1–5–23 Sonezaki, Kita-ku; 361–1100. Seven minutes' walk from Osaka Station. 202 rooms. ¥5,000 (inclusive of service and tax).

Hotel Sun Life. 3–3–6 Utsubohonmachi, Nishi-ku; 443–1231. One minute walk from Awaza subway station. 63 rooms. ¥4,800 (inclusive of service and tax).

New Oriental Hotel. 2–6–10 Nishimoto, Nishi-ku; 538–7141. One minute walk from Awaza subway station. 120 rooms. ¥4,570 (without bath); ¥5,270 (with bath, inclusive of service and tax).

Osaka Green Hotel. 2–8–5 Shinmachi, Nishi-ku; 532–1091. Five minutes' walk from Yotsubashi subway station. 100 rooms. ¥5,300 (inclusive of service and tax).

Shin Osaka Sen-i City Hotel. 2–2–17 Nishimiyahara, Yodogawa-ku; 394–3331. Eight minutes' walk from Shin Osaka Station. 70 rooms. ¥4,180 (without bath) (inclusive of service and tax).

Toko Hotel. 1–3–19 Minamimoricho, Kita-ku; 363–1201. One minute walk from Minamimorimachi subway station. 300 rooms. ¥5,500 (inclusive of service and tax).

HOW TO GET AROUND. Osaka, like Tokyo, is a city whose streets are congested with cars practically the whole day long. However, again like Tokyo, Osaka has an excellent public transportation system. **Subways** criss-cross the city and recommended as the fastest and most convenient means of transportation.

Several overhead railways as well as subway lines have their terminals or stations in Umeda and as a result Umeda has become synonymous with the names of the stations themselves. These are the main Osaka Station for the JNR Tokaido line; Hankyu Umeda Station for the Hankyu lines to Kobe, Takarazuka, and Kyoto; Higashi Umeda Station for the Tanimachi subway line to Osaka Castle and Tennoji; Umeda Station for the Midosuji subway line to Namba and Tennoji; Nishi Umeda Station for the Yotsubashi subway line to Namba; and Hanshin Umeda Station for the Hanshin line to Kobe. All the stations are connected by underground passages.

The *Midosuji subway line* is the trunk line in the city's transportation, conveniently linking the station complex in Umeda with both the JNR's Shin Osaka Station (which is where the Shinkansen bullet trains stop) and three key downtown terminals, namely Shinsaibashi, Namba, and Tennoji. Shinsaibashi can be reached in 12 minutes, Namba in 14 minutes, and Tennoji in 20 minutes. Thanks to the typical sound planning of the Japanese, each subway line and the elevated railways are colored separately and distinctively in different colors. This plus the fact that all station names are written in English should make it very easy for even the absolute newcomer to use public transportation armed with a map of the subway and overhead transit system. The maps are available at most stations. Subways and trains operate from about 5:00 A.M. to midnight.

Taxis are available in plenty. The minimum fare for the medium-sized taxi is ¥470 for the first 2 kilometers. After that, the meter goes up by ¥80 for every additional 390 meters. Somewhat smaller-sized taxis charge ¥450 for the first 2 kilometers, but these are not as numerous as the medium-sized taxis.

Car rentals. There are a number of rent-a-car companies in Osaka, including: *Japaren Company Limited,* 2–18 Nipponbashi Nishi 1-chome, Naniwa-ku, 632–4881; *Mitsubishi Rent-A-Car,* 5–23 Minami-Horie 1-chome, Nishi-ku, 538–2428; *Nissan Rent-A-Car,* Asahi Hoso Building, 2–2 Oyodocho Minami, Oyodo-ku, 458–7391; *Nippon Rent-A-Car Service Inc.,* 2–25 Sonezakishinchi, Kita-ku, 364–1671; and *Toyota Rent-A-Car,* 3–1 Dojimakami, Kita-ku, 344–6831.

TOURIST INFORMATION. *Osaka Tourist Association:* c/o Trade and Tourist Department, Osaka Municipal Office, Semba Center Building (No. 2), 1–4 Semba-chuo, Higashi-ku; 261–3948. Open 9:15 A.M. to 5:00 P.M. weekdays and until 1:00 P.M. on Saturdays (closed Sundays and holidays). *Osaka Tourist Information Office:* 1–1 Umeda 3-chome, Kita-ku; 345–2189. *Japan Travel Bureau (JTB):* JTB has counters in Osaka Station (open 9:00 A.M. to 6:00 P.M. all the year round; 361–5471); in Hotel New Osaka, 441–4801; Hotel Osaka Grand, 202–1212; and Asahi Building, 203–1921. The latter three are open from 9:00 A.M. to 5:00 P.M., except on Sundays and holidays.

COMMERCIAL INFORMATION. Visitors who are interested in trade with Japan could find the following institutions of use to them. *Osaka Prefectural*

Foreign Trade Institute. This trade promotion center provides the best opportunity for manufacturers and trading companies to promote sales abroad by exhibiting their products.

Osaka International Trade Fair. Asashiobashi subway station. This international fair, held every other year in April, hosts scores of business representatives from countries from all over the world. The latest and finest quality products are exhibited.

Osaka International Trade Center. Dojima-ohashi bus stop; next door to Royal Hotel. A joint venture of Osaka Prefecture and the business community, this trade center has a permanent trade exhibition. Trade information is available and foreign exhibits are accepted.

Osaka Merchandise Mart. Tenmabashi Station on Keihan line or subway. This 22-story building was built along the Yodo River in the center of Osaka City in 1969. It accommodates over 280 wholesalers and business enterprises in textiles, furniture, interior decoration, and general merchandise. Exhibitions and business fairs are also held here.

USEFUL ADDRESSES. *U.S. Consulate General:* Sankei Building, 4–9 Umeda 2-chome, Kita-ku; 341–2754. *British Consulate General:* Hong Kong and Shanghai Bank Building, 45 Awaji-machi 4-chome, Higashi-ku; 231–3355/7. *Osaka Immigration Office:* 2–31 Tanimachi, Higashi-ku; 941–0071.

MEDICAL SERVICES. In general, it is best to seek the assistance of your hotel or inn when you need a doctor, dentist, or medical supplies. Many Japanese practitioners are American- or European-trained, and the pharmaceutical supplies in this country are up to Western standards.

Yodogawa Christian Hospital, Awajihonmachi, Higashi-yodogawaku (322–2250/4), is accustomed to foreign patients, as is the *International Catholic Hospital* at 5–26, Yamasakacho, Higashi-Sumiyoshi-ku (791–0939). *Osaka National Hospital,* Hoenzaka-cho, Higashi-ku (942–1331), is excellent.

SEASONAL EVENTS AND FESTIVALS. January. *Senbonzuki Festival* on the 3rd. At Mizuma Temple near Mizuma Station on the Mizuma line. A happy annual event, during which steamed rice is pounded into a cake. At this temple, in the south of the prefecture, Mochi, the pounded rice cake, is served to visitors as an amulet against evils.

Tohka Ebisu Festival from the 9th–11th. At Imamiya-Ebisu Shrine in Ebisu-cho, Naniwa-ku, near Imamiya Station on the Nankai line. A popular festival dedicated to the God of Wealth and Fortune. The festival, complete with an elaborate procession, is held on January 10 at Ebisu shrines all over the country. In the Tohka Ebisu Festival of the Imamiya Shrine in Osaka City, one can see ample demonstration of the easygoing, gay, and optimistic nature of the natives of Osaka.

Doya-doya Naked Festival on the 14th. At Shitennoji Temple near Tennoji Station. Two teams of young men wearing only loin cloths parade, compete in cold water austerities, and jostle for a sacred stick around the central pillar of the Rokuji-do Hall. The red team represents sailors, fishing, and the sea; the white team farmers and the land. The winners are said to be blessed with good harvests. In recent years, the participation in, and enthusiasm for this 300-year-old basically Shinto rite have rapidly declined.

March. *Higan-e* (Holy Service of Nirvana) runs from the 18th–24th. At Shitennoji Temple near Shitennoji-mae subway station. Hundreds of little stalls are set up to sell to the crowds making pilgrimages to their family graves.

April. *Ashibe Odori* takes place between the 1st and 10th. Annual dance program given by Osaka's geisha quarter at Asahi-za, the Bunraku theater at Dotonbori. Twice daily from noon, four times on Sundays.

Between April 14th and May 2nd. is the *Osaka International Festival of Music and Drama*. Leading artists from all over the world plus Japanese classical theater. Held at the Festival Hall in Nakanoshima.

Shoryo-e takes place on the 22nd. At Shitennoji Temple, near Shitennoji-mae subway station. A holy service held for Prince Shotoku, the founder of the temple. On this occasion, the ancient court dance of Bugaku is performed on the Ishi-Butai (stone stage) in the sanctuary. The dance is solemn and dignified, and the elegant costumes and colorful masks worn by the performers are of great beauty.

Cherry Blossoms at the Mint Bureau can be seen in mid-April. The precinct of the Mint Bureau along the Yodo River is open to the public for viewing of the double petaled cherry blossoms. Well known and well frequented, the Mint garden is open to the public every year at the time of cherry viewing.

June. *Otaue Shinji Rice Planting Festival* is held on the 14th. At Sumiyoshi Shrine near Sumiyoshi-Taisha Station on the Nankai line. This festival, also called Sumiyoshi Folk Dance, is celebrated by the people, who plant young rice plants ceremoniously in the sanctuary. The folk dance is dedicated to the god for good harvest, and is performed in a circle by children. Wearing peasants' traditional working clothes in brilliantly contrasting white, black, and red, they dance in imitation of rice planting to the accompaniment of ancient music. This folk dance is also performed at the Sumiyoshi Festival on August 1.

July. *Aizen Festival* on the 1st. At Shoman-in Temple, Tennoji-ku, near Shitennoji subway station. As a branch of Shitennoji Temple, Shoman-in Temple and its main cathedral, the Aizen-do, are dedicated to the God of Fire, Aizen. Held first among all the summer festivals in Osaka, this festival is especially well patronized by the people. On the night of June 30, *yamabushi* (itinerant mountain priests specializing in magic) build a bonfire with rituals to exorcise evil. The temple treasures are shown and geisha parade. People turn out in new summer kimonos on this occasion.

Setomono Matsuri or Ceramic Ware Festival runs from the 22nd–26th. At Zama Shrine near Hommachi subway station. A large-scale fair of chinaware is held during the festival period.

Tenjin Matsuri or Festival of Tenmangu Shrine takes place on the 24th–25th. Perhaps Osaka's biggest and considered one of the best festivals in Japan, it features a spectacular procession of over a hundred gorgeously decorated boats carrying mikoshi (shrine palanquins) from Nakanoshima to Osaka Castle accompanied by fireworks, dances, and parades. There is a special stand for foreigners as well as special boat tickets through JTB and major hotels.

Sumiyoshi Matsuri Festival is held from the 30th to August 1st. At Sumiyoshi Taisha Shrine near Sumiyoshi Taisha Station on the Nankai Line. This festival features a parade of half-intoxicated youths carrying a 2½-ton palanquin down to the Yamato River (late on the night of the 31st) and then back to the shrine on the evening of the 1st. In Ohama Park, there is an enormous all-night bazaar with fireworks and folk dancing. This festival is held for the safety and prosperity of fishermen and (since 1962) of automobile drivers also.

August. *Noh Performance* at Ikutama Shrine, Tennoji-ku, from the 11th–12th. A classical dance drama of Buddhist inspiration, Noh is one of the most traditional and powerful esthetic art forms of Japan. As in Bugaku, the performers wear masks that combine an abstract symbolism with a realistic portrayal of different types of character. These masks unite in a strange and moving way the beauty of abstract design with a profound expression of human emotion. Springing from Buddhist philosophy, with its emphasis upon the tragic and fleeting character of human existence, the spirit of Noh is a deeply pessimistic one. The Ikutama Noh is held in the sanctuary of the shrine at night and performed on the stage under a mysterious illumination provided by burning kindlewood.

November. *Shinno Festival* on the 22nd–23rd. At Sukuna-Hikona Shrine in Doshomachi, Higashi-ku. Near Kitahama subway station. The shrine is dedicated to Shinno, legendary Chinese king of medicine, and Sukuna-Hikona-no-Mikoto, Japanese god king of medicine. Over a period of 270 years, the merchants and manufacturers of medicines and chemicals have been concentrated in the Doshomachi area of the city. The festival originated in 1822 when cholera broke out and pharmacists distributed pills and papier-mâché tigers among the public at the shrine. Papier-mâché tigers are still distributed during the festival.

INDUSTRIAL TOURS. Osaka, which is one of the most developed industrial and commercial cities in the world, actively promotes factory tours by visitors. The Osaka City Government organizes factory visits for both citizens and tourists.

Tours are operated in March, April, July, August, and October for about ten days in each month. A tour visits a couple of plants or factories of various industries such as a beer brewery, an automobile factory, a broadcasting center, a dairy products factory, the Mint, the Osaka Port, and so on. Information about schedules and reservations can be obtained from the City Tourist Information Office or the Osaka Tourist Association. The telephone number of the *City Tourist Information Office,* located at JNR Osaka Station, is 345–2189. The number of the *Osaka Tourist Association,* located in the Semba Center Building (No. 2), is 261–3948.

Some manufacturers are willing to accept visitors to their plants in Osaka. *Matsushita Electric Company* (National), for example, admits up to 50 persons at a time to its factory at 1006 Oaza Kadomacho, Osaka-fu. English-speaking guides are provided. Enquiries can be made through your hotel, the *Japan Travel Bureau;* the *Trade and Tourist Section,* Economic Bureau, Osaka City Office, located at 1–4 Nakanoshima, Kita-ku; or the *Osaka Tourist Association Office* at the address given above.

HOME VISIT SYSTEM. Osaka has a home visit system designed to give foreign visitors a chance to visit a Japanese family at home. In Osaka, a certain number of families voluntarily receive foreign guests without any monetary compensation. English is spoken in most host families and other languages in some of them.

Visiting hours usually are limited to a couple of hours on weekends or holidays. Or, in the case of weekdays, usually after supper. There is no charge except for the cost of transportation to and from the host's home. The number of visitors must be less than five. For making arrangements, call, visit, or write to the following office, preferably four days in advance: Osaka Tourist Association, c/o Trade and Tourist Department, Osaka Municipal Office, Semba Center Building (No. 2), 1–4 Semba-chuo, Higashi-ku, Osaka; 261–3948.

414 JAPAN

PARKS. Tennoji Park. Near Tennoji Station on the JNR loop line or subway. This park, quite conveniently located within the city area, has been provided for recreation and relaxation. It has various facilities like the Tennoji Zoo, playground, flower and botanical gardens, a typical Japanese garden called Keitaku-en, and a modern art museum and concert hall. Families come out here in their leisure time to relax and entertain themselves. The park was laid out in 1909 on the site of the fifth industrial exposition.

The Green Park of Hattori. Near Sone Station on the Hankyu Takarazuka line. Conveniently located in the suburbs of Osaka, an extensive area of 54 square miles was laid out with facilities for recreation and sports, an open-air concert hall, and the Local House Museum. Dotted with woods, bamboo groves, and scores of ponds, this park is full of picturesque variety.

HISTORICAL SITES. Osaka Castle; 941–3044. Fifteen minutes' walk east of Tanimachi 4-chome Station on the Tanimachi and Chuo subway lines. Most famous of all Osaka's attractions. A reproduction of the massive 16th-century castle built by Toyotomi Hideyoshi. Castle tower open from 9:00 A.M. to 5:00 P.M. (up to 8:30 P.M. during the summer). Admission ¥300. An additional ¥100 is charged for admission to the grass-covered Nishinomaru Garden of the castle.

Shitennoji Temple; 771–0066. Seven minutes' walk south from Shitennoji-mae Station of Tanimachi subway line. Open 8:30 A.M. to 4:00 P.M. every day. Admission ¥200 for adults and ¥100 for children. On the 22nd of each month, from 9:30 A.M. to 3:00 P.M., one can visit the shrine's gallery of paintings of Prince Shotoku as a young prince. Admission to this gallery is free.

Sumiyoshi Shrine; 672–0753. Exactly in front of Sumiyoshi Taisha Station of the main Nankai line. Open daily from 6:00 A.M. to 5:00 P.M. Admission free.

Temmangu Shrine; 353–0025. Five minutes' walk to the south from Minami Morimachi Station on the Tanimachi and Sakaisuji subway lines. Open daily from 9:30 A.M. to 5:00 P.M. Admission free.

MUSEUMS. Japan Handicraft Museum. 7–6 Namba Naka 3-chome, Naniwa-ku; 641–6309. Ten minutes' walk from Namba subway station. Folk arts and crafts. Open daily from 10:00 A.M. to 5:00 P.M. Closed on Mondays. Admission: ¥300.

National Museum of Ethnology. EXPO Memorial Park, Suita City; 876–2151. Twelve minutes by bus from JNR Ibaraki Station. On display are articles of the daily life of the world's nations. Open daily from 10:00 A.M. to 5:00 P.M. Closed on Wednesdays. Admission: ¥250.

Osaka Municipal Art Museum. Tennoji Park, 121 Chausuyama, Tennoji-ku; 771–4874. Three minutes' walk from Tennoji Station. Art objects, both ancient and modern. Open daily from 9:30 A.M. to 5:00 P.M. Closed on Mondays. Admission: ¥150.

Osaka Municipal Museum. 1–1 Osaka Castle, Higashi-ku; 941–7177. Ten minutes' walk from Morinomiya Station. The museum is located just outside the castle tower and consists of nine rooms with different themes, all illustrating the history and culture of the city. On display are materials and records connected with the city's past. Open daily from 9:15 A.M. to 4:45 P.M. Closed on the second and fourth Mondays of each month. Admission: ¥150.

Osaka Museum of Science and Technology; 443–5821. Seven minutes' walk from Hommachi Station on the Midosuji, Chuo, and Yotsubashi subway lines.

The museum occupies the first and second floors of the Osaka Science and Technology Building, which also contains a fine convention hall. Open daily from 10:00 A.M. to 4:00 P.M. on weekdays, and from 10:00 A.M. to noon on Saturdays. Closed on Sundays and national holidays and from December 28 to January 4. Admission free.

Traffic Science Museum; 581–5771. Bentencho Station, JNR loop line or Chuo Line subway. This museum was established together with the Traffic Museum in Tokyo in 1962 for the purpose of scientific and historical studies on traffic and transportation. Locomotives and other means of transportation are exhibited systematically to aid study in traffic science. Open 9:30 A.M. to 5:00 P.M. Closed on Mondays and from December 29 to January 3. Adults, ¥250; Middle school students and under, ¥100.

Electric Science Museum; 531–1181. Near Yotsuhashi Station on the Yotsuhashi subway line. The museum also houses a planetarium. The museum is open daily from 9:30 A.M. to 4:45 P.M. Closed on Mondays and from December 28 to January 4. Adults, ¥120; children ¥60. The planetarium is open daily, four times a day, for about an hour at a time, from 10:00 A.M. to 3:45 P.M. on weekdays and from 11:15 A.M. to 3:45 P.M. on Sundays. Adults ¥180; children ¥90. Closed on Mondays and from December 28 to January 4.

Natural Science Museum; 697–6221. Situated inside Nagai Park near Nagai Station on the Midosuji subway line. Open from 9:30 A.M. to 4:30 P.M. Closed on Mondays, national holidays, and between December 28 and January 4. Adults, ¥150; under 16, ¥70.

The Fujita Art Museum; 10–32 Amijima-cho, Miyakojima-ku 351–0582. Former residence of Baron Fujita. See how a Japanese millionaire lived—his art collection, tea ceremony utensils, and garden. Open between mid-March and the beginning of June and again from mid-September to mid-December. Closed on Mondays (except national holidays).

STAGE. Bunraku. An ancient form of dramatic art. Life-like puppets act out historical tales and love tragedies, accompanied by a chanted text and classical music on the *shamisen,* the traditional 3-stringed Japanese instrument. Performed seasonally, for 2–3 weeks at a time, at the *Asahiza Theater,* 2–18 Dotombori 1-chome, Minami-ku; 211–6431. Five minutes by car from Nipponbashi subway station. The usual schedule is from January 2 to 22; April 9 to 25; July 15 to 31; and October 14 to 30, but allow for slight changes from year to year. There are two performances daily, each lasting from between three and a half to four hours including an intermission. Ticket prices for the all-reserved seats are ¥3,500 and ¥2,800. There are also six performances a year of bunraku at the new *Kokuritsu Bunraku Gekijo* (National Puppet Theater), 1–12–10 Nihonbashi, Minami-ku; 212–2531. Each of the six performances lasts for three weeks.

Kabuki. The "song and dance art." A brilliant spectacle, even if you can't follow the story (a written English text often is available). Developed by a woman in the late 16th century, this art form features high-passioned melodramas performed by male actors in heavy makeup and gorgeous costumes. *Shin Kabukiza Theater,* 3–25 Namba 4-chome, Minami-ku; 631–2121. Five minutes' walk from Namba Station. There is usually one performance series a year, lasting for 25 days. Sometimes other forms of Japanese drama are performed and there may be a whole year with no kabuki performances.

416   JAPAN

SHOPPING. Osaka has nine department stores. The hours of business are normally from 10:00 A.M. to 6:00 P.M. However, during the mid-year and year-end bonus seasons, store hours are extended, sometimes up to 9:00 P.M., and the weekly off days done away with.

Opposite Osaka Station are *Hankyu* (8–7 Kabutacho, Kita-ku; 361–1381. Closed Thursdays) and *Hanshin* (13–13 Umeda 1-chome, Kita-ku; 345–1201. Closed Wednesdays). To the east at Tenmabashi is *Matsuzakaya* (2–35 Kyoba-shi, Higashi-ku; 943–1111. Closed Wednesdays), and at Koraibashi is *Mitsuko-shi* (63–1 Koraibashi 2-chome, Higashi-ku; 203–1331. Closed Mondays). At Shinsaibashisuji and on Midosuji Boulevard are *Daimaru* (1–118 Shinsaiba-shisuji, Minami-ku; 271–1231. Closed Wednesdays) and *Sogo* (1–38 Shinsaiba-shisuji, Minami-ku; 271–2221. Closed Thursdays). To the south at Namba is *Takashimaya* (6–14 Nambashinchi, Minami-ku; 631–1101. Closed Wednes-days). Farther south are the *Kintetsu* store at Abeno, near Tennoji (1–43 Abenosuji 1-chome, Abeno-ku; 624–1111. Closed Thursdays) and *Kintetsu* at Ueroku to the east (1–1 Uehommachi 6-chome, Tennoji-ku; 779–1231. Closed Thursdays).

In addition to these excellent and well-stocked department stores, Osaka has a large number of popular shopping areas, many of which are rambling under-ground arcades.

Those looking for bargains in electrical appliances should go to the Nippon-bashi underground shopping area, which lies between Namba Station on the Midosuji, Sennichimae, and Yotsubashi subway lines and Nipponbashi Station on the Sakaisuji and Sennichimae subway lines. For bargains in clothes, one should go to the Dobuike area between Hommachi Station on the Chuo, Tanimachi, and Yotsubashi subway lines and Sakaisuji-Hommachi Station on the Chuo and Sakaisuji subway lines. Another inexpensive shopping area is the Jan-Jan Yokocho (Jan-Jan Lane) in the southeastern part of the Shinsekai downtown amusement quarter.

One of the more sophisticated spots for shopping is the *Shinsaibashisuji* center in the Minami area, which is well known for its arcade and marble pavements. The center is close to Shinsaibashi Station on the Midosuji Subway Line. On either side, there are elaborately decorated shops, with eye-catching window displays. Even if you don't plan to make any purchases, this is a very attractive place for window shopping.

Yet another concentration of stores can be found in the newly-opened 27-story *Acty Osaka Building* atop Japan National Railways' Osaka Station. Housed in this fifth tallest building in Osaka are an assortment of shops with well-known names, in addition to a branch of Daimaru Department Store.

DINING OUT. Listed below is a selection of restaurants, all of which belong to the Japan Restaurant Association. These restaurants have a high standard and provide ex-cellent service. They are well accustomed to catering to overseas visitors. Some—not all—accept international credit cards. They are American Express Card, Diners Club and MasterCard, indicated after the restaurant's name by the abbreviations AE, DE, and MC respectively.

The specialties of a given restaurant are indicated in the listings. A number of restaurants serve both Japanese and Western style food.

JAPANESE STYLE

Expensive (¥ 10,000 and above per person, depending on frills)

Aioiro. 1–16–12 Tenjinbashi, Kita-ku; 351–6508.

Amihiko. 2–86 Kitahama, Higashi-ku; 201–5315. Kabayaki (broiled eel).

Chikuyotei Honten. 3–5–3 Nakanoshima, Kita-ku; 441–1883. Kabayaki. AE, DC.

Edogiku. 2–41 Kawaramachi, Higashi-ku; 231–5858. Sukiyaki and steaks. DC.

Gansuiro. 2–49 Kawaramachi, Higashi-ku; 231–5570.

Hanasaku. 5–20 Imabashi, Higashi-ku; 231–3925.

Hon Miyake. 3–2–4 Nakanoshima, Kita-ku; 231–3188. Sukiyaki and steaks.

Honmorita. 1–6–18 Namba, Minami-ku; 211–3608. Sukiyaki and steaks. DC, MC.

Iroha. 48 Soemoncho, Minami-ku; 211–4529.

Kagairo. 1–29 Kitahama, Higashi-ku; 231–0272. DC.

Kitamura. 46 Higashi-Shimizucho, Minami-ku; 245–4129. Sukiyaki and steaks. DC.

Kitano Yamatoya. 9–18 Doyamacho, Kita-ku; 315–8111.

Kitcho. 3–23 Koraibashi, Higashi-ku; 231–1937.

Matsumoto. 1–8–3 Dotonbori, Minami-ku; 211–4521.

Nadaman. Osaka Royal Hotel, 5–3–68 Nakanoshima, Kita-ku; 443–7101.

Nishiki. 52 Soemoncho, Minami-ku; 211–4722.

Rogetsu Bekkan. 1–7–10 Sonezaki-Shinchi, Kita-ku; 341–1188.

Sakaguchiro. 51 Chausuyamamachi, Tennoji-ku; 771–3522.

Sakau. 4–4 Hiranocho, Higashi-ku; 231–2225.

Sakura Kadan. 2–1–6 Higashi Kobashi, Higashinari-ku; 981–0630.

Sangen. 31 Kasayamachi, Minami-ku; 211–5292. DC.

Shigenoya. 5–11 Awajicho, Higashi-ku; 231–3049.

Shin-ichi. 27 Soemoncho, Minami-ku; 213–0180.

Shin Kiraku. Shin-Hanshin Bldg., 2–2–25 Umeda, Kita-ku; 345–3461.

Shoben Tango-tei. 1–7–12 Dotombori, Minami-ku; 211–3208.

Takouki. 2–5–14 Sennichimae, Minami-ku; 631–2535. Tempura specialty.

Tsurutei. 1–2–21 Sonezaki-Shinchi, Kita-ku; 341–1295.

Yamatoya. 16 Soemoncho, Minami-ku; 211–0058.

Moderate (¥ 5,000–6,000 per person)

Dojima Suehiro. Dojima Grand Bldg., 2F, 1–5–17 Dojima, Kita-ku; 345–1212. The Suehiro chain is noted for its sukiyaki and steaks.

Hachisaburo. 1–3–9 Namba, Minami-ku; 211–3201. Sushi.

Hanafusa. 5–2 Kita-Kyuhojimachi, Higashi-ku; 251–1838. Sukiyaki and steaks. DC.

Hiranomachi Suehiro. 3–24 Hiranomachi, Higashi-ku; 231–4773. Sukiyaki and steaks.

Hon Fukuzushi. 1–12 Shinsaibashisuji, Minami-ku; 271–3344. Sushi. DC.

Izumoya. 2–47 Shinsaibashisuji, Minami-ku; 211–1531. Kabayaki.

Kitahachi. 2–25 Imabashi, Higashi-ku; 231–0267. Tempura.

Maiko Kitashinchi-ten. 1–6–10 Sonezaki-Shinchi, Kita-ku; 344–2913.

Maruman Honke. 30 Unagidani Nakanocho, Minami-ku; 252–0651. DC, MC.

Minokichi Semba-ten. Yagi Bldg., 2–10 Minami-Kyutaromachi, Higashi-ku; 262–4185. AE, DC.

Semba Suehiro. Itochu Bldg., 4 Kitakyutaromachi, Higashi-ku; 252–2140. AE, DC.

Sentei. 5–2 Kita-Kyuhojimachi, Higashi-ku; 251–1830.

Shiruyoshi. 50 Higashi-Shimizucho, Minami-ku; 251–8971.

Shori. 1–1–9 Sonezaki-Shinchi, Kita-ku; 345–3604. Tempura. AE, DC.

Soemoncho Suehiro. Yamatoya Bldg., 2F, 14 Soemoncho, Minami-ku; 213–8571. Sukiyaki and steaks. AE, DC.

Suehiro Navio Hankyu-ten. 1–18 Kakuta-cho, Kita-ku; 316–1422. Sukiyaki and steaks.

Sushiman. Daimaru Department Store. 1–118 Shinsaibashisuji, Minami-ku; 252–2873. Sushi.

Tenkin. 2–13 Fushimicho, Higashi-ku; 231–2529. Tempura.

Yoshinozushi. 4–13 Awajicho, Higashi-ku; 231–7181.

WESTERN STYLE

Expensive (¥ 10,000 and above per person, depending on frills)

Bistrot Vingt-Cinq. 25 Taihoji-cho Nishino-cho, Minami-ku. 30 meters west of Sogo and Daimaru department stores in Minami-ku; 245–6223. Serves French cuisine.

Edoyasu. 5–33 Kitahama, Higashi-ku. 231–2113.

Restaurant Hook Osaka-ten. 10–20 Toganocho, Kita-ku; 312–3050. AE, DC.

Moderate (¥ 5,000–6,000 per person)

Bonheur Tezukayama. 1–3–16 Naka Tezukayama, Sumiyoshi-ku; 672–1210.

Esquire Club Soemoncho-ten. 14 Soemoncho, Minami-ku; 213–7871. AE, DC.

Esquire Club Umeda-ten. 1–5 Komatsubaracho, Kita-ku; 312–6882. AE, DC.

Gourmet l'Omelette. Osaka Maru Bldg., 2B, 1–9–20 Umeda, Kita-ku; 346–0681. DC.

Hollyhock. 5–14–12 Fukushima, Fukushima-ku; 453–4530. Located on third floor of Plaza Building in front of Fukushima Station. Serves home-made Italian dishes.

Mato. 16 Soemoncho, Minami-ku; 211–5406. AE, DC.

Restaurant Kagairo. Meiji Seimei Bldg., 5–1 Fushimimachi, Higashi-ku; 231–2386. AE.

CHINESE

Chugoku Daihanten. Osaka Eki-mae Dai-san Bldg., 33F, 1–1–3 Umeda, Kita-ku; 344–2937. Chinese and especially Shanghai cuisine. Stewed shark's fin, regular ¥4,500. Prawn cooked in chili sauce, regular ¥3,900.

Mandarin Palace. Sumitomo Nakanoshima Bldg., 13F, 3–2–18 Nakanoshima Kita-ku; 444–0800. Peking cuisine. More than 200 different kinds of Chinese dishes, including roasted Peking duck. ¥4,000–15,000 per person.

Botan-en Bekkan. 10th Floor, Hanshin Department Store, Umeda; 344–3601. ¥650 per person (noodles in soup) to ¥10,000 per person.

INDIAN

Ashoka Restaurant. Osaka Dai-ichi Hotel, 2B; 346–0333. Tandoori chicken, kabab, and curries.

Moti. Doton Bldg., 3F, 1–6–15 Dotombori, Minami-ku; 211–6878. Tandoori chicken and curries. Close to Namba Station in the Dotombon entertainment area. ¥650 and up for curry to ¥4,000 for full tandoori meal.

NIGHT LIFE. In Osaka, nightclubs range from the biggest and splashiest, through mass-production drink dispensaries down to tiny intimate places for regular clients. There are many relatively inexpensive drinking joints in the Dotombori and Shinsaibashi areas. You can do an evening on the town in Osaka for anywhere from ¥3,600 to ¥36,000, or more. And then sober up with the bathing and "relaxing" massage of a Toruko Buro or Turkish Bath (the *New Japan* is Osaka's leading one, Dontonburi, Midosuji-nishi). Try the *Fuji, Bijinza,* and *Metro* cabarets, all in Minami-ku. The *Golden Mikado* is one of Osaka's most expensive clubs. *St. Tropez* is a restaurant-theater. ¥6,000 buys all you can eat and drink. *Club Arrow,* 88 Dojima, Kita-ku puts on three shows nightly. *Adult Disco* in Umeda has "50% rock, 50% slow." *Royal Horse* is a "genuine, down-to-earth jazz lounge." *Petit Theatre Claude* is a lounge-type disco. *Metropolitan* is a dance hall for 1,000 persons. *Spankey,* Kakusho Bldg., likes to have couples whatever the mix. *The Love Machine,* also in Kita-ku, has extravagant laser, and is cheaper. At *Hatch 1 & 1,* near Nanba Stn., you can eat, drink and dance all night. *Maggi,* top cosmopolitan disco, ¥1,000.

WESTERN HONSHU AND

SHIKOKU

by
MIRANDA KENRICK

Miranda Kenrick is co-author of the book, Too Far East Too Long. *She is a free-lance writer, whose pieces on travel and Japan have appeared in* Far East Traveler, *the* Mainichi Daily News, Tour Companion, *and the* Tokyo Week-Ender.

The national parks, distinctive coastlines, and rugged mountains of the west of Japan beckon the visitor. Ancient castles, temples, and shrines snuggle into the scenery, and no matter which month you plan your trip, the odds favor your happening upon a local festival.

Japan's superlative public transportation system earns the praise of residents and visitors alike. Plot your own course and you'll probably be able to get wherever you want to go—on land, anyway!

The Inland Sea

Geologists theorize that volcanic activity eventually cracked Honshu, Kyushu, and Shikoku, once a single land mass, into three separate

420

islands. The long, shallow stretch of water separating them is called Seto Naikai, literally The Sea Within Channels—popularly known as the Inland Sea. It is divided into six bodies of water—the Bay of Osaka, and the seas of Harima, Bingo, Aki, Iyo, and Suo.

The Inland Sea's spectacular beauty extends some 500 kilometers from the Bay of Osaka in the east to the Straits of Shimonoseki, its western extremity. Sixty-four kilometers at its widest, and less than 7 at its narrowest, it is crammed with hundreds of islands, some highly developed and many entirely uninhabited. Numerous ferry boats criss-cross the water, and a 4-day cruise, "Love Boat" Japanese-style, chugs from the port of Kobe to Nagasaki and back. Much of the Inland Sea sparkles within the boundaries of the wide-spread Seto Naikai National Park, first designated in 1934 and later expanded several times to include deserving picturesque spots and places of historical and religious importance.

The Inland Sea has a long, colorful history. In 660 B.C., the first Emperor, Jimmu, made a triumphant passage through it en route to settle in present-day Nara Prefecture. The 9th-century scholar-priest, Kukai, lingered as he traveled on its shores, founding temples and shrines as he went. In the 12th century, the city of Shimonoseki at its western outlet witnessed the final victory of the Minamoto clan over their arch-rivals the Taira. The memory of the annihilation of the Taira and the drowning of the child Emperor Antoku motivates April ceremonies at Shimonoseki's Akama Jingu Shrine.

Awaji, the largest and most developed Inland Sea island, is a ferry boat journey from Kobe (one hour or two depending on your craft). Bunraku, the traditional puppet theater of Japan, has 200 years of history here. And the whirlpools at Naruto Straits between Awaji and Shikoku perform four times a day every day without ever missing a show. At each change of the tide, water crashes through the straits, raising or reducing their level a good 1½ meters, with eddies up to 25 meters across. Front-row seats can be had at Cape Naruto, and the best time to see the whirlpools is an hour before or after the change of tides.

Regular ferry services connect Shodo, the next largest island, with Uno and Okayama on Honshu, and Takamatsu on Shikoku. Soybean sauce and olive production provide local livelihood while the capriciously-formed peaks and rocks of Kankakei Gorge entice tourists.

Kobe

Let's start our journey along the Inland Sea coastline in the cosmopolitan port city of Kobe, Osaka's immediate western neighbor. Just 3½ hours from Tokyo by bullet train, Kobe is Japan's seventh largest city and her busiest port. She has invested in Japan's first convention and exhibition complex on the man-made Port Island. Port Island is so advanced, in fact, that the Portliner train that covers the 10-minute journey to Sannomiya (Kobe's shopping area) manages without a driver. Although it is a modern city, Kobe retains the appeal of centuries of cultural influences from China and Korea.

The city divides itself along the JNR elevated railway tracks, with sophisticated shopping streets to the south and a bright entertainment district to the north. Seek out Chinese food in Kobe, as excellent as the city's famed beef and Nada sake (rice wine).

In the north of Kobe in Kitano-cho are preserved a number of "ijinkan" residences of early foreign settlers, some dating back to the end of the 19th century. Few buildings in Tokyo, by contrast, survived the Great Earthquake of 1923 or, later, the bombs of the Second World War.

Popular as a residential city, Kobe has wooded mountains behind it that protect the port from northern winds and provide a scenic, natural leisure land. Over the last 80 years Mt. Rokko, the highest peak in the Rokko range, has, inevitably, been developed as a summer resort, complete with cable cars, driveways, observation terraces, hotels, restaurants, and parks. Mt. Rokko and the other mountains of the Rokko range form an integral part of the area's beauty, history, and legends. Mt. Maya was named after the mother of Gautama Buddha, and Tenjoji Temple on the peak was dedicated to her. Tairyuji Temple, on the summit of Mt. Futatabi, dates from the 8th century. Spreading over the mountains is the Mt. Rokko Pastureland, which is an alpine botanical garden, and Japan's oldest golf course (1903), constructed by an Englishman, Arthur Groom.

The hot-spring inns of Arima Spa, an ancient resort on the other side of Mt. Rokko, characteristically nestle along a gorge amongst cherry and maple trees at the foot of the mountain. From Mt. Rokko's 1000-meter-high summit, there is a famous view of Kobe, the harbor, Awaji Island, and the mountains of Shikoku.

The Suma district, in the west of the city, was a 12th-century battlefield for the Minamoto (Genji) and Taira (Heike) clans. The Rokko range sweeps down to the sea here, creating a natural barrier that the 17th-century Tokugawa warriors capitalized upon. Today the only battles at Suma Beach are those with the waves.

Along the Inland Sea Route

Himeji, an hour west by local train from Kobe, glories in its majestic Shirasagi-jo, the Castle of the White Heron. This structure demonstrates a combination of grace and strength that is unique, and very Japanese. Originally a 14th-century fortress, its five-story donjon and three-story keeps are connected by covered passageways. Designated an important National Treasure, Himeji was repaired and rebuilt over a period of eight years ending in 1964. It illustrates, particularly, the Japanese skill with wood—two 26-meter-high wooden pillars support the donjon, whose soaring lines bristle with sculptured detail. Pause in the suicide tower, way up in the castle. Once upon a time samurai proudly invited their family and friends here to witness their ritualistic ending of life.

Today, the castle grounds are a showplace for the happy display of plum and cherry blossom trees, azaleas, and wisteria, all vying for seasonal prominence.

About twenty-two kilometers southwest of Himeji is Ako, original home of the 47 *ronin* (masterless samurai) who executed appropriate revenge in Tokyo on the feudal lord who killed their lord, Naganori

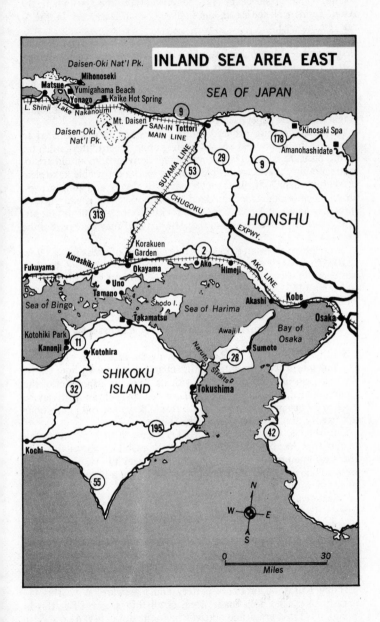

INLAND SEA AREA EAST

Daisen-Oki Nat'l Pk.

SEA OF JAPAN

Mihonoseki

Matsue

Yumigahama Beach

Yonago   Kaike Hot Spring

L. Shinji   Lake Nakanoumi

Mt. Daisen

Daisen-Oki Nat'l Pk.

SAN-IN MAIN LINE

Tottori

9

178   Kinosaki Spa

Amanohashidate

SUYAMA LINE

29

53

9

CHUGOKU

313

HONSHU

EXPWY.

Korakuen Garden

Kurashiki

2

AKO LINE

Fukuyama

Okayama

Ako

Himeji

Uno

Tamano

Shodo I.

Akashi

Kobe

Sea of Bingo

Takamatsu

Sea of Harima

Osaka

Kotohiki Park

11

Kanonji

Kotohira

SHIKOKU ISLAND

32

Awaji I.

Naruto Straits

28

Sumoto

Bay of Osaka

Tokushima

42

195

Kochi

55

N

W   E

S

0   30

Miles

Asano. Today a shrine in Ako commemorates the spot where the Asano residence once stood, and in Tokyo, each December 14, the 47 are remembered.

Continuing west beyond Ako, stop in Okayama, a former castle town that conveniently groups several of its best features close together. Korakuen, only minutes away from the railway station by taxi, is one of Japan's top trio of model gardens (the others are in Kanazawa and Mito). Tsunamasu Ikeda, lord of the Bizen clan, ordered the garden's construction in 1686, and for the next fourteen years his retainer Nagatoda Tsuda supervised its laying.

Korakuen, private property until 1884 when it was donated to Okayama Prefecture and opened to the public, means "the garden for taking pleasure later." This curious name derived from an old aristocratic morality that decreed "bear sorrow before the people; take pleasure after them." Stroll through bamboo groves and pine groves, around ponds and along crooked streams, past woodland shrines, spreading lawns, and gigantic granite rocks. Notice how the distant Mt. Misao and Mt. Keshigo fit into the view just as if they were part of the garden.

Over the river from Korakuen lie the ruins of Okayama's Crow Castle. Completely black, it deliberately contrasts with the dazzling whiteness of Himeji's Heron Castle. Only two turrets remain from Okayama's 1573 structure, both of which are Important Cultural Properties.

For souvenirs, look for stoneware, known as Bizen-yaki, and cotton textiles. *Tai* (sea bream) is a regional speciality, and in season you could live on Okayama peaches.

South of Okayama is Uno, a port serving the Inland Sea and Shikoku. Takamatsu (covered later in this chapter) is only an hour away. West of Uno lies Washuzan Hill with its stunning panorama of the island-studded, emerald-colored Inland Sea. Washuzan Hill can be reached by bus in an hour and a half from Okayama, and in one hour and twenty minutes from Kurashiki Station.

Kurashiki is 16 kilometers south of Okayama, thirteen minutes away on the JNR local train. Unlike Kyoto, Kurashiki does not keep its historical monuments down every side street and all over the town. It preserves one special district as a showplace, like a beauty spot in an otherwise ordinary face.

A watercourse, with swans and weeping willows, distinguishes the district. The half-circle of each bridge across the canal becomes, with its reflection, a full circle. Old houses and old rice granaries, belonging to an age that ended a century or more ago, line the streets on both sides of the waterway. In feudal times the village of Kurashiki collected rice and raw cotton from the surrounding countryside, and its little port thrived from handling rice shipments to Osaka.

Today Kurashiki produces pottery and glassware, as well as tablemats, bags, and dolls made from, of all things, grass! But this is special, this Igusa grass, and noteworthy for its durability. Also special are the delicious muscat grapes, pears, and mandarin oranges grown in this region.

Kurashiki's Archaeological Museum is housed in a heavy-beamed former rice granary, its white walls decorated with the square black tiles characteristic of the area. Inside the museum are pre-historic artifacts of Japanese, Persian, and Incan civilizations. The Folkcraft Museum that occupies four old rice granaries on the opposite side of the river exhibits basketwork, ceramics, textiles, and wooden ware from different countries, including Japan. It also displays the folk furniture of Japan. The Folk Toy Museum, adjacent to the Folkcraft Museum on its south side, has vast collections of ingenious creations in paper, straw, and clay.

In its Greek temple building, the nearby Ohara Art Gallery houses Western paintings and sculptures, including works by Rodin, Picasso, and El Greco. Immense Shoji Hamada pots, impressive Kanjiro Kawai pots, and charming Bernard Leach pots are exhibited together in the Japanese department.

Tomonoura Bay, south of Fukuyama, is another port serving the island of Shikoku. In the spring, fishermen concentrate on catching *tai*, and should you be overcome with a desire to observe the traditional net-fishing, excursion boats *(tai-ami)* will oblige. These boats chug out of Sensui Island, stopping also at a Kannon (Goddess of Mercy) temple.

Kosanji Temple on Ikuchi Island merits a detour. Short of Hiroshima, de-train at the port of Mihara and from here (50 minutes by steamer, 20 minutes by faster craft) cross to Setoda Port. A 10-minute walk eastward, average speed, brings you to Kosanji, built in 1946 by an islander named Kozo Kanemoto. Its ornate gate resembles Nikko's famous Yomeimon (Sunlight Gate) sufficiently to earn it the title Nikko of the West. The buildings are modeled on Nara's Horyu-ji and Osaka's Shittenoji temples. Kosanji houses a number of Important Cultural Properties.

Hiroshima

Hiroshima is internationally known for the tragedy of 8:15 A.M. August 6, 1945, when the world's first atomic bomb devastated the city, killing some 200,000 people. Read John Hersey's account, *Hiroshima,* published in 1946. Today, except for the gutted frame of the Atomic Bomb Dome, Hiroshima has experienced a complete metamorphosis, rebuilt as the City of Peace. Its hospitals and clinics, however, continue to treat A-Bomb victims, and the Atomic Bomb Casualty Commission, established in 1947, studies the long-range effects of radiation.

August 6 is still the most important day of the year here, with Buddhist, Shinto, and Christian memorial services, thousands of peace ralliers, and white doves that flutter over the city.

Every day of the year bells chime in the Peace Memorial Hall and in the Memorial Cathedral for World Peace. A German Jesuit priest, Father Superior LaSalle, who survived the Bomb, inspired the building of the Memorial Cathedral in 1954. Several countries contributed, and Germany sent the bells and organ. During the first papal trip to the Far East, in early 1981, Pope John Paul II visited the Cathedral.

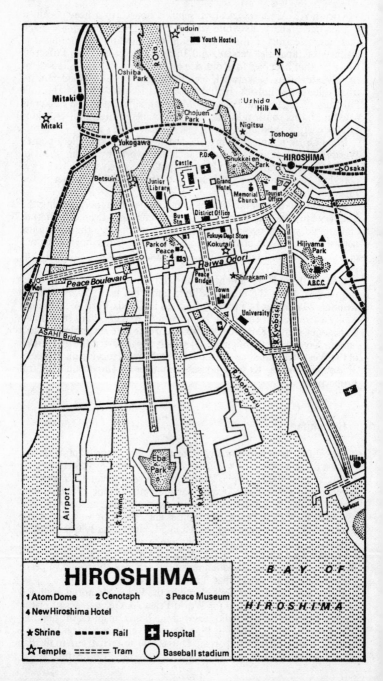

HIROSHIMA

1 Atom Dome   2 Cenotaph   3 Peace Museum

4 New Hiroshima Hotel

★ Shrine   ▬▬▬ Rail   ✚ Hospital

☆ Temple   ═════ Tram   ◯ Baseball stadium

Relics of the explosion are set out in a straightforward, unemotional display in the Peace Memorial Museum within the Peace Memorial Park, their impact all the stronger for their understatement. Also within the park are the Peace Memorial Hall and the Memorial Cenotaph, within which are listed the names of known A-Bomb victims. Its optimistic epitaph reads in Japanese "repose ye in peace for the error shall not be repeated."

Of course Hiroshima, today a bustling commercial center, offers more than its immediate sad history. Its castle, 10 minutes by bus from the main railway station, dates back to the 16th century. It had been a National Treasure until the Bomb obliterated it, but 1958 saw the construction of a copy. Shukkeien Garden, another short bus ride from the station, was originally designed in 1620 and is today registered as a Scenic Place. It faithfully reproduces Si Hu (West Lake) in southern China.

Miyajima

Itsuku-shima, better known as Miyajima (Shrine Island), is an easy day's outing from Hiroshima. A fast electric train will take you from Hiroshima to Miyajima-guchi on the shore opposite the island in about half an hour, but if you have time to spare it is worth going there by bus or car from the center of Hiroshima. By this route you will enjoy some superb views of the islands and the oyster and seaweed beds, as well as some attractive little fishing harbors. The Japanese, with their penchant for labeling, rate Miyajima in the Inland Sea as one of their Scenic Trio, along with Amanohashidate on the Japan Sea coast, and Matsushima, the Pine Island, in Sendai.

In the early centuries, neither the beginning nor the ending of human life was permitted on the sacred island—the pregnant and the dying were rushed to the mainland. Although the Meiji Restoration (1868) revised this edict, Miyajima still has no cemetery. Burial or cremation takes place on the mainland, and mourners, returning to Miyajima, must first be purified.

The shrine, founded fifteen centuries ago, honors three female deities, the daughters of the thunder god. The shrine itself is built on supports that extend into the sea where the huge (17 meters) famous red *torii* stands. At low tide you can amble out to it, but at high tide *torii* and shrine seem to float on the surface of the water.

The Main Shrine opens only one of its three parts to the public. Shrine dances are performed here, and festival dances outside, on an open-air platform. For a donation to the shrine, which you can arrange in advance through your guide or hotel, *bugaku* (ancient Chinese court dances) and *kagure* (ordinary Shinto dances) are presented.

The corridors and principle structures—the Main Shrine (Honden), Offering Hall (Heiden), Hall of Worship (Haiden), and Purification Hall (Haraiden)—are National Treasures. Japan's oldest Noh stage (1568) is here, as well as such gems as Noh drama costumes, bugaku dance wooden masks, and medieval armor.

INLAND SEA AREA WEST

SEA OF JAPAN

Daisen-Oki Nat'l Pk.

Izumo Taisha

Izumo

Oda

9

375

Hamada

SAN-IN MAIN LINE

186

HONSHU

CHUGOKU EXPW'Y.

Hagi

9

(under construction)

54

191

316

Yamaguchi

Miyajima I. (Itsukushima)

Hiroshima

Onomichi

Mihara

Hofu

KURE LINE

2

185

Shimonoseki

Kure

Sea of Suo

188

196

Imabari

Sea of Iyo

Matsuyama

11

KYUSHU

Yawatahama

56

33

194

197

SHIKOKU ISLAND

56

N

W E

S

Nakamura

0   30

Miles

You may want an overnight stay on Miyajima to see the lighting of the stone lanterns—again, for a fee, this can be done just for you—and early morning dances at the shrine.

There's a certain amount of climbing (there always is!) to reach Gumonji Temple, 530 meters straight up on the island's highest point. A cable car helps you only so far. If you enjoy scenery, though, the view rewards the effort, extending as it does over the Inland Sea with its seductive coves, bays, and islets.

Miyajima is singularly lovely, with its swimming beaches, pines, cedars, cypresses, springtime cherries, and autumn maples. The drawback is that hordes of domestic tourists think so too, and swarm over the island, especially in the spring and the autumn.

The Japan Sea Coast

Now we sweep northeast to Izumo, near the coast of the Sea of Japan. Izumo is the home of Izumo Taisha (the Great Shrine), Japan's oldest Shinto shrine, predating the advent of Buddhism. Rebuilding has been necessary over the centuries and today the oldest, original building dates back less than 250 years, to 1744. Dignified pine trees line the avenue that leads to the beautiful shrine.

Mythology united in matrimony a god, Susano, and a maiden, Inada, at Izumo Taisha. They then lived where Yaegaki Shrine now stands. Consequently young couples today flock to Yaegaki Shrine to be married, then visit Izumo Taisha to ask for the gods' blessings. Shinto gods congregate at Izumo in October, its busiest month.

One hour's ride from Izumo on the San-in Line is Matsue. Matsue's willow-fringed canals and castle moat earn it the title of the City of Water. Matsue will forever be linked with Lafcadio Hearn, the Irish-Greek teacher and writer who married a Japanese woman, changed his name to Yakumo Koizumi, and became a Japanese citizen. Although Hearn lived in Matsue only briefly in 1890, his Japanese-style home, near the moat of the city's old castle, has been preserved. The Memorial Hall next door contains many of the manuscripts, letters, and papers he wrote that show his efforts to interpret Japan to the rest of the world.

Walk from Lafcadio Hearn's House to the castle, built in 1611 by Hideyoshi's general Yoshiharu Horio. Some of the original structures remain. Lake Shinji, nearby, is Japan's sixth largest lake, where a motorboat will whisk you from Matsue Ohashi to the islet of Yomega-shima, with its small shrine.

On the bus again for an hour to Mihonoseki, out on the eastern tip of the Shimane Peninsula, within the Daisen-Oki National Park. A fishing port, Mihonoseki long ago did double duty as a barrier station where travelers were subjected to searches. Walk 15 minutes to Gohon Matsu (5 Pines) Park to see the last of the five original pines celebrated in the folk song "Seki no Gohonnatsu." Well over 350 years old, the tree measures some 4 meters in circumference, and excites considerable local veneration.

Less than 32 kilometers east of Matsue, Yonago, with its domestic airport and its trains and buses, is the logical jumping-off point for the nearby spa of Kaike, Yumigahama swimming beach, and Mt. Daisen.

The hot springs of Kaike offer relief to the rheumatic, the anemic, and the asthmatic. Pine trees beautify its beaches as they do at neighboring Yumigahama.

The Daisen-Oki National Park is split up into several areas around the region. One centers itself on the mountains surrounding Mt. Daisen; another spreads out as far as the Oki Archipelago, embracing the Shimane Peninsula and the harbor of Mihonoseki; a third takes in the area around Izumo Taisha, and a fourth includes Mt. Sambe with its extinct volcano.

Mt. Daisen, an hour's bus ride from Yonago, is 1,711 meters high and famed for winter skiing and summer camping. Its smiling western slopes, graceful and conical, evoke appreciative cries of "Oh, another Mt. Fuji!," but the mountain's craggy northern and southern profiles are grim and forbidding.

From Daisenguchi Station it's a half-hour bus ride to the Daisenji Temple high up on the mountainside. Founded in 718 by the Tendai sect, it once boasted over a hundred temples and monasteries that eventually disappeared in flames. Today it features a bronze statue of the Eleven-Headed Kannon and other Buddhist images.

Should you want to tackle Mt. Daisen's summit, you're on your own—for 5½ kilometers straight uphill. Allow a good four hours up and half that down again. Recommended for hardy folk who find superlative views intoxicating.

Tottori, about 132 kilometers east of Matsue, belongs to the San-In Kaigan National Park, which extends some 77 kilometers to Amino on the Okutango Peninsula. The town is a busy trading and market center (lumber, rice, fruit—try the Nijusseiki pears) and only 20 minutes by bus from the famous expanse of sand dunes that is such an unusual feature in Japan. Just as Matsue is linked with Lafcadio Hearn, so is Tottori synonymous with Hiroshi Teshigahara and his film *Woman of the Dunes*, shot on this incredible 16-kilometer stretch of "desert." On scorching summer days there is no shade at all along the seashore here. Sand skiing is popular as is summertime camping, and sunsets turn the sky crimson every night. Tourist facilities include cafeterias, game centers, and a kiddyland.

Farther east along the Japan Sea coast, but still within the San-in Kaigan National Park, Kinosaki Spa has been a favorite in the Kansai area since the 7th century. In the past the town had six large public baths set in natural hot springs, but today all the *ryokan* have their own baths. These hot springs, like those of Kaike, are credited with medicinal properties that relieve gastroenteric disorders and female complaints.

Just beyond the boundaries of the San-In Kaigan National Park is the Heavenly Bridge, Amanohashidate, another of Japan's Scenic Trio. The sandbar, several kilometers long and 110 meters at its widest point, is covered with pine trees that have been contorted into remarkable shapes.

Don't be surprised at the number of people who turn around and bend over to peer at Amanohashidate from between their legs. This traditional position gives the sandbar the effect of being suspended in air and supposedly makes it easier to imagine gods gathered on it as they created Japan. Some people climb onto a ledge before looking backwards through their legs. Although it is not as unnerving as kissing the Blarney Stone in Ireland, you still need good balance to view Amanohashidate "properly."

Shikoku

Dropping down to the south of Honshu now, we cross over the Inland Sea to the island of Shikoku. On Shikoku 88 holy shrines and temples honor the scholar-priest Kukai, who devised the hiragana alphabet of Japan and introduced a Chinese sect of Buddhism into the country. A proper pilgrimage to all 88 holy places has to be made on foot, which takes about two months, depending on the state of your feet, of course. Beginning in Tokushima, pilgrims proceed clockwise around the island, visiting the shrines in a prescribed order. They wear simple white cotton robes and straw hats, and carry canes. Today many pilgrims whip around by bus instead of walking.

North of Tokushima, Takamatsu is Shikoku's gateway, with a domestic airport and regular ferry service to ports such as Kobe, Osaka, Uno, and Hiroshima.

Originally a castle town and feudal capital, Takamatsu still administers Shikoku. Its shops specialize in patterned fans and umbrellas, paper products, and lacquerware.

Within the city visit Tamano Park—site of the original castle whose surviving three turrets and gate are Important Cultural Properties—and Ritsurin Park, as lovingly laid out as Korakuen in Okayama. Its six ponds and thirteen hills are divided into north and south sections, blending into a background of pine trees. Keep the ponds on your left and walk in a counterclockwise direction fully to appreciate the garden. Also within Ritsurin Park are a zoo, folk art gallery, and museum.

Yashima, half an hour by bus from Takamatsu, was once an island but is now connected to the mainland. A cable car whisks you up to the summit with its marvelous views and Buddhist temple, Yashimaji, full of relics of the Minamoto/Taira clashes of the 12th century.

The small island of Megi (also known as Oniga Shima, or Demons' Island) is a 20-minute ferry journey from Takamatsu. Associated with the children's story of Momotaro, the boy who was born from a peach, it is the island where he, a dog, a pheasant, and a monkey routed a den of demons.

An hour southwest of Takamatsu by train is Kotohira with its Kotohiragu Shrine, also known as Kompira. Sailors of old appealed to the sea gods here for protection and safe passage. Kompira is halfway up Mt. Zozu but your climbing has only just begun when you face the 785 steps to and within the shrine. First comes the Great Gate (Daimon) then the Parlor (Shoin) then the Tea Hall, the Rising Sun Hall, and Central Shrine. The Inner Shrine itself is a further half-hour journey straight uphill. All of the magnificent shrine should be seen, an hour's worth of step climbing though it may be.

Kotohiki Park, on the seashore, has enormous pine trees with gnarled roots that have thrust themselves far aboveground. Climb Kotohiki Hill to look down on the *zenigata,* 17th-century ditches dug to resemble coins. "Be frugal," the town folk told themselves and dug the ditches as a reminder.

An hour and a half southeast by train from Takamatsu is Tokushima, the starting point for religious pilgrimages around Shikoku. It is also—with Awaji and Osaka's Bunrakuza Theater—known for its puppet theater. Farmers put on the shows between planting seasons. Shops display wooden chests of drawers and mirrors and cotton products, such as the fabric worn during the August 15–18 Awa Odori. During this festival the town vibrates as people sing and dance in the streets.

The late 19th-century Portuguese consul Wenceslao de Moraes is buried in Tokushima. Like Lafcadio Hearn, he married a Japanese woman, settled, and spent his last years writing books about Japan.

Tokushima has its beautiful Tokushima and Bizen parks. Outside the city the gorges of Oboke and Koboke overlook the meandering Yoshino River, Japan's last vine suspension bridge sways in Iya, and the sea crashes through the Naruto Straits that just barely separate Shikoku and Awaji.

Kochi is situated at the center of Shikoku's southern coastline. It produces processed marine products, notably a dried bonito seasoning called *katsuobushi.* Kochi is famous for its *Onaga-dori,* cocks with 8-meter-long tails, the result of crossbreeding pheasants and fowls 300 years ago. The prefectural government has also designated sanctuaries to protect the near-extinct Japanese otter, which lives in the rivers here.

Kochi Park encompasses the site of the city's 17th-century castle, while Godaisan Park has beautiful gardens and Chikurin-ji. Chronologically the 31st of Shikoku's 88 sacred places, Chikurin-ji is Kochi's oldest temple. Katsurahama (Katsura beach) flaunts white sands, rocks, reefs and pines, while Murotozaki, 2½ hours away by bus, at Shikoku's southeastern extremity, boasts a wild, untamed rocky coast.

In the northwestern portion of Shikoku, Matsuyama, the island's largest city, is another old castle town. Its castle was built in 1602, and is well-maintained, with four gates, plus buildings housing palanquins and armor that was once the property of the Matsudaira daimyo. The castle, smack in the city center, surrounds itself with parkland that extends to Katsuyama. Three minutes by ropeway and you're on the summit.

Visit nearby Dogo, one of Japan's oldest spas with a number of natural hot springs that fuel the public bathhouses. Behind the main bathhouse is a smaller one built in 1899 for the exclusive use of the Imperial family but open today to any old body. During the Hot Spring Festival of March 19–21 people parade in fancy dress.

The prefecture exports its oranges—*iyo-kan,* the spring varieties, and *natsu-mikan,* the summer ones. The persimmons of Tobe, 12 kilometers south of Matsuyama, enjoy nationwide popularity, and Tobe-yaki, a porcelain ware, finds its way into the shops of America and Europe.

Omogokei Gorge, 2½ hours away from Matsuyama by bus, entices walkers with numerous tempting trails.

PRACTICAL INFORMATION FOR
WESTERN HONSHU AND SHIKOKU

 WHEN TO GO. Spring and autumn are the most comfortable times to visit Japan—no winter overcoats to carry nor muggy heat to contend with—but the typhoons of late August and September can disrupt ferry services in the Inland Sea and trains everywhere. Furthermore, in spring and autumn you must be prepared for school excursions above and beyond the usual crowds. Expect standing room only at the popular beaches during the summer. The ski resorts in western Japan often have hot springs, too, and aren't as formidably crowded as those in the Japan Alps. Whenever you visit and wherever you go, wear comfortable shoes.

 HOW TO GET THERE. *Western Honshu.* **By boat.** You may enter Japan through the international port of Kobe. At present, it is served by irregularly scheduled freighters and some tour liners. Pearl Cruises of Scandinavia in San Francisco offers a number of luxury cruises from Hong Kong to China, Korea, Kobe, and back to Hong Kong.

By air. International flights serve Osaka's Itani Airport, but most tourists to Japan enter through Narita Airport, 66 km from central Tokyo. You may change at Narita for Haneda, then go directly on to Osaka, another 55 minutes by jet. Or, if you stop in Tokyo, the most convenient way is to come by super express train to Shin-Kobe station, a trip of about 3½ hrs.

By train. By JNR's super expresses, Okayama is 4 hrs. 10min. (¥13,800) from Tokyo, 50 min. (¥4,600) from Shin-Osaka. Hiroshima is 5 hrs. 8 min. (¥15,300) from Shin-Osaka. Hakata, gateway to Kyushu, is 6 hrs. 56 min. away from Tokyo.

By bus. Bus services on the Trans-Chukogu Expressway connect Osaka with Tsuyama, Yumura Spa, Yonago and Tottori, and Kobe with Kinosaki Spa.

Shikoku. **By air.** Osaka is the nearest international airport to Shikoku. There are daily flights from Tokyo and Osaka to Takamatsu, Tokushima, Kochi, and Matsuyama.

By boat. There are numerous ship routes, luxury package cruises, and small commuter ferryboats traveling to Shikoku. See also *How to Get Around,* below.

By train. You can go from anywhere in Japan to Shikoku by train. The main line to Shikoku runs from Tokyo through Osaka to Okayama's port town of Uno, where the passenger cars are loaded onto *Japanese National Railways* ferries for the one-hour boat trip to Takamatsu. The fastest time from Osaka to Takamatsu by train is 3 hours by super express Hikari.

The first of ten projected bridges to link the main island and Shikoku is already completed. Both vehicles and trains use it.

 TELEPHONES. Area codes: Kobe 078; Himeji 0792; Okayama 0862; Kurashiki 0864; Hiroshima 082; Izumo 0853; Matsue 0852; Yonago 0859; Tottori 0857; Takamatsu 0878; Tokushima 0886; Kochi 0888; Matsuyama 0899. *International Calls:* From area code 078, dial 0051 only. **Emergencies.**

Police, 110 throughout Japan; *Fire and Ambulance,* 119 throughout Japan. *Ship Information.* To call your boat in Kobe, dial 331–8181 and give the operator the name of the ship. To locate any ship at berth, call the *Harbor Master* at same number.

 **HOTELS AND INNS.** By and large, the hotels of western Japan and Shikoku fall into the categories of *Expensive* and below. Although reputable chains such as the Prince Hotels and the New Otani have hotels throughout the country—and almost all Western hotels have heating and air conditioning, private bathrooms with hot showers, telephones, and television—you may be dismayed at the dimensions of your room. There's not much to spare after you and your luggage are installed, and the bathrooms could induce severe claustrophobia.

Japanese versions of Western food still leave a lot to be desired, and the system of some *ryokan,* where you eat breakfast in a dining room, is to telephone you when your breakfast is ready. They mean that literally, for they make and serve the food before calling you, so you will find cold toast and coffee and congealed eggs waiting.

Still, Japan scores where it matters: you won't be mugged either in your hotel or on the street; if you misplace wallet and camera they'll probably be returned; and hotel maids don't hover for tips.

There are usually reasonable Western-style hotels around the main railway stations, and in most provincial towns the main shopping streets are conveniently within walking distance. *Expensive* Japanese *ryokan,* which usually offer an inclusive price for overnight accommodation, dinner, and breakfast, pamper you with meals served in your room. There are also kokumin shukusha (lodgings offering Japanese dinner, bed, and breakfast), Kokumin Kyukamura (government-run vacation villages), and the good old YMCA, YWCA, and YHA. For details on the various kinds of accommodations see *Facts at Your Fingertips* in the front of this book.

WESTERN-STYLE

Fukuyama

Grand. 2–7–1 Nishimachi, Fukuyama, Hiroshima Pref. 720; (0849) 21–5511. Near the railway station, gift shop, beauty parlor. Also convenient for Tomonoura Bay, Kosanji Temple, and Onomichi in the Inland Sea. 90 Western, 8 Japanese rooms. Single ¥5,500–7,500, Japanese style for two ¥10,000.

Himeji

Himeji Castle Hotel. 210 Hoji, Himeji City; (0792) 84–3311. 243 comfortable rooms. Single ¥7,000–7,500; double ¥12,000–14,000.
Hotel Sun Route Himeji. 195–9 Ekimae-cho, Himeji City; (0792) 85–0811. Also opposite the railway station. 94 rooms. Single ¥5,500–7,000; double ¥10,000–12,000.
New Osaka. 198–1, Ekimae-cho, Himeji City; (0792) 23–1111. Opposite the railway station. 38 rooms, some Japanese-style. Single ¥6,500–7,500; double ¥11,000–13,000.

Hiroshima

Grand. 4–4 Kami Hatchobori, Naka-ku, Hiroshima City 730; (082) 227–1313. Chinese and Japanese restaurants, cocktail lounge, nightclub, gift shop, barber and beauty shop. 379 Western, 6 Japanese rooms. Single ¥8,300–9,800, double ¥13,000–15,500.

Hokke Club. 7–7, Naka-machi, Naka-ku, Hiroshima City 730; (082) 248–3371. One of Japan's reasonably priced hotel chains.

Kokusai. 3–13 Tate-machi, Naka-ku, Hiroshima City 730; (082) 248–2323. Japanese restaurant, revolving bar, cocktail lounge, bowling alley, gift shop, barber and beauty shops. 68 Western, 11 Japanese rooms. Single ¥5,500–6,500, double ¥10,000–13,500.

Station Hotel. 2–37 Matsubara-cho, Minami-ku, Hiroshima City 730; (082) 262–3201. Convenient location, snack bar, grill, shops. 147 Western, 9 Japanese rooms. Single ¥4,400–5,000, double ¥6,500–11,000.

Kobe

Kobe International. 8–1–6 Goko-dori, Chuo-ku, Kobe 651; (078) 221–8051. Centrally located, on the 6th and 7th floors of Sannomiya's Kokusai Kaikan Bldg. 48 rooms.

New Port Hotel. 6–3–13 Hamabe-dori, Chuo-ku, Kobe 651; (078) 231–4171. Faces the Flower Road that is lined with flowers, plants and the famous Flower Clock. 207 Western rooms, Single ¥5,500–7,000, double ¥11,000–15,000.

Oriental. 25, Kyomachi, Chuo-ku, Kobe 650; (078) 331–8111. Modern, with coffee shop, grill, sky restaurant. Reputable. 190 Western rooms. Single ¥7,000; double ¥12,000–14,000.

Portopia Hotel. 6–10–1 Minatojima, Naka-machi, Chuo-ku, Kobe 650; (078) 302–1111. On the futuristic man-made Port Island, this is a world-class, resort-type hotel. Overlooks parkland, sea, mountains. 10 minutes by Portliner to Sannomiya. 32 stories, 529 Western, 4 Japanese rooms. Single ¥9,000–13,000; double ¥14,000–21,000.

Rokko Oriental. 1878 Nishi Taniyama, Rokkosan-cho, Nada-ku, Kobe 657–01; (078) 891–0333. On Mt. Rokko, with city views, outdoor restaurant, Genghis Khan barbecues. 48 Western, 12 Japanese rooms. No singles, double ¥13,000–20,000.

Rokkosan. 1034 Minami Rokko, Rokkosan-cho, Nada-ku, Kobe 657–01; (078) 891–0301. Also on Mt. Rokko, near upper terminal of railway. Good food, rooftop beer garden. 74 Western, 4 Japanese rooms. Single ¥6,000; double ¥8,000–13,000.

Sannomiya Terminal Hotel. 8-chome Kumoidori, Chuo-ku, Kobe; (078) 291–0001. Conveniently inside the JNR Sannomiya Railway Station, opposite the underground Santica Shopping Town. 190 Western rooms. Single ¥5,700–7,500; double ¥10,000.

YMCA. 2–7–15 Kano-cho, Chuo-ku, Kobe 650; (078) 241–7201.

YWCA. 1–10 Kami Tsutsuki-dori, Chuo-ku, Kobe 650; (078) 231–6201.

Kochi

Dai-ichi. 2–2–12 Kitahon-machi, Kochi City 780; (0888) 83–1441. Has ambience. 118 Western rooms. Single ¥5,200–5,800, double ¥9,000–13,000.

Josei-Kan. Kami-machi; (0888) 75–0111. First-class hotel, with a bar. Convenient location. 63 rooms. Single ¥5,000–6,500; double ¥8,500–11,000.

Sansuien. Takajomachi; (0888) 22–0131. 133 rooms, all with baths. Single ¥5,500–6,000; double ¥9,000–12,000.

Kurashiki

Kokusai. 1–1–44 Chuo, Kurashiki, Okayama Pref. 710; (0864) 22–5141. Near the museums, pretty Japanese garden, gift shop. 66 Western, 4 Japanese rooms. Single ¥5,800, double ¥10,500–14,000.

Mizushima Kokusai. 4–20 Mizushima-Aobacho, Kurashiki, Okayama Pref. 710; (0864) 44–4321. Sports facilities, gift shop, tea ceremony room. 73 Western, 1 Japanese room. Single ¥4,000–10,000, double ¥6,500–13,000.

Matsue

Ichibata. 30 Chidori-cho, Matsue, Shimane Pref. 690; (0852) 22–0188. Very attractive hotel with hot springs bath, golf, boating, beach, access to golf. 97 Western, 41 Japanese rooms. Single ¥5,000–6,000, double ¥9,000–42,000.

Matsuyama

ANA Hotel. 3–2–1 Ichiban-cho, Matsuyama, Ehime Pref. 790; (0899) 33–5511. Opposite the city-center castle, Japanese and Chinese restaurants, bar, shopping arcade, beauty parlor. 240 Western, 3 Japanese rooms. Single ¥6,500–7,300, double ¥12,000–18,000.

Oku-Dogo. 267 Suemachi, Matsuyama, Ehime Pref. 791–01; (0899) 77-1111. At Dogo Hot Springs, with own hot springs baths, extensive Japanese garden, bowling alley, cabaret, zoo, ropeway, and fishing! 166 Western, 77 Japanese rooms. Single ¥2,500–5,000, twin ¥5,000–10,000.

Okayama

Kokusai. 4–1–16 Kadota Honmachi, Okayama City 703; (0862) 73–7311. In Higashiyama Natural Park, with Japanese garden, indoor and outdoor pools, gift shop. 192 Western, 2 Japanese-style rooms. Single ¥7,000–9,000, double ¥13,000–25,000.

Plaza. 2–3–12 Hama, Okayama City 703; (0862) 72–1201. Offers recreation facilities—boating, fishing, skating, golf course. 83 Western, 2 Japanese rooms. Single ¥4,500, double ¥8,000–8,500.

Royal. 2–4 Ezucho, Okayama City 700; (0862) 54–1155. Near the station and city center. Gift shop, beauty parlor bowling alley. 198 Western, 4 Japanese rooms. Single ¥6,000, double ¥11,000.

Takamatsu

Grand. 10–5–1 Kotobuki-cho, Takamatsu, Kagawa Pref. 760; (0878) 51–5757. Convenient location, gift shop, beauty parlor. 136 Western rooms. Single ¥4,700–5,600, double ¥9,100–16,000.

International. 2191 Kitacho, Takamatsu, Kagawa Pref. 760; (0878) 31–1511. Belongs to the Tokyo Dai-ichi Hotel chain. 10 minutes by car from the station. Pool, gift shop, Japanese garden, sports facilities. 102 Western, 5 Japanese rooms. Single ¥5,800–7,500, double ¥9,500–18,000.

Keio Plaza. 5–11, Chuo-cho, Takamatsu, Kagawa Pref. 760; (0878) 34–5511. Belongs to the Tokyo Keio Plaza family. Near the pier, Ritsurin Park, entertainment district. Gift shops, access to beach, fishing, golf. 178 Western, 2 Japanese rooms. Single ¥5,200, double ¥9,000–16,500.

Takarazuka

Takarazuka Hotel. 1–46 Umenocho, Takarazuka, Hyogo Pref. 665; (0797) 87–1151. Comfortable, with pool, Japanese garden. 159 Western, 6 Japanese rooms. Single ¥7,000–7,500; double ¥8,000–16,000.

Tokushima

Astoria. 2–26–1 Ichiban-cho, Tokushima City 770; (0886) 53–6151. Convenient location. 24 Western, 1 Japanese room. Single ¥4,000–5,000, double ¥6,000–10,000.

Awa Kanko. 3–16–3 Ichiban-cho, Tokushima City 770; (0886) 22–5161. Long experience in welcoming foreign visitors. Conveniently located, gift shop, beauty parlor. 23 Western, 12 Japanese rooms. Single ¥5,200. double ¥10,000.

Park. 2–32–1 Tokushima-cho, Tokushima City 770; (0886) 25–3311. City location, but quiet. Japanese garden, good service. 75 Western, 6 Japanese rooms. Single ¥5,200–8,200, double ¥10,000.

Tottori

New Otani. 2–153, Ima-machi, Tottori City 680; (0857) 23–1111. Joint venture of the New Otani Hotel in Tokyo and the Hino-Maru Motor KK group in Tottori. Several restaurants, gift shop, barber, beauty parlor. Access to beach, fishing, sailing, skiing, golf. Traditional good service and international-class facilities. 140 Western, 3 Japanese rooms. Single ¥6,800–7,500, double ¥11,500–22,000.

JAPANESE-STYLE

Arima Spa

Arima Grand Hotel. 808 Arima-cho, Kita-ku, Kobe 651–14; (078) 904–0781. A Japanese inn, its name notwithstanding. Noted for its hot springs baths with their medicinal properties. Single with 2 meals ¥17,000–25,000.

Takayama-so. 400–1 Arima-cho, Kita-ku, Kobe; (078) 904–0744. A lovely Japanese inn set against hot springs. Manager Takeshi Surukawa speaks English, is eager and helpful. Single rooms ¥3,800–4,500, twin ¥7,000–8,000, triple ¥9,000–10,500.

Himeji

Banryu. 135 Shimodera-machi; (0792) 85–2112. Near the dazzling white castle, has 18 rooms, 11 with bath. Single with 2 meals ¥15,000–20,000.

Hiroshima

Ikedaya. 6–36 Dobashi-cho, Naka-ku, Hiroshima; (082) 231–3329. A Japanese family inn, a short bus ride from the station, near the Peace Memorial Park. AE, Visa, and yen traveler's checks accepted.

Mikawa. 9–6 Kyobashi-cho, Minami-ku, Hiroshima; (082) 261–2719. Only 7 minutes walk from the station. Single room ¥3,000, double ¥5,600, triple ¥8,400. Breakfast ¥500, Dinner ¥1,500.

Kaike Spa

Tokoen. 2155 Kaike, Yonago City 683. Noted for its healing hot springs baths. Single with 2 meals ¥20,000–25,000.

Kobe

Shichifuku. Miyamae-cho, Hyogo-ku. 35 rooms.

Kobe. 5–2–31 Kumochicho, Chuo-ku 651; (078) 221–5431. Single with 2 meals ¥13,000.

Kurashiki

Shimoden. 1666–2 Ohata, Kurashiki; (0864) 79–7111.

Tokusankan. Over 200 years old, former residence of a village headman.

Matsue

Minamikan. Suetsuguhon-cho, on the shores of Lake Shinji, 14 rooms.

Suimeiso. 26, Nishicha-machi, Matsue 690; (0852) 26–3311. Conveniently located in town. 50 rooms. Single with 2 meals ¥30,000–50,000.

Matsuyama

Funaya. 1–33 Dogo-yuno-machi 790; (0899) 47–0278. One of the better inns at Dogo Hot Springs in the suburbs of Matsuyama. Looks like a Western hotel

438 JAPAN

from the outside but inside are Japanese rooms, gardens, public and private hot springs baths. Single with 2 meals ¥18,000–20,000.

Kasugaen. 3–1, Dogo-sagidani-machi 790; (0899) 41–9156. Similar to Funaya, with good service. Single with 2 meals ¥18,000–20,000.

Miyajima

Iwaso. (08294) 4–2233. 20 rooms. ¥10,000–30,000 with 2 meals.

Kamefuku. 849 Miyajimacho, Saeki-gun; (08294) 4–2111, Very near the shrine. 49 rooms, most with baths. ¥15,000–20,000 with 2 meals.

Okayama

Shin Matsunoe. 3–21–29 Ifuku-cho; (0862) 52–5131. Near the magnificent Korakuen Garden. 50 rooms, 39 with bath. Single with 2 meals ¥12,000–30,000.

Takamatsu

Kawaroku. 1–2 Hyakkencho; (0878) 21–5666. Old established, comfortable inn. 75 rooms, all with bath. Single with 2 meals ¥15,000–20,000.

Ryokan Miyuki. 262 Sakaemachi, Kotohiri-cho, Nakatado-gun, Kagawa; (08777) 5–3457/1302. 4 minutes walk from Kotohira Stn. on national railways. Belongs to the Japan Economy Accommodation Federation. Single ¥3,500. Breakfast ¥500.

Tokiwa Honkan. 1–8–2 Tokiwa-cho; (0878) 31–5577. Mixture of Oriental and Occidental, good service, attractive garden. 24 rooms. Single with 2 meals ¥15,000–18,000.

Tokushima

Bizan. 1–9 Higashi-yamatecho; (0886) 22–7781. Popular during the Awa Odori festival mid-August. Single without meals ¥4,000–6,000.

BUSINESS HOTELS
(¥3,500 and up)

Fukuyama. *Fukuyama Kokusai,* 1–1–26, Shiromi-machi, Hiroshima Pref. 26 rooms.

Kobe. *Minakami,* 1–1–15, Mizuki-dori. 52 rooms. *Green Hill,* Ikuta-ku.

Kurashiki. *Kurashiki Station,* 2–8–1, Achi. 136 rooms.

Matsuyama. *Business Hotel Taihei,* 3–1–15, Heiwa-dori. 85 rooms.

Okayama. *Okayama New Station,* 18–9, Ekimotocho. 44 rooms.

Takamatsu. *Tokuju,* 3–5–5, Hanazono-machi. 121 rooms.

Tokushima. *Business Hotel Tokushima,* 1–15, Shin-Kura-machi. 40 rooms.

KOKUMIN SHUKUSHA

(Standard room charge with two meals about ¥5,000)

Hiroshima Pref. *Ondo Lodge,* Ondo-no-Seto Park, Kure-shi. *Miyajima Lodge,* Omotoenchi, Miyajimacho, Saeki-gun. *Yuki Lodge,* 2563 Tada, Yuki-cho, Saeki-gun. *Iwakura Lodge,* Tsuda, Saekicho Saeki-gun. *Okuno-shima,* Tadanoumimachi, Takehara City.

Hyogo Pref. *Aioiso,* 5321 Kanagasaki, Aioishi. *Shinguso,* 1093 Shingu, Shingucho, Ibo-gun. *Akatomboso,* Daiyama, Tatsunocho, Tatsuno-shi. *Sasayamaso,* 474 Kawaracho, Sasayamacho, Taki-gun.

Kagawa Pref. *Shimanoyado,* 1460–3 Ko, Tonoshocho, Shodo-gun. *Shokinkaku,* Matsubara, Tsudacho, Okawa-gun.

Okayana Pref. *Ojigadake,* 1421–1 Tokincho Kojima, Kurashiki-shi. *Tamanoso,* 2–12–1 Shibukawa, Tamano-shi. *Kinzanso,* 274, Okutsugawa Nishi,

Okutsucho, Tomata-gun. *Mimasakaso,* 903, Yunogo, Mimasakacho, Aida-gun. *Toriso,* 1553–5, Toyosaka, Yubaracho, Maniwa-gun. *Hiruzen,* Kami Fukuda, Kawakami-mura.

Shimane Pref. *Sambeso,* Shigaku, Sanbecho, Oda-shi. *Seiranso,* 161–1, Kawate, Yoshidamura, Iishi-gun. *Kunigaso,* Urago, Nishi-noshimacho, Chibugun.

Tokushima Pref. *Umigameso,* Hiwasaura, Hisacho, Kaibu-gun.

Tottori Pref. *Suimeiso,* 132, Asahi, Togocho, Tohaku-gun. *Sekiganeso,* 1397, Sekiganeyado, Sekiganecho, Tohaku-gun. *Misasa Onsen Kaikan,* 388–1, Misasa, Tohaku-gun. *Kaigaraso,* Hamamura, Kedakacho, Kedaka-gun. *Sakyuso,* Toriuchi, Hamasaka, Tottori-shi. *Daisen Kagamiganaru,* Efumachi, Hino-gun.

KOKUMIN KYUKAMURA

Goshikidai, Ohya Tomimachi, Sakaide City, Kagawa Pref.
Tohyo, Sakura Kaigan, Imabara City, Ehime Pref.

 YOUTH HOSTELS. Ashiya. 1–309, Okuyama, Ashiya City 659; (0797) 38–0109. 20 min. by bus from Ashiya Sta. and 10 min. on foot. 100 beds. Closed Dec. 29 thr. Jan. 3. **Tarumi Kaigan YH.** 5–58, Kaigan-dori, Tarumi-ku, Kobe City 655; (078) 707–2133. 8 min. on foot from Tarumi Sta. 28 beds. **YH Yamada Mudoji.** 100, Shinchi, Fukuchi, Yamada-cho, Kita-ku, Kobe City 651–12; (078) 581–0250. 8 min. by bus from Minotani Sta. and 15 min. on foot. 31 beds.

YH Tegarayama Seinen-No-Ie. 58, Nishi-nobuse, Himeji City 670; (0792) 93–2716. 5 min. by bus from Himeji Sta. and 8 min. on foot 48 beds. Closed Dec. 28 thr. Jan. 3. **YH Okayama-ken Seinen Kaikan.** 1–7–6, Tsukura-cho, Okayama City 700; (0862) 52–0651. 20 min. on foot from Okayama Sta. 65 beds. Closed Jan. 18 thr. 24. **Kurashiki YH.** 1537–1, Mukaiyama, Kurashiki City 710; (0864) 22–7355. 10 min. by bus from Kurashiki Sta. and 10 min. on foot. 80 beds. **Washu-Zan YH.** 1666–1, Obatake, Kurashiki City 711: (0864) 79–9280. 1 hr. 20 min. by bus from Okayama Sta. and 3 min. on foot. 60 beds.

Hiroshima YH. 1–13–6, Ushita-shin-machi, Higashi-ku, Hiroshima City 730: (082) 221–5343. 10 min. by bus from Hiroshima Sta. and 8 min. on foot 104 beds. **Hiroshima Saka-Machi YH.** Ueda, Saka-machi, Hiroshima City 731–43: (082) 885–0700 20 min. on foot from Saka Sta. 25 beds. **YH Makoto Kaikan.** 756, Sairen-cho, Miyajima-machi, Saiki-gun, Hiroshima-ken 739–05: (08294) 4–0328. 10 min. by boat from Miyajima-guchi and 5 min. on foot. 75 beds. **Tachikue-Kyo YH.** Tachikue, Ottachi-machi, Izumo City 693–03: (0853) 45–0102. 30 min. by bus from Izumo-shi Sta. and 5 min. on foot 50 beds. **Matsue YH.** 1546, Kososhi-machi, Matsue City 690–01: (0852) 36–8620 30 min. by bus from Matsue Sta. and 15 min. on foot 82 beds.

Yonago-Minami YH. 780, Kitakata, Saihaku-cho, Saihaku-gun, Tottori-ken 683–03: (085966) 3410. 25 min. by bus from Yonago Sta. and 15 min. on foot. 11 beds. **Daisen YH.** Daisen, Daisen-cho, Saihaku-gun, Tottori-ken 689–33: (085952) 2501. 50 min. by bus from Yonago Sta. and 3 min. on foot. 102 beds. **YH Kohoji.** 195, Shimo-asozu, Hawai-cho, Tohaku-gun, Tottori-ken 682–07. Tel (085835) 2054. 10 min. by bus from Kurayoshi Sta. and 10 min. on foot. 35 beds. **Wakasa Hyonosen YH.** 631–10, Tsukuyone, Wakasa-cho, Yazu-gun, Tottori-ken 680–07: (08588) 2–1700. 25 min. by bus from Wakasa Sta. and 20 min. on foot. 96 beds.

Amanohashidate. 905, Manai, Nakano, Miyazu City 629–22: (07722) 7–0121. 17 min. by boat from Amanohashidate Sta. and 10 min. on foot. 60 beds.

YH **Amanohashidate Kanko Kaikan.** 22, Ogaki, Miyazu City 629–22: (07722) 7–0046. 17 min. by boat from Amanohashidate Sta. and 2 min. on foot. 70 beds. **Naruto YH.** 149–12, Kitatono-cho, Hayasaki, Muya-cho, Naruto City 772: (08868) 6–4561. 5 min. by bus from Naruto Sta. and 7 min. on foot. 50 beds. **Awaji YH.** Ama, Nandan-cho, Mihara-gun, Hyogo-ken 656–07: (07995) 2–0460. 10 min. by boat from Fukura Port. 116 beds.

Takamatsu Yashima-Sanso YH. 77–4, Yashima-naka-machi, Takamatsu City 761–01: (0878) 41–2318 8 min. on foot from Yashima Sta. 50 beds. **YH Takamatsu Yuai-Sanso.** 2–4–14, Nishiki-cho, Takamatsu City 760: (0878)22–3656. 10 min. on foot from Takamatsu Sta. 32 beds. **Takamatsu-Shi YH.** 531–3, Okamoto-cho, Takamatsu City 761: (0878)85–2024. 15 min. on foot from Okamoto Sta. 52 beds. **YH Kotohira Seinen-No-Ie.** 1241, Kawanishi-otsu, Kotohira-machi, Nakatado-gun, Kagawa-ken 766: (08777)3–3836. 15 min. on foot from Kotohira Sta. 68 beds.

Tokushima YH. 7–1, Hama, Ohara-machi, Tokushima City 770: (0886) 63–1505. 30 min. by bus from Tokushima Sta. and 3 min. on foot. 80 beds. **Kochi-Ekimae YH.** 3–10–10, Kita-hon-cho, Kochi City 780: (0888)83–5086. 7 min. on foot from Kochi Sta. 104 beds. **Hitsuzan YH.** 30–4, Koishiki-cho, Kochi City 780; (0888)33–2789 10 min. by bus from Kochi Sta. and 20 min. on foot. 50 beds. **Shinsen-En YH.** 22–3 Dogohimezaka Otsu, Matsuyama City 790: (0899) 33–6366. 8 min. on foot from Dogo-Onsen Sta. 47 Beds.

HOW TO GET AROUND. Generally speaking, it is possible to get just about anywhere in Japan—long hauls and inter-city—by public transportation. Taxis cruise in the cities too, although their prices have become prohibitive.

By air. There are domestic airports, with many daily flights, in Osaka, Okayama, Hiroshima, Izumo, Yonago, Tottori, and on Shikoku in Takamatsu, Tokushima, Kochi, and Matsuyama.

By train. There are four types of trains—super express (Shinkansen or "Bullet"), limited express, ordinary express, and local. All are clean, reliable, frequent, and fast. Super express trains have special stations so that from Shin Kurashiki, for instance, you need a local train to Kurashiki.

By bullet train from Tokyo, Kobe is 3½ hours, Okayama is 4 hours 10 minutes, Kurashiki 4 hours 45 minutes, Hiroshima 5 hours 8 minutes.

For east-west travel in **Kobe**, take the JNR or any one of a number of private train lines. For north-south trips, take taxis. Portliner connects Port Island with Sannomiya, and a subway links Suma New Town with the western business section.

Private inter-urban rail lines connect Kobe with Osaka, Takarazuka, Nara, and Kyoto. *JNR* links Kobe with Himeji, Okayama, Kurashiki, and Hiroshima. From Hiroshima, Miyajima is ½ hour by JNR, 63 min. by Hiroshima Electric Railway or 37 minutes by bus, and then 10 minutes by ferry. Trains and buses connect the Inland Sea route with the Japan Sea coast. It's only ½ hour on the train from Izumo to Matsue, and the same again to Yonago, then 2½ hours on to Tottori. Change at Toyooka (2 hours) for Amanohashidate (1 hour 20 minutes). Back to Osaka from Amanohashidate takes 3 hours 40 minutes by express train. It's 2 hours 20 minutes from Amanohashidate to Kyoto by limited express.

JNR runs many trains on Shikoku. From Takamatsu it's 1½ hours to Tokushima, 3 hours to Kochi, 3 hours to Matsuyama.

By bus. Buses complement the trains everywhere on Honshu, as well as on Shikoku. The bus from Hiroshima to Izumo on the Japan Sea coast is less complicated than the train. Change at Miyoshi (1 hour 45 minutes from Hiroshima) for Izumo (2½ hours).

By boat. Numerous daily commuter ferries connect Honshu and Shikoku. The main ports on Honshu are Osaka, Kobe, Akashi, Okayama, Uno, Fukuyama, Onomichi, Mihara, Kure, and Hiroshima. They serve Takamatsu, Marugame, Niihama, Imabari, and Matsuyama on Shikoku. From Uno to Takamatsu is 23 minutes by hovercraft, 55 by ferry. From Hiroshima to Matsuyama is just over an hour by hydrofoil; Kure to Matsuyama is 50 minutes.

JNR operates a direct 6-hour Tokyo-Takamatsu service. The super express Hikari whooshes you to Okayama, where you change to the JNR Uno line to the ferry that connects with Shikoku. From Osaka the same train-ferry journey takes but 3 hours.

The *Kansai Steamship Co.* (in Tokyo 03–274–4271) operates a 4-day round trip luxury cruise between Kobe and Nagasaki, stopping at Shibushi and Kagoshima. The *Sunflower I* offers shipboard sports, parties, films, and disco dancing, and optional sightseeing tours of Kagoshima and Nagasaki. Three nights and 4 days on board, including 8 meals, costs between ¥45,000 and ¥120,000.

There are several long-distance ferry services covering the Inland Sea—unfortunately, most of them sail overnight. The Osaka/Kobe/Matsuyama/Beppu route, operated by the Kansai Steamship Co., leaves Osaka daily at 4:30 P.M., reaching Beppu the next morning at 7:30. The entire journey costs ¥11,400 first class; ¥5,700 second.

The *Hiroshima Green Ferry* leaves Osaka Nan-ko Ferry Terminal (a 15-minute walk from Suminoe Koen Station on the Yotsubashi Line) each night at 8:20 P.M., reaching Hiroshima's Dejima Port at 7:10 the next morning. In reverse, it leaves Hiroshima at 8:20 P.M., reaching Osaka at 7:20 A.M. Special class costs ¥12,000; first class ¥8,200; second class ¥4,100. Bookings can be made in Tokyo (03) 542–0096, Osaka (06) 532–3121, or Hiroshima (082) 228–1665.

The car-ferry route from Tokyo to Kochi via Nachi Katsuura, is operated by the *Nihon Kosoku Ferry Co.* (Tokyo 03–274–1801, Kochi 0888–31–0520). It leaves Tokyo on the odd-numbered days of each month and Kochi on the even-numbered days. Leaving Tokyo at 6:20 P.M., it reaches Nachi Katsuura in Wakayama Prefecture at 8:10 A.M., then proceeds in daylight to reach Kochi at 3:40 P.M. Special class fare is ¥37,800; first class ¥27,000, second class bed ¥17,000; and second class floor ¥13,500.

The Tokyo/Tokushima/Kokura (Kyushu) route is operated by the *Ocean Tokyu Ferry Co.* (Tokyo 03–567–0971, Tokushima 0886–62–0489). It leaves Tokyo at 6:00 P.M. and reaches Tsuda Port, Tokushima, at 1:40 the next day. Sailings both from Tokyo and Kokura are on the even-numbered days of each month.

There are also a number of mini cruises within the Inland Sea. The *Seto Naikai Kisen Co.* (Tokyo 03–567–8740, Hiroshima 083–351–5291) offers its Splendid Tour of the Seto Inland Sea. It plies between Miyajima and Ikuchi Island, visiting several islets, whirlpools, the Oyamazumi Shrine on Omishima Island, and Kosanji Temple on Ikuchi Island.

TOURIST INFORMATION. Kobe. *Tourist Information Center,* 2nd floor, Kobe Kotsu Center Bldg., west exit of JNR Sannomiya Stn.; (078) 392–0020. *Japan Travel Bureau,* Sannomiya Stn.; (078) 231–4111. *International Tourist Association,* 14th floor, Shoko-Boeki Center Bldg.; (078) 232–1010. *Good Will Guide* is a nationwide organization to help tourists overcome language difficulties. Over 600 volunteers in Osaka and Kobe. In Kobe: 3rd floor, Kobe Sannomiya Kotsu Center Bldg., Chuo-ku; (078) 331–3351.

Okayama. *Prefectural Gov't Tourist Section,* Uchisange; (0862) 24–2111.

Kurashiki. *Railway Stn. Information Office,* 1-chome Achi; (0864) 26–8681. *Japan Travel Bureau,* 2-chome Achi; (0864) 22–5601. *City Tourist Dept.,* Nishi Nakashinden; (0864) 26–3411.

Hiroshima. *Japan Travel Bureau,* Kamiya-cho; (082)247–5131.

Takamatsu. *Kagawa Prefectural Gov't, Tourist Section;* (0878) 31–1111. *JNR Tourist Center;* (0878) 51–1335.

Matsuyama. *Matsuyama City Office, Tourist Section,* 7–2 Niban-cho, 4-chome; (0899) 48–6557.

Useful Addresses. *United States Consulate,* 6–3–1 Kano-cho, Chuo-ku; (078) 331–6865. The only consulate of an English-speaking country in Kobe.

 MEDICAL SERVICES. Kobe, with its large foreign settlement, has the Franciscan-operated *Kaisei Hospital,* 3–11–15, Shinohara Kita-machi, Nada-ku; (078) 871–5201. *American Pharmacy* dispenses most medicines. Otherwise, should you need medical attention, appeal to the information desk of your hotel.

ELECTRICAL CURRENT. The electric current in western Japan and Shikoku is 100 volts and 60 cycles (hertz) A.C.

 PLACES OF WORSHIP. Kobe. *Rokko Catholic Church,* 1–21 Akamatsu-cho, 3-chome, Nada-ku; (078) 851–2846. *Evangelical Lutheran Church,* 2–11, Makajima-dori 2-chome, Chuo-ku; (078)242–0887. *Kobe Union Church,* 6–15, Ikuta-cho 4-chome, Chuo-ku; (078) 221–4733. *St. Michael's Cathedral* (Anglican), 15 Shimo Yamate-dori 5-chome, Ikuta-ku; (078) 351–4378. **Hiroshima.** *The Christian and Missionary Alliance Japan Mission,* 11–20, Kako-machi, Naka-ku; (082) 241–6450. **Tokushima.** *Finnish Lutheran Mission,* 5–36, Atake 3-chome; (0886) 23–5534.

LOCAL BUSINESS HOURS AND HOLIDAYS. Most offices operate from 9:00 A.M. to 5:00 P.M., close on Sundays and about a dozen annual public holidays. Most department stores are open from 10:00 A.M. to 6:00 P.M. and choose a mid-week day to close.

 SEASONAL EVENTS AND FESTIVALS. As usual, please beware of the sudden changes in dates caused by rain, inauspicious omens, and the vagaries of the lunar calendar. Always check with your hotel before setting out, or telephone the place directly.

WESTERN HONSHU

February. *Naked Festival,* Saidaiji Temple, Okayama. One of the largest of such observances in Japan. Several thousand young men fight for possession of one of two batons tossed into their midst by priests. To make it difficult, the action takes place inside the blacked-out court, and the wands are scented camphorwood. To prevent injuries, it is said, the youths are not allowed to wear any clothing except for the traditional Japanese loincloth. Those who manage to smuggle the baton out of the temple to the waiting priests are rewarded with blessings and some large prize. Evening, and very crowded. Third Saturday of the month.

April. *Gumonji-do,* Mt. Misen, Miyajima. Fire-walking ceremonies on the 15th. Take cable car from Maple Valley to the top of Mt. Misen, 580 meters. A 10-minute walk into the woods higher up the mountain leads to the temple set among granite ledges and founded by Kobo Daishi, who brought the teachings of the Shingon sect from China 1,200 years ago. Fire-walking usually lasts about two hours, from 1:00 P.M. Stay for the spring *bugaku,* ancient sacred dances from central Asia that now survive only in Japan.

May. *Izumo Taisha Grand Festival* from the 14th–16th sees crowds of starry-eyed Japanese from all over the country gather at this shrine of blessed weddings.

June. *Kangensai* (Music Festival), Miyajima, Hiroshima. The Itsukushima Shrine on Miyajima island holds its most elaborate ceremonies on the 17th. The shrine deity is taken from the sacred resting place, put on board a special boat and ferried across to the mainland, where he spends the night. At dawn, he is brought back. There are occasional performances of *bugaku* (similar to the Imperial court's *gagaku* dances) and extra services at the temples and the main shrine itself.

July. *Toro Nagashi* takes place on the 16th–17th in Matsue City. A part of the Bon Festival; the rites here see people casting thousands of lighted lanterns on the waters of Lake Shinji and along the city's many canals.

August. *Peace Festival* is held on the 6th in Hiroshima. Solemn ceremonies to commemorate the atom bombing of the city in 1945 begin with services at 8:15 A.M., the fateful hour, before the Cenotaph in Peace Park. Fireworks in the evening.

Dance Festival for Chugoku region is held from the 15th–16th in connection with *O-Bon* at the Hiroshima stadium. Features dance groups from all over Japan, who perform regional dances.

Tamatori Ennen Festival is held in mid-month in Miyajima, Hiroshima. During the day, there is a scramble in the water around the floating *torii* for a lucky wooden ball tossed into the crowd of waiting youths by the priests. Whoever retrieves the ball and swims with it to the priests is rewarded with blessing and a prize.

September. *Izumo Taisha Grand Festival,* on the 15th is a repeat of May ceremonies.

October. *Quarrel Festival* at Himeji in mid-month. At Matsubara Shrine, the bearers of three giant portable shrines (o-mikoshi) begin to carry them around the town and thence back to the main shrine. En route, at one or more places agreed upon, the bearers attempt to be first in line, and the three groups come together with a gigantic clash. The crowds of men rush each other with their heavy burdens, smashing at full speed.

November. *Fire-walking ceremonies* at Gumonji-do, Mt. Misen, Miyajima on the 15th. Repeat of April ceremonies but without the *bugaku* dances.

SHIKOKU

August. *Yosakoi Festival,* on the 10th–11th, is a modern innovation devised by the people of Kochi City to celebrate the popularity of the song *Yosakoi,* which goes to show that some people will start a festival on the weakest excuse. Dancing in the streets. Yosakoi means "Come in tonight."

Awa Odori, Tokushima City, around the 15th. Also called the Fools' Dance, it is the most colorful display of public emotion in Japan, the townspeople and visitors dancing through the streets all night, singing the same tune over and over. "Fools we are who dance, fools they are who watch us prance. Since fool I must be, I want to be a dancing fool." Everyone is welcome to join, and all wear kimono and dance a kind of modified mambo. If you can't visit Tokushima at this time, you may perhaps be able to watch the spectacle on television, thus becoming a looking fool. Remotely related to the O-Bon dances.

October. *Kompira Shrine Grand Festival* runs from the 9th–11th. This shrine and its gods are patrons to those traveling on water. Therefore, sailors, fishermen, and travelers in general have great faith in the efficacy of a visit here. In addition to ceremonies at the shrine, you can see *Kemari,* ancient Japanese court football played here in costumes of the Heian period. Many elaborate floats are paraded through the compound.

Ushioni Matsuri, the Ox-Devil Festival, Yoshida, Ehime Prefecture. Takes place on the 28th–29th. Two stations before Uwajima City, Yoshida is the site of Uwatsu Shrine, where the grotesque bulls are paraded and large figures of bulls are carried through the streets. Rustic color.

All year. Throughout the year, you may see many groups of white-clad pilgrims at various points on Shikoku Island. They are making the trip around the island to visit its 88 sacred spots. Those who do so will surely achieve salvation, it is held by devout Buddhists. Recently, some of the less pious make the trip by auto or bus, but the truly faithful still do it by foot, as did a recent prime minister, who is said to have cured a severe illness by making this pilgrimage some years ago.

 **TOURS AND SPECIAL INTEREST SIGHTSEEING.** Most local tours are in Japanese, although *JTB* offers some with English-speaking guides. Many tours of western Japan originate in Kyoto or Osaka. A full-day *Sunrise Tour* takes in Hiroshima and Miyajima: ¥34,000 without lunch. A 2-day tour carries on through the Inland Sea: ¥69,000. A 3-day tour goes on to Tomonoura, Kurashiki, and Okayama: ¥99,000. All begin on Sunday, Tuesday, Thursday, from March to November. Not all meals included.

 THE HOME VISIT SYSTEM. Operated entirely on good will, in several cities, this enables foreign visitors to meet local people in their homes. Apply to the tourist information bureau the day before you want to go. In **Kobe:** Tourist section, Kobe City Gov't., 6–7 Kano-cho, Chuo-ku; (078) 331–8181.

 PARKS AND GARDENS. Daisen-Oki National Park. In northwestern Honshu, this park encompasses the mountains surrounding Mt. Daisen, the Oki Archipelago, the Shimane Peninsula and the harbor of Mihonseki, the area around Izumo Taisha, and Mt. Sambe with its extinct volcano. Mt. Daisen is famed for winter skiing and summer camping.

Korakuen. One of Japan's top trio of model gardens. 5 mins. from Okayama Station, Okayama, by taxi. Open 8:30 A.M.–5:30 P.M., Apr.–Sept.; 9:00 A.M.–4:30 P.M., Oct.–Mar.

Makino Botanical Garden. In Kochi on Shikoku. Named after the late collaborator of the famous botanist Maximowiczi, displays all kinds of flowers, fungi, plants.

Peace Memorial Park. Encompasses the Peace Memorial Museum, Peace Memorial Hall, and Memorial Cenotaph. 15 min. by bus from Hiroshima Station.

Ritsurin Park. Rivals Korakuen in Okayama. Also contains zoo, folk art gallery, and museum. 10 min. by bus from Takamatsu Station on Shikoku.

San-In Kaigan National Park. On northwestern Honshu, extends some 77 kilometers from Tottori to Amino on the Okutango Peninsula. Includes the famous desert sand dunes, unique in all Japan. Sand skiing and summer camping.

Shukkeien. Designed in 1620, registered as a Scenic Place. 5 min. by bus from Hiroshima Station. Open 9:00 A.M.–6:00 P.M., April 1–Sept. 30; 9:00 A.M.–5:00 P.M., Oct. 1–Mar. 31. Admission ¥ 100.

 BEACHES. Popular beaches everywhere are crammed in the summer, and very commercialized. *Suma, Maiko,* and *Shioya* in **Kobe** are attractive, and some foreign residents find their own coves on **Awaji.** On that island *Ohama* is popular. The Japan Sea coast has many swimming beaches, including *Yumigahama, Tottori,* and *Amanohashidate.*

Shikoku has the least crowded sea coast. *Katsurahama,* 40 minutes by bus from Kochi Station, is lovely.

 HOT SPRINGS. Hot springs in Japan are believed to contain medicinal properties. **Arima,** 40 meters above sea level, about 1 hour northwest of Kobe through the magnificent Rokko mountains. **Dogo,** 20 minutes by bus from Matsuyama on Shikoku, has a bathhouse, now public, that was once exclusively for the use of the Imperial Family. **Kaike,** 20 minutes by bus east of Yonago on the Japan Sea coast, has pine trees fringing its shores. **Kinosaki,** in the San-In Kaigan National Park, ½ hour by bus from Toyooka, has been known since the 7th century.

 PARTICIPANT SPORTS. During the short **skiing** season special trains run from Osaka to Mt. Kannabe, Hyogo Prefecture, and Mt. Daisen, Tottori Prefecture. The skiing ground at *Mt. Kannabe* may be reached easily from Ebara Station on the San-in line. There are lift systems at nine places in the Kannabe area. *Mt. Hyonosen* and *Mt. Hachibuse* skiing grounds are 1 hour and 15 minutes by bus from Yoka Station. *Oeyama,* in Kyoto Prefecture, has one lift system and may be reached from Miyazu Station on the Miyazu line. At *Mt. Daisen,* 60 minutes by bus from Yonago Station, there are four lift systems and extensive skiing grounds.

 SPECTATOR SPORTS. Both **Kobe** and **Hiroshima** have major-league baseball teams and regularly scheduled games between April and October. The *Koshien Stadium,* Naruo-cho, Nishinomiya (Kobe) and the *City Stadium,* Hiroshima, are the places to go. Pick up a "Play Guide" in each town, ask at your hotel front desk, or go to the stadium itself.

 HISTORICAL SITES. Amanohashidate. The Heavenly Bridge. On the Japan Sea coast. Walking distance from Amanohashidate Stn., but seen to its best advantage from a mountain-top over the water. A few minutes by ferry, then a cable car.

Miyajima. The Shrine Island with its "floating" red torii. 20 minutes from Hiroshima on the JNR Sanyo Line to Miyajima-guchi, then 10 minutes by ferry.

Izumo Taisha. Japan's oldest Shinto shrine. 25 minutes by bus from Izumoshi Station, northwestern Honshu.

446 JAPAN

Matsuyama Castle. Built in 1602, this is one of the best preserved castles in Japan. On Katsuyama in the center of Matsuyama on Shikoku.

Himeji Castle. Originally an early 14th-century castle, this was rebuilt in the 1960s. Demonstrates Japanese skill with wood. In Himeji, 1 hr. west of Kobe by local train.

Ijinkan. Residences of foreign settlers, dating back to the late 19th century. Kitano-cho in Kobe.

Kotohiragu Shrine. One of Japan's most sacred Shinto shrines, also known as Kompira. One hr. southwest of Takamatsu by train.

Architectural Interest. *White Heron Castle,* Himeji. Demonstrates Japanese genius with wood. The patterns of the castle moats, gates, roofs, and the 26-meter pillars should be seen from the top of the castle. A 10-minute walk from Himeji Station.

 MUSEUMS. In **Kobe,** the *Municipal Art Museum* houses some 4,000 pieces relating to the influence of Western art on Japan during the period 1549–1858. At 35–1 Kumauchi-cho, Fukiai-ku. Daily 9:00 A.M.–5:00 P.M., cl. Mon. and in August. The *Hakutsuru Art Museum* specializes in ancient Chinese art. At 1545 Ochiai, Sumiyoshi-cho, Higashi Nada-ku. Open Tues-Sun., 9:00 A.M.–5:00 P.M. In **Fukusaki,** the house of Kunio Yanagida, pioneer folk historian, is preserved as a museum of his works. The house is relocated in the compound of Suzumori Shrine. The *Thomas "Weathercock" House* in **Kitanocho** is open as an "Ijinkan," residence of early foreign settlers. *Eikoku-kan,* nearby, is another restored residence. *Persia House* contains Persian Art. Near Urokono-ie; (078) 222–0081. At **Takarazuka,** the Seichoji Temple, Kiyo-shikojin, specializes in the works of Tessai Tomioka, a Japanese-style painter.

Kurashiki offers the best museums in the region. Most interesting is the *Folkcraft Museum,* containing an excellent selection of items, mostly ceramics, woodcraft, and textiles designed by the common people of previous eras. 9:00 A.M.–4:00 P.M. closed Mons. Admission, ¥300. Nearby is the *Archeological Museum,* which contains 1,400 artifacts of Japanese civilization. Open 9:00 A.M.–4:30 P.M., except Mon. Entrance ¥300. Finally, you have the *Ohara Art Museum,* gift of local millionaire who decided the countryfolk of west Japan should have a chance to see originals by El Greco, Rodin, and other Western masters. Hours for the above are: 9:00 to 5:00. Closed Mondays. Entrance ¥300.

Ancient swords and armor are the major attractions at the *Hayashibara Museum in* **Okayama.** *Okayama Municipal Orient Museum* displays 2,000 pieces of pottery, glassware and excavated articles. The Yasuhara Collection is housed in the new *Near East Arts Museum,* near Korakuen. *Bizen Ceramics Hall* (Bizen Togei Kaikan) has modern and *Bizen Old Ceramics Art Museum* (Bizen Koto Bijutsukan) antique Bizen ware, dating back to the Nara Period. Open 9:30 A.M.–4:00 P.M. daily except Monday.

The *Hiroshima Peace Memorial Museum* keeps the records of the 1945 atomic explosion. 1–3, Nakajima-cho, **Hiroshima City.** Open 9–5. *Museum of Art,* collection of the Bank of Hiroshima. Closed Mons. ¥500.

In **Tottori,** there is a *Folk Art Museum,* with handicraft items of the Japan Sea coastal areas. Open 10:00 A.M.–4:00 P.M. Closed Mondays. *Folk Toy Museum.* Adjacent to Folkcraft Museum. 5,000 folk toys from around the world. Open 8:00 A.M.–5:00 P.M., year-round. Admission, ¥200.

PERFORMING ARTS. The all-female troupes of Takarazuka, celebrated by James Michener in *Sayonara*, have been presenting revues and light opera in their home town since 1914. The opera house seats 4,000 people. North of Kobe; 34 minutes by express train from Hankyu Umeda Station on the Hankyu Railway Line to Takarazuka. When you get off the train, ask the way to the theater—it is well known.

SHOPPING. Kobe has its shopping streets, Sannomiya and Motomachi, with many arcades and department stores in between. Santica Town is an enormous underground complex in front of JNR Sannomiya Station. Hankyu, Daimaru, Sogo, and Mitsukoshi department stores maintain the standards set in Tokyo. Look for kimono, silk, curios, bamboo ware, and tortoise-shell ware.

Okayama is the home of Bizenyaki stoneware, which dates back 1200 years. You can buy directly from the workshops at Bizen Ware Center: 974 Bizen City; (0862) 4–2453. 45 minutes by train (Ako Line) from Okayama to Imbe. Open daily except Sunday and national holidays, 8:30 A.M.–5:15 P.M.

Kurashiki specializes in pottery, papier mache toys, and table mats, dolls, and handbags woven from igusa grass.

Hiroshima produces Japanese clogs, writing brushes, and musical instruments such as the koto.

Paper, near-sacred in Japan, comes from **Tottori** and **Yonago,** as do wooden ware and raw silk.

Marugamecho, Hyogocho, Minami Shimmachi, and Katahara-cho are shopping districts of **Takamatsu** on Shikoku. Best buys include lacquer and bamboo ware, Japanese parasols and fans.

Tokushima, on Shikoku, has its folk art, particularly Awa, Deko, and Kokeshi wooden dolls. Bamboo goods are attractive, too, as are mirror stands and Awa-chijimi (cotton crepe).

Kochi, on Shikoku offers ornamental hair pins and combs, as well as coral artcraft. **Ino,** west of Kochi, produces lovely handmade paper.

The prefecture of Ehime on Shikoku specializes in towels. In **Matsuyama** consider those with identifiably Japanese designs, beautifully dyed, for your souvenirs and gifts.

DINING OUT. Seafood is good in most parts of Japan. Try *tai* (sea bream) in Okayama, oysters in Hiroshima, and *fugu* (blow fish—poisonous in its unprepared state, so beware) in Shimonoseki.
The appropriate price ranges given below are per person for dinner.

KOBE

Western

Aka Noren. 3–9–5 Sannomiya, Chuo-ku; (078) 391–2154. Also specializes in steak, but of Matsuzaka beef. About ¥8,000.

Arakawa. 2–9 Nakayamate-dori, Chuo-ku. Open from mid-afternoon. Known for its steaks, of the famous Kobe beef. About ¥8,000.

Attic. Ijinkan Club Bldg., 4–30–2 Kitano-cho; tel. (078) 222–1586. Features Kobe beef and Australian wine. ¥4,000–5,000.

Coco a coco. 4–7–11 Kano-cho, Chuo-ku; (078) 392–4031. Offers 89 varieties of sandwiches. Lunchtime special of sandwich, soup, and coffee. ¥550 to

¥880 between 11:00 A.M. and 2:00 P.M. In the evenings, prices range from ¥500–1,000 for sandwiches alone. Open 11:00 A.M.–9:00 P.M. Tuesday to Friday, 11:00 A.M.–10:00 P.M. Saturday, 11:00 A.M.–8:00 P.M. Sunday and national holidays.

Cosmopolitan. 1–3–16 Sannomiya-cho, Chuo-ku; (078) 331–1217. Brunch and confectionery. ¥1,000–2,000 for light meals.

Escargot. 1–22 Sannomiya-cho, Chuo-ku; (078) 331–5034. Excellent French food, but correspondingly high prices. ¥7,000–10,000.

The King's Arms. 4–2–15 Isobe-dori, Chuo-ku; (078) 221–3774. An English pub, complete with dartboard and draft beer. Good roast beef. About ¥5,000.

Liberty Bell. 6th floor, You Bell Bldg., 1–4–6 Nakayamate-dori, Chuo-ku; (078) 332–2020. An American country pub, with dishes of the old American West. Features live country and bluegrass music. You buy 10 Liberty Bell coins for ¥2,500 and use them to pay for food and drink.

Misono. 1–7–6 Kitanagasa-dori, Chuo-ku; (078) 331–2890. Near the west exit of Sannomiya Station. Reputable, though pricey, steak house. ¥6,000–8,000.

Restaurant Hook. 2–9–11 Sakaemachi-dori, Chuo-ku; (078) 332–4129. Known for its charcoal grilled steaks. ¥4,000–5,000.

Yesterday. 5–1–5 Kagoike-dori, Chuo-ku; (078) 242–5227. Old-fashioned decor, open Monday - Thursday 11:00 A.M. to 2:00 A.M., Friday–Saturday 11:00 A.M. to 4:00 A.M., Sunday and national holidays 9:00 A.M. to midnight. ¥2,500–5,000.

Japanese

Blanc de Blancs. 7th floor, Shinyei Bldg., 77–1 Kyo-machi, Chuo-ku; (078) 321–1455. Tempura, sukiyaki, French food.

Chiyo-zushi. South of Center-Gai, Sannomiya. Very good sushi. ¥100–200 per piece; platters ¥800–1,500.

Gombei. Under the tracks at Motomachi Station. Good, reasonably priced sushi. ¥100–200 per piece; platters ¥800–1,500.

Mitsuwa. 3–5 Nakamichi-dori, Chuo-ku; (078) 341–0615. Famed for its sukiyaki, top prices. ¥6,000–8,000.

Ohnishi. 3rd floor, You Bell Bldg., 1–4–6 Nakayamate-dori, Chuo-ku; (078) 332–4029. Specializes in teppan-yaki with a tasty dip sauce. Open 5:30 P.M. to 2:00 A.M.; closed Wednesdays. ¥3,000–5,000.

Okagawa. 3–4–1 Motomachi, Chuo-ku; (078) 331–6154. Over 30 years of experience, known for tempura and sukiyaki. Expensive. ¥6,000–8,000.

Chinese

Botan-en. 1 Motomachi-dori, Chuo-ku; (078) 391–5141. Cantonese specialties. ¥4,000–6,000.

Daiichi-ro. 94 Edo-cho, Chuo-ku; (078) 331–0031. Excellent Peking-style cooking, separate cubicles for small, private parties. ¥4,000–6,000.

Hai Whan. Ohnishi Bldg., 3 Ninomiya-cho, Chuo-ku. Imperial Chinese atmosphere, good food. ¥4,000–6,000.

Kinryukaku. Kobe Shimbun Kaikan Bldg., 7–4 Kumori-dori, Chuo-ku; (078) 221–1616. Also good Cantonese dishes. ¥4,000–6,000.

Mandarin Palace. Near Ikuta Shrine. Features the cuisines of Szechuan and Canton. ¥4,000–6,000.

Indian

Gandhara. Babylon Towers, 2–6–5 Kitano-cho, Chuo-ku; (078) 242–3377. Good curries. Open 11:00 A.M. to 10:00 P.M., closed Wednesdays.

Gaylord. Two locations: *Basement, Meiji Seimei Bldg.,* opposite the City Hall's Flower Clock in Sannomiya; 251–4359. Lunch from 11:30 A.M. to 2:30 P.M., dinner 5:00–9:30 P.M. Open daily. *Daiei Shopping Center,* opposite Chuo Shimin Byoin on Port Island; (078) 302–5728. Open 11:00 A.M. to 10:00 P.M., closed Wednesdays. Kobe's oldest Indian restaurant, very popular. ¥2,000–4,000.

Kashmir. Japan House Motoyama Bldg., 3–4–12 Motoyama, Kita-machi, Higashi Nada-ku; (078) 452–0701. Good Indian food.

Maya. I.T.C. Bldg., 4–1–8 Isobe-dori, Chuo-ku; (078) 231–0703. Beautiful restaurant, superb food. Lunch 11:30 A.M.–2:30 P.M., special lunch ¥900, buffet ¥1,500 and ¥1,000 for children. Dinner 5:00–10:00 P.M., closed Mondays.

OKAYAMA

Kogyo Kaikan. Good Japanese grill.

Miyoshino Kaikan. 1–3–1 Ekimae-cho. Japanese and Western dishes, at reasonable prices.

Sangyo Kaikan. Good, reliable Japanese grill.

Yoshikawa. A good range of Japanese dishes.

HIROSHIMA

Amagi Honten. 10–10 Kami Noboricho; (082) 221–2375. Elegant, expensive restaurant, serving only Japanese food. ¥5,000 and up.

Hada Besso. 26 Funairi-cho. Japanese and Western dishes.

Hanbei. 8–12 Honura-cho; (082) 282–7121. Mostly Japanese food, ¥2,000–3,000.

Hyotei. 6–16 Dobashicho; (082) 232–0143. Pure Japanese food, very good fish. ¥2,000–3,000.

Issa-en. 10 Onomachi, Fukae. Japanese and Western food.

Kanzashi. 18 Mikawa-cho. Specializes in tempura.

Kushi-no-bo. Kanjingura. Another tempura restaurant.

Lira. 1–4–7 Kamiyacho; (082) 247–2151. Italian specialties. ¥2,000–3,000.

Mitakiso. 1–7 Mitaki-cho. International food.

Suehiro. 1–21 Tatemachi; tel. (082) 247–7175. Belongs to the steak house chain. Also sukiyaki. ¥2,000–3,000.

Suishin. 6–7 Tatemachi. Great variety of rice based dishes, excellent fish.

Zakuro Mingei. 1–15 Horikawa-cho; (082) 241–0396. Traditional food, traditional restaurant. ¥5,000 and up.

MATSUE

Minami. 14 Suetsugu Honmachi; (0852) 21–5131. Many Japanese specialties. ¥5,000 and up.

TAKAMATSU

Kawaramachi. 2–10–12 Kawaramachi, (0878) 31–2590. An expensive, but good, steak restaurant. ¥5,000 and up.

TOKUSHIMA

Kotoshidake. Good Japanese food. ¥5,000 and up.

New Tokushima. Keizai Center Bldg., Nishi Shinmachi, near the ropeway station. An excellent grill.

Shunjuen. Higashi Shinmachi, near the ropeway station. Chinese and Western food.

MATSUYAMA

Komadori. On main shopping street near the castle. Specializes in steak and Indian curry. ¥2,000–3,000.

NIGHT LIFE. Nightclubs, bars, and cabarets are to be found everywhere, but the good ones in western Japan are in the **Kobe** metropolitan area. By far the best is the *Kitano Night Club and Restaurant.* Situated on the mountainside above Kobe, it has plenty of parking space for cars and, if you can spare the time for it, a magnificent view of the city and harbor. The quality of the entertainment is high and, of course, so are the prices. A very suitable place for couples to go to, which is more than you can say for some of the others. In Kobe the *Moonlight,* 1, Kitanagata-dori, Ikuta-ku is very similar. The *Club Night and Day,* Shimoyamato-dori, not far from the Moonlight, is average. You can go as a couple if you like. *Club Cherry,* Sannomiya, is also good, and provides English-speaking hostesses. Newer is *Club Manhattan,* opposite the City Hall; it claims to be "good for your own relax" and to have "informal" prices. 6:00 to 11:30 P.M. A large and variegated collection of bars, clubs, and restaurants extends cheek-to-jowl for several blocks north from Sannomiya Station, e.g. *Copacabana,* with a Samba band from Brazil; *Uplands,* with draft beer and live music; and *Ken-Rich,* for country music. *Shekinah,* disco for adults, is on Kitanozaka-dori.

The only other place with any pretensions to providing high-class entertainment of this kind is **Hiroshima,** where *Hong Kong* is best.

Night life is quiet on the sleepy island of **Shikoku,** but it is amusing for foreigners with a taste for cultural exchange. Foreigners are so rare in this part of Japan that a friendly smile will elicit the most amazing responses (and always innocent ones) from people who desire to practice their English. One of the best ways to meet the people is to drop into one of the better bars or coffee shops in the four large cities on the island and let them tell you all about life in Shikoku.

KYUSHU

by
CLIFF PARFIT

Cliff Parfit is an educational adviser and director of the English Centre translation and teaching agency in Shimonseki.

For Kyushu, Japan's second most important island, the most significant recent incident has been the completion of the last part of the Chugoku expressway, allowing in vehicular traffic from the country's main population centers. An increase in tourism is confidently expected, and Kyushu is well prepared to meet tourist needs of all kinds. It often seems that Kyushu people in hotels and shops have just a little more time to be helpful and friendly in this most friendly of countries, so that tourists are sure of a warm welcome and a comfortable stay.

Kyushu was the site of Japan's first significant contact with the West, in the 16th century. The Portuguese, and later the Dutch, settled here, but the Portuguese were driven out, and Christianity, which was spreading across the whole island, was ruthlessly stamped out by the Bakufu government. The Dutch were tolerated, though confined to the tiny fan-shaped island of Deshima in Nagasaki. There they maintained a toehold in Japan until the opening of the country, which came shortly before the Meiji restoration of 1868.

Both Portuguese and Dutch have left their mark in Kyushu in the shape of historical monuments, museum exhibits, institutions, customs, and even products of the region.

Although it was Kyushu's Satsuma men, from the area around Kagoshima, who posed the most serious threat to the early Meiji government in a revolt led by Saigo Takamori, the struggle left little bitterness, and Satsuma gave Japan its greatest naval leaders, including the immortal admiral Togo (the Nelson of Japan).

Kyushu has some of the most easily accessible scenic beauty of Japan. There are beautiful islands off the coasts, nature parks with volcanic setpieces as in the Mt. Aso and Kagoshima areas, and hot springs in abundance, with all the atmosphere of holidays and honeymoons that is so typical of Japan's hot-spring areas. Beppu has the added attraction of bubbling sulphurous pools, crocodiles, and a famous hot-water geyser.

Perhaps the best introduction to the natural beauty of Kyushu might be obtained by a trip on the Trans-Kyushu Sightseeing Route (Yamanami Highway) from Beppu to Mt. Aso with extensions to Nagasaki.

People who have read the book or seen the film *Shogun* will want to see Hirado, Shimabara, Hirado Island, and Nagasaki to reenact the scenes of the book in their minds. They may well wonder whether anything of the old atmosphere still remains—and of course it does. In spite of the modern hotels and pylons, in many places you can find vignettes that will recall those stirring times.

But beautiful as they were, we would not wish to ride on one of those hard wooden saddles, or sit for hours in one of the tiny palanquins in which the local lords jogged their way to Edo (Tokyo). Modern Kyushu is comfortable and convenient, with reliable transport services and excellent hotels—the ideal place for a holiday.

Kyushu's Largest City—Kitakyushu

The huge industrial conurbation of Kitakyushu ("North Kyushu") has engulfed a number of smaller cities and towns. However, some of these, such as Moji, Kokura, and Kurosaki, manage to retain their individual character. Moji is a port and fishing area at the nearest point on Kyushu to Honshu, the main island of Japan. Many tourists visit the island from this spot through one of the Kanmon tunnels, over the fine Kanmon Bridge (one of the longest in the Orient), by ferry, or by ship. Visitors often come to Shimonoseki in western Honshu by ferries from Korea and China, and then go on to Kyushu. Moji is not a very interesting shopping center, but it has one of the island's oldest and finest golf courses. Kokura is Kyushu's most important shopping area. Kokura Castle is a reconstruction, but the impressive walls with their massive stones are original. The castle contains a museum of samurai weapons and armor as well as an exhibition of folk crafts. There are many good shops and department stores in the area around the castle. Another busy downtown area is Kurosaki, especially the section around the Sogo Department Store. But Kitakyushu is not all industry. There are some beautiful mountain regions not far out of town.

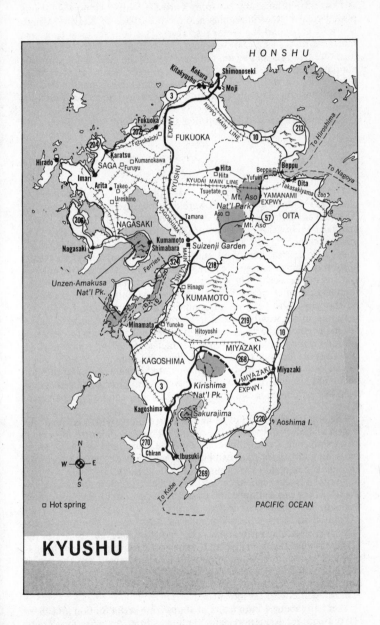

□ Hot spring

KYUSHU

Thirty-five minutes by car from Kurosaki Station along a well-sign-posted road in the mountains is the craft village of Kyushu Mingei Mura (it is beyond the Otani reservoir). This is a beautiful spot, and functions rather as a craft university for weaving, pottery, glasswork, furniture making, and so on, but it is open to the public on Saturdays, Sundays, and public holidays. The craftspeople work in full view of the public. There are also craft showrooms, restaurants, a small hotel, and a craft museum. The glass-blowing department under Mr. Funaki is especially famous.

Kita-kyushu has recently opened a fine modern monorail system.

Fukuoka

The Shinkansen line terminus is at Fukuoka (Hakata Station). At one time Fukuoka and Hakata were two towns separated by the river Nakagawa, Fukuoka being the samurai quarter, and Hakata the commercial area; but these divisions are now of historical interest only. The modern city of Fukuoka is by far the most important city of Kyushu. It has a dock area, a busy international airport, and a modern system of subway trains—surely one of the cleanest and best organized subway systems in the world. The subway connects with a huge underground shopping precinct known as Tenjin Shopping Centre, which is a mecca for shoppers. The Tenjin is air-conditioned, making it comfortable for shopping in all weathers, and it is connected by escalator to half a dozen or so fine department stores. It is well policed and is for pedestrians only, though a large car-park is attached. Smoking is not allowed, and dogs are not admitted, so it is clean and safe.

The local souvenirs are beautifully painted Hakata dolls, but they are bulky and easily broken, so other souvenirs might be preferred. There is no lack of choice in the many Fukuoka shops and large department stores.

The city is very proud of its fine new art gallery, which is one of the largest and best equipped in the country. There are frequent important loan exhibitions from galleries all over the world, and as the Japanese are willing to pay for such exhibitions, they really do draw the crowds. The gallery is beside the grounds of the old castle.

Fukuoka is an excellent center from which to explore all parts of the island. There are a number of guided bus tours. (You can get details from the bus depot near Hakata Station.)

Popular short trips from Fukuoka include those to the famous pottery towns: Karatsu for Karatsuyaki, Onda for Ondayaki, Imari for the world famous Imari china, and Arita for Aritayaki. Imari china is multicolored painted ware, often with designs drawn from the period of Dutch influence in Japan, and Arita is the place where (traditionally) translucent porcelain was first made in Japan. Typical Arita porcelain is milky white with designs in red.

There are about 4 kilometers of shops from Arita Station and there is a museum for Arita porcelain 10 minutes from Arita Station. Traditional sales of pottery are held at Imari April 1st through 5th and Arita May 1st through 5th each year. Prices are usually half shop prices.

Kumamoto

Kumamoto is roughly in the center of the island about 1½ hours by car from Fukuoka. Kumamoto city is a busy modern city, but it has been partially destroyed several times in its checkered history.

Kumamoto Castle, originally built in 1601, was reconstructed in 1960 and the walls heavily restored, but the site is perfect; and, musing on the cyclopean masonry of the defense works, one can readily imagine how life might have been for the daimyo and his court in the timeless days before Japan was dragged into competition with the industrial world. The keep of the castle contains a fine collection of ancient Japanese weapons, and other relics of bygone lords of the castle.

Kumamoto's Suizenji Garden is one of the most famous gardens of Japan (the two others are in Kanazawa and Okayama). Suizenji is a Momoyama-style garden of hillocks, rocks, pine trees and water. By the artificial lake is a teahouse where one may watch the tea ceremony and drink frothy green tea while enjoying the beauty of the garden.

Madame Butterfly City

There is an inherent danger in visiting Nagasaki, as the charm and haunting beauty of Japan's first international city may cause the visitor to fall in love, or to be disappointed in the rest of Kyushu, or of Japan, for that matter. The beauty, as in all Japanese urban areas, comes in little patches surrounded by great expanses of ugly factories and poorly designed buildings and shops.

There is no getting away from Cho-cho san in Nagasaki. There's a statue, and she appears on advertising material and shop signs. Of course she is a fictional character; but in Pierre Loti's famous book *Madame Chrysanthème* we can glimpse a little of Lt. Pinkerton's heartless viewpoint in Loti's real-life descriptions of the "rent-a-wife" service in early Meiji-era Nagasaki.

The city is superbly sited on a virtually landlocked harbor with buildings perched on the hillsides all around. The best-known house is certainly the lovingly-preserved Glover Mansion. Thomas Glover was one of the first English traders in 19th-century Japan. In his later years he used to hint darkly that it was he who had won the war against the Tokugawa Shogunate because he had supplied the modern-style rifles with which the Satsuma and Choshu troops easily defeated the much larger, but poorly equipped, Tokugawa armies.

Glover was no Lt. Pinkerton. A glance at the comfortable house in which he lived with his highly respected Japanese wife will show that he had come to Japan to stay. The excellent view from this site includes the harbor entrance, and across the way, the huge Mitsubishi shipyards (this is what the atom bombs were aiming at, but missed). Perhaps the moving walkways in the otherwise beautiful garden add a rather bizarre touch, but they make it possible for visitors to see the whole of Nagasaki's Meiji village in comfort. In addition to Glover's house, there are a number of other fine old houses of the Meiji period in an

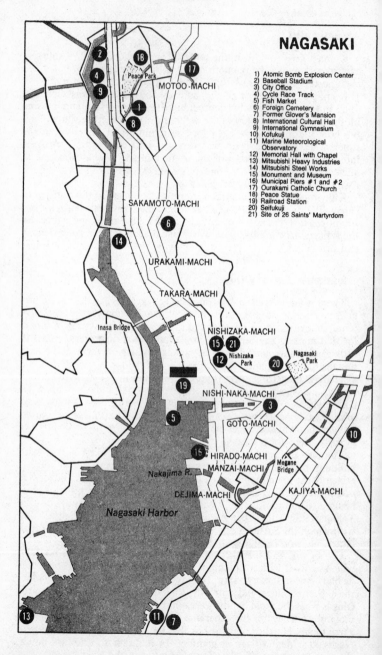

NAGASAKI

1) Atomic Bomb Explosion Center
2) Baseball Stadium
3) City Office
4) Cycle Race Track
5) Fish Market
6) Foreign Cemetery
7) Former Glover's Mansion
8) International Cultural Hall
9) International Gymnasium
10) Kofukuji
11) Marine Meteorological
    Observatory
12) Memorial Hall with Chapel
13) Mitsubishi Heavy Industries
14) Mitsubishi Steel Works
15) Monument and Museum
16) Municipal Piers #1 and #2
17) Ourakami Catholic Church
18) Peace Statue
19) Railroad Station
20) Seifukuji
21) Site of 26 Saints' Martyrdom

Peace Park

MOTOO-MACHI

SAKAMOTO-MACHI

URAKAMI-MACHI

TAKARA-MACHI

NISHIZAKA-MACHI

Nishizaka Park

Nagasaki Park

NISHI-NAKA-MACHI

GOTO-MACHI

HIRADO-MACHI

MANZAI-MACHI

Nakajima R.

Megane Bridge

DEJIMA-MACHI

KAJIYA-MACHI

Nagasaki Harbor

Inasa Bridge

excellent state of preservation, and furnished with pieces from the period. Some have been moved here from other locations in the city.

The Sixteenth Mansion, on the route out of the Glover estate, is reputed to be the oldest Western-style wooden house in Japan (built 1860). Well worth a visit, it contains a fine collection of early Christian relics, together with a collection of Dutch and early Meiji glassware and pottery.

The Oura church, farther down the street, was built in 1864 and is the oldest Gothic-style church in Japan. It was built in memory of twenty-six Japanese Christian saints who were crucified in 1596 during the first wave of anti-Christian persecutions.

The Portuguese, and later the Dutch, were confined to the tiny fan-shaped island of Dejima. This was once on the coast, but is now some distance inland. Here, by an astonishing freak of fortune, the land developers and the atom bomb have spared one of the original Dutch houses of the settlement. Though sadly neglected, this unique relic should not be missed by anyone interested in the history of the area. Near Dejima are "The Dutch Slopes." These ancient stone-paved streets, with their colonial style houses are the oldest streets of the city.

Though living and trading under tight control, the Dutch provided the only channel through which modern medical and other knowledge came into Japan. The doctors of this tiny outpost also gave the world its most reliable early information on Japan. The fine books by Kaempfer, Thunberg, and Siebold are still important standard works on Japan.

Modern Nagasaki, of course, has its attractions. There is a splendid shopping center, and the Hamacho arcade is equipped with a sliding roof for all-weather shopping. There are, in addition, the usual large department stores found in most other Japanese cities.

The principal souvenirs of the area are objects fashioned from turtle shell, and though in some cases it seems sad that turtles should have been slaughtered to produce such tasteless junk, there are items such as the traditional combs in which the material has been used with elegance and skill.

Most visitors also take away a box of Castella, a plain spongecake made originally in Castille but brought to Japan by the Portuguese. The boxes are decorated with *namban* pictures of the Portuguese merchants and priests with their black servants.

An essential visit for all political leaders who may come to the area is to the atom bomb exhibition in the International Cultural Hall at Urakami, where they may see what most of the civilized world may look like if their statesmanship fails. The Roman Catholic Cathedral of Urakami is where the second atomic bomb exploded on August 9, 1945. Today visitors can see the new Urakami Cathedral and the Peace Park with its massive symbolic statue commemorating the estimated 75,000 dead from the bomb.

Other well-known sights of Nagasaki are the Spectacle Bridge (Megane-bashi), built in 1634 over the Nakashima River; Sofukuji, the Chinese-style temple dating from 1629; and Suwa Shrine, a Shinto shrine that still maintains a white horse, which may only be ridden by one of the gods. Various events, such as demonstration tea ceremonies and pop music shows, are held in Suwa Park during the year.

Near the port area one can find the night spots of Nagasaki. Bills at "hostess bars" tend to be geared to the pockets of expense-account company men or sailors with several months' pay, so caution is urged; but the atmosphere of the area, with its winking lights, is quite friendly, and the tiny restaurants for eels or noodles are delightful and not too expensive.

Many of Japan's Christians live in the Nagasaki area. In spite of decades of persecution, which extended into the Meiji Period, Christianity was never completely wiped out, and these days Christian institutions abound in Nagasaki. Another place of early Christian interest in the same part of Kyushu is the island of Hirado. About 2 hours by car, north along a pleasant road from Nagasaki. These days it is reached via a handsome modern bridge. It has a finely sited castle, a Dutch bridge, a Dutch wall, and other relics; but by far the most impressive and interesting feature is the superb Matsuura Museum housed in the former residence of the Matsuura family, which once ruled the island. The museum is filled with magnificent exhibits, formerly the household property of the lord. Also, a new attraction in Nagasaki is the Holland Village, complete with a windmill, and offering Dutch goods and foods.

Unzen and Amakusa National Park is an area of natural beauty in Nagasaki Prefecture. There are golf courses, camping sites, horse-riding tracks, tennis courts, and so on. In early summer one can enjoy the beauty of the azaleas, in fall the colors of the "fire" maples, and in winter the patterns of frost in the trees in higher spots. There are hotels to suit all pockets.

Beppu—A Geothermal City

Beppu, situated on Kyushu's northeastern coastline, seems to have everything—sea, mountains, streams, fresh air, and hot springs—it really deserves better architecture and town planning. However, it's a very comfortable place. Invalids come from all over Japan for the hot-spring baths, but even if you are perfectly well, a bath in hot water bubbling from the depths of the earth is a most enjoyable experience.

This is the place for a quiet holiday. The impressive sights of Beppu can be seen in a day. They are known locally as "hells." There is a hot geyser that erupts at 25-minute intervals, a "sea" pool, a pool of "blood," in which the water is colored by mineral deposits, and several bubbling pools. The local taxi drivers are prepared to make a round-trip at a reasonable price that should be agreed upon beforehand. Fortunately in Japan, visitors are spared the nuisance of tipping, and there is less fear of a "rip-off" at every turn than in almost any other country in the world.

The thing to do in Beppu is to eat some eggs that have been boiled in the waters of the "Umi-jigoku" or "Sea Hell." They are delicious.

There are hotels here to suit all tastes. The European-style rooms are adequate. One hotel, The Suginoi, is so large that a bus service is run between the two main wings. The well-run hotel museum is excellent, showing antiquities from the Edo Period, armor, picture scrolls, pottery, lacquerware, and other items. The museum shop is also highly recommended. All the hotels have geothermal baths and there are treatment centers for many complaints. Patients going to Beppu for treatment can get reliable information and excellent advice from Beppu City Hall, near the yacht harbor in south Beppu.

Beppu Marine Aquarium (at the foot of Takasaki-yama) is one of the largest in Japan, and has a spectacular display of fish; though perhaps the most surprising sight is the young woman who enters one of the main tanks in flippers and mask to feed fish almost as big as herself.

For those interested in monkeys, and who don't mind the smell, there is a mountain with three troops of semiwild monkeys at Takasaki. There is also the African Safari Park at Ajimu Kogen, about 1 hour by car northwest of Beppu.

The mountain scenery around Beppu is superb. At Kijima Kogen, 45 minutes from Kitahama Station in Beppu, there is a mountain resort center with a play park for children, a hotel, and a huge restaurant. It can hardly be said to contribute to the beauty of the area, but it is very convenient. The restaurant specialty is barbecued wild boar meat grilled on charcoal grills at the table.

Sports of the area include deep-sea fishing, hang gliding, and golf. Information can be obtained in English from the local tourist office.

The Mount Aso Area

There is fine scenery in this area, but though Mt. Aso, situated southwest of Beppu, is the largest active volcano in the world, with a crater of about 20 kilometers in diameter, it is not a beautiful mountain. It is perhaps best seen from a distance. Ropeways go to points near enough to the crater for most purposes, and there is a mountain bus service. Walkers who enter the off-limit areas are warned that there is always the risk of danger from noxious gases. People have been killed by the volcano within recent memory.

For naturalists (particularly bird lovers) this is an area of great interest, but the wild boars that formerly inhabited the area in great numbers must be extremely uncommon these days. The only boars normally seen are stuffed specimens in the wild boar restaurants.

The area is crossed by the Trans-Kyushu or Yamanami Highway, from which one can enjoy the scenery—mile after mile of grassy uplands.

Miyazaki

Miyazaki is on the southeast coast of Kyushu, and therefore enjoys very favorable weather for much of the year. With its palm-lined roads, it is a typical holiday resort. Children particularly may enjoy a holiday in Miyazaki. It has camel rides and a huge amusement park. There are also beautiful, scrupulously clean beaches (unusual these days in Japan). Other places of interest include a safari park, the fascinating Saboten Cactus Garden, and a subtropical horticultural garden. Tiny Aoshima island, about 13 miles away and reached by a causeway, is a geological curiosity with its unusual "washboard" formation rocks. A similar geological formation can be found on several parts of the nearby coastline.

Miyazaki can be very hot indeed during mid-summer; take plenty of lotion if you plan any sunbathing.

The Miyazaki Safari Park is at Sadohara. It seems that tropical animals live comfortably in this part of Japan, as common species breed here without difficulty. The park is much the same as other safari parks, but very well run.

At Oyodogawa River there is a beautiful golf course within driving range of the ocean.

On warm summer evenings, downtown Miyazaki is an exciting place, full of winking neon lights, but be prepared for a whopping bill if you spend time in one of those friendly hostess bars.

With its warm climate, good hotels, and diverse attractions, Miyazaki is one of the best places in Japan to go for a late seaside holiday when the rest of mainland Japan is cold.

Kagoshima

Often referred to as the "Naples of the Orient," Kagoshima enjoys a sunny spot at the southern end of Kyushu. For many Kagoshima people, their introduction to the Western world came in 1863 when a British fleet shelled the town. Many ships were sunk, and much of the town was destroyed. Astonishing to relate, this action was not resented by the Satsuma clan (the great clan of the area, headed by the Shimazu family). It wasn't long before their chief men were cheerfully plotting with the British legation staff against the Bakufu government so soon to be replaced by leaders from Satsuma and Choshu in the first Meiji government.

Satsuma men held the chief posts in the Meiji navy, where British naval influence remained strong. Admiral Togo, the victor of the Battle of Tsushima, in which the Russian Fleet was destroyed in 1905, was a Satsuma man. He was trained in an English naval academy. His ships, including his flagship the *Mikasa,* which can still be seen at Yokosuka dockyard south of Tokyo, were built in English shipyards.

Of course Kagoshisma has uniforms and personal objects that belonged to Togo, as well as those connected with Takamori Saigo, one of the founders of the Meiji state, who was once called a rebel, but has many fans among Japanese people.

Things to see in Kagoshima include the elegant Shimazu museum, Shokoshuseikan, which was a stone-built Meiji-era machine factory; the Iso Teien, the villa of the Shimazu family; and the Samurai residences in Chiran, midway between Kagoshima and Ibusuki.

You can also visit Mt. Sakurajima, a 20-minute ferry ride from Kagoshima Port's Sakurajima Pier. Shopkeepers in Kagoshima sometimes have to sweep up the fine volcanic dust that still comes from this active volcano. The mountain with its plume of smoke can be seen from most parts of the city.

About 45 kilometers south of Kagoshima at Ibusuki there are twenty different hot springs. In Surigahama Beach, a 5-minute bus ride from

Ibusuki Station, there are special slimming baths in which the bather is covered in hot sand. As in Beppu, medical advice is available. It is warm and comfortable throughout the year in this corner of Japan.

Kirishima National Park is between Kagoshima and Miyazaki (go by the Kirishima "Sky Line" toll road). It's famous for azaleas in summer, and maples in autumn.

PRACTICAL INFORMATION FOR KYUSHU

WHEN TO GO. In summer much of Kyushu has subtropical weather, but even so it is quite pleasant along the coastline where there is a breeze from the sea. June and part of July is apt to be wet and muggy as in the rest of Japan, and in September there is a risk of typhoons, but October and November are usually beautiful months. In South Kyushu even early December can be a pleasant month for a holiday.

HOW TO GET THERE. By train. The gateway to Kyushu is Shimonoseki on the western tip of Honshu. The Shinkansen route leads through Shimonoseki and the Kanmon tunnel to Kokura and Hakata, with links to other parts of the island. The Shinkansen from Osaka to Fukuoka takes 3 hours and 20 minutes. Hakata can be reached from Tokyo in under 7 hours by Shinkansen. Nagasaki is 2½ hours from Hakata by limited express, and Kagoshima is 6 hours from Hakata.

By car. Motorists can pass over the massive Kanmon Bridge or through the Kanmon road tunnel.

By air. There are international airports at Fukuoka and Kagoshima, with flights from Hong Kong, Formosa (Taiwan), Guam, and Hawaii into Fukuoka. There are other airports for domestic flights at Kita-Kyushu, Nagasaki, Kumamoto, Miyazaki, and Oita.

Flight times are about 1 hour 40 minutes from Tokyo to Fukuoka and about an hour from Osaka to Fukuoka.

From Tokyo to Kagoshima the flight time is 1 hour 45 minutes, while the time from Osaka to Kagoshima is 1 hour 10 minutes.

By boat. There are excellent ferry services to and from Kagoshima, Nagasaki, Beppu, and Oita. The car ferry services provide a restful start and finish to a motoring holiday in Kyushu. The boats are comfortable and air-conditioned though often crowded at peak holiday times. Kobe to Kagoshima is 14 hours, Nagoya to Oita 20 hours, Kawasaki (near Tokyo) to Hosojima (Miyazaki Prefecture) 26 hours. Bookings may be made through local travel agents who can also advise on schedules that vary with seasons.

Regular international ferry services connect Pusan in Korea with Shimonoseki, which is a convenient junction for visitors planning a shopping holiday in Fukuoka.

TELEPHONES. As in the rest of Japan, there are telephones within easy reach all over Kyushu. The following are the area codes for some of the main cities: Beppu, 0977; Fukuoka, 092; Imari, 09552; Kagoshima, 0992;

Kitakyushu, 093; Kumamoto, 0963; Miyazaki, 0985; Nagasaki, 0958; Oita, 0975; Saga, 0952; Sasebo, 0956.

Emergencies. Police 110; Fire 119. Spoken English is very poor on the whole, however the operators may understand *Fire!* or *Police!* and the address if given very carefully.

HOTELS & INNS. Western-Style Hotels. The hotels listed have adequate Western-style accommodation. Most rooms are with bath and toilet and there is often a television and a refrigerator—even in the cheaper rooms. Most larger hotels offer a choice of Western-style of Japanese breakfast.

Business Hotels. The dividing line between normal hotels and business hotels is not always absolutely clear, but is becoming more so as more large business hotels are being built. They are particularly popular with businessmen and young people, and have lots of single rooms.

The accommodation is fairly basic, but the tiny rooms invariably have private bath and toilet. They usually have a television, telephone, and refrigerator as well. No service is offered; patrons have to carry their own luggage. Japanese breakfast is often available but Western-style breakfast more seldom. Prices are reasonable. Location is usually convenient rather than beautiful.

Japanese-style Hotels & Inns (Ryokan). For a change of atmosphere, a stay at a Japanese inn is recommended. You will sleep on the tatami with Japanese-style bedding (futon). The smaller inns will probably not have a private bath, but you can feel very near to traditional Japan. It is customary to give a tip (cha-dai) at the start of your stay—perhaps ¥1,000 when the maid brings in the obligatory tea and cakes on your arrival.

Prices are not cheap, but might work out favorably for a family occupying one large room. Prices normally include two meals.

Roadside Hotels & Motels. Travelers by car may often see a string of colored lights or a gaudy sign at the roadside in most places in Japan. These indicate the roadside hotels and motels. Some of these are the so-called "love" hotels. They usually offer a garage next to a simple room with a bathroom and toilet. Pay television and refrigerator with beer, soft drinks, etc., for sale, are standard. For travelers on a budget (particularly families) they offer good value. At most hotels of all grades a sleeping kimono is available free of charge, so pajamas are not needed. (Japanese families are reluctant to use these hotels.)

Kokumin Shukusha (Japanese National Hotels). These are government-owned hotels. They are a little simpler in standards than normal hotels and there are usually communal baths. They are often used for group tours but individual rooms are available. Prices might be attractive for a family group occupying one large room. In addition to those we list, there are about forty others on Kyushu. Inquiries through JTB.

Kokumin Kyukamura (also called Kokumin Kyukason) are rather similar organizations, but often provide camping space. Good sports facilities usually are available. These are excellent for cheap family vacations, and are busiest during school holidays.

Youth Hostels. In Japan these are clean and friendly but most facilities are communal. It is essential that guests pay close attention to the rules of the Japanese Y.H.A. On the whole the hostels are as good as those of any country in the world, and they are cleaner than average. Bookings may sometimes be made through JTB.

About Costs. Business hotels cost *about* ¥5,000 per night (no breakfast); Japanese inns vary. They usually provide an evening meal and breakfast. Single about ¥8,000. If you travel with a family it is possible to stay cheaper at an inn (all sleeping on tatami in a single room). Large hotels cost about ¥6,000–10,000 per night (double rooms cheaper). Information on accommodations geared to your budget can be provided at the station information centers. Local tourist information offices in JNR stations are also helpful in suiting the accommodations to individual pockets.

Major credit cards are accepted by most large hotels, but on the whole they are not yet popular, especially in smaller hotels and inns. Fortunately, there is little fear in Japan of pickpockets or muggers, so it isn't dangerous to carry cash.

Getting There. You will want to telephone, or have someone who speaks Japanese telephone your destination for directions.

WESTERN-STYLE

Beppu, Oita and Mt. Aso National Park

Most Beppu hotels have excellent hot spring baths available free to guests.

Aso Kanko Hotel. 40 minutes by car from Kumamoto station and 35 minutes from Kumamoto airport; 15 minutes from Mt. Aso. Convenient for touring in the Mt. Aso National Park.

Beppu New Grand Hotel. 20 minutes by car from Beppu Station; (0977) 22–1161. 111 rooms. Situated right in the center of Kijima Kogen. Close to the amusement area and golf course.

Hotel Hakuun Sanso. 8 minutes by car from Beppu Station; (0977) 23–1151. Comfortable hotel. 138 rooms.

Kamenoi Hotel. 3 minutes by car from Beppu Station; (0977) 22–3301. A comfortable hotel in central Beppu. 88 rooms.

Kuju Lakeside Hotel. 50 minutes by car from Beppu Station and on the Yamanami Highway; (09778) 4–3151. 71 rooms. A lakeside, mountain hotel. Beautiful scenery.

Ninago Hotel. 5 minutes on foot from Beppu Station; (0977) 22–1111. 74 rooms. Old established hotel. Conveniently situated.

Oita Daiichi Hotel. 1 minute from Oita Station; (0975) 36–1388. 139 rooms.

Oita Nishitetsu Grand Hotel. 5 minutes by car from Oita Station. (0975) 36–1181. Convenient for trips to Mt. Aso and Beppu. 219 rooms.

Suginoi Hotel. 8 minutes by car from Beppu Station; (0977) 24–1141. A huge hotel beautifully situated on Kankaiji Hill overlooking Beppu Bay. 608 rooms. The hotel has a very large and busy shop, an equally big amusement center, and a well-run museum. Fine hot spring baths.

Fukuoka City (includes Hakata)

Hakata Miyako Hotel. Facing Hakata Station and convenient to the business area of the city; (092) 441–3111. 269 rooms with 210 singles. Modern but not expensive.

Hakata Shiroyama Hotel. In the center of downtown Fukuoka; (092) 281–2211. 126 rooms. There is a fine night view of the city from the sky lounge.

Hakata Tokyu Hotel. In the Tenjin area (Central Hakata) and well up to Tokyu hotel standards; (092) 781–7111. 226 rooms.

Hakata Zen-Nikku Hotel. Convenient to Hakata Station; (092) 471–7111. An All Nippon Airways hotel. 360 rooms with 215 singles. Modern and comfortable.

Hotel New Otani Hakata. 5 minutes from Hakata Station; (092) 714–1111. Over 400 rooms. *Sky Lounge* restaurant and seven other restaurants, and a shopping plaza. Every comfort. Parking for 430 cars.

Lions Hotel. 7 minutes on foot from Hakata Station; (092) 451–7711. 88 rooms. Specially recommended for members of the worldwide association of Lions Clubs.

Nishitetsu Grand Hotel. 10 minutes by car from Hakata Station but near the Fukuoka (private) railway station; (092) 771–7171. 308 rooms. Old, established.

Station Plaza. A handy hotel. 1 minute from Hakata Station; (092) 431–1211. 248 rooms.

Takakura Hotel Fukuoka. 10 minutes by car from Hakata Station in a quiet residential area; (092) 731–1661. 60 rooms.

Tokyo Dai-ichi Hotel Fukuoka. 5 minutes by car from Hakata Station; (092) 281–3311. 229 rooms. Not expensive.

YWCA Hotel. 15 minutes by car from Hakata Station; (092) 741–6485. 30 rooms. English-speaking staff.

Kagoshima

Kagoshima Tokyu Hotel. 10 minutes by car from Nishi-Kagoshima Station; (0992) 57–2411. 206 rooms. This hotel has an excellent view of Sakurajima Volcano.

Kagoshima Hayashida Hotel. 3 minutes by car from Nishi-Kagoshima Station; (0992) 24–4111. 200 rooms. This hotel is situated right in the center of Kagoshima. Close to the business and shopping district.

Kagoshima Sun Royal. 10 minutes by car from Nishi-Kagoshima Station. 50 minutes by car from Kagoshima Airport; (0992) 53–2020. 337 rooms. This hotel has a marine restaurant (5 mins on foot from the hotel) and you can see fish (regardless of their fate) enjoying themselves as you dine.

Shiroyama Kanko Hotel. 10 minutes by car from Nishi-Kagoshima Station; (0992) 24–2211. 621 rooms. This hotel is situated on Shiroyama Mountain and has a wonderful view of the Sakurajima Volcano. The restaurants are excellent. Recommended.

Kita-Kyushu City (includes Kokura)

Kokura Hotel. Central Kokura, convenient to the shopping center; (092) 531–1151. 101 rooms. It has a friendly restaurant and coffee bar for footworn shoppers.

Kokura Station Hotel. Very close to Kokura Station. (093) 521–5031. 182 rooms. Reasonable.

Kokura Tokyu Inn. 8 minutes on foot from Kokura Station; (093) 521–0109. Comfortable hotel. 190 rooms. Normal Tokyu standards.

New Tagawa Hotel. In the center of Kokura. 3 minutes by car from Kokura Station; (093) 521–3831. The Japanese-style garden is famous.

Sun Sky Hotel. 5 minutes by car from Kokura Station and close to the Kita-Kyushu expressway exit; (093) 521–0123. 167 rooms. There is a splendid view of the mountains from the sky lounge.

Kumamoto

Kumamoto Hotel Castle. Pleasantly situated by the castle grounds; (0963) 53–6111. 225 rooms.

New Sky Hotel. 3 minutes by car from the station; (0963) 53–2111. 201 rooms. Situated near the Kumamoto Castle, Suizenji Park and other places of interest.

Togiya Hotel. 5 minutes by car from Kumamoto Station. (0963) 54–3131. 65 rooms. Special arrangements available for long stays.

Miyazaki

Hotel Plaza Miyazaki. 5 minutes by car from Miyazaki Station. 20 minutes by car from Miyazaki airport; (0985) 27–1111. 183 rooms. Fine sky restaurant.

Hotel Phoenix. 2 minutes by car from Miyazaki Station; (0985) 23–6111. 118 rooms. Close to downtown Miyazaki. Elegant modern hotel.

Miyazaki Kanko Hotel. 5 minutes by car from Miyazaki Station; (0985) 27-1212. 200 rooms. Situated along the Oyodo River and the center of the city; close to the business and shopping center.

Seaside Hotel Phoenix. 15 minutes by car from Miyazaki Station; (0985) 39-1111. 193 rooms. Close to all the tourist spots. Excellent service. International conference hall and fine sky restaurant. Next to Phoenix Country Club golf course.

Nagasaki

Bus Terminal Hotel. 5 minutes by car from the station and close to the bus terminal; (0958) 21-4111. 161 rooms. Reasonable prices.

Harbour Inn Nagasaki. 2 minutes by car from the station. (0958) 27-1111. 175 rooms. Recommended.

Nagasaki Grand Hotel. 5 minutes by car from the station. (0958) 23-1234. Convenient for downtown Nagasaki. 70 rooms.

Nagasaki Tokyu Hotel. 7 minutes by car from the station, near the Glover Mansion; (0958) 25-1501. Fine modern hotel with every convenience. 214 rooms. Excellent restaurant with seafood specialties.

New Nagasaki Hotel. A handy hotel. 2 minutes walk from the station; (0958) 26-6161. 60 rooms.

New Urakami Hotel. 3 minutes walk from Urakami Station; (0958) 45-1117. 89 rooms. Convenient for Peace Park.

Unzen Kanko Chalet Hotel. 60 minutes by car from Isahaya Station. 90 minutes by car from Nagasaki Airport; (095773) 3263. 2,165 ft. above sea level in the National Park. 65 rooms.

Saga

Hotel New Otani Saga. 10 minutes by car from Saga Station; (0952) 23-1111. Fine hotel. Well situated facing the remains of the castle. 100 rooms.

Saga Tokyu Inn. A convenient hotel. 1 minute on foot from Saga Station. (0952) 29-0109. 134 rooms. Normal Tokyu Hotel standards.

BUSINESS HOTELS

Beppu & Oita

Beppu Daiichi Hotel. 1 minute on foot from Beppu Station; (0977) 24-6311. 62 rooms.

Business Hotel New Hayashi. 1 minute on foot from Beppu Station; (0977) 24-5252. 63 rooms.

Business Hotel Oita. 8 minutes on foot from Oita Station. (0975) 32-6111. 87 rooms.

Groria Hotel. 3 minutes by car from Oita Station. (0975) 34-6421. 100 rooms.

Hokke Club Oita. 7 minutes on foot from Oita Station. (0975) 32-1121. 205 rooms.

Nippaku Hotel. 3 minutes by car from Beppu Station; (0977) 23-2291. 73 rooms.

Oita Daiichi Oriental Hotel. 10 minutes on foot from Oita Station. (0975) 32-8238. 100 rooms.

Hakata

Ark Hotel Hakata. 10 minutes by car from Hakata Station; (092) 781-2551. 360 rooms.

Business Hotel Hakata Nichibo. 7 minutes on foot from Hakata Station; (092) 441-7411. 120 rooms.

Daimyo Personal Hotel. 15 minutes by car from Hakata Station. (092) 711–9111. 179 rooms.

Hakata Daiichi Hotel. 1 minute on foot from Hakata Station. (092) 411–3501. 125 rooms.

Hakata Green Hotel. 2 minutes on foot from Hakata Station; (092) 451–4111. 500 rooms.

Hakata Park Hotel. 5 minutes on foot from Hakata Station; (092) 451–1151. 174 rooms.

Hokke Club Fukuoka. 7 minutes on foot from Fukuoka Station. (092) 271–3171. 292 rooms.

Mitsui Urban Hotel Fukuoka. 7 minutes on foot from Hakata Station; (092) 451–5111. 310 rooms.

New Reisenkaku Hotel. 5 minutes on foot from Hakata Station. (092) 441–8601. 213 rooms.

Sun Life Hotel. 1 minute on foot from Hakata Station. (092) 473–7111. 240 rooms.

Tokyo Daiichi Hotel Fukuoka. 7 minutes by car from Hakata Station; (092) 281–3311. 221 rooms.

Kagoshima

Hokke Club Kagoshima. 3 minutes by car from Nishi Kagoshima Station; (0992) 26–0011. 129 rooms.

Hotel New Nishino. 8 minutes by car from Nishi Kagoshima Station; (0992) 24–3232. 90 rooms.

Kagoshima Gasthof. 4 minutes on foot from Nishi Kagoshima Station; (0992) 52–1401. 87 rooms.

Kagoshima Kuko Hotel. Next to the Kagoshima Airport; (09955) 8–2331. 115 rooms.

Station Hotel New Kagoshima. 3 minutes on foot from Nishi Kagoshima Station; (0992) 53–5353. 117 rooms.

Kokura

Kita-Kyushu Daiichi Hotel. 5 minutes by car from Kokura Station. (093) 551–7331. 105 rooms.

Kyushu Rico Hotel. 2 minutes on foot from Kokura Station; (093) 521–4444. 265 rooms.

Tetsubil Hotel. 5 minutes on foot from Kokura Station; (093) 551–6231. 80 rooms.

Yutaka Business Hotel. 2 minutes on foot from Kokura Station; (093) 511–0101. 96 rooms.

Kumamoto

Businessman Shin-Kumamoto Hotel. 10 minutes by car from Kumamoto Station; (0963) 64–6151. 60 rooms.

Hotel Sun Route Kumamoto. 10 minutes by car from Kumamoto Station; (0963) 22–2211. 88 rooms.

Hokke Club Kumamoto. 5 minutes by car from Kumamoto Station. (0963) 22–5001. 153 rooms.

Kumamoto Business Hotel. 1 minute by car from Suizenji Station; (0963) 84–1144. 87 rooms.

Kumamoto Daiichi Hotel. 5 minutes on foot from Kumamoto Station; (0963) 25–5151. 84 rooms.

Kumamoto Tokyu Inn. 5 minutes by car from Kumamoto Station; (0963) 22–0109. 140 rooms.

Miyazaki

Hotel Sun Route Miyazaki. 10 minutes by car from Miyazaki Station; (0985) 53–1313. 105 rooms.

Miyazaki Business Hotel. 5 minutes by car from Miyazaki Station; (0985) 28–6161. 188 rooms.

Miyazaki Daiichi Hotel. 5 minutes by car from Miyazaki Station; (0985) 24–8501. 152 rooms.

Miyazaki Green Hotel. 6 minutes by car from Miyazaki Station; (0985) 26–1571. 74 rooms.

Miyazaki Leman Hotel. 3 minutes by car from Minami Miyazaki Station; (0985) 53–1131. 105 rooms.

Miyazaki Oriental Hotel. 1 minute on foot from Miyazaki Station; (0985) 27–3111. 96 rooms.

Sunnyside Hotel. 3 minutes by car from Miyazaki Station; (0985) 25–3822. 82 rooms.

Nagasaki

Business Hotel Mitsubishi Kaikan. 2 minutes by car from Nagasaki Station; (0958) 24–4176. 76 rooms.

Business Hotel Motofuna. 5 minutes on foot from Nagasaki Station; (0958) 21–2400. 86 rooms.

Business Hotel New Port. 10 minutes on foot from Nagasaki Station; (0958) 21–0221. 75 rooms.

Hotel Nakajima Kaikan. 4 minutes by car from Nagasaki Station. (0958) 21–6060. 80 rooms.

Nagasaki Plaza Hotel. 7 minutes on foot from Nagasaki Station; (0958) 24–5151. 60 rooms.

New Urakami Hotel. 5 minutes by car from Nagasaki Station; (0958) 45–1117. 89 rooms.

JAPANESE INNS (RYOKAN)

Beppu

Hotel New Showaen. 0977–22–3211. Has a beautiful Japanese garden. The seafood is excellent.

Fukue City

Suisen Kaku. 5 minutes on foot from the harbor; 09597–2–2161. The inn is in the old castle grounds. It has the atmosphere of an ancient castle.

Kagoshima City

Hotel Shusuien. 09932–3–4141. There is a huge bath. Local Satsuma cooking is the speciality of the house.

Hotel Tsurumaru. 0992–22–4131. Speciality is lobster dishes.

Karatsu City

Ryokan Jonaikaku. 09557–2–4151. Serves excellent seafood.

Kitakyushu

Hotel New Tagawa. 10 minutes on foot from Kokura station; 093–521–3831. This hotel has a beautiful Japanese-style garden.

Kumamoto City

Hotel Tsukasa Honten. 10 minutes by car from Kumamoto Station; 0963–52–5101. Located in the shopping center.

Miyazaki

Takachiho. Next to Takachiho shrine; 09827–2–3232. An excellent place to enjoy fresh river fish.

Takeo Hot Spring

Nakamasu Ryokan. 09542–2–3118. This is a long-established inn. It has an alkaline spring and is decorated with antique pottery.

Ureshino Hot Spring. 09554–3–1100. This inn has a garden bath. During summer, a swimming pool is available.

Unzen Hot Spring

Unzen Miyazaki Ryokan. 095773–3331. Near the entrance of the "hell." There is a Japanese garden. Some Western rooms are available.

Yanagawa City

Ohana. 09447–3–2189. The house once belonged to the local daimyo. There is a spring bath in the house. There are also many treasures of former times, and the garden is the haunt of wild ducks.

HOLIDAY VILLAGES (KOKUMIN KYUKAMURA)

Ibusuki Kokumin Kyukason. 10 minutes by bus from Ibusuki Station; (09932) 2–3211. North of Ibusuki hot spring, near the beach. Tennis courts are available.

Minami Aso Kokumin Kyukason. 10 minutes by bus from Takamori Station; (09676) 2–2111. Conveniently situated for touring Kumamoto, Aso, Takachiho, and Miyazaki.

Shikanoshima Kokumin Kyukason. 1 hr 10 mins by bus from Hakata Station; (092) 603–6631. Near the beach; 4 tennis courts.

Unzen Kokumin Kyukason. By bus from Isahaya Station. Change at Obama and get off at Suwano-ike; (09577) 4–9131. Near Suwanoike Lake, close to Unzen hot spring resort.

KOKUMIN-SHUKUSHA

Aoshima. 2–12–36, Aoshima, Miyazaki City, Miyazaki; (0985) 65–1533.

Kaimonso. 5390 Kawajiri, Kaimon-cho, Ibusuki-gun, Kagoshima; (09332) 3151.

Nakamura. 1442–5, Bochu, Aso-cho, Aso-gun, Kumamoto; (09673) 4–0317.

Yataro Inn. 2–1 Futocho, Nagasaki City; (0958) 21–8269.

Yobiko Lodge. 1413 Onoue, Yobiko-cho, Higashi Matsuura-gun, Saga; (09558) 2–3006.

Yufu Sanso. 2927–1 Kawakami, Yufuin-cho, Oita-gun, Oita; (09778) 4–2105.

Yurin so. 320 Unzen, Obama-cho, Minami Takaki-gun, Nagasaki; (095773) 3355.

 HEALTH SPAS AND BATHHOUSES. The principal health spa with modern facilities is Beppu. This city also contains many establishments for leisure bathing. The Japanese have always associated hot springs with "having a good time," so wherever there are hot springs there are likely to be facilities for adult enjoyment. Other recommended hot springs are at:

Amagase, a hot spring resort surrounded by mountains. There are several open-air baths on the river bank. 1½ hours by express train from Hakata

KYUSHU 469

Station. Two neighboring springs are Yunotsura Onsen and Tsuetate Onsen. *Amagase Kanko Hotel Seitenkaku* (097357–2350); *Sky Hotel Sesuien* (097357–2380).

Ibusuki (It means "a place rich in water"), with more than 700 springs at a temperature of 60 – 80°C. The sand baths on the shore are especially well known. There is a unisex Jungle Bath at *Ibusuki Kanko Hotel*. Ibusuki is 50 minutes by train from Nishi-Kagoshima Station. *Ibusuki Seaside Hotel* (09932–3-3111); *Phoenix Hotel* (09932–3-4111). Roykan *Shusui-en, 27–27, 5-chome, Yunohama; 57–3700 or (09932) 3–4141. Expensive.* Across from hot-sand beach; 45 rooms or suites.

Kirishima with its 400 springs is 3 hours by car from Miyazaki Station and 1 hour from Kagoshima Airport. *Kirishima Prince Hotel* (8–2831); *Kirishima Kanko Hotel* (8–2531).

Unzen, popular since the Nara period. 2 hours by bus from Nagasaki Station. *Unzen New Grand Hotel* (095773–3291); *Unzen Kanko Hotel* (095773–3263).

Yamaga City in Kumamoto. On Route 3. The Sanko bus from Kumamoto Station takes 1 hr. 10 min. to Yamaga. *Yamaga Ground Hotel* (3–4171); *Yamaga Seiryoso Hotel* (3–2101).

Remember the sign for a hot spring *(onsen),* which is a little cauldron with three waves of heat coming up from it. You might see it in many other places all over the island. For convenience on alphabetical list of other spas on the island is given below:
Akune; Amakusashimoda; Aso; Aso-Uchinomaki; Beppu; Chikugogawa; Furuya; Futsukaichi; Harazuru; Hayato; Hinagu; Hita; Hitoyoshi; Kumanokawa; Minamioguni; Obama; Takeo; Tomana; Tsuetate; Ureshino; Yufuin; Yunoko.

 HOW TO GET AROUND. By train. The Shinkansen (super express) stops in Kyushu are Kokura (in Kita-Kyushu) and Hakata (Fukuoka City). Nonsmokers are advised to take the first carriage in Shinkansen trains, as this is a nonsmoking carriage. More non-smoking carriages are promised for 1985.

From Hakata, JNR services extend throughout the island. Beppu is about three hours from Hakata by limited express, and Hakata to Nagasaki takes about the same time.

By bus. The bus station is very close to Hakata railway station, and from here there are excellent bus services and a number of special tour buses. Local travel agents can offer a range of special tours to places of interest. On a smaller scale the same is true of most other towns and cities in Kyushu. The local railway station connects with local bus services and there is usually a wide selection of local tours. For some tastes the charming bus couriers talk (and sing) too much, but there is no mistaking their desire to please. If planning to spend any appreciable time in one place, it is worth writing beforehand for tourist literature. A letter addressed to the local town hall generally finds its way to the appropriate tourist office.

There are express sightseeing buses between Nagasaki and Unzen, and between Nagasaki and Beppu. Many sightseeing bus services operate from Kumamoto and Nagasaki over the Amakusa Five Bridges. The bridges link formerly isolated subtropical islands so that a bus tour is possible with a ferry link to Unzen on the Trans-Kyushu Sightseeing Route (the Yamarami Highway). Fares are moderate, and information can be obtained from bus stations in Beppu and Kumamoto.

By car. As elsewhere, rent-a-car services are fairly expensive. Nippon Rent-a-Car operates from Fukuoka. However motoring is often rather frustrating for non-Japanese as the roads are usually badly signposted.

Motorists in their own cars who have a reasonable amount of time to spare can usually get about without too much difficulty, but it is important to remember that outside the main cities, Japanese people, though endlessly kind, seldom have sufficient command of the English language to give directions.

By air. Plane services are available from Fukuoka Airport to Kagoshima and Miyazaki.

By boat. The Kansai Kisen's Inland Sea Trip to Beppu is recommended. Boats run three times a day between Osaka, Kobe, Matsuyama, and Beppu, taking 14 hrs. between Osaka and Beppu. For information (in Beppu) call 0977–22–1311.

 TOURIST INFORMATION. For information and bookings, contact Japan Travel Bureau at the addresses below. **Beppu:** International Tourist Building (Kokusai Kanko Kaikan), 2943 Kitahama; 0977–24–5111. Beppu also has a Tourist Information Center; 0975–32–7305.

Fukuoka. Daiwa Seimei Kaikan Building, 1–14–4 Tenjin, Chuo-ku; 092–771–5211.

Kagoshima. Kagoshima Hayashida Hotel, 12–22 Higashi Sengoku-cho; 0992–23–8516.

Kitakyushu. J.T.B. Building, 1–1–1 Sakai-machi, Kokura Kita-ku; 093–551–5121.

Kumamoto. J.T.B. Building, 1822 Shimodori; 0963–22–4131.

Nagasaki. 1–95 Onoe-cho; 0985–24–5194.

Most cities and lots of smaller places have lively local tourist boards that are very ready to supply detailed local information. The pamphlets are beautifully illustrated but the English is usually terrible, though one can get the general drift of meaning. Address your letter to the tourist board of whichever town or district you plan to visit.

For their Driving and Sightseeing Map of Kyushu, contact *Japan Guide Map Co., Ltd.,* 72, Tateno, Naka-ku, Yokohama; 045–621–2424.

At any rest center along the main toll roads, it is possible to get free maps and motoring information.

 SEASONAL EVENTS AND FESTIVALS. Anyone who has seen the brilliant film *Rickshaw Man,* by Kurosawa, will remember Mifune's exciting drumming scene and all the fever of excitement at the Gion Festival at Kokura. People who think they know the Japanese without ever having seen a *matsuri* (festival) know only one side of Japanese nature. Most festivals are perhaps best seen at night. The colored lanterns, the long lines of dancers, and the insistent drumming, create an unforgettable impression.

The more famous festivals are excellent for trade and tourism. There is a saying, for example, about the Kokura Gion Festival, that if there is no rain, money will fall instead.

Only the major festivals and events are noted here, but there are many other less important local festivals.

January. The 15th is "coming-of-age" day in Japan and young people who have reached the age of 20 during the previous year, attend a town hall ceremony. Afterwards there are informal gatherings for the girls to show off their finery. If the weather is fine, the castle grounds at Kokura show a wonderful spectacle with hundreds of girls in brilliant kimono and white fur tippets. The flashbulbs pop and there is a true festival atmosphere all over the city.

April. *Beppu* Hot Spring Festival runs from the 1st – 3rd. Devil dances and so on.

From the 1st – 5th is the special *pottery market* for Imari china in Imari City.

Nagasaki Kite-flying Festival. (Time depends on winds and weather). Nagasaki has had a Chinese quarter from early times, and the kites flown are obviously Chinese in inspiration. Teams of young men compete in flying their huge decorative kites.

May. *Arita Chinaware and Pottery Fair* runs from the 1st – 5th. There is an immense display, and people come from far and wide as the wares are all at half price.

Beppu Yacht Race (Kitahama Yacht Harbor) takes place in early May.

Hakata's Dontaku Festival goes from the 3rd – 5th. (The best day is May 3.) The word "Dontaku" comes from the Germanic word "Donnertag," signifying Maundy Thursday, the pre-Lent festival. There are parades and dances through the center of the city, with drums and shamisen players on decorated trucks. May 3 and May 5 are public holidays, so of course there are crowds from all over the area.

June. In mid-June is the *Peiron Festival at Nagasaki.* This is a rowing boat festival with a peculiarly Chinese atmosphere. The long boats are propelled through the water at a tremendous speed by their crews of young men, with the coxswain keeping time with a drum. Inquire locally, because the races depend on the weather, and sometimes are held in July or August.

July. On the week following the last Saturday in July is the *Oku-Beppu Summer Festival.* Fireworks, processions – lots of fun.

Kokura Gion Festival is held on the 10th – 12th. There is a statue of the drummers in front of Kokura Station.

Other *Gion* festivals are held throughout the month. There are processions, dances, and decorated trucks with drummers, musicians, and singers. Modern amplifying equipment ensures that the noise can be heard all over the area. The matsuri seem to be more magical after darrk. July 10 –12: Usuki; July 14 and 15: Wakamatsu, Tobata, and Hita; July 23 – 25: Kashiwazaki and Nakatsu; July 26: Saga.

August *Aso Kite-flying Festival* takes place on the 5th on the high grassy plains of Mt. Aso. You can see kites from all over the world. A magnificent spectacle.

Kumamoto Yamaga Lantern Festival is on the 16th. Women dance through the night with lanterns on their heads. It's a charming and colorful sight.

October. *Nagasaki Kunchi* runs from the 7th – 9th. October is a very pleasant month in Nagasaki and this is one of Japan's major festivals. The festival was originated by the Nagasaki Chinese community and the atmosphere is still largely Chinese. Portable shrines and floats are carried through the streets and there are dances in which the heavy shrines with people standing on their platforms are whirled about in a seemingly very dangerous manner. Then there are dragon dances with the dragons always in pursuit of a jewel, which always just eludes them. Reserved seats are available for the ceremonies and it is wise to make hotel reservations in good time for the festival.

If you are unable to go to Nagasaki at festival time you can see an exciting film of the festival at the Municipal Exhibition Hall on the way out of the Glover House and Meiji Village. The hall also contains the ship floats, the dragons, and other items used.

Kyushu has a galaxy of ancient festivals, in addition to those already discussed. The more important are listed chronologically here: *Tamaseseri,* January 3, Hakata; *Tsuinasai,* January 7, Dazaifu; *Hadaka Matsuri,* mid-January, Aoshima; *Hiburi Shinji,* March 19, Aso; *Nagasaki Matsuri,* April 27–29, Nagasaki; *Ohtsunahiki,* June, first Sat. and Sun., Yobiko City, Saga Pref.; *Hakata Gion Yamakasa,* July 1–15, Hakata (best day is 15th, 5:00 A.M.); *Urabon Kai,* Aug. 13–15, Nagasaki; *Toimisaki Himatsuri,* Sept. 10–11, Miyazaki; *Miyazaki Gingu Taisai,* Oct. first Sat. and Sun.; *Karatsu Kunchi,* Nov. 2–4, Karatsu; *Ohara Matsuri,* Nov. 2–3; *Saitobaru Kofunsai,* Nov. 1;

TOURS. Bus tours are strongly recommended in Kyushu, though one might occasionally wish that the charming lady guides would sit down and let visitors look in peace.

One important tour center is at the bus garage very close to Hakata Station. Excellent and inexpensive tours are available throughout the island, but as these tours are seasonal, local inquiry is advised.

PARKS. Among the many lovely parks and gardens in Kyushu, the following are well worth a visit:

Sasebo Tropical Plant Garden; Jinganji Park and *Iso Park* in Kagoshima; *Miyazaki Cactus Garden; Tachibana Koen* (the park by the Oyodogawa River); *Suizenji* in Kumamoto; and *Kizankoen* in Hita.

The fascinating undersea world may be observed in Kyushu's underwater parks. There are three on Amakusa Island; *Amakusa Undersea Park, Tomioka,* and *Ushibuka* undersea parks. There is another such park on the southern tip of Kyushu—the *Satamisaki Undersea Park.*

In Nagasaka Prefecture, *Unzen and Amakusa National Park* has campsites, horseriding trails, and tennis courts.

ZOOS & SAFARI PARKS. African Safari Park. 40 minutes by bus from Beppu Station. 69 kinds of animals with a total of 1300. Open 9:00 A.M.–5:00 P.M.; 4:00 P.M. during winter.

Aso Kuma Bokujo. 15 minutes on foot from Aso Station. 7 different kinds of bears and a total of 200 animals. Open 8:00 A.M.–6:30 P.M.

Cable Rakutenchi. 10 minutes west of Beppu Station by bus. There is a zoo, a science museum, an open stage, a playground, etc. Cable car service from 9:00 A.M.–6:00 P.M.

Kodomono-kuni (Children's Country). 30 minutes by bus from Miyazaki Station. There is a zoo and a botanical garden. Camel riding, rowing boats can be enjoyed. Open 8:00 A.M.–5:30 P.M.

Miyazaki Safari Park. 45 minutes by bus from Miyako City Terminal. (The terminal is very close to Minami Miyazaki Station.) Open 9:00 A.M.– 5:00 P.M. No closing day.

Nagasakibana Parking Garden. Southwest of Ibusuki in Kagoshima. 20 minutes by bus from Yamakawa Station. 30 different species of birds are kept free among subtropical plants. Open 8:00 A.M.–5:00 P.M.

Takasakiyama Shizen Dobutsuen (Takasakiyama Natural Zoo). 15 minutes by bus from Kitahama Station, Beppu. About 2000 wild monkeys. Open 8:00 A.M.–5:30 P.M.; 5:00 P.M. in winter.

THEME PARKS AND AMUSEMENT CENTERS. *Kirishima Kogen Kokuminkyuyochi.* 1 hour 10 minutes by bus from Kagoshima Airport. A Japanese-style holiday camp. Horseback riding, tennis, camping, and cyling can be enjoyed here.

See also "Zoos and Safari Parks."

 CHILDREN'S ACTIVITIES. Children can go through a surprising amount of money in a short time at the amusement parks in every holiday resort and the "game centers" in every resort hotel, but there are lots of other, more wholesome activities which cost little. Camping and hiking can be enjoyed at little cost in the many campsites and at most of the Kokumin-Kyukamura.

It is wise to make bookings for youth hostels and Kokumin Shukusha—especially at holiday periods. For further information see the "Hotels and Inns" section or contact the JTB.

Free fishing is available in many places around the coast, though it is unwise to assume that any fish caught is edible. Blowfish need expert preparation to be safely edible.

For a more expensive late holiday with children, the Miyazaki area with its safari parks, its pleasure parks, its amusements, and its beaches is ideal.

 SPORTS. Participant sports. Kyushu contains a number of very fine *golf* courses. (Check with your hotel if you would like to have a game.) Perhaps the two best-known are Koga, near Fukuoka, and Moji in Kita-Kyushu. The Moji Club has an excellent clubhouse. Near Kagoshima there is the Ibusuki Golf Course and the old established Yoshimo course. In Miyazaki there is the Miyazaki Oyodogawa Golf Course (48–1934) and Phoenix Country Club and Golf Course (39–1301). In Beppu there is the Kuju Golf Club. Practice golf ranges can be found in virtually every town.

Ten-pin bowling has become less popular these days in Japan, but in its place *tennis* clubs are springing up wherever there is space, while for the indolent there is pachinko (pinball) and the game centers.

There are areas for *walking* and exploring in Mt. Aso, Unzen National Park, and the Ibusuki peninsula, while in the hills above Beppu *hang gliding* is the popular sport.

Sea *fishing* is excellent on many parts of the long coastline while in Moji, Nagasaki, and some other areas it is possible to hire a small boat for fishing. Cormorant fishing may be seen at Hita on the Misumi River between Fukuoka and Beppu. The fishing begins at the end of May and goes on until the end of October. For inquiries telephone 09732–3–3111.

Swimmers will find beautiful clean beaches at Miyazaki and Momoji Matsubara which as the name suggests is a beach shaded by pine trees. Momoji Matsubara is a half-hour drive from Hakata or may be reached by ferry in 1 hour from Hakata.

Spectator sports. A popular sporting festival at Fukuoka City is the Sumo Tournament (Basho) which takes place in November each year.

 HISTORICAL SITES. *Dazaifu Tenmangu.* 40 minutes by train from Fukuoka. Shrine of the God of Learning. Students go here to pray for success in their examinations.

Fukuji Temple. 45 minutes by bus from Takada Station. The oldest building in Kyushu Island. Late Heian period. Open 8:30 A.M.–6:00 P.M. Closed if it rains.

Hakozaki-gu. 15 minutes by bus from Hakata station. One of the largest shrines built in honor of the deified prince Hachiman, god of war.

Honmyoji. 10 minutes by bus or tram car from Kotsu Centre, Kumamoto. Northwest of Kumamoto Castle. A fine temple built for the Kato family. There are hundreds of stone lanterns. Open 9:00 A.M.–4:00 P.M. Closed on Mondays.

The Ijinkan. It was built by order of the Shimazu family as a guest house for English experts who had come to teach spinning. 25 minutes by bus from Nishi-Kagoshima Station. Open 9:00 A.M.–5:00 P.M. Closed Wednesdays.

Kashii-gu. North of Hakata. 10 minutes on foot from Kashii Station. Because of the ancient building method employed in its construction, this shrine is one of the important treasures of Japan.

Kofukuji and Sofukuji. It is 10 minutes on foot between the two Chinese-style temples. 5 minutes by bus from Nagasaki Station. Open 8:00 A.M.–5:00 P.M.

Miyazaki Jingu. 20 minutes by bus from Miyako City Terminal. A well-known shrine in an ancient building style. There is an old house and a museum on the grounds of the shrine. Museum open 9:00 A.M.–4:30 P.M.

Ohana. 10 minutes by bus from Yanagawa Station. This house once belonged to the Lord Tachibana. A whole houseful of antiques is exhibited. Open 9:00 A.M.–5:00 P.M.

Usa Jingu. 10 minutes by bus from Usa station in Usa City. The principal shrine of the 15,000 Hachiman shrines of Japan.

Udo Jingu. 1 hour 20 minutes by bus from Miyazaki Station. The shrine is in a cave and is usually visited by newly married couples to pray for good fortune.

Usuki Sekibutsu. 1 hour 20 minutes by bus from Oita Station. About 60 stone Buddhist images made in the Heian and Kamakura periods. Open 8:30 A.M.–5:00 P.M.

Chiran. Between Kagoshima City and Ibusuki. A neighborhood of Samurai residences, many open to the public, preserved as it was 200 years ago.

Architectural interest. Japan treasures its ancient monuments, and in almost any shrine or temple some item of architectural interest is preserved. Castles, even when reconstructed, usually preserve some features of the original, and the massive ramparts remain. Sadly, however, as in the rest of Japan, most of the fine Meiji buildings have been swept away. Fortunately many of these extremely interesting buildings have been preserved in excellent condition in **Nagasaki.** The Meiji Village near the Glover Mansion gives an excellent idea of how rich European merchants lived in the 1860s and 1870s. A Christian church from the period is also preserved here.

MUSEUMS & ART GALLERIES. The fine modern *Fukuoka Art Museum* (near Fukuoka Castle grounds) is of international standard. Though the painting and sculpture collection here is not outstanding, there are frequent visiting exhibitions of the highest importance. The museum has a restaurant and comfortable areas for rest and study.

At Nagasaki, the *Sixteenth Mansion,* a fine old pre-Meiji house on the way out of the Nagasaki Meiji Village, has one of the finest collections of Meiji glassware in Japan.

In Kagoshima the residence of the daimyo of Satsuma has been turned into a museum of the beginnings of the Industrial Revolution in Japan in Meiji times: the *Shoko Shusei-kan* in Senganen Garden.

In the island of Hirado (three hours drive from Fukuoka) is the beautiful *Matsuura Museum*—formerly the residence of the local daimyo. This contains a fascinating collection of Eastern and Western antiquities.

All the *castles* on the island of Kyushu (sadly, for the most part, concrete reconstructions) contain fine collections of samurai weapons and armor, showing the fine quality workmanship and impeccable taste of the Edo Period craftsmen.

Also in Kagoshima is the *Municipal Art Museum,* located 10 minutes by streetcar from Nishi-Kagoshima Station. Houses works by famous Japanese painters born in Kagoshima Prefecture. There is also folk art and tools. Open 9:00 A.M.–4:30 P.M.; closed Mondays and national holidays.

In Kita Kyushu The *Art Gallery* is a beautifully situated modern building with frequent splendid exhibitions.

PERFORMING ARTS. Tickets for ballet, music and live performances of every kind can be obtained at the major department stores in **Hakata** and other bigger cities. Most stores have a special counter for this purpose and precise details of forthcoming events can be obtained.

 SHOPPING. When traveling in Kyushu there are temptations to spend money at every turn, and things are not necessarily expensive. This is proved by the number of people who come to Kyushu from all over Southeast Asia for the shopping.

Serious shopping is best done in **Fukuoka** where standards are virtually as good as those of Tokyo or Osaka, and where items are perhaps just a little less expensive. Clothes and most household goods are available in a bewildering array in the large department stores in the Tenjin area, and there are many excellent speciality stores near the city center.

For souvenirs and impulse shopping there are large souvenir shops attached to most of the large hotels, especially in resort areas. Guests can saunter about in the evenings when there is little else to do, and buy at their leisure. Perhaps some of the "souvenirs" are rather junky, but local craftwork is often a good buy.

In **Kokura, Nagasaki,** and **Kagoshima,** big-store standards are much the same as in Hakata, and most towns have at least one shopping arcade. These shopping arcades are glass-roofed pedestrian streets lined with shops and restaurants. They are ideally suited to Japanese weather conditions in that they are comfortable for shopping in the wet or hot weather, as well as in the cold of winter. The main arcade in the Hamamachi Shopping Center in Nagasaki has the additional refinement of a roof that can be rolled back in fine weather.

The small castle town of **Karatsu** (about 1½ hours by car from Fukuoka) is noted for its pottery. The old Japanese saying "Ichi Raku, Ni Hagi, San Karatsu," suggests that in all Japan the third most important place for pottery is Karatsu.

Arita, also not far from Fukuoka, is the home of the famous red and white Arita china, while **Imari City,** which is also within reach of Fukuoka, is the home of the traditional multi-colored Imari china. Be sure that you understand what you are about when buying "old" Imari at high prices. Of course some old Imari is available, but most likely these days it is found in reputable antique shops.

Specialty Shops. For traditional Japanese paper visit the old established shop *Kukkodo,* Shintencho Arcade, Hakata; (092) 712–2252. (The arcade is at the back of the Iwataya Department Store.)

Traditional Hakata dolls may be seen in great variety in the station shopping center attached to Hakata Station.

For flower perfumes, perfumed teas, and even meals that appeal to the nose, visit *Koryoen* at the foot of Kaimondake, Kagoshima; (099332) 3238.

For the traditional Castella cake of Nagasaki, go to the famous and old established shop *Fukusaya*—though many other Nagasaki shops will assert that theirs is just as good.

At the *Hamacho arcade* in Nagasaki try one of the dozen specialty shops for turtle-shell rings, combs, picture frames, and so on.

Kagoshima is famous for boxes, bowls and other objects made from the ancient cedars of Yakushima island (Yakusugi). Try some of the shops in the *Tenmonkan Dori Arcade*.

Vases and other objects fashioned from bamboo are excellent in Beppu. Try some of the shops in *Ekimae-dori*.

 DINING OUT. Adequate Western-style food can be found in most hotels but the visitor who eats only Western food will miss much of the pleasure of travel in Kyushu. If you can't be bothered to look for a special restaurant, try any *Robatayaki*. It's a restaurant with counter seats where you can choose just what you want from the counter display. Fish, potatoes, and other foods are grilled on a charcoal grill. The meal can cost as much or as little as you like.

For a very cheap meal try an *Okonomiyaki* restaurant. Okonomiyaki are Japanese savoury pancakes, which you cook for yourself at the table.

One of the cheapest lunches is *Nagasaki Champon* (noodles and vegetables in soup). It is said that they taste better when slurped noisily.

Eel restaurants offer a tasty and nourishing meal that is typically Japanese. They are not cheap, but are usually good value. Eels can be eaten all the year-round, but are best in summer.

One of the most expensive meals at Japanese restaurants is *fugu*, or blowfish. These fish are caught in the waters off Kyushu and are eaten uncooked (November to March only). The flesh is sliced into thin slivers, which are arranged on a large plate in the form of a chrysanthemum. It is possible to be poisoned by fugu that have been prepared by inexperienced amateurs, but the danger is exaggerated. It is impossible to come to harm on account of fugu prepared at any normal Japanese restaurant. There remains the danger of heart failure when you see the bill.

Mizutaki is another specialty of the region. This is a tasty chicken dish cooked at the table in an earthenware pot.

Korea is very close to Kyushu, so Korean restaurants can be found in most towns. The most popular meal is *yakiniku*, thinly sliced meat cooked at the table on gas barbecue pans. It is eaten with garlic flavored pickles and rice. With this hot and spicy food, beer is the best drink. Most Korean restaurants serve the popular Kirin beer.

In the Mt. Aso area you can eat wild boar barbecued at the table. From the quantity eaten one might imagine that all the wild boars would have been hunted down long ago, but even if some of the meat is really quite tame pig, it is extremely tasty.

Chinese influence is still strong in Nagasaki, so it is worthwhile to sample some of the Chinese-style dishes when in the Nagasaki area. *Nagasaki Shippoku* is an elaborate Chinese/Japanese meal that needs at least half-a-dozen diners. A version in wax may be seen in the municipal museum.

In addition, there are the usual popular dishes such as *Jingisu Khan* (meat cooked at the table on an iron replica of Genghis Khan's hat), and sukiyaki.

As elsewhere in Japan, hamburger restaurants and quick-food stands abound —perhaps to the despair of parents who wish to educate their children about food. Children also seem to enjoy hot corn-on-the-cob sold from tiny roadside stalls in all parts of Kyushu, and of course there are plenty of roadside fruit stalls.

It is perhaps worth mentioning that establishments bearing the name "Snack" in neon lights do not serve snacks. They are bars dispensing weak whiskey and sympathy to tired company men. From the numbers that seem to thrive, they obviously fill a long-felt need. Your bill in such a place will certainly raise your eyebrows unless you are traveling on an expense account.

Travelers in Kyushu are advised that outside the major hotels it is virtually impossible to obtain a Western-style breakfast. Coffee shops don't normally open until 10:00 A.M. So if you are staying at business hotels, have some fruit handy for an early breakfast.

About cost. In all the restaurants given it is possible to get a set meal from about ¥ 3,000, or even less in restaurants marked "reasonable," but it is possible to pay very much more of course. Look at the wax model display usually shown outside almost every restaurant. The models show just what you can expect to eat and the price. More expensive restaurants also add a service charge and a tax.

JAPANESE FOOD AND LOCAL DISHES

Kagetsu. 2 Maruyama, Nagasaki City; (0958) 22–0191. Established 1624. The house and its garden are historical monuments. Shippoku is the specialty here. (See introduction above.) Open 12:00 P.M.—7:30 P.M. Closed once a week. Cost for two about ¥ 30,360. Telephone beforehand.

Kumasotei. 6–10 Higashi Sengoku-cho, Kagoshima City; (0992) 22–6356. Specialty *Tonkatsu* dishes (pork and vegetables). Open 11:00 A.M.–10:00 P.M.Highly recommended also for local specialties.

Matsukawa. 3–2 Matsubara, Saga City; (0952) 24–5285. Established at the end of Edo Period. The oldest inn in Saga Prefecture, but today the house is used as a restaurant rather than an inn. 12 Japanese rooms. Excellent fish dishes. Open 11:00 A.M.–9:00 P.M. daily.

Ohana. Shingai-cho, Yanagawa City, Fukuoka Prefecture; (09447) 3–2189. The house is a national treasure. It belonged to the Tachibana family who were lords of Yanagawa-han. The house has many antique art objects. Specialties are fish and poultry. Cost per person ¥ 10,000. Open 10:00 A.M.–8:00 P.M. Telephone beforehand.

Satsuma. 10–4, Chuo-cho, Kagoshima City; (0992) 52–2661. In front of Nishi Kagoshima Station. Specialties are fish and shochu. The second floor has a fine display of antiques. Prices reasonable. Open 11:30 A.M.–10:00 P.M.

Shimamoto. Imayashiki, Izuhara-cho, Shimokata-gun, Nagasaki; (09205) 2–5252. A large tank contains live fish of various kinds. Fish are baked on a stone. There is also *Mokonabe,* a dish of cooked fish and vegetable. Open 11:00 A.M.–9:00 P.M. Closed 1st and 3rd Sundays each month.

Takamori Dengaku Hosonkai. 2639 Kamishikimi, Takamori-cho, Aso-gun, Kumamoto; (09676) 2–0234. Food is cooked over charcoal fires. Many vegetable dishes; also *Kappo zake* (sake heated in bamboo—very tasty). Open 10:00 A.M.–8:00 P.M. daily. Prices reasonable.

Tamanoyu Ryokan. Yufuin, Yufuin-cho, Oita-gun, Oita Pref.; (09778) 4–2158. Located on a 450-meter-high plateau. There are 12 little teahouses in the

garden. Specialty vegetable dishes. Around ¥ 10,000 per person. Open 11:30
A.M.–8:30 P.M. daily. Reservation advised.

WESTERN-STYLE FOOD

Gas-Light. Albergo Quarto (Yonban-kan), 2–23 Aioi-cho, Sasebo City;
(0956) 25–7833. Specialties are homemade pasta and seafood. Open 10:00 A.M.–
10:00 P.M. daily.

Ginrei. 2–11, Kajiya-cho, Nagasaki City; (0958) 21–2073. Open 10:00 A.M.–
9:00 P.M. daily. The owner of this restaurant has spent over 50 years assembling
a museum of antique glass, paintings, lamps, and Dutch pottery, which you can
enjoy as you dine. Specialties are prawn and veal dishes.

Kamogawa. 2–3–3 Yakuin, Chuo-ku, Fukuoka City; (092) 731–4825. Take
off your shoes and sit at a circular grill bar. The chef serves from the center,
and steaks and chops are grilled to perfection in front of the customers. Open
11:30 A.M.–2:00 P.M., and 5:00 P.M.–10:30 P.M. Closed Tuesday.

Matsuzaka. 1st Floor, B.S. Building, 3–19 Ekimae, Hakata-ku, Fukuoka
City (near Hakata Station); (092) 441–4413. Meat is grilled on a charcoal fire.
Japanese beef is more expensive than imported, but both are available. Open
11:30 A.M.–10:00 P.M. daily; national holidays and Sunday, 4:00 P.M.–10:00 P.M.;
closed 1st and 3rd Sundays each month.

On Green. 5–4–8 Tenjin, Chuo-ku, Fukuoka City; (092) 712–6886. Delightful pinewood restaurant specializing in seafood cooked in the Mediterranean
style. Also homemade pasta. Open 11:00 A.M.–10:00 P.M. Closed Mondays.

Paris Sanku. 6th Floor, Tachibana Park Building, Nishi 1, Miyazaki City;
(0985) 27–7633. This restaurant has a pleasant evening view with the lights of
the town reflected on the Oyodo River. French-style fish and meat dishes. Open
12:00 midday–3:00 P.M., and 5:00 P.M.–9:30 P.M. Closed Mondays.

Peppermint Park. 1–7–27, Akasaka, Chuo-ku, Fukuoka City; (092) 721–
4980. This restaurant has its own vegetable garden and uses naturally cultivated
vegetables only. Specialties are omelettes and paella.

NIGHT LIFE. In the Kyushu countryside, the bright
lights are the on/off neon lamps of the fireflies—except
at festival times when the area erupts into noise and
gaiety. In most towns however, there is a night life cen-
ter. Usually the area is compact, with lots of tiny bars and "snacks" crammed
into a few streets.

Without doubt the best area for plush night life is Hakata, but almost every
town has its amusement area with brilliant neon displays and touts offering
optimistic estimates of what an evening in their club or strip show will cost.
Unless entry is by ticket, it is wise to inquire about the cost before relaxing in
a place of entertainment.

TOHOKU

by
NORMAN SKLAREWITZ
and
JAN BROWN

For hundreds of years, urban Japanese have referred to the northern prefectures of Japan's main island of Honshu as the *Michinoku*. That translates variously as "deep North," or, more precisely, as "back country." It wasn't exactly a complimentary description, for residents of the Tohoku region were long considered country bumpkins.

Because it was physically isolated by mountains and a lack of good transportation from the more advanced and relatively prosperous southern two-thirds of the island, Tohoku remained less developed even into recent years.

But that same relative isolation, even neglect, has today made the Tohoku region among the more attractive areas of the entire nation. City folks aren't making fun of Tohoku residents anymore.

Here tradition, folk arts, festivals, and old-fashioned customs and virtues remain strong. The pace of life is less hectic. Small countryside towns and villages still feature thatched roof cottages, terraced rice paddies and dramatic vistas of mist-shrouded mountains, pine forested hillsides, and a rugged seacoast where tiny fishing communities cling to narrow shelfs of flatland.

It is such attractions that bring Japanese and foreigners on holiday up north. There visitors enjoy the pleasure of countless hot springs resorts, quiet mountain trails, and the centuries-old shrines, temples, and historical properties that reflect the rich cultural heritage of the Tohoku.

Like New England or the Pacific Northwest, the Tohoku isn't an actual political region at all; it's just a convenient geographic grouping of adjoining prefectures. These are: Fukushima, Miyagi, Yamagata, Akita, Iwate, and Aomori.

Sendai

The biggest city in the area and its unofficial capital is Sendai, capital of Miyagi Prefecture. Once a castle town, Sendai today has a population in excess of 670,000 and is Tohoku's commercial and educational center. Because there are so many woods around the city and local government has planted so many trees along its wide boulevards, Sendai enjoys the reputation of being a "city of trees."

The earliest history of the immediate area and what was to become the city of Sendai is wrapped up in the life and exploits of the 16th-century feudal lord named Date Masamune. It is his statue in full armor, astride his horse, that dominates the strategic heights over the Hirose River, original site of Lord Masamune's Sendai Castle.

Known as the "one-eyed dragon," because of his valor as a warrior and the loss of an eye through smallpox, Date Masamune is credited with being a skillful administrator (he had constructed a canal that linked two rivers and greatly facilitated transportation of rice and other commodities through the area), an artist, and a scholar.

Sendai figures in one of the more bizarre instances of early contact between Japan and Europe. In 1613, a small party of samurai warriors sailed from Tsukinoura Bay, just up the coast from Sendai, with the goal of visiting Pope Paul V in Rome. They hoped also to be received by Philip III of Spain.

The voyage was made under the auspices of Date Masamune for reasons history has left unclear. They could have been religious or purely commercial. The two-masted, 500-ton galleon crossed the Pacific, landing first in California, then proceeding on to Acapulco, Mexico, where the group broke up. Some returned to Japan but the leader persisted, traveling overland to Vera Cruz and then by ship on to Cuba and from there to Spain.

The journey lasted seven years and before the expedition's leader, a samurai named Hasekura, returned to Japan, the Tokugawa shogunate had outlawed Christianity. Hasekura was baptized in Spain and made a citizen of Rome. As a gift from the Pope to Date Masa-mune, he brought back a pair of crystal candlesticks exhibited on occasion in the Sendai City Museum or in Matsushima's Zuiganji Temple's museum.

Sendai is widely known for its lavish Tanabata Festival, held August 6–8 each year. The streets in the city center become a riot of color and action as countless paper displays festoon shops and avenues.

The town's main shopping center is the glass-arcaded Ichibancho, running straight from the City Hall to the university campus, which

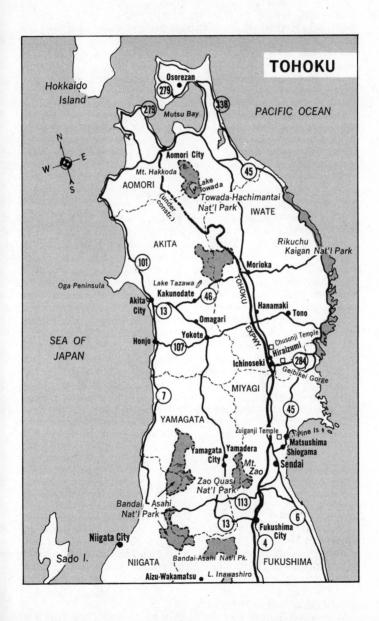

TOHOKU

Hokkaido Island

Osorezan
(279)
(279)   (338)
Mutsu Bay   PACIFIC OCEAN

N
W   E
S

Aomori City

Mt. Hakkoda
AOMORI   Lake Towada   (45)
(under constr.)   Towada-Hachimantai Nat'l Park
IWATE

AKITA   Rikuchu Kaigan Nat'l Park

(101)
Morioka
Oga Peninsula   Lake Tazawa
Kakunodate   (46)   Hanamaki
Akita City   (13)   Tono
Omagari   TOHOKU EXPWY
Honjo   Yokote
(107)   Chusonji Temple
Hiraizumi   (284)
Ichinoseki   Geibikei Gorge
(7)   MIYAGI

YAMAGATA   (45)

Zuiganji Temple   Pine Is
Matsushima
Yamagata City   Yamadera   Shiogama
Mt. Zao   Sendai
Zao Quasi Nat'l Park
Bandai-Asahi Nat'l Park   (113)
(13)   (6)
Fukushima City
Niigata City   (4)
Sado I.   NIIGATA   Bandai-Asahi Nat'l Pk.   FUKUSHIMA
Aizu-Wakamatsu   L. Inawashiro

SEA OF JAPAN

has been adorned by some well-designed modern buildings. The Ichibancho is linked to another busy center round the railway station by a long, animated street of fascinating shops, including some good kimono stores. The street is called Chuo-dori, and it leads into Nakake-cho and the station square. In Chuo-dori the visitor can find very modern and attractive shops specializing in all kinds of folk art from the Tohoku region, in particular dyed cloth, lacquerware, wooden toys, pottery, bamboo, and bog-oak souvenirs and *kokeshi,* limbless wooden dolls unique to and a symbol of the Tohoku region.

The loveliest, and (except at the time of the iris flowers, in June), the quietest place in Sendai is the exquisite landscape garden of Rinnoji, reached from the center in ten minutes by taxi.

The other sights in Sendai include the ruined castle on Aoba Hill, of which only the massive moat and retaining walls and part of a gateway survive. From this loffty viewpoint one can enjoy a wide panorama of the Hirose River and the city, with the Pacific beyond and the mountains to the north.

There is also the Osaki Hachiman Shrine, a national treasure, where every January 14 the Festival of the Burning of New Year Decorations is celebrated. A quiet little Buddhist temple called Sengakuin is noted for its stone Buddha and its painted screens and scrolls; it is situated near the Toshogu Shrine at the end of another swarming shopping-street, Miyamachi. The city museum, the prefectural museum and the Zuihoden, Date Masamune's elaborate mausoleum, are all west of the station near the Hirose River.

Forty minutes beyond Sakunami, on the Senzan rail line, is Yamad-era. One should visit the shrines and temples and curious rocky crags of this little village preferably in the last week of October, when the autumn tints of the leaves are at their best, a really stunning display of color covering the mountainsides and hanging down over the torrents in the rocky gorges. At the end of this line, about 90 minutes by semi-express from Sendai, is the mountain city of Yamagata, a pleasant, leisurely place where good trout fishing can be found. There is a university with many enthusiastic speakers of English, and the charming pottery village of Hirashimizu on its outskirts.

Matsushima

Up the coast from Sendai is, what many feel, the quintessential Japanese scenic experience—Matshushima, the Pine Islands. Centuries of wind and wave action have carved myriad tiny and not-so-tiny islands into bizarre formations. Matsushima is historically one of Japan's three loveliest sights, today attracting throngs of tourists.

In Matshushima town is the great Zuiganji Temple with its series of natural caves and grottos filled with Buddhist statues and memorial tablets. An adjoining museum contains rare scrolls and exhibits from the Date Masamune household. Many of the magnificent features of the temple are national treasures.

Matsushima-Kaigan (sea coast) may be reached from Sendai in about 40 minutes via the Senseki line or in about an hour by bus. One popular way to view the Pine Clad Islands is to go from Sendai by bus or train to Shiogama City on Matsushima Bay. There at the wharf visitors may catch an excursion boat that crosses the bay, passes many of the more prominent islands, then docks at the Matsushima-Kaigan Pier, It's a pleasant walk from there to all the city sights.

Finally, if it is a clear day you should take a short taxi trip to one of the surrounding heights and enjoy a bird's-eye view of the panorama. A word of advice: connoisseurs of Japanese landscape-viewing consider that Matsushima is seen at its best in extremes of weather. They have seen it in howling typhoons, under snow, and, most poetic of all, through slanting rain, when it looks like an old print by Hiroshige.

Other Regional Attractions

Much of the early history of the Tohoku region with the exploits and personalities of a succession of warlords sent north into this "frontier" territory to cope with insurgents. These *daimyo* built shrines and temples as well as castles as they and their retainers settled the forbidding land.

The town of Kakunodate, about 200 kilometers northwest of Sendai, provides visitors with a rare glimpse of their life in the 17th and 18th centuries. Once a castle town, Kakunodate today still has 15 houses occupied by *samurai* during the Tokugawa Period (1603–1867). Four of these residences are open to the public, permitting visitors to get an intimate feeling of life during that era.

A local museum, the Denshokan, features handicrafts and historical remnants of that colorful feudal era. Kakunodate is on the Tazawako line and may be reached from the town of Omagari, a stop on the Ou Main Line, in 30 minutes.

There are, throughout the region, other special little centers of particular beauty and historical, religious or cultural significance. Hiraizumi, 90 kilometers north of Sendai near Ichinoseki on the Tohoku Shinkansen line is the most historically significant spot in Tohoku. It was intended to be a northern capital of 12th-century Japan, a city like Kyoto, built on the classical Chinese model. Although it failed to achieve such glory, Hiraizumi did serve as a respected center of culture and Fujiwara clan power. The Konjikido, or Golden Hall, located here, was built in the early 12th century as part of the Chusonji Temple complex of 340 buildings. The hall embodies elements of Indian, Persian, Greek, Chinese, and Korean cultures. It is a small building, one story high, but is covered in gold leaf and ornately decorated.

Ichinoseki, a short distance due south of Hiraizumi, was a castle town in the Edo Period and is now a pleasant commercial and timber center. Gembikei Gorge is about 30 minutes away by bus and is a popular scenic attraction for Japanese tourists. Tono, along the Kamaishi line east of the Hanamaki Shinkansen Station, is a stunningly picturesque mountain-locked basin of thatched-roofed farmhouses (including the Minshuku Margariya that takes in overnight guests) and legend-rich country temples and shrines. It is best explored by rental car or taxi.

Of all regions of Japan, Tohoku represents the "great outdoors," for here are located a network of ski resorts, prefectural parks, national parks, and what the Japanese government terms "quasi" national parks, rated the next highest to national parks in terms of attractions, facilities, and scenery. Accommodations are often only Japanese-style and booked solid in July, August, and October. Among these parks and distinct geographic attractions, each posessing a different character and scenic specialty, are the Rikuchu Kaigon National Park along Iwate Prefecture's Pacific coast; Bandai-Asahi National Park in Fukushima; the Towada-Hachimantai National Park in Aomori and Iwate; Lake Tazawa and the Tazawako Plateau in Akita; and Zao Quasi-National Park in Miyagi and Yamagata, famed for its fine skiing facilities, its hot springs resorts and its so-called "snow monsters" which are snow-covered trees.

Hot springs resorts ranging from rustic to modern high-rise hotels cover the entire region. Most interesting are those at Narugo in Miyagi, Higashiyama in Fukushima, Hanamaki in Iwate, and the Hakkoda Mountains in Aomori.

Aomori, with a population of 291,725, is capital of Aomori Prefecture and home of the annual Nebuta Festival as well as center for lumbering and apple growing. It is at the northern end of the Tohoku Region and is situated on Mutsu Bay.

Morioka, capital of Iwate Prefecture, south of Aomori, is now the northern terminus of the Tohoku Shinkansen, which is enhancing its role as an easy-to-reach destination city. Once a castle town, Morioka is most well known among Japanese as the place where the distinctive iron kettles known as *nambu-tetsubin* are made. Visitors are welcome at the factory. Morioka's castle is a ruins now, but its folkcrafts, and its pleasant mix of country town/big city ways, make it a popular destination of foreign visitors.

Akita, on Honshu's west coast, was also once a castle town. Today it is the capital of Akita Prefecture and has a population of close to 290,000. It's here that the spectacular Kanto Festival is held in August. Visitors also enjoy visiting the bustling Citizen's Market, which is a fun combination of supermarket and village market, and has the feel of "old Japan."

Aizu-Wakamatsu, an island city near Lake Inawashiro and the Bandai-Asahi National Park in Fukushima is Tohoku's most interesting city for foreign visitors. It has a replicated castle, a sprawling samurai manor/museum called Buke-yashiki, folk museums, feudal-era storefronts and a pottery village, making it well worth a visit.

PRACTICAL INFORMATION FOR TOHOKU

 WHEN TO GO? Tohoku's climate is similar to that of New England, and it is at its most beautiful in spring and autumn. The winters are cold and snowy, and Japanese-style accommodations use kerosene space heaters rather than central heat. Summers are refreshingly cool, attracting hordes of Japanese visitors from the sweltering south. Japan's most famous summer festivals are all held the first week of August in the Tohoku cities of Sendai, Akita and Aomori. Accommodations during the festivals are tight and the cities are crowded, but the festivities are unforgettable.

HOW TO GET THERE. By air. *All Nippon Airways* (ANA) operates from Tokyo with jet flights to Akita five times a day; to Sendai with four flights a day; and to Hanamaki with two flights a day. *Toa Domestic Airlines* (TDA) operates three flights daily from Tokyo to Aomori; four flights to Misawa; and four flights to Yamagata.

By train. Since their openings in August 1982, the *Tohoku Shinkansen* and *Joetsu Shinkansen* bullet train lines have drastically reduced travel time from Tokyo to Tohoku, a giant first step in the "mainstreaming" of the remote district. Both trains temporarily leave from Omiya, a 25-minute "relay train" ride from Tokyo's Ueno Station until the Shinkansen tracks are extended to Ueno, at press time scheduled for March 1985.

The Tohoku Shinkansen terminates in Morioka, near the center of the Tohoku district in Iwate Prefecture. The trip from Tokyo to Morioka that used to take 6½ hours will be reduced by March to 2 hours and 45 minutes. At Morioka connecting trains on the Tohoku Honsen line reach Aomori City on the shore of Mutsu Bay in the far month in another 2 hours and 35 minutes.

The Joetsu Shinkansen reaches Niigata City, on the Sea of Japan just south of Tohoku, in 1 hour and 53 minutes. At Niigata, long distance trains coming north from Osaka and Kyoto carry visitors into Tohoku along the Uetsu Honsen's western coastal route to Aomori City. On Tohoku's eastern side, the Tohoku Honsen and the Joban Honsen connect Tokyo's Ueno with Aomori City; the Ou Honsen branches from Fukushima in southeastern Tohoku to connect interior and western cities with Aomori.

By car. The nearly completed Tohoku Expressway is missing only one short leg north of Morioka before it connects Tokyo and Aomori City. Because driving time from Tokyo is several times over that of the Shinkansen, visitors who want to drive should consider combining train and rental car travel. Major Tohoku train stations have national rental car chain branches such as Toyota, Nissan, and Nippon. *JNR*, the national railways, operates a Shinkansen and drive system which offers a 20% discount on rental cars to Shinkansen ticket holders. Even with a discount, rental cars and gasoline prices are high in Japan.

By ferry. A good way to combine travel to Tohoku and Hokkaido is to fly to Hokkaido's Chitose Airport from Tokyo, see the northern island, and then come to Tohoku by ferry across the Tsugaru Straits. *JNR Seikan Renraku* ferries from Hokkaido's Hakodate arrive in Aomori City in under 4 hours. The private *Higashi Nippon Ferry Company* has an overnight ferry (8 hours, with 4-person staterooms available) between Tomakomai, a 2-hour bus ride south of Sapporo, and eastern Aomori Prefecture's Hachinohe. Other Higashi Nippon ferry terminals in Tohoku are in northernmost Oma and Mutsu Bay's Noheji.

TELEPHONES. The prefixes for cities in the Tohoku district are: Sendai 0222; Aizu-Wakamatsu 0242; Morioka 0196; Akita 0188; Aomori 0177; Yamagata 0236.

HOTELS AND INNS. From late October to late April, the Western-style hotels are recommended, since Japanese inns may lack adequate heating. During the balance of the year, a stay at one of the inns listed below can be a most pleasant and unique experience. Compared with most other parts of Japan, accommodations in the Tohoku are moderately priced.

Business hotels are designed almost exclusively for businessmen on limited expense accounts. Rooms, are by Western standards, extremely small; literally, it's often not possible to open a suitcase inside such a room. Dining rooms in business hotels serve only Japanese food; menus are limited. Staff will not speak English. Rooms are, however, generally quite clean and priced considerably under those rates charged in a full-service Western-style hotel.

Larger cities and resort areas also offer Western-style tourist hotels (kanko hotels) with steeper prices and more frills. They are often crowded with Japanese bus-tour groups, but you may find their added amenities, such as plusher Western-style dining rooms and larger rooms, worth the extra expense. Similarly, Japanese-style inns range from basic to luxurious with corresponding prices.

Japan Travel Bureau has a network of service offices throughout Tohoku, but it cannot be assumed that such offices are staffed by English-speaking employees. Unless you can enlist the services of a Japanese-speaking person, you should make detailed travel plans with JNTO in Tokyo and transportation and room reservations through a Tokyo JTB office (see Tourist Information). Reservations are essential Aug.-Oct. and highly recommended at all times.

WESTERN-STYLE
Sendai

Rich Sendai. In the heart of the nightlife district. 2–2–2 Kokubuncho; 62–8811, 242 rooms.

Sendai Tokyu. The largest in Sendai, 302 rooms. 2–9–25 Ichibancho; 62–2411.

Sendai. 1–10–25 Chuo; 25–5171. Two minutes' walk from the station. 89 rooms. Excellent service, including an English-language morning paper.

Sendai City. An old timer, 3 minutes from the station. 58 rooms. 2–2–10 Chuo; 23–5131.

Sendai Plaza. New, first rate, 2–20–1 Honcho; 62–7111.

Tokyo Dai-ichi. Has the flair of the chain. At 2–3–18, Chuo; 62–1355.

Morioka

Hotel Higashi Nihon. 3–3–18, Odori, Morioka; 25–2131. Modern facility, with 209 rooms and 8 restaurants.

Hotel Royal Morioka. Has 100 rooms at walking distance from the station, 1–11–11 Saien; 53–1331.

Morioka Grand. 1–10 Atagoshita; 25–2111. On a hill overlooking Kitakami Plain and the entire city. 44 rooms western and Japanese.

Morioka Terminal. 1–44 Ekimaedori, Morioka; 25–1211. A JNR project with 194 rooms, inside the station.

New Carina. 2–6–1, Saien Morioka; 25–2222. Centrally located and moderately priced. 249 rooms.

Akita

Akita Castle. First-rate location opposite moat. 206 rooms. 1–3–5 Nakadori; 34–1141.

Akita New Grand. 5–2–1 Nakadori; 34–5211. 114 rooms.

Hachinohe

Hachinohe Grand. 14 Bancho; 46–1234. 127 rooms.

Hachinohe Park. 2–14 Fukiage, Saiwaicho; 43–1111. 62 rooms in a beautiful garden.

Washington. 7 Jusannichi-machi; 46–3111. On main shopping street, 149 rooms.

Aomori

Aomori. Commanding views of the Mutsu Bay and the Hakkoda Mountains. 1–1–23 Tsutsumi-machi; 75–4141. 100 rooms.

Aomori Grand. 140 rooms near the station. 1–1–23 Shin-machi; 23–1011.

Yamagata

Yamagata Grand. Central, 1–7–40 Honcho; 41–2611. 120 rooms. Hotel New Otani group member.
Onuma. In the city. 72 rooms. 2–1–10 Kojirakawa-machi; 23–4143.

Mt. Zao

Hotel Sunroute Zao. Togatta Onsen, Zao-machi, (02243) 4–2321. 52 rooms, pool, tennis, near Zao ski slopes. 30 min. by bus from Shiroishi Station.

BUSINESS HOTELS

Akita. *Akita Park.* 4–5–10, Sanno; 62–1515. 197 rooms. 204 rooms. *Hawaii* 2–2, Senshu Kubotamachi. 360 rooms; 33–1111. *Hawaii New Wing.* 5–1–5 Nakadori, 33–1110. 240 rooms.
Aizu-Wakamatsu. *Fuji Grand.* 1–12, Naka-machi, Aizu-Wakamatsu, Fukushima Pref. 75 rooms. *Green Hotel Aizu.* Ekimae; 24–5181. 48 rooms.
Morioka. *Morioka Rifu.* 18–5, Nasukawa-machi; 54–4151. 57 rooms. *Star.* 2–7–6 Chuo-dori; 52–3730. 207 rooms. *New City Hotel.* 13–10 Ekimae-dori; 54–5161. 119 rooms. *Hotel Sunroute Morioka.* 3–7–19 Ohdori; 25–3311. 118 rooms. *Ace.* 2–11–35 Chuo-dori; 54–3811. 139 rooms.
Sakata. *Sakata Green.* 1–6–10, Honcho, Yamagata Pref. 69 rooms.
Sendai. *Green.* 2–5–6, Nishikimachi. 147 rooms. *Sendai Oroshi Center.* 2–15–2, Oroshi-machi. 52 rooms. *Sendai Royal.* 4–10–11, Chuo. 70 rooms. *Hotel Sun Route Sendai.* 173 rooms at 4–10–8 Chuo. *Washington,* 2–3–1 Ohmachi. 611 rooms. *Mitsui Urban.* 2–18–11 Honcho. 212 rooms.
Tsuruoka. *Sanno Plaza.* 6–8 Sannocho, Tsuruoka City, Yamagata Pref. 109 rooms.
Yamagata. *Tokyu Inn.* 1–10–1 Kasumicho; 33–0109. 100 rooms. *Green.* 1–3–12, Kasuniiche. 64 rooms. *Yamagata.* 1–1, Saiwaicho. 86 rooms.

JAPANESE-STYLE

Sendai

Miyako, 43 rooms; Takenaka Bekkan, 32 rooms.

Matsushima

Futabaso, 47 rooms; *Matsushima Dai-Ichi,* 32 rooms; *Matsushima Kanko; Taikan,* 32 rooms. All have the advantage of beautiful location.

Morioka

Aishin-kan. At Tsunagi Onsen; 89–2111. An inn with a touch of antiquity. 105 rooms. (35-minute bus ride from Morioka).

Akita

Eitaro, 35 rooms, 33–4151.

Aomori

Sakamoto, 28 rooms, 76–1481. In Misawa, *Komaki Onsen,* huge complex of hotels, museums, hot baths, 3–5151.

Yamagata

Ryokan Goto Matabei, 30 rooms. At Zao Spa, *Hotel Jurin,* 30 rooms, (0236) 94–9511; *Hotel Zao,* 55 rooms, a few western, 94–9191.

Fukushima

In the city: *Ryokan Tatsuki,* 12 rooms.

At Tsuchiyu Spa: *Sansuiso,* 53 rooms; *Yamaneya Ryokan,* 34 rooms; *Mukadaki,* 86 rooms.

At Iizaka Spa: *Akagawaya,* 30 rooms; *Hashimotokan,* 20 rooms; *Ichirakuso,* 27 rooms; *Masuya,* 41 rooms; *Tenryukaku,* 48 rooms; *Wakaki Bekkan,* 83 rooms; *kotakikan,* 31 rooms.

At Ura-Bandai: *Ura Bandai Kogen,* 59 rooms.

KOKUMIN SHUKUSHA

These Japanese-style, government-sponsored lodges are extremely popular with Japanese travelers because of their beautiful natural settings and low prices. Thus, early reservations are essential, especially for August–October.

Nishi-Towadaso, 72–1, Aza Toyama, Oaza Fukuro, Kuroishi-shi, Aomori Pref.

Iwakiso, Oaza Momosawa, Iwakicho, Naka-Tsugaru-gun, Aomori Pref.

Sannokaku, No. 4 Chiwari, Oaza Nibu, Tarocho, Shimohei-gun, Iwate Pref.

Onikobe Lodge, 23–38, Moto Miyahorn, Onikobe, Narugomachi, Tamatsukuri-gun, Miyagi Pref.

Hachimantai Onuma Lodge, Aza Kumasawa, Hachimantai, Kazuno-shi, Akita Pref.; (01862) 3–7041.

Komakusaso, 2–1, Obonai Komagatake, Tazawako-machi, Senboku-gun, Akita Pref.

Towada Caldera, Okawatai, Towada-ko, Kosaka-machi, Akita Pref.; (017675) 2821.

Okinajimaso, 1048, Gotenyama, Okinazawa, Inawashiro-machi, Yama-gun, Fukushima Pref.

Zao Bodai San-so, Zao Bodai, Kaminoyama-shi, Yamagata Pref.; (023679) 2121.

KOKUMIN KYUKAMURA

Iwate Sanroku, Shizukuishi-machi, Iwate-gun, Iwate Pref.; (01969) 2–2425.

Tazawako Kogen, Komagatake, Tazawako-machi, Akita Pref.;(01874) 3–1141.

Ura Bandai, Hibara-so, Kita-shiobara-mura, Yama-gun, Fukushima Pref.; (024132) 2421.

Pension Bear Garden is in Iwate Kogen ski area, near Koiwai Farm. Tel: Japan Pension Information Counter, TOKYO (03) 407 2333; OSAKA (06) 375 1601.

 YOUTH HOSTELS. Shimokita YH. 2–20–3, Chuo, Mutsu City 035; (01752) 4–1012. 15 min. on foot from Shimokita Sta. 60 beds. **Jonenji YH.** 4–8, Tanabu-cho, Mutsu City 035; (01752) 2–1891. 5 min. on foot from Tanabu Sta. 50 beds. Closed Nov. thr. Mar.

Uto YH. 13–9, Chaya-machi, Aomori City 030; (0177) 41–7416. 13 min. by bus from Aomori Sta. and 3 min. on foot. 160 beds. **YH Asamushi.** 203–6, Yamashita, Asamushi, Aomori City 039–04; (0177) 52–2865. 15 min. on foot from Asamushi Sta. 160 beds. **Oirase YH.** Yakeyama, Towadako-machi, Kamikita-gun, Aomori-ken 034–03; (01767) 4–2031. 2 hrs. 46 min. by bus from Aomori Sta. and 10 min. on foot. 80 beds. **YH Hakubutshu-kan.** Yasumiya, Towadakohan, Towada-machi, Kamikita-gun, Aomori-ken 018–55; (017675)

2002. 75 min. by bus from Aomori Sta. and 2 min. on foot. 200 beds. Closed Nov. 11–Apr. 14.

Nishi-Towada YH. 18, Nagasakashita, Itadome, Kuroishi City 036–04; (01725) 4–8265. 25 min. by bus from Kuroishi Sta. and 4 min. on foot. 60 beds. **Hirosaki YH.** 11, Mori-machi, Hirosaki City 036; (0172) 32–5833. 10 min. on foot from Daigaku-byoin-mae Bus Stop. 40 beds. **Fukaura YH.** 154, Okamachi, Fukaura-machi, Nishi-tsugaru-gun, Aomori-ken 038–23; (01737) 4–2459. 7 min. on foot from Fukaura Sta. 30 beds. **Morioka YH.** 1–9–41, Takamatsu, Morioka City 020–01; (0196) 62–2220. 15 min. by bus from Morioka Sta. and 3 min. on foot. 96 beds.

Hachimantai YH. 5–2, Midorigaoka, Matsuo-mura, Iwate-gun, Iwate-ken 028–73; (019578) 2031. 50 min. by bus from Obuke Sta. and 2 min. on foot. 150 beds.

Iwatesanroku-Shizukuishi YH. 19–1, Hayasaka, 10th Chiwari, Nagayama, Shizukuishi-cho, Iwate-gun, Iwate-ken 020–07; (0196) 93–2854. 20 min. by bus from Shizukuishi Sta. and 2 min. on foot. 30 beds. **Noda YH.** 3–6, Tamagawa, Noda-mura, Kunohe-gun, Iwate-ken 032–02; (019478) 2314. 20 min. on foot from Noda-tamagawa Sta. 86 beds. Closed Nov. thr. Apr. **YH Suehiro-Kan.** 7–27, Suehiro-machi, Miyako City 027; (01936) 2–1555. 3 min. on foot from Miyako Sta. 70 beds. Closed Dec. 31 thr. Jan. 7. **Miyako Kimura YH.** 1–28, Kuroda-machi, Miyako City 027; (01936) 2–2888. 7 min. on foot from Miyako Sta. 70 beds.

Rikuzen Takata YH. 176–6, Sunamori, Kesen-machi, Rikuzen-takata City 029–22; (01925) 5–4246. 25 min. on foot from Rikuzen-takata Sta. 96 beds. **Tono YH.** 13, Tsuchibuchi, Tsuchibuchi-cho, Tono City, Iwate-ken 028–05; (01986) 2–8736. 10 min. by bus from Tono Station and 7 min. on foot. 24 beds. **Hanamaki YH.** 26–4, Okubo, Kudashizawa, Hanamaki City 025–02; (01982) 5–2458. 40 min. by bus from Hanamaki Sta. and 5 min. on foot. 70 beds. **Motsuji YH.** 58, Osawa, Hiraizumi-machi, Nishi-Iwai-gun, Iwate-ken 029–41; (019146) 2331. 8 min. on foot from Hiraizumi Sta. 90 beds. Closed Dec. 30 thr. Jan. 3.

YH Takishima Ryokan. 28–1, Shinyashiki, Narugo-machi, Tamatsukuri-gun, Miyagi-ken 989–68; (02298) 3–3054. 6 min. on foot from Narugo Sta. 50 beds. **Karakuwa YH.** 2–8, Nakai, Karakuwa-machi, Motoyoshi-gun, Miyagi-ken 988–05; (02263) 2–2490. 50 min. by bus from Kesennuma Sta. 17 beds. **YH Kinkazan Jinja.** 5, Kinkazan, Ayukawahama, Oshika-machi, Oshika-gun, Miyagi-ken 986–25; (02254) 5–2264. 15 min. on foot from Kinkazan Port. 50 beds. Closed Dec. 28 thr. Jan. 3. **Matsushima YH.** 94–1, Minami-akazaki, Nobiru, Naruse-machi, Mono-gun, Miyagi-ken 981–04; (02258) 8–2220. 25 min. on foot from Nobiru Sta. 124 beds. **Sendai Chitose YH.** 6–3–8, Odawara, Sendai City 983; (0222) 22–6329. 6 min. by bus from Sendai Sta. and 3 min. on foot. 70 beds. Closed Dec. 31 thr. Jan. 3.

YH Sendai Akamon. 61, Kawauchi-kawamae-cho, Sendai City 980; (0222) 64–1405. 10 min. by bus from Sendai Sta. and 5 min. on foot. 51 beds. Closed Dec. 30 thr. Jan. 3. **Sendai Onnai YH.** 1–9–35, Kashiwagi, Sendai City 980; (0222) 34–3922. 15 min. by bus from Sendai Sta. and 2 min. on foot. 25 beds. **Sendai-Dochuan YH.** 31, Kitayashiki, Onoda, Sendai City 982; (0222) 47–0511. 25 min. by bus from Sendai Sta. and 1 min. on foot. 20 beds. **Minami-Zao YH.** 59–17, Kashiwagiyama, Shichigashuku-cho, Katta-gun, Miyagi-ken 989–05; (02243) 7–2124. 80 min. by bus from Shiroishi Sta. and 3 min. on foot. 50 beds.

Towada YH. Hakka, Towada-kohan, Kazuno-gun, Akita-ken 018–55; (017675) 2603. 70 min. by bus from Towada-minami Sta. 100 beds. **Kuromori-So YH.** 63, Kaminoyu, Towada-oyu, Kazuno City 018–54; (01863) 7–2144. 17 min. by bus from Towada-minami Sta. and 2 min. on foot. 50 beds. **Hachiman-**

tai **Onuma YH.** Onuma-onsen, Hachimantai, Kazuno City 018–51; (01862) 3–7042. 50 min. by bus from Hachimantai Sta. and 5 min. on foot. 78 beds. Closed Nov. 6 thr. Apr. **Tazawa-Ko YH.** 33–8, Kami-ishikami, Obonai, Tazawa-ko-machi, Senboku-gun, Akita-ken 014–12; (01874) 3–1281. 15 min. by bus from Tazawa-ko Sta. and 2 min. on foot. 98 beds.

Oga YH. 85–1, Nakazato, Kitaura-yumoto, Oga City 010–06; (018533) 3125. 50 min. by bus from Hadachi Sta. and 3 min. on foot. 120 beds. **Oga Chorakuji YH.** Monzen, Funakawa-minato, Oga City 010–05; (01852) 7–2611. 50 min. by bus from Oga Sta. and 5 min. on foot. 80 beds. **Fukushima YH.** Takayu-onsen, 1–49, Jin-no-mori, Machiniwasaka, Fukushima City 960–22; (0245) 91–1412. 40 min. by bus from Fukushima Sta. and 8 min. on foot. 96 beds. **YH Bandai-So.** Yokomuki-onsen, Inawashiro-machi, Yama-gun, Fukushima-ken 969–27; (024272) 2911. 40 min. by bus from Inawashiro Sta. 200 beds.

Ura-Bandai YH. Goshikinuma, Ura-bandai, Azuma-kyoku, Fukushima-ken 969–27; (024132) 2811. 30 min. by bus from Inawashiro Sta. and 7 min. on foot. 100 beds. **YH Bandai Yuai-Sanso.** 7105, Hayama, Inawashiro-machi, Yama-gun, Fukushima-ken 969–31; (02426) 2–3424 15 min. by bus from Inawashiro Sta. and 3 min. on foot. 70 beds. **Misato YH.** 45–7, Hirohata, Shimo-oguni, Ryozen-machi, Date-gun, Fukushima-ken 960–08; (02458) 6–1828. 40 min. by bus from Fukushima Sta. and 4 min. on foot. 15 beds.

Tsuruoka YH. 1–1, Miya-no-mae, Sanze, Tsuruoka City 999–74; (023573) 3205. 15 min. on foot from Sanze Sta. 96 beds. **Azuma YH.** 3934, Seki, Yonezawa City 992–14; (0238) 55–2002. 50 min. by bus from Yonezawa Sta. and 15 min. on foot. 50 beds. **Yamagata YH.** 293–3, Kurosawa, Yamagata City, Yamagata Pref. 990–23. 5 min. on foot from Kurosawa-onsen bus stop. 20 beds.

HOW TO GET AROUND. Most visitors use a combination of trains, buses and sightseeing boats to explore Tohoku. Rental cars are available, but, except on the Tohoku Expressway, road signs are not in roman letters. The expressway runs from Tokyo to Aomori City, except for a short leg north of Morioka yet to be completed. Off the expressway, the driving pace is leisurely and the roads are generally good and uncrowded. The *Tohoku Shinkansen* bullet train connects Tokyo and Morioka with stops at Fukushima City, Sendai, Ichinoseki, and other main cities on the eastern side of the district. The *Tohoku Honsen* follows the same route and then goes on to Aomori City. The *Ou Honsen* covers the interior and western side of Tohoku from Fukushima City to Aomori City with stops at Yamagata City, Omagari, Akita City, Hirosaki, and others. The *Uetsu Honsen* runs along the Sea of Japan to Aomori City.

Bus routes cover all but the most remote areas, although many run on infrequent schedules in less populated locations. A new private train line, the *Sanriku Teitsudo,* has joined JNR local lines along the rugged Pacific coastline of the Rikuchu Kaigan National Park, and sightseeing boats also connect several points within the park. Comfortable sightseeing buses (with Japanese commentary only) from nearby cities cover the Towada-Hachimantai and Bandai-Asahi National Parks. Get train, bus and boat schedules at the Japan Travel Bureau in Tokyo.

TOURIST INFORMATION. A note of caution. English is not widely spoken in outside Tohoku, particularly the major cities. There are, for all practical purposes, no local sightseeing tours in which English-speaking guides are available. So while local residents will be more than eager to help the visitor find his or her way around, some advance research is advised.

The *Japan National Tourist Office* has a tourist information center in Tokyo, located on Harumidori, between Hibiya Park and the elevated tracks of the Japanese National Railroad. The center staff can provide guidance on getting around the Tohoku, and assist with details on transportation and local accommodations. TIC hours are: 9:00 A.M. to 5:00 P.M. on weekdays; Saturday from 9:00 A.M. to noon; closed Sunday and national holidays.

Japan Travel Bureau (JTB) has a network of service offices throughout the Tohoku. These can make reservations for accommodations and transportation for foreign visitors, but it cannot be assumed that such offices are staffed by English-speaking employees.

Aomori. 2–8–7, Shinmachi, Aomori City; (0177) 23–2411. Located on the main street.

Morioka. Inside Morioka Station; (0196) 51–1311. Also 2–5, Uchimaru, Morioka City; (0196) 51–3331. Opposite side of Iwate Prefectural Library.

Hanamaki. 1–9024, Ohdori, Hanamaki City; (0198) 23–6321. In front of Hanamaki Station.

Ichinoseki. 152 Ohte, Ichinoseki City; (0191) 23–4000. 3 blocks northwest from Ichinoseki Station.

Akita. 3–2–5 Ohmachi, Akita City; (0188) 63–6616. 8 blocks west west from Akita Station.

Sendai. Inside Sendai Station; (0222) 64–3461. Also 3–6–1 Ichibancho, Sendai City; (0222) 22–5243. 6 blocks from Sendai Station, next to Dai-Ichi Kangyo Bank.

Fukushima. Inside Fukushima Station (0245) 23–3311. Also 4–4 Ohmachi, Fukushima City; (0245) 23–2851. Located in Tohou Building on Chuo-dori Street.

SEASONAL EVENTS. January. *Donto-sai Festival* in Sendai on the 14th–15th. The Festival of the Burning of New Year Decorations is celebrated at the Osaki Hachiman Shrine with an enormous bonfire and Shinto ceremonials conducted with easy dignity and unpompous reverence in a gay fairground atmosphere. Evening.

In mid-January throughout Japan *hadaka mairi* or naked festivals are held at local shrines, including those in the snowy north. In most cases, crowds of men clad only in loincloths participate in parades and games in the snow to demonstrate their piety and fortitude.

February. *The Iwate Snow Festival,* Feb. 3–12, is held on the snowy slopes of Mt. Iwate near Morioka. Ice sculptures and snow huts (kamakura) cover the summertime pastures of Koiwai Ranch.

Bon-ten or Kamakura Festival, Yokote City, from the 15th–17th. Kamakura is the name given in Yokote to the little snowhouses which are scooped out of the large drifts and piles of snow at the sides of the streets, or in private gardens. Women and children wearing fine *kimono* or hooded cloaks of straw sit inside the kamakura. There is *tatami* on the snowy floor, and they sit round a brazier, their legs covered with pretty *futon* or quilts. On the brazier they heat pots of sweet sake, called *ama-zake* and rice cakes. In the back wall of each kamakura is a little niche for a *Shinto* shrine, with lighted candles and offerings of oranges, *sake,* apples and ricecakes; these are gifts to the God of Water, so important for the rice fields in spring and summer. On the morning of the 16th there is the Bon-ten Parade, one of the most colorful in all of Japan. A similar festival is observed at Miyoshi Shrine, Akita, on February 17.

April. *Cherry Blossom Festival* begins at Hirosaki and continues for about two weeks, from April 24th–May 7th. Differs from other cherry festivals throughout the country only in the relative lack of commercialism. Neighborhood processions and plenty of unorganized merriment by the farmfolk under the trees. All day and night.

May. The 3rd is the final day of the *Uesugi Festival* in Yamagata's Yonezawa where a half-mile-long procession of costumed samurai warriors honor the city's former castletown days. *The Spring Fujiwara Festival* in Hiraizumi, Iwate Pref., May 1–5, features outdoor Noh performances at Motsuji and Chusonji temples on the 5th, and a costume parade of 12th-century samurai on the 3rd.

June. *Chagu-Chagu Umakko,* Horse Festival, in Morioka on the 15th, At this festival, colorfully decorated horses are led from Sozen Shrine to Hachiman Shrine.

July. *Nomaoi,* or Wild Horse Chasing, on Hibarigahara, Hara nomachi, Soma, Fukushima Pref., July 23–24. A crowd of riders in ancient armor vie for three shrine flags, and men in white costumes try to catch horses chased into an enclosure by the horsemen.

August. *Bon Odori,* the Summer Dance Festival, is celebrated throughout the region with folk dancing practically every evening from mid-month. The dances in Sendai's Kozenji-dori, lit by lanterns imaginatively painted by school children, and the one outside Sendai Station are good examples of this traditional festival.

Lantern Floating and Fireworks Festival, Abukuma River, Fukushima City on Aug. 1st. Associated with the Buddhist Festival of the Dead, the casting of lighted lanterns on the river denotes the farewell ceremonies in which the family returns the souls of the deceased ancestors to their proper places in paradise. The lanterns are supposed eventually to reach the sea.

Port Festival, Shiogama Town on the 5th. The annual celebration at the town, located halfway between Sendai and Matsushima, is blessed by colorful ceremonies. The portable shrine of Shiogama is carried through the streets and then placed on a large decorated boat in the shape of a Phoenix. The boat then sails to the Matsushima pine-covered islands and back, surrounded by hundreds of gaily decorated fishing boats.

Hirosaki Neputa Festival, Aug. 1–5. Aomori Prefecture's former castle town is the scene of evening processions of huge and elaborate fan-shaped floats made of bamboo and rice paper and lighted from inside. Main features in Hirosaki are the figures of mythical warriors, demons and brave samurai, carried by as many as 50 persons. The children almost always carry small goldfish lanterns.

Aomori City's *Nebuta Festival,* Aug. 2–7, is one of Tohoku's Big Three summer festivals held the first week in August. (Tanabata and Kanto listed below are the other two.) The three lure two million Japanese visitors north for a frenzied week of color and crowds. Nebuta is like Neputa, but on a grander scale with giant, gaudily painted illuminated floats and thousands of chanting, sake-laden dancers.

Kanto (Lantern) Festival, Akita City, from the 5th–7th. Every afternoon the festival begins with a parade of *kanto* is a long bamboo pole with 8 crossbars from which hang about 50 paper lanterns. Weighing about 130 pounds, the 50-foot high pole-and-lanterns mass is shaped like a pile of rice bales, the lanterns representing sacks of grain. Each kanto is carried by one young man representing his own neighborhood, school, or place of employment. At twilight kanto handlers begin their balancing acts to the accompaniment of drum and bamboo fife music and the rousing cheers by their partisan supporters. A winner is announced around midnight when everyone, except perhaps the by now completely inebriated performer, is exhausted.

Star Festival, the Tanabata Matsuri, from the 6th–8th, is the most celebrated display of color and popular enthusiasm to be found in Japan. Visitors from all over the land flock to Sendai to see the decorations, which turn the streets into whispering arcades of brilliantly hued blossoming paper streamers. These papers, on smaller versions of which love poems and secret wishes are written and exchanged, are suspended from huge balls of paper flowers which in turn hang from long bamboo poles arching high over the roadway. This festival commemorates the romantic Chinese legend of the Weaving Princess and the Peasant Shepherd. *Hanagasa Festival,* Yamagata City, from the 6th–7th. Thousands of folk dancers in summer cotton kimono (yukata) and flower-decorated straw hats (hanagasa) parade through downtown Yamagata after dark for what is sometimes called Tohoku's 4th big summer festival.

September. *Kokeshi Festival,* Narugo, Miyagi Pref., from the 7th–9th. Narugo's kokeshi folkcraft tradition is celebrated with a lantern and costume parade on the 7th, a competition of kokeshi artisans on the 8th, and folk dances on the 9th. Also a memorial service is held for imperfect wooden dolls that had to be destroyed over the year. *Aizu Byakko Festival,* Aizu-Wakamatsu, Fukushima Pref., from the 22nd–24th. At 10:00 A.M. each day a procession of samurai warriors leaves Tsuruga Castle to parade through city streets.

October. *Lantern Festival,* Nihonmatsu City from Oct. 4th–5th. In the evening in this small mountain town, the inhabitants and anyone who cares to join parade the streets carrying every sort of lantern. There are prizes for the most elaborate and the most ingenious. Some of the lanterns are strikingly original in design. Many of the homemade ones can be purchased after the festival.

November 1–3. *Autumn Fujiwara Festival,* Hiraizumi. Like the spring festivities, there is a parade on the 1st and Noh performances at Chusonji Temple on the 3rd.

TOURS. Get details at the TIC or JTB in Tokyo. Morioka, Sendai and Aizu-Wakamatsu offer bus tours of their cities. Some Sendai tours include Matsushima Bay. Buses with tour guides leave from Amorori City and Misawa for Lake Towada, from Aizu-Wakamatsue and Fukushima City for the Bandai-Asahi National Park, and from Akita City for the Oga Peninsula.

To Matsushima. At Shiogama's wharf, there are tour boats that cross Matsushima Bay. The tour operators offer a choice of boats for the ride; there are the familiar harbor-tour type boats or, for a higher price, a small fleet of quite garishly decorated "dragon boats." Descriptive narrations over the ship's loudspeaker, on any of the excursion boats, is only in Japanese.

PARTICIPANT SPORTS. *Skiing* and *ice skating* are the favorite sports in winter, and Mt. Zao the best location for both. Make Sendai your base, and arrange with your hotel or the local travel agency for reservations at the ski grounds. You will find every slope covered with Japanese enthusiasts, ranging from the amateurs to the experts. Try to avoid weekends, when crowds make intelligent skiing impossible.

MUSEUMS. At **Aizu-Wakamatsu,** *Bukeyashiki* is an ancient samurai mansion complex open for viewing: an authentic recreation of a grouping of ten buildings of a 17th-century feudal estate. **Hiraizumi,** two and one-half hours by express from Sendai, boasts two small museums and a picture gallery. A modern fireproof museum at the top of the hill, near Chusonji Temple, contains many gorgeous relics of robes, screens, fans, and scrolls from the time of a famous warlord's exile. A large gallery of paintings reconstructs the life of Yoshitsune's times. Open from 9:00 A.M. to 5:00 P.M. except on special observance days at the temple. The treasure House of the temple contains an interesting display of the costumes and jewelry taken from the mummies of several Fujiwara lords, whose bodies were discovered resting beneath the Konjiki-do (Golden Temple) shortly after World War II.

Akita has several collections of note. At Senshu Park is the *Hirano Art Museum* that houses contemporary Japanese paintings as well as works by Goya, Picasso and Van Gogh. The *Prefectural Museum* and the *City Museum* are small, but occasionally schedule special exhibitions. In **Aomori City,** the *kyodokan* and *keikokan* (short taxi rides from the station) display folk articles. In **Morioka,** the city museum, *Kyodo Shiryokan,* is a new building in a feudal-era garden. The *Morioka Museum of Modern Arts,* near Mount Iwa, is the one-man effort of painter Yaoji Hashimoto. At **Kagano,** the museum is modelled after a Tohoku farmhouse, and has sculptures and paintings, many of them of local scenes.

In **Iwaizumi,** Iwate, is the nation's first science museum, utilizing a newly found natural stalactite cave. Its murals are controversial reproductions *(Ryusen Shindo Science Museum).*

The *Tenkyo Kaku Villa,* where the Emperor and Empress honeymooned in 1924, has been restored and opened to the public. Built in 1908 as a summer resort house for Prince Arisugawa, the villa is on the shore of Lake Inawashiro, **Fukushima.**

 SHOPPING. Folkcraft specialties are the shoppers' delight in Tohoku. Kokeshi dolls, limbless cylindrical wooden dolls, were originated in Tohoku and here you can find all types. The widest selections are in Sendai craft shops, but in hot spring towns, such as Sakunami and Narugo in Miyagi Pref., you can see the process and make your own doll. Cast-iron kettles *(tetsubin)* are Morioka's specialty and excellent handmade paper is Sendai's, along with the famous Sendai chests and fine antiques. Prefectural showrooms in Sendai, Morioka, Akita, Yamagata, and Aomori display local handicrafts.

 DINING OUT. For Western food, the hotel restaurants are generally the best with the exception of Sendai where a selection of international restaurants can be found. American-style fast food chains are slowly creeping northward into the larger cities. The adventurous traveler will not be satisfied unless he has an opportunity to try the local specialties, especially the delicious Matsushima oyster, the Morioka noodles, and other Tohoku specialties. Below is a listing of the best eating establishments in the area, excluding the hotels.

Sendai

Fukizushi. The best *sushi* restaurant in Sendai. Located farther up Kokuncho street. Slightly more expensive than usual in Tohoku.

Seiyoken. 1–1 Omachi; Offers good European dishes at reasonable prices.

Akita

Akita Club. Nakadori, specializes in sukiyaki.

Hamanoya. 4, Ichikawahan, Akita City. Specializes in baked or raw *hata hata* fish, a local specialty.

Kurabu. In the Meitengai downtown district. Another specialist in *shotsurunabe* and *kiritampo.*

Plaza Miyako. 9–25 Yanagi-machi. In Noshiro City (between Aomori and Akita), claims to have the best French-style chicken in Tohoku, a distinction about which there is probably little argument.

Aomori

Suiraku. 3–3–4 Honcho, specializes in sea urchin and fresh scallops. The scallops *(hotategai)* are cooked, fried, or served raw from mid-July to March.

Itamacho. 3–3–8 Honcho, well-established. Japanese seafood the specialty.

Ezashi

Matsuya Shokudo and **Manya Shokudo.** These restaurants specialize in the noodle, lifting it to a place of honor. The town is located about halfway between Sendai and Morioka City, and if you get tired of traveling, you can always get off for some noodles and catch the next train. Both are located at Ezashicho, Ezashi-gun.

Hiraizumi

Chusonji Temple. Their special mushroom dish, called *shiautoryori,* is a typical monastic food in that it is vegetarian, but quite delicious.

Morioka

Chokuri-an. 1–12–13, Nakanohashi-dori; 24–0441. Serves soba.

Jubei. 3–11, Nagata-cho; 54–5235. Sushi.

Nambu Robata. Hachiman-cho; 22–5082. Regional specialties served at traditional hearth-side.

Yamagoya. 2–6–23 Saien; 52–5672. Serves country dishes of traditional food. The name means "mountain hut."

Shiogama

Janomezushi. Specializes in oysters and *fugu* (globe-fish) served *sukiyaki* style. Inexpensive. Inarishita. Also a *sushi* shop.

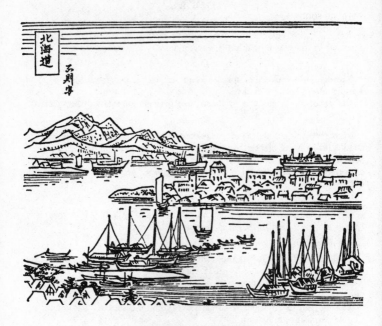

HOKKAIDO

By
WALTER W. MILLER

Hokkaido, Japan's northernmost main island, is unlike any other place in this island nation. The island is big—83,500 square kilometers (32,240 square miles); it's rugged, formed by violent volcanic eruptions, which created soaring mountains and rolling plains. The landscape and climate is very similar to New England's. The Japanese call it their "Last Frontier." Despite its massive size and wide-open spaces, Hokkaido, with a population of about 5.6 million people, is Japan's least populated island. There is a frontier spirit in the people here; they are generally more relaxed and open, friendlier than their counterparts to the south. And like most people raised in an open, "frontier" environment, they exude a degree of confidence that is welcome.

Many tourists coming to Japan bypass Hokkaido, which is too bad. Although full-scale development didn't begin on the island until the Meiji era, from 1868–1912, Hokkaido has natural wonders that make a journey to the island worth the time and expense. And its rewards are offered year-round—go in the winter for the best skiing in Asia or to attend the world-famous Sapporo Snow Festival, which is held for five days in early February every year; spring, summer, and early autumn are ideal for hiking, backpacking, and mountain climbing. In addition, the island is noted for its numerous hot springs where you can bathe in soothing waters any time of the year. Hokkaido also is famous for its beer—some claim Sapporo beer is the best in Japan—and its cuisine, such as its delicious salmon; Genghis Khan, a mutton barbecue with a special sauce; *Kegani* (hairy) crabs, which are mainly caught off the coasts of the island and simply boiled to bring out their subtle flavor; and the tasty corn on the cob, which is grilled with a special sauce at street stands.

Hokkaido is home to the Ainu, a people native to the island, who have not fared well against the encroaching tide of modern life. By the last decade of the 19th century their way of life was nearly destroyed and they themselves faced extinction. The Japanese government stepped in, however, and began implementing a policy aimed at assimilating the Ainu into the mainstream of Japanese life. The first Ainu arrived on the island about 800 years ago, displacing a race of people who apparently had occupied the land for a much longer time. The Ainu also used to live on Honshu, with their territory reaching nearly to present-day Sendai. But this peaceful people stood no chance against the more warlike Yamato Japanese, who pushed them back to the wilderness of Hokkaido.

Little is known about the Ainu. Their roots might possibly be traced to tribes in Siberia, but experts remain puzzled over just where the Ainu originally came from. Traditionally they were a race with slight Caucasian traces, for example, abundance of facial and body hair, and of course their language was different from that of the Japanese. Being so physically different and speaking a different language, they were severely discriminated against. As a result, many have adopted Japanese names, language, and customs, and most do not advertise the fact that they are of Ainu descent. Today there are perhaps 15,000 full-blooded Ainu on Hokkaido. A few wear traditional dress for tourists and can be seen at Shiraoi, Noboribetsu-onsen, Asahikawa, and in the area around Akan-ko and Kussharo-ko.

The government seriously began opening up Hokkaido in the Meiji Era encouraging residents of the lower islands to migrate to the north. They were greeted by a rugged frontier and harsh climatic conditions, similar to what settlers in the United States experienced when they began moving across the Mississippi and opened the West. But their efforts paid off to a considerable extent and today, through its fishing industry and agriculture, Hokkaido has become one of Japan's major sources of food. Unlike on the southern islands, farming is practiced on a large scale and there are expansive dairy farms. Major crops are potatoes, sweet corn, wheat, and beans. In addition to fishing, forestry is also a key industry. More than 70 percent of the island is under timber, and the amount of annual lumber production is a quarter of the nation's total.

You can reach Sapporo, capital of Hokkaido, either by flying or taking the train and ferry, which, if you have the time, is a terrific way to see a lot of the Japanese countryside. The flight from Tokyo's Haneda or Narita airports to Chitose Airport, which services Sapporo, takes 1 hour and 25 minutes.

By train you take the Tohoku or Joban lines from Tokyo's Ueno Station to Aomori on Honshu's northern coast, about a 9-hour journey.

Or, if you don't mind changing trains at Morioka, you can save over 3 hours travel time by taking the Tohoku Shinkansen bullet train north to its Morioka terminus. You can make the trip to Sapporo all in one day, but it's easier to spend the night in Aomori. There are several hotels near city's ferry pier. The next morning you board the Seikan-renraku ferryboat for the 3-hour, 50-minute voyage to the port city of Hakodate, located on the southern tip of Hokkaido. Then you get the Hakodate Line train from Hakodate to Sapporo, a journey that takes about 4½ hours.

For more than fifteen years Japanese workers have been drilling and blasting their way through volcanic rock 790 feet below the sea, building the world's longest tunnel, intended to link the main island of Honshu with Hokkaido. Some 3,000 workers have been working on the 32.3-mile Seikan tunnel, designed for the Shinkansen, Japan's famed "Bullet Train," which could conceivably whisk passengers between Tokyo and Sapporo in 5 hours, 50 minutes, slicing 11 hours off the current train travel time. But the staggering $800 million cost of the project has more than tripled and there are serious doubts that the tunnel will ever be used for passenger train service.

Hakodate

Hakodate is not a city where you need to spend a lot of time, but nevertheless it offers some interesting blends of East and West. The city fans out from the base of Mount Hakodate on the tip of Oshima Peninsula, which juts out into the Tsugaru Straits off the coast of southwestern Hokkaido. It's the jumping off place for the rest of the island. Hakodate flourishes as an important fishing port, although the fishermen here as elsewhere in Japan have sharply felt the limitations Moscow has placed on their fishing activities in Soviet waters.

You can get to the top of the 335-meter-high Mount Hakodate by walking or by riding the cable car. The summit provides a breathtaking view of the city, especially at night.

Hakodate was one of the first three ports in Japan opened for foreign trade in 1859. In the old section of the city are numerous American and European-style buildings, some quite impressive. This area is good for an easy early morning of wandering. To get to the old section of Hakodate, which is centered around the Japan Orthodox Hakodate Resurrection Church, take the streetcar to Juji-gai stop in Motomachi. You see the church when you get off the streetcar. The church was established by a Russian prelate in 1862. The present Byzantine-style building was constructed on the site in 1916 after the original was destroyed by fire. It is not open to the public.

Nearby is the Hakodate-koen park, a lovely wooded area with hundreds of cherry trees. Here, too, is the Hakodate Museum, which has a good collection and a modern display of artifacts of the aboriginal races of the island.

Goryokaku, Japan's only Western-style fort, is located in the center of the city, a 10-minute walk from Goryokaku streetcar stop. The star-shaped fort was built in 1864. It was the site of a siege for more

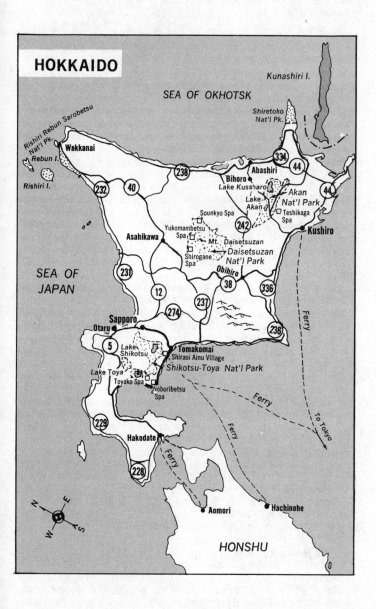

HOKKAIDO

Kunashiri I.

SEA OF OKHOTSK

Shiretoko Nat'l Pk.

Rishiri Rebun Sarobetsu Nat'l Pk.

Rebun I.

Wakkanai

Rishiri I.

238

Bihoro
Lake Kussharo
Lake Akan

Abashiri

334

44

44

232

40

Akan Nat'l Park

Teshikaga Spa

Kushiro

Sounkyo Spa

Yukomambetsu Spa

Asahikawa

242

Mt. Daisetsuzan

Shirogane Spa

Daisetsuzan Nat'l Park

SEA OF JAPAN

231

12

274

237

Obihiro

38

336

236

Sapporo

Otaru

5

Lake Shikotsu

Tomakomai

Shiraoi Ainu Village

Shikotsu-Toya Nat'l Park

Lake Toya

Toyako Spa

Noboribetsu Spa

Ferry

Ferry

To Tokyo

229

Hakodate

Ferry

Ferry

228

N E W S

Aomori

Hachinohe

HONSHU

than a month in 1868, when supporters of the Tokugawa shogunate resisted the Meiji restoration.

Sapporo

Sapporo, home to about 1.4 million people, is a fairly new city, beautifully laid out in a Western-style chessboard pattern, which makes it an easy place for strolling. The city was founded in 1869 by Yoshitake Shima, the first commissioner of the Hokkaido Colonization Commission. It's pleasantly cool here in summer, and the harsh winter temperatures don't arrive until mid-December.

Sapporo gained worldwide fame in 1972 when it was headquarters for the Winter Olympics, which were played out at various places on the island. Many new Western-style hotels and restaurants were built then, making this city an especially comfortable place for Westerners who can't adjust to the sleeping and eating habits of the Japanese.

Sapporo's transportation system is excellent. The bus system is extensive; the subway has two lines, the North-South and the East-West, respectively, running underground in the downtown area and aboveground in the suburban areas; and there is one streetcar line in operation.

The city has numerous parks, the most famous and popular being Odori Park, which runs east and west through the city's center, dividing it north and south. On sunny days people flock here to enjoy the sun and eat their lunches on the lush green grass. During the February Snow Festival, the park is taken over by giant ice and snow statues carved in the shape of animals, cartoon characters, and famous buildings, such as the White House in Washington, D.C.

The people who own Sapporo Beer's original brewery had the good sense not to tear it down. Instead, it has been transformed into a German-type beer hall, located 1.7 kilometers east of the train station. In winter it's a great place to go to enjoy a roaring fire, eat, and drink beer; and during the summer there is a huge outdoor beer garden where you can sit at tables, drink cool, refreshing beer and listen to music.

Although Sapporo isn't very old, it does have some sites of merit. For example, adjacent to the City Hall, about 400 meters south of the train station, is the Clock Tower (a National Cultural Treasure) built in 1878; today the building houses a museum of Hokkaido history. The Old Hokkaido Government Building is also a National Cultural Treasure. Originally built in 1873 to house the Colonization Commission, the Western-style red-brick building was rebuilt at its present site, about 200 meters southwest of the train station, in 1888. The city is also home to Hokkaido University, located about 500 meters north of Sapporo Station. The campus itself is a lovely park and a good place for a quiet stroll.

Going in the other direction from the station, 500 meters to the southwest, is the Botanical Gardens, which contains some 5,000 varieties of plants collected from all over the island. Here also is the Ainu Museum, with some 20,000 items, including costumes, canoes, and other objects used by the Ainu.

The beautiful new Hokkaido Museum of Modern Art, a five-minute walk from the Tozai subway line's Nishi 18 Station, has displays of local, national and foreign modern art, as well as special exhibits.

Nakajima Park is located 2.5 kilometers south of the station, or easily reached from Nakajimakoen subway station. It contains a Japanese garden, the Nakajima Sports Center, a swimming pool and two cultural treasures of merit: the Hasso-an teahouse, originally built in the 17th century by Enshu Kobori, noted master of the tea cult; and the Hoheikan guest house, once used to receive the Imperial families and other distinguished guests.

About 10 kilometers south of Sapporo Station is Hitsujigaoka Observation Hill, a vast expanse of grass fields stretching over sloping hills on the outskirts of the city. A super place for an easy hike and for a terrific view of the city.

The best way to see the rest of Hokkaido is to use Sapporo as a base and rent a car to take day- or one- or two-night trips out into the countryside. Another way is to go by train, a journey that isn't difficult and provides an excellent way to see the island.

Shikotsu-Toya National Park

About 70 kilometers southwest of Sapporo, is an area of lakes, mountains, forests, volcanoes, hot springs, and other sights. Shikotsu-Toya National Park is the playground for both Hakodate and Sapporo, and as such, it is relatively tamed.

Lake Toya is noted for its natural design—it's an almost completely circular caldera lake. The enormous Toyako Spa, located on the lakeshore, is jammed with hotels, inns, restaurants, and gaudy souvenir shops.

From the lake you can enjoy a clear view of Mount Yotei, called the Mount Fuji of Hokkaido. There are good hiking trails in the nearby hills, and several camping grounds. Toya Spa is on the south shore, and a 7-minute bus ride away is the smaller, quieter Sobetsu spa, which also has accommodations.

The Jozankei Spa is only about an hour southwest by bus from Sapporo Station. Lodged between high cliffs soaring above the upper reaches of the Toyohira River, this popular spa has numerous hotels, both Japanese and Western-style, and restaurants. It also is a fine base for exploring Lake Toya. Good hiking trails into the mountains can be found here too, and 25 minutes by bus will bring you to the Jozankei Kogen International Skiground.

Jozankei is the center of winter sports in this area. It has the most developed of the island's many ski resorts; however, it still doesn't compare with what you may be used to in Europe or the United States. The best thing to remember is that if you are coming to Hokkaido to ski, don't expect to find many modern mechanical ski amenities. You will, however, find excellent slopes and good snow conditions.

About 46 kilometers by mountain roads from Toyako Spa, or 1 hour and 30 minutes by train from Sapporo, is Noboribetsu Spa, the most famous in Japan. It is especially noted for its hot spring baths and the "Valley of Hell," described below. The Dai-ichi Takimoto Hotel-Inn has both Western and Japanese-style rooms and public hot-spring mineral baths. Its "grand bathroom" is reputedly the largest in Japan. A vast, tiled room, it contains baths of various shapes and sizes filled with hot-spring water of different chemical compositions. This is one of the few spas left in Japan where mixed nude public bathing still prevails. But don't get too excited or alarmed—the men cluster at one end of the giant hall, the women at the other; eyes are modestly lowered.

A few minutes' walk from the village is Jigokudani, or Hell Valley, a bow-shaped valley 400 feet deep and about a mile around, full of fufalores, boiling streams, nearly overwhelming smells of sulfur, and tourists taking pictures.

Shiraoi is a small village south of Lake Shikotsu, 40 minutes by bus or car, or 30 minutes by train from Noboribetsu. This is probably the largest single settlement of Ainu found on the island. Here, you will see typical Ainu grass houses and listen to an Ainu chieftain, perhaps; actually, what you will see are the last remnants of a dying people and their culture.

From Shiraoi, by turning inland at the port city of Tomakomai, you can reach Lake Shikotsu where the small spa of Marugoma is located. Here you can fish—the lake trout are reportedly delicious. Few people here speak English, but you can easily find a Japanese inn in which to spend a night or two. If you are driving, it takes about 2 or 3 hours to reach Sapporo.

Akan National Park

Located due east of Sapporo on the other side of Hokkaido is Akan National Park, a magnificent wilderness area marked by dense forests, three major lakes, and several volcanoes. Allow at least two or three days for a trip to this region. Probably the best way to reach the park is to take a train or plane to one of the towns nearby and then rent a car to travel through the park itself.

At the northeastern edge of the park is Abashiri, a pleasant little town with an excellent collection of genuine Ainu arts and crafts in the town's museum. Here also are clean lake beaches, a natural botanical garden, and good camping sites.

Entering the park through Bihoro, about 30 kilometers southwest of Abashiri, is the most interesting route. South from Bihoro the road crests the Bihoro Pass, nearly 2,000 feet above sea level and one of the mere handful of places in all Japan where you can get a feeling of really open space. The sweeping views over the Abashiri Plain and over most of Akan National Park are breathtaking. The drive down from the pass is through an alpine forest which in October bursts with color.

Each of the park's three lakes—Kussharo, Akan, and Mashu—has its own distinctive characteristics. Kussharo is Japan's largest mountain lake, but its shores are relatively flat and well developed. There are hot springs with good Japanese-style accommodations, a youth hostel and a campground.

Lake Akan is surrounded by dense forest. The town of Akan is a provincial resort with a number of Japanese inns and a lovely view of the mountains. The lake is famous for *marimo*—lovely green two- to five-inch balls of duckweed, which absorb oxygen from the water and rise slowly to the surface. There they release their oxygen and sink quietly to the bottom again. They occur in only three lakes in the world—one in Switzerland, one in the Siberian island of Saghalien, and here. Once almost destroyed by greedy tourists, marimo now are strictly protected by law.

Just about an hour's drive from Akan is Mashu, a deep crater lake of dark, almost black, blue water. It is one of the deepest lakes in Japan. Curiously, no water flows in or out of this lake, and at 136 feet it has the second highest transparent depth in the world. About 45 minutes southwest of Lake Mashu is Teshikaga Spa, a small hot spring town with a number of pleasant Japanese inns.

Daisetsuzan National Park

Daisetsuzan National Park is the largest of Japan's national parks, and is located almost right in the center of Hokkaido. The park attracts tourists who come to enjoy its lofty mountains covered by forests and wild flowers in profusion; numerous gorges and ravines carved by the huge Ishikari River; and popular spas such as Sounkyo, Shirogane, Yukomambetsu, and Shikaribetsu.

The word "Daisetsuzan" means "Great Snow Mountains" and refers to the park's five major peaks, all of them more than 6,500 feet in height. The major jumping off place for a visit to the park is Asahikawa, an ugly industrial city. You would have a more pleasant stay in either Sounkyo or Shirogane spas.

Sounkyo, a 2½-hour drive from Asahikawa, has a number of good Japanese inns and is located on the Sounkyo Gorge.

Shirogane also has numerous hot spring inns, located not far from Mount Tokachi, a volcano which last erupted in 1962. The lava from this eruption formed a massive blanket down one face of the mountain and in winter this now provides an excellent base for skiing. Shirogane is about a 3½-hour drive from Asahigawa.

At Yukomambetsu spa you can take a cable car part of the way up Mount Asahi, the highest mountain in Hokkaido at a height of 2,290 meters, then make about a 2-hour hike to reach the summit, which provides a rewarding panoramic view. The spa is southeast of Asahikawa, about 1 hour, 30 minutes by bus.

The Northeast Coast

Along the northeast coast of Hokkaido is the Abashiri Quasi-National Park. The highlights of the park are sand dunes on the Sea of Okhotsk coast and natural flower gardens along the swampy shore of Lake Saroma. An example is the Koshimizu Gensei Kaen (Natural Flower Garden), reached in 30 minutes by bus from Abashiri city station. Abashiri is the center of the park and the largest city on the northeast coast.

In winter, innumerable ice floes jam together and stretch from the coast out to sea as far as the eye can see. Also during the winter months the annual flight of swans from Siberia to Tofutsu Lagoon, attract bird watchers as does the government-protected Tancho-zuru swamp, near Kushiro on Hokkaido's southeast coast.

PRACTICAL INFORMATION FOR HOKKAIDO

WHEN TO GO? The standard Hokkaido season is from May to October. During July and August Hokkaido is jammed with vacationing students, tour groups, affluent Japanese and resident foreigners fleeing the heat of the cities in Honshu. Hotel space is difficult and scenic spots are crowded and noisy. To a lesser degree, Japanese tourists come north again in early October for fall foliage viewing and again, in full force, during the first week of February for Sapporo's fantastic Snow Festival. The best months are probably May and October. May is spring in Hokkaido and the cherry blossom is out; October is autumn and the forest land that covers much of the island is a mass of autumn colors. Both months have cold nights, but generally warm up during the day. However, chilly spring and fall days are not unusual and may even bring fresh snows in the higher parts of the national parks. Winter sports enthusiasts, of course, should visit the island between December and March, when the "five whites" are unfailing attractions: winter festivals, ice floes, white cranes, migrant swans, and skiing.

HOW TO GET THERE. By air. *Japan Air Lines* (JAL), *All Nippon Airways* (ANA) and *Toa Domestic Airlines* operate about 20 flights a day between Tokyo's Haneda International Airport and Chitose airport, which services Sapporo, capital of Hokkaido. JAL also has flights to Chitose from Tokyo's New International Airport at Narita. Flights from Narita and Haneda airports to Chitose take 1 hour, 25 minutes. There are flights from Tokyo to Hokkaido's southern port city of Hakodate; and flights from most other large cities on Honshu and Kyushu to Chitose.

By train. Travel to Sapporo from Tokyo by train-ferry: Tohoku line or Joban line takes 9 hours by limited express from Ueno Station, Tokyo to Aomori. The new Tohoku Shinkansen bullet train saves over 3 hours travel time, but you must change trains at Morioka. Seikan-renraku ferry takes 3 hr. 50 min. from Aomori to Hakodate, Hakodate line limited express takes 4 hr. 30 min. from Hakodate to Sapporo. Beautiful scenery along the way, both through northern Honshu (Tohoku) and from Hakodate to Sapporo make the long trip worthwhile. Other Tohoku-Hokkaido ferries leave from Hachinohe (an overnight ferry to Tomakomai) and Noheji on the Tohoku line and remote Oma, Honshu's northernmost point, only 2 hours across the Tsugaru Straits from Hakodate.

By boat. There is the 9,000-ton luxury ferryboat *Marimo,* which sails the Tokyo-Kushiro (near Akan National Park) route twice weekly, taking about 30 hours. Operated by the Kinkai Yusen Co. The 7,800-ton *Shireto-ko,* operated by the Japan Coastal Ferry Co., sails between Tokyo and Tomakomai taking about 30 hours.

TELEPHONES. Hakodate, 0138; Sapporo, 011; Noboribetsu, 01438.

HOTELS AND INNS. There are numerous Western-style hotels in Sapporo. Those listed below are all in central city. Japanese business hotels are in most cases very modern, Western-style, all rooms with bath and in most cases phones and TV's.

WESTERN-STYLE

Alpha. 1 Minami Nishi-5 Chuo-ku, Sapporo; 221–2333. Splendid service; swimming club; Playboy Club Sapporo. 147 rooms. ¥ 9,000–20,000.

The Hotel Alpha Tomamu. Aza Naka Tomamu, Shimukappu-mura, Yufutsu-gun, Hoddaido 079–25. Telephone Sapporo Reservation Center, 011–251–7117. At the foot of Mt. Tomamu in the Sekisho Plateau, two hours east of Sapporo by train, Sekisho line. This is the sister hotel of the Hotel Alpha Sapporo. The hotel has its own skiing ground that is the largest in Asia, with four chairlifts and one gondola. It is part of the Alpha Resort Shimucup project, modeled after Aspen in Colorado. ¥ 8,000–20,000.

Century Royal. 5 Nishi Kita-5 Chuo-ku; 221–2121. 336 rooms. ¥ 7,500–14,500.

New Miyakoshi. 3 Nishi Kita-2 Chuo-ku; 221–2141. 124 rooms. ¥ 5,500–12,000.

Sapporo Grand. 4 Nishi Kita-1 Chuo-ku Sapporo; 261–3311. 519 rooms. ¥ 7,000–20,000.

Sapporo International. 4 Nishi Kita-4 Chuo-ku; 222–3811. 100 rooms. ¥ 7,000–15,000.

Sapporo Park. 3–11 Nishi Minami-10 Chuo-ku; 511–3131. 223 rooms. ¥ 7,000–20,000.

Sapporo Prince. 11 Nishi Minami-2 Chuo-ku; 231–5310. ¥ 7,000–18,000.

Sapporo Royal. 1 Higashi Minami-7 Chuo-ku; 511–2121. 88 rooms. ¥ 6,500–14,600.

Sapporo Tokyu. 4 Nishi Kita-4 Chuo-ku; 231–5611. 263 rooms. ¥ 7,500–18,000.

JAPANESE-STYLE

Hotel Maruso. 3–3 Kitaichijo Nishi Chuo-ku; 221–0111 86 rooms (most western). ¥ 18,000.

Sapporo Daiichi Hotel. 10 Odori Nishi Chuo-ku; 221–1101. 70 rooms. ¥ 8,500–10,000.

BUSINESS HOTELS

Sapporo. *Business Hotel Lilac,* 17 Kita-Ohdori Nishi. 46 rooms; *Business Hotel Marumatsu,* 3–7 Minami Nishi. 42 rooms; *Marushin,* 4–1 Minami Nishi. 75 rooms; *Business Hotel Soen,* 14–16 Kita, Nishi. 162 rooms; *Washington Sapporo,* 4–1–8, 4 Kita, Nishi. 524 rooms.

Otaru. *Business Hotel New Minato,* 2–10–10 Inaho. 73 rooms.

Obihiro. *Green,* 12 Nishi-Ichijo-Minami. 65 rooms.

Muroran. *Muroran Royal,* 2–21–11 Nakashima-machi. 61 rooms.

Kitami. *Kitami Towa,* 6 Nishi 5. 54 rooms.

Asahikawa. *Asahikawa Prince,* 1 Hidari, 7 Ichijo-dori. 129 rooms. *Green,* 6 Hidari, 8–1. 110 rooms. And a *Tokyu Inn,* at 6 Showa-dori.

YOUTH HOSTELS. *Sapporo House, 721–4235; Sapporo Miyagoka, 611–9016; Nakanoshima, 831–8752; Sapporo Shiritsu Lions, 611–4709.* You can also call Sapporo Tourist Association, 221–0013, for information about youth hostels and campgrounds in Hokkaido.

SPAS, RESORTS, AND HOT SPRINGS. Akan Kohan Spa. Most of this area in Akan National Park is taken up with volcanoes and virgin forest. Three major lakes: Kusshara, Akan, Mashu. Park has convenient bus service to scenic spots. Directions or destinations should be written out in Japanese. *Hotel Akankoso.* 1 hr., 50 min. by bus from Kushiro City train station; (015467) 2231. 97 Japanese and Western rooms. ¥18,000–20,000 per person with 2 meals.

Jozankei Spa. Located west of Sapporo, about 1 hour bus ride. In the mountains, amidst hot springs. *Jozankei Hotel.* 4–340–1 Nishi, Jozankei Onsen, Minami-ku; (011) 598–2111. 250 Japanese and 14 western rooms. ¥12,000–15,000.

Noboribetsu Spa. Located in Shikotsu-Toya National Park, which is southwest of Sapporo. Noted for volcanoes, caldera lakes, and hot springs. Bus and train connect it to Sapporo. *Daiichi Takimotokan.* 55 Noboribetsu Onsen, Noboribetsu City. 13 min. by bus from Noboribetsu St.; (01438) 4–2111. 364 Japanese and western rooms. ¥10,000–30,000.

Toyako Spa. Located in Shikotsu-Toya National Park. *Hotel Manseikaku.* 21 Aza Toyako-Onsen-machi, Abutacho, Abuta-gun. 15 min. by bus from Toya St.; (01427) 5–2171. 200 Japanese and Western rooms. ¥12,000–18,000.

Yunokawa Spa. Near Hakodate. *Hanabishi Hotel.* 1–16–18 Yunokawa-machi, Hakodate City; (0138) 57–0131. 15 min. by car from Hakodate St. 105 Japanese and Western rooms. ¥6,000–15,000.

HOW TO GET AROUND. For most people, plane and automobile will be the best way of traveling in Hokkaido. Two airlines, *Toa Domestic* (TDA) and *Nippon Kinkyori Airways,* fly within Hokkaido. They connect Sapporo with Wakkanai, Hakodate and Kushiro. From July–October there are also daily flights between Wakkanai and Rebun and Rishiri. For information on local and tour bus service, as well as for car rental, call Sapporo Tourist Association, 221–0013.

TOURIST INFORMATION. *Consulates:* American Consulate, 28 Nishi 1 Kita, Chuo-ku, 641–1115–7. *General Information:* Japan Travel Bureau, Nihon Seimei Bldg. 4–1 Nishi 3 Kita, Chuo-ku, 271–4011. Sapporo Tourist Association, 221–0013. Sapporo City Office Tourist Department, 221–2376.

SEASONAL EVENTS. Dates often vary from year to year so be sure to check with T.I.C. **February.** *Sapporo Snow Festival.* The biggest event of the year, attracting thousands and thousands of Japanese and foreign tourists in early February. Features huge snow sculptures, plus fireworks and sports. Located in the heart of the city, goes on day and night.

June. *Sounkyo Gorge Festival.* A sacred fire is relayed to the festival site, making remarkable reflections in the gorge.

July. *Hakodate Port Festival.* Features a parade, floats, and decorations on boats. *Orochon Fire Festival* is celebrated by the Ainu at Abashiri. Includes traditional aborigine dancing.

August. *Hakodate Hachiman Festival,* at the temple of the same name.

October. *Akan Marimo Festival* at Lake Akan. Celebrates the discovery by local merchants of the commercial value of marimo plants. The *Ainu Iyomante bear festival.*

 MUSEUMS. Ainu Museum is located in the Botanical Gardens, about 500 meters southwest of Sapporo Station. Good collection of costumes, canoes, and other items. Hrs: 9:00 A.M.–4:00 P.M. (Apr. thru Sept.) 9:00 A.M.–3:30 P.M. (Oct. thru Nov.). Closed on Mondays, and Nov. 4 thru Apr. 28.

Clock Tower, with its museum of Hokkaido history, is adjacent to City Hall in Sapporo, 400 meters south of the train station. Hours: 9:00 A.M.–4:00 P.M. Closed Mondays and holidays.

Hokkaido Museum of Modern Art, a 5-min. walk from Nishi 18 subway stop on the Tozai line. Opened in 1977, the impressive modern building with soaring rooflines houses a collection of Hokkaido-related art, Japanese and foreign modern art and changing special exhibits. Hrs: 10:00 A.M.–5:00 P.M. Closed Mondays and national holidays.

Hakodate Museum. Has a good collection and modern display of artifacts of the aboriginal races that lived in Hokkaido. It is close to the last two stops on the tram line 2, and not too far from the junction stop Horaicho (line 10).

The outlying cities of Kushiro, Asahikawa, and Abashiri also have museums of local interest featuring prehistoric relics and historical displays.

 PARKS. Niseko-Shakotan-Otaru-CoastQuasi National Park. West of Sapporo. *Niseko* is 1 hr., 50 min. by express train from Sapporo. Noted for its mountains and hot springs. Good skiing in winter. *Otaru.* 30 min. by express from Sapporo. Largest port city on west coast and starting point for traveling in park. *Shakotan Peninsula* features views of rugged shoreline and Sea of Japan.

Shikotsu-Toya National Park. About 1 hr., 20 mins. by bus from Sapporo. Features lakes Shikotsu and Toya, Noboribetsu spa, and Shiraoi Ainu village. Has volcanoes, caldera lakes, and hot springs. Good bus and train network links it to Sapporo.

Akan National Park. Located on far western part of the island. Has large volcanoes, three major lakes of Kussharo, Mashu, and Akan. Hot springs.

Abashiri, Shiretoko, and Nemuro parks. These extend along the west coast of Sea of Okhotsk. Noted for natural fields of wild flowers and coastal scenery.

Daisetsuzan National Park. Japan's largest national park, located in central part of the island. Noted for lofty mountains, as well as its forest and the sheer cliffs and waterfalls of Sounkyo Gorge. Also has Mt. Asahi, 2,290 meters, the largest mountain in Hokkaido. Park can be reached by train or plane from Sapporo.

Rishiri-Rebun-Sarobetsu National Park. Located in extreme northern coast of Hokkaido. 1 hour by air from Sapporo. Main features are Sarobetsu Natural Flower Gardens and volcanic island of Rishiri. Regular bus circles the island in 2 hours. The flower garden is in the central part of the park. June–July is best time to see the flowers.

508 JAPAN

SPORTS. *Skiing* (Best places are near Sapporo). **Furano.** 2 hr., 15 min. by express train (JNR Nemuro line) from Sapporo Station to Furano; 10 min. bus ride to ski ground. Season: early December–early April. 13 lifts; lights for night skiing. *Furano Prince Hotel.* 01672–3–4111. ¥13,000 and up.

Hotel Kuroda (0167) 23–4135. ¥10,000 and up.

Teine Olympia. 50 min. by bus from Sapporo. Season: late Nov.–mid April. 2 ropeways, 18 lifts, night skiing.

Teine Highland. 1 hr. by bus from Sapporo. Season: mid Nov.-early May. 1 ropeway, 5 lifts, cross-country skiing, night skiing.

Niseko Kokusai Hirafu. 1 hr., 40 min. by express train (JNR Hakodate Line) from Sapporo to Kutchan. 20 min. bus ride to ski ground. Season: late Nov.–early May. 14 lifts, night skiing. *Hirafu Kanko Hotel,* (01362) 2–2350. ¥11,000 and up. *Alpen Sanso.* (01362) 2–1105. ¥6,500–10,000. *Niseko Prince Hotel.* (01362) 3–2239. ¥5,000–10,000.

SHOPPING. Most of its modern shops and department stores are clustered near the eastern part of Odori Park, both at street level and in the underground arcades of Aurora Town and Pole Town. More shopping is in the Sapporo Station area. Tanukikoji (Badger Alley) is a lively 10-block-long covered arcade with shops, restaurants and several folkcraft stores. It is south of Odori Park, running parallel to the park's eastern section.

DINING OUT. Hokkaido's regional specialties include Hokkaido salmon; Genghis Khan, which is a mutton and vegetable barbecue; Sapporo Ramen, a version of Chinese noodle soup; corn, which is a local product, usually grilled; Hairy Crabs, served boiled or steamed; and dairy products.

A favorite dish in winter is *Yosenabe,* a fish stew containing salmon, crab, and much more. *Ishikarinabe* is a river salmon stew cooked in earthenware pots. During the summer, an evening barbecue of mutton is held on the Tsukisappu sheep farm 4 miles outside of Sapporo. Reservations are best made through the Japan Travel Bureau.

There are countless Japanese restaurants in the central part of Sapporo, as well as those serving Western-type food. **Muscat,** 3 Nishi Kita-Nijo, Sapporo, is good for European dishes. **Sapporo Bier Garten,** almost 2 kilometers east of the train station (221–9191), is a lot of fun for beer and good food. **Taj Mahal,** in the Kotsu Kosha Building basement (231–1168) has tandoori dishes and curries.

The better Western-style hotels have excellent dining rooms. Inexpensive meals, both Western and Japanese, can be found in abundance in the shopping arcades and department stores. In Hokkaido's outlying areas, the fare is much less cosmopolitan, but more Westernized than other Japanese hinterlands, with potatoes, corn, and dairy products often featured. Akan National Park's buttered, grilled potatoes are unforgettable.

THE RYUKYU ISLANDS

by
MIRANDA KENRICK

The Ryukyus are a rope of some 70 subtropical islands, tossed care-lessly into the sea between southern Japan and Taiwan. Divided into four main groups—Okinawa, Miyako, Yaeyama, and Daito—they are sun-basked islands, steeped in the sea. Colors predominate—cobalt, purple, and opal in the water, reds of earth and hibiscus, white of sand and coral, blazing orange and molten gold of sunset.

Okinawa Island

Okinawa, 1,220 square kilometers in area, is the largest and most important island. Its vulnerable position between powerful neighbors—Tokyo to the north, Manila to the south, and Shanghai only 700 sea kilometers away—probably gave it the nickname "keystone of the Pacific." Over the centuries the island has taken in people from Southeast Asia, China, and Japan, with a recent dash of America added.

Okinawa's written history dates back to 600 A.D., and Chinese influ-ence has been strong since the late 14th century. For 250 years Okina-wa paid homage and symbolic tribute to China, and in return reaped the benefits of trade, technology, and culture. In 1609 the barons of nearby Satsuma (southern Kyushu) moved in and allegiance shifted to

Japan, although China continued to receive the payment of tribute. By the 19th century the Dutch, British, French, and Americans vied to establish trading posts on Okinawa. In 1872 tribute to China ended when Japan gobbled up the Ryukyus and incorporated them into her empire. The year 1879 saw the end of the Okinawan monarchy. After the Second World War the United States claimed Okinawa and administered it until its reversion to Japan in 1972.

Okinawa has a long history, but the devastating battles starting in April 1945, when American forces flattened all resistance, almost completely wiped out the physical heritage of preceding centuries, and replaced it with memorials to war.

The south of the island still bears the scars of Okinawa's immediate history. At Mabuni is Suicide Cliff where in June 1945 Japanese General Ushijima and his followers voluntarily and ritualistically died. Here too is Kenji-no-To, the tomb of students, young lads who ran messages for the army and went on patrol for the soldiers. Not far away is the memorial to the unknown soldier, especially in remembrance of the Hokkaido 10,000 who died on Okinawa. Also nearby is the Cave of the Virgins (Himeyuri-no-To or Lily Tower) where nurses attached to the Japanese Army took their own lives, and Shiraume-no-To (White Plum) where girl students and their teachers died.

Naha, the port and capital of Okinawa, has built over her wounds in efforts to get on with the compelling business of living. The famous shopping street Kokusai Odori (International Avenue) is almost 2 kilometers long, lined with restaurants as well as department stores and souvenir shops. Nearby Okinawa City has sophisticated American-style plaza shopping centers.

Look for pottery, lacquerware, coral, and *bingata* textiles. The bingata weaving employs hundreds of patterns of birds and flowers and streams, an art that is complicated, time-consuming, and ancient. The vegetable-dye colors, though, do not fade, however bright the sun, strong the wind and rain, salty the spray. If you want to see the process, the Shuri district in the east of Naha has the workshops.

From ancient times, islanders have been potters with village kilns, producing their craft of overglaze enamel on stoneware and white slip patterns. For their *awamori* (a fiery distilled rice wine) they make stoneware jars that they leave unglazed. For 500 years the Okinawans have been lacquerware makers. To some work they add relief pictures; in some, they fill surface-carved patterns with gold foil; for others they decorate red and black lacquer with inlays of mother-of-pearl. They make pictures of coral and twist necklaces of shell; and since snakes slither on these islands, they use snakeskin for purses and belts.

Onoyama Park's baseball and track facilities occupy the sites of the prewar Gokoku Temple and Yomochi Shrine in Naha's southwestern section. At Sogenji Temple, mausoleum of the kings of Shuri from the 12th century, part of the original stone wall still remains. Once it was decreed the most beautiful stone structure in the Ryukyus.

At Nami-no-ue is Naha's waterfront shrine dedicated to the three gods believed to be ancestral deities of the Imperial family. An amusement complex here looks one way to Naha Port, the other way to Tomari Port, and straight ahead to the unfailing magnetism of the East

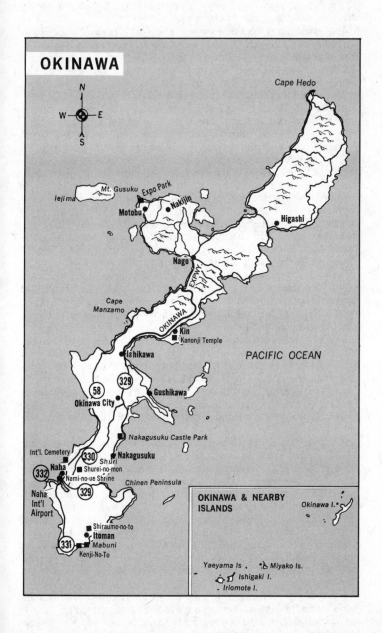

512   JAPAN

China Sea. Sunsets here stain the sky and drip into the sea, slowly draining away as darkness closes in.

In this district is the Teahouse of the August Moon, not the original teahouse, but an enterprise that knew a good name when it heard it. The teahouse caters parties and presents entertainment of lively Ryukyuan dancing that calls for the accompaniment of voices and stringed and percussion instruments.

To the east is the Shuri district, capital of the Ryukyus for 700 years until the mid-19th century. Today Shuri is the center of politics, education, religion, and the arts. The University of the Ryukyus is here, where for 500 years Shuri Castle proudly stood. The castle's razing represents one of the most grievous losses of the 1945 campaign. In Shuri Museum opposite the castle site, the few pieces of castle masonry that have been salvaged and assembled seem more pitiful than if there were none.

Shurei-no-mon (the Gate of Courtesy), dating back to the 16th century and once designated a National Treasure, also succumbed to bombs. The reproduction, resembling a two-story Chinese tower, has been here since 1958. Its name draws attention to the traditionally pliant, eager-to-please nature of the Ryukyuans, once called by Chinese ambassadors the people of the Nation of Courtesy.

To some, Okinawa seems an island of the dead, and that is not entirely because of its recent sad history. Its countryside proliferates with tombs, the turtle-back, or lock-and-key type (the roof resembles the shell of a turtle), and the *hafu,* or cave type. Explore caves on the beaches and you might stumble over the occasional human bone. At least 20th-century cremation has, for the most part, dispensed with the traditional "wind burial"—disinterring the body six years later and scraping away any remaining flesh for the wind to disperse.

Hire a car and whisk yourself around Okinawa. Or make short trips out of Naha by bus. Southwest 12 kilometers is the fishing village of Itoman, with traditions that include an annual June Dragon Boat race, February porpoise hunts, and temples dedicated to the gods of the sea and of fertility.

The stalactite cave of Gyokusendo is also southwest of Naha, about 12 kilometers. The third-largest cave in Japan (after Shuhodo in Yamaguchi and Ryusendo in Iwate), it meanders underground for more than 2 kilometers. Don't attempt to count the stalagmites and stalactites—there are over 900,000. Clear streams trickle underground. Stay alert for fluttering bats.

Farther along Okinawa's west coast, Kudaka Island off Chinen Peninsula believes itself to be the original place of the creation of the world. Its annual Ura Uri (Fire Descent) Festival lights up July. At another festival, held only once every 12 years, all locally born females between the ages of 30 and 70 become holy women who serve the deities.

North of Naha the completely Americanized Highway 58 passes the city's International Cemetery where a few of Commodore Perry's sailors are buried. Leave the main highway near Gusukuma and travel east about four kilometers if you want to see the tombs of Yuduri, the burial place of 13th-century Okinawan kings.

Only 45 minutes by car northeast of Naha is the site of Nakagusuku Castle, now a children's playground. The castle dated back to 1454, but today only its sun-bleached stone walls remain, stretching some 900 meters around the castle site.

Nearby is the Nakamura House, a representative old private house that miraculously survived the war and is kept as it has been for 200 years. Built without a single nail, it also has a *godown* (warehouse) with an anti-rat device called *nezumi-gaeshi*. The house is designated an Important Cultural Property.

Past Nakagusuku the country grows freer, with sweeping expanses of sugar cane and pineapple plantations. Roadside stalls sell the fruit.

Bullfights are Gushikawa's Sunday attraction. Two bulls enter a ring, lock horns, and push. As in sumo wrestling, the winner is the one who forces his opponent out of the ring. These bullfights have ancient origins and large followings of loyal fans who cheer on their favorite bulls. Gushikawa is northeast of Nakagusuku and almost nine kilometers northeast of Okinawa City.

Heading northwest from Gushikawa for about 10 kilometers, you'll come to Nakadomari, where Route 58 follows the western seacoast while the New Okinawa Expressway, built especially for Expo '75, takes to the mountains. Okinawa has beaches, beaches, and still more beaches, each one seductive and alluring. Follow the shore and linger at Yokuda, Moon Beach, Tiger, or Tanchame. At beautiful Moon Beach glass-bottom boats open up an underwater world of brilliant tropical fish, swishing seaweed, and curiously formed coral.

Precipices protect the cove and beach of Manza at rocky Cape Manzamo and mark the beginning of the Okinawa Coastal National Park. Feudal kings of old battled here for possession of the northern provinces.

Route 58 and the Okinawa Expressway reunite just short of Nago, a provincial town replete with banks, offices, pineapple processing factories, and its own Long Beach. The ruins of Nago Castle are just 15 minutes' walk from the center of town. Long stone steps lead to the castle site where cherry blossoms are in their glory during an annual January festival.

After Nago the roads divide again, one over the hills of red soil and pineapples, the other around the winding shore and through attractive villages. Notice the low-roofed country houses that are built to withstand typhoons. Amongst the red tiles on the roofs squat ceramic *shisa* (lion-dogs). Each is of different form, each is a talisman descendant of the original lion-dog that came from ancient China to create an Okinawan sea legend. The first shisa, favorite of a Ryukyuan king, flew in the sky to fight a marauding dragon. He won and the dragon fell in the sea to become an island. And today ceramic shisa crouch where tiles are red, trees are glossy green, and bougainvillea trail over clay walls.

Both the sea and the mountain roads lead to Toguchi and the Motobu Peninsula, site of the world's first International Ocean Exposition of 1975. Before Expo, Motobu was a lonely, wild land, crossed by rough tracks, the haunt of butterflies and snakes, smothered in wind-torn palms, scarlet hibiscus, and wild morning glories. Expo developed the area and after 1975 it became a park. Cherry blossoms flower in January, canna lilies in April, and the national flower, the deigo, in May. Each season has its flower and Christmas produces giant scarlet poinsettias. Here, though, you must beware of the *habu*, a deadly poisonous snake that still lives in the undergrowth and in stone walls.

Iejima lies a short ferryboat ride away from Motobu. A World War II battlefield, it is today a quiet little island, with a disused airfield and a monument carrying a simple inscription "at this spot the 77th Infantry Division lost a buddy, Ernie Pyle, 18 April 1945." A movie theater in Tokyo was, for a number of postwar years, named for the distinguished war correspondent.

Iejima charms, with its semi-tropical greenery and lovely beaches. Hire a bicycle and pedal around, or spend a day camping, swimming, or fishing. Climb Mt. Gusuku, if you feel you have the energy. It's a testing climb but worthwhile for its view of this green island, with the mainland eight kilometers away.

Back on Okinawa, proceed northeast beyond Motobu to the ruins of Nakijin Castle, also known as Hokuzen (North) Castle. It was destroyed over 500 years ago, when Ryukyu was three kingdoms, each constantly waging war on the others.

Cape Hedo, the northernmost point of Okinawa, and only a four-hour journey from Naha, is a wild outpost where storm clouds gather, ponder, and stalk off. On a clear day you can see as far as Amami-Oshima to the north.

The unadventurous traveler should return to Nago on Route 58. The intrepid might choose the little-traveled west coast, where the beaches are inhabited by sea birds. In 1981 an unknown species, given the Japanese name of *yambaru-kuina*, was spotted in the region. Small villages here have hardly been touched by modernity. According to age-old folk custom, tides still determine the timings of weddings, and fishing villages hold festivals that are designed to ensure safe sailing, good catches, prosperity.

From Nago, Route 329 takes you across the narrow neck of the island from the East China Sea coast to the Pacific Ocean, known here as the Philippine Sea.

A few miles south on Highway 13 stop in Kin, famous for its Kannonji Temple, its gigantic stalactites and grottos. Nearby Ishikawa has another of those lovely beaches. Highway 8 goes to the tip of the Katsuren Peninsula where the sun goes down in flaming colors. Fantastic tides allow, given perfect timing, for cars to be driven the 12 kilometers to the offshore islands of Yabuchi and Higa.

Miyako Island

Some of the islands in the Ryukyuan chain are accessible from Okinawa only by ship. Others have small airfields. From above each looks sun-blessed and indolent, yellow-beached, and rocky. Waves that curl and break on the shores seem motionless, as if no more than splotches of white paint.

Miyako, just an hour by air from Naha, is the largest of the eight islands comprising the Miyako Islands. Flat and unscathed by the war, it is covered with sugarcane fields. Most of the houses are low slung, poised to resist the typhoons that blow their way with monotonous regularity.

Buses cover the island and four hours in a taxi provides a comprehensive look around. Hirara, the main center, has Miyako jofu cloth and coral jewelry. Harimizu Shrine, in Hirara, is dedicated to the founder of the island. The Monument of Philanthropy here was a gift from a grateful Emperor Wilhelm I of Germany, in appreciation of the rescue of the sailors of his trading vessel *Robertson*. The Miyako islanders even sent the Germans all the way safely home in a government ship. The Poll Tax Stone is 1.4 meters high. Between the 17th and 19th centuries islanders were measured against it and taxed when they achieved the stone's height. Over 1,200 kinds of tropical flowers and trees flourish in a tropical botanical garden near the Tax Stone. Another monument honors five men who long ago did a Paul Revere by alerting the island of the approach of the Baltic fleet during the Russo-Japanese War.

The Yaeyama Islands

In 1972 the Yaeyama Islands became Japan's 25th national park, Iriomote. Coral reefs surround the nineteen islands of the group, which includes Ishigaki, Taketomi, and Iriomote. All the islands support jungle vegetation, and bird and animal life.

Festivals have always played a vital part in Japanese village life. Nirai Kanai, the abode of the gods, lies beyond the horizon where sea and sky meet. The gods come to visit at certain times of the year. In the Yaeyama Islands, at festival time, young men dressed in leaves and grasses and wearing masks of paper or wood portray the visiting gods.

Ishigaki is the administrative center of the Yaeyama Islands, and it is rich in folk art and old customs. Buses and taxis cross the island, and as on Miyako, a four-hour taxi journey offers a good look around. The residence of Miyara Donchi, built in 1819, is designated an Important Cultural Property. It indicates the lifestyle of the nobility of the former Ryukyuan Kingdom, and its rock and sand garden is one of a kind. Torinji Temple, built in 1614, is known for its two wooden images of Deva Kings, both of which are Important Cultural Properties. Gongen-do Hall is the oldest (1614) shrine in Okinawa Prefecture, and is dedicated to Kumano-Gongen deity.

At 525 meters Mt. Omoto is the highest peak in Okinawa Prefecture. Fishermen in dazzling Kabira Bay collect black pearl oysters. During festivals at Kabira, young men assume godly roles. They don bamboo hats, straw capes, and cover their faces. Then they make nocturnal visits to village houses, purifying, promising, blessing.

The tiny island of Taketomi, also part of Iriomote National Park, is but 12 kilometers in circumference. It maintains a population of about 300 but attracts some 40,000 tourists each year. Many of them leave with little pouches of *hoshisuna* (star sand). Taketomi has its own hoshisuna beach where the sand is found in coral rock. Helping yourself is prohibited, but local enterprise offers it for sale.

Village life in the Yaeyamas has always been simple, a blending with nature. Homes are, predictably, low slung, and the inevitable snarling shisa statue wards off evil spirits. Women have traditionally applied themselves to the weaving of minsa cloth. Look for sashes and belts in the natural indigo dyes.

Iriomote lies just one degree north of the Tropic of Cancer. Its forests are almost untouched and mangroves grow right down to the water's edge. Ferry along the Urauchi River and you may well wonder if you haven't suddenly been transplanted to the Amazon. Baby sharks live in the river and the denseness of the undergrowth conceals snakes.

The area near Mariyudo and Kanpira Waterfalls is the natural habitat of the Iriomote Wildcat, a "living fossil" that has hardly changed for some 5 million years. They are nocturnal creatures, though, as well as being on the verge of extinction, so your chances of happening upon one are virtually nil. Sighted in 1965, the cats are believed to be unique to the island forests.

PRACTICAL INFORMATION FOR THE RYUKYUS

WHEN TO GO. In general the tourist season is October–April. Though Okinawa's climate does not vary too widely year round, winter (Dec.–Feb.) is often cloudy, with temperatures in the 60's (16° C). Spring (Mar.–May) is the best season, when everything is in flower. Avoid late May and June, the rainy season. Summer (June–Oct.) is long, the season when the swimming is best, the local color most typically Okinawan, and typhoons frequent but brief. Autumn is the shortest season (Oct.–Nov.). Average year-round temperature is 73° F (23° C).

HOW TO GET THERE. By air. The terminal at Naha Airport was built specifically for the accommodation of visitors to the 1975 International Ocean Exposition. It has parking space for five jumbo jets, and 1,000 cars. *ANA* and *JAL* have 7 daily flights to Naha from Tokyo. Nagoya, Osaka, Fukuoka, and Kumamoto, Kagoshima, Amamioshima have regular services to Naha. Flying times vary with the type of aircraft used.

Coming in from Hong Kong or Taipei, *Northwest Orient, TWA,* and *JAL* stop at Okinawa. *Japan Airways* has a Taipei-Naha service.

From Naha to Miyako takes 50 minutes by air. Naha–Ishigaki is 55 minutes, ¥14,720. Naha–Iriomote is an hour, ¥18,030.

By boat. Five shipping lines operate regular sea services to Naha from Tokyo, Osaka/Kobe, Kagoshima and other ports. These lines are: *Ryukyu Kaiun* (RKK), (03) 281–1831, *Oshima Unyu,* (03) 273–8911, *Kansai Kisen,* (03) 274–4271, *Terukuni Yusen,* and *Arimura Sangyo.* Vessels include very modern passenger liners and deluxe car ferries. Several ships have swimming pools; all have clean and attractive accommodation, game rooms, social lounges, and bars. All have medical and other emergency facilities.

The sailing time from Tokyo to Naha is about 40 to 46 hours; between Kagoshima and Naha it is about 20 hours. Some ships go direct, while others call at smaller islands *en route.*

It's an hour by sea from Ishigaki to Iriomote, 20 minutes from Ishigaki to Taketomi. Daily services: 9 summer, 7 winter.

TELEPHONES. Area codes: Naha 0988; Okinawa City 09893; Ishigaki 098082. **Emergencies. In Naha and Okinawa City:** *Police,* 088–3450; *Fire department,* 088–3444; *Ambulance* **(Naha)** 088–5358; **(Okinawa City)** 077–2533.

HOTELS AND INNS. On the main island of Okinawa, hotels and inns are of international standard. The Hilton offers the uniform quality for which it has a world-wide reputation. Some beach resorts are luxurious and all have such sports facilities as tennis, cycling, and anything to do with the sea. If you stay anywhere other than the main cities or the beach resorts, expect only the basics without frills. On some of the outer, smaller islands, Japanese-style accommodation might predominate.

OKINAWA

Manza Beach

Manza Beach Hotel. 80 minutes' drive from Naha Airport, is a nine-story hotel shaped like a pearl shell. Each of its 401 rooms has an unobstructed sea view. The hotel is the major facility in the newly developed Manza Beach Resort. ANA operates eight tour plans from Tokyo, Nagoya, and Osaka. Each plan includes air fare, hotel, breakfasts, and dinners. Apply to your nearest ANA agent, or the ANA Sky Holiday Holiday Center: Tokyo, (03) 580–8600; Nagoya, (052) 971–8600; Osaka, (06) 261–8600.

Motobu

Royal View. 938 Ishikawa, Motobu-cho, Kunigami-gun, Okinawa Pref. 905–03; (09804) 8–3631. 92 Western rooms. Twin ¥12,000–14,000.

Naha

Hotel Ekka. 1068–9, Ameku, Naha, Okinawa Pref. 900; (0988) 68–3135. 220 Western, 10 Japanese rooms. Single ¥7,000. Twin ¥11,000–13,000. Japanese style (for 2) ¥13,000.

Naha Tokyu. 1002, Ameku, Naha, Okinawa Pref. 900; (0988) 68–2151. Only a kilometer from downtown, splendid sea views. 278 Western, 2 Japanese rooms. Single ¥8,500. Twin ¥12,500–14,500. Japanese style (for 2) ¥13,000.

Okinawa Fuji. 1–6 Nishi, Naha, Okinawa Pref. 900; (0988) 68–1118. 185 Western rooms. Twin ¥8,000–14,000.

Okinawa Grand Castle. 1–132–1 Yamakawacho, Shuri, Naha, Okinawa Pref. 903; (0988) 86–5454. Part of JAL's hotel chain. 304 Western, 1 Japanese room. Twin ¥13,000–16,000. Double ¥15,000–16,000. Japanese style (for 2) ¥45,000.

Okinawa Harbor View. 2–46, Izumizaki, Naha, Okinawa Pref. 900; (0988) 53–2111. 341 Western, 5 Japanese rooms. Single ¥9,000. Twin ¥14,000–17,000. Double ¥19,000. Japanese style (for 2) ¥19,000

Okinawa City

Hilton International Okinawa. 1478 Kishaba, Kitanakagusuku-son, Okinawa Pref. 901–23; (09893) 5–4321. Overlooking the China Sea and the Pacific from a hill in Kita Nakagusuku, the 310-roomed hotel has resort facilities, excellent restaurants, and is set in an historic, 40-acre park called the "10,000 years' garden." The garden, which contains ancient family tombs of the Old Kingdom, is the site of an annual festival dedicated to a bygone feudal warlord. The Hilton runs three shuttle buses between the hotel and the airport, stopping on the way at the Mitsukoshi Department Store in Naha City. Single, ¥12,000–16,000; twin and double ¥16,500–20,000.

Koza Palace Hotel. 1–43 Goya 2-chome, Okinawa City 904; (09893) 3–4590. 67 rooms, moderately priced. Single ¥4,500–7,000; double ¥8,000–11,000.

IEJIMA

Hilltop Hotel. Small, moderately priced, and friendly.

YAEYAMA ISLANDS

Hotel Miyahira. 4–9 Misaki-cho, Ishigaki, Okinawa Pref. 907; 158 Western, 6 Japanese rooms. Twin ¥16,000. Double ¥16,000. Japanese style (for 2) ¥12,000–16,000.

 YOUTH HOSTELS. Naha YH. 51, Onoyama-cho, Naha City 900; (0988)57–0073. 15 min. on foot from Naha Port. 100 beds. **YH Harumi-so.** 2–22–10, Tomari, Naha City 900; (0988)33–3218. 15 min. by bus from Naha Port and 3 min. on foot. 40 beds. **YH Tamazono-so.** 54, Asato, Naha City 902; (0988)33–5377. 15 min. by bus from Naha Port and 5 min. on foot. 30 beds. **YH Yashima Ryokan.** 117, Tonojo, Ishigaki City 907; (09808)2–3157. 5 min. on foot from Ishigaki Port. 20 beds. **Ishigaki-Shi-Tei YH.** 287, Shinkawa, Ishigaki City 907; (09808)2–2720. 13 min. on foot from Ishigaki Port. 13 beds. **Trek Ishigakijima YH.** 165–12, Hoshino-mura, Ishigaki-shi, Okinawa-ken 907–02; (09808) 6–8257. 30 min. by bus from Ishigaki Port and 1 min. on foot. 12 beds. **YH Takana Ryokan.** 499, Taketomi, Taketomi-machi, Yaeyama-gun, Okinawa-ken 907–11. 10 min. on foot from Taketomi Port. 31 beds. **YH Iriomote-Jima Midori-so.** 870, Uehara, Taketomi-cho, Yaeyama-gun, Okinawa-ken 907–11; 098096–2526. 20 min. on foot from Taketomi Port. 15 beds.

 RESORTS. Okuma Beach Resort at Hentona, on the northwest coast of Okinawa Island, is a small former U.S. Army housing complex. Japan Air Lines converted it into a beautiful resort, complete with speedboats, rowboats, yachts, kayaks, and surf boards. Bungalow accommodation is delightful and the food lavish, with morning and evening buffets as well as barbecues and à la carte menus. A 4-day, 3-night package including air fare, accommodation, and unlimited mileage car rental is available from ¥113,800. For details, telephone (03) 454–3549 in Tokyo and (06) 227–0775 in Osaka.

The **Hilton Hotel** periodically offers similar package tours to their luxurious Okinawa hotel, which, although it is in town, is very much a resort; (09893) 5–4321. The Tokyo Hilton International has details.

The **Moon Beach Hotel** in Maegane-ku, Onna district, has its own magnificent beach and also offers residential arrangements. Moon Beach is on Okinawa's west coast, about 30 km northwest of Okinawa City; (09896) 4–3480.

 HOW TO GET AROUND. There are no trains on Okinawa, only buses and taxis. Self-drive hire cars are reasonable and perhaps the best way for seeing the island. Bicycles are an alternative on the outer islands.

TOURIST INFORMATION. Okinawa Tourist Service: 1-2-3 Matsuo, Naha City, Okinawa Pref. 900; (0988) 62-1111. **Okinawa Tourist Association:** 41, Asahi-cho, Naha.

The magazines *This Week on Okinawa* and *Life on Okinawa* tell you what's going on.

USEFUL ADDRESSES. American Consulate General. Naha: 2129 Aza Gusukuma, Urasoe City, Okinawa 901-21; (0988) 77-8142, 8627, 8651, 8677. It is open Monday to Friday, 9:00 A.M. to noon and 1 to 5 P.M. Except for renewal of passports and other minor problems, an appointment should be made in advance.

MEDICAL TREATMENT. There are several American doctors and many Okinawan doctors with American training in the islands, and they can all be reached through your hotel front desk. Convenient, perhaps, is the *Seventh Day Adventist Medical Center* in Naha 165 Aza Uenoya; (0988) 67-0107. The *American Drug Company,* on Highway 5, Awase Meadows, offers European and Stateside drugs and cosmetics. For an *ambulance* in Naha, telephone 088-5358, and in Okinawa City, telephone 077-2533.

ELECTRICAL CURRENT. The electrical current is 100 volts and 60 cycles (hertz) A.C.

PLACES OF WORSHIP. *Church of God in Christ.* 1705 Chibana, Okinawa City; (0989) 37-2506. *Kadena Christian Center.* 1291 Matsumoto, Okinawa City; (09893) 7-5001. *Anglican Episcopal Church of Japan (Nippon Sei Ko Kai).* 935 Makiminato, Urasoe City, Okinawa; (0988) 77-4931.

BEAUTY PARLORS & BARBERS. *Awase Meadows Beauty Parlor,* in the shopping center of Awase Meadows, in the southwest district of Okinawa City, and the *Ryubo Beauty Parlor* in the Ryubo Department Store, downtown Naha, have English-speaking operators and good reputations.

LOCAL BUSINESS HOURS AND HOLIDAYS. As on the mainland, most offices operate from 9:00 A.M.–5:00 P.M., closed on Sundays and about a dozen annual public holidays. Department store hours are usually 10:00 A.M. –6:00 P.M. and they usually close one mid-week day.

SEASONAL EVENTS AND FESTIVALS. Ryukyuan festivals follow the traditional East Asian lunar calendar (not the Western, solar one) so that the exact date on which an event falls will vary somewhat from year to year (like Easter). In addition, the weather and local circumstances often cause dates to be changed.

January. The Western New Year (Jan. 1) is for townspeople and government offices. For farmers and country people, the lunar New Year (variable, early **February**) is the chief holiday of the year, 3–5 days of feasting and family visiting.

February. (lunar Jan. 20) *Juriuma Festival,* a procession of Okinawan *geisha* near the *Teahouse of the August Moon* (yes, one does exist, though it's not the original). Tsujimachi, afternoon and evening.

March. *Porpoise Roundup,* Nago village. The fishermen use their own peculiar methods to catch large schools of porpoises. A bit bloody, but spectacular.

June. (lunar May 4) *Dragon Boat Races,* called *Haryusen.* Revealing the distinct Chinese background of the island's customs, this is an exciting event, especially for those who bet on the outcome. Biggest race at Itoman Village, others at Naha and Nago.

July. *Fire Descent Festival (Ura Uri)* is a pyromaniac's delight. Details change, so enquire before setting out. Kudaka Island.

Eisa, from the 14th-16th. The biggest festivity of Okinawa, Eisa is a lively mass dance, accompanied by the shouting of dancers and spectators, "Eisa, Eisa, Eisa . . . "

August. *Tsunahiki Matsura* takes place in late August. This involves a giant tug of war between two villages, and the exact site is apparently a matter of some discussion up to the last minute. Yonabaru village, about 3 miles from Naha.

August Moon Festival, based on the theory that the 15th day of August (lunar calendar) is the right time to sit up all night watching the lunar orb, hire geisha, and drink plenty of *sake,* or *awamori,* Okinawa's brandy.

September. The festival of the feudal *Lord Gi-Hon* takes place on the 13th, on the grounds next to the Okinawa Hilton. Bullfights are held every Sunday of summer in the villages of northern Okinawa. Bullfights are held each Sunday at Gushikawa, on Okinawa's east coast, 8.8 km northeast of Okinawa City.

 TOURS AND SPECIAL INTEREST SIGHTSEEING. The *Okinawa Bus* and *Ryukyu Bus* companies offer full day and half-day tours of the island. Travel agencies include *International Travel Service,* 3-5-5 Kumoji, Naha; *Okinawa Travel Agency,* 259-1 Matsuo, Naha; and *Central Travel Agency,* 1371 Koya, Okinawa City. *Susie's Tour,* American-owned and operated, and *American Express* both operate from Awase Meadow Shopping Center.

 BEACHES. If Okinawa has anything to offer, it's beaches. This is one of the few places in Japan where you really can find your own. Should you want facilities, however, the well known beaches include Yokuda, Moon Beach, Tiger, and Tanchame. Motobu has a spectacular sea coast, as do the outer islands of Iejima, Miyako, Ishigaki, Taketomi, and Iriomote.

 THEME PARKS AND AMUSEMENT CENTERS. Expo '75 with its theme "The Sea We Would Like To See" transformed the Motobu Peninsula. After the 6-month ocean exposition the vast area was converted into a low-key amusement center, with many of the existing buildings left intact. Alas, it is little patronized, perhaps because of its distance from Naha—2 hours by car; 2½ hours by bus.

 PARTICIPANT SPORTS. Swimming is the most popular sport in Okinawa, where the sand is white and the sea changes color through every shade of blue. Resorts, such as Okuma, offer a range of water activities from **wind surfing** to **yachting.** There are organized **diving clubs** including Hama Fishing Tackles, (09893) 7-1611; Naha Suien, (0988) 55-0434; and Dive

World, (09889) 7-2636. Boats for **deep sea fishing** may be hired in Naha, Itoman, Tomari, Baten, and Yakana. Your hotel or travel agent can provide details.

SPECTATOR SPORTS. Bullfights are popular in Okinawa and scheduled on an irregular basis in many villages. Gushikawa, northeast of Okinawa City, however, offers one each Sunday. Okinawans love **wrestling,** too, as well as a kind of Oriental football, **kemari,** bamboo sword **fencing,** and the deadly, native sports, **karate** and **jodan omote.** *Karate* is familiar to many Westerners, and is literally translated "Open hand." *Jodan omote* is a variation of the same barefisted boxing and means "smiling face." Experts in these sports must register their names with the local police station, because their fists are considered deadly weapons.

HISTORICAL SITES. Okinawa was a World War II battlefield, and the south of the island was almost completely devastated. *Suicide Cliff* at Mabuni is where General Ushijima and his followers ended their lives. Also at Mabuni is *Kenji-no-To,* commemorating students who ran messages and went on patrol for the army. *Himeyuri-no-To,* nearby, is the cave where young Army nurses died. *Iejima Island* was a battleground, too, where the correspondent Ernie Pyle died in the final days of the war.

Sogenji Temple, the mausoleum of the former kings of Okinawa from the 12th century, was for more than 400 years one of the most sacred temples in the Ryukyus. Persons passing the gate in vehicles had to dismount and show respect by walking. Ambassadors from China visited Sogenji Temple before making state visits. The temple and most of the wall were destroyed during the second World War. Today only part of the original stone wall remains. Sogenji is in the north of Naha.

On Ishigaki Island, *Gongen-do Hall* is Okinawa Prefecture's oldest shrine (1614). *Torinji Temple,* built also in 1614, is famous for its two wooden images of Deva Kings. Both are Important Cultural Properties. The residence of *Miyara Donchi,* dating back to 1819, is an Important Cultural Property with an unusual rock and sand garden.

Architectural Interest. The 200-year-old Nakamura House was built without a single nail. It survived the war and is maintained in its original form. It is near the site of the 1454 Nakagusuku Castle, south of Okinawa City.

MUSEUMS. *Okinawa Prefectural Museum,* Onaka-cho, Shuri. Art objects of the locality, including paintings, sculptures, and calligraphies. Open daily, 9:00 A.M.–5:00 P.M. Closed Mondays and national holidays.

SHOPPING. Kokusai Odori (International Avenue) is Naha's main shopping street, with almost 2 kilometers of department stores and souvenir shops. Ryubo Department Store is worth investigating. Nearby Okinawa City (formerly Koza) has sophisticated shopping centers laid out American style in plazas. Local specialties include ceramics, lacquerware, coral and seashell jewelry. Okinawan handicraft is supported by 600 years of tradition and the family skills of a score of generations. Bingata fabrics (also called Ryukyu kasuri), stencil-dyed and patterned, are produced throughout Okinawa and sold for kimono, mats, screens, wall hangings and cards. Tourists may see the process, as well as buy the products, at the shop of *Shokyu Kayo,* 2–137, Ona-cho, Shuri,

Naha. The weaving of kasuri fabrics is mostly a cottage industry. The village of Haebaru outside Naha specializes in kasuri production.

For lacquer, try *Okinawa Shikki,* just off the east end of Kokusai St. Lacquerware workers use seasoned *deigo,* a soft light wood, or red sandalwood, both indigenous to Okinawa. The finished ware may be a rich black, or red, brown, white or blue. Mother-of-pearl inlay may be used for ornamentation. Also recommended is the *Kakuman Lacquerware Company* 1–124, Maegimacho, Naha.

For ceramics go to *Tsuboyacho,* just off Himeyuribashidori. Retail outlet is *Okinawa Toki;* but wander through the tiny streets where for generations 12 families of hereditary potters have maintained the island's traditional art. *Kobayashigawa* is the most noted of these workshops. All sell directly retail.

 DINING OUT. An Okinawan proverb says, "Make the most of what your farm produces." Since Okinawa is often visited by devastating typhoons, the people have learned to maximize the food available to them. Many dishes use pork, and almost all parts of the pig are used in cooking. Other main dishes are made from *taro* and sea bream. The special drink is *awamori,* a brandy made from rice or sweet potatoes, and rather powerful. It is drunk in the same way as *sake* or Chinese *lao chu.* On the smaller islands, expect to live on rice and noodle dishes, and fish.

The restaurants listed below are all on Okinawa. Most are in the ¥2,000–4,000 price range per person for dinner. Fast food places are about ¥800 to ¥1,500 per person.

Okinawa Hilton. The Mingei Coffee Shop in the Hilton is reminiscent of a Japanese country inn. Lunch or dinner, about ¥1,000–3,000 per person. The Genji has a *tempura* corner and stone-cooked steaks. The Castle Grill features *haute cuisine* and French service. Dinner at these latter two restaurants costs about ¥5,000 per person.

Ryotei Matsunoshita. 2–10–5, Tsuji, Naha, famed as the "Teahouse of the August Moon." Reservations. One-hour program of Ryukyuan dances presented from 8:00 P.M. Cost, from ¥2,500 to ¥5,000 per person, including the dance program.

Fuji. 2–6–6, Kume, Naha; and **Mie,** 1–10–4, Kumoji, Naha; and **Tsukigase,** 205, Matsuo, Naha, are Ryukyuan specialty restaurants without the dance programs.

Rai-Rai-Ken. Serves both good Japanese and Chinese food, reflecting the island's double culture, but the Chinese is better. Fascinating blend of the architectural styles of the two countries. Prices moderate to slightly high.

Sam's Anchor Inn. Route 58 in Ginowan, between Naha and Okinawa City. Kobe beef, rum and coconut cream pie, dinner only.

Hernandos. Makiminato on Route 58. Steak house with a great old southwest atmosphere conjured by Texas dress. Dinner only.

The Pizza House. Urasoe, north of Naha and short of Ginowan. Pizza at low rates.

Suehiro. On the top floor of the Hotel Sun Route at Sogenji. Good meat, reasonably priced.

Seikoen. Route 58, opposite the Bei-Ryu Housing area. Korean food. 11:00 A.M.–11:00 P.M.

Sam's by the Sea. Near the Okinawa yacht harbor. Polynesian splendor, tropical drinks. Char-broiled steaks, sea food, dinner only. Sandwich lunches.

Paradise Gardens. Near the Hilton. Chinese and other kinds of moderately priced food.

On Kokusai-dori in Naha are branches of Kentucky Fried Chicken and Baskin-Robbins ice cream. Dunkin Donuts in the Ryubo Department Store claims to be the biggest one in the world! Try Fort Jiro Bakery for the cakes, pastries and bread, and for its ice skating, bowling and beer garden.

Along the shore of the Okinawa Coastal National Park are many drive-ins and snack bars. Of superior interest is the China Seas Drive-In and the Hukilau.

McDonald's Hamburger has a stand next to the Million Shopping Center (which is open from 10:00 A.M. to 2:00 A.M.) at Makiminato. A stone's throw away is the Big Dip Dairy Bar, which has cottage cheese as well as ice creams and milk shakes.

 NIGHT LIFE. Naha has three amusement sections. The **Tsuji** area has a military atmosphere, rather tawdry, full of strip shows and short-term hotels. **Jukkanji-cho,** east of the Asato River, is an out-and-out licensed quarter, narrow alleys, tiny cubicles, and *tokushu fujin* ("special women"). Poverty can be pretty grim. For real Ryukyuan tea house atmosphere, **Sakurazaka** area is best. (The Sakurazaka Kanrakugai runs south from Kokusai O-dori, just east of and parallel to Heiwadori, bus stop: Bokushi.) Try the *Kappa Inoue, Salon Napoleon,* and *Cabaret Showboat.* For authentic Okinawan plays, skits, and music hall-type entertainment, go to the *Okiei Gekijo.* The *Ryukyus Hall* and *Cabaret Uruwashi* often get foreign acts in their bookings. *Club Miss Ginbasha,* Route 58, is a daughter venture of *Mama Ginbasha,* Roppongi, Tokyo.

In Okinawa City, the *Playboy Club* and the *Mikado* are the best-known cabarets. With the opening of the Okinawa Hilton, two more night spots brighten Okinawa City. The *Castle Grill* at the hotel provides occasional entertainment; and the *Den,* which is a discotheque/nightclub with a Western mood and a radio station mockup.

FIVE-MINUTE JAPANESE

No one can hope to get very far with any language in five minutes. The purpose of the following vocabulary is not so much to make you into a linguist as to help you have a little fun. Whenever you are in a fix, someone whose English is better than your Japanese is sure to come forward to save you. Remember in Japanese that every syllable has equal stress. Pronounce the vowels as: *a* as in father; *e* as in pen; *i* is somewhere between ink and machine; *o* as in rope; and *u* as in put. Good luck!

English	Japanese	English	Japanese
Good morning	o-ha-yo	go back (turn around)	modote
Good afternoon	kon-nichi-wa		
Good evening	kon-ban-wa	hurry	hayaku
Goodnight (on retiring)	o-yasumi-nasai	go slowly	yukkuri
		stop	tomatte
Goodbye	sayonara	left	hidari
Thank you	domo arigato	right	migi
I'm sorry, please excuse me	sumi-masen	next	tsugi
		corner	kado
Yes	hai	toilet	toi-re
No	i-ie	information desk	an-nai-sho
Maybe	tabun	hotel	ho-teru
Wait a minute	chotto-matte	room	heya
I don't understand	wakarimasen	key	ka-gi
I	watakushi (for a lady)	eat	tabe-masu
	boku (for a man)	drink	nomi-masu
		meat	niku
You	anata	fruit	kudamono
he	ka-re	water	mizu
she	ka-no-jo	hot water	oyu
today	kyo	coffee	co-hi
tomorrow	ashita	tea	o-cha
yesterday	kino	money	kane
how much?	ikura deska?	One	Ichi
expensive	takai	Two	Ni
Anything cheaper?	Motto yasui no wa?	Three	San
		Four	Shi
I'll buy this	Itadakimasu or Kaimasu	Five	Go
		Six	Roku
telephone	denwa	Seven	Shichi
Please telephone and ask	Denwa de Kiite kudasai	Eight	Hachi
		Nine	Ku
taxi	tak-shi	Ten	Ju
bus	bus-u	Eleven	Ju-ichi (10 + 1, etc.)
train	densha		
subway	chika-tetsu	Twenty	Ni-ju (2 × 10, etc.)
station	eki		
ticket	kippu	Thirty, etc.	San-ju (3 × 10, etc.)
airport	hi-ko-jo		
street	michi	Hundred	Hyaku
Where is . . . ?	. . . doko deska?	Thousand	Sen
shop	mi-se	Ten thousand	Man or Ichi-man (thus, 25,000 is ni man go sen)
stamp	kit-te		
police box	koban		

HISTORICAL AND CULTURAL CHRONOLOGY OF
JAPAN

Beginning about 5,000 B.C.   *Jomon* culture (hunting and gathering) began its spread.

Around 300 B.C. to 200 A.D.   *Yayoi* agricultural society supplanted *Jomon.*

CHINA: The great Han Empire (206 B.C. to 220 A.D.), a period of Chinese expansion and stable military power. From around the time of Christ Chinese records show evidence of awareness of the existence of Japan.

THE WEST: The zenith of Roman civilization.

Around 400 A.D.   Appearance of *tumuli* (earthen burial mounds for nobles, containing *haniwa* pottery figures).

CHINA: A period of civil wars and barbarian invasions.

400 to 500 A.D.   Rulers of the Yamato area (Nara and Ise in southern Honshu) established hegemony throughout the southern area. In the early fifth century relations were established between Yamato and China; in 405 Chinese ideograms were accepted as the official written language of Japan.

THE WEST: The Roman Empire broke up; usually dated as 476 A.D.

538 to 552 A.D.   Buddhism was introduced to the Japanese (Yamato) court and nobility through contact wuth Kudara, a Korean kingdom. Confucian ideas also flowed into Japan via Korea.

CHINA: The establishment of the Sui Dynasty in 581 A.D., which led to the reunification of the Chinese Empire.

604 A.D.   Prince Shotoku issued a constitution. The first official embassy was sent to China shortly thereafter. This period saw the first Japanese emperors as such.

CHINA: The great T'ang Dynasty succeeded the Sui in 618 A.D. (it was then to hold sway until 907 A.D.)

THE WEST: The Hegira of Mohammed, in 622.

645 A.D.   The Taika Reform consolidated the Yamato states' move toward organization along Chinese lines.

710 A.D.   A permanent capital was established at Nara.

THE WEST: Charles Martel halted the advance of the Muslims into Europe at the Battle of Tours, 732.

794 A.D.   The capital was moved from Nara to Heian (Kyoto).

THE WEST: The coronation of Charlemagne in 800.

995 A.D. Fujiwara Michinaga gained control of the government. Lady Murasaki began writing *The Tale of Genji* in 1004.

CHINA: The Sung Dynasty was founded in 960 A.D.

THE WEST: The Holy Roman Empire was founded in 962. The Normans conquered England in 1066 A.D. The First Crusade began in 1096.

1159 A.D. The Heike (or Taira) military family took power away from the rival Genji (or Minamoto) family and inaugurated a despotic reign in Kyoto.

1192 A.D. The Kamakura Shogunate *(Bakufu)* government was established by Minamoto-no-Yoritomo. ("No" is possessive, so the name means "Yoritomo of the Minamotos.") The town of Kamakura, south of modern Tokyo, gradually became the nation's center of power and authority. The warrior code of *bushi* (virility and plain-living) came to supplant the aristocratic graces of the Heian period of Kyoto. In 1191 the priest Eisai brought the Rinzai Zen sect to Japan; its austere tenets appealed to the Kamakura Shogunate spirit.

THE WEST: The Magna Carta, 1215.

1227 A.D. The Soto sect of Zen Buddhism was transplanted in Japan from China by the priest Dogen.

CHINA and THE WEST: From about 1200 to 1260 A.D. the Mongols achieved domination of much of the Eurasian continent, led primarily by Genghis Khan.

1274 and 1281 A.D. The Mongolian invasions of Japan were repulsed.

CHINA: In 1271 A.D. Kublai Khan, a Mongol, established the Yuan Dynasty, after the overthrow of the Sung by the Mongol hordes.

THE WEST: Marco Polo traveled from Venice to the China of Kublai Khan.

1333 A.D. The Kamakura Shogunate was overthrown by a group led by Emperor Daigo II, who had chafed at being a mere figurehead under the Shogunate. The general Ashikaga, who had been sent by the Shogunate to quell the revolt, had switched to the side of the revolt.

1338 A.D. The Ashikaga Shogunate (so-called Muromachi Period) was established, with its capital back in Kyoto, as General Ashikaga pushed Emperor Daigo aside. In 1397 the Kinkaku (Golden) Pavilion was built in Kyoto.

CHINA: The Ming Dynasty supplanted the Yuan in 1368, and restored ethnic Chinese rule.

THE WEST: The Hundred Years' War began in 1339. Chaucer died in 1400. In 1453 the Ottoman Turks captured Constantinople.

1492 A.D. THE WEST: Columbus discovers the West Indies. In 1517 Martin Luther openly challenged the authority of the Papacy. The first voyage around the world, begun by Magellan, was completed in 1522. In 1537 some Portuguese settled at Macau off the southern Chinese mainland.

1543 A.D.   The Porguguese landed at a Japanese island. In 1549 Francis Xavier brought Christianity to Japan.

THE WEST: Queen Elizabeth I was crowned in 1558.

1573 A.D.   Oda Nobunaga, having taken the capital, overthrew the Ashikaga rule, beginning the Momoyama Period. Upon Nobunaga's assassination in 1582 his lieutenant Toyotomi Hideyoshi started his rise to power, which ended successfully in 1590. In 1582 ambassadors from authorities in Kyushu, the southwestern Japanese isle, reached Rome.

THE WEST: The Spanish Armada was destroyed by England in 1583.

1592–1598 A.D.   Hideyoshi attempted unsuccessfully to conquer Korea. He died in 1598.

THE WEST: Henry IV of France published the Edict of Nantes in 1598, guaranteeing Protestants freedom of worship.

1603 A.D.   The Tokugawa Shogunate government (*bakufu,* or feudal)—destined to endure for about 250 years—was founded by Tokugawa Ieyasu. Edo (now Tokyo) became the de facto capital when Ieyasu moved his headquarters there. In 1609 Dutch merchants were permitted to trade in Japan.

THE WEST: Shakespeare died in 1616. In 1620 the *Mayflower* reached America.

Around 1640 A.D.   The *Bakufu* effectively closed Japan off from the outside world. Christianity was suppressed with violence.

CHINA: The Ching Dynasty, of the Mongol Manchus from the north of China, began in 1644.

THE WEST: Galileo's major work on science was published in 1638.

1716 A.D.   The death of the great artist Ogata Korin.

THE WEST: Isaac Newton died in 1727.

1796 A.D.   The first Japanese–foreign language dictionary (Dutch) was completed.

THE WEST: The American Revolution began in 1776.

1805 A.D.   The woodblock artist Utamaro died.

THE WEST: The French Revolution began in 1789.

1823 A.D.   Hokusai created his woodblock-print series "Thirty-six Views of Mt. Fuji."

THE WEST: The first railroad was completed, between Liverpool and Manchester.

1833 A.D.   Hiroshige completed his woodblock-print series "Fifty-three Stages of Tokaido."

CHINA: The First Opium War, 1839 to 1842, between the Western powers and the Manchus.

THE WEST: The first steamship crossed the North Atlantic.

1853 A.D.   Commodore Perry of the U.S. arrived in Japan. The first treaty of amity with the U.S. was signed in 1854, and Townsend Harris opened the first U.S. consulate in Japan in 1856.
THE WEST: The U.S. Civil War ended in 1863.

1867 A.D.   The Tokugawa government's long reign ended with the ascension to the imperial throne of Emperor Meiji, who oversaw sweeping modernization that abolished *bakufu* feudalism. (The Meiji Era officially began in 1868.)
THE WEST: Karl Marx began publishing *Das Kapital.*

1894 A.D.   The outbreak of the Sino-Japanese War.
CHINA: The Boxer Rebellion of the Chinese against the Western occupying powers broke out in 1900.

1904 A.D.   The Russo-Japanese War began.

1912 A.D.   Emperor Meiji died.
CHINA: The First Chinese Republic of Sun Yat-Sen brought an end to the Ching Dynasty.
THE WEST: World War I, 1914–1918.

1937 A.D.   War in China and on the mainland between Japan and Chinese forces. World War II began in Europe in 1939, with Japan attacking Pearl Harbor in 1941.

1945 A.D.   Japan surrendered to the Allied Forces, after first Hiroshima and then Nagasaki were atom-bombed.

1952 A.D.   The occupation of Japan by the Allied Forces formally ended.

JAPANESE ART-HISTORY PERIODS

5000 B.C.–   **Jomon**
Hunting/Gathering.

300 B.C.–   **Yayoi**
Agriculture.

300 A.D.–c. **Fifth Century** A.D.   **Tumuli**
Toward the end of this period the Yamato area in southwestern Honshu (the main Japanese island) rose to ascendancy; relations were established with China, and Chinese characters were adopted as the official written language.

552–646 A.D.   **Asuka**
Continued building and crystallizing of strong Chinese influence—and the advent of Buddhism. The beginning of "imperial" thinking.

646–710 A.D.   Early Nara
Prince Shotoku of the Yamato area led a political and legal reorganization, consolidating the advances of the Asuka Period.

710–794 A.D.   Late Nara
The new capital, Nara, was established in 710, embodying many of the Asuka and Early Nara Periods' developments. The great Nara temples were constructed.

794–897 A.D.   Konin
In 794 the capital was moved from Nara to Heian (the present-day Kyoto). The building of the great Kyoto Buddhist temples began, to be accelerated later by the Fujiwaras.

897–1086 A.D.   Fujiwara (Heian)
The ascendancy of the Fujiwara family, in providing wives and chief ministers to the emperors, created a period in which the aristocrats had both the wealth and the unthreatened leisure time for refined cultural pursuits. Stimulus from China lessened and Japanese cultural elements came into prominence.

1086–1185 A.D.   Late Fujiwara (Late Heian)
The power of the Fujiwaras was lessened by the strengthening of the emperors and by over-reliance on other military clans. Chinese cultural development again became a major factor in Japan.

1185–1249 A.D.   Kamakura
Military values replaced refined aristocratic and courtly values as the measure of virtue. Dryer and more rigorous forms of Buddhism—especially Zen—came to the fore. The great Kamakura temples were built, as power and wealth shifted away from Kyoto.

1249–1392 A.D.   Late Kamakura
A period of instability and discontent with the Kamakura government, leading to the reestablishment of the emperor's power, and then rapidly to a new military regime under one of then-Emperor Daigo's generals, Ashikaga Takauji.

1392–1568 A.D.   Ashikaga (Muromachi)
The rise of regional centers of power under various *daimyo* (military lords) led to a number of commercial and cultural flowerings around the country. This facilitated contact between the feudal powers and the growing number of artisans and middle-class merchants in those towns. But the same rise of regional power led to rivalries and ultimately to political instability. There was a renewed influx of Chinese influence (Yuan and Ming); this was also perhaps the height of the power of Zen Buddhism and its astringent qualities, soon to pale somewhat with the rise of the commercial middle class.

1568–1603 A.D.   Momoyama
Oda Nobunaga and Toyotomi Hideyoshi reunified the country under central control after the unravelling of the Ashikaga Shogunate control of the country. Gorgeous artistic display became common among the

overlords, and spread to the merchant classes with the continued growth of commercial development.

1603–1867 A.D.   Tokugawa

The deep entrenchment of feudalism, begun in 1603 by Tokugawa Ieyasu, one of the *daimyo* under Nobunaga and Hideyoshi, is the single great theme of this period. The *bakufu* returned with a vengeance, with tightened central control of the country plus isolation from the outside world—though the latter weakened much toward the end of the period. This period saw many of the warrior-class *samurai* out of work. There was continued growth of towns and cities, hence the middle class, hence popular culture, such as woodblock prints.

1867–1912 A.D.   Meiji

The startling—almost overnight—turn away from feudalism and toward the useful offerings of Western science, education, and art, and toward political and financial reorganization of the country along Western lines but by Japanese choice.

INDEX

The letter H indicates Hotels and other accommodations. The letter R indicates Restaurants.

General Information

See also Index below for detailed information for areas, cities, and towns

Geographical